POLITICS, POWER
AND THE COMMON GOOD

POLITICS, POWER
AND THE **COMMON GOOD**

AN INTRODUCTION TO POLITICAL SCIENCE
Third Edition

ERIC MINTZ

Grenfell Campus,
Memorial University of Newfoundland

DAVID CLOSE

Memorial University of Newfoundland

OSVALDO CROCI

Memorial University of Newfoundland

Pearson Canada
Toronto

Library and Archives Canada Cataloguing in Publication

Mintz, Eric
  Politics, power and the common good: an introduction to political science / Eric Mintz, David Close, Osvaldo Croci.—3rd ed.

Includes index.
ISBN 978-0-13-138477-4

  1. Political science—Textbooks. 2. Canada—Politics and government—Textbooks. I. Close, David, 1945– II. Croci, Osvaldo III. Title.

JA66.M56 2012   320   C2010-905919-0

ISBN 978-0-13-138477-4

Vice-President, Editorial Director: Gary Bennett
Editor-in-Chief: Ky Pruesse
Senior Acquisitions Editor: Lisa Rahn
Executive Marketing Manager: Judith Allen
Senior Developmental Editor: Darryl Kamo
Project Manager: Richard di Santo
Production Editor: Susan Broadhurst
Copy Editor: Susan Broadhurst
Proofreader: Camille Isaacs
Compositor: MPS Limited, a Macmillan Company
Permissions Researcher: Debbie Henderson
Art Director: Julia Hall
Cover Designer: Miriam Blier
Cover image: Getty Images

2 3 4 5   15 14 13 12 11

Printed and bound in the United States of America.

BRIEF CONTENTS

CONTENTS

PREFACE

Politics is a fascinating subject and one that affects all of our lives. Unfortunately, some students are turned off by politics because they see it as an activity involving people who seek personal benefits or glory. The overblown rhetoric, distortions, and lies of government leaders, the exaggerations and unfulfilled promises of the politicians who seek our votes, and the violence and wars that have been justified by dubious political ideals are sufficient to lead us to adopt a skeptical view of politics.

However, there is another side to the story. Politics can and should be about how we might best achieve what is good for our communities and for the world as a whole. Humanity faces many important challenges—for example, how to establish and expand human rights, protect the environment, reduce poverty, and create a more peaceful world. Political actions and decisions are very important in dealing with such challenges. In order to act effectively in political life, it is essential to understand how the political world works. We need to examine different views about how political communities should be organized and the values they should pursue.

Ten years ago, we decided to write a textbook that would provide students with an interesting, easy-to-read, and straightforward introduction to the discipline. With this third edition of *Politics, Power and the Common Good*, we continue to endeavour to present a clear explanation of the basics of politics, while at the same time raising challenging questions that will encourage students to think deeply about the contemporary political world.

In this book, we provide the basic knowledge that every citizen should have, from understanding the political parties that seek our votes to understanding the way that Canada's parliamentary system works. While readers need to understand the politics and political structure of our own country, politics is about more than the institutions of government. Globalization makes it important to understand what is happening in the world at large and how this affects our lives in Canada. Readers will learn about the contending perspectives that are used to understand the world, the problems of the five-sixths of the world that live in poverty, the global political system of the twenty-first century, and much more.

As the authors of this book, we do not claim to have all of the answers to political problems. Nor do we want to promote a particular political perspective. Instead, our goal is to introduce our readers to the analysis of politics and government and raise important political questions to ponder and discuss.

HALLMARK FEATURES

Chapter-Opening Vignettes

An interesting and often provocative story introduces each chapter and its content. Among the book's vignettes are the controversy surrounding whether Catalonia and Quebec are nations, the struggle for universal health care coverage in the United States, the Canadian Parliament's efforts to find out the truth about the torture of detainees handed over to Afghan authorities, and the massive oil spill in the Gulf of Mexico in 2010.

Boxes

Appearing in every chapter, the boxed material emphasizes key theoretical issues and focuses on global and Canadian examples. These boxes deal with such topics as the near collapse of the global financial system, Aboriginal protests in Canada, why the majority of young people don't vote, and the extent to which the position of women has improved.

Key Terms

Important terms are set in bold-face in the narrative, appear in the margin for instant reference, are listed at the end of each chapter, and can be found in the end-of-book Glossary.

Chapter Objectives

The chapter's learning objectives situate the material and help students to structure their reading effectively.

Summary and Conclusion

Each chapter ends with a summary and conclusion, providing a quick recap of the chapter's contents.

Discussion Questions

Questions located at the end of each chapter spark critical thought and conversation.

Further Reading

This section steers students toward references that will expand their understanding of the chapter's topics.

Weblinks

Web addresses found in the margins provide additional research resources.

Text Design

The text's colour design showcases photos, figures, tables, and cartoons to illuminate concepts discussed in the text and to capture students' interest.

NEW TO THIS EDITION

This third edition of *Politics, Power and the Common Good* provided us with an opportunity not only to update the textbook, but also to make a number of additions and changes to improve the book, including:

- A new chapter on freedom, equality, and democracy (Chapter 3)
- An expanded discussion of environmentalism (Chapter 5)
- Analysis of data from recent World Values Surveys (Chapter 6)
- Discussion of the 2008 elections in Canada and the United States and the 2010 British election (Chapter 8)
- The Tea Party movement, which developed in 2009 to challenge what it deemed to be "big government" (Chapter 9)
- The differences between democratic and non-democratic government (Chapter 11)
- An expanded discussion of the courts and legal systems (Chapter 12)
- The major changes to the European Union in December 2009 (Chapter 13)
- The development of the parliamentary system (Chapter 14)
- The "miracle economies" of India and the People's Republic of China (Chapter 17)
- Radical and constructivist approaches to understanding international politics (Chapter 18)

In response to reviewer feedback for a more concise textbook, the organization has been modified to reduce the number of chapters:

- Discussion of the relationship between politics and the economy has been moved to Chapter 16.
- The democratic ideal is now discussed particularly in Chapters 3 and 11.
- Analysis of the communications media is included in Chapter 9.
- Non-democratic systems and the transition to democracy are analyzed in Chapter 11.

SUPPLEMENTS

The supplements package for this book has been carefully created to enhance the topics discussed in the text.

Instructor's Resource CD-ROM (IRCD)

This instructor's resource CD includes the *Instructor's Manual, Test Item File,* and *PowerPoint Presentations.*

Instructor's Manual

For each chapter of the text, this manual provides sample lecture outlines, clarification of potentially confusing terms and ideas, and a description of the major themes. In addition, it includes sample course outlines and lecture schedules.

PowerPoint Presentations

This instructor resource contains key points and lecture notes to accompany each chapter in the text.

Test Item File

This test bank contains more than nine hundred multiple choice, true/false, short answer, and essay questions.

MyTest

The test bank is also available as a MyTest, a powerful assessment generation program that helps instructors easily create and print quizzes, tests, and exams, as well as homework or practice handouts. Questions and tests can be authored online, allowing instructors ultimate flexibility and the ability to manage assessments efficiently anywhere, at any time. The MyTest can be accessed by visiting **www.pearsonmytest.com.**

Companion Website

This student resource features chapter objectives and study questions, as well as links to interesting material and information from other sites on the Web that reinforce and enhance the content of each chapter. The companion website can be accessed at **www.pearsoncanada.ca/mintz.**

CourseSmart

CourseSmart goes beyond traditional expectations to provide instant, online access to the textbooks and course materials. Instructors can save time and hassle with a digital eTextbook that allows you to search for the most relevant content at the very moment that it is needed. Whether it's evaluating textbooks or creating lecture notes to help students with difficult concepts, CourseSmart can make life a little easier. See how when you visit **www.coursesmart.com.**

Technology Specialists

Pearson's Technology Specialists work with faculty and campus course designers to ensure that Pearson technology products, assessment tools, and online course materials are tailored to meet your specific needs. This highly qualified team is dedicated to helping schools take full advantage of a wide range of educational resources, by assisting in the integration of a variety of instructional materials and media formats. Your local Pearson Education sales representative can provide you with more details on this service program.

ACKNOWLEDGMENTS

Writing a textbook is somewhat of a parasitic activity. We have ransacked the books and articles of our esteemed colleagues for ideas that we hope we have explained in an interesting and accessible way to readers unfamiliar with the theories and jargon of the discipline. We have attempted to cite what we have borrowed from the extensive literature of political science and related disciplines. If we have overlooked someone's contributions, we extend our apologies and ask that we be informed so that proper acknowledgement can be made in the next edition.

We would like to thank the many political science professors who provided detailed and helpful suggestions by reviewing the second edition of this book and the draft chapters of the third edition. Among these reviewers were the following individuals (in alphabetical order): Caroline Andrew, University of Ottawa; Louise Carbert, Dalhousie University; Paul Hamilton, Brock University; Joshua Hjartarson, University of Toronto; Paul Nesbitt-Larking, Huron University College; Michael A. O'Neill, University of Ottawa; Stephen Phillips, Langara College; Paul Prosperi, Langara College; and Mitu Sengupta, Ryerson University.

We would also like to thank the many people at Pearson Canada whose professional expertise and enthusiasm have been essential in developing this text. In particular, we would like to thank Darryl Kamo, Developmental Editor; Lisa Rahn, Acquisitions Editor; Susan Broadhurst, Production Editor and Copy Editor; and Camille Isaacs, Proofreader.

Eric Mintz would like to thank Diane Mintz for her continuing support and the Grenfell Campus of Memorial University of Newfoundland for granting a sabbatical during which this edition was written. David Close and Osvaldo Croci would like to acknowledge the support of the colleagues and staff of the Political Science Department at Memorial University of Newfoundland.

Finally, we would like to thank Tami Thirlwell, whose original cartoons were specially designed for this book.

We look forward to receiving comments and suggestions from students, teaching assistants, professors, and other readers to help us in writing the next edition. Please send comments to emintz@swgc.ca with the subject line "politics text."

A Great Way to Learn and Instruct Online

The Pearson Canada Companion Website is easy to navigate and is organized to correspond to the chapters in this textbook. Whether you are a student in the classroom or a distance learner you will discover helpful resources for in-depth study and research that empower you in your quest for greater knowledge and maximize your potential for success in the course.

[www.pearsoncanada.ca/mintz]

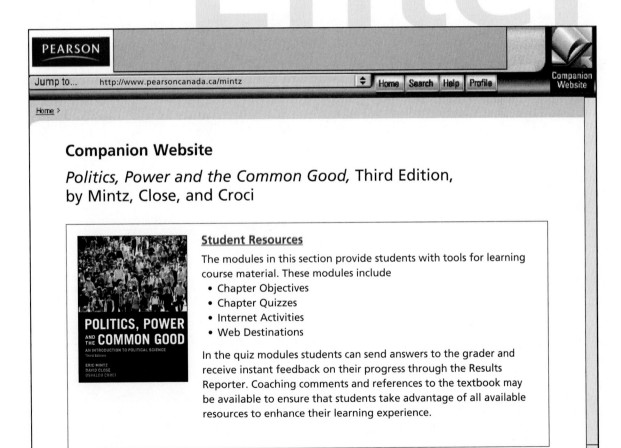

PEARSON

Jump to...   http://www.pearsoncanada.ca/mintz   Home Search Help Profile

Companion Website

Home >

Companion Website

Politics, Power and the Common Good, Third Edition, by Mintz, Close, and Croci

POLITICS, POWER
AND THE COMMON GOOD
AN INTRODUCTION TO POLITICAL SCIENCE
Third Edition

ERIC MINTZ
DAVID CLOSE
OSVALDO CROCI

Student Resources

The modules in this section provide students with tools for learning course material. These modules include
- Chapter Objectives
- Chapter Quizzes
- Internet Activities
- Web Destinations

In the quiz modules students can send answers to the grader and receive instant feedback on their progress through the Results Reporter. Coaching comments and references to the textbook may be available to ensure that students take advantage of all available resources to enhance their learning experience.

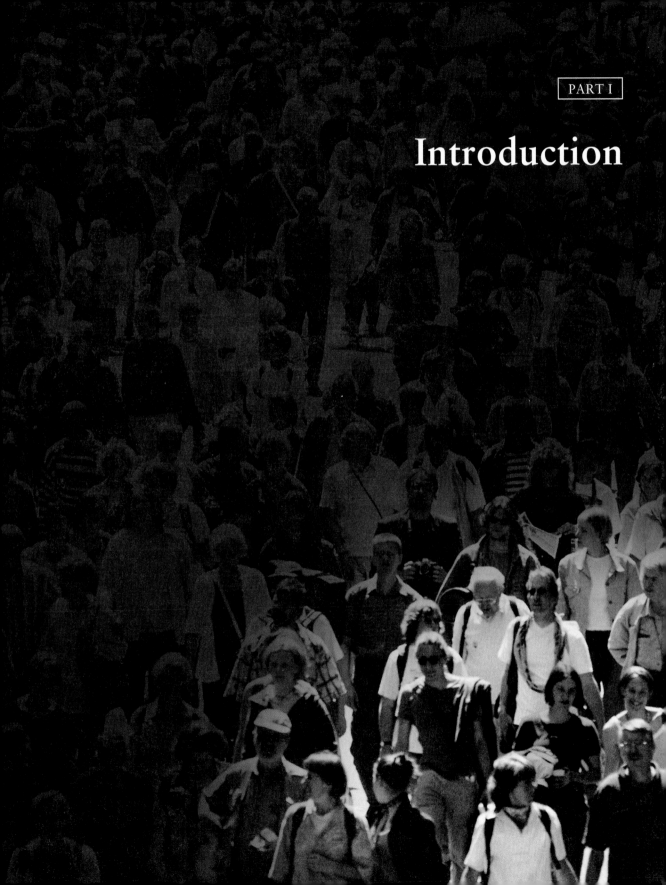

PART I

Introduction

Chapter 1

Understanding Politics

PHOTO ABOVE: Protesters in Copenhagen engage in political action seeking to draw attention to the lack of effective government action to deal with the critical problem of global climate change.

CHAPTER OBJECTIVES

After reading this chapter you should be able to:

1. discuss the importance of politics
2. define the concepts of power, authority, and legitimacy
3. discuss whether seeking the common good is a meaningful goal of political life
4. explain the difference between the empirical and normative analyses of politics

Climate change, the biggest threat facing humanity, is a critical political issue. If effective action is not taken, the effects of climate change several decades from today could be horrific. For example, a huge decline in the ability to grow food in much of the world would lead to mass starvation, riots, wars, and unprecedented population migrations to areas still able to produce food (Dyer, 2008).

Carbon dioxide in the atmosphere has increased from 280 parts per million (ppm) prior to the Industrial Revolution to 384 ppm in 2009 (Blasing, 2009). The atmospheric concentration of other greenhouse gases (such as methane) is also increasing rapidly. Already the negative effects of climate change are being felt in tropical areas and in the Arctic. Although it is difficult to determine precisely the effects of increasing greenhouse gases (GHGs) in the atmosphere, there is a strong scientific consensus that when the level of carbon dioxide reaches 450 ppm (if not earlier), the result will be an increase in the average global temperature of about two degrees Celsius. At that point, there would likely be an irreversible acceleration of global warming.

A massive reduction in the emission of GHGs is needed to avoid a potential global catastrophe. However, despite widespread awareness of the problem since the early 1990s, global GHG emissions have *increased* by more than 40 percent in the past decade. Although some of the richer countries have reduced their emissions, other countries—including Canada, the United States, and Australia—have increased emissions substantially. As well, emissions in developing countries have been increasing rapidly, with China now the largest single emitter of GHGs.

Reducing GHG emissions involves resolving important political disputes. When the prime ministers and presidents of most of the world's countries met in Copenhagen, Denmark, in December 2009 for the United Nations Climate Change Summit, they failed to reach agreement on a treaty to reduce GHG emissions. Developing countries pointed out that the richer countries have been responsible for most of the GHG emissions. Developing countries generally oppose reductions of or limitations on their emissions because this would undermine their efforts to achieve economic growth and improve their standard of living. However, some of the richer countries, particularly the United States, have been unwilling to take actions that would reduce the global competitiveness of their products unless the developing countries make binding commitments to limit their emissions. Corporations that produce fossil fuels have pressured governments to avoid any measures that would limit emissions and to continue to provide their industry with subsidies and tax breaks amounting to US$550 billion annually (Macdonald, 2010). Measures to encourage reduced use of fossil fuels, such as carbon taxes, are often unpopular.

Overall, short-term concerns about corporate profits and economic growth, winning elections, and continuing to live or seek a lifestyle that results in increasing GHG emissions often outweigh long-term concerns about the consequences later in our lives and in the lives of our children. Difficult questions exist about how the costs of addressing the problem should be distributed and how a coordinated response can be achieved in a world characterized by power conflicts and a highly unequal distribution of wealth. Determined political action, skilful political negotiations, and effective public policies are necessary to solve this challenging problem.

WHY IS POLITICS IMPORTANT?

Politics sometimes seems to be a trivial or undesirable activity. When we see political party advertisements that are devoted to personal attacks on leaders of other parties, politics may seem like a game played by those seeking to gain or maintain power. When we hear about elected representatives serving time in jail for defrauding government of millions of dollars, we may view politics as characterized by corruption. When politicians avoid fulfilling their promises and seem to spout empty rhetoric, we may wonder why anyone would bother to spend time following politics.

The ancient Greek philosophers viewed politics as the "master science." This depiction of politics may seem strange, but it reflects an important reality. The laws and policies of government can affect all aspects of our lives and our society. The opportunity of many students to receive a higher education is affected by the funding of educational institutions, the availability of loans and grants to students, and the tuition fees (directly or indirectly set by government) that students must pay. If you are unable to find work or become disabled, your ability to live a decent life may depend on the level of support that governments have provided. Political decisions affect the economy, the quality of the environment, the freedoms you can enjoy, and whether your country will send troops to fight in another part of the world.

BASIC CONCEPTS

It is important to recognize that there are no universally accepted definitions for many of the concepts used in analyzing politics. Those with different perspectives about politics will often define concepts in different ways. For example, while democracy is often defined primarily in terms of the procedures for holding elections to choose among competing parties and candidates, others define democracy as involving direct control of governing decisions by the people, or even "government that is by or for the common people" whether or not that government is chosen by a competitive election (Macpherson, 1965, p. 5). Similarly, there is no single generally accepted definition for the concepts of politics, power, and the common good, which are discussed in this chapter. Nevertheless, clear definitions of basic concepts are important if we are to analyze, understand, and discuss politics in a meaningful way.

Politics

Politics can be viewed as a feature of all organized human activity (Leftwich, 1983). Whether in a family, a business, or a sports group, decisions about what the group should do need to be made. Different members of the group will often have different views and efforts may be made by members of the group to try to persuade others about a particular course of action. Power relationships will likely have an effect on what the group does. Thus we can analyze the politics of any group to assess how decisions are made, which people tend to get their way, and whose ideas and interests the group's decisions tend to reflect.

Some political scientists view the study of politics as including all relationships that involve power (Hay, 2002). Generally, however, political science focuses primarily on the making of decisions that relate to the governing of a political community. David Easton's definition of politics as the "authoritative allocation of values for a society" (1953, p. 129) is used by many political scientists. The "allocation of values" refers to how the limited resources of a society (more generally, those things that are desired or valued) are allocated (distributed). By referring to the *authoritative* allocation of values, Easton suggests that what is distinctive about the allocation of values through governmental institutions is that this allocation is generally accepted as binding on all persons in the community. Politics, in this view, "concerns all those varieties of activity that influence significantly the kind of authoritative policy adopted for a society and the way it is put into practice" (Easton, 1953, p. 128). However, while many government decisions are authoritative, governments also take actions that are not considered binding on the members of the political community. For example, governments may try to persuade us to adopt healthier lifestyles.

For the purposes of this book, we define **politics** as activity related to influencing, making, or implementing collective decisions for a political community (whether a country, a local community, or the loosely organized global community). Political activity includes individuals and groups trying to influence the collective decisions and policies of governments and mobilizing support for political parties seeking to gain or maintain control of the government, as well as the interactions among various governing institutions in developing and implementing public policies. Raising awareness of problems affecting the political community and efforts to change political values, attitudes, and opinions can also be viewed as political. In addition, taking action concerning problems that affect society or the world as a whole might also be considered political regardless of whether the action is directed at influencing government (as discussed in Box 1-1, A Broader View of Politics).

POLITICS Activity related to influencing, making, or implementing collective decisions for a political community.

Power

Discussion and analysis of politics often focuses on power. Statements such as "the prime minister is very powerful," "big business is more powerful than ordinary citizens," and "the United States is the most powerful country in the world" are very frequently made. Determining the validity of such statements, however, can be difficult and controversial. Nevertheless, power is important in affecting political decisions.

Power is often defined as the ability to achieve an objective by influencing the behaviour of others (Nye, 2004), particularly to get them to do what they

POWER The ability to achieve an objective by influencing the behaviour of others, particularly to get them to do what they would not have otherwise done.

BOX 1-1
A Broader View of Politics

We often think of political activity as involving the struggle for political power and the attempts to influence the decisions of government. But this may be too limited a focus. Consider the following examples.

Various environmental groups have sought to end the clear-cutting practices of forest companies in British Columbia. Having had limited success in persuading the B.C. government to pass stricter logging regulations, they turned to other methods to achieve their objective. Europeans were encouraged to participate in a boycott of products made with B.C. lumber, and pressure was put on retail businesses such as Home Depot to sell only lumber produced in an environmentally friendly manner. These activities had considerable success, and a number of B.C. forest companies began to change their logging practices.

In 2010, environmental groups, including Greenpeace and Forest Ethics, reached an agreement with the Forest Products Association of Canada. The major forestry companies agreed to stop logging about thirty million hectares of boreal forest that is the prime habitat of endangered caribou herds, to reduce GHG emissions to become carbon neutral, and to meet or exceed the high sustainability standards set by the independent Forest Stewardship Council. In return, environmental groups promised to suspend their boycott campaigns and help the industry market itself as "green" (Mittelstaedt, 2010).

In many ways, these activities by environmental groups are similar to what we normally consider political. People were mobilized to try to achieve an objective that was viewed as being in the public interest. Rather than influencing government to adopt a policy that might change the actions of forestry companies, environmental groups directly pressured some of the companies to change their actions to deal with a public problem. The activities of environmental groups, therefore, could be considered political, even though the groups decided to try to affect the decisions of private businesses rather than the decisions of government.

would not have otherwise done.[1] Power, in this definition, is a relationship among different individuals and groups. As such, it is not easily quantifiable and changes depending on the objective being pursued and the circumstances involved. For example, the president of the United States may be very powerful in decisions concerning the deployment of armed forces, but less powerful when trying to persuade the American Congress concerning agricultural or housing policies.

Political power can be exerted in several different ways.[2] *Coercion* involves using fear or threats of harmful consequences to achieve an outcome. For

---

[1] Some political scientists prefer to use the term *influence* for the general ability to affect behaviour, leaving the term *power* to refer to the use of coercion, inducements, or manipulation to get people to act against their own desires or interests (Dahl, 1984).

[2] Power can be significant even when there is no intentional exercise of power. Political actors may change their behaviour because they *anticipate* that there will be negative consequences from those with greater power if they act in a particular way, even if no direct threat has been made. For example, knowing that the United States has imposed severe economic sanctions on Cuba, other Caribbean countries may be reluctant to act in ways that could result in similar consequences.

"Don't they understand that politics is about power?"

example, Nazi Germany's threat to invade Czechoslovakia in 1938 was successful in convincing the Czech government to allow Germany to annex part of its territory. If your employer threatens to fire you unless you work on behalf of a certain candidate in an election, coercive power has been used to intimidate you. *Inducements* involve achieving an outcome by offering a reward or bribe. For example, if your employer promises to give you a promotion should you decide to support a particular candidate, power has been exercised in the form of an inducement. *Persuasion* is a very important aspect of political life, as people are often involved in trying to persuade other people to think and act in particular ways. Persuasion may involve the use of truthful information to encourage people to act in accordance with their own interests or values, or the use of misleading information to manipulate people. In practice, it is often difficult to distinguish between persuasion based on truthful information and persuasion involving manipulation, as exaggeration and selective presentation of the facts are often used to make a persuasive argument. Power can also be exercised through *leadership*. For example, a country that is successful in providing wealth and harmony to its population may be able to convince other countries to follow its example (Nye, 2004).

Power does not necessarily mean that one actor controls or dominates others, although the term is generally used to refer to situations where one person or group is in a stronger position than others. Politics often involves considerable bargaining and negotiating among different political actors. Although bargaining sometimes involves exchange among equals (as when two legislators agree to support each other's proposals for new legislation), the type of bargain achieved often reflects differences in power among the parties to the bargain. For example, rich countries may be in a better position than poor countries to negotiate an international trade agreement favourable to their interests because of their greater power, even if some concessions are made to poorer countries to gain their agreement or to legitimate the agreement.

It is difficult and often contentious to determine who is powerful in any political community, and whether power is concentrated in a small number of hands or widely dispersed. Even if through careful analysis we were able to determine who influenced various decisions that we considered important, this would not necessarily give us a full picture of who is powerful. If those who are powerful are able to prevent important issues from being raised, then power has been exercised through "non-decisions" (Bachrach & Baratz, 1962). For example, the owner of a polluting factory may be said to be powerful if discussion of the pollution problem is deliberately avoided by the political leaders of the community or by the media. In other words, power can be exercised through control of the **political agenda**, that is, the issues that are considered important and are given priority in political deliberations.

POLITICAL AGENDA The issues that are considered important and given priority in political deliberations.

In addition, those who are able to shape the dominant ideas in a society may have a general, long-term effect on the politics of that society and the decisions that are made. If those dominant ideas work against the interests of the weaker groups in society and result in the weaker groups acting against their own "true" interests, then it could be argued that power has been exercised in an indirect manner (Lukes, 1974). Take, for example, societies where women are expected to confine themselves to domestic responsibilities such as cooking, cleaning, and raising children, while men are involved in public activities, including politics. Ideas that these "separate spheres" are "natural" or that women do not have the qualities necessary to participate in public life might lead many women to believe that their proper role is different from that of men, and thus lead them not to challenge that system. In this case, power has been exerted through the dominant ideas that favour the interests of men, rather than through deliberate efforts to affect specific decisions.

This "third face" of power (see Table 1-1) moves us away from power being defined solely in terms of a relationship in which a person or group directly influences another person or group. Instead, this approach tends to assume that decisions will reflect the interests of the dominant groups in society. Subordinate groups may be unlikely to act in their own interests because they have accepted the ideas that benefit the dominant groups. However,

FIRST FACE	Ability to affect decisions
SECOND FACE	Ability to ensure that issues are not raised
THIRD FACE	Ability to affect the dominant ideas of society

TABLE 1-1
**THE THREE FACES
OF POWER**

determining what is in the "true interests" of an individual or group is often contentious because it assumes that the preferences of an individual (for example, which party a person votes for) are not necessarily the same as what is good for that person.

THE DISTRIBUTION OF POWER   In any society, the resources that give individuals and groups the potential to exert political power are unequally distributed. Wealth, control of important aspects of the economy, social status and prestige, official position, control of information and expertise, the ability to mobilize supporters, control of the means of force, and the ability to influence people are some of the resources that can be used for advantage in politics. Although all citizens in a democracy have some potential power through their right to vote, other resources are less equally distributed.

Analyzing the distribution of power involves more than adding up the resources available to different groups. Groups differ in how effectively they use their power resources. Some groups are more successful than others in mobilizing potential supporters, forming alliances with other groups, and appealing to the values and beliefs of the community to achieve their objectives. As Box 1-2, People Power, illustrates, mobilizing ordinary citizens around a popular cause can sometimes bring about fundamental changes.

The political power of different individuals and groups is not only a product of their skill in mobilizing resources. Political institutions may be organized and operate in ways that advantage or disadvantage certain groups. For example, the U.S. Senate, which contains two senators elected from each state, gives the representatives of small states the power to reject proposals favoured by those representing a substantial majority of the American population.

Overall, different analysts come up with different depictions of how power is distributed in particular countries. When considering democratic countries like Canada and the United States, some see power as highly concentrated, particularly because decisions tend to reflect the interests and involvement of a small number of persons, such as government and business elites (Domhoff, 2009; Mills, 1956; Panitch, 1995). Others note the influence of a wide variety of groups that promote many different interests and argue that power is quite dispersed throughout society, with no group or interest dominant (Dahl, 1961). Similarly some view political power as widely dispersed in a democracy because voters will affect the general direction of government through their choice among the political parties that compete for their support (Downs, 1957).

BOX 1-2
People Power

Those who control large corporations, occupy top government positions, or head major social organizations clearly have many resources that can be used to affect governing and collective decisions. Occasionally, however, groups and individuals with seemingly few resources are able to bring about major changes in the way the political community is governed.

The dictatorial Philippine government of Ferdinand Marcos was successfully challenged in 1986 when a very large number of people, including praying nuns, sat down in front of the army's tanks and refused to move. In Eastern Europe, peaceful demonstrations by ever-larger numbers of people helped to bring down communist regimes in 1989. Black South Africans, by engaging in a determined struggle against the white minority-controlled government and organizing international support for their cause, were eventually successful in challenging the oppressive system of apartheid. Canadian Aboriginals, who in the past were ignored by the political system, have been able to make their voices heard through successful legal cases in the courts, confrontation with Canadian authorities, and building a strong moral case that they have been treated unjustly. In each case, ordinary or disadvantaged people were able to challenge the powerful through determined and skilful action, even though serious personal risks and sacrifices were involved.

"People power" is not always successful. For example, student-led actions to support demands for democracy in the People's Republic of China were brutally suppressed by the army on orders from the Communist party leadership in 1989. Despite the outrage in many parts of the world when news coverage revealed the suppression of peaceful protest, the Chinese government did not back away from its hard-line stance.

People power. Citizens of Prague, Czechoslovakia, turned out by the hundreds of thousands in November 1989 to protest the communist regime led by General Secretary Milos Jakes. Just one month later, the regime toppled peacefully, and the formerly communist Assembly elected Václav Havel, leader of the pro-democracy Civic Forum, as the country's president.

THE POSITIVE AND NEGATIVE SIDES OF POWER Power is often viewed negatively because of its association with efforts to dominate or exploit others. Governments, at times, have used the power they wield to establish, promote, or defend systems of economic, social, and military domination and exploitation. As well, there are tendencies for individuals with political power to use their power for their own benefit rather than for the good of the political community. In addition, those in powerful positions may become arrogant and unresponsive to the needs and desires of the population. As former American Senator William Fulbright put it, "power has a way of undermining judgment, of planting delusions of grandeur in the minds of otherwise sensible people and otherwise sensible nations" (cited in Lobe, 2002, p. 3).

Power is often thought of in terms of some people, groups, or countries having *power over* others, which is then used to the benefit of those holding the power. However, we can also think about power (particularly in the form of authority, discussed below) in a more positive way as the *power to* achieve worthwhile collective goals. Power is often necessary to induce people to co-operate in order to achieve objectives that benefit themselves and the political community as a whole, such as developing the economy, providing security, and protecting the environment. Such objectives may not be easily achieved by individuals, but might be achievable by using the collective power of the community organized by government. This can be illustrated by what is known as the **free rider problem**. Imagine that all persons in a community agreed they would each contribute to building a road that would benefit everyone. One miserly individual might decide not to contribute to the cost of building the road, knowing that the road would still be built with the contributions of others. However, if enough people followed this self-interested logic, the road might never be built and everyone would suffer. The use of the coercive power of government (for example, to enforce the payment of taxes) is often useful or necessary to achieve goals that benefit the community as a whole. However, as Box 1-3, The Tragedy of the Commons, illustrates, there are sometimes alternatives to the use of coercive action by government to achieve the common good.

FREE RIDER PROBLEM A problem with voluntary collective action that results because an individual can enjoy the benefits of group action without contributing.

Authority and Legitimacy

Authority, the right to exercise power that is accepted by those being governed as legitimate, is of special importance in understanding politics. Those with political authority claim that they have been *authorized* (whether by God, tradition, legal rules, election, or some other source) to govern. If a person's right to make governing decisions is generally accepted by those being governed, then that authority is often viewed as **legitimate**. More generally, we can assess whether the system of governing is accepted as legitimate.

ESTABLISHING AND MAINTAINING LEGITIMACY How is the legitimacy of a system of governing established and maintained? Why do most Canadians accept the right of a few people in government to make decisions for the political community, even though they may not agree with the decisions that are being made? German sociologist Max Weber (1864–1920) described three basic types of authority, each of which could try to establish its legitimacy in its own way:

- charismatic authority
- traditional authority
- legal–rational authority

In practice, there are often combinations of these types of authority.

AUTHORITY The right to exercise power that is accepted by those being governed as legitimate.

LEGITIMACY Acceptance by the members of a political community that those in positions of authority have the right to govern.

The Tragedy of the Commons

In a famous article Garrett Hardin (1968) asks us to imagine a situation where herders allow their flocks to graze on a common pasture (that is, a pasture available freely to all members of the community). To make more money, each herder may find it profitable to purchase more cattle to graze on the common land. Eventually, the pasture will be overgrazed and all will suffer. One solution would be to privatize the commons, with the owner then charging a fee to allow each head of cattle to graze there. This would, however, not necessarily lead to the common good, as only those who could afford the fee could then graze their cattle. It might also result in the owner converting the pasture to another, more profitable endeavour, thereby depriving herders of their livelihood. The alternative that Hardin favours involves a coercive government ensuring that the commons is not overused.

However, American political scientist and Nobel economics prize winner Elinor Ostrom (2000), looking at a variety of real-world situations, points out that under the right circumstances co-operation among the users of a common resource, such as water or pastures, can result in the proper management of that resource. These conditions include the development of a sense of community, shared values, and mechanisms to monitor and enforce the use of the resource to ensure that no cheating occurs. In contrast to Hardin's bleak outlook, which included the idea that a dictatorial, overbearing global government might be needed to solve global environmental problems such as overpopulation, Ostrom's analysis points to the possibility that co-operation to achieve solutions potentially can be arrived at even when individuals are concerned with their own interests, provided that there is trust and discussion among the members of the community. To what extent this can apply to global problems remains an open question, although Ostrom suggests that co-operative institutions in combination with governments and markets can be useful in dealing with global environmental problems (Dietz, Ostrom, & Stern, 2003).

CHARISMATIC AUTHORITY
Authority based on the perception that a leader has extraordinary or supernatural qualities.

Charismatic authority is based on the personal qualities of the leader. These qualities might include exhibiting extraordinary or supernatural qualities through such means as performing miracles, issuing prophecies, or leading a military victory (Weber, 1958). Charismatic leaders, such as Mao Zedong, leader of the Chinese communist revolution, have inspired intense devotion in their followers. Some democratic leaders such as Pierre Trudeau, John F. Kennedy, and Barack Obama have also been described as charismatic, although this has not been the basis of their authority.

TRADITIONAL AUTHORITY
Authority based on customs that establish the right of certain persons to rule.

Traditional authority, whether exercised through the elders of a tribe or a ruling family, is based on customs that establish the right of certain persons to rule. The traditional authority of monarchs who inherited their position was often buttressed with the idea that rulers had a divinely created right to rule that was sanctified by religious authorities. Japanese emperors, for example, claimed to be descended from the sun goddess. The legitimacy of traditional authority can be based on beliefs that a certain family has always ruled and that customs are sacred practices that will bring evil consequences if violated (Weber, 1958). Queen Elizabeth II exercises traditional authority, although

Charismatic leaders, such as Mao Zedong, leader of the Chinese communist revolution, inspire intense devotion in their followers. Charismatic authority rests upon the belief of followers in magical powers, revelations, and hero worship. The Chinese media depicted an elderly Mao supposedly performing the heroic feat of swimming across the Yangtze River to maintain his charismatic image.

her authority is very limited. As the saying goes, "The monarch reigns, but does not rule."

Modern societies, in Weber's view, are characterized by efficient management and bureaucratic organization. The **legal–rational authority** of modern societies is based on legal rules and procedures rather than on the personal qualities or characteristics of the rulers. Authority is impersonal in the sense that it rests in official positions such as prime minister or president, rather than in the individuals holding such positions. The right of those in governing positions to rule is based on being chosen by a set of established and accepted legal procedures. Those holding official positions are expected to act in accordance with legal rules and procedures. Thus, their authority is limited. The legitimacy of the system of governing is based on a belief in the legality of the procedures for selecting those who have official duties and the legal "correctness" of the procedures that are used in governing (Weber, 1958). This type of authority is "rational" in that it is logically connected to what Weber saw as the goal of governing: maintaining public order (Nelson, 2006).

Holding free and fair elections involving all adult citizens to designate those authorized to make governing decisions is often considered to be the most effective way of establishing the legitimacy of government. Nevertheless, a "legitimacy crisis" can occur even in democratic systems (Habermas, 1975). Although an unpopular government in a democracy can be voted out, if governments are persistently ineffective in dealing with serious problems, citizens

LEGAL–RATIONAL AUTHORITY The right to rule based on legal rules and procedures rather than on the personal qualities or characteristics of the rulers.

might question the legitimacy of the democratic institutions and processes in their country. For example, if the policies of successive governments led to widespread poverty and unemployment or to a collapse in the value of the currency, then the legitimacy of the system of governing might be challenged. Legitimacy can also be reduced if some groups feel that there is a long-term pattern of mistreatment by the government. In other words, the legitimacy of a democratic government not only may require an acceptance of the procedures by which governing authorities are chosen and actions are taken, but also may depend on the perceived rightfulness of how government (or, more generally, the system of governing) exercises its authority (Barnard, 2001). In particular, the governing authorities will have a higher level of legitimacy if their actions are perceived as being consistent with the general principles and values of the political community (Gilley, 2006).

In addition, a system of governing that is imposed on a country or on a part of the population without its consent might be viewed by as illegitimate, even if it establishes democratic procedures. For example, when a democratic system of governing was established in Germany after World War I, some Germans doubted its legitimacy, partly because they viewed it as being imposed on the country by the victors in that war. The problem of legitimacy, combined with the failure of German governments to deal effectively with the problems the country faced, eventually contributed to the demise of the democratic system and the takeover by Adolf Hitler and the Nazi party. Likewise, conquered peoples are often unwilling to accept the legitimacy of the governing authorities imposed by the foreign rulers regardless of how well the authorities govern.

THE SIGNIFICANCE OF LEGITIMATE AUTHORITY   Effective governing depends not only on governing institutions having the power to force people to act in certain ways, but also on their ability to establish and maintain legitimate authority. A government that is not accepted as legitimate by a significant proportion of the population will have to devote much of its energy and resources to persuading or coercing the population to obey its laws and maintain order. All governments rely on coercion and other forms of power to some extent, but generally most people feel an obligation to obey a legitimate government. Thus, a government whose rule is considered legitimate can rely more on authority than on coercion to get people to obey the laws it adopts.

Having legitimate authority gives government a powerful resource to achieve its goals. People usually obey laws, even when they find those laws to be against their interests or values, because they view the source of those laws as legitimate. This can potentially allow the government to act for the good of the community as a whole, even when some may object to the policies adopted. However, even though most people would agree that political authority is a necessary and desirable feature of an orderly society, questions can arise concerning whether there are circumstances in which authority should be resisted or disobeyed. What would you do if you were drafted to fight in a war that you considered unjust? Would you resist the authority of a democratically elected government that was persecuting an unpopular minority, even if that persecution were done in a legal manner?

The Common Good

Political philosophers have often viewed politics as different from other activities in that it is concerned with what is common to the community as a whole. Ensuring the good functioning of the basic activities of governing—such as maintaining order and security, providing for a just settlement of disputes, and taking actions to promote a prosperous, sustainable economy—potentially benefits all members of the political community (Wolin, 1960). Ideally politics is about pursuing the **common good** of a political community.

On the surface, the concept of the common good (similar to the concept of the public interest) seems uncontroversial. Who would not agree that political activity should be directed toward the common good of the political community? However, in practice, determining and achieving the common good can be contentious as members of a political community have different interests and values.

For classic political philosophers such as Aristotle (384–322 BCE), governing ideally involved working toward achieving a good society in which citizens could lead a virtuous life. Jean-Jacques Rousseau (1712–1778) argued that citizens should put aside their personal interests and through discussion determine what is in the general interest, which he termed the "general will." The general will did not represent simply the views of the majority, but rather the true interests of all citizens. For Rousseau, acting in accordance with the general will was true freedom, as citizens have made the law themselves (Nelson, 2006; Thiele, 1997). Rousseau's critics point out that the concept of a general will that all citizens are obliged to obey can be used to justify a totalitarian system—one in which there is total control of society and people's lives and thoughts in pursuit of a collective goal that is proclaimed as being in the general interest of all. A more pragmatic approach to the public interest was advocated by American philosopher and educational reformer John Dewey (1859–1952). In his view social problems represented the reality that there were conflicting interests in society. However, through an open process of discussion and scrutiny, the merits of different solutions to problems could be assessed in terms of the public's "more inclusive interests" (cited by Bozeman, 2007, p. 113).

For those who have an **individualist perspective** on politics, the idea of the common good and how it can be achieved is rather different. This perspective assumes that human beings act primarily in accordance with their own interests—in other words, selfishly. A community is a collection of individuals each pursuing his or her own interests. Thus, it is naive or hopelessly idealistic

COMMON GOOD What is good for the entire political community.

INDIVIDUALIST PERSPECTIVE A perspective that views human beings as acting primarily in accordance with their own interests.

to expect people (whether as voters, politicians, or government officials) to deliberately act for the common good, particularly when that involves sacrificing their own interests.

Those who hold the individualist perspective often argue that if every person is free to pursue his or her own interests, the result will lead to the best overall result for the members of the community. For example, Scottish philosopher Adam Smith (1723–1790) suggested that if individuals pursue their own self-interest in a free-market system, the result will be maximization of the wealth of society. The common good, in this perspective, is simply the aggregate of the preferences or interests of individuals. Since there is no collective or community interest beyond that of the interests of individuals, the implication of this perspective is that government should be restricted to the minimum needed to provide security and protection for individuals and the free market.

Are we concerned only with our own good? If individuals pursue their own interests, will the good of the entire community be served? Are the communities that we live in no more than a collection of independent individuals? Critics of the individualist perspective argue that humans are social beings who flourish through harmonious interaction with others. Connected to our social nature is the capability to care about others. This capability initially develops within our own family, but can extend to the social groups to which we belong, to citizens of our country, and potentially to the world as a whole. The outpouring of assistance by people around the world to Haiti following the devastating earthquake there in January 2010 suggests that individuals exhibit a concern for the well-being of others that is not motivated solely by self-interest.

Further, the communities to which we belong—including political communities—help to shape our sense of ourselves, that is, our identity. A sense of belonging to and participating in a community (or a set of communities) could be considered an important part of a fulfilling and meaningful life. People have an interest not only in their own material well-being, but also in the quality of their community and the social relations that are a part of that community (Lutz, 1999). Individuals engage in political activity not only to advance their own interests, but also to pursue the values they think should guide the actions of government (Lewin, 1991).

Contemporary political communities often feature considerable diversity such that a consensus on what is the common good may be difficult or impossible to achieve. The values of a particular religion no longer provide a widely accepted guide as to what constitutes a good society or a virtuous life. Even if a number of general values such as freedom, equality, order, and justice are shared by people within the community, these values may be thought of in different ways and different people or groups may give these values different priorities.

As well, the costs and benefits of actions to achieve the common good are often unequally distributed. For example, most people would agree that reducing air pollution would be for the common good of the political community.

However, the costs of reducing pollution to achieve this objective may fall more heavily on some, such as factory owners and automobile users, than on others. Likewise, a free school breakfast program primarily benefits those whose parents are very poor. Nevertheless, we might view such a program as being for the common good if we assume that being part of a community involves caring about others in that community and supporting policies that help others to enjoy the benefits of the community. However, in political communities where there are sharp divisions (based, for example, on economic inequality, religion, or cultural identities), the sense of being members of a shared community and a willingness to be concerned about others may be weak or non-existent. In such political communities, the notion of the common good may not be very meaningful.

ACHIEVING THE COMMON GOOD?   We often look to government to achieve the common good. But how can we be assured that government will pursue the common good rather than the particular interests of those in government? In *The Republic*, the ancient Greek philosopher Plato (c. 429–347 BCE) sketched out an ideal of how the common good might be achieved. This involved placing political authority in the hands of a wise philosopher–king who had been thoroughly educated in the art of governing. To ensure that such a leader would rule for the common good rather than out of personal interest, leaders would be prevented from having a family or owning property.

What might this suggest for governments and their citizens operating in the real world and not in a great thinker's utopia?

In the contemporary world, democracy is often seen as the form of government most likely to actually pursue the common good. Ideally, through discussion among citizens, an informed consensus can be reached about the policies that are desirable for the common good. However, meaningful discussion is often difficult to achieve outside of small groups and small communities. Instead, there is often an expectation that decisions in a democracy will tend to reflect the opinions of the majority of the population. Even if this is the case, it does not ensure that the common good of the community will be achieved. The majority is not necessarily oriented toward the common good of all members of the community, and at various times majorities have supported policies that oppress minorities.

Some suggest that a **pluralist system**, one in which a large number of groups put forward the demands of a wide variety of people and interests and government tries to satisfy as many groups as possible, will result in the common good. A potential problem here is that even if government is responsive to groups representing a wide variety of interests, this does not necessarily result in the common good. Providing particular benefits to various groups that are able to exert effective pressure may not be the same as acting for the common good. If each group pursues its own interests, the good of the entire community may be ignored.

PLURALIST SYSTEM A political system in which a large number of groups representing a wide variety of interests are able to influence the decisions of government. Government tries to satisfy as many groups as possible and no group has a dominant influence on government.

Although seeking the common good is a worthwhile objective for political life, it should be kept in mind that the claim to be acting for the common good (or other ideals) can be deceptive. Ruthless leaders have tried to justify brutal actions in the name of the long-term good of the political community. For example, the Soviet leader Joseph Stalin tried to justify his actions, which resulted in the starvation of millions of peasants, with the ideal of creating a "classless society." Fascist leaders such as Adolf Hitler and Benito Mussolini used the appeal of the good of the nation to suppress dissent and justify wars of aggression. Even in those democratic countries where individual rights are valued, appeals to the common good are sometimes made to justify repressive government actions in order to fight terrorism, subversion, and crime. In general, there is a real danger that government leaders claiming to pursue the common good of the political community as a whole will act in ways that are oppressive to some members of that community.

A QUESTION OF COMMUNITIES   The common good is often thought of in terms of the country in which we live. But the common good of the country may not necessarily be the same as the common good of the other political communities to which we belong, such as provincial or local communities. Indeed, some argue that we should be concerned about the common good of humanity. The processes of globalization (discussed in Chapter 2) are creating increased interaction and interdependence among the peoples of the world. However, despite greater awareness of and concern about what happens in other parts of the world, for most of us our sense of being part of a global political community is much weaker than our sense of being Canadian. Major differences among the peoples of the world in culture and circumstances mean that there are fewer shared interests and values upon which a consensus about the common good of humanity could be based.

Some environmentalists suggest that the common good should include not only humanity (including future generations), but also the Earth as a whole, including plants, animals, and the ecosystems upon which life is based (Daly & Cobb, 1994). Protecting the environment is ultimately essential for humanity as well as for plants and animals. But, when faced with the issue of protecting the jobs of loggers or protecting the habitat of an endangered animal or plant, should the good of human beings be given greater priority than the good of other life forms? Or as parts of an interrelated whole, are all life forms, including humans, of equal inherent worth (Devall & Sessions, 1998)?

WHAT IS POLITICAL SCIENCE?

POLITICAL SCIENCE The systematic study of politics.

The term **political science** may sound confusing, as politics and science seem to be very different. Indeed, some universities and colleges prefer to use terms such as *political studies*, *politics*, or *government* rather than political science. However, keeping in mind that the word *science* is derived from a Latin word

BOX 1-4

The Development of Political Science

The origins of political science are often traced back about 2400 years to the works of ancient Greek philosophers Plato and Aristotle, although even before that the Chinese thinker Confucius also developed influential political ideas (Tremblay et al., 2004). Classical political philosophy focused on how the common good could be achieved through the organization of governing and society. Based on their understanding of human nature and the realities of politics, political philosophers are concerned with important normative questions: Who should rule? Are we obligated to obey the decisions of those in positions of political authority? What values, such as freedom and equality, should be pursued in politics? Is a just society possible? As well, political philosophers analyze the meanings attached to key concepts of political analysis such as justice, freedom, power, and democracy.

Political science as an academic discipline distinct from economics, philosophy, and law developed in the late nineteenth century and often focused on the description of governmental institutions and constitutional law. In the mid twentieth century, a different approach, termed behaviouralism, was developed particularly by political scientists educated in the United States. Behaviouralism focuses on examining the actual behaviour of political actors such as voters and legislators, typically by using quantitative methods such as survey research (a sophisticated version of public opinion polls). The goal of behaviouralism is to develop a value-free scientific approach to understanding politics. Political science, like the other

social sciences, is concerned with human actions. Therefore, unlike the physical sciences, political science cannot definitively predict what will happen in specified circumstances. Instead, the scientific study of politics develops generalizations that can explain various political phenomena.

Political science today uses a variety of approaches and methods and has become more of a global endeavour than one centred in the United States. There is increased interest in qualitative as well as quantitative methodologies. Rational choice models based on the assumption that individuals will act rationally to maximize their interests have been widely used to try to explain political behaviour. The behavioural emphasis on rigorous scientific testing of hypotheses with empirical data has been complemented by an interest in a broader understanding and theorizing about politics and its relationship with society, the economy, and historical development. For example, the subfield of political economy focuses on explaining politics in terms of the inter-relationship of politics and the economic system. Other researchers focus on the significance of political institutions in affecting political behaviour and public policies. Instead of looking at the politics of a single country, the scientific study of politics often takes a comparative approach of explaining political phenomena through a detailed analysis of similarities and differences among countries. Political philosophy has been reinvigorated in recent times by major works and debate on topics such as justice, the accommodation of diversity, and deliberative democracy.

meaning knowledge, we could define political science simply as the systematic study of politics. As Box 1-4, The Development of Political Science, indicates, political science includes a diverse set of ways to approach the study of politics.

A distinction is often made between empirical analysis and normative analysis (see Table 1-2). **Empirical analysis** involves explaining various aspects of politics, particularly by using careful observation and comparison

EMPIRICAL ANALYSIS Analysis that involves explaining various aspects of politics, particularly by using careful observation and comparison to develop generalizations and testable theories.

TABLE 1-2
EMPIRICAL, NORMATIVE, AND POLICY ANALYSIS: AN EXAMPLE

EMPIRICAL ANALYSIS	Why are women less likely than men to run for Parliament?
NORMATIVE ANALYSIS	Should legislatures be a microcosm of society?
POLICY ANALYSIS	What is the best way of increasing the proportion of women in Parliament?

NORMATIVE ANALYSIS
Analysis that includes examining ideas about how the community should be governed and what values should be pursued through politics.

POLICY ANALYSIS Analysis that involves evaluating existing policies and assessing possible alternatives to deal with particular problems.

to develop generalizations. The goal of empirical analysis is not simply to gather data to describe various features of politics and government, but also to develop testable theories that will help us to understand how politics works. **Normative analysis** includes examining ideas about how the community should be governed and what values should be pursued through politics.

In practice, the distinction between empirical and normative analysis is not as clear-cut as it seems. Political scientists are part of the world they study, and inevitably the empirical questions they choose to study and the way they go about researching those questions will be affected by their values and perspectives. Likewise, normative analyses are based on understandings of human nature and how the political world works. The combination of empirical and normative analysis is particularly evident in **policy analysis**, which involves evaluating existing policies and assessing possible alternatives to deal with particular problems. In providing practical advice, policy analysts have to consider what is feasible rather than ideal, which calls for an understanding of political realities. That is, they need to consider how best to achieve desired values under particular circumstances.

Why Study Politics?

Understanding politics is essential in order to take effective action to achieve our goals and ideals. Imagine that you are concerned about global climate change and would like governments to take actions to reduce the use of fossil fuels. Or perhaps you think that university tuition fees are too high and should be lowered or eliminated to allow greater accessibility to higher education. Or you heard that a friend has been killed by someone who was drinking and driving and you decide that stricter laws are needed. How would you go about trying to achieve your goals? Would you write a letter to the prime minister, your member of Parliament, your member of the provincial legislature, or your local municipal council? Join a group that is taking up your cause? Organize a protest demonstration? Vote for a party that appears sympathetic to your concerns? Run for public office? Sit back and hope that decision-makers in government make the right decision?

Understanding politics can help you to think about the issues that arise in politics, how to achieve what is best for yourself and your community, and how to recognize some of the obstacles that hinder the achievement of your goals.

CAREER TIES   Students often ask how taking political science courses or getting a degree in political science will help them to find employment and pursue a career. Political science would obviously be useful for anyone contemplating a career in politics, but most of those who study politics are not budding politicians. Nevertheless, about one-fifth of Canadians work for government or its agencies. Those who work for business or non-profit organizations often interact with government and governmental agencies. Knowledge of government policies and regulations is useful in almost every field of endeavour. And, in an increasingly globalized world, knowledge of foreign political systems and international organizations and agreements is very important for doing business. Taking political science courses or a degree in political science provides a good background to a wide variety of career choices.

Political science courses can also be helpful in developing general intellectual skills that are useful in one's personal development and eventual career. Such skills include developing the ability to communicate effectively, read carefully, do good research, and think critically. Political science contains a great diversity of perspectives and approaches. This diversity helps to make political science interesting, challenging, and useful in the development of general intellectual skills.

Canadian Political Science Association
www.cpsa-acsp.ca

Political Science Resources
www.psr.keele.ac.uk

Summary and Conclusion

Politics plays a vital role in our lives, our communities, and the world as a whole. Whether or not we are interested in politics, we are affected by political decisions. Because of disagreements about what political communities should do, political activity involves mobilizing people to advance their interests and values. As well, politics involves trying to resolve conflicts in order to achieve the co-operation needed to achieve collective goals.

Politics is a complex activity. To understand what goes on in political life and the policies that result from political activity, it is necessary to examine the interests that people and groups pursue, the ideas and values that affect their activities and decisions, the identities that are important to them, and the institutions, rules, and processes that shape political activities and lead to the actions and policies of government. As well, politics in any particular political community is affected by the economic, social, and historical context and the international system in which it operates (with government policies, in turn, affecting economic and social systems as well as individual behaviour). Of particular importance in determining the actions that governments take is the distribution of political power.

People often have a negative view of politics. When a job or a promotion goes to a person because of their contacts and family connections, or because they have flattered their employer, others often grumble that the decision was "political." Likewise, if a politician makes a decision based on trying to gain power or a personal benefit, win re-election, or reward supporters, rather than on a careful analysis of what is best for the country, the decision is often criticized for being "political." Politics, in other words, is often thought of as involving the selfish or competitive pursuit of one's own interests, without concern for others or the community as a whole.

Politics is also often viewed negatively because many people distrust governments and politicians. Governments are often criticized for being inefficient, wasteful, and prone to corruption. Some governments have supported or acquiesced in the domination and exploitation of the weak within the society that they govern. The laws and policies adopted by governments may reflect the interests and values of the dominant groups in society, resulting in the harassment, persecution, or neglect of the less powerful. As well, some governments have pursued the conquest, control, and exploitation of other countries. Because power and authority are easily abused, it is important to ensure that those in governing positions are held accountable for their actions and that excessive concentration of power is resisted. As the famous saying of nineteenth-century British historian Lord Acton warns, "Power tends to corrupt and absolute power corrupts absolutely."

There is, however, also a positive side to politics. Many people engage in political activity not only to advance their own interests or to pursue power for its own sake, but also with the hope of advancing the common good of the political community. Many governments have been able to work toward the common good by such measures as establishing peace and security within the political community, creating a fair and impartial system of justice, helping to develop their country's economy and infrastructure, and providing accessible education and health care. Governments can also promote the common good by regulating and checking the power wielded by various social and economic institutions, and thus help to protect and assist the weaker or disadvantaged members of society.

Political science, the systematic study of politics, has its roots in thousands of years of discussion and analysis about what is good for the communities we live in and how this good can best be achieved. Contemporary political science is building a systematic, theoretically based understanding of politics while continuing to examine fundamental questions about the values upon which governing should be based. Many political scientists also use their research to provide practical advice about the political processes and public policies that are for the common good.

Key Terms

Discussion Questions

1. What are the major political issues in your local, provincial, and national communities? What about in the global community? Do the most talked-about issues reflect the most serious problems that each of these communities faces? Are any important issues ignored?

2. Should we be concerned if political power is highly concentrated? Can we trust government to look after the common good?

3. Is it meaningful to talk about the common good in a diverse society?

4. How important is the study of politics? Is it an essential component of a good education?

5. Do all citizens have a responsibility to keep themselves informed about politics?

Further Reading

Aristotle. (1973). *Politics of Aristotle* (E. Barker, Trans.). New York: Oxford University Press.

Dahl, R.A., & Stinebrickner, B. (2002). *Modern political analysis* (6th ed.). Upper Saddle River, NJ: Prentice Hall.

Etzioni, A. (2004). *The common good*. Oxford: Polity Press.

Leftwich, A. (1983). *Redefining politics: People, resources and power*. London and New York: Methuen.

Marsh, D., & Stoker, G. (Eds.). (2010). *Theory and methods in political science* (3rd ed.). New York: Palgrave Macmillan.

Theodoulou, S.Z., & O'Brien, R. (Eds.). (1999). *Methods for political inquiry: The discipline, philosophy, and analysis of politics*. Upper Saddle River, NJ: Prentice Hall.

A number of novels provide interesting and provocative descriptions of politics in the past, present, and possible future:

Achebe, C. (1966). *A man of the people*. London: William Heinemann.

Allende, I. (1987). *Eva Luna*. New York: Bantam Press.

Anonymous. (1996). *Primary colors*. New York: Warner Books.

Atwood, M. (1985). *The handmaid's tale*. Toronto: McClelland & Stewart.

Kapuściński, R. (1989). *The emperor: Downfall of an autocrat* (W.R. Brand & K. Mroczkowska-Brand, Trans.). New York: Vintage International.

LeGuin, U.K. (1974). *The dispossessed*. New York: Avon Books.

Orwell, G. (1948). *1984*. New York: New American Library.

Warren, R.P. (1959). *All the king's men*. New York: Bantam.

Chapter 2

The Nation-State and Globalization

PHOTO ABOVE: After intense controversy, the Spanish legislature in 2006 recognized the Catalan nationality and gave expanded self-governing powers to the region of Catalonia.

1. explain the difference between a nation and a state
2. discuss the nature of the modern state
3. explain the nature and significance of nationalism

4. examine the meaning of citizenship
5. outline the nature and significance of globalization

On June 18, 2006, 74 percent of Catalans voting in a binding referendum supported the adoption of a revised Statute of Autonomy of Catalonia (a region of northeastern Spain with 7.2 million people who have a distinct language, history, and culture). The revised statute recognized the Catalan nationality and expanded the self-governing powers of Catalonia's government. Recognizing this distinct nationality came after an intense debate within Spain and a close vote in the Spanish legislature.

A few days later, Canadian Prime Minister Stephen Harper and his Cabinet attended the *Fête Nationale* celebrations in Quebec City. When reporters asked Harper if he would describe Quebec as a nation, he evaded the question, responding that "if the National Assembly [the Quebec legislature] wants to make such a declaration, that's its right." However, in December 2006, Harper introduced a motion that the Canadian House of Commons "recognize that the Québécois form a nation within a united Canada." Although the motion, which passed by a 266–16 margin, has no legal significance, it stirred up considerable controversy. Michael Chong resigned from the Cabinet, stating that he believed that Canada is one nation—a view widely shared by English-speaking Canadians. Other Cabinet ministers differed on the meaning of recognizing the Québécois as a nation: did it refer only to French-speaking Quebecers, most of whom share a common culture and ancestry, or did it refer to all residents of Quebec? Harper did little to clarify the meaning of the motion by stating that the Québécois are a nation "bound together by a common language, culture, and history" and that "recognition of Quebec as a nation is part of the Canadian identity" (*Globe and Mail Online*, December 19, 2006).

In June 2010, Spain's constitutional court struck down provisions of the Autonomy Statute that gave preferential status to the Catalan language and declared that there was no legal basis to recognize Catalonia as a nation. In response, more than one million Catalans marched in protest in Barcelona chanting the slogan: "We are a nation."

Disputes about whether Catalonia and Quebec are nations are not simply about the extent to which these regions are different than other parts of their countries in history, language, and culture. Rather, the term *nation* is a highly charged political term because the major form of political community in the modern world is the nation-state. Declaring a region or a group within a country to be a nation is viewed by some as undermining efforts to build a strong national identity in the country as a whole and leading eventually to the breakup of the country. Others argue that recognition that countries like Canada and Spain contain different nations that should have considerable self-governing powers enhances the stability of those countries and the legitimacy of the state.

A basic political question is whether the world should be divided into self-governing countries, each based upon a people that consider themselves a nation. Or can stable and well-governed countries be built on the recognition and political accommodation of different nations?

We begin this chapter by examining the nature of the modern state. Then we look at the concept of nation, which is often viewed as the basis of the modern state, along with the related topics of nationalism, citizenship, and political identity. Finally, we discuss the processes of globalization, which many observers believe is eroding the significance of nation-states.

THE STATE

STATE An independent, self-governing political community whose governing institutions have the capability to make rules that are binding on the population residing within a particular territory.

A **state** is an independent, self-governing political community whose governing institutions have the capability to make rules that are binding on the population residing within a particular territory.[1] In Max Weber's classic definition, the state successfully claims "the monopoly of legitimate use of physical force within a given territory" (Weber, 1970, p. 78).

The state can be viewed as a more extensive and permanent expression of the political community than the **government**, the set of institutions that makes decisions and oversees their implementation on behalf of the state for a particular period of time (Heywood, 2002).[2] The Canadian state, for example, includes not only the Canadian government and the governments of the provinces and territories, but also, the military and police forces, the employees of the various levels of government, and state-owned corporations (termed Crown corporations in Canada). Some state institutions (such as the courts and the Bank of Canada) are autonomous in the sense of being free of direct government control.

GOVERNMENT The set of institutions that makes decisions and oversees their implementation on behalf of the state for a particular period of time.

Overall, states play a major role in modern societies. In addition to their traditional functions of providing for law, order, and security, modern states are very active in activities such as regulating business activity; fostering economic development; stabilizing the economy; providing health, education, and social services to the public; assisting the disadvantaged; and protecting the environment. As Table 2-1 indicates, government spending (including transfers to individuals, businesses, and other organizations) accounts for a substantial proportion of a country's income. Generally, government spending as a proportion of the total economy is higher in the richer countries than in the poorer countries, although some exceptions to that pattern exist.

Sovereignty and the State

SOVEREIGNTY The principle that states are the highest authority for their population and territory and are not subject to any external authority.

States are often described as being sovereign. The **sovereignty** of states has two basic related dimensions. First, states claim to be the highest authority for their population and their territory. Second, states are not subject to any external authority, but rather are able to act independently in the world. They may make agreements with other states for various purposes, but they remain sovereign because they can cancel those agreements.

Although some forms of political organization resembling the state have existed in different times and places, the modern state is generally viewed as

---

[1] The term *state* as used in political science is often misunderstood because regional political units within some countries (including the United States, Australia, and India) are called states.

[2] The term *government* refers, in the Canadian context, particularly to the prime minister and Cabinet at the national level, although the public service that works under their direction could also be considered part of the Canadian government.

COUNTRY	GOVERNMENT EXPENDITURE AS % OF GDP	COUNTRY	GOVERNMENT EXPENDITURE AS % OF GDP
Cuba	68.2	United States	37.4
Sweden	52.5	Japan	36.0
France	52.3	Nigeria	34.3
Denmark	51.0	Australia	34.2
Hungary	49.7	Russia	33.4
Belgium	48.3	Switzerland	32.2
Italy	47.9	Egypt	29.8
Netherlands	45.3	South Korea	28.9
Germany	44.2	Argentina	28.5
United Kingdom	44.0	South Africa	27.8
Czech Republic	42.6	Turkey	23.9
Poland	42.1	Mexico	22.2
Norway	40.9	China	19.9
Brazil	40.7	Pakistan	19.3
New Zealand	40.3	Indonesia	19.1
Canada	39.1	Chile	18.6
Spain	38.1	Bangladesh	14.3

TABLE 2-1

TOTAL GOVERNMENT SPENDING IN SELECTED COUNTRIES

Notes: *GDP* is gross domestic product. *Government expenditure* includes direct government spending and transfers to individuals.

SOURCE: *Compiled from the* 2010 Index of Economic Freedom *by The Heritage Foundation, 2010; retrieved from www.heritage.org/research/features/index.*

developing in Europe over the past several centuries and spreading to other parts of the world in more recent times. In particular, as the feudal system declined in Europe, various monarchs strove to establish themselves as the highest authority in the territory that they controlled by limiting the authority of lords and nobles. Similarly, various rulers challenged the authority of the Catholic Church. The treaties comprising the Peace of Westphalia (1648), which ended the devastating Thirty Years War (based, in part, on conflicts between Protestants and Catholics), established the idea that states and their rulers were the supreme authority in their territory. Devastating civil wars led to the idea (expressed, for example, by Thomas Hobbes, as discussed in Chapter 3) that a single absolute power with the means of coercion was needed to maintain order.

The development of bodies (such as Parliament) that represent different parts of the country and important elements of the population provided rulers with a means to levy and collect the taxes needed to wage wars and to develop an administrative structure (McGovern, 2007). The development of the capitalist economic system and the Industrial Revolution also were important in the development of the modern state. Costly infrastructure (such as canals, roads, railways, and ports) needed to be built by or with the financial support of the state. Markets needed to be created by removing internal barriers to trade within a country. A common language, an educational system, and an extensive array of laws governing business activities were needed to service the needs of business and industry.

Prior to the development of the modern state, the territories controlled by monarchs were often viewed as their own property able to be disposed of as they saw fit. Territory sometimes passed from one set of rulers to another as a result of royal marriages as well as through conquest. Although the term *sovereign* referred to a monarch with absolute authority, legislatures and the people challenged the absolute power claimed by monarchs. In Britain, the Glorious Revolution (1688) resulted in Parliament's removal and replacement of a monarch and established the idea that Parliament is the supreme authority. The leaders of the French Revolution (1789) proclaimed that sovereignty rested with the people. Regardless of whether sovereignty is viewed as resting in the hands of a single individual (such as a monarch), Parliament, the constitution, the people as a whole, or some combination of these, the modern state itself is viewed as sovereign. More generally, the idea developed that the state is an impersonal authority separate from particular individuals and from society—that is, "an independent structure of laws and institutions which rulers are trusted to administer on behalf of the community" (McGovern, 2007, p. 23).

Although the state is sometimes depicted as a powerful, unified body with a particular purpose, the various institutions that make up a state do not necessarily work co-operatively in pursuit of a common interest or goal. This is particularly the case in federal political systems such as Canada's where the national and provincial governments each have their own important legislative (law-making) powers entrenched in the constitution and substantial financial and administrative capabilities to implement their own policies.

The concept of state sovereignty is particularly important when we look at the relationship among states. A central principle of international law is that the states of the world are the legal equals of one another, and thus states should not interfere in the affairs of other states unless invited to do so. In other words, states are expected to respect each other's sovereignty. States, whether large or small, powerful or weak, rich or poor, are viewed as being self-governing.

TODAY'S STATES   Most of the contemporary world's people and land mass (and some of the adjoining ocean) are divided among the individual states of the world. The empires that ruled over conquered territories and peoples have been dissolved. However, some former colonies, such as French Polynesia, New Caledonia, Bermuda, Puerto Rico, and Greenland, have not gained full independence but instead have varying degrees of self-government or are considered part of the former imperial power. As well, some states dominate areas whose people claim the right to be self-governing states; examples include Tibet (part of China) and the Chechen Republic (whose independence drive was suppressed by Russia).

Overall, the number of sovereign states has increased substantially. As of 2010, 192 states are members of the United Nations (see Figure 2-1), ranging

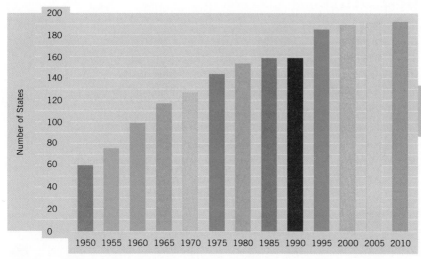

FIGURE 2-1

THE INCREASING NUMBER OF SOVEREIGN STATES: MEMBERSHIP IN THE UNITED NATIONS

Note: Almost all recognized sovereign states are members of the United Nations.

SOURCE: United Nations, Growth in UN Membership. Data retrieved from www.un.org/en/members/growth.shtml. Reproduced with permission.

from China with a population estimated at more than 1.3 billion to the island of Tuvalu with a population of about 12 000 people.

Civil wars, extreme corruption, uncontrolled violence, and economic collapse have occasionally shattered states, resulting in no effective governing authority. In these countries, often referred to as **failed states**, governments cannot enforce laws, maintain order, protect the lives of citizens, or provide basic services (see Box 2-1, Somalia: A Failed State). A number of countries are in the process of developing states, but ones where the central government has a limited capacity and tribal or other groups have greater importance and legitimacy than the state itself.

In addition, control of some territory is contested or its future is uncertain. For example, Israel occupies some of the territories that it captured in wars with neighbouring countries, India and Pakistan have clashed over control of Kashmir for decades, and the People's Republic of China (mainland China) claims that the island of Taiwan (which refers to itself as the Republic of China) is an integral part of China. As well, the independence of some territories, including South Ossetia (from Georgia) and Kosovo (from Serbia), is disputed.

Although there is widespread acceptance of the principle that states are sovereign, sometimes weaker countries have found their sovereignty limited because of the great disparities in power among the states of the world. The United States, for example, has a long history of involving itself in the affairs of Caribbean and Latin American countries, including invading and overthrowing the governments of Grenada (1983) and Panama (1989). The former Soviet Union exercised tight control over the countries of Eastern Europe.

At times, various elements of the international community have intervened in sovereign states to protect human rights. For example, the North Atlantic

FAILED STATE A state that is unable to enforce laws, maintain order, protect the lives of citizens, or provide basic services.

The Failed States Index
www.foreignpolicy.com/articles/2010/06/21/the_failed_states_index_2010

BOX 2-1

Somalia: A Failed State

Somalia, in East Africa, became an independent country in 1960 following the merger of a British protectorate and a United Nations trust territory controlled by Italy. After President Sharmarke was assassinated in 1969, General Siad Barre took power in a coup and governed Somalia until ousted by leaders of rival clans in 1991. With clan leaders unable to set aside their differences, Somalia has lacked an effective central government since 1991. Somaliland in the northwest declared itself independent in 1991 and Puntland in the northeast declared itself autonomous in 1998. The rest of the country became a lawless territory with the means of coercion held by warlords, clans, militias, and a variety of armed gangs.

A U.S.-led, United Nations–sanctioned international peacekeeping mission in 1992 ended after two Black Hawk helicopters were shot down and news coverage showed a dead American being dragged through the streets of the capital. Many attempts have been made to establish a central government in Somalia. The most recent effort saw the establishment of a United Nations–backed Transitional Federal Government in 2004. However, this government was pushed out of most of the country by the loosely organized Council of Islamic Courts. Although the Transitional Government was able to regain some control with support from Ethiopian troops in 2006, the more militant Islamic al-Shabab (with connections to al-Qaeda) has since taken control of much of southern Somalia. In 2009, the Transitional Government selected Omar Sharmarke (a dual Canadian–Somali citizen who studied political science at Carleton University and is the son of the assassinated president) as prime minister. However, as of mid 2010 this government controlled only a small area within the capital of Mogadishu.

Although Somalia has managed to function without an effective government since 1991, citizens have lived in constant fear of violence and banditry. Pirates have had a safe base from which to attack international shipping. Al-Shabab has instituted an extremely harsh form of justice, including (according to Amnesty International) the stoning to death for adultery of a 15-year-old girl who was raped.

Treaty Organization (NATO), which includes Canada, bombed Serbia (then known as Yugoslavia) in 1999 to end Serb mistreatment of ethnic Albanians in the province of Kosovo. Such actions are often controversial because of differences of opinion about whether the actions are justified and whether they will have the desired effects. For example, Serbs argued that their actions in Kosovo, which resulted in large numbers of Albanians fleeing the country in fear for their lives, were taken to deal with the terrorist activities of Albanian separatists.

In 2001, the Canadian-sponsored International Commission on Intervention and State Sovereignty (ICISS) concluded that in certain circumstances the responsibility to protect the people of a country justified international action, particularly through the Security Council of the United Nations, despite the principle of state sovereignty:

> *State sovereignty implies responsibility, and the primary responsibility for the protection of its people lies with the state itself. Where a population*

◄ With no effective government to maintain order, militants with guns ride freely through Mogadishu, the capital of the failed African state of Somalia.

is suffering serious harm, as a result of internal war, insurgency, repression or state failure, and the state in question is unwilling or unable to halt or avert it, the principle of non-intervention yields to the international responsibility to protect. (ICISS, 2001, p. xi)

At the UN World Summit in 2005 it was agreed (and reaffirmed by the UN Security Council in 2006) that there is a collective international responsibility to protect if genocide, war crimes, ethnic cleansing, and crimes against humanity are involved. However, many non-Western countries are concerned that military intervention could be used by Western countries to promote their own interests. But, to date, the UN Security Council has not authorized any interventions despite evidence that Sudan was not protecting the people of the Darfur region of the country. This raises a controversial question about whether intervention by individual states or groups of states is justified when the UN Security Council fails to authorize intervention.

THE NATION-STATE

The basis for dividing the world into about two hundred states is that each state claims to represent a particular nation. By having its own state, a nation can be self-governing rather than being controlled by a foreign power. Thus modern states are often referred to as **nation-states**, sovereign states based on people living in a country who share a sense of being a member of a particular nation. In reality, however, many states are not based on a single nation.

NATION-STATE A sovereign state based on people living in a country who share a sense of being a member of a particular nation.

Nation

The term *nation* is often confused with that of the *state*, but the two terms have different meanings. A **nation** is a group of people who have a sense of common identity and who typically believe they should be self-governing within their homeland (Suny, 2006).[3] To be self-governing does not necessarily mean that members of the nation believe they should have their own sovereign state. Self-government can involve a degree of autonomy within a country. For example, even though a majority of Quebecers view themselves as members of a distinct nation, many prefer to have a strong Quebec government within Canada rather than a fully sovereign independent Quebec.

How does a sense of national identity develop among a large group of people who do not know each other? A national identity can be based on people located in a particular territory who share common characteristics such as ethnicity[4] (that is, a belief in a common ancestry), language, culture, and religion. There are some countries (for example, Japan, Norway, Iceland, and Bangladesh) in which most people have the same ethnicity, language, culture, and religion. However, most countries feature a diverse population, to varying extents.

A feeling of belonging to a nation can also develop over time from the shared experiences of living in a particular region or country and from sharing the values, particularly the basic political values, common to the people of that area (sometimes referred to as a "civic nation"). States often try to promote this sense of national identity among their citizens through their educational systems, national holidays, and the promotion of a national culture. It can also develop through feelings of patriotism that are often associated with war or international sporting events such as the Olympics. It may be difficult, however, to create a strong, inclusive national identity in countries with deep social divisions based on characteristics such as ethnicity, language, or

---

[3] A distinction is sometimes made between a nation in a sociological sense (that is, a people having shared characteristics and culture) and a nation in a political sense of a people in a geographical area that has or wants self-government or their own sovereign state. See, for example, Trudeau (1993).

[4] The terms *ethnic group* and *ethnicity* are rather vague. Although an ethnic group is often defined as a group with common ancestry ("blood"), most ethnic groups are composed of people who have different ancestries, given the intermingling of peoples in most parts of the world. Beyond a belief in having a common ancestry, ethnic groups are often characterized as sharing such features as a common language, religion, culture, and history (Dowty, 2005). In this usage, an ethnic group is similar to a nation except that a nation, as we have defined it, includes the political objective of self-government, which an ethnic group does not necessarily seek. For example, Canadians of Polish, Chinese, and Greek ancestry may view themselves as members of distinct ethnic groups, but do not consider themselves members of distinct nations within Canada.

religion, particularly if those divisions are connected to a history of discrimination, persecution, or inequality among groups located in different regions.

Overall, whether a result of ethnic, racial, linguistic, religious, cultural, historic, or regional differences, there are many countries where substantial numbers of people view themselves as having a different national identity than their fellow citizens. Even in Western Europe, where the idea of the nation-state originated, there are countries (for example, Belgium, Spain, Switzerland, and the United Kingdom) that could be considered **binational or multinational states**. Other European countries, while continuing to have a dominant nationality, have become more diverse as a result of immigration from countries that have different cultures and religions.

BINATIONAL AND MULTINATIONAL STATES States whose populations are composed of two or more nations.

Because there are different bases for a sense of national identity (that sometimes change over time) and because there are important implications for the governing of a country, the question of whether a country is a nation-state can be the subject of serious political controversy, as discussed in Box 2-2, Is Canada a Nation-State?

The Development of National Identities

Until modern times, people tended to view themselves mainly in terms of their clan, tribe, or local community. Except in small city-states, most people felt little connection to those who ruled their territory. In many parts of the world, clan, tribal, and local or regional identities continue to be stronger than broader national identities.

Although elements of national identity can be found before modern times, historians generally view the French Revolution of 1789 as sparking the development of a sense of nationhood among the general public. The French Revolution was based on the idea that the state is an instrument of the people (that is, the nation), with the people having the right to overthrow rulers who do not reflect the will of the people. The subsequent Napoleonic Wars helped to create a sense of unity and pride in the French nation and its citizen army (which replaced reliance on foreign mercenaries). In reaction to the French conquest of much of continental Europe, other European peoples developed their own sense of national identity.

To some extent, the process of developing a national identity has involved building upon existing ethnic identities and cultures. However, states have often made deliberate efforts to replace local and regional dialects, cultures, and identities with a national culture, language, and identity. National myths have been created and histories written to create national heroes and support claims that the state was built upon a long-standing nation. For example, in the latter part of the nineteenth century the government of France created a French identity in the rural areas of the country by instilling patriotism through the educational system and encouraging the use of Parisian French throughout the country instead of the very distinct dialects that were spoken in various parts

BOX 2-2

Is Canada a Nation-State?

Canada was largely built on the foundations laid by three peoples: Aboriginals (who are themselves very diverse in language and culture), the French colonists of the seventeenth and eighteenth centuries, and persons of English, Scottish, Welsh, and Irish ancestry, many of whom came to Canada from the United States after the American War of Independence. Added to this diverse foundation are large numbers of persons from various countries in Europe, Asia, Africa, and Latin America, particularly since the latter part of the nineteenth century. Because of Canada's lingering ties to Britain, a sense of Canadian identity was slow to develop. Indeed, until a few decades ago, Canada lacked specifically Canadian symbols of identity such as a flag, national anthem, or even citizenship.

Most English-speaking Canadians view Canada as a nation-state, based on each resident of Canada having the same rights. With more than one-third of Canada's population tracing their ancestry to neither the British Isles nor France, Canadian governments since the early 1970s have promoted the view that Canada is a multicultural nation (that is, one nation composed of a variety of different cultural groupings) with two official languages. However, many French Quebecers view Quebec as a distinct nation with a substantial minority favouring the establishment of an independent Quebec nation-state. Aboriginal Canadians resent the privileging of those of British and French ancestry in such ideas as "two founding peoples" and "two

nations." Instead, many Aboriginals view Canada as ideally being a partnership between Aboriginal First Nations and the descendants of subsequent settlers.

Thus, Canada can be considered a nation-state, a multicultural nation-state, a nation-state with one or more minority nationalities, a binational state, or a multinational state, depending on one's perspective. The complexity of the concept of *nation* is illustrated by the fact that many Quebecers view themselves as both Québécois and Canadian without necessarily seeing one national identity as subordinate to the other.

The question of whether Canada is a nation-state is not only a definitional argument, but also a political dispute of potentially great significance. If, for example, Quebecers are officially recognized as members of a distinct nation, this suggests that the Quebec government may need greater powers to act on behalf of the Quebec nation. Proposals in the 1980s and 1990s that the Canadian constitution recognize Quebec as a distinct society met with vigorous opposition from those who view Canada as one nation with all provincial governments having the same powers. Likewise, recognition of Aboriginal nations can lead to expectations that Aboriginal governments should be treated as equals to other governments in Canada, that Aboriginals be guaranteed representation in Parliament and the Supreme Court of Canada, and that Aboriginals be subject to their own laws.

of France (Weber, 1976). In the United States, where persons from a variety of countries settled, American governments devoted considerable effort to the creation of a common sense of American identity, although blacks and Native Americans were largely excluded from the American "melting pot." Creating a national identity has often involved trying to persuade different groups to adopt the culture, language, and values of the dominant group.

Instead of encouraging or persuading different ethnic, cultural, and linguistic groups to give up their distinctiveness and assimilate into the dominant

In recent decades, Canada's multicultural policy has encouraged persons of different cultures to retain their culture and traditions. Pictured here is a performer at Toronto's Caribana festival, which is enjoyed by as many as one million people each year.

group, Canada and a number of other countries in recent times have adopted a policy of **multiculturalism**. This involves recognizing and respecting different cultures and providing encouragement and support for different groups to retain their cultures and traditions.

Advocates of multiculturalism view diversity as desirable and argue that tolerating and accommodating differences strengthens national unity. Critics argue that multiculturalism can conflict with individual rights (for example, by protecting cultural traditions that discriminate against women) and interferes with the integration of immigrants into society. Multiculturalism has been particularly controversial in a number of European countries where the immigration of substantial numbers of Muslims has been viewed by some as a threat to the values and culture of the society (see Box 2-3, Multiculturalism and the Niqab). For example, Geert Wilders, the popular leader of the Party for Freedom in the Netherlands, has called for a ban on the immigration of persons from "non-Western" countries, has been strongly critical of Islam, and has proposed that Muslims be paid to leave the country. His party increased its support from 5.9 percent in 2006 to a close third-place finish with 15.5 percent of the vote in the country's 2010 election.

MULTICULTURALISM The idea that different cultures within a country should be recognized and respected and provided with encouragement and support to help them retain their cultures and traditions.

Difficulties in Creating Nation-States

In the nineteenth century, the concept of popular sovereignty (that the people should be able to govern themselves) became transformed in Europe into the idea that nations defined in cultural terms should be self-governing. After World War I, the principle of **national self-determination** (that nations should be able to choose to be self-governing) was applied to the establishment of

NATIONAL SELF-DETERMINATION The idea that nations should have the right to determine their political status, including choosing to have their own sovereign state.

Multiculturalism and the Niqab

Multiculturalism has often been viewed positively as enriching a country with the cuisine, music, dance, dress, and customs of peoples from around the world. However, there has been increasing criticism of multiculturalism policy by those who argue that it interferes with the integration of immigrants into society.

Although only a very small number of Muslim women in North America and Europe wear a niqab (face covering), the Netherlands and Belgium have made covering one's face in public illegal and, while this text was being written, France's National Assembly passed similar legislation. In Quebec, a woman was expelled from a publicly funded French-language class for covering her face. Subsequently, in March 2010, the Quebec government introduced a bill that would prevent any person from obtaining or delivering government services while covering his or her face.

Those who support banning the niqab in public places argue that this garment symbolizes the subservience of women and undermines contemporary values of gender equality. Opponents of the ban view it as a means to single out Muslims for discrimination, a threat to multiculturalism, and an unnecessary restriction on rights and freedoms.

several new states in central and eastern Europe out of the empires that had collapsed. It was recognized, however, that it would be unrealistic to establish states strictly on the basis of the location of national cultures. Thus, attempts were made (generally unsuccessfully) to persuade new states to protect minority nationalities that resided in their territory (Harty & Murphy, 2005). The United Nations International Covenant on Economic, Social, and Cultural Rights, which came into force in 1976, establishes that "all peoples have the right to self-determination," which involves the right to "freely determine their political status and freely pursue their economic, social, and cultural development."

The idea of dividing the world into states based on where people with a particular national identity reside is hard to achieve. Persons sharing such an identity often do not live in well-defined geographical areas. In many parts of Eastern Europe and the Balkans, for example, different nationalities are so highly interspersed that it would be very difficult to draw boundaries that would include each nationality within its own state.

The attempt to create a single national identity within a diverse country has not been very successful in many parts of the world. The countries of Africa, for example, have retained the boundaries that resulted from conquest by various European empires. These political boundaries generally bear little relationship to the geographical location of peoples, languages, cultures, and religions. In other words, the boundaries are artificial, often combining very dissimilar peoples into the same country. Despite efforts by the leaders of independence movements and post-independence governments to create new national political identities, severe tensions often exist among peoples sharing the same country. This has helped to fuel the wars that have plagued a number of African countries.

Is the Nation-State the Most Desirable Form of Political Community?

In a nation-state, people have a bond with each other, and thus are more likely to feel a commitment to advancing the good of the political community. A sense of trust in government and other institutions may be easier to develop. Political compromises that are acceptable to different social groups may be easier to achieve because an appeal can be made to a common national interest (Keating, 1996). In a nation-state, rule is by members of the nation who can claim to have the good of the nation at heart and to share the basic values of the other members of the nation. The legitimacy of the state and governing authorities is less likely to be questioned when the state is based on people who consider themselves part of a common nation. A stable democratic system may be more likely to be sustained in a nation-state. Democratic dialogue is facilitated by having a common language, culture, and basic political values. Deep divisions and the lack of a common sense of nationhood can hinder efforts to develop or maintain democracy. Nevertheless, some democratic countries such as Canada and Spain that might be considered binational or multinational have survived and flourished despite occasional "national unity" crises and the presence of separatist movements.

The development of separatist movements seeking to create a new nation-state out of a region of an existing state raises questions about whether it is desirable that nations with small populations and located in small geographical areas have their own self-governing state. Certainly, there are advantages to larger states in terms of having large internal markets, spreading the costs of government services over a large population, and being able to defend the country militarily. However, some small states such as Singapore and Luxembourg have been successful economically and able to maintain their sovereignty. The development of economic agreements and military alliances composed of a number of countries has helped to offset some of the problems that might otherwise face small nation-states. Nevertheless, some nations are so small and lacking in economic capabilities (such as the many Aboriginal First Nations in Canada) that establishing a sovereign state for each group that considers itself a nation is unrealistic.

NATIONALISM

Nationalism is based on the view that the nation-state is the best form of political community and that a nation should have its own self-governing state. Nationalists seek to promote the interests, culture, and values of their

NATIONALISM The idea that the nation-state is the best form of political community and that a nation should have its own self-governing state.

▶ Nationalism continues to be a powerful force in the modern world. For instance, Basque nationalists, whose homeland is divided by the international border between France and Spain, have resisted outside domination since the tenth century. Basque nationalists have sought to create an independent state through both conventional political action and terrorism.

Internet Modern History Sourcebook: Nationalism
www.fordham.edu/halsall/mod/modsbook17.html

The Nationalism Project
www.nationalismproject.org

particular nation, and believe that people's loyalty to their nation should take precedence over their other loyalties, such as to their family, tribe, clan, local community, or religion.

Nationalism has been one of the most influential political ideas of modern times. Nationalism played a crucial role in the creation of new nation-states such as Germany and Italy in the second half of the nineteenth century and Poland and Ukraine in the twentieth century. The struggle of various peoples to free themselves from exploitative foreign rule in the name of "national liberation" led to the breakup of powerful empires. Nationalism continues to inspire a variety of movements that have arisen in opposition to existing states among those seeking to create their own independent state. For example, Basque nationalists seek to create an independent Basque state in areas of Spain and France that they consider their homeland. Nationalism can also take the form of trying to strengthen and unify an existing state by promoting a common culture, limiting foreign influences, and protecting domestic ownership and control of the economy. For example, Canadian nationalists have advocated limiting American economic and cultural influence through such measures as restricting foreign ownership of business and requiring that the broadcast media carry considerable Canadian content.

Types of Nationalism

A distinction is often made between ethnic nationalism and civic nationalism. **Ethnic nationalism** views common ancestry along with the cultural traditions and language associated with a particular ethnic group as the basis for a nation-state. By attempting to base a state on a particular ethnic group, ethnic nationalism can result in harassment, discrimination, and the oppression of those who do not share the characteristics of the dominant group. In some cases, as in the former

ETHNIC NATIONALISM
Nationalism based on common ancestry along with the cultural traditions and language associated with a particular ethnic group.

Yugoslavia and Rwanda in the 1990s, it can lead to "ethnic cleansing," the forcible removal and even the massacre of people whose ethnicity differs from that of the dominant ethnic group. Ethnic nationalism can also result in war if attempts are made to seize areas in other countries where members of the ethnic group live or areas that are considered the traditional homeland of the ethnic group.

Civic nationalism views shared political values and political history as the basis of a nation-state. Civic nationalism tends to be more inclusive than ethnic nationalism as it treats all permanent residents of a state as equal citizens regardless of their characteristics. Civic nationalists often want to create a sense of nationhood among its citizens by encouraging the adoption of a common set of political values and beliefs and promoting loyalty to the nation-state through patriotic rituals.

In practice, it is often difficult to separate the two types of nationalism. For example, contemporary Quebec nationalists often claim that their nationalism includes all residents of Quebec and is therefore civic nationalism. However, occasional comments by some prominent Quebec nationalists implying that only those descended from the original French settlers are "true" Quebecers suggests that there is also an element of ethnic nationalism.

CIVIC NATIONALISM
Nationalism based on the shared political values and political history of those who are citizens of a country.

Evaluating Nationalism

Nationalism can be viewed positively in terms of fostering the establishment and maintenance of self-governing nation-states. Throughout Africa, Asia, and Latin America, nationalist ideas encouraged people to challenge domination and exploitation by Europe's imperial powers. Contemporary nationalists suggest that nationalism can be useful in maintaining diversity in the world against the pressures for a homogeneous American or Western-dominated world. As well, nationalism may encourage the development of a sense of solidarity with others beyond one's family and local community, thus providing legitimacy for the state.

On the negative side, nationalism has been an important cause of many wars and conflicts. Although some new nation-states have been created in a peaceful manner (for example, Czechoslovakia split peacefully into the Czech Republic and Slovakia in 1993), attempts to create new nation-states have frequently involved violent conflicts.

Nationalism has often fostered a sense of superiority that can lead to efforts to dominate weaker countries and peoples. Indeed, the sense of superiority of one's nation has been used to justify the building of empires. The European powers that dominated and exploited most of the world justified their actions by claiming that they were bringing their "civilized" values to what they considered to be "primitive" or "backward" peoples. Through the doctrine of *terra nullius* (land belonging to no one), European settlers tried to legitimate their occupation of the Americas, Australia, New Zealand, and other areas inhabited by indigenous peoples.

As well, nationalism may encourage uniformity within a country and make it less cosmopolitan and vibrant. An exclusive focus on the interests of the nation can provide a justification for the authoritarian (non-democratic) rule of those who claim to speak on behalf of the nation. Nationalism has often been used to justify the trampling of the rights of minority groups and critical individuals. Extreme forms of nationalism can also encourage xenophobia, fear or hatred of other nationalities.

Although nationalism can encourage people to consider the common good of their own political community, it does not encourage people to think of the good of humanity as a whole.

CITIZENSHIP

CITIZENSHIP The idea that a country's permanent residents are full members of the political community with certain duties and rights.

Connected to the development of the modern nation-state is the idea of **citizenship**—that a country's permanent residents are full members of the political community with certain duties and rights. A citizen is not only subject to the laws passed by the governing institutions of that state, but also shares in the power of the sovereign state (Rousseau, 1762/1968).

Those who are born in a particular country with at least one parent who is a citizen are usually considered citizens automatically. Citizenship also usually derives from having at least one parent who is a citizen even if a person was not born in the country. In many countries the spouse of a citizen is granted citizenship (although in some countries this depends on gender). Most countries have a naturalization process by which those resident in a country for a period of time and able to demonstrate knowledge of the country and its official language can become citizens upon taking an oath of allegiance.[5] A number of countries (including Germany, Russia, China, and Israel) have special procedures to facilitate the granting of citizenship to those having an ethnic relationship to the country. Although we often think of citizenship as involving an exclusive loyalty to one country, many persons are citizens of two (or more) countries (as discussed in Box 2-4, Who Is a Citizen?).

Citizenship is often discussed in terms of the rights for individuals. T.H. Marshall (1950) portrayed the concept of citizenship rights as expanding, often as a result of considerable political struggle, from civil rights (such as freedom of speech and religion) to political rights (such as the right to vote and hold elected office) to social rights (such as the right to free education, health care, and employment).[6]

---

[5] Some countries, including Saudi Arabia, Kuwait, and the Gulf States, make it virtually impossible for foreigners (and their children) to obtain citizenship. This has resulted in only a minority of residents having citizenship and the majority of workers having no rights.

[6] In practice, civil and social rights are often provided to all permanent residents of a country, not just to those who are citizens. The provision of a variety of government services to the large number of illegal immigrants (and their children) who form an important part of the labour force has become a contentious issue in the United States.

BOX 2-4
Who Is a Citizen?

As Israeli planes bombarded Hezbollah strongholds in Lebanon in July 2006, the Canadian government attempted to bring its citizens to safety in Canada. To the surprise of many, this potentially involved not just a relatively small number of tourists and business travellers, but up to fifty thousand persons, many of whom had dual Lebanese and Canadian citizenship and Canadian passports. Some argued that the Canadian government should not help persons who had, in some cases, never set foot in Canada or paid Canadian taxes (although most of those evacuated at government expense were tourists or business travellers). Others argued that treating those with dual citizenship differently than other Canadians was discriminatory and would create two classes of citizens.

A more fundamental question is whether individuals should be required to have citizenship status in only one country or whether dual citizenship (as allowed by Canada's Citizenship Act, 1977) is an appropriate response to increased migration and the reality of globalization. Some countries allow dual or multiple citizenships while others do not.

At times, questions of conflicting loyalties have arisen when governmental or military leaders have retained dual citizenship. For example, when Michaëlle Jean (who came to Canada from Haiti as a child) was appointed as Canada's governor general in 2005, controversy erupted when it was revealed that she was a citizen of both France and Canada. Although France requires that foreign leaders give up their French citizenship, this was not required because the French government considered Jean's position to be ceremonial. Nevertheless, to avoid controversy within Canada, Jean voluntarily gave up her French citizenship. Subsequently, controversy arose when Stéphane Dion was elected as Liberal party leader in 2006 while retaining French citizenship based on his mother's nationality. In contrast, little notice was taken of Liberal leader (and, briefly, prime minister in 1984) John Turner's British citizenship. In the United States, California Governor Arnold Schwarzenegger has both Austrian and U.S. citizenship. The Australian Constitution prohibits those holding a foreign citizenship from being a member of Parliament.

Does citizenship involve only individual rights or does it (as Marshall suggested) also involve obligations to the political community? For example, citizens may be expected to defend their country in times of war. Governments have used this argument to justify compulsory military service and to draft men (and likely women in the future) to fight in wars, even those that are not strictly defensive in nature. As well, since citizenship is associated with being a member of the political community, some have argued that citizens have an obligation to become informed participants in politics. For example, several countries (including Australia and Italy) require that all citizens vote in elections and penalize those who do not. Indeed, it has been suggested that citizens should put aside their personal interests and act in political life for the common good of their country (Pierson, 1996).

The concept of citizenship is generally based on the view that all citizens should be equal members of the political community regardless of social status, ethnicity, gender, wealth, or other characteristics. In the past, citizenship was limited to a small segment of the population, such as males, property owners, and those born in the country. The struggles for equal political rights in the past century and a half have been successful in most countries in expanding citizenship to include most of the population.

There has been increasing discussion about whether members of certain groups should have different citizenship rights because of their particular circumstances (termed "differentiated citizenship") such as historic rights, a legacy of oppression and discrimination, or exclusion of the group from the mainstream of society. For example, many Aboriginal First Nations in Canada have various rights established by treaties and other agreements between Aboriginal chiefs and the British Crown or the Canadian government, rights that are now recognized in the Canadian Constitution.

Some have argued that the special rights of Aboriginals eventually should be extinguished so that they can be treated in the same manner as other Canadians (as was proposed by the Canadian government in 1969). Others have argued that Aboriginals should be self-governing nations within Canada. This could imply a form of dual citizenship in which Aboriginals are both citizens of their Aboriginal nation and citizens of Canada (Harty & Murphy, 2005). Political scientist Alan Cairns (2000) has tried to find a middle ground, termed "citizens plus," in which Aboriginal differences are recognized, but not at the expense of a strong common citizenship that would bind Canadians together.

Overall, the question of whether the conventional meaning of citizenship as equal membership in a particular political community with all persons having the same duties and rights has increasingly been raised, particularly in multinational states (Carens, 2000).

GLOBALIZATION

The Globalization Website
www.emory.edu/SOC/globalization

Some analysts claim that the modern state is declining in significance. Globalization is making the boundaries of states less relevant, eroding state sovereignty, and reducing the ability of governments to determine the direction of their countries. Indeed, one author predicted that by 2025 we will see the end of the nation-state, to be replaced by small units subordinate to a global economy (Ohmae, 1995).

GLOBALIZATION The processes that are increasing the interconnectedness of the world.

Globalization is often described in terms of the processes that are, in effect, shrinking the world. The obstacles of space and time are being rapidly overcome by contemporary technology, such as high-speed, low-cost communications. This is increasing the interconnectedness of the world and creating a greater awareness of the world as a whole. American journalist Tom Friedman (2000, p. 9) describes globalization as

> *the inexorable integration of markets, nation-states and technologies to a degree never witnessed before—in a way that is enabling individuals,*

corporations and nation-states to reach around the world farther, faster, deeper and cheaper than ever before, and in a way that is enabling the world to reach into individuals, corporations and nations farther, faster, deeper, and cheaper than ever before.

Globalization is often described as an inevitable process. However, various circumstances, including the policies adopted by governments, can accelerate, slow down, or even reverse the trend. For example, the economic globalization that developed in the late nineteenth and early twentieth centuries was reversed by World War I and later by the rise of economic and political nationalism during the Great Depression of the 1930s. On the other hand, globalization accelerated beginning in the 1980s as many governments adopted policies aimed at promoting free trade, free markets, and a reduction in the role of government.

Economic Globalization

A key aspect of globalization that has important political implications is the development of a global economic system in terms of production, trade, and finance. Many business corporations have become global in their activities; they move or contract out their production facilities to wherever goods and services can be produced at the lowest cost and sell their products and services in a variety of countries. Global trade has increased greatly in the past half-century (see Figure 2-2). The process of economic globalization has been most pronounced in the international financial markets that provide a substantial proportion of the money and credit needed by business and government. Approximately $2 trillion is traded daily on the currency markets, much of it for speculative purposes (Harmes, 2004). Capital can flow instantaneously in and out of countries connected to the global financial markets. However, there is no global free market in labour, as most workers in the poorer countries cannot easily move to countries that offer high wages and full employment.

Economic globalization potentially can increase overall economic efficiency by increasing competition and allowing countries to focus on the products and services they can produce at the lowest cost and using trade to obtain products and services that can be obtained more cheaply elsewhere. As well, consumers can benefit from lower prices and a wider selection of goods and businesses and governments have a broader source of finance.

However, economic globalization has important risks as economic problems in one country can quickly spread around the world. For example, the serious global financial crisis that began in 2007 started when U.S. housing prices dropped sharply, resulting in many persons who had bought their homes with little or no down payment defaulting on their mortgages. In turn, leading financial institutions around the world that held mortgage-backed securities

FIGURE 2-2

**TOTAL VOLUME OF
MERCHANDISE EXPORTS
(WORLD), 1950 TO 2008
(INDEX: YEAR 2000=100)**

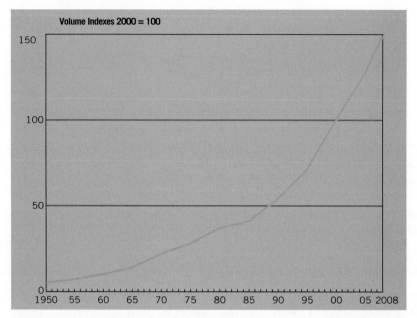

SOURCE: *Compiled from World Trade Organization, International trade statistics, 2009, World merchandise exports, products and gross domestic product, 1950–2008 from www.wto.org/english/res_e/statis_e/its2009_e/ its09_appendix_e.pdf.* Courtesy of The World Trade Organization.

and complex related derivative instruments faced bankruptcy, threatening the global economy. The life savings and pension plans of many individuals were decimated by the resulting stock market crash while governments around the world amassed large debts in order to stimulate the economy and avoid a severe global economic depression.

Overall, economic globalization reduces the ability of national governments to manage their own economies and tends to concentrate power in the hands of the largest corporations. It also tends to increase global inequality, weakens labour, and can facilitate tax evasion.

Cultural Globalization

Globalization also involves the spreading of cultural products and values around the world. Advances in communications, such as the Internet, have greatly increased the interaction of people, businesses, and other organizations worldwide. Leading brands such as Coke, Pepsi, McDonald's, Taco Bell, and Nike have become familiar to people around the world. American movies, television shows, and music videos are the leading sources of entertainment in many parts of the world. CNN and BBC World are major sources of news in many countries (although Qatar-based Al Jazeera has been increasing its global coverage in recent years).

Cultural globalization is often viewed as a process in which Western (and particularly American) culture is spread globally. Although the transformation of communication has given us increased access to cultures in other parts of the world, the flow of cultural communication outward from Western countries is substantially greater than the flow in the reverse direction.

Cultural globalization has some important political effects. The spread of democracy is often attributed, in part, to the information revolution that has both spread democratic values and presented challenges to the attempts of non-democratic governments to control information and ideas. The portrayal on television of the wealth of Western societies is thought to have contributed to the collapse of communist regimes in Eastern Europe as people compared their situation to that of their Western neighbours.

However, there are substantial cultural differences among various regions of the world that movies, television shows, music, fast foods, and brand labels cannot easily erase. Indeed, Islamic fundamentalists may have their negative views of Western societies reinforced by what they perceive as the decadence portrayed in Western-produced movies and television.

Political Globalization

Many contemporary problems, including the regulation of global business and finance, global climate change, international crime and terrorism, and the spread of diseases, cannot be dealt with effectively by individual states alone. A variety of institutions have developed to try to coordinate the actions of states, promote trade, and deal with global problems. The European Union (discussed in Chapter 13) has created a level of governing above that of the state. In other cases, such as the North American Free Trade Agreement (involving Canada, the United States, and Mexico), Mercosur and the Andean Community (South America), and the Asia-Pacific Trade Agreement, countries have reached agreements that affect the policies they adopt. In fact, with the development of a number of regional economic, political, and military agreements, the growing interconnectedness of the world can be said to involve a substantial degree of regionalization rather than globalization.

At the global level, the United Nations and its agencies have had some success in helping states deal with global issues, although with only limited success in dealing with war and other forms of violence. Three major international financial institutions (discussed further in Chapters 17 and 18) are of considerable importance in regulating the global economy. The World Trade Organization, with 153 member states and 30 observer states, is dedicated to pursuing free trade, resolving trade disputes, and overseeing trade agreements. The International Monetary Fund, with 186 member states, oversees the global financial system and provides loans to countries facing financial crises. The World Bank, which also has 186 member states, focuses on providing assistance to developing countries. In addition, annual summits of the leaders of countries with some of the largest national economies (the G7, the G8, and, beginning in 2010, the G20) provide a forum for discussion of the global economy and other important international issues.[7]

Global Policy Forum
www.globalpolicy.org

International Forum on Globalization
www.ifg.org

Many non-governmental organizations operate on a global scale seeking to influence policies in such areas as human rights, the environment, the status of women, and peace as well as being directly involved in projects to aid developing countries. Greenpeace, for example, has grown from a small Vancouver organization concerned with nuclear weapons testing in Alaska to a large international organization involved in environmental causes around the world. A concerned American, Jody Williams, made extensive use of email to mobilize a wide variety of groups and individuals around the world that successfully pressed for an international treaty banning anti-personnel land mines (although forty countries, including the United States, Russia, and China, refused to sign the treaty). International business, labour, and religious groups are also important actors on the global political stage.

Globalization and the State

Is globalization seriously eroding the power of states? The heightened pressures of economic competition may encourage countries to adopt policies that focus on removing barriers to the global free market, reducing the role of government in regulating the economy and cutting the taxes that are needed to provide social benefits. The rules of trade adopted by bodies such as the World Trade Organization are aimed at trying to establish a "level playing field" in which government policies that protect domestic products and services and place barriers to trade and investment are expected to be eliminated.

Nevertheless, there is diversity among the policies adopted by different countries, reflecting continuing differences in cultures and circumstances. The relatively prosperous countries of Western Europe, for example, generally have continued to maintain a wider range of social benefits for their populations as well as higher environmental and health standards than other countries.

---

7 The G7, established in 1975, includes Canada, France, Germany, Italy, Japan, the United Kingdom, and the United States. Russia was invited to join in 1997, creating the G8. The G20 consists of countries responsible for about 85 percent of the global economy, including several major developing countries. Although it originally consisted of finance ministers and central bank governors, the G20 now includes meetings of government leaders and is expected to become more important than the G7 and G8. None of these groups has a permanent organizational structure.

The governments of the newly industrialized countries of East Asia are more heavily involved in directing their industries than is the case in the United States and Canada. Generally, countries have tended to adapt to globalization in different ways, and have chosen to integrate into the global economy to differing extents (Garrett, 1998).

Despite some downsizing of government, reduction of business regulation, and privatization of some government services in a number of countries beginning in the 1980s, governments are still far more active than they were in the past. Indeed, concerns about security have increased the role of the state in some areas, including increased surveillance of the population. The developing countries generally have had to reduce state control of imports and investment in order to gain access to the global economy. However, they have needed greater state action to provide better education and training, a stronger framework of laws concerning property rights and business activities, various public services, and a competent administrative structure (Wolf, 2001). Therefore, although globalization creates new challenges, the state remains strong in developed countries while many countries in the developing world have been strengthening their state apparatus.

It has been argued that globalization is eroding the power of the nation-state not only by shifting power upward to global institutions, global markets, and global corporations, but also by indirectly challenging the nation-state from below. If states are less able to provide for the well-being of their people, this may stimulate separatist movements. The development of organizations such as the European Union and the North American Free Trade Agreement makes it possible for some people in smaller areas, such as Scotland, Quebec, and Catalonia to think that belonging to such organizations will offset the disadvantages they would face by separating from a large country.

Finally, people's sense of identification with the nation-state may be reduced as an increasing proportion of people have multiple identities. This is not an entirely new phenomenon, as religious, cultural, regional, local, and ethnic identities have often coexisted or competed with national identities. However, the substantial number of immigrants, "guest workers," and refugees with different religious, cultural, and ethnic or racial characteristics in many countries has modified and challenged the meaning of nationhood. Nevertheless, despite growing concerns about human rights for all people, global poverty, international financial crises, and global environmental problems, it is doubtful whether more than a small proportion of the world's population has developed a cosmopolitan or global sense of identity. Similarly, despite the growing importance of various international institutions, they have not developed a significant degree of legitimacy among the general population. Most people continue to expect their own state to deal with the issues and problems that are of greatest concern to them.

Summary and Conclusion

The nation-state is often considered to be the primary basis for the way the modern world is organized. Modern states claim to be the highest authority within a particular, well-defined territory. State sovereignty is the legal principle that states have the right to govern their populations and territories without outside interference, and that they should be treated as equals on the world stage. Questions have been raised, however, as to whether outside intervention is justified in some instances, such as when state authorities violate or are unable to protect the basic human rights of the people they govern.

The rationale often given for state sovereignty is that states are the political expression of a nation, and that nations should have the right to govern themselves. However, not all nations have their own state and many states are not based on a single nation. The determination of what constitutes a particular nation is often controversial. Nations are often thought of in terms of the common ancestry, language, culture, and other characteristics of a people. However, a sense of belonging to a nation can also develop among people of diverse backgrounds and characteristics living in a particular country. Governments, along with intellectuals and artists, have often developed myths of nationhood to try to unify the people of their country and create a common culture.

Many states are not based on a people with a single, common identity or set of characteristics. Although some binational and multinational states are stable and successful, the determination of the common good in these states can be difficult because the good of each nation needs to be taken into account to maintain the legitimacy of the state.

The political doctrine of nationalism—with its goals of trying to establish or maintain a self-governing state based on a particular nation and promoting the interests and values of that nation-state—continues to have great significance for the politics of the modern world. From a nationalist perspective, the state should look after the common good of the nation upon which it is based. However, in a number of cases, nationalism has led to discrimination or oppression against those within a country who are not viewed as part of the nation.

Associated with the development of the nation-state is the concept of citizenship. The idea that all permanent members of a political community should be equal citizens with the same rights and responsibilities has been challenged, particularly by minority nationalities that wish to have a different relationship to the state than other citizens. This raises controversial questions as to whether efforts should be made to strengthen a sense of common citizenship or whether recognizing differences and incorporating them into the organization of the state would help to overcome the alienation that may be felt by minority nationalities (Harty & Murphy, 2005).

The contemporary state faces challenges from globalization as well as from regions and groups within the state that would like to gain greater autonomy or independence. Economic globalization reduces the ability of states to manage their economies, cultural globalization may reduce the significance of national cultural differences, and political globalization can limit state sovereignty. However, states are still the most important political unit, although they do need to take globalizing tendencies into account. The governing institutions of the state continue to play a crucial role in providing order and security; economic regulation; justice, social, health, and educational services; and other highly important aspects of our lives.

Nevertheless, politics and governing are becoming more complex as a variety of organizations beyond the state are assuming increased importance. Although a global or cosmopolitan sense of identity has been slow to develop, the development of multiple identities may be reducing the significance of the nation-state as the primary source of political identification (Castells, 2004).

Globalization presents important political challenges; in particular, how to regulate global forces so that they work for the common good of the world rather than concentrating unaccountable power in the hands of large multinational corporations or certain powerful states. Effective political institutions at the global level are needed to direct economic and technological globalization for the common good of humanity (Valaskakis, 2001). "Civilizing globalization"—in other words, trying to make globalization more equitable, environmentally sustainable, democratic, controllable, and less threatening to cultural diversity—is a key political challenge in the twenty-first century (Sandbrook, 2003). To make progress toward achieving the common good of humanity, the development of a consciousness of being part of a global community as well as citizens of a particular state may be necessary.

Key Terms

Discussion Questions

1. Should each nation be self-governing?

2. Is Canada a nation-state?

3. What should be the rights and obligations of citizens? How should citizenship be determined? Should a person be allowed to be a citizen of more than one country?

4. Is multiculturalism a positive feature of countries such as Canada?

5. Is globalization reducing the importance of the state?

Further Reading

Barber, B. (1995). *Jihad vs. McWorld: How globalization and tribalism are reshaping the world*. New York: Ballantine.

Bosworth, R.J.B. (2007). *Nationalism*. Harlow, UK: Pearson.

Brawley, M.R. (2003). *The politics of globalization: Gaining perspective, assessing consequences*. Peterborough, ON: Broadview.

Friedman, T. (2005). *The world is flat: A brief history of the twenty-first century*. New York: Farrar, Straus and Giroux.

Giddens, A. (2000). *Runaway world: How globalization is reshaping our lives*. New York: Routledge.

Harmes, A. (2004). *The return of the state: Protestors, power-brokers and the new global compromise*. Vancouver and Toronto: Douglas & McIntyre.

Harty, S., & Murphy, M. (2005). *In defence of multinational citizenship*. Vancouver and Toronto: UBC Press.

Hay, C., Lister, M., & Marsh, D. (Eds.). (2006). *The state: Theories and issues*. New York: Palgrave Macmillan.

Held, D., & McGrew, A. (Eds.). (2003). *The global transformations reader: An introduction to the globalization debate* (2nd ed.). Cambridge: Polity Press.

Hirst, P., & Thompson, G. (1999). *Globalization in question: The international economy and the possibilities of governance* (2nd ed.). Cambridge, UK: Polity Press.

Ignatieff, M. (1993). *Blood and belonging: Journeys into the new nationalism*. Toronto: Penguin.

McBride, S. (2005). *Paradigm shift: Globalization and the Canadian state* (2nd. ed.). Halifax: Fernwood.

Nelson, B.R. (2006). *The making of the modern state: A theoretical evolution*. New York: Palgrave Macmillan.

Smith, A.D. (2001). *Nationalism*. Cambridge, UK: Polity Press.

Stevenson, G. (2006). *Parallel paths: The development of nationalism in Ireland and Quebec*. Montreal: McGill-Queen's University Press.

Weiss, L. (1998). *The myth of the powerless state*. Ithaca, NY: Cornell University Press.

Chapter 3

Freedom, Equality, and Democracy

PHOTO ABOVE: Winston Blackmore with a few members of his very large family in Bountiful, British Columbia, where polygamy is widely practised as part of the community's religious beliefs.

CHAPTER OBJECTIVES

After reading this chapter you should be able to:

1. explain the meaning of negative freedom and positive freedom
2. discuss the extent to which there should be limits on freedom
3. distinguish among the different versions of equality
4. evaluate the argument that members of disadvantaged groups should receive special preference in education, employment, and political representation
5. examine and evaluate the different versions of democracy

Winston Blackmore, a 52-year-old man living in Bountiful, British Columbia, allegedly has married 25 women and fathered 101 children. As a former bishop of the Fundamentalist Church of Jesus Christ of Latter Day Saints, he believes that having multiple wives is an essential doctrine of his faith and a requirement for entry into the highest kingdom of heaven. Although the Church of Jesus Christ of Latter-day Saints (Mormon) that was founded in the United States originally believed in taking multiple wives, in 1878 the U.S. Supreme Court upheld the law against polygamy on the grounds that constitutional guarantees of religious freedom did not extend to the practices of this religion. This led the Mormon Church to ban polygamy in 1890 and to excommunicate fundamentalists who continued this practice.

Polygamy (having more than one wife or more than one husband) has been an offence under the Criminal Code of Canada since 1892. However, prosecutions have been rare and governments have generally avoided interfering in the affairs of tightly knit religious communities. However, after negative publicity in the media about life in Bountiful, the B.C. government decided to prosecute Winston Blackmore and William Oter, another Bountiful leader alleged to have three wives. After two special prosecutors refused to take the case on the grounds that the law against polygamy violates the Charter of Rights and Freedoms, the case presented by the third special prosecutor was dismissed on the grounds that "prosecutor shopping" by the government was improper (CBC News, 2009, September 29). The B.C. government then asked the Supreme Court of the province for its opinion on whether the law against polygamy violates the Charter's protection of freedom of religion that became part of Canada's Constitution in 1982.

Leaving aside the issue that some of the marriages in Bountiful may have involved underage girls, the question of whether banning polygamy is a violation of freedom of religion remains. Is the government justified in banning a practice that many people consider abhorrent or undesirable? Should freedom of religion override the value of women's equality that such patriarchal practices challenge? While some women have divorced their husbands and left Bountiful, others have expressed support for the practice of plural marriage. If this support is not coerced, should government step in to prevent them from engaging in what many believe is an unequal and oppressive relationship and, in effect, force them to be free?

The issues raised in the Blackmore case extend far beyond Bountiful's small, isolated community. As immigration brings large numbers of people with different religions, customs, and practices to Western countries, questions about whether such persons should be free to live their lives in ways that may be inconsistent with contemporary Western values have become increasingly controversial. In France, for example, polygamous marriages have become a hot political issue, as an estimated two hundred thousand persons (mainly Muslims from Africa) live in polygamous families there (*The Economist,* 2010, May 8–14).

In this chapter, we will examine some key ideas and values—including freedom, equality, and democracy—that affect the way people think about politics, how governments should act with regards to these values, and who should make governing decisions.

FREEDOM

Individual freedom is a key political value, particularly in Western democracies such as Canada and the United States. Freedom, or liberty,[1] is often defined in terms of the ability to act as one wants without interference, restraints, or coercion. In any functioning political community, some limits are placed on what individuals can do, particularly so that harm is not done to others. Few would see laws forbidding murder, assault, and theft, along with appropriate punishments, as violations of individual freedom. More controversial are laws that limit various forms of expression that do not cause direct physical harm to others but could be emotionally harmful or may lead to harm if they mobilize people to take certain actions (see Box 3-1, Nazis in Skokie).

In modern societies, governments have been quite active in placing some restrictions on individual behaviour, even when direct harm to other individuals is not involved. For example, laws requiring the use of seat belts in automobiles and helmets by motorcyclists are intended to reduce the likelihood of harm to oneself in an accident. In addition, it may be beneficial to society as a whole if it reduces government spending on hospital care for the injured.

Arguments Regarding Freedom

What arguments are used to defend freedom? One argument is that all individuals have a natural right to freedom. John Locke (1632–1704) assumed that individuals had been free and equal in the state of nature (that is, before the establishment of government) but lacked the means to settle disputes fairly. Therefore, through what he termed the "social contract," people agreed to establish government for specific purposes—namely, the protection of life, liberty, and property. Government should be limited in its powers, acting as a trustee to protect the rights of the people, and removable by the people, by force if necessary, if it infringes on the liberties that it is supposed to protect.

Thomas Hobbes (1588–1679) began with the same basic assumptions that individuals were free and equal in the state of nature and capable of rationally pursuing their own interests. However, he argued that the state of nature involved a war of "all against all," leading to lives that were "solitary, poor, nasty, brutish, and short." Therefore, people quickly contracted to form a government and transferred absolute, undivided authority to a sovereign power (government or a ruler) to preserve order. There was no right to individual freedom; whether any freedom was enjoyed would depend upon the

---

[1] Although the words *freedom* and *liberty* have different origins that carry somewhat different meanings (Fischer, 2004), they are often used interchangeably in contemporary discussions.

BOX 3-1

Nazis in Skokie: Freedom for Racists?

In 1977, the National Socialist Party of America (NSAP), a neo-Nazi group led by Frank Collin,* planned a march in Skokie, Illinois, a suburb of Chicago that has a large Jewish population, including many survivors of the Nazi Holocaust (discussed in Chapter 4). A county court granted an injunction requested by the village of Skokie prohibiting the NSAP from parading in Nazi uniforms, displaying the swastika, and distributing material promoting hatred against Jews and blacks.

The American Civil Liberties Union (ACLU) took up the cause of the right to free speech and free assembly, citing the U.S. Bill of Rights, which prohibits laws "abridging the freedom of speech, or of the press; or the right of the people peaceably to assemble." David Goldberger, a Jewish lawyer representing the ACLU, successfully convinced the Illinois Supreme Court to overturn the injunction and allow the march. An appeal to the U.S. Supreme Court was unsuccessful. The city of Chicago, which had originally denied the NSAP a permit, decided to allow the group to parade in a park thus avoiding a potential confrontation in Skokie.

The courts in the United States have tended to be more vigorous in upholding the right to free expression than is the case in many other democratic countries. In Canada, for example, the Supreme Court has upheld the provision of the Criminal Code that provides serious penalties for those who incite hatred against an identifiable group.

The case of Skokie illustrates the controversies that can arise concerning whether freedom should be an absolute right. Should the right to express one's views take precedence over the right of people to be free to enjoy their lives without being subjected to hateful views directed against the group to which they belong? Does the possibility of confrontation and violence justify the banning of political demonstrations? Is the banning of freedom of speech and freedom of assembly the "thin edge of the wedge" that could allow governments to take away the freedom to criticize government? Are universities justified in establishing "speech codes" that prohibit the expression of words or ideas that are deemed to be offensive or demeaning to any group or deemed to create a hostile environment?

---

* It was later revealed that Frank Collin had a Jewish father who claimed to have been a prisoner at the Dachau concentration camp.

will of the sovereign power in taking action to maintain order. Nevertheless, since the goal of the sovereign was to maintain order, Hobbes assumed that it would not interfere unnecessarily in people's private lives, thus leaving them free, for example, to buy and sell goods and to instruct their children as they see fit.

The state of nature was a fictional assumption used by Locke and Hobbes to develop their analyses. Hobbes's argument regarding the need for an absolute sovereign power was based on the English Civil War that was occurring while he wrote *Leviathan*. Indeed, studies of "primitive" tribes have found that people in these tribes generally exhibit sociable behaviour rather than being highly self-interested.

Government clamps down on unhealthy eating.

UTILITARIANISM An alternative basis for individual freedom is **utilitarianism**, the view that "actions are right in proportion as they tend to promote happiness, wrong as they tend to produce the reverse of happiness" (Mill, quoted in West, 2006, p. 223). Although the idea of utilitarianism can be traced back to the ancient Greek philosopher Epicurus, its development is usually associated with nineteenth-century English thinkers Jeremy Bentham and John Stuart Mill. Bentham assumed that humans are self-regarding animals whose behaviour could be explained as an effort to maximize pleasure and to minimize pain: "Nature has placed mankind under the governance of two sovereign masters, pain and pleasure . . . They govern us in all we do, in all we say, in all we think." (quoted in Qualter, 1986, p. 14). Combined with this view of human behaviour was a simple moral theory: that which causes pleasure is good and that which causes pain is bad. Individuals need only measure whether an action promotes their own happiness in order to decide what it is desirable to do.

Bentham applied the same standard to government actions. That is, government should always act to achieve the greatest happiness for the greatest number. Utilitarianism does not involve any inherent limits on the scope of government to protect freedom. However, Bentham and his followers generally assumed that a high level of individual freedom would lead to the greatest happiness of the greatest number since each individual knew best what brought him or her pleasure.

UTILITARIANISM The view that humans seek to maximize pleasure and minimize pain and that government should act to achieve the greatest happiness for the greatest number.

▶ John Stuart Mill, a leading advocate of individual freedom.

Those who are critical of a high level of individual freedom often argue that liberty is simply a licence to engage in undesirable behaviour. In this view, liberty is equated with self-indulgence and is undesirable for the individual and the community as whole. A modified version of utilitarianism developed by John Stuart Mill attempted to address this criticism by distinguishing among different kinds of pleasures. According to Mill, pleasures that involve the higher faculties—for example, art, literature, and music—are better than those that involve the satisfaction of basic desires. Indeed, Mill asserted that "it is better to be a human dissatisfied than a pig satisfied; better to be Socrates dissatisfied than a fool satisfied" (Mill, 1871, p. 14). Further, Mill argued that once individuals learned to enjoy the higher pleasures, they would value these more than the lower pleasures. More generally, Mill viewed liberty as necessary for the development of the individual rather than simply for the satisfaction of desires. For Mill, "the end of man . . . is the highest and most harmonious development of his powers" (Mill, 1859/1912, p. 71).

The view that some actions are better than others could lead to the conclusion that government is justified in limiting freedom in order to lead individuals to live better lives or to prevent them from doing undesirable things. However, Mill argued that liberty is necessary for the full development of each individual's capabilities: "Developing one's perceptions, judgements, discriminative feeling, mental activity, and even moral preference are only exercised in making a choice" (Mill, 1859/1912, p. 72). Therefore, even if government had the good of the people in mind, by limiting choice its actions could interfere with the development of their individual capacities to think and act—that is, with their individuality.

Liberty is useful not only in terms of the development of the individual, but also to society as a whole. The competition and interplay of different ideas is necessary, Mill argued, for people to get closer to the truth. Over the long run, Mill assumed, the more valid ideas will show their worth and the less valid ideas will fall by the wayside, just as in the marketplace good products eventually outsell poor products (Hagopian, 1985, p. 174). Maximum freedom is needed so that all ideas can be tested.

Mill doubted that any individual, group of individuals, or government could possess knowledge of absolute truth. Therefore, suppression of any opinions cannot be justified because those opinions may contain an element of truth. Even if we could obtain knowledge of what is true, the suppression of untrue opinions would not be socially desirable because the expression of untrue ideas helps the holders of true opinions to understand the basis for holding those opinions. More generally, Mill argued that being challenged by different ideas is desirable if society is to avoid stagnation and if individuals are to exercise their capacity for reason.

FREEDOM AND MORALITY   Should certain types of behaviour be banned because of their immoral nature? Those who favour restricting and punishing immoral behaviour argue that tolerating such behaviour undermines the morality of society as a whole. For example, traditional principles of morality included the belief that sex outside of a marriage between one man and one woman is immoral. Indeed, in many countries homosexual acts and sex outside of marriage are severely punished, and it is only in recent decades that sodomy has been removed from the criminal codes of many Western countries. However, as discussed in Box 3-2, Sex for Sale, prostitution remains a controversial issue even in countries that no longer have laws regarding sex between consenting adults.

Some who argue that there should be no restrictions on behaviours that do not cause significant harm to others claim that there are no absolute moral standards because different people have different values or because the values of different cultures are equally valid. With no consensus about what is immoral, the imposition of a particular view of morality is undesirable. Therefore, using this perspective, those in Bountiful, B.C., should be free to practise polygamy (unless the marriages were coerced) because society cannot claim that the general practice of monogamy is morally superior.

In modern, diverse societies, the imposition of moral standards associated with a particular religious or cultural group will be unacceptable to many people. Imposing one set of moral principles can often lead to bitter conflict with those who hold different beliefs and values. However, some religious and

BOX 3-2

Sex for Sale: Morality, Safety, and Prostitution

In October 2009, three current and past sex-trade workers went to court to challenge Canada's laws concerning prostitution. Although prostitution technically is not illegal in Canada, almost all activity related to prostitution is illegal. The Criminal Code makes it illegal to communicate in a public place for the purposes of prostitution, to live off the avails of prostitution, to operate or be found in a common bawdy house (brothel), or to engage in sex in a public place (including an automobile). These laws, the sex-trade workers argued, should be struck down because they make it difficult or impossible to work in the sex trade in a safe fashion and thus violate the workers' right to security guaranteed in the Charter of Rights and Freedoms. On the other side, groups such as the Catholic Civil Rights League and REAL Women of Canada argued that prostitution should be illegal because most Canadians belong to religions that view it as an immoral activity.

There are a variety of dimensions to the issue of legalizing prostitution. The lawyer representing the Attorney General of Ontario argued in court that the existing laws prevent the "normalization" of a harmful activity (Alcoba, 2009). Others who weighed in on the issue favoured an outright ban on prostitution, pointing out that most parents would not want their daughters to become prostitutes. Prostitution is also viewed as encouraging negative attitudes toward women in general. Public health issues concerning the spread of diseases are often raised when prostitution is discussed. And prostitution is seen as potentially undermining marriages, although perhaps considered less harmful in that respect than having an extramarital affair. Further, prostitution is often strongly opposed by those in the neighbourhood where it exists because of the nuisance it can create as well as the exposure of children to the practice. Finally, prostitution often has unsavoury connections, including links to organized crime, illegal drugs, pimps who exploit prostitutes, the trafficking of women and children from poor countries who are enticed or coerced into commercial sex, and the encouragement of "sex tourism."

Those who favour removing the restrictions on activities related to prostitution (as has occurred in the Netherlands, Denmark, and Germany) argue that the current system in Canada and some other countries puts women, particularly "streetwalkers," at risk as evidenced by the substantial number of murders and other acts of violence perpetrated against prostitutes. Government regulation of licensed brothels would provide protection, reduce the spread of disease, and help to ensure that underage or coerced sex slaves are not employed. Since the so-called "world's oldest profession" will be practised whether legal or illegal, it is argued that government should do what it can to protect the often vulnerable people (such as young women, Aboriginals, and the poorly educated) who are involved in the sex trade. Reference is often made to the banning of alcohol early in the twentieth century on the grounds that it led to immorality, including the disruption of family life. In the case of alcohol, prohibition in the United States did not stop its use, but rather had the negative consequences of funding gangs and organized crime.

The issue of prostitution illustrates the complex mix of moral and practical issues that often are involved in questions about whether certain activities should be allowed or banned.

cultural practices are cruel, barbaric, or disrespectful of human dignity and even a very tolerant society will find them unacceptable.

FREEDOM AND ORDER   Freedom and order are often considered to be opposing values. Dictatorial regimes frequently invoke the value of order to justify the suppression of dissent. Even in countries that value freedom, governments and security forces often try to limit marches and demonstrations by raising fears that peace and order could be threatened. However, as discussed in Chapter 10, the rights of those suffering from discrimination or oppression have often been advanced through unconventional protest activities that could be considered disorderly and disruptive.

Nevertheless it can be argued that freedom can only be securely maintained in an orderly political community that maintains the rule of law. Anarchists have held out the ideal of a peaceful, co-operative society that can be developed after the coercive power of the state is ended and the capitalist system (or other economic systems based on inequality) is overthrown. In a society where there is a strong sense of solidarity and sharing among the people, it is suggested that social pressure would be sufficient to prevent individuals from harming others. While such a society is possible in small-scale communal settings, it is questionable whether the world could be organized in such a way, at least at the present stage of human development. In countries such as Somalia

◀ Police arrest protesting cyclists in downtown Toronto during the G20 summit, June 27, 2010. More than 900 persons were arrested, but most charges were eventually dropped.

where an effective state apparatus able to maintain law and order has not existed in recent decades, violence has been rampant. Much of the population there would likely be willing to give up their freedoms to a group that is able to restore law and order regardless of how harshly that group would rule. Therefore, meaningful freedom realistically requires some degree of order based on just and enforceable laws. Among those who value freedom, however, there is a fear that to achieve order and security, people may be willing to accept policies that unduly infringe upon their freedoms. Indeed, governments and persons who are less committed to the value of freedom may exaggerate threats to security in order to justify restrictions on freedom.

Negative and Positive Freedom

NEGATIVE FREEDOM The absence of physical and legal restraints on the actions of individuals.

POSITIVE FREEDOM The capacity to do something worth doing or enjoying.

Government is often viewed as the enemy of individual freedom. However, English philosopher T.H. Green (1836–1882) argued that government action is often needed to provide the basis for people to be free to develop their individuality. The absence of physical and legal restraints on our actions (**negative freedom**) does not necessarily make us free. If we think of freedom as a "positive power or capacity of doing something worth doing or enjoying" (termed **positive freedom**), then individuals in a primitive society with little or no government are less free than modern citizens, who are subject to the many laws and regulations of governments (quoted in Qualter, 1986, p. 98). Although modern society presents greater opportunities to be free in Green's positive sense, there are many obstacles that can prevent people from fully developing themselves, such as poverty, ill health, illiteracy, and long hours of work. Government, by helping to ensure that individuals have the means to live a life of dignity and self-respect, can help to make freedom meaningful for all rather than a special privilege for a few.

Therefore, Green argued, government has a responsibility to remove the social and economic obstacles that can hinder individual development in order to establish a meaningful right to freedom. A somewhat active government is needed in order to establish the conditions in which individuals can freely develop their capabilities. While individuals should be responsible for their own development, government can aid individuals in the pursuit of freedom. Fighting poverty, protecting the health and safety of workers, improving the quality of cities, providing a good education to all persons, and ensuring that everyone has adequate housing are, therefore, proper activities of government.

PROPERTY RIGHTS AND ECONOMIC FREEDOM   The idea of positive freedom suggests that some limits on property rights and economic freedom are necessary to ensure that all individuals can be truly free, particularly in the sense of being able to develop themselves. While rights to life and liberty can apply to all persons, the right to property is more exclusive since many people do not have a significant amount of property. As a result, there has often been considerable controversy concerning property rights and economic freedom.

John Locke viewed the Earth as having been given by God to humanity in common. However, he argued that through their labour (for example, by tilling the soil) individuals gained the right to possess property. Others argue that property or wealth is often not gained through hard work but through conquest, exploitation of the labour of others, or inheritance. Locke's argument that people without property in his time could go to America and use the vacant land there ignored the occupancy of that land by indigenous peoples.

Eighteenth-century Scottish philosopher Adam Smith provided an influential utilitarian argument for an economic system in which property rights were protected and government left individuals free to act as they saw fit in the economic marketplace. Smith argued that a free, competitive economy is the most efficient system of production and distribution because it maximizes the total wealth of a country. It can therefore be considered an application of Bentham's advocacy of the greatest good for the greatest number, if one makes the contentious assumption that maximizing wealth maximizes happiness.

Smith's basic argument in *The Wealth of Nations* (1776) was that a free, competitive economy is the most efficient way of producing goods and maximizes the total wealth of the community. Individuals pursuing their own economic interests will be guided by the "invisible hand" of the marketplace to act in a way that is in the interests of the community as a whole. As Smith wrote, "It is not from the benevolence of the butcher, the brewer, or the baker that we expect our dinner, but from their regard to their self-interest" (Smith, 1776/2004, p. 105). Competition among producers results in the production of goods at the lowest possible price. The signals of the marketplace lead to a balance between what goods are produced and what goods consumers desire. The free marketplace, in other words, is self-regulating. Intervention by government lowers the overall level of wealth and creates special privileges for those who are able to influence government at the expense of the society as a whole. The common good is best achieved by allowing individuals to pursue their own economic self-interest.

Smith also advocated the removal of barriers to international free trade. Tariffs (taxes) on imports designed to protect domestic industries result in higher prices for consumers and special privileges for protected industries. In Smith's view, pursuing the interests of the nation-state through protectionist policies, the granting of monopolies to particular companies, and the extraction of wealth from colonies (the mercantilist policies common in the seventeenth and eighteenth centuries) hindered the development of a prosperous and peaceful world.

For Smith, the proper role of government was to provide protection from foreign invasion, protect property, and maintain order through a system of laws. Involvement in the economy should be limited to providing certain "collective goods," such as roads, canals, education, and street lighting that are unlikely to be provided by private business (Ball & Dagger, 2004). Although Smith wanted to free the market from government regulation, he believed that a community needed to be based on shared moral principles to limit greedy and selfish behaviour that could harm the common good (Lipschutz, 2004, p. 143).

Critics argue that an unregulated free-market system leads to a concentration of economic power in the hands of a small number of large corporations, rather than the economy being guided by the "invisible hand" of the marketplace. Greed often seems to be the guiding principle of some of the top executives at the leading corporations. As well, maximizing wealth for a community may be undesirable if it is associated with great inequalities, exploitation, poverty for some, and environmental degradation.

Advocates of a free-market economy with a minimum of government involvement also argue that such an economic system protects and enhances individual freedom. A free-market economy is seen as freeing people from dependence on the arbitrary decisions of others (such as kings and feudal lords). Individuals make their own economic decisions; they are "free to choose" how to operate their businesses, what work they will do, or what goods they will buy (Friedman & Friedman, 2001). The material well-being of individuals is determined by the impersonal "natural" forces of the marketplace rather than by the arbitrary decisions of those with political power. Further, it is argued that with the economy in private hands, government will be less able to take away liberties, as supporters of freedom will have the resources needed to make their opposition known.

EQUALITY

Equality, like freedom, is an influential ideal in the modern world. Freedom and equality are, at least in part, complementary ideas. For example, we would not view freedom as established in a country if some persons in that country were so poor that they agreed to be slaves. However, extreme versions of equality may be incompatible with individual freedom. For example, we might not view a society to be free if everyone is required to live in the same way and all forms of competition are banned to ensure that everyone is perfectly equal.

Types of Equality

EQUAL RIGHTS The same legal and political rights for all persons.

The idea of equality has various different meanings and applications. **Equal rights** involve all persons having the same legal and political rights. Equal legal rights consists of applying the laws equally to all persons regardless of whether they are rich or poor, black or white, male or female, and so on. Likewise, political equality includes the equal right to vote, to seek public office, and to voice one's opinions.

Equality of opportunity consists of seeking to give all persons an equal chance to get ahead in life, regardless of their backgrounds or characteristics. For example, providing the same opportunity to obtain a good education to all persons is important in achieving equality of opportunity. Determining who attends university or receives a good job based on merit rather than on the wealth or connections of one's family is an important application of this principle.

Equality of outcome consists of trying to reduce or eliminate differences in the distribution of wealth, income, power, and other goods. Greater economic equality can be pursued by measures designed to redistribute income and wealth. For example, many governments use a system of graduated (progressive) income tax in which those in higher income brackets pay a higher percentage of their income in taxes. In practice, however, tax exemptions and differential treatment of various kinds of income (for example, treating capital gains and dividends differently than employment income) often offset the redistributive characteristics of the graduated income tax. Estate taxes (a feature of many countries, but not Canada) also limit the accumulation of wealth in a small number of hands over time. Likewise, various forms of assistance to the less advantaged as well as the provision of various services without cost (such as primary and secondary education and, in some countries, university education and health care) can reduce inequality of outcome. Similarly, the provision of basic necessities at low cost or the rationing of scarce necessities (as occurred during the two world wars and as occurs in communist countries) can provide a degree of equality of outcome.

EQUALITY OF OPPORTUNITY
The equal chance for all persons to get ahead in life, regardless of their backgrounds or characteristics.

EQUALITY OF OUTCOME
An equal distribution of wealth, income, power, and other goods.

The Development of the Ideal of Equality

Historically, equality was not a generally accepted value. Society was often tightly structured, with one's position largely determined by the position and status of one's parents and ancestors as well as one's gender. Politics was a matter for elite groups; the political activity of the masses, if any, tended to consist of resistance or rebellion. Individuals were seen as substantially unequal in their intelligence and capabilities and the division of society into different classes was frequently viewed as natural because of these differences among individuals. An orderly society was one in which those in different classes knew their place and did not seek equality.

The French Revolution of 1789 included an attack on the dominance and privileges of the monarchy, the nobility, and the Catholic Church. Contrary to the norm of ordinary persons being subjects of the ruling groups, the revolutionaries adopted the idea that all persons were citizens with equal rights and responsibilities. Based on this notion of natural rights, the National Assembly established during the French Revolution proclaimed the Declaration of the Rights of Man and Citizen. Similarly, the American Declaration of Independence (1776) included the following statement: "We hold these truths to be self-evident, that all men are created equal, that they are endowed by their Creator with certain unalienable Rights, that among these are Life, Liberty and the pursuit of Happiness." These rights were subsequently defined by the Bill of Rights, which was ratified in 1781 as an amendment to the U.S. constitution. Despite the glowing declarations of citizens' rights, these rights were not extended to women in either France or the United States. As well, the United States excluded slaves from the rights of citizens while, in France, the abolishment of slavery in 1784 was later reversed.

Many nineteenth-century political thinkers favoured equal rights in principle, but worried about the consequences of granting equal political rights to all persons (see Box 3-3, Plural Voting). Some believed the poor would use their voting power to elect those committed to taking away the wealth of the middle and upper classes. Others feared the less educated would be intolerant and therefore their voting strength would be a threat to individual liberty. British parliamentarian Edmund Burke (1729–1797) argued that ordinary people did not know what was in the interests of the nation. Therefore, political power should be exercised by the "natural aristocracy" (including the nobility, who had inherited substantial property, as well as men of law, science, and the arts and "rich traders") who had the education and leisure time to discern what was in the true interests of the nation and could represent the people as a whole (Macpherson, 1980, p. 47).

In the contemporary world, the ideas of equal rights and equal opportunities have become widely accepted, even if equal rights are not always applied in practice and equal opportunities have been difficult to achieve. Indeed, millions of women, men, and children in a number of countries continue to live in conditions of slavery that are sometimes tolerated or not vigorously combated by governments. Although reducing inequality in the distribution of wealth and income is often seen as interfering with the pursuit of economic growth, there is evidence that greater equality of outcome improves people's quality of life and leads to a better society (Wilkinson & Pickett, 2009).

Group Equality

Equality can be thought of in terms of equality not only among individuals, but also among groups sharing some common characteristics. Establishing equal legal and political rights for individuals may be insufficient to change long-established attitudes and practices and create meaningful equality for those in groups that have suffered from discrimination or oppression. Laws that try to prevent discrimination based on various characteristics such as age, race, religion, gender, and gender orientation can be useful in reducing inequalities, but they, too, are often insufficient to establish meaningful equality for indigenous (Aboriginal) peoples, women, and various racial and ethnic minorities. Various forms of encouragement and support may be needed

Plural Voting: More Votes for the Educated?

The utilitarian perspective developed by Jeremy Bentham presented a strong argument for the extension of the right to vote to all adult persons. In this perspective, individuals pursue their own interests to increase their happiness. If only one part of society is represented in government, then government will be concerned about the interests of that part of society. Therefore, the goal of the greatest happiness for the greatest number would not be achieved. The greatest happiness principle can be achieved only if government is truly representative of all people and if all people are careful to monitor and criticize government to ensure that their interests are taken into account.

John Stuart Mill also opposed the idea that an elite minority should be responsible for governing the community. In addition to Bentham's argument about the need to protect the interests of all, Mill viewed democracy as positive in terms of his ideal of self-development. Participation in political life would help people to develop their capabilities by encouraging them to become more informed, to discuss and debate issues with others, and thereby to become more reasonable and responsible. Indeed, unlike most men of his time, Mill argued that women should have the same right to vote as men since women had the same intellectual capabilities as men.

However, Mill was uneasy about movements that sought to gain the right to vote for all adult citizens. Because the majority was potentially intolerant of the views of minorities, the extension of the right to vote was a possible threat to liberty, which Mill viewed as the highest value. The dilemma, then, was how to give most people the opportunity to develop themselves through participation in politics while avoiding the risks involved in allowing a basically uninformed majority to control the community.* One suggestion put forward by Mill was plural voting. Workers would each get one vote, business people might each get two or three votes, while those with a university education along with artists, writers, and others who had more fully developed their capabilities might each get five or six votes. Indeed, plural voting existed to a limited extent in the United Kingdom until it was abolished by the Labour Party government in 1948. Until then, UK voters who had some affiliation to a university could each cast two votes in an election: one in a university constituency and the other in the constituency in which they resided.

---

* In addition, Mill argued that those on welfare, those who did not pay direct taxes (because they might make reckless demands on government), and those who could not read, write, or reckon should be excluded from voting rights. However, by advocating universal education and direct taxes, Mill hoped to reduce the number of people excluded from voting.

if members of disadvantaged groups are to overcome obstacles and achieve equality of opportunity. Beyond encouragement and support, moving toward greater equality of outcome among groups may involve legislation or policies that give preference to or reserve places in education and employment for members of groups that are disadvantaged or under-represented. As discussed in Box 3-4, A Woman's Place Is in the House, there has been considerable discussion about the under-representation of women in government and legislative bodies.

A Woman's Place Is in the House: Equal Representation in the House of Commons

Although women have had the right to vote and seek election to Canada's House of Commons since 1920, only about one-fifth of the members of Parliament are female. Despite the educational and professional achievements of women in recent decades and the efforts of some political parties to recruit more female candidates, women continue to be under-represented in the House. To achieve equal representation some women's groups have advocated that one-half of legislative seats be guaranteed to women by requiring each district to elect one male and one female candidate. Such equality of outcome, it is argued, would allow the concerns and views of women to be given proper weight. However, a proposal to establish this system in the Legislative Assembly of Nunavut was rejected in a 1998 Nunavut referendum.

**AFFIRMATIVE ACTION/
EMPLOYMENT EQUITY**
Policies designed to increase the proportion of persons from disadvantaged or under-represented groups in various positions.

Some governments have adopted **affirmative action** or **employment equity** programs[2] to increase the proportion of persons from disadvantaged or under-represented groups (such as women, Aboriginals, persons with disabilities, and visible minorities) in various positions. Canada's Charter of Rights and Freedoms specifically allows laws, programs, or activities designed to ameliorate the conditions of disadvantaged individuals or groups (s. 15). This may involve giving preference in hiring when candidates for a position are substantially equal, or establishing targets or quotas for hiring members of under-represented groups. Not surprisingly, quotas and preferential hiring policies have often created a backlash, as some members of non-disadvantaged groups feel that they are being discriminated against and limited in their opportunities.[3] Further, some members of disadvantaged groups feel that if hired because of a quota or a strong preference policy, they will be looked down upon as being hired for their race or gender rather than because of their qualifications and competence. While policies that give preferential treatment to certain groups may be viewed as limiting equality of opportunity in terms of treating individuals the same, they may have the positive effect of enhancing diversity in the workforce. Efforts to increase the diversity of the Toronto police force have helped to increase the force's effectiveness in dealing with diverse ethnic and racial groups and to overcome the distrust of police among groups that suffered harassment by a previously predominantly white police force (Appleby, 2010).

---

[2] The term *employment equity* was adopted in Canada on the recommendation of the *Report of the Commission on Equality in Employment* (1984) because of the intense controversies that accompanied quota-based affirmative action programs in the United States.

[3] In July 2010, the Canadian government ordered a review of its employment equity process after a white woman was prevented from applying for a particular government job that was open only to Aboriginals or members of a visible minority. While Cabinet ministers argued that hiring should be based on merit rather than race, critics were concerned that that the review would undermine employment equity programs.

Affirmative action policies have also become quite common in educational institutions, particularly to increase the proportion of women and Aboriginals in various professional programs. In the United States, the Supreme Court has upheld law school admission policies that give preference to racial minorities (particularly by admitting those with lower grades or test scores than unsuccessful white applicants) but rejected the use of quotas based on race. Nevertheless, because many people are opposed to racial preference policies, several U.S. states have passed initiatives to ban preferential admission policies.

DEMOCRACY

The term **democracy** comes from ancient Greek words that can be translated as "rule by the people." The democratic ideal is that all adult citizens should have an equal and effective voice in the decisions of the political communities to which they belong. Like all ideals, it may be impossible to fully realize the democratic ideal. Nevertheless, by analyzing the political systems of different countries we can examine the extent to which they are democratic and the different ways in which the democratic ideal is pursued. In addition, because the idea of democracy is popular, there are many countries that claim to be democratic but that we would consider undemocratic, semi-democratic, or undergoing a transition to democracy. In particular, although democracy is often associated with the holding of elections, we would not consider a country to be democratic if only advisory bodies with little decision-making capability are elected, if there are restrictions on which individuals and parties can contest elections, if elections feature coercion and intimidation of voters, or if the results of an election do not reflect the choice of voters. As well, claims of democracy made by unelected rulers who argue that they are acting in the interests of their people are not what we normally think of as democracy.

DEMOCRACY Rule by the people.

Democracy in Ancient Athens

About 2500 years ago, the important Greek city state of Athens adopted a system of **direct democracy**, that is, a system in which citizens themselves make the governing decisions. The citizens of Athens (which did not include women, slaves, and the foreign born) met in an open assembly about ten times a year. After a discussion in which all citizens could participate, the decisions governing this powerful political community were made through a vote by those present. Many officials were randomly selected for short terms in office through a lottery system (as were juries). The Athenian statesman Pericles defended this system, saying that "instead of looking on discussion as a stumbling-block in the way of action, we think it an indispensable preliminary to any wise action at all" (Thucydides, *The Peloponnesian War*, II, 40; quoted in Warren, 2002, p. 174).

DIRECT DEMOCRACY A system in which citizens themselves make the governing decisions.

TABLE 3-1

ARISTOTLE'S BASIC CLASSIFICATION OF TYPES OF RULE

RULE BY	LAWFUL RULE FOR THE COMMON GOOD	ARBITRARY RULE FOR THE RULERS' OWN INTERESTS
One	Kingship	Tyranny
Few	Aristocracy	Oligarchy
Many	Polity	Democracy

In contrast, the Greek philosopher Plato (c. 428–347 BCE) viewed democracy as involving leaders of the mass of people plundering the rich and distributing some of their wealth. Democracy, he argued, would degenerate into tyranny, as the mass gives up its freedom to a popular leader who would become a despotic tyrant. Plato's student Aristotle (384–322 BCE) examined 158 political communities and classified them in terms of whether there was rule by a single person, rule by a few, or rule by the many. Rule by one, a few, or many were good forms of government if the rulers worked toward the common good and governed in a lawful manner. Alternatively, if the ruling individual or group acted arbitrarily for its own interests, rule by one, a few, or the many could be considered a bad or "perverted" form of government. Aristotle's analysis is often summarized using a table that depicts six types of government (see Table 3-1).

Aristotle viewed democracy as a perverted form of government in which the poor, being the majority, governed in their own interests by taking away the property of the rich. Therefore, democracy did not work for the common good. As well, Aristotle was concerned that the masses could be swayed by passion and demagogic speakers rather than by reason, and might not act in accordance with established laws. However, he viewed citizen participation in politics as desirable and suggested that rule by the many could be a good form of government (which he termed "polity," or constitutional government) if it abided by the laws and governed for the good of all. Although rule by a virtuous few (aristocracy) would be best, in most cases it was not practical because of the small number of virtuous men.[4] Instead, the best form of governing that could be established in most cases would be a combination of democracy and oligarchy (rule by the wealthy), particularly if there was a large middle class that could moderate the tensions between the rich and the poor. With a large middle class, the polity form of governing would reflect neither the arrogance of the rich nor the enviousness of the poor (Hollowell & Porter, 1997).

---

[4] Virtue, which could be thought of as "the full and proper development of a human's faculties," requires leisure, or "time spent in the cultivation of the mind." In Aristotle's view, women, along with manual workers and slaves, did not have the time necessary to develop their minds and thus (along with the foreign born) could not be considered citizens and be involved in governing (Hollowell & Porter, 1997, pp. 62, 80).

Modern Democracy

Aristotle's analysis points to the reality that democracy has often been associated with struggles for greater social and economic equality. However, except in revolutionary situations, democratic forces have generally sought to pursue equality in a lawful manner and have avoided seizing the property of the rich.

Working class and women's movements were eventually successful (generally in the early twentieth century) in winning the right to vote for all adult citizens. However, although democratic governments (particularly in the richer countries) have adopted measures to provide assistance to the disadvantaged and to place higher taxes (sometimes with loopholes) on the rich, social and economic inequalities continue to be important. Indeed, in recent times there has been a tendency in many democratic countries for income differences to increase. For example, in 1995, Canada's top 50 corporate chief executive officers earned 85 times as much as the average worker; in 2008, the average income of this group was 243 times that of the average worker (Mackenzie, 2010). Politics often continues to focus on differences in the distribution of wealth and income among different groups and classes. Although voting potentially gives power to ordinary citizens, large corporations, the wealthy, and other elites have often been able to find ways to exert strong influence over the policies adopted by democratically elected governments.

Canadian Centre for
Policy Alternatives
www.growinggap.ca

Arguments for Democracy[5]

Those who promote the democratic ideal argue that it is the best way to achieve the common good. By involving the population as a whole in governing, the interests and values of different parts of the population are more likely to be reflected in decisions than if decision making is left in the hands of a single individual or a particular group. As well, by encouraging people to be freely involved in making governing decisions, those decisions can potentially benefit from the discussion and deliberation of persons with a wide variety of viewpoints. Even if the public as a whole is not directly involved in governing, democratic procedures such as elections can help to ensure that those holding governing positions are held accountable to the people and serve the good of the population as a whole.

Governments that have been chosen by the people are more likely to be accepted as legitimate by their populations. Because the people have a role in the political process, they are more likely to accept what government does, even if they happen to disagree with particular decisions. Therefore, democratic governments may be more effective than non-democratic ones, even though the processes of democratic decision making are often complex. As well, democracies have the positive feature of allowing for a peaceful transition

---

[5] Arguments against democracy are discussed in Chapter 11.

of power. Citizens can remove a government with which they are dissatisfied without having to resort to violence. Democracy may also encourage people to be more civic minded. Through involvement in politics, people may feel a greater attachment to the political community and be more likely to assume a sense of responsibility to their fellow citizens. Citizens may derive a sense of fulfillment and meaning through sharing in the governing of their community.

Finally, as discussed above, democracy is often associated with the promotion of equality. Although the adoption of democratic procedures does not necessarily result in greater social or economic equality, democracy has the potential to give some influence to those who would otherwise be powerless. This influence may encourage elected politicians to develop policies to aid the disadvantaged.

Types of Democracy

DIRECT DEMOCRACY   Direct democracy, in which citizens meet to discuss and make governing decisions, is generally considered impractical in large modern political communities. Nevertheless, some New England towns and small Swiss cantons have maintained this version of democracy.

LIBERAL, REPRESENTATIVE DEMOCRACY A political system that combines a high level of individual freedom and the election of representatives to a legislative body.

LIBERAL, REPRESENTATIVE DEMOCRACY   The type of democracy that Canadians are most familiar with can be termed **liberal, representative democracy**. As discussed in Chapter 11, this type of democracy involves the free competition of candidates and political parties to elect representatives to a legislative body (such as Canada's House of Commons)[6] that is empowered to pass legislation and approve government spending and taxing proposals. It also incorporates the ideology of liberalism (see Chapter 4), which advocates a high level of individual freedom, limitations on the power of government, the rule of law, and protection of individual rights.

Liberal, representative democracy is sometimes viewed as a limited form of democracy. Although citizens are free to vote for their representatives and directly (in a presidential system) or indirectly (in a parliamentary system) determine who will lead the government, they are not involved directly in discussing and making collective decisions. The political freedoms characteristic of liberal, representative democracies allow opportunities for people to try to influence the decisions made by their representatives and governments through various forms of independent political organization and expression. Nevertheless, governments and representatives do not necessarily follow the wishes of the people. Thus advocates of plebiscitary democracy and deliberative democracy seek to modify liberal, representative democracy to provide for greater direct citizen involvement in the making of governing decisions.

---

[6] As discussed in Chapter 14, Canada, like some other democratic countries, does not fully match this description, as Parliament includes an unelected Senate that also has to approve legislation, government spending, and taxing proposals.

PLEBISCITARY DEMOCRACY   **Plebiscitary democracy** uses such devices as referendums, initiatives, and recall elections to give citizens greater control over collective decisions and over their elected representatives.

Referendums give citizens the opportunity to vote on a particular issue or a proposed law.[7] A number of countries require that changes to their constitution be approved by a referendum. Referendums can also be used in some countries to repeal a law that has been passed by a legislative body. Many American states and municipalities make frequent use of referendums, although there has never been a national referendum in the United States. In Canada, there have only been three referendums at the national level, concerning the prohibition of liquor (1898), conscription (1942), and a package of constitutional changes known as the Charlottetown Accord (1992). Provinces and municipalities have held a number of referendums. Particularly notable have been two referendums in Quebec related to independence, including the 1995 referendum that by a margin of less than 1 percent rejected giving the Quebec government a mandate to negotiate sovereignty.

Although referendums involve a vote by the people, the decision to hold a referendum and the wording of a referendum are generally set by those in control of the government or the legislature. Some referendums have been used to manipulate the people through misleading wording. Indeed, many non-democratic governments have used referendums to try to legitimate their rule. For example, some dictators have held referendums asking for approval of their continued rule without allowing a choice among alternative candidates and without providing an opportunity for public criticism of the leader.

A stronger means of giving the public a direct say in decision making is the **initiative**. This procedure gives citizens the right, by obtaining a sizable number of signatures on a petition, to have a proposition that they have drafted put to a vote by the electorate for approval. This right for laws to be proposed and approved by the people has been established in Switzerland, Italy, and a majority of American states. A weak form of the initiative has also been adopted by British Columbia (see Box 3-5, The "No HST" Initiative in British Columbia). For example, during the American presidential election in 2008, voters in 36 states passed or rejected a total of 153 initiatives on proposals for state laws on such topics as abortion, same-sex marriage, and legalization of marijuana for medical purposes, as well as various tax proposals. As with referendums, the wording of initiatives can be complex and misleading. In addition, the gathering of a large number of signatures can be a costly endeavour and campaigns for initiatives as well as referendums may favour those who are well-financed, including large corporations.

PLEBISCITARY DEMOCRACY A form of democracy in which citizens have greater control through the use of such devices as referendums, initiatives, and recall elections.

REFERENDUM A vote by citizens on a particular issue or a proposed law.

INITIATIVE A procedure that gives citizens the right, by obtaining a sizable number of signatures on a petition, to have a proposition that they have drafted put to a vote by the electorate for approval.

---

[7] A distinction can be made between referendums whose results are binding on government and those that are only advisory (the latter sometimes referred to as plebiscites). However, even if a referendum is not legally binding, governments will often accept its results.

BOX 3-5

The "No HST" Initiative in British Columbia

During the 2009 provincial election campaign, the media asked political parties in British Columbia whether they were opposed to harmonizing the federal goods and services tax (GST) with the provincial sales tax. The Liberal party responded that "a harmonized GST is not something that is contemplated in the BC Liberal platform" (Spector, 2009). Three days after winning the May 12 election, the Liberal government began discussions with the federal government on the Harmonized Sales Tax (HST), which came into effect on July 1, 2010. As of June 2010, more than 700 000 citizens had signed an initiative petition to scrap the HST created by former Social Credit premier Bill Vander Zalm and backed by the opposition NDP.

British Columbia adopted an initiative procedure in 1991. If, within 90 days, at least 10 percent of registered voters in each electoral district sign a petition supporting a proposed bill, a legislative committee must decide whether that bill will be voted on in the legislature or whether a province-wide vote will be held. If the second option is chosen and more than half of the registered voters in the province and in at least two-thirds of the electoral districts vote in favour of the bill, a legislative vote on the bill is required.

Difficulty in obtaining a sufficient number of signatures and the provisions that allow legislators rather than voters to have the final say on initiative proposals has discouraged the use of this procedure. Nevertheless, the strong public outrage regarding the introduction of the HST in B.C. resulted in the collection of more than enough petition signatures in every electoral district. This led the B.C. government to consider cancelling the HST rather than holding a public vote on the initiative, and contributed to the resignation of Premier Gordon Campbell in November 2010.

RECALL A procedure that allows citizens to remove representatives from office. By gaining a sufficient number of signatures on a petition, citizens can require that their representative seek re-election before the term of office is over.

Initiative & Referendum Institute
www.iandrinstitute.org

Initiative and Referendum Institute Europe
www.iri-europe.org

DELIBERATIVE DEMOCRACY A political system in which decisions are made based on discussion by free and equal citizens rather than by elected representatives alone.

Recall procedures allow citizens to remove representatives from office. As with the initiative, a recall involves gathering a sufficient number of names on a petition and then holding an election to determine whether the majority of voters wish to remove their representative and hold a new election. Recall procedures are available in some American states and Swiss cantons, Venezuela, the Philippines, and British Columbia. For example, a recall election in 2003 saw Arnold Schwarzenegger replace Gray Davis as governor of California. In British Columbia, no recall attempts have been successful since recall procedures were adopted in 1991, although one provincial legislator resigned rather than suffer a likely defeat in a recall election. In June 2010, plans were being developed to try to recall twenty-four Liberal members of B.C.'s legislature in an attempt to rescind the harmonized sales tax.

DELIBERATIVE DEMOCRACY   In recent years, there has been considerable discussion among political theorists about the possibility of a **deliberative democracy** in which decisions are made based on discussion by free and equal citizens (Elster, 1998). Through involvement in deliberative processes, it is hoped that people will become better informed, more active citizens. Through dialogue, people will come to understand the viewpoints of others and then, ideally, work together constructively to propose policies that are for the common good. Unlike representative and plebiscitary versions of democracy, deliberative democracy brings citizens into decision making through discussion, rather than primarily through voting.

Advocates of deliberative democracy often envision it as operating primarily among citizens at the local level, where face-to-face dialogue is possible and the issues being discussed may have direct relevance to the lives of those involved. Making people in local communities responsible for managing their resources (such as rivers, forests, or coastal fisheries) or establishing community Parliaments (Resnick, 1997) may encourage deliberative decision making.

Citizens' juries are another possible way to involve ordinary citizens in deliberation and decision making. The citizens' jury brings together a group of randomly selected citizens. Like the juries used to determine the outcome of some court trials, citizens' juries are composed of persons without any special knowledge of the topic under consideration. Trained facilitators are used to guide the deliberation, jurors are provided with information, and witnesses are called to explain and justify different viewpoints. In British Columbia, an extensive process of deliberation along with public hearings was used by a randomly selected Citizens' Assembly to recommend whether a new system should be used to elect provincial legislators. The recommendation for a single transferable vote electoral system (see Chapter 8) was put to the citizens of the province in a binding referendum in 2005. Although 57.7 percent voted in favour of the new system, this was short of the required approval by 60 percent of voters and by majorities in 60 percent of the province's electoral districts. The proposal was soundly defeated in a second referendum in 2009. A similar process was used to develop a recommendation for change to Ontario's electoral system. However, the proposal to adopt a mixed member proportional representation (discussed in Chapter 8) was supported by only 37 percent of voters in a 2007 referendum.

The Deliberative Democracy Consortium
www.deliberative-democracy.net

◄ The British Columbia Citizens' Assembly discusses its recommendations for changing the province's electoral system.

Summary and Conclusion

Freedom, equality, and democracy are popular political values in many countries in the contemporary world. A high level of freedom allows individuals to pursue their own interests and develop their own capabilities. The freedom to engage in political activity is also an essential element of liberal democracy. Nevertheless, questions often arise as to what limits on individual freedom are desirable to preserve order and security, to prevent harm or offence to others, and to promote the common good of society.

Although an active government is often thought to be the enemy of freedom, some argue that for freedom to be meaningful for all members of the political community, government should ensure that all persons have the capability and resources to develop themselves and live a life of dignity. Finding a balance between negative freedom (the absence of restraints) and positive freedom (the capacity to do something) is often controversial because an active role for government in helping and protecting the disadvantaged often requires some limits to economic freedom and property rights. In advancing the goal of greater equality, some limitations of individual freedom, particularly economic freedom, may be necessary.

In analyzing equality, it is important to distinguish between three basic types of equality: rights, opportunity, and outcome. Pursuing equality of opportunity and, even more so, equality of outcome requires active rather than minimal government. Generally, most countries have come to accept the principle of equal rights in their laws. In practice, however, there are often formal or informal barriers to achieving equal rights. Likewise, although progress toward equality of opportunity has been made in a number of countries through universal education and attempts to end discrimination against those with particular characteristics, inequalities in income and wealth and the negative attitudes that are often held concerning those with particular characteristics make full equality of opportunity difficult to achieve. Finally, although the economically developed democratic countries generally feature lower levels of economic inequality than many of the poorer countries, there has been a tendency for inequality in income and wealth to grow as the top personnel in large corporations have been able to sharply increase their compensation.

Controversy exists concerning the inequality among different groups. Clearly, members of some groups have been seriously disadvantaged because of discrimination or oppression in the past that, to varying extents, continues in the present. Measures to rectify past injustices, to overcome inequalities in the present, and to increase the diversity of different occupations, educational institutions, and political positions can cause a backlash among those in the dominant groups who feel their opportunities may be limited because of their characteristics. Reconciling the focus of liberal democracy on individual rights and opportunities with preferential policies to create greater group equality can be difficult.

Democracy is based on the ideal of rule by the people. Liberal, representative democracy provides citizens with indirect control of laws and policies through the election of persons and parties to make decisions on their behalf. By providing political freedoms, individuals can express their views, organize to influence the laws and policies of government, and have a free and informed choice in elections. However, liberal, representative democracy is viewed by some as not providing a fully democratic political system. In particular, some argue that citizens should be given a more direct ability to make or ratify decisions through mechanisms of plebiscitary or deliberative democracy.

Overall, by establishing and protecting equal rights for all persons, liberal democracy provides a way of combining freedom with some degree of equality. Nevertheless, there are often important differences between those who believe that a democratic government should pursue social and economic equality and those who favour limited government and economic freedom. Different viewpoints about freedom and equality are central to the ideological perspectives discussed in Chapter 4.

Key Terms

Discussion Questions

1. Should "hate speech" such as the expression of negative views concerning different races, religions, or genders be banned on college and university campuses?

2. Should extremist political parties be prevented from contesting elections?

3. Should government try to create greater equality by levying very high taxes on those whose incomes are more than $1 million a year?

4. Should each electoral district elect one male and one female candidate to create gender equality in Canada's House of Commons?

5. Is plebiscitary democracy or deliberative democracy a worthwhile modification of liberal, representative democracy?

6. Does liberal, representative democracy provide an appropriate combination of freedom and equality?

Further Reading

Berlin, I. (2002). *Liberty*. Oxford: Oxford University Press.

Dahl, R.A. (1998). *On democracy*. New Haven, CT: Yale University Press.

Goodwin, B. (2007). *Using political ideas* (5th ed.). West Sussex, UK: John Wiley & Sons.

Held, D. (2006). *Models of democracy* (3rd ed.). Cambridge, UK: Polity Press.

Resnick, P. (1997). *Twenty-first century democracy*. Montreal: McGill-Queen's University Press.

Sandel, M.J. (2009). *Justice. What's the right thing to do?* New York: Farrar, Straus and Giroux.

Thiele, L.P. (1997). *Thinking politics: Perspectives in ancient, modern, and postmodern political theory*. Chatham, NJ: Chatham House Publishers.

Tinder, G. (2004). *Political thinking: The perennial questions* (6th ed.). New York: Pearson Longman.

Wilkinson, R., & Pickett, K. (2009). *The spirit level: Why equal societies almost always do better*. London: Penguin.

PART II

Ideals and Ideologies

Chapter 4

Liberalism, Conservatism, Socialism, and Fascism

PHOTO ABOVE: Vladimir Lenin's brother was arrested and then hanged for plotting to assassinate Tsar Alexander III. On learning of the execution, Vladimir promised to "make them pay for this!" Soon thereafter, he began studying the works of revolutionary thinkers Karl Marx and Frederick Engels and later, as the leader of the Bolsheviks, advocated revolutionary action.

CHAPTER OBJECTIVES

After reading this chapter you should be able to:

1. explain the meaning and significance of political ideology

2. discuss the ideas of liberalism, conservatism, socialism, and fascism

3. outline the development and major variations of each ideology

4. apply the terms "left" and "right" to the analysis of political perspectives

After his brother was arrested for concealing a bomb in a medical encyclopedia, Vladimir Ilych Ulyanov— and ultimately world politics—underwent a profound change. Vladimir was still a teenager when his older brother Alexander was hanged for planning to assassinate Russia's Tsar Alexander III. On learning of the execution, Vladimir proclaimed, "I'll make them pay for this! I swear it!" (Shub, 1966, p. 16).

Expelled from university for supporting student demands, Vladimir began studying the works of revolutionary thinkers Karl Marx and Frederick Engels and passed the examinations needed to become a lawyer. Later, in exile in Switzerland, he adopted the name Lenin. He became the leader of the Bolshevik party (later known as the Communist party), which advocated revolutionary action.

With Russia suffering extreme hardships and military defeats in World War I, Tsar Nicholas II was forced to abdicate in March 1917. A provisional government continued the devastating war and did little to alleviate the dire circumstances faced by much of the population. Using the slogan "peace, bread, land," the Bolsheviks led a successful attack on the seat of government in Petrograd (now St. Petersburg). After a bitter civil war, Lenin was able to gain control of Russia, which was renamed the Union of Soviet Socialist Republics.

In many ways, the communist regimes of Lenin and his successor Stalin were even more oppressive than the tsarist governments that had ruled Russia for centuries. Dissent of any kind was brutally repressed. Forced labour camps were set up in remote regions of Russia. Whole populations were exiled from their homelands. And millions of peasants died of starvation as a result of the policies adopted by the Communist government.

Strongly held ideas and beliefs, whether religious or political, can have a profound effect on the world and on our lives as well as shaping the way that we understand the world. In this chapter and the next chapter, we will examine various important political perspectives, termed political ideologies.

POLITICAL IDEOLOGIES

POLITICAL IDEOLOGY A package of interrelated ideas and beliefs about government, society, the economy, and human nature that inspire and affect political action. Each ideology provides a different perspective that is used to understand and evaluate how the world actually works. Most ideologies also provide a vision of what the world should be like and propose a means of political action to achieve their objectives.

A **political ideology** is a package of interrelated ideas and beliefs about government, society, the economy, and human nature that inspire and affect political action. Each ideology provides a different perspective that is used to understand and evaluate how the world actually works (Sunderlin, 2003). Marxism, for example, looks at the world through the lens of class conflict, feminism sees the world in terms of male dominance, and liberalism views historical development as involving the struggle for individual freedom.

Most political ideologies also provide a vision of what the world should be like and propose a means of political action to achieve their objectives. Some ideologies challenge and seek to transform the existing basic power arrangements; other ideologies provide justifications for the existing order. Ideologies are often associated with social movements and political parties. For example, democratic socialism has been closely associated with the labour movement and with political parties such as the New Democratic Party in Canada and Social Democratic parties in Europe.

ENLIGHTENMENT An intellectual movement that developed in the mid eighteenth century, emphasizing the power of human reason to understand and improve the world.

The development of political ideologies is associated with the ideas of the European **Enlightenment** and with the economic and social upheavals associated with the development of capitalism and the Industrial Revolution. The mid-eighteenth-century Enlightenment involved a major shift from traditional religious beliefs toward an optimistic belief in the power of human reason to make the world better. Setting the tone for the modern world, Enlightenment thinkers argued that through reason and science, people could understand the world. Progress could be achieved by consciously shaping the world and its institutions. Human beings could create a better society on Earth, rather than waiting for the life after death promised by religion. The French Revolution of 1789, influenced in part by Enlightenment ideas, involved a fundamental challenge to the traditional bases of authority: the monarchy, the aristocracy, and the Catholic Church. New and competing sets of ideas developed about how society and the state should be organized and run. Likewise, the rise of capitalism and the Industrial Revolution disrupted previous patterns of economic and social life, leading to intense disputes over the desirability of the capitalist system. The political ideologies that developed in Europe spread to the rest of the world, although they have often been modified by different cultures and circumstances.

Ideological conflict has been at the centre of political life for more than two centuries. Intellectuals, politicians, and political activists often have a particular ideological perspective. Controversies over a variety of public policy issues often reflect differences among those who have different ideological perspectives. Many people do not consciously hold an ideological perspective, but nonetheless are affected in their thinking by elements of one or more ideologies. Whether in a subtle or explicit manner, ideological perspectives are often conveyed to the public by governments, various political and social groups, the educational system, and the mass media. Ideas related to particular ideologies are often used in political life to mobilize support for particular causes, movements, parties, policies, and governments.

The Negative Side of Ideology

The term *ideology* originated to describe efforts to develop a science of ideas. However, the term is often used to describe certain sets of ideas and ways of thinking in a negative way. For Karl Marx, the key developer of communism, ideology was the instrument of the ruling class used to justify the harsh realities of the capitalist system. Others use the term to describe what are viewed as extremist perspectives such as communism and fascism. Political figures often describe themselves as "pragmatic" (that is, practical and relying on common sense) and characterize their opponents as "ideologues."

There is some validity to the negative characterizations of ideology. Some people treat the leading texts of their ideology as if they were the absolute truth and refuse to consider seriously any criticisms of their perspective. In this respect, some political ideologies can resemble fundamentalist religions. Further, ideological thinking can be simplistic and ideological adherents may provide distorted depictions of reality to fit their mental model of the world. More importantly, ideologies have been used to justify the unjustifiable, such as the extermination of the European Jewish population by the Nazis and the mass murder of educated city residents in Cambodia in the 1970s.

However, ideologies are the belief systems of not only fanatics, extremists, and simplistic thinkers. Some of those whose ideas reflect the mainstream ideologies of liberalism or conservatism are dogmatic in their thinking. As well, those who view themselves as practical or pragmatic may, often unknowingly, be influenced by an ideological perspective. In particular, the leading or dominant ideology in a community will often seem to be "common sense."

◀ Ideologies have been used to justify the unjustifiable, such as the death of about one-fifth of the population of Cambodia from 1975 to 1979. In an attempt to create an agrarian communist utopia, Pol Pot's Khmer Rouge regime evacuated the cities and undertook a deliberate campaign of destroying the educated part of the population through starvation, slave labour, and executions. Some Western intellectuals, blinded by the regime's ideology, tried to deny the reality of the Cambodian "killing fields."

On the positive side, an ideology can provide some coherence, consistency, and direction to a person's political thinking and actions As Boris DeWeil (2000) argues, the ongoing debate among different ideologies is an inherent and desirable aspect of democratic politics, resulting from the fact that people have different value priorities (for example, whether equality or freedom is more important). Ideologies provide us with different ideas about the common good and how it may be achieved. "Without ideology, politics becomes the pursuit of power as its own reward" (DeWeil, 2000, p. 5).

Examining Ideologies

When examining ideologies, we should keep in mind that each ideology is a broad perspective containing many variations that evolves over time. It is not always easy to distinguish clearly between one ideology and another because differences between them may be subtle. However, each of the major ideologies has some distinguishing themes (see Table 4-1).

TABLE 4-1
IDEOLOGIES: KEY THEMES

Note: These are only broad characterizations that do not capture the diversity and evolution of each ideology.

	LIBERALISM	CONSERVATISM	SOCIALISM	FASCISM
Human nature	Individuals able to think and act according to reason	Humans imperfect with capacity for evil	Humans co-operative and social	People motivated by emotion rather than reason
Key value	Individual freedom	Order, stability, social harmony	Equality	Loyalty to nation-state
Political system	Liberal, representative democracy	Traditional institutions	Egalitarian democracy	Authoritarian leadership
Rights	Protect individual rights	Rights balanced by duties	Provide universal social and economic rights	Subordinate individual to the state
Morality	State should not impose morality	Maintain traditional moral values	Promote equalitarian values	Promote heroic virtues
Economy	Free market with equality of opportunity	Free market with social harmony	Planned economy	Corporate state
Political analysis	Struggle for freedom	Radical changes undesirable	Class conflict and struggle for equality	Racial or national conflict

FIGURE 4-1

POLITICAL IDEOLOGIES ON THE LEFT–RIGHT DIMENSION

Political parties with ideological names, such as Liberal or Conservative parties, do not *necessarily* reflect the ideology corresponding to their name. Political parties are often, but not always, founded on a set of ideological principles. However, in the pursuit of electoral success, they may find it desirable to modify or ignore those principles.

Left and Right

A simple way of depicting ideological positions is in terms of left and right, as illustrated in Figure 4-1. The terms *left* and *right* originated in the seating arrangements of the French National Assembly established after the French Revolution of 1789. Those who favoured the old order sat to the right of the chairman of the Assembly. Those who opposed the absolute authority of the monarch, demanded that the power and privileges of the Catholic Church be reduced or eliminated, and favoured redistributing the property and wealth of the nobility sat to the left (Needler, 1996). The seating arrangement of parties of the left and right continues to this day in the semi-circular French National Assembly and in the European Parliament.

In contemporary usage, the **left** is associated with the pursuit of greater social and economic equality, while those on the **right** generally see inequality as a natural feature of human society. A secondary meaning is that those on the right believe that traditional (usually religious-based) moral values should be reflected in laws and supported by community institutions, while those on the left generally oppose state support for religious institutions and favour laws based on universal human rights rather than traditional morality. In other words, equality and freedom are often associated with the left while traditional morality and elite authority tend to be associated with the right.

While liberalism is typically depicted as being in the centre of the ideological spectrum, we need to be careful about the meaning of the centre. Because being in the centre is often viewed positively, assessing what is the centre can often be controversial. Fascists often claimed that they represent a middle way between communism and capitalism. Conservatives often suggest that liberals in North America are left wing rather than centrist, while liberals often view conservatives as being far to the right.

Although the terms *left* and *right* are often used in political discussion, portraying political perspectives along a single dimension can be misleading, as the differences among the ideologies are multi-dimensional. For example, although communism and fascism are very different in their views on equality, communist and fascist states exhibit some similarities in their efforts to exert tight control over their societies. Furthermore, some perspectives such

LEFT The general ideological position associated with advocacy of greater social and economic equality, laws based on universal human rights rather than traditional morality, and opposition to state support for religious institutions.

RIGHT The general ideological position associated with opposition to imposing greater social and economic equality and with maintaining traditional (usually religious-based) moral values and institutions.

as nationalism and environmentalism do not fit easily on the left–right dimension because their focus is on a different set of concerns.

LIBERALISM

Your ideological position: an easy, anonymous, five-minute quiz www.politicalcompass.org

The ideology of liberalism emphasizes the desirability of a high level of individual freedom, based on a belief in the inherent dignity and worth of each individual. Individuals are assumed to be capable of using reason and taking rational actions in pursuit of their interests. Thus, individuals should take responsibility for their own lives with as little interference as possible. Establishing a set of basic rights for all individuals allows people to live their lives as they see fit (Barry, 1996). Because of the human capacity for reason, freedom allows individuals to develop their capabilities. This makes progress a characteristic of free societies.

Historically, liberalism developed out of the struggles against the arbitrary power of absolute monarchs, restrictions on free business activity, the imposition of one set of religious values on the population of a country, and the granting of special privileges to particular groups—such as churches, aristocrats, and business monopolies.

Although liberals see a need for government, they are concerned that those in governing positions will abuse their power to pursue their own interests. Therefore, a central goal of liberalism is to ensure that the rights of individuals are firmly protected so they cannot be taken away by government. Liberals advocate the **rule of law**; that is, government should act only in accordance with established laws rather than in an arbitrary fashion, and all persons should be equally subject to the law. Liberals also believe that the scope of government activity should be limited. This involves distinguishing a substantial area of private activity, where government should not be involved, from matters of public concern, in which government may be involved. As former Canadian Liberal Prime Minister Pierre Trudeau argued, "The state has no place in the nation's bedrooms." What goes on between consenting adults, in this perspective, should be left to their own moral judgment.

RULE OF LAW The idea that people should be subject to known, predictable, and impartial rules of conduct, rather than to the arbitrary orders of particular individuals. Both the rulers and the ruled should be equally subject to the law.

Religious belief, in the liberal view, is a private matter based on the conscience of the individual. A policy of tolerance should be adopted concerning those holding different beliefs. Government should not require or promote adherence to any particular religion, and laws should not be based on any particular religious perspective. Government is not a creation of God to promote or enforce moral values, but rather a human creation for more limited purposes, specifically to provide the rules and procedures under which individuals can enjoy freedom.

Liberalism is also associated with the view that government should be based on the consent of the governed. Contemporary liberals are strongly committed to the principles of liberal democracy, and generally prefer representative democracy to the plebiscitary forms of democracy discussed in Chapter 3.

Classical and Reform Liberalism

Liberalism is often analyzed, particularly in English-speaking countries, in terms of an evolution from classical to reform liberalism. Based on the ideas of John Locke (discussed in Chapter 3), **classical liberalism** viewed government as established for limited purposes—namely, the protection of life, liberty, and property. As well, classical liberalism is associated with support for a **laissez-faire economic system**—that is, an economic system (advocated by Adam Smith) in which workers, consumers, and privately owned businesses freely interact in the marketplace with little government interference. The proper role of government is limited to such activities as maintaining order, enforcing contracts, and providing a means for impartially settling disputes.

Reform liberalism (also referred to as social liberalism, welfare liberalism, or modern liberalism) combines support for individual freedom with a belief that government action may be needed to help remove obstacles to individual development. Reform liberalism developed in the latter part of the nineteenth century as many liberals became concerned that the laissez-faire system established in countries such as Britain seemed to offer little to develop the capabilities of workers and disadvantaged sectors of society. Life was harsh for the majority of the population, who worked long hours in unsafe conditions to eke out a living with no protection against sickness, disability, unemployment, or old age.

Reform liberals argue that government should play a role in assisting the disadvantaged through such measures as unemployment insurance, old age pensions, health care, and subsidized education. This creates a more meaningful freedom for the less fortunate members of society by ensuring that a basic standard of living is available to all. In other words, reform liberals have viewed freedom as a matter of not simply limiting government interference in people's lives. Rather, some government action is needed to ensure an equal right to freedom. In addition, reform liberalism tends to place greater emphasis on equality, particularly equality of opportunity, than does classical liberalism.

Reform liberals generally share with classical liberals a belief in the virtues of a free-enterprise system. However, reform liberals argue that property rights may need to be limited, to some extent, in order to advance the rights and freedoms of others. For example, the freedom of a factory owner may need to be limited by government regulations in order to protect labourers from unsafe working conditions, consumers from harmful products, and the environment from the discharge of pollutants

British economist John Maynard Keynes's analysis that a laissez-faire system based on the pursuit of self-interest does not necessarily lead to the common good has influenced reform liberalism. In Keynes's view (discussed in Chapter 16), government needs to use its powers to help make the economy run more smoothly, particularly by adopting policies that foster full employment, while leaving private businesses unhindered in their individual operations.

CLASSICAL LIBERALISM A form of liberalism that emphasizes the desirability of limited government and the free marketplace.

LAISSEZ-FAIRE ECONOMIC SYSTEM A system in which privately owned businesses, workers, and consumers freely interact in the marketplace without government interference.

REFORM LIBERALISM A version of liberalism that combines support for individual freedom with a belief that government action may be needed to help remove obstacles to individual development.

Liberal International
www.liberal-international.org

Furthermore, some contemporary reform liberals take what is known as a communitarian rather than an individualist approach to liberalism. For example, Canadian political philosopher Will Kymlicka (1991, p. 208) argues that it is membership in a cultural community that "enables individual freedom . . . [and] enables meaningful choices about how to live one's life."

Neo-Liberalism

NEO-LIBERALISM A perspective based on a strong belief in the free marketplace and opposition to government intervention in the economy.

Although the ideology of liberalism has evolved over time, some of the ideas associated with classical liberalism have continued to be very influential. In particular, the idea of moving toward a laissez-faire economic system (including global free trade) with a limited role for government, often labelled **neo-liberalism,**[1] is an important ideological perspective in the contemporary world.

The neo-liberal perspective is based on the idea that individuals are motivated by self-interest, particularly material self-interest. Individuals should be free to choose and pay for the services they wish to receive, government services should be privatized wherever possible, taxes should be substantially reduced, and access to welfare should be strictly limited. Although labelled "neo-liberal," this strong belief in the free-market system and limited government is often associated with contemporary conservatism, particularly in the United States and Canada. In continental Europe, the term *liberal* generally refers to a belief in a free-market economy, limited government, and a separation of religion from laws and governing.

CONSERVATISM

CONSERVATISM A perspective or ideology that emphasizes the values of order, stability, respect for authority, and tradition, based on a view that humans are inherently imperfect, with a limited capacity to reason.

REACTIONARY A conservative who favours a return to the values and institutions of the past.

Conservatism, particularly in its traditional form, emphasizes the values of order and stability in the community. Conservatives are usually critical of those who advocate rapid and fundamental change. Conservatism as a distinctive perspective or ideology developed particularly in response to the French Revolution (1789), which challenged the privileges of elites, promoted equality and popular sovereignty, proclaimed the "Rights of Man," and sought to reorganize society along rational principles.

Some conservatives (labelled **reactionaries**) responded to the failures of the French Revolution by advocating a return to the values and institutions of the old order. Other conservatives, such as British member of Parliament Edmund Burke (1729–1797), took a more moderate position, arguing that change, when necessary, should be slow, gradual, and consistent with the particular traditions of a country.

---

[1]Although the terms *neo-liberalism* and *neo-conservatism* are often used interchangeably, neo-liberalism focuses on the desirability of a free-market economy while neo-conservatism focuses more on cultural and moral values and a strong military. Neo-liberalism can also be distinguished from libertarianism, which emphasizes the desirability of freedom from all forms of government intervention in the lives of individuals.

Conservative thinkers view humans as inherently imperfect, with a great potential for evil and a limited capacity to use their reasoning abilities. To maintain civilized values against the ever-present tendencies of evil, laws need to be respected and vigorously enforced by government, and respect for those in positions of authority must be maintained. Therefore, conservatives have generally favoured a strong government with strong leadership able to protect order and stability and to pursue national interests. As well, conservatives often argue that traditional, religion-based moral values need to be maintained in order to prevent the collapse of civilized society.

Because of the individual's limited capabilities to reason and because of the complexity of society, conservatives argue that we should respect the wisdom that has slowly built up over the ages. This wisdom, they argue, is reflected in traditional customs and practices. Conservatives tend to be critical of attempts to improve society by deliberate political effort.

Conservatives view the institutions of private property, religion, marriage, and the family as the bulwarks of the social order. They generally oppose government policies designed to move society in the direction of greater equality (for example, by redistributing income, wealth, and property from the rich to the poor) based on the view that people are naturally unequal. Attempts to impose equality are disruptive and undermine the natural leadership of elite groups. Instead, conservatives have traditionally looked to the upper classes to help, protect, and provide moral guidance to the poor.

Conservatism tends to differ from liberalism in being less concerned with the rights of individuals. Instead, as Edmund Burke put it, society should be viewed as a living organism in which the well-being of the individual is dependent on the well-being of the whole, or as a tapestry composed of interwoven threads. Society and the state are not simply based on a temporary contract among individuals, but rather are a permanent partnership "between those who are living, those who are dead, and those who are to be born" (Burke, 1790/1955, p. 110). Governments, along with an official, established religion, are important features of human society that are needed to restrain the passions of individuals. Instead of proclaiming the universal rights of all humanity, Burke argued that the traditional liberties of particular countries should be defended. Nevertheless, conservatives place a high priority on law and order rather than on individual freedom and stress the responsibilities of individuals to society.

The Canadian Conservative Forum
www.conservativeforum.org

Historically, conservatism was often associated with the landowning, hereditary aristocracy, which viewed itself as preserving civilized values and having an obligation to lead society. The relentless pursuit of profit by entrepreneurs in the growing industrial and commercial sector of the economy was frequently viewed with disdain. Some conservatives worried that the revolutionary impact of the modern free-market economy and associated global free trade could undermine the local values and particularisms that conservatives cherish. Further, some conservatives were concerned that a pure free-market capitalist system created deep social divisions between capitalists and workers that could threaten national unity and social order.

As conservatism evolved, it became less oriented to the views of the declining aristocracy. Instead, conservatism has often been associated with the values and interests of the business community, and has thus supported the free-market capitalist system against the challenges posed by the equality-seeking ideologies of communism, socialism, and reform liberalism. In addition, conservatives have become concerned about the decline of the work ethic, which they believe is caused by the development of the **welfare state**. Many conservatives have continued to defend traditional moral values in opposition to what they view as the permissiveness of modern, secular societies.

The New Right

An influential contemporary version of conservatism, termed the **New Right**, developed in the 1970s combining, in various ways, the promotion of free-market capitalism and limited government (neo-liberalism) and traditional cultural and moral values (social conservatism). Although this combination of ideas among conservatives was not new, the vigorous promotion and application of this perspective since the 1970s helped to make this the leading version of contemporary conservatism in many countries, as discussed in Box 4-1, The "Iron Lady."

The New Right was also a reaction to the "New Left," a perspective that views the marginalized in society (such as ethnic and racial minorities, students, youth, women, and the poor) as oppressed groups whose liberation would lead to fundamental changes in society. For the conservative-minded, the New Left and radical criticism of the status quo posed a threat to Western values, while the "counterculture" of 1960s youth promoted immorality.

The New Right has opposed affirmative action programs, arguing that legal equality and laws preventing discrimination are sufficient to provide equal opportunities for all. Attempting to ensure equal outcomes creates unrealistic expectations and an overly activist, coercive government (Medcalf & Dolbeare, 1985). In addition, government encouragement for groups to develop their distinctive cultures and identities is viewed by the New Right as weakening the nation-state by undermining the common interests and values of the nation (Whitaker, 1997).

In the New Right's view, Western civilization faces a cultural crisis because of the decline of traditional moral values. The overbearing nature of big government has undermined the ability of communities to maintain moral norms (Frum, 1996). Liberal social values have fostered a permissive society in which "anything goes" while moral principles are ignored.

The New Right (particularly the element known as the Christian Right) has often focused on the promotion of traditional family values, which it

WELFARE STATE A state in which government ensures that all people have a decent standard of living and are provided protection from hardships resulting from circumstances such as unemployment, sickness, disability, and old age.

NEW RIGHT A perspective that combines, in various ways, the promotion of free-market capitalism and limited government and traditional cultural and moral values.

BOX 4-1

The "Iron Lady": Margaret Thatcher

In 1984, the National Union of Mineworkers began a year-long strike in Britain to protest the closure of twenty state-owned coal mines and the loss of twenty thousand jobs. Conservative Prime Minister Margaret Thatcher took a tough stance against the strike. Strikers on the picket line were subject to attacks by police and thousands of picketers were arrested; laws were passed to curb strikes and end closed shops and sympathy strikes; and welfare benefits were denied to the spouses and children of strikers, leading to accusations that Thatcher wanted to starve strikers back to work. In the end, the dejected and divided miners returned to work with no concessions. Over the following years, more mines were closed and the once powerful British labour movement greatly weakened.

Margaret Thatcher, the daughter of a grocery store owner and mayor of Grantham, England, received a degree in chemistry from Oxford and practised law. First elected to Parliament in 1959, she gained notoriety as Minister of Education for eliminating free milk for schoolchildren. After defeating former Prime Minister Edward Heath to become Conservative party leader, she led her party to electoral victory in 1979. She served as prime minister until forced out by her party caucus in 1990. She was known as the "Iron Lady" for her toughness and determination and sometimes described as the "only real man" in her all-male Cabinet. Under her direction, the British government greatly reduced the regulation of business, privatized state-owned industries and public housing, and reformed education, health, and welfare systems. In addition, Thatcher was an advocate of traditional moral values, hard work, and individual responsibility; introduced legislation to prevent the promotion of homosexuality; and took tough measures against criminal behaviour. In international affairs, she was a strong ally of American President Ronald Reagan in the fight against communism and ordered British troops to retake the disputed Falkland Islands (Malvinas) in the South Atlantic that had been captured by Argentina.

Thatcher changed the course of British politics and revitalized the conservative ideology throughout the world by adopting a strong free-enterprise orientation. Unlike traditional conservatives, Thatcher had a strongly individualistic perspective, claiming that "there is no such thing as society." Instead of the moderate, consensus-oriented approach favoured by many Conservative politicians, Thatcher forcefully pursued a new direction, for better or worse. While many conservative thinkers claim that conservatism is not an ideology, being pragmatic rather than pursuing a vision of society, few would doubt that Thatcher's tough-minded conservatism was ideological in nature.

contends are threatened by abortion, homosexuality, premarital sex, divorce, and sexually explicit television, movies, and music. The traditional moral views of the New Right can also be seen in their views on crime. Unlike the liberal-minded, who tend to view crime as a result of societal injustices and seek to rehabilitate criminals, the New Right argues that criminals need to take full responsibility for their crimes. Therefore, they favour harsh punitive measures to deter criminal behaviour.

The New Right (particularly the element labelled "neo-conservative") is also associated with taking a hardline approach in international relations.

In the 1980s, key figures in the New Right advocated defeating communism rather than merely containing it. The New Right has advocated strong action against what American President George W. Bush in 2002 termed the "axis of evil" (Iran, Iraq, and North Korea). The United States and its allies should exercise global leadership and use its strength to promote Western values—including democracy, freedom, and the free-market capitalist system—worldwide. This involves ensuring that the United States has overwhelming military superiority and a willingness to take unilateral military action with its allies against "rogue regimes" and those who support terrorism, with or without the approval of the United Nations.

Understanding Neo-Conservatism
www.publiceye.org/conservative/
neocons/neocon.html

TENSIONS WITHIN THE NEW RIGHT   There are important tensions within the New Right perspective, which generally advocates a free economy in a strong state (Gamble, 1994). Those contemporary conservatives who have adopted the individualistic, market-oriented perspective of neo-liberalism typically want the role of government kept to a minimum. In particular, "economic" or "fiscal" conservatives focus on reducing government spending, cutting taxes, and eliminating government debt and deficit. Social conservatives, in contrast, focus on criticism of the individualism, freedom, and materialism of modern society and support laws and government action to help create a moral community.

Traditional Conservatism and the New Right

In some ways, the New Right is not entirely new. Conservatives have always been defenders of property rights and have supported the idea of limited government while favouring laws to punish "immoral" behaviour. Both traditional conservatives and the New Right have been strongly critical of socialism and the redistribution of wealth by government. Many traditional conservatives, however, do not accept the pure free-market and minimal-government perspective associated with some elements of the New Right.[2] In addition, the activist approach of the New Right to foreign policy, particularly in exporting democratic values, tends to differ from traditional conservatism, which was often concerned with maintaining a stable "balance of power" in international politics (discussed in Chapter 18) and, in the United States, sought to limit foreign involvements.

Traditional conservatism emphasizes the need to respect authority and thus, in modern times, tends to favour limited forms of democracy. In contrast, the New Right has a substantial element of populism that is critical of authority and believes that the common people should be in more direct control of decision making through such devices as referendums, initiatives,

---

[2] The strong anti-government perspective is particularly evident within contemporary American conservatism. European conservatives (aside from exceptions such as Britain's Margaret Thatcher) tend to see a need for a paternalistic state and favour a somewhat active role in managing the economy and providing some social benefits (*The Economist*, 2010, February 13).

and recall. New Right populists claim that politicians, government officials, and judges have undermined traditional values, have catered to what the New Right considers to be "special interests" (such as various equality-seeking groups), and do not reflect the views of the majority. Plebiscitary democracy is viewed by some contemporary conservatives as a way of ensuring that political decisions reflect the views of the "silent majority" that holds traditional or conventional moral values.

More generally, many traditional conservatives preach the virtues of moderation and gradual change. The New Right, by contrast, has tended to pursue its convictions with greater ideological zeal.

SOCIALISM

Socialism, like reform liberalism, developed as an important political ideology in reaction to the harshness of the early capitalist system. Socialists view human beings as basically social rather than self-interested. Socialists are critical of the capitalist system not only for what they consider its exploitative nature, but also for its emphasis on competition, which undermines the co-operative and community-oriented nature of humanity. Inequality is viewed as largely the result of the power relations in society and the economy rather than of the inherent differences in the capabilities of individuals. A more equal society in terms of the distribution of wealth, income, and power will lead to a greater sense of community and solidarity and will facilitate co-operation rather than conflict (Heywood, 2003). Social justice can be achieved by reducing inequalities and ensuring that all persons have the rights and resources needed for a life of dignity.

Within the socialist ideology, there are a variety of views as to what an ideal society would be like and how such a society could be achieved. Generally, socialists favour some form of social (collective) rather than private ownership of the major means of production so that many of the decisions that affect the life of the community are no longer in the hands of the owners of corporations. Some have envisaged the establishment of small, self-sufficient communes in which property would be collectively owned, all would work co-operatively, and material goods would be shared equally (see Box 4-2, Utopian Socialism). Others have looked to the state to own the major means of production and operate them for the good of society as a whole. Still others envision a system of worker-run co-operative enterprises. Many contemporary socialists look to some form of mixed economy where government plays a substantial role in planning and regulating the economy as well as providing various free or low-cost public services.

Marxism and Communism

The ideology of socialism developed from a variety of sources and has numerous variations. The ideas of Karl Marx (1818–1883) and Frederick Engels

SOCIALISM An ideological perspective based on the view that human beings are basically social in nature and that the capitalist system undermines the co-operative and community-oriented nature of humanity. Socialism advocates the establishment of an egalitarian society.

Socialist International
www.socialistinternational.org

BOX 4-2

Utopian Socialism

In his classic book *Utopia*, English writer Thomas More (1478–1535) condemned the evils of pride, envy, and greed that result "wherever men have private property and money is the measure of everything" (1516/2004, p. 198).

In existing societies, More asserted, the rich "serve their own interests under the name of the common good" while in reality they look after only their private good. Instead of only a few being prosperous and happy "while all the rest live in misery and wretchedness," More imagined a society in which all things are owned in common, money is no longer used, and everyone is free to take from the common storehouses all the necessities that are needed to live a meaningful life. In such a society, people would be concerned with the "common affairs" of the society, rather than worry about earning a livelihood (More, 1516/2004, pp. 198–202).

More did not intend *Utopia*, which literally means "nowhere," to be a blueprint for society. However, a number of socialists, particularly in the nineteenth century, developed elaborate models of an ideal communal society. These "utopian socialists" were criticized by other socialists, including Marx and Engels, for having the naive view that fundamental changes could occur by developing visionary schemes or establishing model communities instead of taking political action to transform the capitalist system.

Nevertheless, a number of small-scale communes have been established at various times. Israel's kibbutzim, although involving only a very small proportion of the population, are one of the few successful secular communal societies. Various religious sects, such as the Hutterites, have maintained a communal lifestyle that they view as following the teachings of Jesus Christ.

HISTORICAL MATERIALISM The view that historical development and the dynamics of society and politics can be understood in terms of the way society is organized to produce material goods.

(1820–1895), often termed Marxism, have been particularly important in terms of both providing a perspective for understanding the dynamics of societal change and providing the doctrine adopted by the revolutionary movements that established communist regimes. Their analysis, termed **historical materialism**, starts with the assumption that historical development can be understood in terms of the way society is organized to produce material goods. In every society except the most primitive ones, production involves the exploitation of a subordinate class by a smaller, dominant class. The leading ideas, beliefs, and morals of a society serve the interests of the dominant class, by limiting awareness of their exploitation among the subordinate class. However, each of the major systems of production—slave-owning, feudal, and capitalist—has internal tensions ("contradictions") that eventually become irresolvable. This eventually leads to an overthrow of that system and its replacement by a new system of production.

In their examination of the capitalist system of production, Marx and Engels argued that the profits obtained by the owners of capital (the bourgeoisie) were based on the exploitation of the workers (the proletariat). The capitalist system appeared to be free, as goods and labour could be freely bought and sold in the marketplace. It was, however, only the appearance of

◄ This statue of Marx and Engels in the former East Berlin is a reminder of the importance of the communist ideology in the past century.

freedom. Workers, in reality, had little choice but to sell their labour power to survive. In addition, the emphasis on competition, profit, and selfishness in the capitalist free-market system violated what Marx and Engels viewed as the essentially social and creative nature of humanity.

The capitalist system in the Marxist view is an important, but not the final, stage of historical development. Conflict between the working class and the bourgeoisie will intensify because the two classes have incompatible interests. The large working class that was developing in Marx and Engels's time as a result of industrialization would eventually organize itself into a revolutionary force. This class would overturn the capitalist system and replace it with a system based on social, rather than private, ownership of the means of production. Although the capitalist system is much more productive than earlier systems of production, its unplanned nature meant that it could not fully unleash the power of human productivity. In particular, capitalism, Marx and Engels believed, was prone to ever-increasing crises of severe unemployment and depression. In addition, free competition among capitalists would be undermined as weaker capitalists were forced out of business, leaving the remaining capitalists with monopoly control of the marketplace.

Because the state generally acts in the interests of the capitalist class, the working class would have to capture control of the state and then use the state apparatus to transform the capitalist system into a socialist system. This would likely necessitate a revolution, as capitalists will be unlikely to give up their control voluntarily or peacefully. However, as workers in Europe began

Marxists Internet Archive
www.marxists.org

to gain the right to vote in the late nineteenth century, Marx and Engels saw a possibility that in some countries working-class control of state power *might* be achieved through the election of socialist political parties, provided that police and military forces were not used to suppress the socialist movement.

After the revolution, the workers would control the state in the interests of the working class ("the dictatorship of the proletariat") and would use the state to expropriate the property of the capitalists. *Eventually*, Marx and Engels argued, the selfishness that is characteristic of economic systems based on private ownership would disappear. The increased production of an economy devoted to human needs rather than private profit would lead to material abundance that could fulfill the basic needs of everyone. A further transition from socialism to **communism** would then occur. In a communist society, everyone would be free to take from society what they need. Although production would be highly organized, the need for a coercive state would diminish or disappear because, in the Marxist perspective, the need for a coercive state arises out of the need to use coercion to maintain private property and the inequality that it entails.

COMMUNISM A system in which private property has been replaced by collective or communal ownership and everyone is free to take from society what they need.

LENINISM Vladimir Lenin (1870–1924), the Russian Communist leader, modified the ideas of Marx and Engels. In Lenin's view, the capitalist system could be overthrown only by force—but the workers themselves could not spontaneously overthrow the system. What was needed was a tightly disciplined party firmly controlled by a revolutionary vanguard.

Because nineteenth-century Russia was largely a peasant society with a relatively small working class, the Communist party that was in the vanguard of the proletariat was particularly important in leading the revolution and directing the subsequent course of revolutionary change. Instead of putting power in the hands of councils of workers and peasants, as many of those involved in the Russian Revolution had hoped, Lenin, and even more so his successor, Joseph Stalin (1877–1953), established a tight grip on Soviet society and established a totalitarian regime dedicated to rapidly building an industrialized economy. Similarly, tight party control has also been characteristic of government in China, where the Communist party under Mao Zedong (1893–1976) was successful in capturing power in 1949 after a lengthy guerrilla war.

LENINISM The version of Marxism that includes the belief that the capitalist system can be overthrown only by force, by means of a tightly disciplined party controlled by a revolutionary vanguard.

THE COMMUNIST SYSTEM COLLAPSES Communist party control of the Soviet Union and Eastern Europe collapsed at the end of the 1980s. A loosening of the tight control exercised by Communist leaders allowed the people to overthrow their governments with a minimum of violence. Although China is still controlled by the Communist party, it has abandoned efforts to create an egalitarian communist society and instead has become a major force in the global capitalist economic system (as discussed in Chapter 17). Various versions of Marxism continue to provide important perspectives on the world. However, communism, as developed and implemented by Lenin, Stalin, and Mao, is no longer a powerful political force.

Democratic Socialism

Unlike communism, **democratic socialism** is based on the belief that only democratic methods should be used to work toward a socialist society. Democratic socialists reject the notion of the dictatorship of the proletariat, arguing instead that political rights and freedoms should be respected. Likewise, although they believe that an active government is needed to provide for the well-being of the citizenry, they argue that governments should abide by the rule of law, protect civil liberties, and not act in an arbitrary manner.

Rather than complete state ownership of the means of production, democratic socialists have favoured measures such as public ownership of some key industries, encouragement for co-operative enterprises, requirements that workers have a voice in the decisions of the businesses that employ them, the right of workers to unionize and bargain collectively, and government planning and regulation of the economy. To achieve greater equality, democratic socialists advocate government provision and subsidization of various services, along with some redistribution of income and wealth from the rich to the poor, particularly through the tax system.

Social Democracy

Over time, ideas about nationalizing (having the government take over) the "commanding heights" of the economy, or about replacing the capitalist system, have generally moved to the fringes of democratic socialist parties. Indeed, many leading figures within democratic socialist parties prefer to call themselves social democrats[3] to indicate that they no longer believe in a socialist economic system (that is, one with a high level of state ownership or control).

Instead, contemporary social democracy generally includes the belief that the capitalist economy can be reformed to ensure that it works for the common good. Social democrats also advocate greater social and economic equality to achieve a meaningful democracy. As Ed Broadbent (2001), a former leader of Canada's New Democratic Party, puts it, market economies have "generated the wealth needed to provide effective social rights," but its unequal distribution of income and power "runs counter to the democratic goal of equal citizens." For Broadbent, democracy involves not only political and civil rights, but also entitlements that ensure that various social and economic rights such as health, education, employment, and child care are available to all persons. In other words, social democrats believe that the excesses of the free-market

DEMOCRATIC SOCIALISM
The perspective that socialism should be achieved by democratic rather than revolutionary means, and that a socialist society should be democratic in nature with political rights and freedoms respected.

---

[3] The term *social democracy* has had different meanings. In the nineteenth century, European socialist parties called themselves social democrats even though many adopted a Marxist approach. After the establishment of the Soviet Union, there was a split between Marxist-Leninists, who called themselves communists, and social democrats, who rejected the revolutionary path to socialism. In recent decades, the term *social democracy* has often been applied to those who no longer advocate the goal of a socialist economy.

capitalist system can be curtailed by government action to provide a welfare state, greater equality, and regulation of the market economy.

Social democratic ideas provided much of the basis for the consensus concerning the welfare state and the relations between business and labour that developed in many of the countries of the Western world after World War II. However, globalization and neo-liberalism have created challenges for social democrats, who have generally looked to a strong nation-state to provide a variety of public services and a substantial degree of control of the market. In Western Europe, some social democrats played a key role in developing the European Union and ensuring that its free-market policies were combined with guarantees of human rights and environmental protection. In the United Kingdom, former Labour Party Prime Minister Tony Blair sought to modernize social democracy through the "Third Way," which involved greater acceptance of the free market, globalization, individualism, and personal responsibility. Other social democrats, while favouring global social justice and the development of democratic global institutions, are critical of economic globalization, emphasize the importance of social solidarity rather than individualism, and see a continuing need for the market economy to be controlled for the common good (Leggett, 2007).

Anarchism

ANARCHISM An ideology that views the state as the key source of oppression and seeks to replace the state with a system based on voluntary co-operation.

Anarchy Archives
http://dwardmac.pitzer.edu/
Anarchist_Archives/

Anarchism, which literally means "without rule," seeks to eliminate the state, which it views as a key source of oppression. Socialist anarchism (or anarcho-communism) advocates the elimination of both the state and private property. In its place, socialist anarchists advocate a co-operative or communal society based on what they see as the natural principle of mutual assistance. Instead of large and powerful states, they envision a world based on voluntary co-operation among a network of local communities.

Anarchists generally favour "direct action" such as demonstrations, civil disobedience, street theatre, and general strikes, rather than the establishment of political parties (which they view as an instrument of power) and voting to achieve their objectives. Although many anarchists oppose all forms of violence, including participation in wars, some anarchists have used violence and selected assassination of business and government leaders in the hope of encouraging a popular uprising to "smash the state." Whether members of the "Black Bloc," who have clashed with police and smashed windows at various protests (including during the G20 summit in Toronto in June 2010 and the 2010 Winter Olympics in Vancouver), are truly anarchists or simply "hooligans" is a matter of debate.

Various forms of socialist anarchism were important in the international socialist movement in the latter part of the nineteenth century as well as in the Spanish Civil War (1936–1939). However, anarchism has generally been overshadowed by communism, democratic socialism, and social democracy in the past century. Nevertheless, anarchism continues to have some significance—for example, as an element of the anti-globalization movement.

FASCISM

The ideology of **fascism** developed in the period between World War I and World War II based, in part, on the views of various thinkers who were critical of the ideas of the Enlightenment. Fascism combines an aggressive form of nationalism with a strong belief in the naturalness of inequality and opposition to both liberal democracy and communism.

FASCISM An ideology that combines an aggressive form of nationalism with a strong belief in the naturalness of inequality and opposition to both liberal democracy and communism.

Nationalism and Racism

Loyalty to the nation-state is extremely important in fascist thought. In the fascist view, the well-being of the individual is based on the well-being of the nation-state to which the individual belongs. Individuals owe absolute loyalty to the state, and the state has the right to control all activities in order to promote its interests. Further, the state is seen by fascists as a cohesive or organic whole that is based on the bonds of a common culture or ancestry. Foreigners and those of minority cultures are typically viewed as a hindrance to the creation of a homogenous society based on the dominant nationality.

Related to the extreme nationalism of fascist ideology is a belief in the superiority of particular nationalities and races. This superiority is exhibited not only in cultural achievements, but also in such characteristics as bravery and heroism. War allows that superiority to be realized, and the conquest and subordination of "inferior" nations and races is justified.

NAZISM   The ideas of racial superiority and racial conflict were particularly evident in **Nazism**. Building on some nineteenth-century theories that viewed racial differences as profound, the Nazis proclaimed their belief that the Germans and some related Nordic peoples were the heirs of an "Aryan master race" that could be restored through careful breeding. As a "culture-creating" master race, a revived Aryan race would exert dominance over other "inferior" races. The Nazis viewed the Jews as their key racial enemy and sought to rid Europe of the Jews. This resulted in the systematic genocide known as the **Holocaust** (see Box 4-3, The Holocaust).

NAZISM A version of fascism associated with Adolf Hitler, the Nazi leader of Germany, emphasizing racial conflict and the superiority of the "Aryan race."

Belief in a Natural Inequality

Fascists also believe that there is a natural inequality within society between the masses and their natural leaders. The masses can be mobilized by skilful leaders through the use of slogans and symbols. Democratic leaders are seen as weak because they pander to the masses to gain their support. Instead, fascists often argue that a heroic leader with a creative "will to power" will arise above the masses in exceptional circumstances. Such an exceptional leader, fascists

HOLOCAUST The systematic extermination of six million European Jews by the Nazis during World War II.

The Holocaust History Project
www.holocaust-history.org

BOX 4-3

The Holocaust

The racist ideology of the Nazis that viewed Jews as "subhuman" had horrific consequences.

In the 1920s and 1930s, stirring up anti-Semitic prejudices was an important part of the Nazi appeal. After gaining power, the Nazis began taking away the rights of Jews, including their citizenship, and encouraged attacks on Jewish businesses and individuals. As the German armies conquered Eastern Europe in World War II, they began rounding up Jews and shooting them in mass pits or gassing them in mobile gas chambers. Eventually, Adolf Hitler and his top officials decided on what they termed the "final solution" to the "Jewish problem" (that is, the total elimination of the Jewish people). Persons of Jewish ancestry were transported to massive concentration camps for slave labour and systematic, industrial-style extermination.

In all, the Nazis organized the deliberate murder of about six million persons of Jewish ancestry, including about one and a half million children. In addition, about five million other persons were killed, deemed "unfit" because of their nationality, disabilities, sexual orientation, or political views. The Holocaust is particularly horrifying because of the systematic, determined, and state-directed nature of the "extermination." Further, it occurred in modern and so-called civilized societies, often with the acquiescence and involvement of people throughout Europe, despite some heroic exceptions.

The Holocaust should not be viewed as a single, isolated event. The persecution of Jews had a very lengthy history throughout Europe. Likewise, racist views that some peoples are inferior or not fully human were used to justify wiping out most of the indigenous population of the Americas after the European conquest, the massive slave trade, and the massacre of hundreds of thousands of Tutsis in Rwanda in 1994.

believe, embodies the will of the people. Fascism favours strong, authoritarian leadership, arguing that natural leaders should be allowed free rein to rule in the interests of the nation-state, enhancing its unity, culture, and power.

Rejection of the Enlightenment

Underlying the fascist ideology is a rejection of Enlightenment thought. Fascists assume that human beings are motivated by emotion rather than by reason. People are rooted in their ancestry and their territory, and can be mobilized into action through myths and propaganda. As well, fascism rejects the idea that we are all part of a common humanity (Eatwell, 1995). Instead of the liberal and socialist belief that a peaceful world can be created, fascism sees struggle and the use of force as inevitable.

Because fascists see the world as based on a struggle for dominance, they argue that constant preparation for war is necessary. The strength of one's nation-state must be developed to ensure its dominance. Divisions or disagreements within the nation-state cannot be tolerated because they lead to weakness. Fascists believe that it is right and natural that the strong should dominate and subjugate the weak, and that humanitarian policies directed at aiding the disadvantaged lead to weakness. Adapting the **social Darwinist** ideas of English social theorist Herbert Spencer (1820–1903), fascists see war and conflict as a natural process that allows humanity to evolve through the "survival of the fittest."

SOCIAL DARWINISM The use of Darwin's theory of evolution to argue that competition and conflict allow humanity to evolve through the "survival of the fittest."

Corporate State

Fascism is also critical of liberal and socialist systems of thought for their focus on achieving material well-being. Benito Mussolini's Italian fascist regime adopted the idea of the **corporate state**, in which business and labour would work harmoniously to achieve goals established by the state to advance the good of the nation (Heywood, 2003). In practice, this involved the subordination of labour and business to the fascist regime and the suppression of the labour movement.

CORPORATE STATE A system associated with fascist Italy in which business and labour work harmoniously to achieve goals established by the state to advance the good of the nation.

A New Order

Fascism is often depicted as a reactionary ideology. To some extent this is valid, as fascism rejects many aspects of modern society and politics, including individualism and materialism, which fascism views as a cause of moral decay. However, fascism embraces only selected myths from the past, such as the ideal of the heroic Teutonic warrior or the glories of the Roman Empire. The Nazis glorified the ethnically homogenous rural communities of the past, but also celebrated modern technology with a vision of a technological future (Neocleous, 1997). Unlike reactionary conservatives, fascists view themselves as creating a new order rather than restoring the old order in Europe.

Fascism can be described as a radical right-wing ideology. The interwar fascist movement gained considerable support from nationalistic, authoritarian conservatives and other right-wing forces who shared with fascists a belief in order, leadership, and authority and who were anti-Semitic and anti-democratic. However, fascism tends to be distinct in its emphasis on conflict, militarism, total control of society, mobilization of the people behind a populist leader, and its rejection of most moral principles (Mann, 2004).

The Continuing Significance of Fascism and the Radical Right

Fascism is often associated with the dictatorial regimes of the Italian fascist leader Benito Mussolini (1883–1945) and the German Nazi leader Adolf Hitler (1889–1945). However, fascist movements also had substantial followings in a variety of countries in the 1930s, and some non-fascist political leaders privately expressed admiration for Mussolini and Hitler. The decisive defeat of the militarist fascist regimes in World War II and the revelation of the horrors they perpetrated resulted in the discrediting of the fascist ideology. Nevertheless, semi-fascist regimes remained in power in Spain and Portugal until the early 1970s and a number of countries, including Greece, Guatemala, Argentina, Bolivia, Chile, and Paraguay, have at various times come under the control of authoritarian right-wing regimes that have some elements of fascism.

NEO-FASCISM A revival of fascism in contemporary times.

There has been somewhat of a revival of extreme right-wing political parties that are often labelled **neo-fascist** in many European countries. In particular, various parties (including the Front National in France, the Austrian Freedom Party, the British National Party, the Slovak National Party, and Hungary's Jobbik Party) have adopted racist policies, including encouraging or requiring those of non-European ancestry to return to their homelands. For example, the Jobbik Party, which campaigns for Hungarian racial "purity" and is connected to an illegal paramilitary group that uses symbols similar to those used by the Hungarian Nazis, won 16.7 percent of the vote in Hungary's 2010 parliamentary election (Engelhart, 2010). In some cases, the rise of neo-fascist parties has encouraged more mainstream parties to make somewhat similar appeals. In addition, there has been increasing violence by extreme right-wing groups directed at Muslims, Roma, Jews, immigrants, and various other racial, religious, and ethnic minorities. In the United States, groups like the Aryan Nation promote racism and the ideal of an all-white America. As well, various militia groups train for armed resistance to what they believe is a new world order conspiracy (by the United Nations and other international institutions, Zionists, banking institutions, the Illuminati, or Freemasons) to take over the United States. Individuals influenced by militia groups carried out the bombing that killed 168 people at the U.S. government building in Oklahoma City in 1995.

Summary and Conclusion

Political ideologies have had a major impact on politics in the modern era. Most ideologies have a vision of a better world and some ideas about the political actions needed to achieve their vision. Political ideologies provide not only basic sets of values and goals to those who engage in political activity, but also differing ways of analyzing and understanding the world.

Liberalism focuses on the ideal of individual liberty. The coercion of individuals should be minimized.

In the perspective of liberalism, the common good is best achieved by allowing individuals to pursue their own interests, develop their own capabilities and morality, and act on their own values. Those with power are likely to use that power for their own interests. Thus, limiting power, protecting individual rights and freedoms, and establishing the rule of law are important means to achieve the objectives of liberalism. A peaceful and prosperous world can be developed through the promotion of tolerance, adherence to laws, and the facilitation of global interactions through free trade and the free interaction of ideas. For classical liberals, the free market, equal legal rights, and limited government ensure that individuals are not subject to the arbitrary and oppressive power of government and other institutions. Reform liberals are concerned with achieving meaningful freedom for all and believe that government can play a useful role in removing the obstacles to individual development. As well, reform liberals favour the promotion of equality of opportunity so that individuals can compete on a more equal basis and are rewarded according to merit.

Conservatism, because of its pessimistic view of human capabilities, does not generally present an ideal of a better world that can be achieved through conscious political action. The common good is best obtained in an orderly community in which traditional moral values and institutions are maintained. Traditional practices are seen as containing accumulated wisdom. The limitations of human reason suggest that change should be gradual in nature. Individuals should accept their place in society and be encouraged to work for the good of the community. Respect for those in positions of authority should be promoted, and those with wealth and privilege should be encouraged to look after the well-being of society. Because of human frailties and the human capacity for evil, restraints on individual actions are necessary to ensure the common good of the community.

The New Right version of conservatism views the welfare state and the undermining of traditional Western values as the cause of many contemporary problems. The New Right generally favours strengthening the state's ability to fight criminal and immoral behaviour and to promote Western values at home and abroad. As well, many New Right conservatives favour a global laissez-faire capitalist system with minimal government involvement in the economy.

Socialism promotes the ideal of a society based on co-operation and equality. The focus of the capitalist system on the pursuit of profit and individual wealth hinders the achievement of the common good. Eliminating oppression and inequalities and ensuring that the needs of all are fulfilled would allow humans, as social and co-operative beings, to pursue the common good of humanity. For communists, a revolution based on the working class is needed to destroy the oppressive power of capitalism and the capitalist-based state. This will allow for the creation of a classless socialist—and eventually communist—society. Democratic socialists, on the other hand, argue that socialism can be achieved through the election of a socialist party and the gradual evolution of society toward socialism. Contemporary social democrats suggest that the major ideals of socialism can be achieved by reforming capitalism, reducing inequalities, and guaranteeing social and economic rights to all.

Fascism seeks to build a powerful, united, militaristic nation-state that will provide strong leadership and direction to the masses. Order, leadership, and discipline need to be strong in a world characterized by conflict and the struggle for dominance. Fascists view the idea of the common good of humanity as a whole as unrealistic. Instead, the collective good of the state, nation, or race is emphasized in fascist thought.

Key Terms

Anarchism 96

Classical liberalism 85

Communism 94

Conservatism 86

Corporate state 99

Democratic socialism 95

Enlightenment 80

Fascism 97

Historical materialism 92

Holocaust 97

Discussion Questions

1. How important are political ideologies in contemporary political life?
2. Is a particular ideological perspective prevalent in your community, among your friends, or at your university or college?
3. Which ideological perspective has the most realistic view of human nature?
4. Which ideological perspective do you think provides the best perspective on freedom, equality, and democracy?
5. Are socialism and communism still relevant in the contemporary world? Is fascism likely to become a major political perspective again?
6. What are the views of the different ideologies on the common good?

Further Reading

Ball, T., Dagger, R., Christian, W., & Campbell, C. (2010). *Political ideologies and the democratic ideal* (2nd Canadian ed.). Toronto: Pearson Canada.

Eatwell, R. (1995). *Fascism: A history.* New York: Penguin.

Freeden, M. (2003). *Ideology: A very short introduction.* Oxford: Oxford University Press.

Giddens, A. (1998). *The third way: The renewal of social democracy.* Cambridge, UK: Cambridge University Press.

Griffin, R. (1993). *The nature of fascism.* London: Routledge.

Harrington, M. (1989). *Socialism.* New York: Penguin.

Kelly, P. (2005). *Liberalism.* Cambridge, UK: Polity Press.

King, P. (Ed.). (1996). *Socialism and the common good: New Fabian essays.* London: Frank Cass.

Laqueur, W. (1996). *Fascism: Past, present, future.* New York: Oxford University Press.

Mann, M. (2004). *Fascists.* New York: Cambridge University Press.

Nisbet, R. (1986). *Conservatism: Dream and reality.* Milton Keynes, UK: Open University Press.

Pierson, C. (2001). *Hard choices: Social democracy in the twenty-first century.* Cambridge, UK: Polity Press.

Roussopoulos, D. (Ed.) (2002). *The anarchist papers* (rev. ed.). Montreal: Black Rose.

Scruton, R. (1984). *The meaning of conservatism* (2nd ed.). London: Macmillan.

Segal, H. (1997). *Beyond greed: A traditional conservative confronts neo-conservative excess.* Toronto: Stoddart.

Singer, P. (1980). *Marx.* Oxford: Oxford University Press.

Chapter 5

Newer Perspectives: Feminism and Environmentalism

PHOTO ABOVE: Rima Fakih, a 24-year-old Arab American, wins the 2010 Miss America title. Despite feminist protests against beauty contests, they still attract attention.

1. describe and discuss the feminist perspective
2. compare the different versions of feminism
3. explain the different views on equality within the feminist ideology

4. describe and discuss the distinctive features of environmentalism
5. compare the different versions of environmentalism

The year is 1968. A sheep has just been nominated for the title of Miss America, and women are throwing their high heels, girdles, false eyelashes, and other symbols of oppression into a "freedom trash can." This is all part of a much-publicized demonstration against the Miss America Pageant by feminists who attack it as a beauty contest that exploits women. A young female reporter, seeking to link the Miss America demonstration to Vietnam War protests where draft cards and the American flag had been burned, described the women as burning their bras. Although no bras were actually burned, militant feminists will thenceforward be ridiculed by their critics as "bra burners."

The Miss America contest was one of the early targets of the women's liberation movement because it was viewed as a manifestation of how a male-dominated society dehumanizes women by treating them as sexual objects. Some of those involved in this movement developed the radical feminist perspective that holds that the oppression of women is the most basic feature of all societies. Radical feminists believe that a fundamental transformation of society is needed to liberate women and achieve true equality.

Some prominent political commentators have argued that the age of ideologies has ended (Bell, 1998; Fukuyama, 1992). With the collapse of communism and the differences between liberals, conservatives, and social democrats appearing to diminish, political controversy, they said, will involve the details of policy rather than the clash of sharply different perspectives.

However, the perspectives examined in this chapter—feminism and environmentalism—each seek fundamental changes in the values, institutions, and policies of the political community. Feminism raises basic questions about the role of women in society that were in the past often given only very limited attention. Environmentalism, particularly in its stronger versions, presents fundamental challenges to our ways of thinking about humanity and our relationship to nature, the way our institutions operate, and how we should live.

FEMINISM

Feminism is often thought of in terms of achieving equality for women. This involves not only establishing equal rights and opportunities for women and eliminating discriminatory practices, but also challenging the traditional views about women that have often had the effect of confining women to domestic life and restricting their freedom. Beyond seeking to achieve equality with men, many feminists argue that political decisions should give greater emphasis to the different experiences and values of women instead of being based primarily on male values.

According to feminists, all societies are, to varying extents, characterized by **patriarchy**. As explained by Lorraine Code (1988, p. 18), "patriarchal societies are those in which men have more power than women, readier access than women to what is valued in the society and, in consequence, are in control over many, if not most aspects of women's lives." Changing the patriarchal nature of society is a basic goal of feminism.

FEMINISM A perspective that views society as patriarchal and seeks to achieve full independence and equality for women.

PATRIARCHY A system in which power is in the hands of men and many aspects of women's lives are controlled by men.

Background

A sexual division of labour in which women are seen as suited for household duties, including the raising of children, and men are seen as best suited for politics, ruling, and other public activities has often been viewed as natural. Some argued that women needed to be protected from the harsh realities of politics, while others viewed women as more prone to emotion than reason. Even Aristotle, who (like Plato) viewed females as equal to males with the capacity for reason and deliberation, asserted that "the male, unless constituted in some respect contrary to nature, is by nature more adept in leading than the female" (*The Politics*, quoted by Bradshaw, 1991, p. 563). Therefore, he argued, men should rule in both the household and the political community. This view of women has persisted despite occasional examples of strong, powerful, and tough-minded female rulers such as Queen Elizabeth I of England (1533–1603); Catherine the Great, Empress of Russia (1729–1762); and, in recent times, a number of women prime ministers and presidents, including Margaret Thatcher, Angela Merkel, Golda Meir, Indira Gandhi, Michelle Bachelet, and Ellen Johnson-Sirleaf.

Council of Women World Leaders
www.cwwl.org

The *Declaration of the Rights of Man*, a product of the French Revolution of 1789, inspired one of the first statements of feminist ideas. In *A Vindication of the Rights of Woman* (1792), Mary Wollstonecraft rejected the common notion that women's natural role was to please men and to bear and raise children. Wollstonecraft argued that women are human beings with the same capacity for rational thinking as men, and should therefore have the same rights as men. If women appeared more emotional and less concerned about the good of the political community, it was a result of being deprived of adequate education and the opportunities to develop themselves, rather

▶ Angela Merkel, chancellor of
Germany since 2005, is one
of a number of female political
leaders who have proven to be
strong, powerful, and tough
minded.

Feminist Collections
http://womenst.library.wisc.edu/
publications/feminist-coll.html

than being an inevitable product of their nature (Adams, 2001). Likewise, John Stuart Mill argued in *The Subjection of Women* (1869) that freeing women from being subordinate to men, providing equal educational opportunities, and establishing a full set of civil and political rights for women were justified because women had the same capacity for rational thought and action as men.

Although both Wollstonecraft and Mill advocated equal rights for women, they assumed that women were more likely to choose domestic life rather than paid employment. By being educated and equal, women would be better equipped to raise their children, and marriages would be happier if wives could interact intelligently with their husbands. Other early feminists, particularly those involved in the revolutionary politics of Marxism and anarchism in the late nineteenth and early twentieth centuries, went further by advocating the liberation of women from their domestic roles and from traditional sexual constraints.

As with other perspectives, there is a variety of different versions of contemporary feminism. This diversity is often discussed in terms of three basic categories:

1. liberal feminism
2. socialist feminism
3. radical feminism

Liberal Feminism

Liberal feminism extends the struggle of women in the latter part of the nine-teenth century and the first decades of the twentieth century for equal legal and political rights (often termed the "first wave" of feminism) to the advocacy of equal opportunities for women in such areas as education and employment. As the influential American feminist Betty Friedan (1998, p. 317) put it, "My definition of feminism is simply that women are people in the fullest sense of the word, who must be free to move in society with all the privileges and opportunities and responsibilities that are their human and American right." In particular, Friedan discussed the problems of women in American suburbs in the early 1960s and concluded that women suffered by being confined to the role of housewife. Pursuing a career and gaining economic independence would allow women to lead more fulfilling lives (Friedan, 1963).

For liberal feminists, the key problem is the discrimination against women that limits their opportunities. Ending unjust laws and adopting affirmative action programs would allow women to participate fully in the mainstream of society. Liberal feminism thus focuses on ensuring that women have the free-dom and opportunity to engage in politics, business, careers, and employment on the same basis as men. Liberal feminism has been successful to some degree: the laws and policies that discriminated against women have been eliminated in many countries and many women have taken the opportunity to obtain higher education and pursue professional careers. However, although the pro-portion of women in top positions in business and politics is much higher than it was several decades ago, women are still strongly under-represented in important positions in most countries (see Table 5-1).

LIBERAL FEMINISM A version of feminism that advocates equal opportunities for women in such areas as education and employment as well as equal legal and political rights.

Socialist Feminism

Socialist feminism views women as oppressed by both the male-dominated character of society and the capitalist system. Women's housework and child care are unpaid labour that is essential for the profitability of capitalism and to ensure that there is a supply of labour for the future. Women also pro-vide the capitalist system with a "reserve army" of low-cost labour that can be mobilized when needed to maintain the profitability of capitalist enterprises. Socialist feminists argue that male–female relations reflect the exploitative relationships of capitalists to workers. Just as the capitalist boss dominates and exploits workers, so, too, husbands are dominant in the home and exploit the labour of their wives.

Socialist feminists argue that the liberation of women involves both a struggle against patriarchy and the transformation of capitalism into a more co-operative and egalitarian socialist society. The free, public provision of child care and possibly other domestic services would help to create the condi-tions for the liberation of women. Overcoming the sexual division of labour,

SOCIALIST FEMINISM A version of feminism that views women as oppressed by both the male-dominated character of society and the capitalist system. The liberation of women is connected to the transformation of capital-ism into a more co-operative and egalitarian socialist system.

TABLE 5-1
WOMEN IN PARLIAMENTS, SELECTED COUNTRIES

Notes: Percentage of women representatives in lower or single house of Parliament. Data as of May 31, 2010.

COUNTRY	PERCENT WOMEN
Sweden	46.4
South Africa	44.5
Argentina	38.5
Spain	36.6
Germany	32.8
Canada	22.1
United Kingdom	22.0
Italy	21.3
France	18.9
USA	16.8
Russia	14.0
Japan	11.3
India	10.8
Brazil	8.8
Saudi Arabia	0.0
World Average	19.1

SOURCE: *Compiled from International Parliamentary Union, Women in National Parliaments. Retrieved from www.ipu.org/wmn-e/classif.htm*

in which women have primary responsibility for most domestic duties, along with transforming the division of labour in the capitalist system, would also enable everyone to live more creative, fulfilling lives.

For some of those influenced by the Marxist version of socialism, the struggle of working-class women and men to overturn capitalism is needed to achieve women's liberation. However, most other socialist feminists do not accept the idea that the struggle of women should be subordinated to the struggle of the working class. In their view, overturning capitalism would not necessarily liberate women and end the sexual division of labour. For example, the Soviet Union initially exhibited a strong commitment to the liberation of women, but never achieved this ideal in practice.

Radical Feminism

RADICAL FEMINISM A version of feminism that views society as based fundamentally on the oppression of women and seeks to liberate women through the fundamental transformation of social institutions, values, and personal relationships.

In the 1960s, a variety of protest movements (including Black Power, North American Indian, anti-war, and student movements) seeking major changes in society and politics were formed. However, many women involved in these movements found that they were male dominated and often did not treat women and issues concerning women with equal respect. This contributed to the development of the "second wave" of feminism, which included the women's liberation movement. Some of those involved in this movement developed the associated perspective of **radical feminism**.

In the radical feminist perspective, patriarchal values are deeply embedded in culture and affect the way that women, as well as men, see themselves (Millett, 1985). Institutions such as the state, the family, and schools perpetuate male dominance and the subjugation of women. Male supremacy is maintained through the dominant values, ideas, and practices of society, which encourage women to be dependent upon and subservient to men. Beauty contests, feminists argue, are just one example of how women are treated as sexual objects whose role is to satisfy men. Male supremacy is also maintained, according to radical feminists, by the use of force in the form of violence against women, including the threat of rape, to keep women under control and subordinate (Brownmiller, 1975).

Radical feminism views the oppression of women as the oldest, most pervasive, and most deeply entrenched form of oppression. As Robin Morgan, a leading feminist writer and organizer of the 1968 Miss America protest, argued, "Sexism is the root oppression, the one which, until and unless we uproot it, will continue to put forth the branches of racism, class hatred, ageism, competition, ecological disaster, and economic exploitation" (Morgan, 1977, p. 9). The implication is that the struggle of women against oppression is fundamentally revolutionary because it has the potential to end various forms of domination and subordination.

Feminist Theory Website
www.cddc.vt.edu/feminism/enin.html

LIBERATION   The goal of radical feminism is **liberation**. Liberation, whether used in feminist theory, Marxism, or the theories developed by those challenging imperialist power in the colonized Third World, goes beyond the concept of freedom that is at the core of the liberal ideology. Liberation involves freeing the human potential that has been stifled by the organization and values of society. Oppression warps the personality of the oppressed, particularly by forcing them to adopt the values of the oppressor. Indeed, from this point of view, those in the oppressor groups are also deprived of an authentic human existence by being expected to take the dominant role.

LIBERATION Freeing the human potential that has been stifled by the organization and values of society.

In other words, radical feminists argue that the way society defines what it is to be female and male is restrictive to both women and men. Patriarchal values not only are oppressive to women, but also force men to adopt socially defined masculine values and behaviours, rather than develop a fully rounded character. For radical feminists, women as an oppressed class are the revolutionary force needed to bring about liberation by struggling against male dominance and the ideology of male supremacy. Liberation will ultimately be for the good of all.

Liberation, therefore, is not simply a matter of ending male domination of positions of governing authority or of limiting the power of the state over women. Rather, radical feminism seeks a fundamental transformation of social institutions, values, and personal relationships. Because male power is exhibited in all aspects of life, radical feminists view their task as one of challenging male dominance in all of its manifestations. Thus, they are critical of the liberal feminist focus on achieving equal rights and opportunities in education, employment, and government. Removing barriers to women's participation in the public sphere is, in their view, insufficient to overturn the patriarchal nature of society. Likewise, they are often critical of Marxist feminists who focus on a transformation of capitalism rather than challenging male supremacy.

Instead, radical feminists argue that "the personal is political," suggesting that conventional personal and sexual relationships between women and men need to be challenged as part of their struggle against a patriarchal society. Indeed, many radical feminists view male dominance in the family as the root of male social, political, and economic domination. By making the personal political, radical feminists hope to expose and challenge what they view as a major basis of male power (Bryson, 2003).

Many radical feminists argue that women must organize separately from men in order to free themselves from oppression. Even though some men are sympathetic to the cause of women's liberation, men who join women's organizations are likely to take a dominant position, and women will tend to be passive and subordinate. The prevalence of male power and values makes it necessary for women as an oppressed class to organize themselves collectively as women. Further, because those who are oppressed often do not realize that they are oppressed and have internalized the values of the male-dominated society, radical feminists argue that a key task is to raise women's consciousness (awareness) of their oppression and to encourage women to take pride in their identity as women.

Feminism and Male–Female Differences

Although women have often been viewed as more "natural" than men because of their role in reproduction and nurturing infants, most feminists reject the idea that biological characteristics result in differences between women and men in values and behaviour. Instead, feminists typically argue that women's values are based primarily on the roles that society has prescribed for them, such as raising children and caring for sick and elderly family members. In this perspective, different gender roles, such as the expectation that men will be breadwinners and women will look after domestic duties, are socially created and imposed, rather than reflecting inherent biological differences between men and women.

Generally feminists have sought to challenge traditional gender roles that involved a sharp differentiation between masculinity and femininity with the feminine viewed as weaker and more passive. Liberation involves being free of such socially created roles, thereby allowing women and men to adopt or experiment with different roles. Some feminists have sought to create an androgynous society in which male–female differences are virtually irrelevant.

However, many feminists seek to celebrate women's different experiences and values. Female attributes such as nurturing, caring, co-operation, emotion, and spirituality (based on their experiences as women) are undervalued in male-dominated societies, which instead emphasize competition, aggression, and rationality. In this perspective, society needs to be transformed so that female values are given greater importance, either because they are superior to male values (for example, more likely to lead to a peaceful and harmonious world) or because female and male values are complementary if given equal weight. As Barbara Ehrenreich and Deidre English (1979, p. 292) argue,

> The human values that women were assigned to preserve [must] expand out of the confines of private life and become the organizing principle of society. The market . . . must be pushed back to the margins. And the "womanly" values of community and caring must rise to the centre as the only human principle.

For example, American psychologist Carol Gilligan concluded in her book *In a Different Voice* (1982) that men and women tend to have a different, but equally valid, sense of morality. Because women think of themselves more in terms of their relationships with others, they are more likely to base their moral judgments on an ethic of care and on the specific context and circumstances in which moral issues arise. In contrast, men tend to base their moral judgments more on abstract, universally applicable principles of "right" and "wrong." In Gilligan's view, male conceptions of morality have been the standard by which morality has been judged. The "different voice" of women has not been heard (Freedman, 2001).

Promoting Women's Identity

Connected to the emphasis on women's values, feminists have sought to promote the identity of women. By celebrating women and their values, feminists hope to encourage women to be more independent and politically active. The development of a distinctive identity and culture of women is seen, particularly by radical feminists, as an important element in encouraging women to have the confidence to collectively liberate themselves from oppression. Instead of the view that all individuals should be treated the same, many feminists hold the view that women *as a group* should be treated equally to men with their distinctive identity recognized and fostered.

Some feminists, however, have been critical of the notion that women share a common identity arising out of their common experiences as women. Black feminists, for example, have argued that women of colour suffer double oppression based on their gender and their race. The characteristics of sisterhood proclaimed by the largely white, middle-class, educated, heterosexual spokespersons for the feminist movement do not, some feminists argue, adequately reflect the diversity of women's experiences (Code, 1988).

Is Feminism Still Relevant?

The feminist ideology and the women's movement have raised a variety of issues that were previously largely ignored in politics. There is, however, considerable disagreement about the extent to which the women's movement has succeeded in changing the position of women (see Box 5-1, "You've Come a Long Way, Baby"?). Table 5-2 gives an indication of the current circumstances of women in Canada.

Although feminist analyses of politics and society continue to be developed in the academic world, the women's movement seemed to falter in the 1980s. Not only was there a backlash against feminism associated with the rise of the New Right, particularly in the United States (Faludi, 1991), but the women's movement in some countries was wracked with internal tensions. In Canada, for example, the once influential National Action Committee on the Status of Women, which was made up of hundreds of member organizations, tore itself apart in the 1990s. In particular, second-wave organizations were criticized by "women of colour," lesbian and bisexual women, and working- or lower-class women for paying insufficient attention to the problems faced by

TABLE 5-2

THE CIRCUMSTANCES OF CANADIAN WOMEN

Notes: A ratio of 1.0 indicates female–male equality. A value below 1.0 indicates that women have or do less than men, while a value above 1.0 indicates that women have or do more than men.

	FEMALE-TO-MALE RATIO
Earned income (2007)	0.65
In low after-tax income group (2007)	1.04
Total time spent working (2005)	1.01
– Time spent in paid work	0.66
– Time spent in unpaid work (mainly household work)	1.56
Free time (2005)	0.93
Employed full- or part-time (2009)	0.85
Unemployment rate, 25 years or older (2010)	0.76
Average hourly wage (2010)	0.84
University bachelor's level enrolment (2006–2007)	1.38
University master's level enrolment (2006–2007)	1.17
University Ph.D. level enrolment (2006–2007)	0.85

SOURCES: Human Development Report, *2009; Gender-related Development Index, http://hdr.undp.org/en/media/HDR_2009_EN_Indicators.pdf; Persons in low income by sex, www40.statcan.gc.ca/l01/cst01/famil19a-eng.htm; Average time spent on various activities for the population aged 15 and over, 2005, www.statcan.gc.ca/pub/12f0080x/2006001/t/4058341-eng.htm; Average hourly wages of employees by selected characteristics and profession, unadjusted data, by province (monthly), www40.statcan.gc.ca/l01/labr69a-eng.htm; Full-time and part-time employment by sex and age group, www40.statcan.gc.ca/l01/cst01/labor12-eng.htm; Labour Force Survey, January 2010, www.statcan.gc.ca/daily-quotidien/100205/dq100205a-eng.htm; and Statistics Canada data cited in Canadian Association of University Teachers,* CAUT Almanac of Post-secondary Education in Canada 2009–2010, *Ottawa: CAUT, 2010. Calculations by authors.*

BOX 5-1
"You've Come a Long Way, Baby"?

Some years ago, commercials for a brand of cigarette designed for women celebrated the advances made by women. It featured, in language that could be deemed sexist, the slogan "You've come a long way, baby." But there is still debate about whether feminism has achieved its objectives and whether contemporary Western societies are patriarchal and oppressive.

There is little doubt that women continue to suffer from brutal and oppressive treatment in many parts of the world. In a number of countries, women continue to be deprived of adequate education, limited in their employment opportunities, restricted in their personal life, treated as inferior in law, and subject to such cruelties as genital mutilation. However, in many countries there have been some major changes in the position of women, particularly in the past few decades:

- Discriminatory laws have generally been abolished.
- Women have entered the paid workforce in large numbers and mothers with young children are often employed outside the home.
- Females now form the majority of university students in many countries, including Canada and the United States, and many high-status professional programs such as law, medicine, and business administration have more female than male students.
- The tendency for the mass media to portray women in negative terms has diminished. Instead of "dumb blondes" and *Father Knows Best*, some television shows and movies treat males as a subject of ridicule.
- Publishers carefully vet textbooks to eliminate sexist language, many universities have established women's studies programs, affirmative action programs have been created to encourage the hiring and promotion of women, and sexual harassment officers have been hired by universities and some major businesses to try to protect women from being abused by those in positions of power.
- Rights to divorce, contraception, and abortion have allowed women in many countries to free themselves from abusive relationships and to gain control over their bodies.

However, feminists argue that progress toward equality and liberation is still limited, even in Western societies. Women still have only a small share of political power and relatively few women hold top positions in the business world. Many women are employed in jobs that are perceived as "women's work" (such as secretary, nurse, social worker, and schoolteacher), with the average employment earnings of women still substantially below that of men. Women continue to have primary responsibility for raising children in many households, and also often have the task of caring for sick and elderly family members. Women are still often judged in terms of their physical attractiveness, and negative stereotypes of women have not been eliminated.

Do women still have a long way to go to be fully equal? Will the current generation, which includes many highly educated and motivated young women, complete the feminist "revolution," or are obstacles still in their way? Even though the position of women in Western societies has changed considerably in recent decades, the under-representation of women in positions of power will undoubtedly continue to be an issue in politics, the economy, and society.

different groups of women. Second-wave feminists were also accused (fairly or unfairly) of being too middle class, puritanical in their appearance and views on sexuality, and too negative toward women who wanted to experience motherhood.

Beginning in the 1990s, some young women have promoted the development of a "third wave" of feminism that emphasizes the diversity of women's experiences and circumstances; celebrates female values, experiences, and beauty; and challenges confining gender roles. Although third-wave feminism may not differ drastically from second-wave feminism in many of its views, it tends to be distinguished by its view that "differences among women are as substantial as differences between women and men" and that "the category of 'woman' is no longer the only identity worth examining" (Dicker & Piepmeier, 2003, pp. 9–10). To some extent, third-wave feminism represents a stylistic generational difference in feminism arising out of the female punk proclamation of "grrrl power" as opposed to the "political correctness" of many involved in feminism's second wave. Unlike "post-feminists," who view the cause of feminism to be won in some Western societies such that individual women can empower themselves, third-wave feminists argue that society is still patriarchal and in need of collective action to achieve social, political, and cultural change.

ENVIRONMENTALISM

The world faces numerous serious environmental problems. These include the following:

- Increasing emissions of greenhouse gases, such as carbon dioxide and methane, resulting from fossil fuel burning, deforestation, and increased agricultural production. The resulting global climate changes could have profound consequences for all life forms.
- Depletion of many natural resources.
- Contamination and misuse of water supplies. A substantial proportion of the world's population lacks access to clean water, and water shortages may reduce food production in the future.
- Devastation of tropical rainforests, which contain much of the Earth's biological diversity, and the extinction of an unprecedented number of species of animals and plants. The decline in biodiversity may hamper the search for new medicines and hinder the world's capability to maintain agricultural production.
- Pollution of various forms, which is degrading the environment and harming the health of humans and other species.

In 1962, American biologist Rachel Carson's *Silent Spring* eloquently made the case that synthetic pesticides were silencing the voices of birds that

◀ Climate change in the Arctic.

heralded the coming of spring. More generally, Carson pointed out that the fragile ecology of the earth was threatened by the large-scale production and use of dangerous chemicals. A series of environmental disasters, including massive oil spills, further increased concern about environmental problems and led to the development of a large environmental movement. In conjunction with this movement, the perspective of **environmentalism** developed.

Environmentalism is not simply an expression of concern about various environmental problems and support for efforts to clean up the environment and reduce pollution. Rather, environmentalism provides a distinctive perspective on the fundamental causes of environmental problems and a vision of an environmentally sustainable world.[1]

Environmentalism includes the belief that humanity needs to fundamentally change its relationship with nature. Influenced by the science of ecology, which emphasizes the complex interrelatedness of the natural world,

ENVIRONMENTALISM A perspective based on the idea that humanity needs to change its relationship to nature so as to protect the natural environment and ensure that it can sustain all forms of life.

---

[1] Because those who believe that fundamental changes are needed in our relationship with the environment differ considerably from those who think that environmental problems can be handled without major changes, Andrew Dobson (2007) has suggested that the term *ecologism* be used to describe the stronger, more distinctive forms of environmentalism. Similarly, terms such as *dark green* or *radical environmentalism* are sometimes used to distinguish strong versions of environmentalism from what can be termed "reform environmentalism."

environmentalism argues that humanity needs to view itself as part of the intricate and fragile web of nature. Understanding our dependence upon nature is necessary to living in harmony with it. Instead of viewing humanity as being outside of nature with the right to control and dominate it, we need to think of ourselves as part of nature and limit our impact on the Earth (Schumacher, 1973).

As Petra Kelly (1947–1992), a founder of the German Green party, stated,

> We must learn to think and act from our hearts, to recognize the inter-connectedness of all living creatures, and to respect the value of each thread in the vast web of life. . . . We have borrowed the Earth from our children. Green politics is about having just "enough" and not "more," and this runs counter to all of the economic assumptions of industrial society. . . . The industrialized countries must move from growth-oriented to sustainable economies, with conservation replacing consumption as the driving force (quoted in Ball & Dagger, 2004, pp. 442, 445).

Many of those who hold an environmentalist perspective argue that one of the basic causes of environmental problems is the idea that we can control nature and use it for our benefit without concern for the consequences. Instead of a focus on human well-being (termed **anthropocentrism**), environmentalism (particularly in its stronger versions) advocates the adoption of a more **eco-centric** philosophy that views nature as having its own intrinsic value—that is, value in and of itself rather than its value for human use (Eckersley, 1992). In addition, those who hold the stronger versions of environmentalism argue that dealing with environmental problems is not simply a matter of developing better technologies, such as pollution abatement equipment and fuel-efficient automobiles, or applying better techniques for managing natural resources. Instead, fundamental economic, social, and political changes along with changes in the relationship of human beings to the natural world are needed to limit economic growth and achieve a sustainable world (Dobson, 2007).

ANTHROPOCENTRISM The focus on human well-being that is at the centre of most political thought.

ECOCENTRISM The view that nature has intrinsic value and should not be valued only in terms of its use for human beings.

Limits to Growth

Environmentalism views our obsession with economic growth as an important cause of environmental problems. Since the Industrial Revolution, there has been a massive increase in the production and consumption of material goods. People in the developed countries have come to enjoy high levels of consumption, while the production and consumption of goods is increasing rapidly in newly industrialized countries such as China and India. Governments have made the pursuit of economic growth their primary objective, and the success of different countries is usually measured in terms of their annual increase in gross national product (the monetary value of the goods and services produced).

The environmentalist perspective emphasizes that there are limits to growth (see Box 5-2, The Limits to Growth). The Earth has a limited carrying

BOX 5-2
The Limits to Growth: A Famous Bet

In 1972, a group of industrialists, political leaders, and academics known as the Club of Rome predicted that within one hundred years there would be an uncontrollable and disastrous collapse of society when the limits to growth were exceeded (Meadows, Meadows, Randers, & Behrens, 1972).

The scenario appeared in a report called *The Limits to Growth*, which was based on a global computer model that attempted to project a variety of current trends into the future. The growth of the world's population and the accelerating use of non-renewable natural resources, particularly oil, caused by an expanding global economy would mean that the resources needed to provide materials and energy would become very costly and scarce.

The doomsday scenario of the Club of Rome came under considerable criticism. Its computer model simplistically projected current trends into the future, assuming that the accelerating rate of increase in resources and population would continue indefinitely. In reality, the rate of increase in population growth has slowed. In 1980, economist Julian Simon publicly bet Paul Ehrlich, a biologist known for his doomsday scenarios, $1000 that the real price of any set of natural resources Ehrlich chose would be lower in the future. Ehrlich chose the prices of copper, chrome, nickel, tin, and tungsten as of 1990. As it turned out, the price of each of these minerals was lower in 1990 and Simon won the bet (Dryzek, 1997).

Simon argues that there are no limits to growth. Human ingenuity and the competitive marketplace will result in more resources being found, substitutes invented, and pollution problems resolved. The resourcefulness of humanity and the vast resources of the world will allow for indefinite economic growth, provided that governments do not take actions to restrict growth. However, some of the optimistic predictions Simon made in 1984—that by 2000 fish catches would increase and cheap nuclear power would be available while problems such as climate change, water scarcity, soil erosion, and pollution would diminish in significance (Simon & Kahn, 1984)—did not come true. For example, one study estimated that the world's oceans now contain only about one-tenth of the amount of large predatory fish, such as cod, that existed before the adoption of large-scale industrial fishing (Myers & Worm, 2003).

Raising fears about the survival of humanity and life on earth has helped to increase awareness of environmental problems, although exaggerated claims of impending doom can also damage the credibility of some environmentalists. On the other hand, the view that human use of the environment can continue to grow and human ingenuity can deal with any problems that might arise ignores the ever-growing strain on the Earth's ecosystems created by increased production, consumption, and population. Indeed, thirty years after *The Limits to Growth* was published, the authors could claim that their predictions were being proven correct (Meadows, Randers, & Meadows, 2004).

capacity—that is, there are inherent limits to the capacity of Earth's ecosystems to support increasing levels of consumption while absorbing waste. Initial studies of humanity's "ecological footprint" conducted by William Rees at the University of British Columbia suggested that if persons throughout the world had the same impact on the environment as the average person in the richer countries, we would need two or more Earths to sustain the world's existing population (Rees & Wackernagel, 1996). As of 2009, it was estimated that it takes about one year and five months to regenerate what the entire human population uses in one year, with the human footprint increasing rapidly (Global Footprint Network, n.d.). Growth in human use of the Earth's resources cannot continue endlessly. At some point, the Earth will reach the limit of its ability to absorb our effluents and provide the accessible resources and energy for our ever-increasing production of material goods.

A Sustainable Society

A basic goal of environmentalism is that of **sustainability**, particularly in terms of maintaining the integrity of ecosystems. Specifically, renewable resources should not be used at a rate that exceeds the ability of ecosystems to regenerate them. Renewable substitutes should be developed to replace the consumption of non-renewable resources. The emission of pollutants should not exceed the ability of the ecosystem to handle them without damage (Korten, 1996). Instead of continual growth of production and consumption, some of those who hold the environmentalist perspective favour a steady-state (no-growth) economy so as to live within the capacities of the Earth. This would ensure that future generations have the same enjoyment and benefit of the environment that we do.

Ecological Footprint Quiz
www.myfootprint.org

SUSTAINABILITY Maintaining the integrity of ecosystems by ensuring that renewable resources are not being used at a rate that exceeds the ability of ecosystems to regenerate them, developing renewable substitutes to replace the consumption of non-renewable resources, and ensuring that the emission of pollutants does not exceed the ability of the ecosystem to handle them without damage.

▶ An open pit coal mine in Columbia. Large-scale mining creates difficult challenges in terms of achieving a sustainable society.

How can a sustainable society be achieved? Encouraging individuals to change their attitudes concerning nature and adopting more environmentally friendly practices (as summarized by the slogan "reduce, reuse, recycle") can be useful. However, many of those who hold the environmentalist ideology argue that fundamental social, economic, and political changes are also needed to achieve a sustainable society. For example, British environmentalists Jonathon Porritt and Nicholas Winner argue that what is needed is "nothing less than a nonviolent revolution to overthrow our whole polluting, plundering and materialistic industrial society and, in its place, to create a new economic and social order which will allow human beings to live in harmony with the planet" (quoted in Dobson, 2000, p. 9).

A meeting of Green parties from seventy-two countries adopted a statement that set six "guiding principles" for a sustainable world: ecological wisdom, social justice, **participatory democracy**, nonviolence, sustainability, and respect for diversity (Charter of the Global Greens, 2001). Although many Green parties have moved away from their radical positions, the Charter of the Global Greens reflects the environmentalist perspective that combines a concern for the natural environment with other politically relevant ideals.

According to many of those who hold the stronger versions of the environmentalist ideology, the economic, social, and political order should be based, as much as possible, on self-governing and self-sufficient local communities in which all citizens would be able to participate directly in the decisions that affect their lives (that is, a participatory democracy). Although some thinkers have argued that centralized, authoritarian governments are needed to take the strict and unpopular measures needed to protect the environment (Hardin, 1974; Heilbroner, 1974), authoritarian governments tend to be militaristic and concerned with the interests of the rulers and those who maintain them in power. In contrast, the environmentalist ideology generally assumes that the decisions of local communities made on a participatory basis would be sensitive to environmental concerns because residents of the local community can see the direct effects of their decisions on the local environment. As well, the local community, with its possibilities for face-to-face interaction, is seen as a more natural community than large states and global corporations. Deliberation by members of a local community hopefully would be more likely to result in decisions for the common good than decisions made by nation-states and large corporations. Further, decisions based on the participation of citizens are more likely to be generally accepted than decisions made by an authoritarian state. Thus, voluntary compliance with efforts to reduce the environmental impact of individuals might be more likely when decisions are based on the participation of citizens. However, highly restrictive and unpopular measures, such as China's adoption in 1979 of a one child per family policy to limit population growth, would be unlikely to be adopted through citizen participation in decision making.

PARTICIPATORY DEMOCRACY A democratic system in which all citizens are able to participate directly in the decisions that affect their lives.

Charter of the Global Greens
www.global.greens.org.au/
Charter2001.pd

Would decentralizing power to local communities help to solve global environmental problems? Those who hold a radical view of an ideal society argue that coordination among local communities could be better achieved by a loose association of communities in a peaceful, global network than by the existing system of competing nation-states. However, the difficulties in achieving coordination among a large number of local communities could be immense, and there is no guarantee that all local communities would act in a sustainable manner.

Greater self-sufficiency would reduce the amount of energy used for transportation and encourage communities to live within the ecological capabilities of their local areas. In the view of some who hold the environmentalist ideology, large global corporations should no longer be the basis of the economy. Instead, smaller, locally based enterprises, co-operatives, and communes geared toward local needs rather than the global marketplace should be the major basis of production. However, self-sufficient local communities might have an unacceptably low standard of living and lack the knowledge and capability necessary to address environmental problems.

Social justice is generally thought about by environmentalists in terms of greater social, economic, and political equality both within societies and between rich and poor areas of the world. Although greater equality does not necessarily lead to greater sustainability, it can be argued that greater equality is necessary to encourage poor countries and poor people to participate in working toward greater sustainability (Carter, 2007). Because environmental policies such as carbon taxes tend to cause greater hardship for the poor than the rich, offsetting payments to the poor are necessary to gain the support of the poor for such policies. Further, since the poor are often most negatively affected by pollution (for example, by living close to polluting industries or toxic dumps) while the rich tend to profit from pollution, it can be argued that wealthy individuals and rich countries should bear most of the costs of cleaning up the environment. Further, since sustainability likely requires a reduction in consumer purchases, such sacrifices are more likely to be acceptable if there is greater equality (Carter, 2007).

Sustainable Development

SUSTAINABLE DEVELOPMENT Meeting the needs of the present without compromising the ability of future generations to meet their own needs; it involves development to ensure that the needs of the poor are fulfilled and protecting the environment for the well-being of future generations.

A major problem for environmentalism is that limiting economic growth on a global basis could deprive persons in the poorer countries of the opportunity to try to catch up to the standard of living enjoyed by the richer countries, or even to ensure that their basic needs are satisfied. Many environmentalists therefore try to combine the objective of sustainability with the idea of global social justice that involves a more equitable distribution of the world's wealth and a concerted effort to reduce global poverty.

Discussions of how to take action to deal with both environmental problems and global poverty have often focused on the concept of **sustainable development**. The World Commission on Environment and Development

(1987, p. 8), which popularized this concept, defined sustainable development as ensuring that development meets "the needs of the present without compromising the ability of future generations to meet their own needs." There are two elements to this definition:

- First, development is needed to ensure that the needs of the poor are fulfilled.
- Second, the sustainability of the environment needs to be protected for the well-being of future generations.

Although the Commission's report highlighted a number of serious environmental challenges and noted the necessity of maintaining the carrying capacity of the Earth, it did not accept the limits-to-growth argument. Instead, the Commission noted that economic growth was needed for much of the world to overcome poverty. However, the Commission argued that the quality of growth should be changed so as to put less stress on the environment. Economic growth should be more equitable, extreme rates of population growth limited, and the resource base of economies conserved and enhanced. Hope was placed on reorienting technology to deal with environmental problems, integrating environmental and economic objectives in political decision making, and increasing public participation in the decisions that affect their communities.

Discussions of the popular idea of sustainable development have been vague, allowing many businesses, governments, and environmentalists to adopt the general goal of sustainable development while often differing on the meaning of that goal and the actions needed to achieve it. Further, as discussed in Box 5-3, Development and Sustainability, it can be difficult to achieve both economic development and environmental sustainability.

Varieties of Environmentalism

REFORM ENVIRONMENTALISM   The idea of sustainable development as expressed, for example, by the World Commission on Environment and Development could be considered a version of **reform environmentalism.** Reform environmentalism is less distinctive than the stronger versions of environmentalism we have been discussing, and can be found in combination with other ideological perspectives, including liberalism, conservatism, and socialism. Unlike stronger versions of environmentalism that advocate fundamental changes, this perspective views the solution to environmental problems primarily in terms of better science, technology, and environmental management. Developing and using better pollution-control technology, encouraging more recycling efforts, promoting measures to assess and mitigate the negative potential effects of new developments, and taking more care to conserve natural resources are seen as resulting in environmental improvement.

REFORM ENVIRONMENTALISM
A perspective that views the solution to environmental problems primarily in terms of better science, technology, and environmental management.

BOX 5-3
Development and Sustainability

The relationship between economic development and environmental sustainability is complex. The ecological footprint of individuals in the poorest countries is very small compared to that of individuals in the rich developed countries. Nevertheless, poor countries have experienced a reduction of their natural resources through deforestation, desertification, overfishing, and changes in agricultural practices. In poorer countries that are successfully growing their economies (such as China and India), there is a huge negative impact on the environment as polluting industries are set up, often with inadequate government regulation. Many millions of persons in countries such as China and India are now able to purchase consumer products such as cars and refrigerators and have changed their eating habits to include regular meals of meat and fish rather than depending on grains, which generally have a lower environmental impact.

Some economists have claimed that although pollution and environmental degradation increases in the early stages of a country's economic growth, this trend is reversed as income increases. With higher incomes, countries can afford to invest in less-polluting technologies (Beckerman, 1992). Nevertheless, the evidence for this hypothesis* is weak, subject to various qualifications, and may apply only to local short-term pollution rather than to effects on the global environment. As well, if rapid economic growth causes irreparable harm to the environment (for example, by degrading soils or by polluting the water supply), this harm may eventually inhibit a country's economic growth (Arrow et al., 1995; Stern, 2004).

Overall, the sustainability of a world in which people in the poorer and developing countries enjoy an equivalent level of wealth and consumption to that of people in the richer countries is questionable.

Although the rich countries have been responsible for many of current problems of environmental degradation, the newly industrialized countries are quickly adding to global environmental problems. While China, for example, is developing wind power and other forms of renewable energy, this hardly offsets the impact on the Chinese and global environments of its rapid industrialization and the building of hundreds of new coal-burning power plants.

Is there a sustainable model for development that will improve the lives of the people in the poorer countries without unduly adding to the environmental burden on their countries and the Earth as a whole? The free transfer of environmentally friendly production processes to the poorer countries would be useful. Likewise, various forms of financial assistance to the poorer countries so that they do not rely on rapid exploitation of their resources to pay off their debts could be helpful. Measures to improve health, education, and social services in poorer countries, rather than focusing heavily on increasing gross national product, would help to improve the quality of life. Developing self-sufficiency and smaller-scale local economic operations rather than attracting large multinational corporations intent on exploiting resources and low-cost labour might also be useful, even though this is contrary to the trend toward globalization. Nevertheless, as various newly industrialized countries along with some of the less developed countries follow the path of the advanced industrialized countries, the question of global sustainability becomes ever more pressing.

---

* This is known as the "Kuznets Curve," an inverted U-shaped curve that shows pollution increasing and then decreasing as average incomes rise in a country.

Reform environmentalism does not view economic growth and environmental protection as necessarily incompatible. Industry, it is argued, can become more efficient and profitable by incorporating environmental considerations into the production process and adopting more sophisticated, less-polluting technologies (Weale, 1992). Indeed, in a number of countries, considerable progress has been made since the 1970s in adopting a variety of environmental policies, reducing some types of pollution, and using energy more efficiently. However, as Box 5-4, Are We All Green Now? suggests, environmental words are not always matched by environmental action, particularly if environmental action is costly.

FREE-MARKET ENVIRONMENTALISM   In the perspective of **free-market environmentalism**, guarantees of the rights of private property and a free-market economy are crucial to environmental protection (Anderson & Leal, 2001). The argument is that the private owners of farms, forests, or fishing areas are more likely to manage the resources they own in a sustainable fashion than if government owns those resources. However, while this may be valid for some small farmers and private woodlot owners who wish to see the land they own be sustainable for their own children and grandchildren, it is less convincing with regards to large multinational corporations that seek short-term profitability with no particular commitment to any particular location. Supporters of free-market environmentalism also point out that competition encourages businesses to produce goods in the most efficient manner. The pursuit of profits may, however, encourage companies to ignore the environmental effects of their actions if the costs of environmental damage are borne by the communities in which they operate. Despite attempts to create a green image, corporations are in business to sell their products and, through their advertising, seek to encourage increased consumption, which is an important cause of environmental degradation.

DEEP ECOLOGY   Among the stronger and more distinctive versions of environmentalism are deep ecology, social ecology, and ecofeminism. **Deep ecology** views the anthropocentric beliefs that have been at the centre of Western thinking as the fundamental cause of environmental degradation, and advocates the cultivation of an environmental consciousness and a sense of oneness with the world that recognizes the unity of humans, plants, animals, and the Earth (Devall & Sessions, 1998). Deep ecology views all forms of life as being of intrinsic value, with humans having no right to reduce the richness and diversity of life forms except to satisfy vital needs. As well, deep ecology advocates a substantial decrease in the human population, the return to a simpler lifestyle in which human impact on the environment is greatly reduced, and the protection and expansion of areas of wilderness to allow other species to flourish (Naess & Sessions, 1993).

FREE-MARKET ENVIRONMENTALISM The perspective that holds that guarantees of the rights of private property and a free-market economy are crucial to environmental protection.

DEEP ECOLOGY An environmentalist perspective that views anthropocentrism as the fundamental cause of environmental degradation and advocates the cultivation of an environmental consciousness and a sense of oneness with the world that recognizes the unity of humans, plants, animals, and the Earth.

Foundation for Deep Ecology
www.deepecology.org

BOX 5-4

Are We All Green Now?

British Prime Minister Margaret Thatcher once declared, "We're all green now." Politicians, government officials, and business leaders regularly proclaim their commitment to protecting the environment. But despite the passage of environmental laws, the signing of many international environmental agreements, and the establishment of plans for sustainable development, many environmentalists claim that we are still headed toward environmental disaster. For example, although an international agreement that led to the drastic reduction in the use of ozone-depleting chlorofluorocarbons counts as a major success story, reduction of the greenhouse gas (GHG) emissions that can cause climate change continues to be an elusive goal.

Building on a commitment at the 1992 Earth Summit to prevent an increase in GHG emissions, representatives of 160 countries reached an agreement in 1997 to deal with the climate change problem. The Kyoto Protocol requires most of the wealthier industrialized countries to reduce their emission of the greenhouse gases responsible for climate change to a level below their 1990 levels (6 percent below for Canada) by 2008 to 2012. Developing countries are not subject to the same requirements, but are encouraged to limit emissions voluntarily, and there are incentives for the richer countries to help the poorer countries control their emissions.

Although the United States government signed the Kyoto Protocol, the American Senate subsequently refused to ratify it by a vote of 95 to 0. President George W. Bush claimed that studies concerning climate change were not definitive. Further, Bush argued that because developing countries were not required to make a binding commitment to reduce their emissions, the Kyoto Protocol could make American industries uncompetitive and result in job losses.

The Canadian government ratified the protocol in 2002, despite objections from the Alberta government and the petroleum industry. However, GHG emissions in Canada have increased substantially since 1990 (see Figure 5-1); thus Canada will not meet the Kyoto commitment to reduce emissions. Indeed, while not officially rejecting the Kyoto Protocol, the Conservative government led by Stephen Harper cut many of the programs that had been established to try to deal with the problem of climate change. In contrast, some European countries will likely meet or exceed their Kyoto commitments.

Despite mounting evidence that GHG emissions will result in serious and potentially irreversible long-term risks to humanity, many governments have preferred talk to serious action. Worldwide, the rate of GHG emissions has increased from 1 percent per year prior to 2000 to 2.5 percent per year from 2000 to 2006 (Black, 2006). Many petroleum companies have tried to discredit the evidence of global climate change, and business-sponsored think tanks have raised fears about the costs of reducing emissions. However, a British government report prepared under the direction of Nicholas Stern, a former chief economist of the World Bank, estimated that *not* taking action to deal with climate change would cost the world economy US$7 trillion (Black, 2006). Meanwhile, some people continue to buy gas-guzzling vehicles that contribute to GHG emissions. Environmentalists may have been successful in raising our environmental consciousness, but this does not mean that we act in a green fashion.

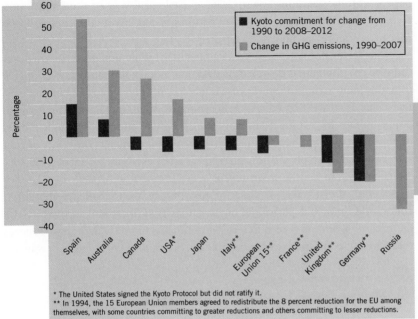

SOURCE: *United Nations Framework Convention on Climate Change, 2009. National greenhouse gas inventory data for the period 1990–2007. Retrieved from http://unfccc.int/resource/docs/2009/sbi/eng/12.pdf*

FIGURE 5-1

CHANGES IN GREENHOUSE GAS EMISSIONS, 1990–2007, AND KYOTO COMMITMENTS, SELECTED DEVELOPED COUNTRIES

Note: If the effects of land use, land-use changes, and forestry were included, the increase in GHG emissions for some countries, including Australia and Canada, would be substantially higher.

SOCIAL ECOLOGY **Social ecology** views social, economic, and political relationships of hierarchy and domination as the cause of both human and environmental problems. Creating an egalitarian and co-operative society is needed to end domination within human societies and the exploitation of nature. Social ecology builds on the ideology of anarchism discussed in Chapter 4. Thus it differs somewhat from eco-socialism, which focuses in the Marxist version on abolishing capitalism and in other versions on using a strong democratic state to deal in an equalitarian manner with environmental problems. Both social ecology and deep ecology favour small-scale, self-sufficient communities in a world in which political power rests with local communities. Social ecology, however, views humans as active and creative stewards of the natural world, while deep ecology promotes a view of humans as being just one of numerous life forms and advocates that humans return to a more natural lifestyle.

SOCIAL ECOLOGY A perspective that views social, economic, and political relationships of hierarchy and domination as the cause of both human and environmental problems.

Institute for Social Ecology
www.social-ecology.org

ECOFEMINISM **Ecofeminism,** a combination of environmentalism and feminism, views male dominance as the basic cause of the degradation of the Earth. Male domination and exploitation of nature is an extension of male domination of women; the "rape" of nature arises out of male desires for control and mastery in a patriarchal society. Women, it is argued, are more closely related to nature and are more likely to understand the world in terms of a

ECOFEMINISM A combination of environmentalism and feminism that views male dominance as the basic cause of the degradation of the Earth.

Activist-educative hub for ecofeminism and ecofeminists
www.ecofem.org

network of interrelationships (that is, an ecological way of thinking). Thus, giving greater importance to women's values, perspectives, and experiences is needed to restore harmony with nature.

Whether or not we accept the argument that male dominance is the basic cause of environmental degradation and that women are more closely related to nature, improving the status of women has positive environmental effects. In particular, providing education to young women, increasing employment opportunities for women, making contraceptive information and choices readily available, and challenging patriarchal traditions has the effect of sub-stantially reducing population growth in less developed countries, thereby reducing pressure on the environment.

Overall, the stronger versions of environmentalism challenge the domi-nant world view that places the highest priority on economic growth, views the natural world as a resource to be used for human benefit, and believes that science and technology are capable of solving all environmental problems (Taylor, 1992).

Summary and Conclusion

The goal of feminism is to achieve a society in which women enjoy independence and equality, with full control over their own lives and bodies. In addition to working toward removing obstacles to the full and equal participation of women in social, economic, and political life, many feminists have sought to affirm the distinct identity of women. Achieving equality and giv-ing greater significance to female values are seen as being not only desirable for women, but also for the common good of humanity. As well, feminist scholars have challenged traditional ways of understanding poli-tics that have largely ignored the importance of gender and the contribution of women.

The ideology of environmentalism raises impor-tant questions about the relationship between human beings and the environment. Environmentalism views human dominance and exploitation of nature as lead-ing to disastrous consequences for the world. Humans need to recognize that they are a part of nature and should learn to live in harmony with it. This involves treading lightly on the Earth and ending the exponen-tial growth in production, consumption, population, and waste. From an environmentalist point of view, the common good should refer not only to the good of human beings, but also to the good of the world as a whole, of which we are an integral part. An important challenge facing environmentalism is the question of how to achieve sustainability while addressing the need to eliminate global poverty.

The perspectives examined in this chapter provide different ways of understanding the world and advocate fundamental changes in society, politics, and our lives. The intensity of the political controversies generated by the stronger versions of these perspectives suggests that the clash of different political perspectives contin-ues to be an important feature of political life.

Key Terms

Discussion Questions

1. Why do some feminists view women as oppressed? Is this a valid depiction of the position of women in Canada?

2. Are fundamental changes needed to improve the position of women?

3. Would a government that had female majority and female leadership act differently than governments dominated by men?

4. How can a sustainable society best be achieved?

5. Do the stronger versions of environmentalism provide a desirable and practical vision for the world?

Further Reading

Carter, N. (2007). *The politics of the environment: Ideas, activism, policy* (2nd ed.). Cambridge, UK: Cambridge University Press.

Dicker, R.C., & Piepmeier, A. (Eds.). (2003). *Catching a wave: Reclaiming feminism for the 21st century.* Lebanon, NH: Northeastern University Press.

Dobson, A. (2007). *Green political thought* (4th ed.). New York: Routledge.

Donovan, J. (2000). *Feminist theory: The intellectual traditions* (3rd ed.). New York: Continuum.

Dryzek, J.S. (2005). *The politics of the earth: Environmental discourses* (2nd ed.). Oxford: Oxford University Press.

Freedman, J. (2001). *Feminism.* Buckingham, UK: Open University Press.

Gillis, S., Howie, G, & Munford, R. (Eds.). (2004). *Third wave feminism: A critical exploration.* Houndmills, UK: Palgrave Macmillan.

Hossay, P. (2006). *Unsustainable. A primer for global environmental and social justice.* London & New York: Zed Books.

McKenzie, J.I. (2002). *Environmental politics in Canada: Managing the commons into the twenty-first century.* Don Mills, ON: Oxford University Press.

Tong, R. (2009). *Feminist thought: A comprehensive introduction* (3rd ed.). Boulder, CO: Westview Press.

PART III

Political Organization, Persuasion, and Action

Chapter 6

Political Culture, Political Participation, and Political Socialization

PHOTO ABOVE: Some people saw the destruction of New York's World Trade Center by al-Qaeda terrorists in 2001 as evidence that there was a "clash of civilizations" between Islam and the West.

CHAPTER OBJECTIVES

After reading this chapter you should be able to:

1. explain the meaning and significance of political culture
2. discuss the differences between the Canadian and American political cultures
3. outline the level of political interest, knowledge, and participation in Western democracies
4. examine the decline of confidence and trust in politicians and governments
5. discuss the low level of voting by young people
6. define political socialization and discuss the agents of political socialization
7. explain the postmaterialist theory of change in political culture

The image of the twin towers of New York's World Trade Center collapsing after they were struck by jets hijacked by al-Qaeda terrorists is one that few people will forget.

The horrific events of September 11, 2001, seemed to confirm the argument of Harvard University political scientist Samuel P. Huntington (1993, 1996) that a "clash of civilizations," such as the clash between Islam and the West, will become the leading source of international conflict. Cultural conflicts, he suggests, have replaced the ideological conflict between communism and capitalism as the major potential source of world war. Huntington (1993) views the world as increasingly divided into seven or eight major civilizations—broad cultural groupings based on differences in history, language, traditions, and particularly religion (Western, Confucian, Japanese, Islamic, Hindu, Slavic-Orthodox, Latin American, and possibly African). In contrast to those who view globalization and modernization as resulting in increased homogenization or Westernization of the cultures of the world, Huntington argues that non-Western peoples are rejecting Western values and building on their own indigenous cultures. "The Western ideas of individualism, liberalism, constitutionalism, human rights, equality, liberty, the rule of law, free markets, the separation of church and state," he writes, "have little resonance in other cultures" (Huntington, 1993, p. 40).

Huntington's analysis has been criticized on a number of grounds. Although there are major differences between Western and non-Western societies on social and moral issues (such as divorce, abortion, gender equality, and homosexual rights), the adoption of tolerant liberal values by Western societies on such issues is a relatively recent phenomenon.

As well, although authoritarian political institutions are firmly entrenched in some non-Western countries, such as most Arab countries, surveys have found that the majority of the population in some of these countries sees democracy as desirable (Inglehart & Norris, 2003; Tessler, 2002). In a number of cases, the problems of developing a democratic political culture can be attributed, in part, to the artificial boundaries imposed by Western powers, the support for dictatorial regimes (such as that of Saudi Arabia) that has been provided by some Western countries, and the vigorous suppression of democratic movements by some regimes (Bellini, 2004; Stephan & Robertson, 2003).

Huntington has also been criticized for exaggerating the similarities among the cultures within each broad civilization. The extreme zealots who wish to impose a strict interpretation of Islamic law and who support terrorism are not representative of the diversity of the Islamic world. Likewise, although there are broad similarities among the peoples of the Western world, there are also important differences in political culture both between and within particular countries.

In this chapter we focus particularly on the political cultures of Western democracies. We also examine political participation, because a vibrant democratic political culture is often thought to be one in which citizens are actively involved in political life. Finally, we consider whether important changes are occurring in the political values of contemporary societies.

POLITICAL CULTURE

The fundamental political values, beliefs, and orientations that are widely held within a political community are often referred to as its **political culture**. One way that political scientists examine political culture is through sample surveys that indicate what proportion of the public has various politically relevant attitudes. Others examine the literature, popular culture, symbols, myths, political institutions, constitution, and policies of a country to gain an understanding of its collective political culture (Bell, 2004). As well, political culture can be analyzed by looking at the nature of political discourse—that is, the language, meanings, and interpretations that are used in political life to discuss and make use of key terms such as democracy, freedom, and equality (Benedicto, 2004).

It is often assumed that each country has a particular political culture based on such factors as the characteristics of the population, its history, and its political experiences. However, in many countries there are different subcultures based on particular class, ethnic, linguistic, religious, regional, gender, or generational groupings. In Canada, for example, not only are there differences between the political culture of the French-speaking people of Quebec and that of the rest of the country, but also the political cultures of Aboriginal peoples are substantially different from that of the non-Aboriginal population. In the United States, there are important regional differences in political culture with the southern states, in particular, having a substantially different political culture than the rest of the country (Grabb & Curtis, 2005). Further, a distinction can be made between elite political culture—that is, the values and beliefs of those most influential in political life—and mass political culture. Indeed, it is often argued that the "political class" of leading politicians, public servants, and political commentators (including journalists and academics) differs significantly from that of "ordinary" people.

Huntington's analysis suggests that there are general similarities among groupings of nations ("civilizations") with similar backgrounds, traditions, and religious beliefs. Others explain the general differences in political culture among the different regions of the world more in terms of different levels of socio-economic development, with more prosperous regions of the world developing the cultural values that emphasize such values as individual autonomy, self-expression, political freedom, and gender equality (Inglehart & Welzel, 2005). Thus development (along with globalization) may reduce the differences in political culture. On the other hand, although many developed Western societies have become more secular, religious values continue to play a powerful role in affecting political values in many parts of the world, including the United States.

Ideological Perspectives

One way to describe the political culture of a political community is in terms of its dominant ideological perspective and fundamental politically relevant values. For example, the political culture of the United States is often described by political scientists as classical liberal (that is, combining protection for the rights and freedoms of individuals with a free-market economy and limited government) while the social democratic ideology with a greater emphasis on equality and support for the welfare state is an important component of the political culture of the Scandinavian countries. The political cultures of Western countries (particularly those influenced by Protestantism) are often described as tending to be individualistic and egalitarian while the political cultures of many Asian countries are said to be more communal or collectivist and accepting of hierarchy and authority.

Louis Hartz (1964) argued that as the societies of Western Europe developed from feudalism to capitalism, traditional conservative perspectives clashed with the liberal perspectives that arose among those seeking a freer society and a free-market economy. This clash between conservative and liberal views led to a synthesis in the form of socialism. The outcome, Hartz concluded, is that Western European political cultures are diverse, with conservative, liberal, and socialist perspectives all important elements of their political cultures. In countries colonized by European settlers, however, only the leading part of the mother country's political culture was carried to the new lands. In Hartz's view, the United States and English Canada are basically liberal "fragments" where such values as individual freedom are predominant.

Others (notably Gad Horowitz, 1966) suggest that the United Empire Loyalists (Americans who left the United States after its War of Independence because of their loyalty to the British Crown) brought to Canada some traditional conservative values (sometimes referred to as a "Tory touch") along with the liberal values characteristic of the American political culture. This in turn made possible the later development and acceptance of an element of socialist values, which in Hartz's theory require the presence of both liberal and conservative orientations. Thus, even though the individualistic values of liberalism are important in both Canada and the United States, liberalism is not the only significant ideological perspective in Canada. Needless to say, the idea that Canada has a "richer" political culture than the United States is popular among Canadian nationalists!

Seymour Martin Lipset (1990) also viewed Canada and the United States as having somewhat different political cultures, which he explained in terms of their different historical experiences. The United States was founded through revolution, while Canada's historical experience was counter-revolutionary. Canadians did not join Americans in overthrowing British rule, which resulted in a more conservative political culture in Canada. Canadians, Lipset argued, are more concerned than Americans about maintaining law and order and are more deferential toward those in positions of authority. Canadians are also less individualistic than Americans and more willing to support collective action for the common good. Thus, he argued, Canadians are more likely to look to government to resolve problems and more willing to trust those in government. Canadian political culture also is characterized by a greater acceptance and tolerance of differences in society than the American political culture. Although Lipset viewed the Canadian political culture as generally more conservative than the American one, he noted that Canadians had become more liberal than Americans in their views on social and moral issues such as abortion, homosexual rights, and decriminalization of marijuana usage. Lipset attributed this to the growing strength of conservative fundamentalist religious groups in the United States as compared to the more liberal direction taken by the major Canadian religions. Further, although he viewed the American political culture as including a strong belief in equality of opportunity so that individuals could advance based on their own merit, he noted that Canadians had become more willing than Americans to support government action to pursue egalitarian policies that redistribute wealth and income to the poor and disadvantaged (Lipset, 1990).

Although some aspects of Lipset's depiction of the differences between the two political cultures are valid, it is questionable whether the Canadian political culture is still more conservative than the American one. In addition to the changes noted by Lipset, survey research has found that Canadians, on the whole, have become less deferential to authority than Americans (Nevitte, 1996). As well, the level of trust and confidence in government tends to be low in both Canada and the United States.

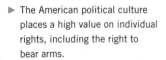

▶ The American political culture places a high value on individual rights, including the right to bear arms.

Democratic Political Culture

Democracy involves various processes and institutions such as elections, political parties, and governments that are accountable for their actions. However, since democracy is ultimately based on the citizenry, it is often suggested that a democratic political culture is needed if democracy is to be sustained and meaningful.

In a classic study based on sample surveys of the population in five countries, Gabriel Almond and Sidney Verba (1963) classified political culture in terms of three basic types. In *parochial cultures*, characteristic of underdeveloped countries, most people are largely unaware of the political system, do not have much in the way of expectations about what government should do, and do not participate in politics. In *subject political cultures*, characteristic of countries that are non-democratic or only recently have emerged from an authoritarian system, citizens exhibit an awareness of the political system and the policies that government adopts but they are not oriented to trying to affect those policies. In *participant political cultures*, citizens are both aware of the political system and have an activist orientation in seeking to affect what government does. In reality, countries generally have a mixture of these political roles. In Almond and Verba's study Mexico was characterized as having a basically parochial political culture; West Germany in the 1950s, a subject political culture; and the United States, a participant political culture.

Although one might think that a participant political culture would be the most suitable basis for a democracy, Almond and Verba argued that a participant political culture could lead to instability as citizens put forward too many demands that governments would be unable to fulfill. In their view, the best political culture (which they termed a "civic culture") features a mixture of participant, subject, and parochial political roles. This allows a balance between the power of government to govern and the responsiveness of government to the people. Almond and Verba's view of democracy has been echoed by those who argue that excessive demands have "overloaded" government. By responding to the demands of the people, governments, it is argued, have been pressured to take actions that do not take into account the long-term well-being of the country. A different viewpoint is expressed by those who view active citizen participation as an essential feature of democracy:

> *An active citizenry is required because it is through discussion, popular interest and involvement in politics that societal goals should be defined and carried out. Without public involvement in the process, democracy loses both its legitimacy and its guiding force. (Dalton, 2006, p. 35)*

In addition to the question of whether democracy functions best with a "civic" or a "participant" political culture, the sustainability of a democratic system may depend on support among the public for the basic principles of democracy and an acceptance of the legitimacy of governments that are elected by the people. As well, a reasonable level of political interest and political knowledge could also be regarded as necessary so that citizens can participate meaningfully in political life and hold government accountable for its actions.

SUPPORT FOR DEMOCRACY   The World Values Survey conducted between 2005 and 2008 found that most people considered it very important to live in a country that is governed democratically. On a scale from 1 (not at all important) to 10 (absolutely important), the mean score for fifty-three countries was 8.6, ranging from 9.6 for Sweden and 9.0 for Canada to 7.4 for Russia and 7.1 for India. Likewise, an average of 91.6 percent of respondents agreed that having a democratic political system is a very good or fairly good way of governing.

However, satisfaction with the way in which democracy works in practice is not quite as strong. Sixty-two percent of Canadians and 64 percent of Americans said they were "very satisfied" or "somewhat satisfied" with the way that democracy works in their country, with lower levels of satisfaction in some other democratic countries (Nadeau, 2002). Further, about one-quarter of persons in the advanced democracies (including Canada) thought that "having a strong leader who doesn't bother with parliament and elections" was very good or fairly good (with about one-third holding this non-democratic view in the U.S. and France). In countries such as Russia, India, Iran, Turkey, and Brazil, a majority of the population indicated a preference for a strong leader (World Values Survey, 2005–2008).

Like other advanced democracies, Canada's political culture is based to a considerable extent on liberal democratic values. Most Canadians share a belief in the desirability of political freedom, individual rights, political equality, and government based on the rule of law. A consensus about general political values is, however, not always matched by a high level of support for the application of these values in practice. For example, although most Canadians support the principle of protecting civil liberties, the majority of people favour suspending civil liberties if there is a national emergency (Sniderman, Fletcher, Russell, & Tetlock, 1996). Likewise, despite a political culture based on individual rights and freedoms, few Americans opposed the stricter measures limiting rights and freedoms that were adopted after the 2001 terrorist attacks on the United States.

VIEWS OF GOVERNMENT AND POLITICIANS   Public confidence and trust in government, elected representatives, political leaders, and political parties has declined in almost all of the advanced democratic countries in recent decades (Dalton, 2006). While 93 percent of Canadians rated firefighters and 87 percent rated nurses as trustworthy, only 12 percent rated local politicians and 7 percent rated national politicians as trustworthy (IPSOS-Reid poll cited in *The Globe and Mail Online*, January 21, 2007). As Figure 6-1 indicates, only a small proportion of people in the advanced democracies said that they

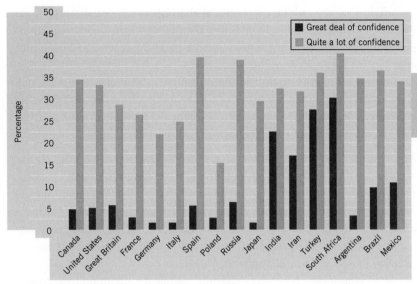

FIGURE 6-1

CONFIDENCE IN THE GOVERNMENT, SELECTED COUNTRIES

Notes: Studies conducted between 2005 and 2008. Those not answering the question or answering "don't know" were excluded from the calculation.

SOURCE: Compiled from World Values Survey, Fifth Wave, 2005–2008. Variable V138.
www.worldvaluessurvey.org

had a great deal of confidence in government. Among Canadians, 3.8 percent said they had a "great deal" and 34.4 percent said they had "quite a lot" of confidence in Parliament. The level of confidence in political parties tended to be even lower while confidence in the civil service was somewhat higher (World Values Survey, 2005–2008).

Canadian Opinion Research Archive
www.queensu.ca/cora

Political efficacy, the attitude that individuals can have an impact on political decisions and that government is responsive to what people want, is also quite low in the advanced democracies. For example, in a study conducted in 2004, 74 percent of Canadians agreed with the statement that "elected officials soon lose touch," 61 percent agreed that "government doesn't care much about what people like me think," and 52 percent agreed that "people like me don't have any say in what government does" (Clarke, Kornberg, & Scotto, 2006).

POLITICAL EFFICACY The attitude that individuals can have an impact on political decisions and that government is responsive to what people want.

What explains the general distrust of government and politicians? In some cases, political scandals and broken promises have created suspicion. However, the fact that increasing distrust is a feature of most advanced democracies suggests that other factors are involved. Citizens have become better informed about the failures of government through the mass media. Interestingly, it is among the more educated and younger parts of the public that the decline in trust has been greatest (Dalton, 2006). A more educated public has higher expectations of government, which leads to disappointment when those expectations are not fulfilled. It has also been suggested that dissatisfaction is a result of the declining capacity of governments to satisfy the needs and desires of the citizenry because of the impact of globalization (Pharr, Putnam, & Dalton, 2000). In addition, the decline in trust and confidence in politicians and political institutions may be part of a general decline in deference toward authority in various forms.

Overall, although citizens have become more critical of government, political parties, and politicians, this does not seem to indicate dissatisfaction with democracy. It may, however, help to explain the increase in protest activity and an increased desire for a greater voice for citizens in decision making.

POLITICAL INTEREST AND KNOWLEDGE   As Figure 6-2 indicates, only a fairly small minority of the population is very interested in politics. Nevertheless, most citizens pay some attention to politics, particularly during election campaigns. For example, about four-fifths of Canadians say that they often or sometimes discuss politics with others, read about elections in newspapers, watch election programs, and are very or fairly interested in elections (Clarke, Jenson, LeDuc, & Pammett, 1996).

As an example of how knowledgeable people are about politics, consider that 84 percent of Canadians polled in 2004 could name Canada's prime minister. (Interestingly, 97 percent of Canadians knew who was president of the United States.) However, only 33 percent knew who the leader of the official opposition was and only 10 percent could name the minister of finance (Canadian Broadcasting Corporation, 2004). Sixty percent of Canadians would fail the test of basic knowledge about Canada that immigrants need to

FIGURE 6-2
INTEREST IN POLITICS, SELECTED COUNTRIES

Notes: Studies conducted between 2005 and 2008. Those not answering the question or answering "don't know" were excluded from the calculation.

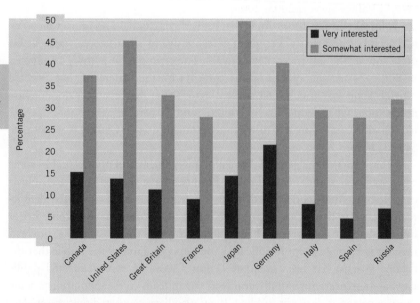

SOURCE: Compiled from World Values Survey, Fifth Wave, 2005–2008. Variable V39. Retrieved from www.worldvaluessurvey.org

pass to become citizens, although 70 percent of a sample of first-generation Canadians passed (IPSOS Reid/Dominion Institute, 2007). The majority of Canadian voters do not know which party has taken a particular stand on most of the important issues during election campaigns (Fournier, 2002). Likewise, only one-third of Americans knew who their representative in the House of Representatives was and slightly more than one-half knew which of the two major parties was more conservative (Milner, 2002).

Although the general level of political knowledge (and sophistication in understanding politics) may be low, most people are knowledgeable (and have a reasonably sophisticated understanding) about those political issues that they consider important to themselves personally (Elkins, 1993). Many citizens are not knowledgeable about the major political issues as defined by politicians, journalists, or academics, but rather focus on understanding the particular issues that interest or concern them. Parents, for example, will likely be more knowledgeable about the education issues that affect their children than about constitutional issues.

> Take a short citizenship test
> www.cbc.ca/cgi-bin/quiz/quiz.
> cgi?quiz=quiz070701

POLITICAL PARTICIPATION

Even though there has been increasing dissatisfaction with politicians and political parties, the majority of people in most countries participate in political life at least to the extent of voting in elections. On average, nearly three-quarters of adults in the established democracies vote in a national election (International Institute for Democracy and Electoral Assistance, 2007b).

Voting

Election turnouts have declined to varying extents in many democratic countries. In parliamentary elections in Europe, for example, voter turnout declined from an average of 82.2 percent in the 1970s and 82.0 percent in the 1980s to 70.9 percent in the first eight years of the twenty-first century (Siaroff, 2009). Turnout in Canada ranged between 70 and 80 percent in the 1960s, 1970s, and 1980s; in the 2008 Canadian election, turnout was only 58.8 percent of registered voters, the lowest in the country's history (see Figure 6-3).

As Table 6-1 indicates, there is considerable variation among democratic countries in turnout for elections. The variation in turnout rates not only suggests that some countries have a more participatory democratic political culture, but also reflects differences in the rules governing elections and the nature of political party competition in particular countries.

EXPLANATIONS Some countries, including Australia, Belgium, and Brazil, require that all citizens vote. Where such rules are enforced through fines or other penalties, voter turnout is, not surprisingly, substantially higher than in other countries. The amount of time and effort that it takes to vote can also affect the turnout rate. For example, about one-quarter of potentially

FIGURE 6-3

TURNOUT IN RECENT CANADIAN NATIONAL ELECTIONS

Notes: Turnout figures represent the total ballots cast as a percentage of electors on the voters' list. Changes in the way the voters' list is prepared and the conduct of elections make comparisons imprecise.

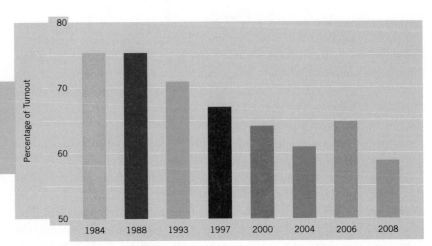

SOURCE: Elections Canada, Voter turnout at federal elections and referendums 1867–2006 and Elections Canada, Official Voting Results Fortieth General Election 2008. Adaptation rests with the authors. Retrieved from www.elections.ca

TABLE 6-1

TURNOUT IN RECENT ELECTIONS, SELECTED COUNTRIES

Notes: Turnout is for parliamentary elections, except for countries marked with an asterisk (*), where turnout is for presidential elections (first round where applicable). Turnout is calculated in terms of the proportion of registered voters, except in the United States where the calculation is based on potentially eligible voters. Some figures are unofficial.

COUNTRY	YEAR	% VOTER TURNOUT	COUNTRY	YEAR	% VOTER TURNOUT
Denmark	2007	86.6	United Kingdom	2010	65.1
France*	2007	83.8	Hungary	2010	64.4
Sweden	2006	82.0	Czech Republic	2010	62.6
New Zealand	2008	79.5	India	2009	59.7
South Africa	2009	77.3	Canada	2008	58.8
Netherlands	2010	75.4	Mexico*	2006	58.6
Spain	2008	75.3	United States*	2008	58.2
Greece	2009	70.9	Nigeria*	2007	57.5
Germany	2009	70.8	Poland	2007	53.8
Russia*	2008	69.7	Switzerland	2007	49.0
Japan	2009	69.3	Pakistan	2008	44.1

SOURCES: *International Foundation for Electoral Systems, Election Guide. Retrieved from www.electionguide.org and various electoral commissions and news sources.*

eligible voters in the United States are not able to vote because they do not take the time to register. Voter turnout in American elections is also substantially higher every fourth year, when there is a presidential election, than in "midterm" elections held every second year to elect members of the House of Representatives and one-third of the members of the Senate. As well, Americans are often faced with a long, complex ballot that includes candidates for a variety of national, state, and local offices, as well as various referendums and initiatives. Accessibility also affects voting rates: countries that make voting possible by mail or Internet and provide alternatives for those who will be absent on election day have substantially higher voter turnout (Blais, Massicotte, & Dobrzynska, 2003).

Countries using proportional representation systems of election (see Chapter 8) tend to have higher voter turnout in part because every vote counts in terms of determining how many representatives each party has in the legislature. As well, countries using a proportional representation system tend to have more political parties likely to gain seats in their legislative body thus offering more significant choices to voters. In countries that use a single member plurality system, such as Canada, many votes could be considered irrelevant, as it does not matter whether a candidate wins by one vote or twenty thousand votes. Thus, some people may not bother to vote if they think that their preferred candidate is well ahead of the other candidates or, alternatively, if they think that the candidate or party they support has no chance of winning.

Countries with well-organized political parties that can mobilize people to vote are also more likely to have high turnout rates. Being contacted by a party worker and persuaded to vote on election day by the party that you support increases the likelihood that you will cast a ballot. Likewise, countries where a high proportion of people have a strong attachment to a political party are more likely to have high turnout rates. The nature of party competition can also affect the level of voter turnout. If the major parties differ significantly in ideological terms or on major policy issues, a higher proportion of citizens will likely vote. As well, voter turnout tends to be higher in elections that feature a close race among the leading parties or candidates. If elections occur too frequently (as occurred, for example, with the 2008 Canadian election), turnout will generally tend to be lower.

Other Types of Political Participation

Only a small proportion of the public is actively involved in politics through working for a party or candidate during an election. As well, membership in political parties has been declining in many countries. However, citizen involvement in a wide variety of issue-oriented public interest groups has been increasing. For example, the proportion of Americans who said that they belonged to civic associations, environmental groups, women's groups, or peace groups increased from 6 percent in 1980 to 33 percent in 1999 (Dalton, 2006). Other countries have also seen a substantial increase in membership in such groups, although generally to a lesser extent than in the United States. By participating in public interest groups and social movements, citizens can try to affect government policies and promote social change. Various forms of protest activity have also become more common in contemporary political life (see Table 6-2).

International Institute for Democracy and Electoral Assistance
www.idea.int

TABLE 6-2

POLITICAL PARTICIPATION, SELECTED COUNTRIES

Notes: Studies conducted between 2005 and 2008. Those not answering the question or answering "don't know" were excluded from the calculation.

COUNTRY	ACTIVE MEMBER POLITICAL PARTY	ACTIVE MEMBER ENVIRONMENTAL ORGANIZATION	EVER SIGNED PETITION	EVER PARTICIPATED IN BOYCOTT	EVER ATTENDED LAWFUL DEMONSTRATION
Canada	5.1%	6.6%	72.5%	23.5%	26.3%
United States	16.3%	6.1%	70.4%	19.7%	15.1%
Great Britain	3.3%	6.0%	68.2%	17.2%	16.6%
France	2.6%	6.3%	66.7%	14.1%	37.5%
Italy	3.4%	1.4%	54.0%	19.7%	36.0%
Spain	1.1%	1.1%	23.4%	7.0%	35.9%
Japan	2.1%	2.4%	59.9%	7.0%	10.2%
Russia	0.8%	0.4%	8.3%	2.6%	15.9%

SOURCE: *Compiled from World Values Survey, Fifth Wave, 2005–2008. Variables V28, V29, V139, V140, and V141. Retrieved from www.worldvaluessurvey.org*

Civic Engagement

Despite the increase in some types of political participation, concerns have been expressed about the apparent decline of citizen involvement in the organizational life of communities (as discussed in Box 6-1, Bowling Alone?). In this view, a democratic political culture and effective democratic governing rest on a citizenry that is not only politically active, but also active in the non-political associations within the community.

Who Participates?

AGE A particularly striking feature of political participation is that young adults are much less likely to vote and participate in election campaign activity than are middle-aged and older voters. For example, in the 2008 Canadian election, only about 37 percent of those aged eighteen to twenty-four voted (Elections Canada, n.d.). Similarly, 37 percent of those aged eighteen to twenty-four voted in the 2005 United Kingdom election compared to 61 percent in the population as a whole and 75 percent of those aged sixty-five and older (Market and Opinion Research International, 2005). As explained in Box 6-2, Why Do So Few Young People Vote?, both the **life cycle effect** and the **generational effect** contribute to this low level of voting. Younger people are more likely than older people to engage in some protest activities, and they participate in issue-oriented groups at almost the same rate as older persons (Dalton, 2006). However, those who engage in non-electoral political activities are generally more likely to vote, and thus the low level of voting among youths cannot be attributed to decisions to engage in forms of political participation other than voting (Blais & Loewen, 2009).

LIFE CYCLE EFFECT The effect of one's age on one's attitudes and behaviour. As people grow older, their attitudes and behaviours may change due to changing circumstances (such as education, marriage, employment, and retirement) related to age.

GENERATIONAL EFFECT The effect on attitudes and behaviour of the views of different generations that persist throughout the life cycle.

BOX 6-1
Bowling Alone?

In his travels in the United States in the 1830s, French aristocrat Alexis de Tocqueville (1805–1859) found a high level of involvement by ordinary citizens in a variety of civic associations. This, he concluded, provided a firm basis for American democracy that did not exist in the hierarchical societies of Europe (Tocqueville, 1835/2000). Likewise, Robert Putnam (2000, p. 19) found that voluntary associations provided social capital, "the social networks and the norms of reciprocity and trustworthiness." These attitudes and networks provided the basis for democracy to function effectively. Participation in groups such as community choirs, bowling leagues, and service organizations developed trust in others, mutual co-operation in pursuit of common goals, tolerance, and leadership skills. Communities with high levels of social capital tend to be healthier, more prosperous, have higher levels of civic engagement, and are better governed (Putnam, 1993, 2000).

However, in the contemporary United States, Putnam found that involvement in a variety of social organizations was declining. For example, membership in bowling leagues had declined sharply; instead, people were bowling with friends or family.

Putnam attributed the decline in the membership of social organizations, in part, to the individualizing effects of television viewing. Spending much of our free time watching television reduces the time available for involvement in social organizations. Declining involvement in social organizations, he argued, is leading to a decline in the vitality of democracy (Putnam, 2000).

However, there has been some dispute about whether civic involvement has declined. Even though involvement in organizations such as Scouts, parent–teacher associations, and bowling leagues has declined, membership in other organizations, such as conservation and environmental groups, has increased substantially (Dalton, 2006; Ladd, 1999). Likewise, in Canada, membership in most types of voluntary organizations has increased (Baer, Curtis, & Grabb, 2001).

Regardless of whether involvement in social organizations has declined or increased, Putnam's analysis suggests that a well-functioning democracy requires not only a particular set of political institutions, but also a society and a political culture that foster trust and co-operation.

EDUCATION AND SOCIAL CLASS   Political participation is also related to education and other indicators of social class such as income. That is, those with higher levels of education, higher incomes, and professional or managerial occupations are more likely to engage in various forms of political participation, including both electoral and protest activity (Dalton, 2006). However, in countries where there is a major party that represents the working class, differences in voting participation among those in different class positions are small (Verba, Nie, & Kim, 1978). One might expect that the large increase in post-secondary education enrolment in recent decades would have the effect of increasing the turnout in elections. In fact, the rate of voting participation among university graduates in Canada has declined slightly in recent elections. Voting by those with less education, however, has declined sharply,

BOX 6-2
Why Do So Few Young People Vote?

Studies of voting behaviour in a variety of countries have found that younger people are much less likely to vote than older people.

Canadian surveys have indicated that while most middle-aged and older people felt that they had a moral obligation to vote, this sense of duty tends to be somewhat weaker among younger voters. Those who are younger tend to pay less attention to elections, have less interest in politics, and have less political knowledge (Blais et al., 2002, 2004; Pammett & LeDuc, 2003). The lower level of voting among the young is *not* a result of a more cynical outlook on politics or a higher level of negative feelings concerning all of the political parties (Blais et al., 2002).

To some extent, there is a tendency for people to be more likely to vote as they get older. Termed a life cycle effect, this could be a result of becoming more connected to one's community through work, involvement in community organizations, and raising a family, as well as a result of increased interest and knowledge of politics. Indeed, voting seems to be habit forming: after voting several times, a person is more likely to continue voting (Goerres, 2007).

However, persons reaching voting age in recent times have been less likely to vote than those reaching voting age in the past.

This lower voter turnout among recent generations has continued even as those generations age. In other words, this generational effect suggests that as they grow older, today's younger people will still be less likely to vote than their parents and grandparents. Indeed, the generational effect is the major factor in explaining why overall voting turnout rates have generally dropped in Canada, with this trend likely to continue (Blais et al., 2004).

Considerable concern has been expressed about the low level of voting among young people. Elections Canada has undertaken a variety of activities to inform young people about the process of elections and to encourage them to participate. Although the rules governing elections have been changed to make it easier for people to vote, many young people do not realize that they can vote on election day even if they are not on the official voters' list. There have also been suggestions that schools should provide more (and better) political education to encourage young people to engage in political activity so that their viewpoints and interests are represented and respected in the political process.

thus offsetting the increase that could be expected from the growth in post-secondary education (Blais et al., 2004).

GENDER   Although politics has traditionally been thought of as a male activity, studies in Canada and other advanced democracies have found that differences between women and men in some forms of participation are quite small or non-existent (Dalton, 2006; Mishler & Clarke, 1995). Indeed in some countries (including Canada) women are slightly more likely to vote than men (International Institute for Democracy and Electoral Assistance, n.d.; Elections Canada, n.d.). It is in higher-level political activities, such as seeking and holding national or provincial political office or a top position in a political party or interest group, that women are much less likely to be involved than men.

POLITICAL ATTITUDES, INTEREST, AND KNOWLEDGE Political participation is also affected by various individual political attitudes. Those with a
strong sense of attachment to a political party are more likely to vote and be
involved in election campaign activities (Dalton, 2006). Likewise, those with
a high level of political efficacy, political interest, and political knowledge are
more likely to be active participants in politics.

POLITICAL SOCIALIZATION AND CHANGING VALUES

Opinions about specific political issues and personalities can often change
quickly. However, a person's basic political values, beliefs, and orientations
are more resistant to change. Therefore, **political socialization,** the processes by
which the values, attitudes, and beliefs of the political culture are transmitted
to members of the political community, is important. Socialization can provide
for continuity as the values and beliefs of older generations are passed on to
newer generations. As well, immigrants may want, or be encouraged, to adopt
some of the political values and beliefs that are prevalent in their new country.

POLITICAL SOCIALIZATION
The processes by which the
values, attitudes, and beliefs
of the political culture are
transmitted to members of the
political community.

    Political socialization, however, is not always a process that ensures con-
tinuity in political thinking. Revolutionary regimes often attempt to change
traditional values and beliefs by socializing young people with new values
and resocializing older people. Even in non-revolutionary political systems,
governments or other powerful forces may attempt to modify the political
culture through deliberate socialization efforts so as to promote the legitimacy
of government and other social and political institutions, develop a sense of
national pride, or achieve other objectives. However, political socialization
does not involve only deliberate efforts to indoctrinate people with particular
values and beliefs. It often occurs in a more haphazard fashion—for example,
when young people observe the discussions and actions of adults.

    There are a variety of different agents of political socialization, includ-
ing the family, peer groups, the educational system, the mass media, religious
organizations, the military, unions, and the workplace. Although socialization
is a lifelong process, it is generally assumed that many basic values and orientations are acquired at an early age. Therefore, the family is likely to be a
major agent of political socialization. In particular, parents are very important
in shaping the religious, ethnic, and other group identities of their children.
American studies in the 1950s and 1960s also found that children and young
adults have a strong tendency to adopt the party identification (sense of attachment to a political party) of their parents, although later studies did not find
quite as strong a tendency (Jennings & Niemi, 1968, 1981). The correspondence between parents and young adults in other political attitudes—such as
political trust, political efficacy, orientations toward political participation,
and opinions on public policy issues—is not particularly strong (Jennings,
1984; Jennings & Niemi, 1981; Mintz, 1993).

State-Directed Socialization

Countries vary in the extent to which state institutions make deliberate and vigorous efforts to promote particular political values. Revolutionary regimes such as the former Soviet Union, the People's Republic of China, and Nazi Germany devoted great efforts to socializing the young (as well as the population as a whole) into the new values associated with the revolutionary ideology. Schools, the media, youth groups, and a variety of other organizations were required to promote "correct" values and criticize traditional values.

In liberal democracies, educational systems are often less explicitly political in terms of promoting a particular ideological perspective. Indeed, schools in many Canadian provinces provide only a limited amount of education concerning the political system. Nevertheless, schools often promote various politically relevant values and ideas.

The establishment of public educational systems in the nineteenth century was associated, in many countries, with the goal of creating a unified nation-state (Weber, 1976). In the United States, the school system has been seen as a means of creating a common sense of being American among a diverse immigrant population. American values were promoted (and often continue to be promoted) through required courses in "civics." Public education systems also served the needs of the emerging industrial system for a disciplined workforce through the practices enforced in the classroom.

In the 1960s and 1970s, a more child-centred educational approach was adopted in many jurisdictions in the advanced democracies. This approach focused on developing the potential of each individual in a less structured environment. Values such as respect for differences and cultural diversity were promoted, thus coinciding with the political trend in various countries to recognize and promote multiculturalism.

In recent years, this "liberal" approach to education has been challenged. Concerns about preparing for the challenges of a competitive global economy have led to a renewed emphasis on standards, testing, and basic skills such as mathematics and literacy. Worries about "homegrown" terrorism and the integration of immigrant families with different cultural practices have led some countries such as the United Kingdom, the United States, and France to consider, and in some cases implement, educational policies that reverse the tolerant, multicultural approach of previous decades and instead promote dominant national values and patriotism (Mitchell, 2003). For example, some American states have reinstituted requirements concerning patriotic rituals such as reciting the pledge of allegiance. France, in a move directed at its large Muslim minority, has banned the wearing of religious symbols and clothing, including the hijab (head scarf), in schools.

The success of government-directed socialization efforts in many countries should not be exaggerated. Teachers do not necessarily follow the government-prescribed curriculum. Religious groups and the Western media brought Eastern Europeans messages that contradicted the socializing messages conveyed by the Communist party. The Internet is bringing Western views about freedom and democracy to countries like China and Iran despite efforts by authoritarian governments to try to block these views. As well, young people do not passively accept what they are told. When different socializing agencies provide different perspectives, young people may develop values, attitudes, and beliefs in their own way. Thus, new generations are not copies of older generations in their political thinking, nor do their ideas necessarily reflect the ideas of the dominant ruling groups.

Changing Value Priorities

Ronald Inglehart (1977, 1990) has suggested that modern societies are undergoing a fundamental change in value priorities. According to his **postmaterialist theory**, political socialization is affected by the conditions present when a person is young. The generations that grew up in the relative security and affluence of the Western world since World War II are more likely to give priority to **postmaterialist values** such as freedom of expression, participation, concern about the quality of life, and appreciation of a more beautiful environment. Earlier generations are more likely to have materialistic values such as a concern for economic growth, order, and physical security (see Box 6-3, Are You Materialist or Postmaterialist?). This is not simply a matter of being

POSTMATERIALIST THEORY
A theory that modern societies are undergoing a fundamental change in value priorities because generations that grew up in the relative security and affluence of the Western world since World War II are more likely to give priority to postmaterialist values than to materialist values.

POSTMATERIALIST VALUES
Non-materialist values such as freedom of expression, participation, concern about the quality of life, and appreciation of a more beautiful environment.

Are You Materialist or Postmaterialist?

Read the following statement and answer the two questions to determine if you would be considered materialist or postmaterialist.

There is a lot of talk these days about what the aims of this country should be for the next ten years. Listed below are some of the goals to which different people would give top priority. If you had to choose, which one of these things would you say is the most important? Which would be the next most important?

1. Maintaining order in the nation
2. Giving people more say in important government decisions
3. Fighting rising prices
4. Protecting freedom of speech

If you chose items 1 and 3, you would be considered materialist; if you chose items 2 and 4, you would be considered postmaterialist; and if you chose a different combination, you would be categorized as mixed.

The four items on this quiz do not fully reflect all of the values associated with materialism and postmaterialism, but are often used instead of a twelve-item scale. The other postmaterialist values used in the twelve-item scale are: more say in work/community, more humane society, make cities/country more beautiful, and ideas count more than money. The other materialist values are: a high level of economic growth, a stable economy, fight against crime, and a strong defence (Dalton, 2006).

SOURCE: *Adapted from the World Values Survey, www.worldvaluessurvey.org*

---

more concerned with material and security needs as one grows older. Rather, studies conducted by Inglehart and his associates have found that the increased tendency to give priority to postmaterialist values has persisted among recent generations as they grow older.

Postmaterialism—in combination with the development of a post-industrial, knowledge-based economy, greater access to higher education, and more effective means of mass communications—may be creating major changes in the political culture of the advanced democracies. These changes, argues Russell Dalton (2006), have resulted in a **new style of citizen politics**. This includes greater citizen activism, the questioning of authority, the development of new political parties and new social movements, the raising of new types of issues (such as issues related to the environment and gender equality), and the development of more liberal social values (for example, greater acceptance of homosexual rights). As well, it is argued that the significance of traditional political divisions ("cleavages") based on such group characteristics as class, religion, and ethnicity has been declining. Likewise, the strength of individual and group attachments to particular political parties has generally tended to diminish.

The extent of value change should not be exaggerated. The trend toward greater postmaterialism found in surveys from the 1980s and 1990s was

NEW STYLE OF CITIZEN POLITICS A set of changes including greater citizen activism, the questioning of authority, the development of new political parties and new social movements, the raising of new types of issues, and the development of more liberal social values.

	CANADA			UNITED STATES		
	1990	2000	2006	1990	1999	2006
Materialist	11.9%	8.6%	10.3%	16.4%	9.5%	21.5%
Mixed	62.5	62.0	58.5	61.2	64.9	60.7
Postmaterialist	25.6	29.4	31.2	22.5	25.6	17.8
N (of respondents)	1647	1882	2143	1839	1179	1222

TABLE 6-3

MATERIALIST AND POSTMATERIALIST VALUES, CANADA AND THE UNITED STATES

SOURCE: *Compiled from the World Values Surveys data retrieved from www.worldvaluessurvey.org. The classification is based on the questions and procedure outlined in Box 6-3, combining the first and second priorities of respondents.*

reversed in some countries in more recent surveys[1] (as indicated in the example of the United States in Table 6-3). In most countries, the majority of the population has a mixture of materialist and postmaterialist values, and in many countries there are more people with materialist than postmaterialist values. Interestingly, Canada had the highest proportion of postmaterialists among the fifty-six countries surveyed.

Materialist concerns about unemployment, economic prosperity, health care, and taxes are still often the leading political issues. Postmaterialist issues (such as concern for the environment) have been added to the political agenda, but have not transformed the conflicts and social divisions that typically affect political life. What makes postmaterialism potentially more significant is that postmaterialist priorities are particularly evident among younger generations and among those with more education.

---

[1] Ersson and Lane (2008) point out that the proportion of postmaterialists averaged over the nine countries that were surveyed in all four waves of the World Values Surveys increased from 13 to 20 percent from 1981 to 1995, but then decreased to 14 percent in 2000. This may, however, reflect specific circumstances, such as changes in the level of inflation, at the time the surveys were conducted.

Summary and Conclusion

Examining the political culture of a country can be helpful in understanding the politics and governing of a country. The dominant political values in a country will likely affect how people think and act in political life and, at least to some extent, how its political institutions operate and what kinds of policies its governments tend to adopt. However, it is important to note that there are often substantial differences in the political values, beliefs, and political orientations of different groups (such as those based on religion, ethnicity, and class) within a country. This can contribute to tensions, conflicts, and misunderstandings among different groups. Differences often also exist between the political culture of the political elites and that of the rest of the population.

The political cultures of the advanced Western countries are often viewed as more liberal and individualistic than the political cultures of other parts of the world that are more collectivist and deferential to authority. Whether this is a persistent feature based on religious values, a result of historical circumstances, or the level of socio-economic development is unclear. Within Western political cultures, there are significant differences—for example, the political cultures of Canada and Western Europe generally tend to be somewhat less individualistic and more liberal and secular in social and moral values than the United States. One effect of this difference in political culture has been a lesser acceptance of the welfare state in the United States than in many other Western countries.

Researchers have found that the democratic ideal of an interested, active, and well-informed citizenry is far from realization even in countries where democratic values and institutions have become solidly entrenched. Although there has been increasing interest in politics, a relatively small proportion of the population is highly interested in politics and follows politics closely. Despite increased education, the level of political knowledge of much of the population does not seem particularly high. Voting participation in some countries is lower than it was a couple of decades ago, although participation in citizens groups and protest activities has been increasing. Younger people, in particular, have a low level of voting, which may mean that their viewpoints and interests are not given great attention in the process of political decision making. Although being active in politics does not necessarily mean that a group is influential, avoiding involvement tends to make a group invisible and politically irrelevant.

A high proportion of citizens say that they favour democracy. However, the levels of trust and confidence in government and politicians have become rather low in a number of democratic countries in recent times. Some analysts have argued that this indicates that there is a "crisis in democracy." Increasing demands from citizens have "overloaded" governments, in the sense that governments do not have the resources to meet all of the demands being placed on them by citizens. Dissatisfaction with government has grown, creating a potential problem of legitimacy for democratic governments (Crozier, Huntington, & Watanuki, 1975). Others argue that a more educated, postmaterialist citizenry has higher expectations of government. With increased information, citizens are more aware of what goes on in government. Citizens have become dissatisfied because of the slowness of governments to respond to their desire for more effective participation (Dalton, 2006).

Research concerning political culture and political participation raises some important issues concerning the ability of democratic countries to pursue the common good. On the one hand, the development of a more critical citizenry can be helpful in making government more responsive to the needs and preferences of citizens and in holding government accountable for its actions. The increase in active participation, particularly in citizens groups that seek the common good (or at least their version of the common good), can be viewed as a positive feature of modern, democratic politics. On the other hand, the rather low level of political knowledge among the citizenry raises questions about whether the common good can be effectively pursued through active citizen participation in politics. A tendency for voting participation to decline increases the likelihood that governments will be based on the electoral support of a minority of citizens. This may encourage politicians to be concerned with the good of only a limited part of society rather than all of the community. The low level of voting among young people is particularly troubling. If newer generations continue to find politics "boring" and pay little attention to politics (Blais et al., 2002), there may be long-term implications for the pursuit of the common good and the quality of democracy.

Key Terms

Discussion Questions

1. Do you think that a "clash of civilizations" is inevitable?

2. Is a particular kind of political culture needed to develop and sustain a democratic political system?

3. Does Canada have a distinctive political culture?

4. Why did you vote or not vote in the last election? Why do you think that younger voters are less likely to vote than older voters? Is voting a civic duty that all citizens have a responsibility to perform?

5. Do you have the same basic political values, beliefs, and orientations as your parents, other family members, or your friends? How would you explain the similarities and differences?

6. Is a postmaterialist political culture developing? What would be its implications for political life?

Further Reading

Adams, M. (2003). *Fire and ice: The United States, Canada and the myth of converging values.* Toronto: Penguin.

Almond, G.A., & Verba, S. (1965). *The civic culture: Political attitudes and democracy in five nations.* Boston: Little, Brown.

Dalton, R.J. (2006). *Citizen politics: Public opinion and political parties in advanced industrial democracies* (4th ed.). Washington, DC: CQ Press.

DeBardeleben, J., & Pammett, J.H. (Eds.). (2009). *Activating the citizen: Dilemmas of participation in Europe and Canada.* New York: Palgrave Macmillan.

Huntington, S.P. (1996). *The clash of civilizations and the remaking of world order.* New York: Simon & Schuster.

Inglehart, R., & Welzel, C. (2005). *Modernization, cultural change, and democracy: The human development sequence.* New York: Cambridge University Press.

Lipset, S.M. (1990). *Continental divide.* New York: Routledge.

Milner, H. (2002). *Civic literacy: How informed citizens make democracy work.* Hanover, NH: University Press of New England.

Putnam, R. (2000). *Bowling alone: The collapse and revival of American community.* New York: Simon & Schuster.

Chapter 7

Political Parties

PHOTO ABOVE: Michael Ignatieff, the only candidate, is acclaimed as leader of the Liberal Party of Canada in 2009.
In both Canada and the United States, many people have become alienated from party politics.

CHAPTER OBJECTIVES

After reading this chapter you should be able to:

1. explain the significance of parties
2. distinguish among different types of political parties
3. evaluate the methods used for choosing party leaders
4. outline the characteristics of the major Canadian parties and the nature of the Canadian party system
5. discuss the financing of political parties and election campaigns

Before he ran as Democratic party candidate for president, Barack Obama was critical of intense partisanship and the view that "winning is all that matters," both of which had alienated Americans from party politics (2006, p. 51).

Are political parties of declining importance in contemporary politics (Meisel, 1979; Meisel & Mendelsohn, 2001)? The membership of political parties in many of the established democracies has dropped substantially since the 1960s (Scarrow, 2000). In Canada, only about 1 or 2 percent of adult Canadians are regular members of a political party (Cross, 2004). As well, political parties are viewed negatively by a substantial majority of the population in many countries (Dalton, 2006). Even persons who are members of a political party are often dissatisfied with their limited influence on the development of party policy positions (Cross, 2004). Many citizens have become involved in public interest groups and social movements to achieve their objectives and pursue what they believe to be the common good. Although the theory of liberal democracy contends that competition among political parties allows citizens to influence the policies adopted by government, the link between citizens and government provided by political parties is often weak. The decisions of government do not necessarily reflect the policy positions presented by the party that has been elected to govern.

Because most major parties are focused on gaining and maintaining political power, they may compromise their principles in order to gain support from voters or from their financial backers. Instead of stimulating policy discussion among their members, parties are often concerned with their image and that of their leader, along with discrediting their opponents.

Nevertheless, the decline of parties should not be exaggerated. Parties play a dominant role in elections through recruiting candidates, running election campaigns, and presenting policy platforms to the public. The governing party (or parties) in a parliamentary system determines the agenda of government, oversees the development of public policies, and is usually able to obtain the support of Parliament needed to pass laws and approve the spending and taxing measures of the government. The opposition parties also play an important role in trying to hold government accountable for its actions and raising issues that have not been dealt with adequately by government. In most democratic countries, parties act as disciplined, united teams in Parliament, thereby simplifying the choice voters make in an election. Through debate among parties, voters may be able to obtain an understanding of the issues facing their country and the strengths and weaknesses of alternative approaches to handling important problems.

As president, Obama found that it was only by mobilizing Democratic party members of Congress, rather than by appealing to a broad majority across party lines, that he was able to gain support for reforming the American health care system (discussed in Chapter 15). Likewise, it was only through the determined effort of the Co-operative Commonwealth Federation (CCF) that Saskatchewan was able to adopt Canada's first system of public Medicare in 1961, despite intense opposition from doctors and private insurance companies. We may not like the squabbling and intense partisanship that goes along with party politics, but political parties can be important instruments of change.

THE ORIGINS AND DEVELOPMENT OF POLITICAL PARTIES

Legislative bodies have always had factions composed of individual members with similar interests and perspectives. As legislative bodies, such as the British Parliament, took the power to choose Cabinet ministers away from the monarch, these factions began to take on a more organized form. In particular, the leading **political party** in Parliament was able to choose and support ministers selected from its party (Katz, 2008).

Cadre and Mass Parties

As the right to vote started to expand, parties that emerged from parliamentary factions looked to local "notables" (that is, the local elites) who had the prestige and financial resources to support the party's candidates in elections. These **cadre parties** had little in the way of formal organizational structures or membership outside of Parliament (Duverger, 1964) This left the members of the party in Parliament and its leadership generally free to take positions in Parliament and government as they saw fit (or in accordance with the views of their financial backers and elite supporters). Cadre parties thus provided a limited link between the people and the government.

Mass parties developed in the latter part of the nineteenth century and the start of the twentieth century to challenge the elite domination of political life and organize the mass of the population. Socialist and Labour parties were formed out of working-class movements and pressed to gain the right to vote for all adults. Other mass parties were formed in some countries based on nationalist movements, farmers' movements, and religious movements. Unlike the cadre parties, which usually were created internally within legislatures, the mass parties generally were externally created to represent major sections of the newly enfranchised population such as the working class. Because many of these parties did not have the support of the wealthy, they generally tried to develop a large membership base that supported the party by regularly paying a small membership fee.

Collecting fees from large numbers of people required a large organization based on a network of local branches with a central office. Democratic procedures, including **party conventions** (regular meetings of elected delegates of the membership), were adopted to approve party positions and to choose members for various positions in the party. Because mass parties generally developed outside of the legislature, members elected to the legislature were expected to follow the wishes of the party membership as expressed at party conventions. As well, mass parties typically sought to penetrate and associate with various social groups such as unions and religious organizations (Gunther & Diamond, 2001). Generally, mass parties attempted to involve their members on a regular basis and to educate their members concerning

POLITICAL PARTY An organization that has a central role in the competition for political power in legislative bodies, and in governing.

CADRE PARTY A loosely organized party usually established by members of a legislative body with the support of local notables. Cadre parties are concerned primarily with electing members of the party to legislative bodies, rather than with building a strong, centralized, membership-based organization outside of the legislature.

MASS PARTY A party that draws its support from a regular dues-paying membership and features a strong party organization outside of the legislature.

PARTY CONVENTION A meeting of delegates from party constituency associations as well as the party's legislators and party officials.

their party's perspective (Ware, 1987). In some countries this involved publishing newspapers, sponsoring sports teams, and organizing the lives of their members through recreational and social activities.

Mass parties generally have a stronger link between citizens and political leaders than do cadre parties. Analysts of mass parties have noted, however, that power tends to be concentrated in the party officials (those with paid positions within the party organization) rather than in the mass membership of the party. Based on his observation in the early twentieth century of the German Social Democratic party (a classic example of a mass party), Robert Michels (1911/1962) developed what he termed the **iron law of oligarchy**. This generalization claims that all organizations, even those that appear democratic, inevitably become dominated by a small group of leaders.

As mass parties in a number of countries succeeded in developing large, membership-based organizations, cadre parties eventually found it necessary to respond to this challenge by developing regular membership-based organizations and adopting some of the democratic party procedures pioneered by mass parties. Nevertheless, traces of the difference still remain. For example, parties with cadre origins often consider the party leadership as the final determinant of party positions and tend to rely more than other parties on financing from business and the wealthy. In contrast, parties with mass origins typically place the authority to approve policy positions in the hands of a party convention and tend to involve their members more in policy development.

In recent decades, the development of modern election campaign techniques, such as the use of television advertising and the solicitation of funds through direct mail and the Internet, has reduced the necessity of building and maintaining a large membership organization. In many countries, including Canada, parties are now funded to a considerable extent by the state. Professionals skilled in the techniques of advertising, public relations, fundraising, campaign management, and public opinion research have become increasingly important to parties in their efforts to gain political power. Mass parties, like parties with cadre origins, eventually found it necessary to make use of campaign professionals to try to appeal to the electorate.

CONTEMPORARY POLITICAL PARTIES

Most major political parties today can be described as **electoral–professional parties** (Panebianco, 1988). Such parties are *electoral* in that their dominant concern is winning elections and *professional* in their reliance on experts to market them to the electorate. These parties may mobilize substantial numbers of supporters during an election campaign (and when leaders and candidates are being chosen), but will tend to shrink to a small number of active members at other times. Electoral–professional parties usually attempt to appeal to all or most of the electorate by avoiding clear ideological positions, shifting their policy positions in response to public opinion, and focusing on the personal qualities of

IRON LAW OF OLIGARCHY
A generalization that claims that all organizations, even those that appear democratic, inevitably become dominated by a small group of leaders.

ELECTORAL–PROFESSIONAL PARTY A political party whose dominant concern is winning elections and that relies on professional experts to market the party to voters.

the party's leaders and candidates (Gunther & Diamond, 2001; Kirchheimer, 1966).[1] Similarly, the term **brokerage party** has often been used to describe the leading Canadian parties (particularly the Liberal party) in the sense that these parties have attempted to find compromises to accommodate a variety of interests (particularly regional and ethnic/cultural divisions) so as to try to build broad support across the country in a non-ideological manner. However, despite their efforts to be broad-based and non-ideological, the policies in government of electoral–professional and brokerage parties may tend to reflect business interests and the country's dominant ideological perspective (Brodie & Jenson, 1988).

BROKERAGE PARTY A party that attempts to find compromises to accommodate a variety of interests (particularly regional and ethnic/cultural divisions) so as to try to build broad support across the country in a non-ideological manner.

Differing somewhat from electoral–professional parties are **programmatic parties**, including the New Democratic Party and the former Reform party, that tend to devote greater attention to the development of a coherent party program and view themselves as more principled than other parties. Nevertheless, to remain competitive, programmatic parties have often adopted some of the techniques and strategies of electoral–professional parties.

PROGRAMMATIC PARTY A party that has a distinct ideological perspective or a coherent set of policy goals that are consistently followed over time.

Not all significant political parties have developed a reliance on professional expertise and a heavy focus on winning elections. Some newer parties that have developed out of social movements (such as Green parties) continue to rely, to a considerable extent, on amateur activists to carry their message to the public and retain some elements of "grassroots democracy" even as they become more professional (Rihoux & Franklin, 2008).

Rather than trying to appeal to the electorate as a whole, some parties focus on representing the interests of a particular ethnic or cultural group, nationality, or region within Parliament with no intention of seeking votes from outside their segment of society. For example, the Scottish Nationalist party (which favours independence for Scotland) participates in elections for the United Kingdom Parliament contesting seats only in Scotland. Other examples include Canada's Bloc Québécois, Italy's Lega Nord (Northern League), and Finland's Swedish People's Party. There are also political parties that put forward candidates in elections in order to promote a particular interest or cause rather than to obtain seats in a legislative body (see Box 7-1, Running to Make a Point).

Finally, a few parties have been formed to promote the election of a particular individual as prime minister or president, particularly a leader who can claim to represent the people as a whole. The classic case of a **personalistic party** is the Union pour la Nouvelle République (often referred to as the "Gaullist party") formed to support General Charles de Gaulle, who led the "Free French" government-in-exile during World War II. De Gaulle was seen

PERSONALISTIC PARTY A party established to promote the election of a particular individual as prime minister or president.

---

[1] Similarly the term *catch-all party* is often used, particularly to describe the changes in many European Social Democratic parties from mass parties committed to achieving socialism through the mobilization of the working class to parties that seek broader support to gain or maintain political power.

Running to Make a Point: Minor Political Parties

In the 2008 Canadian election campaign, the leader of the Marijuana party said that there was no reason to vote for his party. The party was not seeking to elect any members to the House of Commons; rather, he said, the party wanted to put the issue of legalizing cannabis a little higher on the political agenda.

In most democratic countries there are a large number of political parties, many of which have little expectation of electing representatives or even gaining more than an insignificant number of votes. Although the media generally pay little attention to these parties, election campaigns do provide an opportunity to try to get their message across. Some of these parties (such as communist, libertarian, and fundamentalist Christian parties) represent distinctive political perspectives that are strongly held by their members but not reflected in the "mainstream" parties. Others have a particular cause, such as the Pirate party (recently established in a number of countries), which wants greater protection for Internet privacy, open government, and reform of patent and copyright laws, including the legalization of non-commercial Internet file sharing. Although some minor parties have only a short-lived existence on the political landscape, others have exhibited considerable staying power. Most notably, the Prohibition Party in the United States, which seeks to ban the production and sale of alcohol, has run a candidate for president in every election since 1872 (although it gained only 643 votes in the 2008 election).

There have also been parties that seek to make fun of parties and politicians. Poland's Beer-Lovers Party managed to elect sixteen members to the Sejm (lower chamber of Parliament) in 2001 before splitting into large-beer and small-beer parties. The Official Monster Raving Loony Party has been a satirical feature of British elections since 1983. Canada's Rhinoceros party, led originally by a thick-skinned resident of the Granby Zoo, managed to win 110 000 votes in the 1980 election. Its successor, the Neorhino.ca party, campaigned in the 2008 election on a promise to keep none of its promises!

as a non-partisan leader who could end the turmoil of French politics that existed for many years after the end of the war. Likewise, in Argentina, the Partido Justicialiste was formed in 1945 to support the presidential candidacy of Juan Perón and continues to be the leading party long after his death in 1974. More recently, billionaire Italian businessman and football club owner Silvio Berlusconi created his own party, Forza Italia, which successfully supported his political ambition to become prime minister.

CANADIAN POLITICAL PARTIES

The Conservative Party

Canada's first organized political party, the Conservatives, originated as a cadre party based on the coalition of factions that supported the union of the British North American colonies in 1867. The party had close relations with elite groups, including big business. The Conservative party—which adopted

Conservative Party of Canada
www.conservative.ca

the name Progressive Conservative (PC) in 1942—was traditionally associated with tariff protection for manufacturing industries and a strong central government. However, in the 1980s it pursued a free trade agreement with the United States and advocated greater provincial government powers. Support for the party collapsed in the early 1990s, with the party winning only two seats in the 1993 election. The Reform party (established in 1987) promoted the populist New Right vision of a greatly reduced role for government and appealed particularly to Western Canadians who were distrustful of the PC government's efforts to satisfy Quebec's demands for constitutional change. The failure of the PC government's constitutional reform efforts resulted in the establishment of the Bloc Québécois in 1990, led at that time by former PC Cabinet minister Lucien Bouchard.

With the conservative or right-wing vote outside Quebec split between the PCs and the Reform party, the Reform party tried to convince the PCs to merge with them. The first attempt—the Canadian Reform Conservative Alliance (commonly known as the Canadian Alliance), established in 2000 with Reformer Stephen Harper as its leader—had limited success since many national PCs were opposed to the strongly ideological views of the Reform party. Nevertheless, in 2003 (over the objections of some of its prominent members), the PC party agreed to merge with the Canadian Alliance to form a new Conservative party, with Stephen Harper subsequently chosen as its leader. Although former Reformers along with strongly conservative former provincial PCs comprise a substantial proportion of the contemporary Conservative party, Conservatives have tried to adopt a more moderate image than that of the Reform party. The new version of the Conservative party generally favours smaller government (although it substantially increased government spending in 2009 to address the serious recession), lower taxes, freer markets, closer relations with the United States, and increased provincial government power. It also supports traditional social values and tougher sentences for criminal offences.

The Liberal Party

Liberal Party of Canada
www.liberal.ca

The Liberal party developed out of a diverse set of factions, including those who supported the establishment of a democratic system of government in which power ultimately rested on the support of the elected representatives of the people; those opposed to the power and privileges of elites, including the established religions (particularly the Catholic Church in Quebec); and Maritimers who had opposed joining Canada. By the 1880s, the Liberal party had become a unified party in Parliament. The Liberal party can be considered a cadre party in terms of its origins. Its extraparliamentary party organization was slow to develop. Indeed, until recently the national Liberal party did not have a comprehensive list of its members.

The early Liberal party generally adopted the positions of classic liberalism favouring free trade and limited government, as well as supporting provincial rights rather than a dominant central government. As with the early Conservative party, it moderated its ideological perspective to gain support. In particular, it became associated with national unity as it gained the support of French-speaking Quebecers as well as English-speaking Canadians. Beginning in the early 1940s, the Liberal party oversaw the gradual development of the welfare state and, particularly when Pierre Trudeau was prime minister (1968–1979 and 1980–1984), supported a strong national government in the face of the growing assertiveness of provincial governments. The party views the adoption of the Charter of Rights and Freedoms (1982) as one of its key accomplishments.

The New Democratic Party

The New Democratic Party (NDP) has its roots in the Co-operative Commonwealth Federation (CCF), which was established in 1932 by delegates from various farmer, labour, and socialist groups during the height of the Great Depression. Its limited support at the national level and weak finances led the CCF to join with the Canadian Labour Congress (the largest umbrella organization of labour unions) to form the NDP in 1961.

New Democratic Party of Canada
www.ndp.ca

Although the NDP has moderated its democratic socialist ideology, it supports welfare state measures and greater social and economic equality. As well, it tends to favour government regulation of business activities, including stronger environmental regulations. It also generally opposes greater military involvement with the United States and favours nationalist measures to limit American economic and cultural influences.

The Bloc Québécois

The other major party at the national level, the Bloc Québécois, was founded in 1990 by some members of Parliament (mainly PC but also Liberal) who were upset that the PC government was considering modifying a proposed constitutional agreement (the Meech Lake Accord) that would have recognized Quebec as a distinct society. The Bloc contests seats only in Quebec and generally has a close relationship with the Parti Québécois, which represents the independence movement at the provincial level. The Bloc is a voice for Quebec nationalism and is primarily concerned with representing Quebec's interests in the Canadian House of Commons. Thus it has no interest in running candidates outside of the province. Like the NDP, it tends to favour social democratic policies and stronger environmental measures.

Bloc Québécois
www.blocquebecois.org

The Green Party

There are more than a dozen smaller parties that regularly contest Canadian elections. However, only the Green party has, since 2004, become a significant part of the Canadian party system. Although distinctive in its focus on

Green Party of Canada
http://greenparty.ca

▶ Environmentalist Elizabeth May, candidate for the Small Party in 1980 and executive director of the Sierra Club of Canada from 1989 to 2006, was elected leader of the Green Party of Canada in 2006.

environmental issues, the Green party has also developed positions on a variety of issues, including human rights, poverty, health care, electoral system reform, and foreign policy. The Green party reached an agreement with the Liberal party for the 2008 election such that each party would not run a candidate to oppose the other party's leader. However, some of the Green party's policy positions (other than its advocacy of a carbon tax) are closer to those of the NDP.

PARTY SYSTEMS

A party system refers to the basic pattern of relationships among political parties (Sartori, 1976). In an influential analysis, Seymour Martin Lipset and Stein Rokkan (1967) argued that the party systems of Western countries developed in response to two major historical turning points. First, the development of the modern nation-state in the eighteenth and nineteenth centuries often involved conflict between the dominant national culture and various minority cultures, particularly in the more remote regions, creating a centre–periphery **cleavage**. As well, conflicts between the developing state and the Catholic Church, which wanted to preserve its privileges and power, sometimes created a cleavage between Catholics and Protestants or between those with a religious orientation to politics and those with a secular orientation. Second, the Industrial Revolution of the nineteenth century created a cleavage

CLEAVAGE A social division that involves those associated with each grouping having a distinct collective identity and distinct interests that can lead to the development of organizations such as political parties that reflect the different sides of the social division.

between agricultural interests and the new industrialists (which Lipset and Rokkan termed a "land–industry" cleavage) and later a cleavage between the owners of industries and the industrial workers (a class cleavage).

Although the national and industrial revolutions affected all Western societies, the specific historical circumstances of each country affected the manner in which the party system developed in particular countries. For example, the modern British party system was strongly affected by the class cleavage (although the centre–periphery cleavage is particularly relevant for Scotland) while the German party system was affected by a combination of class and religious cleavages (as well as the centre–periphery cleavage for Bavaria). In Lipset and Rokkan's view, the basic pattern of connections between the major interests in society and the party system had become firmly established by the 1960s.

Subsequently, the raising of new issues such as concern about the environment and women's rights along with the development of postmaterialist values (see Chapter 6), the creation of new political parties, and the weakening of the relationship between social group membership and voting choice, led some analysts to argue that Western party systems were changing with the alignments between social groups and political parties becoming less important (Dalton, 2006). Nevertheless, the party systems in many Western countries still reflect, to varying extents, the continuing significance of their cleavage structures.

Ideology and the Party System

Although electoral–professional parties generally tend to downplay their ideological positioning, most party systems do feature at least some degree of ideological competition. As indicated in Table 7-1, many countries outside North America feature competition between social democratic parties and conservative or Christian Democratic parties.[2] In Canada and the United States, the ideological differences between the leading parties generally have not been consistent and clear. Nevertheless, a study of the attitudes of the members of different Canadian parties found that there were substantial differences in their perspectives, including, to some extent, differences between the members of the Liberal and the Progressive Conservative parties (Cross & Young, 2002). However, even if parties tend to attract members who have differing perspectives, this does not necessarily mean that parties will differ in the

---

[2] Christian Democratic parties generally combine traditional Christian social and moral views with notions of social solidarity and the common good that reject the individualism of laissez-faire capitalism as well as the class struggle and state planning of classical socialism. Although arising out of Catholic social movements, Christian Democratic parties have also found support among conservative Protestants in some continental European countries.

TABLE 7-1

PARTY IDEOLOGIES IN SELECTED WESTERN DEMOCRACIES

Notes: Leading parties are in bold; parties with generally less than 5 percent of the vote have been excluded. Italian groupings are shifting coalitions of parties. Some of the ideological depictions are imprecise.

COUNTRY	BASIC IDEOLOGICAL PERSPECTIVE
Canada	**Conservative**; **Liberal**; NDP (social democratic); Bloc Québécois (Quebec nationalist); Green
United States	**Democratic** (liberal; centrist); **Republican** (New Right conservative)
United Kingdom	**Labour** (social democratic); **Conservative**; Liberal Democrats (liberal)
Australia	**Labour** (social democratic); **Liberal** (centre-right); National (rural conservative); Green
France	**Union for a Popular Movement** (conservative); **Socialist Party**; Union for French Democracy (centrist); Front National (far right)
Germany	**Christian Democratic Union**/Christian Social Union; **Social Democratic**; The Left (socialist); Greens; Free Democratic (liberal)
Italy	**People of Freedom** (centre-right); **Democratic** (centre-left); Lega Nord (regional); Italy of Values (generally centrist); Union of the Centre (mainly Christian democracy)
Sweden	**Social Democratic**; **Moderate** (basically conservative); Centre (agrarian); People's Party (social liberal); Christian Democrats; Left party (socialist); Green
Spain	**Socialist Workers Party** (social democratic); **People's Party** (conservative/Christian democracy)

images they present to the public in an election campaign or in their actions if elected to govern.

It is often argued that political parties will tend to adopt similar positions as they seek to win elections (as discussed in Box 7-2, Do Parties Tend to Converge in Their Basic Positions?). In fact, researchers have found a tendency for the leading parties to become less ideological as time passes and to drift to the centre of the ideological spectrum (Caul & Gray, 2000). As well, there has been a tendency for parties established to represent particular segments of society to move toward a broader appeal. For example, the British Labour party, under the leadership of Tony Blair, dropped its commitment to public ownership of industry and moved away from a focus on the interests of the working class. However, this was not simply a successful electoral strategy; it also reflected the ideological vision (termed the "Third Way") of Blair and his supporters.

This tendency for parties to move away from an ideological stance is not absolute and, in fact, there have been occasions when electoral–professional parties have moved in an ideological direction. For example, the moderate

BOX 7-2

Do Parties Tend to Converge in Their Basic Positions?

In *An Economic Theory of Democracy* (1957), Anthony Downs argued that in a two-party system, parties will converge in the ideological centre, defined in terms of the ideological position held by the largest number of voters. Assuming that voters are aware of the positioning of the parties and will vote for the party that is closest to their own position, a left-wing party will find that it gains more votes as it moves toward the centre. Likewise, there is a strong electoral incentive for a right-wing party to move to the centre such that the two parties become virtually indistinguishable in ideological terms. It should be noted that Downs's theory does not apply fully to situations where there are more than two parties. If, for example, there is a far-left party as well as a moderate leftist party, the moderate leftist party may lose votes to the far-left party if it moves too close to the centre.

Although Downs's theory provides a simple model of the dynamics of party competition, it has also been subject to criticism. Party members may choose leaders and candidates whose policy positions most closely resemble their own position rather than that of the average voter, thus leading parties to move away from the centre (Adams & Merrill, 2005). Many of those active in a political party are concerned not only with winning elections, but also with implementing their views about what is best for the political community. Thus, some party activists who are committed to a particular perspective may seek to move their party in a more distinctive ideological direction.

Voters not only may be concerned with choosing the party that is closest to them in terms of its ideology and policies, but also may focus on the credibility and competence of the party and the qualities of its leader and candidates. As well, many voters may be unclear about the ideological positioning of the parties, particularly if parties are deceptive concerning their positions and that of their opponents (Grofman, 1996). Finally, voters may choose the party that leans in the same basic ideological direction as they do, rather than choosing a centrist party that may be closer to their ideological position. A vigorous appeal to right-wing or left-wing themes may, in some circumstances, have a greater appeal to voters leaning to the left or right than a bland centrist appeal. Although taking a strong ideological position is often seen as harmful to a party's electoral fortunes, in certain circumstances it can lead to electoral success, as indicated by the examples of the Conservative party led by Margaret Thatcher and the Republican party led by Ronald Reagan.

British Conservative party was turned into an ideological vehicle for the New Right under the leadership of Prime Minister Margaret Thatcher. Likewise, the Republican party in the United States has been strongly influenced by the New Right since the election of President Ronald Reagan in 1980. The provincial PC governments led by Michael Harris (premier of Ontario, 1995–2002) and Ralph Klein (premier of Alberta, 1992–2006) also implemented policies reflecting the New Right ideology rather than the more centrist policies pursued by previous PC governments in those provinces.

NEW PARTIES   The establishment of new parties can also contribute to making the party system more ideological. In recent decades, Green parties promoting an environmentalist perspective along with advocacy concerning social justice, feminism, grassroots democracy, and peace have been established in about seventy countries.

Likewise, in recent decades, new right-wing populist parties favouring major tax cuts and reductions in government (including Denmark's People's Party, Norway's Progress party, and Canada's former Reform party) have at times been able to gain substantial support in several countries. More extreme right-wing parties have developed significant support in countries such as Austria, France, Belgium, and the Netherlands. Thus, even if competition among the leading parties often tends to be more about gaining power than debating different ideological perspectives, new parties may inject different basic points of view into the party system. In some cases, this has encouraged other parties to adopt positions advocated by newer parties in order to avoid losing some of their supporters.

Two-Party, Multiparty, and One-Party Dominant Systems

In addition to characterizing party systems in terms of cleavages and ideological competition, party systems are often analyzed in terms of the number of significant political parties. The number of parties varies considerably. In the United States, there are only two significant parties (the Democratic and Republican parties). In contrast, Israel has twelve parties represented in the Knesset (its legislative body), although seven of those parties received less than 5 percent of the seats in the 2009 election.

A distinction is often made between two-party, multiparty, and one-party dominant systems.[3] In a **two-party system** (as, for example, in the United States, Malta, and Jamaica), the two leading parties typically win the vast majority of seats in the legislature. The difference in support for the leading parties is small thereby allowing each party a reasonable chance to win an election and, in a parliamentary system, form a majority government (that is, one in which the governing party has a majority of the members in the House of Commons).

Multiparty systems feature three or more parties with significant legislative representation. Countries with multiparty systems are often governed by a coalition of political parties. In a *two-plus party system* the two leading parties usually win 80 percent or more of the seats, but one or more of the

TWO-PARTY SYSTEM A party system in which two major parties contend to control the government. Two-party systems are competitive in the sense that a single party does not govern for a lengthy period of time.

MULTIPARTY SYSTEM A political party system featuring several parties that are significant actors in the competition for political power.

[3] There are a variety of ways to operationalize these terms, with some political scientists preferring to characterize party systems in terms of the proportion of votes parties receive or in terms of a combination of votes and seats.

smaller parties has sufficient support to prevent, from time to time, either of the leading parties from gaining a majority of seats. From 1921 to 1993, Canada could be characterized as having a two-plus party system. In what may be termed a *moderate multiparty system* there are usually four or five significant parties, with the two leading parties having less than four-fifths of the seats. Many countries could be characterized as having a moderate multiparty system, including contemporary Canada, Germany, and Austria. Finally, in *fragmented multiparty systems* (such as in Belgium and Israel) there are five or more significant parties, with typically no single party having a large number of seats (Siaroff, 2009). If the fragmented multiparty system is combined with such features as strongly ideological parties, including significant parties that reject the political system of the country, this can lead to political instability because of the difficulties involved in forming and maintaining a coalition government in these circumstances (Sartori, 1976).

In a few cases, liberal democracies have had a **one-party dominant system** in which a predominant party governs for a lengthy period of time because the opposition is divided among a number of parties, none of which have the support needed to mount an effective challenge to the governing party. This has been the case in some Canadian provinces (notably Alberta) and American states (particularly in the South) as well as in Botswana, South Africa, and (until recently) Japan.

As discussed in Chapter 11, many contemporary non-democratic countries are one-party systems in which only one party is allowed or in which opposition parties are prevented from mounting an effective challenge to the governing party (for example, by harassment or imprisonment of opposition party members or by the falsification of election results).

The number of significant political parties is affected, in part, by the electoral system. Countries with proportional representation systems generally have multiparty systems while some countries that have a single member plurality electoral system (which tend to give a boost in representation to the largest parties) have a two-party system (see Chapter 8 for explanations of electoral systems). Canada, which uses the single member plurality electoral system, historically had a two-party system but now has a multiparty system with significant representation in the House of Commons of the Liberal, Conservative, and New Democratic parties along with the Bloc Québécois (see Figure 7-1). With no one party currently dominant, this has made it difficult in recent years for any party to form a majority government. Nevertheless, only the Liberal and Conservative parties have ever formed the government at the national level and, except for an unusual situation during World War I, there have been no national coalition governments. Instead, Canada has had many minority governments (that is, one in which the governing party has less than half of the seats in the House of Commons) since 1921.

ONE-PARTY DOMINANT SYSTEM A party system in which a single party rules for long periods of time and the opposition parties are not likely to gain the support needed to successfully challenge the dominant party for control of the government.

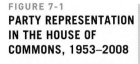

FIGURE 7-1

PARTY REPRESENTATION IN THE HOUSE OF COMMONS, 1953–2008

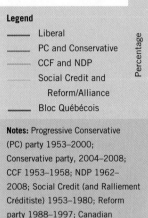

Legend

——— Liberal
——— PC and Conservative
——— CCF and NDP
——— Social Credit and
        Reform/Alliance
——— Bloc Québécois

Notes: Progressive Conservative (PC) party 1953–2000; Conservative party, 2004–2008; CCF 1953–1958; NDP 1962–2008; Social Credit (and Ralliement Créditiste) 1953–1980; Reform party 1988–1997; Canadian Alliance, 2000. Independents not shown.

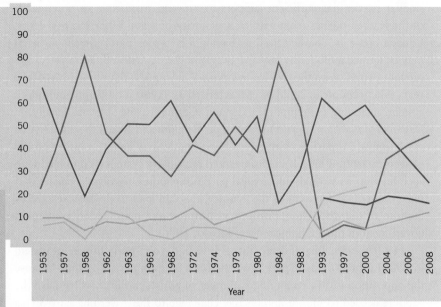

SOURCES: *Calculated from H.G. Thorburn & A. Whitehorn (Eds.),* Party politics in Canada *(8th ed.), Toronto: Prentice-Hall, 2001; and Elections Canada (2004, 2006, and 2008), retrieved from www.elections.ca*

PARTY ORGANIZATION

Imagine that you decide to join a political party. Undoubtedly you would be asked to help the party elect its candidate in your district in the next election. As well, in addition to paying a small membership fee, you would likely be encouraged to make a regular donation to the party. But would your opinions and the opinions of other "ordinary" members of the party have a substantial effect on how the political community is governed? To discuss this question we need to examine the organization and operations of political parties. In particular, we need to look at the extent to which ordinary party members (those not sitting as part of a legislative body) are influential in selecting the party leader and the candidates that represent the party in an election and in developing and deciding on the policy positions that the party takes.

Selecting the Party Leader

Choosing a party leader is a very important task for political parties. Not only is the leader the chief spokesperson for the party but, more importantly in a parliamentary system, the leader whose party gains the most representatives in an election usually (but not always) becomes the head of government (see Chapter 14). In effect, parties choose the most powerful person in government.

Parties use several different methods to choose their leaders:

- *Selection by parliamentary party.* The parliamentary party is used to select the leader in some countries. For example, in 2010 Kevin Rudd, who had led the Australian Labour party to victory in 2007, resigned after it became apparent that he no longer had the support of his party's caucus. Julia Gillard then became party leader (and prime minister) because she was unopposed in the caucus election. Such a system, unlike the alternatives discussed below, ensures that leaders have the support of their colleagues so that they can lead their party effectively in Parliament. Leaders chosen by the parliamentary party are likely to have considerable parliamentary experience, and candidates do not need financial backing to seek the leadership. Selection exclusively by the parliamentary party, however, does not provide a voice for ordinary citizens who are party members.

- *Selection at party conventions.* Party conventions allow various components of the party to participate in the election of the leader. Typically, delegates elected from each constituency, along with the party's legislators, party officials, and representatives of different associations within the party (for example, women, youth, student, and other groups), choose among leadership candidates at a convention. The standard procedure is to hold successive ballots. The candidate with the least number of votes or any candidate not receiving a certain number of votes is dropped from the ballot until one candidate has a majority of the votes cast.

  While party conventions are more representative of the party as a whole than is the parliamentary party, the choice of the convention will not necessarily reflect the choice of all party members. Delegates tend to have a higher socio-economic position than the general membership (in part because of the costs of attending a convention) and the presence of substantial numbers of non-elected delegates may give party elites some ability to influence the results. On the other hand, delegates to a party convention are likely to be committed party members, and party conventions allow those choosing the leader to meet the candidates, hear their speeches, and discuss the merits of the candidates with other delegates. Party leadership conventions also attract considerable media attention, which can potentially boost the party's popularity.

- *Selection by direct membership vote.* In recent times, some parties have decided to choose their leader by a direct membership vote. That is, all party members have the opportunity to choose among the leadership candidates. In some ways, the direct membership vote is the most democratic way of choosing a leader. It not only allows each party member a direct voice in choosing a leader, but also makes it easier for party members who cannot spend the money or devote the time to attend a leadership convention to participate in the choice. As well, the ability of candidates to perform well in an election campaign can be tested by their campaign for party leadership. However, direct membership vote systems can place the power to select a leader in the hands of those with little or no involvement or attachment to the party. During leadership campaigns, party membership often multiplies as each candidate's team aggressively tries to recruit large numbers of new party members—many of whom do not renew their membership after voting in the leadership contest. Although these problems are also evident in the election of delegates in the convention system, they can be more serious in direct membership voting systems.

Canadian parties adopted the party convention method of choosing a party leader in the first decades of the twentieth century. In recent years, the major national parties (as well as many provincial parties) have adopted direct membership vote systems (see Box 7-3, Choosing a Leader). However, although each party member has a vote, the Liberal and Conservative parties use a system in which each electoral district association has an equal weight in the choice of the leader regardless of the number of party members in that district. The NDP reserves one-quarter of the votes for its leader for members of unions affiliated with the party.

A study of eighteen established democratic countries found that 44 percent of parties chose their leaders by a party convention, 24 percent by a vote of the parliamentary party, 23 percent by a vote of party members, and 10 percent by a national party committee[4] (Scarrow, Webb, & Farrell, 2000). As in Canada, there is a general tendency toward including ordinary party members in the selection of a leader (Kenig, 2009).

COSTS   The choice of leaders by either the convention or the membership vote system can be very costly for the candidates. For example, Paul Martin spent nearly $10 million to win the leadership of the Liberal Party of Canada in 2003, while Sheila Copps, the only other contender to stay in the race until the end, spent about $900 000. In 2004, the Conservative party required candidates to pay a deposit of $100 000 to enter the leadership race (half of which was refundable). Stephen Harper, the successful Conservative candidate in 2004, reported spending just over $2 million, while the second-place candidate, Belinda Stronach, spent about $2.5 million. The high cost of mounting a credible campaign has discouraged a number of potential candidates from contesting the leadership of their parties.

---

[4] British Conservative party rules adopted in 1998 involve the party's members of Parliament (MPs) selecting two candidates with party members and then deciding by a majority vote which one will be leader. The British Labour Party chooses its leader and deputy leader using an electoral college in which Labour MPs, affiliated unions, and constituency associations each have one-third of the vote. Candidates need to be nominated by at least one-eighth of the Labour MPs.

Choosing a Leader:
The Liberal Party of Canada

After the defeat of the Liberal party in the 2006 election and the resignation of its leader, Paul Martin, the Liberal party selected Stéphane Dion (a political science professor and Liberal Cabinet minister) as leader even though he was the first choice of only 17.8 percent of those voting at a party convention. As successive ballots were held and other candidates dropped out of the race, Dion came out ahead of the initial front-runners, Michael Ignatieff and Bob Rae.

The Liberal party under Dion's leadership did poorly in the 2008 election. Under pressure from his party's caucus, Dion agreed that he would resign after a new leader was chosen at the party's convention in May 2009. With the three opposition parties angered by the minority Conservative government's budget in December 2008, the Liberals and NDP agreed to form a coalition government with the support of the Bloc to replace the Conservative minority government. Dion would temporarily become prime minister until a new Liberal leader was chosen. As discussed in Chapter 14,

Prime Minister Stephen Harper asked the governor general to prorogue Parliament (end a session of Parliament) rather than face certain defeat in the House of Commons. The Conservatives then mounted a strong attack on the plan for a coalition government. Faced with public opposition to the idea of Dion as temporary prime minister, the Liberal caucus pressured him to resign immediately as party leader. The caucus then chose Michael Ignatieff as interim leader after Bob Rae and Dominic LeBlanc withdrew themselves from consideration. At the 2009 convention, Ignatieff was confirmed as leader since no other candidates decided to seek the leadership.

The procedure used to choose Dion at the 2006 convention will likely not be repeated. At their 2009 convention, the Liberal party voted to adopt a direct membership vote for future leadership selection. Nevertheless, the events of December 2008 indicate that it is important for a party leader to maintain the support of the party caucus even if the caucus is not responsible for choosing the leader.

Canadian party financing law now limits the amount an individual can contribute to leadership candidates and bans contributions from businesses and unions. Even so, each of the leading candidates for the Liberal leadership in 2006 spent about $2 million, particularly by borrowing substantial sums from family, friends, and supporters. Repayable loans are not covered by the limits on donations. Interestingly, during the Liberal leadership race, reporters discovered that eleven-year-old twins had each donated $5400,[5] the maximum individual contribution then allowed under Canadian party financing law, to Joe Volpe's campaign. The children presumably did not open their piggy banks in a demonstration of youthful political interest! Rather, to

---

[5] Changes to the law concerning party financing that came into effect in 2007 limit contributions to leadership campaigns to about $1100 per person, although the provision allowing loans to candidates is unchanged.

▶ Not wanting to appear ageist, Joe Volpe gladly accepts donations from children too.

circumvent the ban on corporate contributions, the top executives of Apotex (a leading Canadian pharmaceutical company) along with their spouses and children donated a total of $108 000 to Volpe's campaign. The embarrassed candidate returned the money to his underage donors even though the donations were legal.

Candidate Selection

Political parties are very important in the selection of candidates for election. Very few candidates are successful in being elected unless they represent a political party. A variety of methods is used by parties in different countries to choose candidates. Some countries conduct a vote among party members. This is generally the case in Canada, although the Liberal party gives its leader the power to appoint a number of candidates without a vote of the party members in the district. Canadian parties also sometimes automatically renominate their sitting members of Parliament. In some other countries, party members select delegates to make the selection. Still others rely on local or regional party officials or a candidate selection committee. Generally, most of the advanced democracies involve the local or regional party organization in the selection process, with the party leader or party executive having the ability to veto the

BOX 7-4
Primary Elections

In the United States, **primary elections** are held to choose each party's candidates for election to almost all public offices at national, state, and local levels. Primary elections are conducted by state governments rather than by the political parties. When American citizens register to vote they can declare themselves to be supporters of a particular party. In some states only registered supporters of a party may vote in their party's primary; other states allow voters to participate in whichever party's primary they want.

The selection of each party's candidate for president is made by a majority vote of delegates at a party's national convention. Primary elections are used in the majority of states to choose delegates, most of whom are committed to supporting a particular candidate at the convention. Some states use a "caucus" system in which registered party supporters meet in each community, discuss the candidates, and select delegates to county and/ or state conventions that then choose delegates to the national party convention. In addition, various party officials also have a vote at the national convention. The dates of the primaries and caucus vary from state to state, with Iowa caucuses and New Hampshire primary held in early January followed by other states or groups of states holding their votes over the following several months. This results in a dwindling number of candidates as time goes on while candidates who do well in the early primaries can gain publicity, financial contributions, and momentum to enhance their campaigns. This system allows some small states to have considerable influence over the choice of presidential candidates. Almost always, in modern times, the winning candidate is known before the party convention that is usually held in late August or early September such that the vote at the convention is a formality.

The primary election system is less party oriented than the process used in most other countries, as most citizens (rather than just party members) can vote to determine who the candidates for election will be. The adoption of this system in the United States in the early twentieth century reflected a distrust of parties and concern about the corrupt practices often associated with party "bosses" and party "machines." However, the primary system weakens political parties since they do not have much control over the selection of party candidates, and it reinforces the tendency in American politics for legislators of each party to act independently rather than as members of a group. The primary election system provides an opportunity for those without a connection to a party to win a party's nomination if they can mount a strong public campaign. The system typically results in potential candidates having to raise very large sums of money to win a nomination, thus making successful candidates dependent on the support of wealthy backers.

---

choice of candidates (Scarrow, Webb, & Farrell, 2000). The procedures for choosing candidates in the United States are somewhat different, as discussed in Box 7-4, Primary Elections.

GENDER QUOTAS The constitutions or laws of fifty-seven countries (for example, France, Argentina, and Mexico) require that parties nominate a certain proportion of women as candidates. Parties failing to nominate the required proportion of female candidates may have the public subsidy for their operations reduced or even have their slate of candidates rejected by election officials.

PRIMARY ELECTION A state-run election in which citizens select the candidates for the party they support prior to the general election.

International Institute for Democracy and Electoral Assistance, Quota Project
www.quotaproject.org/aboutQuotas.cfm

In addition, several countries (including Rwanda and Jordan) reserve a certain proportion of seats in their legislative body for women. Voluntary gender quotas have been adopted by 168 political parties in 69 countries (International Institute for Democracy and Electoral Assistance, 2007a). The use of quotas, while increasing female representation, tends to reduce the ability of local party members to choose their preferred candidate.

In Canada, there are no legally established quotas for female candidates and the proportion of female candidates is rather low (see Table 7-2). Some political parties, however, have undertaken to try to ensure that more female candidates are nominated. The NDP has set an objective of having 60 percent female candidates in "winnable" constituencies (excluding those where the incumbent is seeking re-election) and requires that constituencies prove that they have searched for one or more potential candidates who are female or from other under-represented groups before selecting a candidate. Former Liberal leader Stéphane Dion set an objective of having at least one-third female candidates and succeeded in having substantially more female candidates than the party had had in previous elections.

Party Policy

As we have seen, parties with mass origins generally give formal authority to a party convention to approve the policy positions that the party is supposed to pursue, while parties with cadre origins typically view policies adopted at party conventions as only one source of advice for the leader and the party's

TABLE 7-2

PERCENTAGE OF FEMALE CANDIDATES AND ELECTED MEMBERS OF PARLIAMENT BY PARTY, 2008 CANADIAN ELECTION

PARTY	% OF PARTY'S CANDIDATES	% OF PARTY'S ELECTED MEMBERS
Bloc Québécois	26.7%	40.8%
Conservative party	20.5%	16.1%
Green party	29.7%	—
Liberal party	36.8%	24.6%
New Democratic Party	33.8%	32.4%
Other parties/Independents	18.2%	0.0%
Total	27.8%	22.4%

SOURCE: *Calculated and adapted from* History of Federal Ridings since 1867, Women Candidates in General Elections - 1921 to Date, *Library of Parliament, data retrieved from http://www2.parl.gc.ca/Sites/LOP/HFER/ hfer.asp?Language=E&Search=WomenElection September 14, 2010. Reproduced with the permission of the Library of Parliament, 2010.*

parliamentary members. Indeed, until the 1960s, the Liberal and PC parties of Canada did not hold regular party conventions to discuss policy. Policy resolutions proposed at leadership conventions were not always thoroughly discussed, formally voted upon, carefully recorded, or made accessible.

In some parties there is vigorous debate over policy resolutions at party conventions, providing an opportunity for those active party members to be involved in the discussion of party policy positions. However, the party leader and key party officials often exercise a considerable degree of control over the process of discussing and adopting resolutions at a party convention. Efforts may be made to modify or avoid a vote on resolutions that could harm a party in its attempts to gain public support. Furthermore, the election platforms of parties are typically developed by the party leader, the leader's advisers, and campaign experts concerned with successfully marketing the party to the electorate. In the legislature, the party leader and parliamentary party members often feel free to interpret party resolutions as they see fit. After their party is elected, the prime minister and Cabinet typically argue that they have to make decisions that are for the good of the political community as a whole, rather than acting in accordance with their party's policy resolutions.

Overall, then, party members may be more likely to have an effective voice in candidate and leadership selection than in determining the policies that their party will pursue. Nevertheless, modern political parties do, to varying extents, involve their ordinary members in policy discussion even if control of party policy decisions rests largely in the hands of the party leadership (Scarrow, Webb, & Farrell, 2000).

Party Caucus and Party Government

Parliamentary parties are generally tightly organized. In parliamentary systems, as discussed in Chapter 14, there is a strong expectation that each party's members of Parliament will support the positions that the **party caucus** (a closed-door meeting of the party's parliamentary members) has decided to take. In particular, the party leader typically exercises considerable influence and control over the parliamentary party.

PARTY CAUCUS A closed-door meeting of the party's parliamentary members.

Political parties in modern parliamentary systems play a crucial role in governing. The prime minister and Cabinet are almost always members of a particular parliamentary party (or, in the case of coalition governments, members of the parties forming the coalition) and rely on the support of their parliamentary party to maintain their positions and to approve their legislative and budgetary proposals. However, this does not necessarily mean that the governing party as a whole has a high level of influence on the decisions of the government, as the prime minister and Cabinet (along with various advisers) are crucial in making policy decisions.

PARTY FINANCE

Parties need considerable amounts of money to finance their operations and conduct expensive election campaigns. The financing of political parties and candidates has often been considered a major political problem (see Box 7-5, "Granny D"). There are risks that donors will be able to buy influence through their financial support. In particular, donations may be made to a party or a candidate in the hope of, or as a reward for, a government contract or other benefit. Even when such patronage is not involved, politicians may be more concerned about maintaining the support of their financial backers—often large corporations and wealthy individuals—than about acting for the common good.

Many countries have established limits on election expenses, put restrictions on campaign advertising, provided public subsidies to parties and campaigns, and required public disclosure of significant donations. Generally, this allows for fairer competition among political parties, reduces the likelihood that undue influence will be placed on politicians, and reduces the taint of scandal and corruption that has often been associated with money in politics. Public financing systems, however, can be used to discriminate against smaller or new political parties and thus maintain the dominance of the larger, established parties. As well, the dependence of parties on public funds may reduce their incentive to maintain strong ties with their supporters (Katz & Mair, 1995).

In the United States, there are no limits on campaign spending for Congressional elections and no public subsidies for these campaigns. However, candidates in presidential primaries and presidential elections can receive public money to match individual donations (if they raise money in at least twenty states) provided they are willing to limit their total campaign expenses. In the 2008 election, John McCain accepted the matching public funds while Barack Obama, who had a strong fundraising ability, turned down the public funds and thus was unlimited in his campaign's spending.

Until 2004, there were no limits on contributions to political parties and candidates at the national level in Canada. The Liberal and PC parties relied heavily on contributions from business corporations to fund their parties and their election campaigns. The NDP derived a significant proportion of its funding from unions. Contributions by businesses and trade unions have been banned and individuals are now limited to contributing a maximum of $1100 (indexed to inflation) per year to each of the following: political parties, other party entities (district associations, nomination contestants, and candidates), leadership contestants, and independent candidates. There are also spending limits on election-oriented advertising by groups or individuals that are not parties or candidates.

The restrictions on contributions are offset, to a considerable extent, by payments to parties from public funds. Each year, registered political parties that received 2 percent of the national vote or 5 percent in those districts

BOX 7-5

"Granny D": Raise a Little Hell

"Granny D" fought tirelessly against the corruption of American politics caused by large corporate campaign contributions.

On January 1, 1999, 89-year-old Doris "Granny D" Haddock began a walk across the United States to publicize the need for campaign finance reform. For 14 months, the great-grandmother slogged through deserts, climbed mountain ranges, braved blizzards, and even skied 62 kilometres when the roads were impassable before reaching Washington, DC.

Haddock argued that the American political system had been corrupted by the huge amounts of money corporations give to candidates in return for grants and legislation that make these corporations highly profitable at the expense of ordinary citizens. After her trek, she continued to actively participate in rallies and demonstrations despite being jailed twice. Finally, in 2002, Congress passed a campaign reform bill banning corporations and labour unions from broadcast advertising that explicitly promoted the election or defeat of specific candidates sixty days before an election. Relying on small donations, Haddock ran for the U.S. Senate in 2004, saying, "You're never too old to raise a little hell." She received about one-third of the votes cast.

In January 2010, the U.S. Supreme Court ruled in a five-to-four vote that the protection of free speech in the Constitution meant that political advertising by corporations could not be banned. President Barack Obama called the decision "a major victory for big oil, Wall Street banks, health insurance companies and other powerful interests that marshal their power every day in Washington to drown out the voices of everyday Americans" (quoted by Liptak, 2010). Haddock took the ruling in stride, saying that it provided an opportunity to create a better law than the 2002 law that had not succeeded in cleaning up the problems with campaign finance. Unfortunately, Haddock's voice was silenced on March 12, 2010, when she died at age 100.

in which they ran candidates receive $1.75 (indexed to inflation) from the Canadian government for each vote they obtained in the previous election.[6] As well, these parties are reimbursed for 50 percent of their eligible campaign expenses. Candidates are reimbursed for 60 percent of their expenses if they obtain 10 percent of the vote in their electoral district. There are also limits on the spending of candidates and parties in elections and nomination contests, public disclosure of contributors and expenditures, and generous tax credits for individuals who contribute to parties and candidates.

---

[6] A proposal by the Conservative party to eliminate the party subsidy was dropped after the opposition parties threatened to defeat the minority Conservative government in 2008.

Summary and Conclusion

Political parties play a central role in the competition for political power and in the governing of modern democratic states. Some parties developed out of factions within legislative bodies. Other parties were created by groups outside the legislature to promote a particular ideological perspective or the interests of major sections of the population that were not adequately represented in the legislature. In pursuit of political power, parties have often moved away from representing particular perspectives or interests. Nevertheless, parties often reflect, sometimes in subtle ways, differing perspectives and interests.

Political parties have often been thought of as a crucial link between citizens and government. A competitive party system allows voters to choose which set of politicians should be responsible for governing and which party's platform they prefer. However, parties have often been criticized for being elitist organizations. The involvement of people who join political parties has often been limited to canvassing on behalf of the party's candidates during an election campaign. In recent decades, political parties generally have become more democratic in the processes they use to select their leaders and candidates and in the holding of regular party policy conventions. Changes in the regulation of party finance in Canada and a number of other countries have helped to reduce the influence on political parties of big business and wealthy donors. Nevertheless, parties still tend to be dominated by the leader and a small number of insiders.

Even though many citizens have negative views of political parties and other means of political involvement have become more common, parties are still crucial elements of modern democracies. By choosing among competing parties, voters may be able to hold the government accountable for its actions or inactions and select which general program, direction, and vision for the political community they prefer. Competition among parties can help to prevent the abuse of power and allow ordinary citizens some ability to influence the direction of the political community.

By raising the concerns of those who might not otherwise be heard and developing policies to gain their support, political parties may also facilitate the development of a more inclusive and egalitarian political community. Where parties are strong and well organized, the poor, less educated, and disadvantaged elements of society are more likely to vote and thus, potentially, to be treated as a significant political force. Parties are also important in aggregating (putting together) the interests and perspectives of different sectors of society and trying to develop a coherent program for governing that will have wide support. Other organizations, such as interest groups, can be effective in *articulating* particular interests, but are less concerned about *aggregating* different interests. Thus, it has been argued that parties are essential "to bring interests together for the common good" (Dalton & Wattenburg, 2000, pp. 283–284). Nevertheless, the focus on broad, general appeals to the public often based on the qualities of the party's leader (aided and abetted by the treatment of politics by the mass media) can reduce the significance of parties in putting together a program that aggregates a variety of different interests or provides a vision of the common good.

The conflicts generated by parties in their competitive pursuit for power can divert attention from the real problems that a political community faces. Instead of debating possible solutions to problems, political parties may focus on trivial issues, mislead the public about the positions taken by the contending parties, and turn rational discussion into emotional arguments. On the other hand, by seeking the support of those whose problems would otherwise be ignored in political life and by creating platforms that appeal widely, parties may bridge societal divisions and mobilize those with little political power. Thus, in the pursuit of power, political parties can potentially serve the common good.

Key Terms

Discussion Questions

1. Is there a particular party (or more than one party) that seems to reflect your viewpoints, interests, or identity, or do you feel that none of the major parties really represents you?

2. Are all of the major interests and viewpoints in Canada adequately represented by the major Canadian parties?

3. Is it important for political parties to be democratic in their organization?

4. How should parties choose their leaders?

5. Is the common good better served by two parties with a broad appeal, or by a multiparty system in which a variety of different societal interests and ideological perspectives are represented?

6. Are political parties a necessary and desirable feature of democratic politics?

Further Reading

Bickerton, J., Gagnon, A.-G., & Smith, P.J. (1999). *Ties that bind: Parties and voters in Canada*. Don Mills, ON: Oxford University Press.

Carty, R.K., Cross, W., & Young, J. (2000). *Rebuilding Canadian party politics*. Vancouver: UBC Press.

Cross, W. (2004). *Political parties*. Vancouver: UBC Press.

Gagnon, A.-G., & Tanguay, A.B. (Eds.). (2007). *Canadian parties in transition* (3rd ed.). Peterborough, ON: Broadview Press.

Gunther, R., Montero, J.R., & Linz, J.J. (Eds.). (2002). *Political parties: Old concepts and new challenges*. Oxford: Oxford University Press.

Katz, R.S., & Crotty, W. (Eds.). (2006). *Handbook of party politics*. London, UK: Sage.

Thorburn, H.G., & Whitehorn, A. (Eds.). (2001). *Party politics in Canada* (8th ed.). Toronto: Pearson Education Canada.

Webb, P., Farrell, D., & Holliday, I. (Eds.). (2002). *Political parties in advanced industrial democracies*. Oxford: Oxford University Press.

Webb, P., & White, S. (Eds.). (2007). *Party politics in new democracies*. Oxford: Oxford University Press.

Wolinetz, S.B. (Ed.). (1997). *Political parties*. Aldershot, UK: Ashgate.

Chapter 8

Elections, Electoral Systems, and Voting Behaviour

PHOTO ABOVE: During the 2000 U.S. election, Republican George W. Bush beat the Democratic party candidate, Vice-President Al Gore, even though Bush received fewer votes than Gore, and despite irregularities in the Florida ballots and voting procedures. The U.S. Supreme Court rejected Gore's appeal for a recount—thus awarding the presidency to Bush.

CHAPTER OBJECTIVES

After reading this chapter you should be able to:

1. discuss what is needed for elections to be considered free and fair
2. explain and evaluate the different types of electoral systems
3. evaluate the usefulness of election campaigns in helping people decide how to vote
4. outline the different factors that explain voting behaviour

The 2000 U.S. presidential contest was so close that the outcome was in dispute for many weeks. In the end, Republican party candidate George W. Bush beat the Democratic party candidate, Vice-President Al Gore—despite receiving about 500 000 fewer votes.

When Americans cast their votes for their presidential choice, their votes do not directly result in the election of the president. Instead, the president is selected by members of the Electoral College, who are committed to voting for the presidential candidate who has won the most votes in a particular state.* Even if one candidate wins a state by only a tiny margin, that candidate (in almost all states) will receive all of the Electoral College votes for that state. The votes of the Electoral College are, therefore, a distorted reflection of the votes cast by American voters. As a result of the 2000 election, Bush received 271 Electoral College votes while Gore received 267. A few hundred votes in the state of Florida made the difference in the choice of Bush as president.

Afterwards, arguments raged concerning irregularities in the Florida vote, where the ballots were not properly designed and inconsistent procedures were used for counting ballots. State Republican politicians, led by Florida Governor Jeb Bush, George W. Bush's brother, controlled the election procedures, but were unwilling to allow a full recount of votes.

In the end, the U.S. Supreme Court, in a five-to-four decision, rejected Gore's appeal for a recount, thus in effect awarding the presidency to George Bush. Gore accepted the Supreme Court decision and encouraged Americans to support the president. An analysis of the Florida vote commissioned by some of the major media (although having no legal significance) later concluded that Gore should have received Florida's Electoral College votes and therefore become president.

Elections are a central feature of democracies, providing citizens with the opportunity to choose their representatives and their government. However as the Bush–Gore case illustrates, questions about the fairness of election procedures may arise. Similar concerns have been raised in many countries, including Canada where the representation of parties often does not accurately reflect the choices of voters and where the second-place party occasionally wins the election.

This chapter also discusses whether election campaigns help voters to make informed choices and looks at research concerning the behaviour of voters.

---

* The Electoral College does not actually meet and has no function other than selecting the president and vice-president. Members of the Electoral College send in their vote. Electoral College members, who are selected by each political party, almost always vote for the candidate who won the most votes in their state.

DEMOCRATIC ELECTIONS

Nearly all countries now hold elections. However, elections vary greatly, from those that can be considered democratic in terms of ensuring that voters have a free and fair choice to those that coerce or manipulate voters into endorsing a dictatorial ruler. The practice of elections in many countries, particularly newer democracies, falls between these two extremes. Even long-established democracies do not necessarily provide a completely fair election process.

Meaningful Elections

Elections are only meaningful if those elected have real power. In some countries, elected legislative bodies simply legitimate the decisions of a monarch or dictator. In some other countries, the military will step in if it disagrees with decisions taken by elected officials. Voters should be able to choose freely among candidates and parties seeking office. To protect voters from intimidation, democratic countries use a secret ballot. To ensure meaningful competition, all citizens should have the right to run in elections, and all political parties should have the right to nominate candidates and campaign on their behalf. In other words, an election is not democratic if only those candidates authorized by the state or other institutions are allowed to run, or if some parties are prevented from participating in an election campaign. Sometimes, however, even liberal democracies have banned extremist political parties that are viewed as a threat to the democratic system. For example, in the past Canada banned the Communist party and Germany continues to ban Nazi parties.

UNIVERSAL SUFFRAGE The right of all adult citizens to vote regardless of such characteristics as gender, ethnicity, wealth, or education.

UNIVERSAL SUFFRAGE   Democratic elections are based on the principle of "one person, one vote," with each vote having the same value. Thus, we usually only consider a system of elections fully democratic if there is **universal suffrage**—that is, all adult citizens have the right to vote regardless of such characteristics as gender, ethnicity, wealth, or education. Further, it should be easy for citizens to exercise their right to vote. For example, provisions should be made for students and others who are away from home on election day to vote, and the use of difficult voter registration requirements should be avoided. Ensuring that each vote has the same value can be controversial, as persons in rural and remote areas worry that their interests will not be given due attention because of the large numbers of voters in the major cities. As well, elected representatives will have a more difficult task in meeting their constituents in a large, sparsely populated region.

INFORMATION   Voters need to be provided with useful information if their vote is to be meaningful. Parties and candidates must have the opportunity to get their message to voters. This may involve putting some limits on spending to ensure that one party or candidate does not dominate the campaign, and providing some subsidies to help parties and candidates that do not have the support of wealthy contributors (see Chapter 7). Extensive government advertising during an election campaign should be avoided, as it could give the governing party an unfair advantage. The media should provide fair and extensive coverage of the contending parties and candidates.

INDEPENDENT COMMISSIONS   To ensure that elections are conducted fairly, it is important that the process be overseen by an independent commission. The contending parties and candidates should be able to observe the casting and counting of votes. Foreign observers have played a role in ascertaining whether elections have been properly conducted in many countries that have recently become democratic. If there is evidence that the election rules have not been properly followed, losing candidates should have the right to request a recount and to appeal to the courts or an independent body. The adoption of electronic voting systems in some parts of the United States and elsewhere is raising concerns about the possibility of electoral fraud by tampering with ballot software. Without physical ballots, recounts may be impossible and the accuracy of vote tabulations has been questioned.

Similarly, the drawing of electoral district boundaries should be done by an independent body. In 1812, the term **gerrymander** was coined to describe a sprawling electoral district that looked like a salamander established by Governor Gerry of Massachusetts for partisan advantage. Gerrymandering continues to be practised in many countries including the United States, where electoral districts for the U.S. House of Representatives are drawn by the majority party in most state legislatures. In Canada, independent boundary readjustment commissions, usually headed by a judge, have since 1964 been used to readjust electoral district boundaries after the decennial census.

A REGULAR VOTE   To ensure that those elected to office are held accountable to the people, it is important that elections be held on a fairly regular basis. In most democratic countries, the election of representatives occurs at least once every four or five years. A small number of countries, including Australia and New Zealand, require that elections be held within a three-year period. In some countries, the dates for elections are fixed by law. For example, the election of the president of the United States is always held on the Tuesday following the first Monday of November every fourth year.

In parliamentary systems, the prime minister and Cabinet have to retain the support of the majority of members of the elected legislature. Failure to maintain that support (as exhibited in a vote of non-confidence in the government or the defeat of a crucial aspect of the government's agenda such as the budget) usually results in an election. In the past, Canadian elections were also held when requested by the prime minister, within a five-year period. The Canada Elections Act was amended in 2007 to require that national elections be held on the third Monday in October every four years starting in 2009,

Elections Canada
www.elections.ca

ACE Electoral Knowledge Network
www.aceproject.org

International Institute for Democracy and Electoral Assistance
www.idea.int

GERRYMANDER The manipulation of the division of the country into electoral districts so as to benefit a particular party.

although the governor general retains the discretionary power to dissolve Parliament and call an election. Amid considerable controversy, Prime Minister Stephen Harper (who had promoted the adoption of fixed election dates) requested permission for an election to be held on October 14, 2008, even though his government (elected in 2006) had not been defeated in the House of Commons. British Columbia, Ontario, Newfoundland and Labrador, Prince Edward Island, New Brunswick, and the Northwest Territories have also adopted legislation establishing that elections normally be held on fixed dates every four years.

ELECTORAL SYSTEMS

ELECTORAL SYSTEM The system used to translate the votes that people cast into the composition of the legislature and the selection of the government.

There are a variety of **electoral systems** that are used to translate the votes that people cast into the composition of the legislature and the selection of the government. Electoral systems differ in the extent to which they accurately represent the votes cast for each party, provide a close link between representatives and voters, facilitate the accountability of government, and enable governments and representatives to claim that they have the support of the majority of voters. Because none of the electoral systems is best on every one of these criteria, there has been considerable discussion about which electoral system is most desirable.

There are three major types of electoral systems used to elect members to legislative bodies:

- plurality/majoritarian (including single member plurality, runoff elections, and preferential voting)
- proportional representation
- mixed member proportional

As Table 8-1 indicates, the single member plurality (SMP) and the proportional representation (PR) systems are most common, although the mixed member proportional system has also become quite common.

Plurality/Majoritarian Electoral Systems

Plurality and majoritarian systems typically involve electing a single representative based on which candidate has more votes than any other candidate. In the majoritarian version, the electoral system is designed to try to ensure that the winning candidate has the support of a majority of those voting. Plurality and majoritarian systems often result in a party gaining a majority of legislative seats even if that party did not win a majority of votes.

SINGLE MEMBER PLURALITY (SMP) SYSTEM An electoral system in which voters in each electoral district elect a single representative to the legislature. The candidate with the most votes is elected, even if that candidate did not receive the majority of votes.

SINGLE MEMBER PLURALITY   In a **single member plurality (SMP) system** (also known as "first past the post"), voters in each electoral district elect a

SINGLE MEMBER PLURALITY	RUNOFF	PREFERENTIAL BALLOT	PROPORTIONAL REPRESENTATION	MIXED MEMBER PROPORTIONAL	SINGLE TRANSFERABLE VOTE
Bahamas	Egypt	Australia	Argentina	Bolivia	Ireland
Bangladesh	France	Fiji	Austria	Germany	Malta
Bermuda	Haiti	Papua New Guinea	Belgium	Hungary	
Botswana	Iran		Brazil	Japan	
Canada	Mali		Chile	Mexico	
Ethiopia	Vietnam		Czech Republic	New Zealand	
Ghana			Denmark	Pakistan	
India			Greece	Philippines	
Jamaica			Indonesia	South Korea	
Kenya			Israel	Taiwan	
Malaysia			Netherlands	Thailand	
Nigeria			Poland	Tunisia	
Tanzania			Russia		
UK			South Africa		
USA			Spain		
			Sweden		
			Switzerland		
			Turkey		
			Ukraine		

TABLE 8-1

ELECTORAL SYSTEMS USED TO ELECT MEMBERS OF THE NATIONAL LEGISLATURE, SELECTED COUNTRIES

Note: Elections to a lower or single legislative chamber.

SOURCE: *Compiled from International Institute for Democracy and Electoral Assistance, retrieved from www.idea.int/esd/world.cfm; ACE: The Electoral Knowledge Network, retrieved from www.aceproject.org/ace-en/comparative-data; International Foundation for Electoral Systems Election Guide, retrieved from www.electionguide.org*

single representative to the legislature. The candidate with the most votes is elected, even if that candidate did not receive the majority of votes.

Canada, like the United Kingdom and many of the former British colonies, uses the SMP system. The SMP system provides a simple method for a representative to be chosen from a particular area. However, elections involve more than choosing a representative for a legislative body. They are also very important for choosing a party to form a government for the country, and thus involve choices among competing parties. The SMP system tends to inaccurately translate the votes that a party receives across the country into the seats that it receives in the legislature (see Box 8-1, Distortion in the Single Member Plurality System). In particular, the SMP system usually gives an added boost in representation to the leading party. For example, in the 2005 election in the United Kingdom, the Labour party received 55 percent of the seats in Parliament with only 35 percent of the vote. In the 1993, 1997, and 2000 Canadian elections, the Liberal party received a majority of seats in the House of Commons based on about two-fifths of the votes cast. Table 8-2 indicates that the

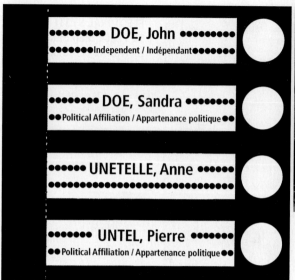

◀ Canadian voters cast a ballot that contains the names and party affiliations of the candidates in their electoral district.

distorting effects of the SMP system are stronger in some elections than others and affect the representation of some parties more than others.

In some cases, the SMP system allows the governing party to completely dominate the legislature, thus hindering the provision of effective opposition to the governing party. For example, the 1987 New Brunswick provincial election resulted in the Liberal party winning all of the seats based on its 60 percent share of the vote. Similarly, in the 2001 British Columbia provincial election, the Liberals won seventy-seven of the seventy-nine seats based on 57.6 percent of the vote.

The SMP system generally favours the most popular party at the expense of smaller parties. However, parties that have their support concentrated in particular geographical areas tend to do much better than parties with modest support spread across the country. For example, the Bloc Québécois has benefited from the workings of the SMP system, while the NDP has received a substantially smaller proportion of seats than votes in every national election. Parties with relatively low levels of support are generally unable to gain representation in the legislature. The Green party did not elect any members to the Canadian House of Commons despite obtaining 940 747 votes in the 2008 election.

The SMP system also tends to exaggerate the regional character of the parties in Parliament. For example, in recent elections the Liberal party has appeared to be more Ontario based and the Conservative party more Western Canada based in terms of their representation in the House of Commons than in terms of the votes they received.

Imagine a very small legislature consisting of five seats. The hypothetical results of voting in each of the five electoral districts are as follows:

Party A would win all of the seats despite having the support of only 40 percent of the voters, while the substantial proportion of the population who voted for parties B or C would be unrepresented.

	District #1	District #2	District #3	District #4	District #5
Party A	40%	40%	40%	40%	40%
Party B	39%	39%	39%	39%	39%
Party C	21%	21%	21%	21%	21%

Occasionally, the distorting effects of the electoral system can result in the most popular party losing the election. The PC party won the 1979 Canadian election with close to a majority of seats based on 36 percent of the vote, even though the Liberal party obtained 40 percent of the vote. Similarly, in several provincial elections, including British Columbia (1996), Quebec (1966 and 1998), Newfoundland (1989), Saskatchewan (1999), and New Brunswick (2006), the party that received the second-highest number of votes won the election and formed the government. The 2000 American presidential election, discussed at the start of this chapter, illustrates the same basic principle: George W. Bush barely won the presidency, even though Al Gore gained

TABLE 8-2

THE IMPACT OF THE SMP ELECTORAL SYSTEM: CANADA, 2004, 2006, AND 2008

Note: "Others" includes independents.

PARTY	2004 ELECTION			2006 ELECTION			2008 ELECTION		
	VOTES	SEATS	DIFFERENCE	VOTES	SEATS	DIFFERENCE	VOTES	SEATS	DIFFERENCE
Liberal	36.7%	43.8%	+7.1	30.2%	33.4%	+3.2	26.3%	25.0%	−1.3
Conservative	29.6%	32.1%	+2.5	36.3%	40.3%	+4.0	37.7%	46.4%	+8.7
NDP	15.7%	6.2%	−9.5	17.5%	9.4%	−8.1	18.2%	12.0%	−6.2
Bloc	12.4%	17.5%	+5.1	10.5%	16.6%	+6.1	10.0%	15.9%	+5.9
Green	4.3%	0.0%	−4.3	4.5%	0.0%	−4.5	6.8%	0.0%	−6.8
Others	1.3%	0.3%	−1.0	1.0%	0.3%	−0.7	1.0%	0.6%	−0.4

SOURCE: *Elections Canada. Calculations and adaptation rest with the authors. Data retrieved from www.elections.ca*

ELECTORAL COLLEGE A body that elects the president of the United States. Members of the Electoral College from each state are expected to vote for the presidential candidate who has won the most votes in their state.

RUNOFF ELECTION An election held if no candidate receives a majority of votes; generally, only the top two candidates appear on the ballot to ensure that the winning candidate has a majority of the votes cast.

PREFERENTIAL VOTING An electoral system in which voters rank candidates in order of preference. If no candidate has a majority of first preferences, the candidate with the least votes is dropped and the second preferences of those who voted for that candidate are added to the votes of other candidates. This process continues until one candidate has a majority.

PROPORTIONAL REPRESENTATION (PR) SYSTEM An electoral system in which the proportion of seats a party receives in the legislature reflects the proportion of votes it has obtained.

slightly more of the popular vote, because the candidate winning the most votes in a state receives all of the **Electoral College** votes for that state regardless of the margin of victory.[1]

RUNOFF ELECTIONS   Many countries, including France, Russia, Brazil, Argentina, Indonesia, and Chile, use a system of **runoff elections** (also known as two-round elections) for the election of a president. If no candidate receives a majority of votes, another election is held in which only the top two candidates appear on the ballot.[2] A few countries use runoff elections to elect representatives to a legislative body. For example, if no candidate to represent a district in the French Assembly obtains a majority of votes, a second election is held. Only the candidates who received at least one-eighth of the votes of the total electorate on the first ballot can remain on the second ballot. The candidate with the most votes on the second ballot wins. The winning candidate often obtains a majority as a result of deals made among parties of the left and among parties of the right so that only the top two candidates appear on the second ballot. The two-round system was designed to reduce the fragmentation of the French party system by leaving smaller parties without legislative representation (Baldini & Pappalardo, 2009).

PREFERENTIAL VOTING   Another type of majoritarian electoral system is **preferential voting** (also known as the alternative vote and instant runoff voting). Instead of marking X beside the name of the candidate one prefers, voters can rank candidates in order of preference. If no candidate has a majority of first preferences, the candidate with the least votes is dropped and the second preferences of those who voted for that candidate are added to the votes of other candidates. This process continues until one candidate has a majority. The effect of preferential voting is generally to make it difficult for parties viewed as extremist to gain representation. As well, it may encourage voters to learn more about different candidates and parties so as to decide on their second and third preferences (Gardner, 2009).

Proportional Representation

The single member plurality, runoff election, and preferential voting electoral systems result in legislatures that do not reflect the overall distribution of support for political parties. To deal with this issue, many countries have adopted some form of **proportional representation (PR) system,** in which the proportion of seats a party receives in the legislature reflects the proportion of votes it

---

[1] In Maine and Nebraska, two electors are selected on a state-wide basis and the remainder are based on the vote in each Congressional district.

[2] In some countries, including Mexico, South Korea, the Philippines, and Taiwan, the candidate with the most votes in a single election is elected as president regardless of whether that candidate received a majority of votes.

has obtained.[3] If, for example, 40 percent of voters supported party A, 39 percent supported party B, and 21 percent supported party C, this would result (in a pure PR system) in 40 percent of the seats going to party A, 39 percent to party B, and 21 percent to party C.

A PR system requires that several representatives be elected from each electoral district. The larger the number of representatives for each district, the more closely the representation of the parties in the legislature will reflect the support each party has in the electorate. In a few cases—the Netherlands, Israel, and Slovakia—the country as a whole is treated as a single district, such that representatives do not represent a particular geographical area.

In some countries (for example, Spain and Norway), a closed-list PR system is used in which individual legislators are selected based on the order of their placement on a list of candidates drawn up by each party. In our hypothetical five-member legislature, the top two names on party A's list of five candidates would become legislators. Other countries with PR systems (for example, Sweden, Poland, and Brazil) use some form of an open-list system that allows voters to indicate which candidate they prefer from the party they have chosen to vote for. Popular candidates who receive a sufficient proportion of votes can be elected even if low on their party's list.

By quite accurately reflecting the support for parties by voters, a PR system almost always results in a situation where no single party has a majority of seats in the legislature.[4] Thus, PR systems typically involve **coalition government**, where two or more parties share in governing. PR systems also often result in a substantial number of parties being represented in the legislature. To try to prevent an overly complex party system in the legislature and keep small extremist parties or parties representing very narrow interests from gaining a voice in legislature, many countries with a PR system require that parties obtain a certain percentage of the popular vote as a prerequisite for gaining legislative seats. For example, the minimum threshold to gain representation is 4 percent in Norway, 3 percent in Greece, and 5 percent in Poland.

Although a PR system provides for more accurate representation of voter support for political parties than other electoral systems, it may reduce the strength of the link between a legislator and his or her district. Multimember districts tend to be much larger than single-member districts, and PR systems tend to focus on representation by party rather than by individual legislators.

COALITION GOVERNMENT A form of government in which two or more parties jointly govern, sharing the Cabinet positions.

Fair Vote Canada
www.fairvotecanada.org

---

[3] For a description of the different formulas that are used to calculate how seats are distributed among parties, see Blais and Massicote (2002).

[4] In 2005, Italy adopted a PR system in which the coalition of parties that wins the most votes is guaranteed to receive at least 54 percent of the seats while the other coalitions and individual parties obtain the remaining seats in proportion to the votes they received provided they have received a certain minimum proportion of votes.

BOX 8-2

Changing Canada's Electoral System

A number of Canadian political scientists and other observers of Canadian politics have advocated modifying or changing Canada's single member plurality (SMP) electoral system. Concerns have often focused on the effects of SMP in heightening regional divisions (Cairns, 1968) as well as distorting the wishes of the electorate.

Adopting a proportional representation (PR) or a mixed member proportional (MMP) system has also been seen as a way of encouraging parties to provide for greater representation for women and minority groups. In countries with such systems, parties are often more likely to make their candidate lists more representative of different social groups than in countries with SMP systems, where district party associations usually have the primary responsibility for choosing candidates.

The leading political parties have had limited interest in electoral system change because the SMP system works to their political advantage. As well, although the Citizens' Assembly in British Columbia proposed the adoption of a single transferable vote system for that province, while the Ontario Citizens' Assembly recommended an MMP system, these proposals were not approved by voters in referendums.

Another Commonwealth country, New Zealand, switched from an SMP system to an MMP system in 1993 after two consecutive elections in which the party with the most votes did not win the election. Changing the electoral system had major effects on politics and government. Since adopting an MMP system, New Zealand has had coalition governments and there has been greater diversity in the legislature since more parties have been able to gain representation (seven parties in the 2008 election). In 2011, New Zealand will hold a referendum to decide whether to retain the MMP system or choose an alternative.

In the United Kingdom, a PR system was adopted in 1999 to elect the country's representatives to the European Parliament. As well, MMP systems are used to elect members to the Scottish Parliament and the Welsh Assembly. As a result of the negotiations that led to a Conservative–Liberal Democratic coalition UK government in 2010, a referendum on whether to replace the national SMP system with an alternative vote (preferential) system will be held on May 11, 2011.

Overall, the choice of electoral system is controversial because it affects the power of different political parties, the basic nature of government (for example, the likelihood of coalition government), and the way the public is represented.

Mixed Member Proportional

To try to combine the benefits of a single member representing a particular electoral district with an accurate translation of votes into seats, some countries have adopted a mixture of SMP and PR systems, termed a **mixed member proportional (MMP) system** (sometimes referred to as an additional member system). Those who advocate changing Canada's SMP system often propose an MMP system (see Box 8-2, Changing Canada's Electoral System).

In the MMP system used, for example, in Germany and New Zealand, voters cast one vote for the party they prefer and one vote for the candidate they prefer. Some legislators are elected to represent particular districts, based on gaining the most votes in that constituency. Others (about one-half of the legislators in the case of Germany) are selected so as to make the overall representation of the parties in the legislature proportional to the votes received by each party in the election. In effect, the selection of representatives by PR in this system is used to compensate parties that were hurt by the workings of SMP (this is termed a *compensatory MMP system*). In another type of MMP system (termed a *parallel MMP system*), part of the legislative body is elected by SMP and the other part by PR without using the PR seats to compensate for the distortions in party representation resulting from the election of representatives for the SMP seats. The parallel system tends to give a boost in representation to the most popular party. For example, in the 2009 Japanese election, the Democratic Party of Japan won 64 percent of the total legislative seats based on only 42 percent of the party vote. Although it won less than one-half of the seats determined by PR, it won almost three-quarters of the SMP seats even though it received only 47 percent of the votes for candidates.

SINGLE TRANSFERABLE VOTE SYSTEM   The **single transferable vote (STV) system** used in Ireland and for Australian Senate elections could be viewed as a variation on the PR system. Voters mark their preferences for candidates in a multimember electoral district. Candidates who receive a certain proportion of the vote are declared elected. The second preferences of voters that are surplus to what the winning candidates need are then transferred to candidates who have not reached the quota. The process is continued until all seats in the district are filled (Blais & Massicotte, 2002). Unlike other PR systems, STV focuses on the choice of candidates rather than parties. Indeed, it encourages competition for votes among the candidates of the same party, thus potentially contributing to tensions within a party. STV does not generally produce as accurate a translation of party votes into party representation as other PR systems, although the distorting effects are usually not large.

SINGLE TRANSFERABLE VOTE (STV) SYSTEM An electoral system in which voters mark their preferences for candidates in a multimember electoral district. Candidates who receive a certain proportion of the vote are declared elected. The second preferences of voters that are surplus to what the winning candidates need are then transferred to candidates who have not reached the quota. The process is continued until all seats in the district are filled.

ELECTION CAMPAIGNS

Parties, leaders, and candidates have many potential ways of appealing to voters for support. Pippa Norris (2002) distinguishes between three basic types of campaigns:

- premodern campaigns
- modern campaigns
- postmodern campaigns

Premodern Campaigns

Premodern campaigns were characteristic of the advanced democratic countries until the 1960s or early 1970s. These campaigns involved considerable personal contact with the voters and campaigning was largely localized. Party volunteers canvassed their neighbourhoods, seeking to determine who supported their candidate so they could ensure that their supporters voted on election day. Leaflets were dropped in mailboxes and supporters were encouraged to put up signs. National leaders traversed the country by train, greeting supporters at the railway stations in small communities and holding rallies in the larger centres. National campaign organizations were small, with the leader and some experienced party advisers establishing the general direction of the campaign.

Despite the localized nature of campaigning, premodern campaigns in the mid twentieth century were oriented, in many countries, to carrying the party's message to voters throughout the country, particularly by appealing to members of groups that supported that party (Plasser & Plasser, 2002).

Modern Election Campaigns

Modern election campaigns are more sophisticated. Public opinion polling is used to provide the basic information needed to develop campaign strategies. Professional consultants, including experts in advertising and marketing, largely determine how the campaign will be conducted and the kinds of appeals that will be made to the voters. Modern campaigns are more centrally coordinated or controlled than premodern campaigns.

The development of television has contributed to the emphasis in modern campaigns on managing the image of the party leader (or, in the United States, candidate). Creating favourable "photo ops" of the leader that will be picked up by the national television news broadcasts is of great importance. As well, short, attention-getting television advertisements are a central feature of modern election campaigns. The typical campaign strategy is to focus on simple, basic themes (Plasser & Plasser, 2002).

Modern campaigns often tend to downplay political party affiliations. Instead of appealing primarily to the party faithful to mobilize them to vote on election day, the goal of the modern campaign is to appeal to a broader, national audience, particularly by focusing on the party leader. The more localized and personalized techniques of the premodern campaign continue to be used, but are not of central importance in the modern campaign (Norris, 2002).

Waging a modern election campaign requires substantial amounts of money and access to professional expertise. Particularly in the United States, an industry of professional campaign consultants has developed. American-based campaign professionals have been hired by parties in many countries to assist in running their campaigns. However, in some countries, legal regulations prevent the full adoption of modern campaign techniques. For example, a number of countries, including the United Kingdom, France, and Belgium, do not allow paid political advertising on television. Instead, many countries provide longer, free-time television broadcasts to the parties (Norris, 2002). In addition, various institutional characteristics (including the nature of the electoral, party, media, and governing systems) and cultural factors affect the ways in which American-developed modern campaign techniques are applied in other countries.

Postmodern Campaigns

Norris suggests that a new postmodern style of campaigning is currently developing. New forms of communication allow a return to more interactive and personalized styles of political communication. Specialized television channels, computerized direct mail and telemarketing techniques, and the use of email allow campaigners to direct specific messages to targeted groups and individuals. In addition to public opinion surveys, postmodern campaigns make extensive use of focus groups to develop their messages to targeted voters and to design effective television commercials. Even more than in the modern campaign, there is a focus on strictly controlling the message and developing the capability to instantly rebut the arguments of opponents (Plasser & Plasser, 2002).

Although televised commercials continue to be the leading means of campaign persuasion, there has been a dramatic increase in the use of the Internet to carry political messages. For example, Barack Obama's campaign (including the nomination campaigns) placed 982 videos online while the McCain campaign posted 376 videos (Owen, 2009). The Obama campaign was particularly successful in using the Internet for fundraising; a substantial proportion of the $656.6 million raised in individual donations was obtained through the use of Internet appeals (Boatright, 2009). However, the ability of campaigns to control the online message is limited: 104 456 videos related to Obama (including the heavily viewed "I've got a crush on Obama" video) and 64 092 related to McCain were placed online during the campaign by individuals and groups not controlled by the candidates' campaigns (Owen, 2009). Canadian parties have also increasingly used the Internet to carry their message through websites, blogs, and social network sites. This allows each party to convey additional material not carried through traditional means (such as specially designed videos). Indeed, in the 2008 Canadian campaign the Conservative party set up the website notaleader.ca to communicate its criticism of Liberal leader Stéphane Dion. However, the use of online media by Canadian political parties has not yet been as extensive and sophisticated as that of campaigners in the United States (Small, 2008).

Norris (2000, p. 147) also argues that we are moving toward "the permanent campaign, in which the techniques of electioneering become intertwined with those of governing." The techniques developed to market the party during an election campaign may also be used by the governing party to try to control the message the government presents to the public. In addition, parties are increasingly using campaign-style advertising, even if an election is not imminent.

▶ Do campaigning politicians tell us what they will really do if elected?

Postmodern campaigning may help the public to become more informed and help parties to be more responsive to specific segments of the public. However, postmodern campaigning that focuses on professional marketing of a political "product" could also be considered manipulative and detrimental to the quality of democratic discussion.

Election Campaigns and Informed Choice

Ideally, elections allow people to choose among parties offering different platforms or directions for the country, and thus affect the way the country is governed. Candidates try to meet as many of their constituents as possible during the election campaign. The mass media provide extensive coverage of election campaigns. Parties carry their basic message to the public through extensive advertising. As well, party platforms, leaders' speeches, and other campaign materials are now accessible online.

◀ Televised leaders' debates provide voters with an opportunity to compare the arguments of different parties and the qualities of the leaders of the major political parties.

However, political parties do not always clearly state their views on major issues during election campaigns. Because parties usually want to appeal to a diverse set of voters, they are often reluctant to take clear positions that might be viewed negatively by a significant group of voters. Instead, vague statements about how they are going to make the political community great are often combined with sharp attacks on their opponents.

PROMISES   Parties usually make a variety of specific promises such as spending money on particular programs and cutting taxes during an election campaign. However, voters cannot be certain that the promises will actually be carried out. For example, during the 2003 Ontario election, Liberal leader Dalton McGuinty signed a written promise not to raise taxes. After the party was elected, the Liberals claimed that the provincial government's finances were much worse than had been portrayed by the defeated PC government. The Ontario government's 2004 budget included an increase in taxes in the form of health care premiums. Legal action against Premier McGuinty was dismissed by Judge Paul Rouleau, who wrote that "anyone who believes a campaign promise is naive about the democratic system" (*Globe and Mail Online*, January 29, 2005).

ADVERTISING   The short (often fifteen- or thirty-second) television advertisements that have become a major feature of modern election campaigns do not provide detailed information. Rather, they often rely on repeating a simple slogan or playing on people's fears (see Box 8-3, Negative Campaign Ads). The emphasis on the party leaders in modern campaigns can mean that consideration of the policy directions proposed by the parties is limited. The televised

BOX 8-3

Negative Campaign Ads

Negative advertising plays on voters' fears—but its success is unclear.

In the 2004 American presidential election campaign, the Swift Boat Veterans for Truth ran a number of strongly worded television ads. They claimed that Democratic candidate John Kerry was unfit to serve as president because he had exaggerated his record as leader of a swift boat unit in the Vietnam War, did not deserve the combat medals he had received, and had betrayed the trust of those in his unit by criticizing the war after his service was completed. However, almost all of the veterans involved in the ad campaign had not served in his unit and most of those who served under him praised his war record. Nevertheless, the smear campaign severely damaged his reputation. In the 2008 American presidential campaign, John McCain's attack ads claimed that Barack Obama would raise taxes on the middle class, even though Obama clearly stated that he would raise taxes only on those earning more than $250 000 a year. An Obama ad claimed that McCain would make an $882 billion cut in seniors' Medicare, even though McCain promised that the level of seniors' benefits would not change (West, 2010).

Negative ads have also been a feature of Canadian campaigns. For example, Liberal ads in 2006 claimed that Harper has a hidden agenda to dismantle the public health care system. The Conservatives did not wait for an official election campaign to begin in running a series of ads in 2007 that stated "Dion is not a leader" and in 2009 that stated "Ignatieff: Just visiting."

A distinction should be made between negative ads that critically assess the promises or performance of another party and those that engage in mudslinging, deception, or unjustified fear mongering (Jamieson, 1992). Negative ads that show the flaws and inconsistencies in another party's positions and performance may be more helpful to voters than ads that rely on platitudes, vague slogans (such as Obama's "change you can believe in"), or general promises.

Overall, negative campaign advertising along with the frequent use of personal attacks on those in opposing parties has become a major feature of election campaigns in many countries (Plasser & Plasser, 2002). Negative advertising is not necessarily more effective in persuading voters than positive ads that focus on the reasons to vote for a particular party or candidate (Lau, Sigelman, Heldman, & Babbitt, 1999). Indeed, negative advertising can backfire if voters view the ads as unfair. However, viewers are more likely to remember an attack ad than a positive one. Researchers have also found that negative attack ads reduce voting turnout, while positive ads slightly increase turnout (Ansolabehere, Iyengar, Simon, & Valentino, 1997). The increasing use of negative advertising may be a contributing factor to the increasing distrust of politicians and political parties.

leaders' debates that have become a regular feature of election campaigns in most countries do potentially provide an opportunity for the voters to compare the arguments of the different parties as well as some of the qualities of the leaders. However, coverage of election campaigns in the mass media has often been criticized for avoiding serious discussion of the issues and focusing more on the horse-race aspect of the election and the qualities (and gaffes) of the party leaders.

Environmental Positions in the 2008 Canadian Election

The 2008 Canadian election campaign featured much more debate about environmental policy than in any previous election. Stéphane Dion had been selected as Liberal leader in 2006 on a "green shift" environmental platform. The Conservative government renounced Canada's Kyoto commitment, promising instead a "made in Canada" approach to greenhouse gas (GHG) emissions. NDP leader Jack Layton proposed the Climate Change Accountability Act (C-377), which was passed by the House of Commons despite the opposition of the Conservative government, but the bill that would require the government to establish regulations to achieve major cuts in GHG emissions did not come to final vote in the Senate before the 2008 election was called.

In the 2008 Canadian election campaign, the Liberal party emphasized its "green shift" environmental plan, which included a carbon tax on the wholesale sale of fossil fuels other than gasoline with the revenues used to reduce individual and corporate income taxes. The Conservative party platform included a proposal to develop "intensity-based" regulations that would reduce emissions per unit of production by large polluters. The NDP proposed a "cap-and-trade" system to limit and reduce industrial emissions along with various incentives to create "green jobs." The Green party advocated the adoption of both carbon taxes and a cap-and-trade system. The Bloc Québécois favoured attempting to meet the Kyoto commitment of a 6 percent reduction in emissions (from 1990 levels) by 2012 through "polluter pays" policies and provincial government action.

Although all parties seemed to have a commitment to dealing with GHG emissions, there were substantial differences in how they would address the issue. Further, the likely consequences of their policy positions (if carried out) would be very different levels of emissions (although likely insufficient to meet their targets). Unfortunately, however, much of the debate on the issue during the campaign did not centre on the strengths and weaknesses of these different approaches, but rather on often misleading claims and counterclaims concerning whether the Liberal carbon tax would be revenue neutral and whether it would result in higher prices for gasoline at service stations.

GLEANING USEFUL INFORMATION Although election campaigns can be criticized for being exercises in manipulation, obfuscation, and dishonesty, those who follow a campaign carefully can often gain useful information about the parties' positions on specific issues and their general values and priorities (see Box 8-4, Environmental Positions in the 2008 Canadian Election). Of course, we have to be careful in interpreting the meaningfulness of the parties' campaign rhetoric. Although parties that are elected to govern may feel it necessary to fulfill or partly fulfill many of their specific promises, the general impression given by vague statements may be misleading. Promises to fix the health care system, reduce pollution, or operate government more efficiently are not very helpful unless there are clear indications as to how such objectives are to be achieved. Likewise, attacks on another party for its proposals,

Canada Votes 2008. Features: Issues & Analysis
www.cbc.ca/news/canadavotes/issuesanalysis

actions, or inactions are not very meaningful unless alternative approaches and policies are presented.

VOTING BEHAVIOUR

Canadian Election Study
www.ces-eec.umontreal.ca

American National Election Studies
www.electionstudies.org

The British Election Study
www.essex.ac.uk/bes

Why do people vote the way they do? Who tends to vote for each party? What affects the outcome of elections? Political scientists have devoted much research effort to such questions, particularly by using survey research techniques. However, the answers tend to be complex because a large number of factors can affect voting behaviour. These factors can be divided into two basic categories (Miller & Niemi, 2002):

- long-term predispositions of voters based on their interests, social characteristics, values, and sense of identification with a particular political party
- short-term factors related to the circumstances of a particular election such as the leaders, candidates, and campaign issues

Long-Term Predispositions

SOCIAL CHARACTERISTICS   Members of a social grouping based on such characteristics as class, religion, ethnicity and race, region, and gender may tend to support a particular party that they associate with the interests or the identity of their group. Thus, one or more major social cleavages (divisions) often affect the long-term patterns of voter support for different political parties. Although social divisions have generally been of declining importance in affecting voting choice in the advanced democracies, there are still some important differences in the voting patterns of different social groupings. In the case of Canada, region, culture (including ethnicity and language), and religion continue to be related to voters' party choices. In the United States, racial, urban/rural, and, to some extent, religious differences are of continuing significance (see Figure 8-1). These differences have been quite consistent over the past few decades.

Class In most countries, there is a tendency for class divisions (divisions based on position in the economy or a combination of income, education, and social status) to affect voting behaviour. Most democratic countries have a social democratic party, allied formally or informally with the labour movement, that is able to gain the votes of a substantial proportion of unionized workers. As well, most democratic countries have one or more conservative parties, often informally allied with business interests, that are able to gain the votes of a substantial proportion of the more affluent and business-oriented segments of society. However, there has been a tendency for such differences in voting by class to decline over time as class distinctions have become blurred, the traditional industrial working class has shrunk, and many workers in the

FIGURE 8-1
VOTE FOR OBAMA (DEMOCRATIC PARTY), U.S. PRESIDENTIAL ELECTION, 2008

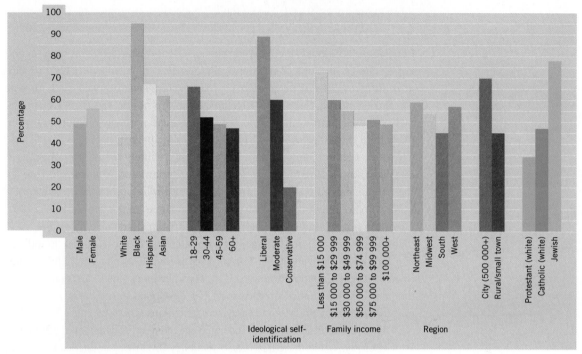

SOURCE: *New York Times. (2008, November 5). Election results 2008. Retrieved from http://elections. nytimes.com/2008/results/president/national-exit-polls.htm*

richer countries have gained the ability to attain more middle-class lifestyles in times of prosperity.

Class voting has not been strong at the national level in Canada, although class differences are significant in affecting voting behaviour in provincial elections in several provinces. Many Canadians think of themselves more in terms of provincial and ethnic identities than in class terms, and political parties (except, to some extent, the NDP) have not been viewed by the majority of voters as connected to particular classes. Nevertheless, the 1999 to 2002 World Values and European Values surveys found that the level of class voting in Canada was about the same as in most other advanced democracies (Dalton, 2006). The NDP tends to do better (other things being equal) among those in union households than among those who are not, with the reverse being the case for the Conservatives. However, the NDP has been unable to gain the support of a majority of union members. Differences in voter support for different parties based on income level are fairly small (Gidengil et al., 2006a). In the United States, union members have quite a strong tendency to vote for the Democratic party with, for example, about two-thirds voting for Barack Obama rather than John McCain in the 2008 election (Moberg, 2008). Although class voting has declined in Britain, those in the lower social classes are still more likely to vote for the Labour party than are those in the higher social classes. For example, the Labour party received 48 percent of the vote of those in the lowest social class in the 2005 election, compared to 28 percent of the vote of those in the highest social class (House of Commons Library, 2005).

Religion In a number of countries there is a relationship between religion and voting choice. Persons of different religious denominations may tend to support different parties; those who are religious are generally less likely to vote for parties on the "left" than are those who are not religious. For example, in the United States, Catholics, Jews, and those with no religion are more likely than Protestants to vote for the Democratic party (see Figure 8-1). Those who attend church regularly are somewhat more likely to vote Republican. In Britain, Catholics are more likely than Presbyterians and Anglicans to vote for the Labour party. In France, those who are not religious are more likely than those who are religious to vote for one of the parties of the left (Dalton, 2006).

In Canada, Catholics (along with non-Christians) are generally more likely than Protestants to vote Liberal (with the opposite the case in Newfoundland and Labrador). However, the Liberal lead among Catholic voters has diminished in recent Canadian elections. On the other hand, the Conservative party (like its Reform/Alliance predecessors) has developed particularly strong support from fundamentalist and evangelical Christians (Gidengil et al., 2009). The NDP tends to do better among those with no religion (Gidengil et al., 2006a).

Generally, while there has been a tendency in various countries for voting differences between different denominations to decline in significance, differences between religious and non-religious voters often continue to be important. This may be the result of the rise of fundamentalism in some countries along with the political attention given to controversial moral issues such as abortion and same-sex marriage in a number of countries (Dalton, 2006).

Ethnic, Racial, and Cultural Groups Differences in voting behaviour are often apparent in countries that have ethnic, racial, and cultural minority groups with distinctive identities. The extremely high support among African-Americans for Democratic candidate Barack Obama not only reflected their support for the country's first black presidential candidate, but also was consistent with very strong African-American support for the Democratic party over the past several decades. For example, 92 percent of black Americans voted for the Democratic Congressional candidates in the 2004 election, compared to 71 percent of Hispanics and 44 percent of whites voting for Democratic party candidates (Dalton, 2006). Similarly, a large majority of Canadians of non-European ancestry vote for the Liberal party (Blais, Gidengil, Nadeau, & Nevitte, 2002), although the Conservative party has made inroads among some non-European groups in recent years.

Region In some countries, there are important regional differences in voting behaviour. For example, support for different parties often varies substantially across Canada, reflecting not only differences in the political culture and economy of different parts of the country, but also a tendency to evaluate governments and political parties in terms of perceptions of how good or bad they are for the interests of one's province or region. Likewise, the Labour party in Britain draws its strongest support from the north of England and from Scotland, while the Conservative party is strong in the south.

Gender   Gender differences in voting behaviour are generally quite small. In some countries, there is a slight tendency for women to be more likely than men to vote for conservative (or religious) parties. In other countries, women, particularly younger women, are more likely to vote for leftist parties (Dalton, 2006).

In the United States, women are somewhat more likely to vote for the Democratic party than the Republican party. In Canada, women have generally been slightly more likely than men to vote for the Liberal party. In recent Canadian elections, women (particularly younger women) have been more likely than men to vote for the NDP, while men have been more likely than women to vote for conservative parties (Blais, Gidengil, Nadeau, & Nevitte, 2002; Gidengil et al., 2006b; Strategic Counsel, 2008).

Some analysts have suggested that the gender gap will widen, in part because of the tendency of women to hold more liberal or leftist views, including a more favourable view of social welfare programs and a less favourable view of pure free-market policies, aggressive military action, and harsh treatment of criminals (Gidengil, Blais, Nadeau, & Nevitte, 2003; O'Neill, 2002).

Other Characteristics   Various other social characteristics are related to differences in voting behaviour in some countries. For example, although age is not usually consistently related to the choices voters make, Green parties have tended to receive greater support from younger voters. In Canada, the NDP has also tended to do better among younger voters than among older ones. In the 2008 U.S. presidential election, Barack Obama drew strong support from younger voters. However, age differences were fairly small in most previous American presidential elections (*New York Times*, 2008).

Voters in rural areas, small towns, and suburban areas tend to be more supportive of conservative parties than are big city voters. For example, in the 2004, 2006, and 2008 Canadian elections, the Conservative party did not win a single seat in Canada's three largest cities (other than in surrounding suburban areas). Likewise, in the United States, the Republican party has tended to draw stronger support from rural areas and small towns than from big cities.

VALUES   Studies in a number of countries have found that general values such as egalitarianism and libertarianism, along with how people view themselves in left/right (or in the United States, liberal/conservative) terms, are related to their voting choices (Miller & Niemi, 2002). For example, a study of voting in the 2004 Canadian election found that those who favoured free-enterprise values were more likely to vote Conservative and less likely to vote NDP. Likewise, those with social conservative values (that is, traditional values on such issues as the rights of gays and lesbians and the role of women) were more likely to vote Conservative and less likely to vote Liberal or NDP (Gidengil et al., 2006a).[5] In Quebec, support for Quebec sovereignty clearly distinguished those who vote for the Bloc Québécois from those who vote for the Liberal party (Blais, Gidengil, Nadeau, & Nevitte, 2002). In the United States, those who consider themselves liberal have a strong tendency to vote for the Democratic party while conservatives heavily support the Republican party. In a number of European countries, there are strong differences in party support between those who consider themselves as being on the "left" rather than on the "right."

PARTY IDENTIFICATION A long-term psychological attachment to a particular political party.

PARTY IDENTIFICATION   Political scientists often use party identification as a major explanation for why people vote the way that they do. **Party identification** can be thought of as a long-term psychological attachment to a particular political party. It is not simply an agreement with the positions that a party is currently taking, or a preference for a particular leader or candidate representing the party. Rather, it is a long-term feeling of closeness to a party that may be developed at quite an early age, similar to one's attachment to a particular religious or ethnic group.

Those that identify with a particular political party will tend to develop a positive view of the party's leader and candidates, prefer that party's position on the issues of the day, and believe that their party is most competent to handle the tasks of governing. Therefore, even though voters typically vote in accordance with their evaluation of the leaders, candidates, and issue positions of the parties, the long-term influence of party identification may lie behind voters' evaluations of the particular features of an election.

The theory of party identification is not meant to suggest that an individual's vote is completely determined by long-term party ties. Voters with weak or non-existent ties to a party will frequently shift their votes from election to election, resulting in changing election outcomes. A particularly unpopular party personality or party issue position may alienate or turn off even some strong party supporters. However, the theory suggests that deviations from voting for one's party will be only temporary. Party identifiers may occasionally vote for another party while still retaining their original party identification.

Although the theory of party identification is useful in understanding voting behaviour and long-term patterns of support for different parties, party identification has been declining in importance in many countries. Fewer

---

[5] These conclusions are drawn from an analysis of voters outside Quebec.

people now view themselves as strong party identifiers, and the proportion of people who view themselves as independent or without a party identification has been increasing in recent decades in the advanced democracies (Dalton, 2000, 2006). For example, in 2009, 39 percent of Americans viewed themselves as "independent" (Pew Research Centre, 2009), a substantially higher proportion than in the 1950s and 1960s.

More than three-quarters of Canadian adults can be considered to have a party identification (Gidengil et al., 2006c; Clarke, Kornberg, & Scotto, 2009b).[6] However, many people do not have a strong party identification or identify with different parties at the national and provincial levels. Those with a party identification do not necessarily vote for "their" party in every election, but nevertheless often retain their party identification (Gidengil et al., 2006c).

Short-Term Influences

While some long-term influences on the vote have declined in significance (although remain very important), short-term factors such as the personalities and issues of an election campaign have increased in significance. Many voters decide how to vote during the election campaign, with some even deciding on election day (Clarke, Kornberg, & Scotto, 2009b). Surveys conducted during the 2000 Canadian election campaign found that about one-third of voters could be considered to have been affected by the campaign (Blais, Gidengil, Nadeau, & Nevitte, 2002).

It is not easy to determine the relative importance of such factors as the quality of leaders and candidates, the issue positions of the parties, and general perceptions of the quality, competence, and performance of the parties, as each factor will tend to influence the others. For example, those who trust a particular party leader may come to agree with the positions that leader's party takes on certain issues, while those who agree with a party's positions may be more inclined to develop a favourable impression of that party's leader and candidates. As well, the importance of various short-term factors may differ from election to election and from country to country, depending on how the parties appeal to the voters and what the mass media emphasize in their coverage of a particular election.

LEADERS   Evaluations of the party leaders can have a significant effect (independent of party identification) on which party a voter chooses to support in an election (Blais, Gidengil, Nadeau, & Nevitte, 2002; Gidengil et al., 2006a; Clarke, Kornberg, & Scotto, 2009a). However, the evaluations of

---

[6] Party identification is usually measured in surveys by a question such as "In federal politics, do you usually think of yourself as a: Liberal, Conservative, NDP, Bloc Québécois, or none of these?"

different party leaders often do not vary widely, thus limiting their effect on the *outcome* of an election (Gidengil et al., 2006a). Having a popular leader can increase the vote for a party, but cannot usually overcome the disadvantages an unpopular party faces.

CANDIDATES   Candidates in an electoral district tend to be less important than party leaders in affecting voting behaviour and election outcomes. Nevertheless, one study found that local candidate preference was a decisive factor for 5 percent of Canadian voters independent of their feelings about the parties and their leaders (Blais et al., 2003). In a closely contested electoral district, a strong candidate can make a difference. In American elections, candidates can have very important effects because they often distance themselves from their party. In doing so, they gain or lose support based, to a considerable extent, on their own characteristics, campaigns, and positions. Incumbent members of the U.S. Congress usually have a strong ability to win re-election.

ISSUES   Although many voters cite issues as the most important reason for their vote choice, the leading parties often do not clearly stake out different positions on what should be done about important problems. Instead, **valence issues**—those on which there is a general consensus—have often been the most important issues in election campaigns (Clarke, Kornberg, & Scotto, 2009a). For example, health care was the leading issue in both the 2000 and 2004 Canadian elections (and a major issue in the 2006 election). However, there was little difference among the parties, as each party proclaimed its commitment to improve the public health care system and to spend more money on health care. Liberal accusations that the Alliance (2000) and the Conservatives (2004) favoured privatization of public health care were met with denials of that claim.

VALENCE ISSUES Issues on which there is a general consensus.

Valence issues may have an impact if voters feel that one party is more competent to handle the problem or if they assign blame or credit for the handling of the problem in the past. However, in many cases (such as the economic problems of unemployment and inflation), voters may feel that "their" party is best able to handle the problem, thus reducing the impact of the issue on the election outcome.

ACCOUNTABILITY   Do voters hold the governing party accountable for its actions in office? An analysis of the 2000 Canadian election found that voters' evaluations of the Liberal government's performance generally had a significant effect on their electoral choice. (In Quebec, however, voters made their choice primarily based on their views about Quebec sovereignty.) Interestingly, though, the Liberal party was re-elected despite considerable voter dissatisfaction with its record on such key issues as health care, taxes, and corruption. Those who were dissatisfied with the Liberal government's record divided their votes among the various opposition parties, thereby limiting the negative impact of their dissatisfaction. A complicating factor was the tendency of many voters to blame their provincial government as well as the federal government for problems with the health care system (Blais, Gidengil, Nadeau, & Nevitte, 2002). In the case of the 2004 Canadian election, the Liberal party's ability to raise fears about the consequences of electing what they described as an extreme right-wing, Harper-led Conservative government may have swung support away from the Conservative party late in the election campaign. Holding a governing party accountable for its actions may be difficult if voters are not comfortable voting for an alternative party.

ECONOMIC CONDITIONS   Voters are concerned about the state of the economy not only in terms of their own economic well-being, but also in terms of the overall economic condition of the country (Kinder & Kiewiet, 1981). There is a large amount of research that (with some exceptions) indicates that the condition of the economy (along with the approval rating of the president or prime minister) has an effect on the outcome of an election. The incumbent party generally tends to do well when the economy is performing well and do poorly when the economy is faltering. For example, some studies have found that Barack Obama's election victory in November 2008 was predictable based on the declining economic situation and the unfavourable rating of the outgoing Republican president.[7] However, although the majority of Canadian voters thought the economy was worsening at the time of the October 2008 election (Clarke, Kornberg, & Scotto, 2009b), the governing Conservatives managed to increase their popular vote and number of parliamentary seats, falling just short of gaining a majority in the House of Commons. In this case, the opposition Liberal party was burdened with an unpopular leader who had trouble explaining and defending his proposed carbon tax. Further, although Stephen Harper was not rated positively by voters, the Conservatives were somewhat more likely to be viewed as the party best able to handle the economy—an issue that was, by far, the most important to voters (Clarke, Kornberg, & Scotto, 2009b).

Overall, although economic conditions have an effect on voters and the outcome of elections, an analysis of voting behaviour in eleven elections in Canada, the United States, and Britain found that that the issue positions adopted by the parties or presidential candidates were a decisive consideration for about twice as many voters as was the case with economic conditions (Blais et al., 2004).

---

[7] See *PS: Political Science and Politics*, vol. 42, no. 1 (2009) for differing analyses.

Summary and Conclusion

Elections are often viewed as the central feature of democratic politics. Elections allow voters to choose who will represent them in the legislature. More importantly, elections can provide an opportunity for voters to maintain or remove a government. If parties take different ideological positions, voters can shift the general direction of the government by their choice of which party to support. Although election campaigns feature manipulation of the voters by the competing parties and politicians, elections also tend to bring politicians into closer contact with voters. In anticipation of an election, parties and politicians ask themselves, "What do voters want?" Appealing to the public may have to be modified, however, to ensure the support of the party's financial backers and party activists.

A basic problem with elections is that we are asked to convey a lot of information by our vote. We may use our vote to express which of the competing platforms we prefer, which candidates and leaders we think are most competent, which party we think is best, what our evaluation is of the current governing party, and so on. However, placing a single X on a ballot cannot really convey our views on a variety of matters.

Voters often express a variety of different attitudes, values, preferences, and judgments when they cast their vote. This can make the interpretation of the result of a particular election difficult and controversial. The messages being sent by voters to politicians through an election are often unclear. Thus, statements by a governing party that it has a mandate to carry out particular policies because it won an election can be misleading.

The single member plurality (SMP) electoral system tends to distort the choices made by voters. By giving a boost to the leading party at the expense of the smaller parties, the governing party often does not have the support of the majority of the voters for the direction in which it plans to take the political community, even if it has the majority of elected representatives on its side. Likewise, although the SMP system provides a single representative for each electoral district, many

representatives are elected by less than a majority of those voting in their district. Representation of diverse viewpoints and interests tends to be inhibited because of the discrimination suffered by smaller parties in SMP systems. Systems of proportional representation (PR), although providing fairer representation, typically result in coalition governments that may be difficult to hold accountable for their actions. Elections using PR systems often result in only small changes in party representation, and major changes in government are less common than in SMP systems. Furthermore, some PR and mixed member proportional (MMP) systems do not give voters the opportunity to get rid of undesirable representatives.

When we consider whether elections serve the common good, we should remember that elections are the culmination of the struggle for political power within a democracy. The contending parties in an election are not engaged in deliberation about what is best for the community, but rather are engaged in a competitive struggle for votes. So it should not be surprising that election campaigns are designed to manipulate rather than to enlighten voters. Nevertheless, election campaigns can serve to mobilize those who support a particular party or candidate to vote and stimulate discussion of political issues even among many who do not ordinarily follow politics. Political campaigns may not live up to the ideal of deliberative democracy, but then neither does political discussion in other forums such as political websites, radio talk shows, or Question Period in the Canadian House of Commons.

In societies with deep social divisions, election campaigns can inflame those divisions, and thus violence sometimes accompanies elections. This is particularly the case for elections that are conducted on a winner-takes-all basis (for example, elections using the SMP system or presidential elections) in countries where some groups fear serious consequences if a party representing an opposing section of society wins.

Despite their limitations, elections are important in enabling voters to hold a government accountable for its actions and to have some ability to affect the direction taken by the political community. In democratic systems, voters do sometimes use the opportunity provided by elections to remove governing parties that have become corrupt, incompetent, unresponsive, or lacking in new ideas. If elections are viewed by citizens as free and fair, those elected to govern normally will be viewed as legitimate authorities. Transitions of political power from one group to another can be accomplished smoothly. Overall, then, the common good is served by a system of free and fair elections. Establishing a legitimate government, providing an incentive for governments to be responsive to those they govern, and providing a peaceful mechanism to remove governments that do not deserve to continue to be in power is good for all members of the political community.

Key Terms

Coalition government 187

Electoral College 186

Electoral system 182

Gerrymander 181

Mixed member proportional (MMP) system 188

Party identification 200

Preferential voting 186

Proportional representation (PR) system 186

Runoff election 186

Single member plurality (SMP) system 182

Single transferable vote (STV) system 189

Universal suffrage 180

Valence issues 202

Discussion Questions

1. Are Canadian elections free and fair? Should voting be modernized by the adoption of electronic or Internet voting?

2. Should Canada change its single member plurality electoral system? If so, what is the best alternative?

3. Should politicians be expected to keep the promises they make in an election campaign? What should happen if they do not?

4. How would you interpret the outcome of the last national, provincial, or local election? Did voters send a clear message about the direction they want their government to follow?

5. What criteria have you used, or do you think you should use, in deciding how to vote? Should you vote for the best leader, the best party, or the best local candidate?

6. Do voters generally make intelligent choices in elections?

Further Reading

Anderson, C.D., & Stephenson, L.B. (Eds.). (2010). *Voting behaviour in Canada*. Vancouver: UBC Press.

Baldini, G., & Pappalardo, A. (2009). *Elections, electoral systems and volatile voters*. New York: Palgrave Macmillan.

Baumgartner, J.C. (2000). *Modern presidential electioneering: An organizational and comparative approach*. Westport, CT: Praeger.

Blais, A. (Ed.). (2008). *To keep or change first past the post? The politics of electoral reform*. Toronto: Oxford University Press.

Campbell, J.E. (2008). *The American campaign: U.S. presidential campaigns and the national vote* (2nd ed.). College Station, TX: Texas A & M University Press.

Clarke, H.D., Kornberg, A., & Scotto, T.S. (2009). *Making political choices: Canada and the United States*. Toronto: University of Toronto Press.

Courtney, J.C. (2004). *Elections*. Vancouver: UBC Press.

Farrell, D.M., & Schmitt-Beck, R. (Eds.). (2002). *Do political campaigns matter? Campaign effects in elections and referendums*. London, UK: Routledge.

Milner, H. (Ed.). (2004). *Steps toward making every vote count: Electoral system reform in Canada and its provinces*. Peterborough, ON: Broadview.

Pammett, J.H., & Dornan, C. (Eds.). (2009). *The Canadian federal election of 2008*. Toronto: Dundurn Press.

Pilon, D. (2007). *The politics of voting: Reforming Canada's electoral system*. Toronto: Edmond Montgomery.

Plasser, F., & Plasser, G. (2002). *Global political campaigning: A worldwide analysis of campaign professionals and their practices*. Westport, CT: Praeger.

West, D.M. (2010). *Air wars: Television advertising in election campaigns, 1952–2008* (5th ed.). Washington, DC: CQ Press.

Chapter 9

Political Influence

PHOTO ABOVE: Lois Gibbs turned political activist extraordinaire when her children fell seriously ill and she realized that the Love Canal toxic dump she lived on top of was to blame.

CHAPTER OBJECTIVES

After reading this chapter you should be able to:

1. discuss the nature and significance of interest groups and social movements

2. examine the organization of interest groups and social movements

3. discuss the extent to which interest groups and social movements help or hinder the achievement of the common good of the political community

4. assess the different perspectives on the mass media

5. evaluate the effectiveness of the mass media in facilitating the achievement of democratic ideals

Lois Gibbs was a housewife who became a political activist when her children fell ill. In 1976, Gibbs learned that the blue-collar subdivision in Niagara Falls, New York, where she lived with her husband and two small children was built on the Love Canal, an unfinished canal that had been used as a chemical disposal site. Over the years, the Hooker Chemical Company, later bought by oil giant Occidental Petroleum, had dumped twenty thousand tonnes (more than eighteen thousand kilograms) of highly toxic chemical waste into the never-completed canal. It was covered over and the land was sold to the municipality of Niagara Falls for one dollar.

In 1978, Gibbs's children became very sick. Her son developed epilepsy and her daughter almost died of a rare blood disease. Talking to other parents in the subdivision, Gibbs found that many children had birth defects, miscarriages were very common, and children often came home from the playground with burns on their hands and faces. Gibbs went around to her neighbours with a petition, asking them if they were as upset as she was. They were, and soon they had formed the Love Canal Homeowners Association. Over the next two years, Gibbs led the association in legal and political battle against Occidental Petroleum and all three levels of government: city, state, and federal. Although the company and the governments all argued that the Love Canal's toxic wastes did not cause the residents' health problems, the community eventually won a settlement of US$120 million and more than eight hundred families were relocated to safe, healthy homes. President Jimmy Carter later declared the Love Canal a national disaster area.

The protest that Lois Gibbs organized and led has left two important legacies. One is the United States Environmental Protection Agency's Superfund, monies used to find and clean up toxic sites throughout the United States. The other is the Center for Health, Environment, and Justice (CHEJ), which Gibbs founded and heads. The CHEJ works with community groups across the United States to protect neighbourhoods from the hazards of toxic wastes.

The Love Canal incident sparked thousands of other grassroots organizations to campaign against toxic sites. By being brave enough to stand up to the powerful and resourceful enough to found and lead a successful political protest, Lois Gibbs showed that even ordinary people can wield a lot of political power when they organize and refuse to take no for an answer.

INTRODUCTION

An important element of political analysis is determining the relative ability of different groups and individuals to influence those in governing positions and the laws and policies that are adopted. Although voters play an important role in deciding which political party and which individuals will be in governing and legislative positions, elections are infrequent events. Voters may have some effect on the general direction taken by government through their choice among parties. However, citizens usually do not have much influence through their vote over the specific policies adopted by governments and legislatures.

In liberal democracies, people are free to voice their opinions and organize into groups in order to try to exert political influence over the public policies that affect their lives. In the liberal democratic ideal, government does not control society and individuals; rather, government is expected to listen to and be responsive to the views of the people in making decisions. In reality, however, questions are often raised about the extent to which government is responsive to the people. Undoubtedly some individuals and groups are more influential than others.

There are a variety of sources of political influence in any political community. In this chapter we will focus on interest groups, social movements, and the media.

INTEREST GROUPS

Interest groups[1] are organizations that pursue the common interests of groups of people, particularly by trying to influence the development, adoption, and implementation of public policies. In recent decades, there has been a great growth in the number of interest groups, the size of their membership, and the diversity of interests that are represented. The growth of interest groups reflects, to a considerable extent, the growth of the activities of government. As governments have become more heavily involved in health care, education, social programs, business regulation, gender issues, and environmental protection, a variety of groups have been formed to promote, modify, or challenge further government actions in such areas (Mahoney & Baumgartner, 2008).

INTEREST GROUP An organization that pursues the common interests of groups of people, particularly by trying to influence the development, adoption, and implementation of public policies.

---

[1] Interest groups are sometimes referred to as pressure groups, particularly to refer to their involvement in influencing government. Young and Everitt (2004) suggest that the term *advocacy groups* is preferable to *interest groups* because many groups are not concerned primarily with gaining benefits for their members but rather promoting their view about issues that may not affect them directly. The term *non-governmental organization* (NGO) is also widely used to include both groups involved in advocacy and those involved in providing services such as humanitarian relief and international development programs.

Many interest groups do not exist exclusively or primarily for political purposes. However, in representing the interests of a particular segment of society, interest groups often find political action necessary or desirable to protect or promote the interests of the group. For example, the major activities of the Canadian Medical Association include the exchange of medical information and the certification of doctors. Nevertheless, because the interests of doctors are strongly affected by government policy, the Canadian Medical Association is also active in developing and promoting a variety of policy positions concerning the medical system.

Self-Interest and Public Interest Groups

The term *interest group* refers to a wide variety of different types of groups. Many groups have been formed by specific economic and occupational interests. Groups to promote various business, agricultural, and labour interests were among the first to be established in many countries. Most professions have also developed well-organized interest groups. Groups based on economic and occupational interests primarily pursue a material interest such as the wages, jobs, or profits of their members. Generally, groups that represent economic and occupational interests as well as groups that want a benefit from government for its members (such as a softball organization that wants to persuade a city council to improve the condition of ball fields) can be considered to be **self-interest groups.**

Public interest groups (also known as citizens' groups) are not primarily concerned with gaining specific benefits for their members, but rather have been formed to promote a position on certain issues or a particular cause that they believe to be in the public interest. For example, in many countries pro-choice and pro-life groups are active in promoting their viewpoints on the issue of whether abortions should be legal. Likewise, Amnesty International mounts public pressure to try to prevent human rights abuses around the world. A variety of interest groups have also been formed to develop, express, and promote the identity, rights, and interests of a particular segment of society (such as those representing different ethnic groups). Many of these groups are members of the Canadian Ethnocultural Council, which promotes the vision of a multicultural country and the elimination of discrimination and racism.

The distinction between self-interest groups and public interest groups is often not clear. Self-interest groups usually argue that the policies they hope to obtain will benefit the whole community. For example, business groups seeking lower taxes claim that such policies will help to create jobs and prosperity for the country as a whole. On the other hand, the claim of some public interest groups that their positions or causes are for the good of the public as a whole are often controversial. Indeed, in some cases, public interest groups have been accused of raising funds for a popular cause primarily to provide

SELF-INTEREST GROUP An interest group whose primary objective is to promote the interests of the group and its members and to seek benefits that are primarily or exclusively for their members.

PUBLIC INTEREST GROUP A group that seeks to achieve goals that the group views as being for the good of the community as a whole rather than specific benefits for their members.

Amnesty International Canada
www.amnesty.ca

Canadian Ethnocultural Council
www.ethnocultural.ca

The Anti-Adams Mine Coalition is an issue-oriented interest group that successfully campaigned against a plan to send Toronto's garbage to an abandoned mine in Kirkland Lake, Ontario.

generous salaries and benefits to the leaders and staff of the organization. Furthermore, some groups combine activities to benefit their members with support for broader public causes. For example, the Canadian Federation of Students not only has involved itself in pursuing lower tuition fees and more government support for higher education, but also has pursued various national and international causes not directly related to the self-interest of students.

Canadian Federation of Students
www.cfs-fcee.ca

Issue-Oriented and Institutionalized Interest Groups

There is a great deal of variation in interest groups, not only in their goals and whom they represent, but also in their organizational development. A distinction is often made between issue-oriented interest groups and institutionalized interest groups (Pross, 1993).

Issue-oriented interest groups often spontaneously develop to express the views of people on a particular issue, concern, or grievance. For example, the Anti-Adams Mine Coalition that fought a plan to send Toronto's garbage to an abandoned mine in Kirkland Lake, Ontario, could be considered an issue-oriented group. Some issue-oriented groups have only a temporary existence and are not concerned about developing a formal organization. When the issue is resolved or passions concerning the issue dissipate, such groups may fold or fade away.

Many other interest groups, particularly those representing economic or professional interests or a major sector of society, have developed a formal

ISSUE-ORIENTED INTEREST GROUP An interest group that spontaneously develops to express the views of people on a particular issue, concern, or grievance.

organization, including such features as a well-established membership base, paid professional staff, permanent offices, and a capability to keep their members, government, and the public aware of their views and activities. Such groups, termed **institutionalized interest groups**, typically develop and promote positions on a variety of issues, monitor the activities of government, and try to develop close working relationships with key government officials (Pross, 1993). For example, the Canadian Chamber of Commerce, the Canadian Federation of Agriculture, and the Assembly of First Nations are regular and long-lasting organizations that are important features of political life. They are generally recognized by government as being the legitimate representatives of a particular segment of society and are often consulted when proposed policies affect their interests.

Issue-oriented interest groups and institutionalized interest groups could be considered as extremes on a continuum of organizational development, with many groups falling somewhere between these two types. Some interest groups concerned with a single issue (such as Mothers Against Drunk Driving) have developed a more professional, structured organization so as to have a more permanent and effective vehicle for their concerns.

Membership in Interest Groups

Organized collective action gives individuals a chance to be influential, which is usually why people join and support interest groups. Modern governments are large and the policy-making process is complex. Few individuals have the contacts and expertise needed to influence decisions. Although your member of Parliament may be willing to listen to your request, and a letter or email to a Cabinet minister or the prime minister may result in a computer-generated response, it is highly unlikely that one individual's demands or opinions will affect government decisions. Most individuals are much more likely to be able to influence political decisions through involvement in an organization than by trying to influence politicians and government officials themselves.

THE FREE RIDER PROBLEM   Mancur Olson (1965) raised the following question: Under what conditions is it rational for individuals to join and support groups to pursue their political interests? In what Olson describes as the *free rider problem*, an individual can often enjoy the benefits of the successes of an interest group whether or not that individual is a member or financial supporter. If, for example, an environmental group is successful in a campaign to reduce air pollution, we all benefit from that action whether or not we supported the group. Rational, calculating individuals may figure that it is to their advantage to let others contribute time and money to the campaign. Of course, if enough people think this way, an interest group will not be able to survive.

The free rider problem is particularly serious for public interest groups because their goals can benefit the political community as a whole. Self-interest groups that seek a specific benefit exclusively for their members find it easier to gain and maintain the support of those who will potentially benefit. Individual companies can anticipate a direct and substantial impact on their profitability if the organization that represents them is successful in persuading government to adopt certain policies that benefit their industry.

In some cases, the free rider problem is largely irrelevant because membership in a group is compulsory. For example, in unionized workplaces, union dues are automatically deducted from paycheques. Likewise, the Canadian Federation of Students, after obtaining a majority vote of students, has convinced university administrations to require that all students pay union dues. Similarly, to practise as a professional (such as a doctor, engineer, or pharmacist) a person is required to be a member of the appropriate professional association.

Further, individuals do not necessarily join an organization for its political activities or its stance on political issues. For example, those who are members of a Canadian church may not even be aware that the Canadian Council of Churches, which represents most Christian denominations, advocates such causes as "just trade" rather than "free trade" as well as founding and sponsoring Project Ploughshares, a group that promotes peace with justice.

The Canadian Council of Churches
www.ccc-cce.ca

Project Ploughshares
www.ploughshares.ca

REASONS FOR JOINING   To some degree, public interest groups can try to avoid the free rider problem by offering particular benefits (termed **selective incentives**) to their members. Some groups provide a glossy magazine, offer merchandise at reduced rates, and arrange for reduced insurance rates and discounts on car rentals and hotel accommodations. However, many public interest groups that provide few selective incentives have developed in recent decades, with some (such as environmental and conservation groups) attracting very large numbers of members. People often join or support public interest groups because of the satisfaction that can be achieved by expressing one's values and contributing to the good of the community. Some people also join interest groups for social reasons, that is, because they enjoy interacting and working with like-minded persons.

SELECTIVE INCENTIVE A particular benefit that is made available to members of an interest group but is not available to the public as a whole.

More generally, an increasingly educated population with greater skills and more leisure time is more likely to pursue various causes through involvement in public interest groups. Nevertheless, many public interest groups experience a high turnover in membership and face large swings in membership and financial support as different causes become more popular. Therefore, they often must devote considerable effort and resources to motivating volunteers and maintaining financial solvency.

Democratic Organizations?

Many interest groups have democratic organizational structures. Institutionalized interest groups typically have some regular method for electing their chairperson and board of directors, who oversee the operations of staff members and set the direction for the organization.

However, the "iron law of oligarchy" (discussed in Chapter 7) applies, to a considerable extent, to many interest group organizations. Although some interest groups do provide for active participation by their members in the group's decision making (for example, by establishing local chapters), there is often not a strong relationship between the members of an interest group and those who act on its behalf. Some of the large national interest groups devote most of their energies to influencing government policy-makers, leaving the "grassroots" members largely uninvolved in the organization (Shaiko, 1999).

Even though many interest groups do not provide a strong vehicle for the voices of their members, there will usually be some shared perspectives between the spokespersons for the group and its members. A group that deviates strongly from the views of its grassroots supporters or members may find that its funds, membership, and ability to mobilize members in support of its cause fade. However, some groups, such as those based on cultural, ethnic, and religious interests, may be able to retain their members even if the political positions they pursue are not fully in tune with the views of the membership.

Government Support for Interest Groups

Government organizations have often provided some financial support and encouragement for the formation and development of interest groups. Beginning in the 1960s, Canadian governments have, at times, encouraged and helped to finance the development of groups representing segments of the population that were largely unrepresented by well-organized interest groups, including Aboriginals, women, and poor people (Pal, 1993).

Why would governments fund groups that represent disadvantaged segments of the population when such groups are often critical of government policies and government's lack of action to deal with their problems? Some governments have hoped to offset the heavy influence that groups representing business and other privileged elements of society are often able to exert on government. This may allow politicians and government officials greater flexibility to act as they see fit. Particular government departments and agencies often find it useful to have active and vocal interest groups in their policy area so as to assist their struggle with other departments or agencies of government for more funds or new programs. Environmental groups, for example, may help Environment Canada to convince the rest of government to treat environmental issues more seriously and gain the resources and policies the government department feels are needed for its programs.

FUNDING AND CRITICISM   It is sometimes thought that interest groups that receive assistance from government will become tame supporters of government. This is not always the case. For example, feminist, Aboriginal, and poor people's groups that have received funding from the Canadian government have, at times, been sharply critical of the policies of the governments that helped to fund them. In response, governments have sometimes reduced or eliminated funding for groups that are critical of government policies and actions. For example, the Harper government sharply reduced the funding of a number of organizations that provide independent policy analysis and advocacy on behalf of the disadvantaged in Canada and in developing countries.

Government funding of public interest groups has been criticized particularly by those who feel that some of the groups are too radical or represent only "special interests." Often ignored is the fact that the promotion of business interests is, in effect, subsidized by government. In calculating their taxes, businesses can deduct contributions to interest groups and other expenses they incur in trying to influence government. In contrast, individuals can only receive a tax credit for contributing to organizations that are deemed to be charitable, which generally in Canada and the United States excludes organizations that devote significant resources (more than 10 percent of their revenues) to political action.

Interest Group Activities

In analyzing how interest groups try to influence public policy, a distinction may be made between inside and outside strategies (Walker, 1991). **Inside strategies** involve interest group leaders developing close contacts with key decision-makers in government and the public service. Presenting briefs to government based on the group's research and participating in advisory bodies also allow influence to be exerted in a quiet fashion. **Outside strategies** involve appealing to the public for support (for example, through the mass media and advertising) and mobilizing members and supporters to put pressure on decision-makers (for example, through petitions, emails, and demonstrations).

Inside strategies have the advantage of directly influencing those responsible for developing government policies. They are less likely to stimulate public opposition and criticism than outside strategies. However, developing a very close relationship with the government may result in interest group leaders becoming influenced by, and associated with, the policy direction and concerns of the government. Outside strategies, if successful in mobilizing the support of the public, may be useful in pressuring politicians who are worried about their chances for re-election. Outside strategies may also be useful in building and maintaining an active membership-based organization. However, governments are often reluctant to be seen as backing down under pressure, and therefore outside strategies can have difficulty exerting influence once government has publicly committed to a particular course of action.

CHOICE OF STRATEGIES Different types of interest groups tend to use different mixtures of strategies. Business and professional associations are

INSIDE STRATEGIES Strategies in which interest group leaders develop close contacts with key decision-makers in government and the public service in order to influence public policies.

OUTSIDE STRATEGIES Strategies in which interest group leaders appeal to the public for support and mobilize members in order to put pressure on decision-makers concerning public policies.

more likely to use inside strategies, although they may devote some attention to outside strategies if they find government unsympathetic to their concerns or if other groups mount strong public campaigns against their interests. Unions, public interest groups, issue-oriented groups, and groups that have developed out of social movements are more likely to use outside strategies. However, they may find that combining these with inside strategies is useful in persuading government to adopt specific policies (see Box 9-1, Campaigning for a Clean Harbour).

The political activities and strategies of interest groups are also affected by the organization and operations of the system of government. Interest groups in the United States, for example, devote considerable effort to trying to influence individual elected representatives in Congress and members of the committees of Congress because of the substantial involvement of Congress in the development of public policies. Canadian interest groups, particularly institutionalized interest groups, tend to direct much of their activity toward influencing those public servants who are important in developing public policy and the particular Cabinet minister whose government department is most relevant to the concerns of the interest group. For example, interest groups representing farmers devote much of their efforts to trying to influence those involved in policy development within the Department of Agriculture and meet regularly with the minister to discuss their concerns and proposals. Canadian members of Parliament do not normally receive the same level of attention from the major Canadian interest groups as senior officials in government departments because of their limited role in developing policy.

In several Western European countries (including, to varying extents, Austria, Germany, Sweden, and the Netherlands), the state actively collaborates with selected major interests (particularly the national organizations of business and labour) to seek a consensus concerning the country's major economic and social policies. State officials guide or facilitate the development of a consensus among the leading interests. In turn, the leaders of these interests persuade those they represent to accept the agreements that have been reached (such as agreements concerning wage and price increases). In such systems (termed **neo-corporatism**[2]), the activities of the leading interest groups and their relationship to government tends to be quite different than in Canada, the United States, or the United Kingdom.

LOBBYING   The inside strategy is often associated with the activity of lobbying. The term **lobbying** arose from the practice by those seeking favours from government or seeking to influence the passage of legislation of congregating in the lobby of the British House of Commons to make their case

NEO-CORPORATISM A political system in which the state actively collaborates with selected major interests (particularly the national organizations of business and labour) to seek a consensus concerning the country's major economic and social policies.

LOBBYING An effort to persuade legislators, executives, or public officials, particularly through direct personal contact, to adopt and implement policies or decisions favoured by an individual, business, or group.

---

[2] Neo-corporatism should be distinguished from the fascist corporate state, which involved authoritarian direction and control of business and labour.

BOX 9-1

Campaigning for a Clean Harbour

Trying to clean up the St. John's harbour has meant dredging up support from far and wide.

The Newfoundland capital was just one of a number of Canadian cities that dump untreated sewage into their harbours. Not only is raw sewage toxic to marine life, it also interferes with the development of the tourist industry and the enjoyment of the harbour. But in the case of St. John's, the substantial cost of building sewage treatment facilities, estimated at $93 million in 1997, was beyond the capability of the city government.

An arrangement to share the costs among the national, provincial, and local governments was worked out in the early 1980s. However, a dispute between the Canadian and Newfoundland governments in 1982 over an unrelated issue (the control of offshore oil) led to the suspension of plans to build a sewage treatment facility. The St. John's city government was subsequently unable to persuade the senior levels of government to carry out their commitments to provide funding.

In 1991, the Canadian government established the Atlantic Canada Action Program (ACAP) to encourage community initiatives, particularly those that would deal with the environmental problems of harbours and coastlines. Based on this, the St. John's Harbour ACAP organization was formed by a group of local citizens. It built on a citizens' group, the Friends of St. John's Harbour, and included representatives of the three levels of government. Partial funding for the organization was provided by Environment Canada.

In addition to carrying out scientific research to document the environmental problems of the harbour, St. John's Harbour ACAP decided that it needed to take political action to clean up the harbour. Its approach involved an outside strategy of mobilizing public support and an inside strategy of collaborating with governments to design the appropriate facilities and negotiate suitable financial arrangements. The group raised the issue in federal, provincial, and municipal elections and kept the public informed of the issue. It lobbied governments and gained the support of local businesses, especially the tourist and convention industries, for its goal.

In 1996, pressure from the St. John's Harbour ACAP helped persuade the three municipal governments in the St. John's area to commit to the project and begin some preliminary work. It was another four years before the provincial government, worried that the Canadian government would not contribute, was persuaded to commit to sharing the costs of the project. The Canadian government was reluctant to commit to the project, fearing that it would be seen as a special handout to one area of the country. Finally, in 2002, as part of a national infrastructure-building program, the Canadian government agreed to provide one-third of the funding.

Although the experience of the St. John's Harbour ACAP suggests that a combined inside/outside strategy is desirable, it has its difficulties. Putting outside pressure on government may result in an antagonistic relationship that may impede efforts to collaborate with government. Although the Canadian government (through Environment Canada) was involved with the formation and activities of St. John's Harbour ACAP, the group had a difficult time persuading the Canadian government to act. On the other hand, an inside strategy of collaborating with government may detract from efforts to mobilize the public support that is often needed to convince governments to act. In this case, over time the two dedicated part-time staff members of the St. John's Harbour ACAP were able to learn the skills of successful interest group activity. They patiently pursued their goal despite years of frustration (Close & Mintz, 2005). In the end they were successful: the primary sewage treatment plant began operations in 2009!

to members of Parliament as they left the legislative chamber. In contemporary usage, lobbying refers to efforts to influence not only legislators, but also those involved in the executive and administrative aspects of government. In particular, lobbying refers to efforts to persuade policy-makers to adopt and implement certain policies or decisions, particularly through direct personal contact.

Lobbying has increasingly become a professionalized activity. In addition to individuals within corporations and interest groups who have developed expertise in lobbying government, a number of consulting firms specialize in lobbying on behalf of a variety of clients, particularly corporations.

Many professional lobbyists are persons who have had high-level experience in government. Their inside knowledge of the workings of government and the thinking of policy-makers, as well as their extensive contacts within government and administration, can make them valuable assets to their clients. However, the revolving door between working in government and working as a lobbyist, as well as the government's hiring of lobbying firms for research and public relations, often leads to ethical questions being raised about whether the relationship between government and lobbyists is too close.

Lobbying often has a very negative image, as it raises the possibility of special deals being worked out in secret to provide benefits, at public expense, to particular individuals, businesses, or groups. Governments in Canada, the United States, and elsewhere have adopted legislation to regulate the activities of lobbyists and to require that lobbyists be registered and publicly disclose some of their activities. It is difficult, however, to ensure that particular interests do not receive unjustified special benefits due to influence exerted behind closed doors. For example, former Canadian Prime Minister Brian Mulroney secretly received envelopes containing several hundred thousand dollars from a notorious influence-peddling lobbyist shortly after leaving office.

INVOLVEMENT IN THE POLICY-MAKING PROCESS   Lobbying is not the only type of "inside" activity engaged in by interest groups. In their interactions with government, many institutionalized interest groups do not simply put forward their demands and pressure government to give them what they want. Interest groups often supply information that government policy-makers need, and work with policy-makers to try to find effective solutions to problems (Montpetit, 2004). The development of government policies is often a product of the discussions among networks of government officials, various interest groups, and experts in a particular policy field. In this situation, interest groups will represent the interest of their members, but as well they will often be involved in trying to find solutions that are acceptable to other interests and to government.

The involvement of interest groups in the policy-making process is often facilitated through the use of "think tanks," non-profit organizations that do policy research and develop policy proposals. The United States has a vast array of think tanks that provide influential policy advice. In Canada, the C.D. Howe Institute and the Fraser Institute have considerable influence on policy discussion and development in Canada. Many think tanks are financed by contributions from the business community. A few, such as the Canadian Centre for Policy Alternatives, are supported by labour unions and individual members.

MOBILIZING PUBLIC SUPPORT   Most interest groups pay some attention to gaining support from the public for their concerns and proposals. For issue-oriented interest groups that have not developed close connections with policy-makers, the "outside" strategy of taking their case to the public may be the only way of effectively influencing public policy. Institutionalized interest groups and individual corporations increasingly seek to create or maintain a good public image to counteract potential public campaigns that might harm their interests.

Mobilizing public support may involve getting the group's message to the public in the hope that a change in public opinion will affect the thinking of policy-makers. In a more active way, interest groups may encourage their members to sign petitions, email their elected representatives, vote for candidates and parties that support their cause, or participate in public demonstrations.

As well, interest groups often try to build coalitions with other interest groups in order to add weight to their claim to speak on behalf of a large number of people on a particular issue. Although some coalitions of groups are only temporary alliances to pursue a particular issue, more permanent groups are often formed to represent the interests of their member groups. For example, the Canadian Council for International Co-operation represents about one hundred organizations seeking to "end global poverty and to promote social justice and human dignity for all."

LEGAL ACTION   Interest groups often make use of the judicial system to advance their interests. For example, environmental groups have had some successes in the courts in forcing the Canadian government to undertake environmental assessments of proposed projects that have potentially negative effects on fish habitats. However, using the court system to pursue interests can be costly. In the past, the Canadian government financed the Court Challenges program to assist equality-seeking groups, particularly women's groups and groups representing linguistic minorities, in challenging laws and policies that are viewed as discriminatory under the provisions of the Canadian Charter of Rights and Freedoms. This program was cancelled by the Conservative government in 2006.

The use of the legal system to pursue interest group objectives is particularly common in the United States, where laws often contain highly specific obligations for government action, and thus provide scope for legal action if the obligations are not fulfilled. In contrast, laws in Canada and elsewhere typically provide considerable discretion to government and administrators in

C.D. Howe Institute
www.cdhowe.org

Fraser Institute
www.fraserinstitute.ca

Canadian Centre for Policy Alternatives
www.policyalternatives.ca

Canadian Council for International Co-operation
www.ccic.ca

determining when and how to carry out the general objectives contained in the law. For example, most environmental laws enable provincial governments or the Canadian government to take action to protect the environment, but do not require that they do so (Boyd, 2003).

Legal actions can also be used to intimidate interest groups. Some corporations have sued public interest groups for millions of dollars based on claims that their reputation has been harmed.

Influence Potential

Interest groups vary in their capabilities to influence public policy. Several factors contribute to the amount of influence a group can exert:

- The size of the group's membership (particularly if it is cohesive) may affect the willingness of politicians to take the group seriously.
- The ability of a group to mobilize its members and supporters and its ability to establish coalitions with other groups to advance its causes are important.
- Financial resources help in maintaining an effective organization, hiring professional lobbyists and political consultants who understand the workings of power and have good contacts with key officials, and conducting research and advertising on behalf of the group's concerns.
- Groups that are able to develop close ties with key government policy-makers are more likely to be influential. This can allow them to get in on the "ground floor" in influencing government as it is developing a policy. Likewise, having allies within government is very helpful.
- Groups that are seen by government, the media, and the public as having expertise and credibility have a strong influence potential.
- Groups whose ideas and proposals coincide with the general thinking of government, the media, and the public are more likely to be successful than groups whose ideas are out of favour or controversial.
- The ability to make credible threats about the adverse consequences of failing to act as the group recommends can be useful.
- A group is more likely to be influential if it does not face powerful competing interest groups in a particular policy area.
- Groups seeking to maintain the status quo are more likely to be successful than those seeking change (Mahoney, 2008).

Although a large number of interest groups have been established in modern liberal democracies, some groups are more influential than others. One study that examined forty-seven different issues in the United States found that trade or business associations and corporations were more likely to have some success in attaining their goals than citizen groups. However, in the very different context of the European Union, the study found that citizen groups were almost as likely as business groups and corporations to have some success (Mahoney, 2008).

The Financial Crisis of 2007–2009

Between 2007 and 2009, many of the largest banks and other financial institutions in the United States and Europe faced bankruptcy, resulting in the worst economic crisis since the Great Depression of the 1930s. Governments felt that these corporations were too big to fail—that is, that their failure could lead to the collapse of the national and global economies. The American government, through various programs (including the US$700 billion Troubled Asset Relief Program), bailed out some leading financial institutions (along with GM and Ford). Governments around the world also initiated major government spending programs (estimated to total $5 trillion) to stimulate failing economies. While successful in preventing a serious economic depression, these efforts resulted in large government deficits and debts.

One of the leading causes of the financial crisis was the deregulation of large financial industry that is the cornerstone of modern economies. Over the past several decades, banks and other financial institutions in the United States were allowed to hide money-losing assets on their financial statements; invest trillions of dollars in complex, highly speculative derivatives rather than in real assets such as houses and manufacturing plants;

decide for themselves how much of their depositors' savings they needed to hold in reserve, and engage in a wave of mergers that created massive financial institutions. From 1998 to 2008, American financial institutions spent more than US$5 billion on political influence, including $1.7 billion in election campaign contributions and $3.4 billion on lobbying federal officials. As of 2007, there were nearly three thousand registered lobbyists working for financial institutions in the United States (Consumer Education Foundation, 2009). Influence was also exerted by the two-way flow of top personnel between the leading financial institutions and the American government, which facilitated the easy access of financial institutions to key policy-makers and regulators (Rothkopf, 2009).

Simon Johnson, the former chief economist of the International Monetary Fund, suggests that the influence of the largest financial institutions was not simply a result of lobbying and campaign contributions. Rather, "the American financial industry gained political power by amassing a kind of cultural capital—a belief system . . . that what was good for Wall Street was good for the country" (Johnson, 2009, p. 2).

It is often argued that business interests have a privileged position from which to influence many aspects of government policy (see Box 9-2, The Financial Crisis of 2007–2009). Business groups and individual large corporations possess considerable financial resources, sources of information, and expertise, and often have close relationships with government that give them considerable influence potential. More fundamentally, the government's desire to retain the confidence of the business community in order to maintain the material well-being of the community means that the interests and policy preferences of business are likely to be highly influential in the development of a wide variety of government policies that affect the activities and profitability of business (Lindblom, 1977). By contrast, the poor and various disadvantaged groups in society often do not have strong and effective interest groups to represent their interests, and their concerns may not be taken as seriously by policy-makers as the interests of business.

SOCIAL MOVEMENTS

SOCIAL MOVEMENT A network of groups and individuals that seeks major social and political changes, particularly by acting outside of established political institutions.

Social movements seek major social and political changes, particularly by acting outside of established political institutions (Martell, 1994). Groups based on social movements may, like other interest groups, seek to change various laws and public policies. However, social movements also have broader goals, such as challenging and transforming the values, power relationships, and institutions of society and politics. A social movement can be thought of as a network of groups and individuals who share a common cause. As well, social movements are often based on, or seek to develop, a sense of collective identity among a substantial segment of society and seek to inspire collective action by this segment of society. For example, the women's movement has sought to raise the consciousness of women not only to increase awareness of the problems women face, but also to create a sense of solidarity among women and to encourage collective action to promote women's values and identity in politics and society.

The distinction between social movements and interest groups is not always clear because many public interest groups originated in, and are associated with, social movements. There are, for example, many environmental interest groups that focus on influencing public policy concerning particular problems. While some members of these groups are concerned only with remedying a specific environmental problem, others view themselves as part of a broader environmental movement that believes that major social, economic, and political changes are needed to deal with environmental problems.

Social Movements & Culture: A Resource Site
http://culturalpolitics.net/social_movements

Old and New Social Movements

Social movements have a lengthy political history going back at least to the beginning of the industrial age in Europe (Heberle, 1951). One of the earliest movements was for the abolition of slavery in Britain in the late eighteenth century (Coupland, 1964). Another early British movement, the Chartists, pressed for the expansion of democratic rights in the 1830s, including the right to vote for all men (Thompson, 1984). Other nineteenth-century movements in various countries sought basic democratic rights for ordinary people (especially the emerging industrial working class), national independence (for example, in Greece and Hungary), and voting and legal rights for women (the suffragette movement).

A wave of protest and discontent that reached its peak in the late 1960s was associated with the development of a variety of new social movements, including the American civil rights movement, the women's movement, the environmental movement, Aboriginal movements, the gay and lesbian movement, the anti-war movement, and various new nationalist movements (including a Quebec nationalist movement). Later, the global social justice movement (often referred to as the anti-globalization movement) developed.

BOX 9-3

The Tea Party Movement

The Tea Party movement that developed in the United States in 2009 is often described as a radical right-wing populist movement. The movement drew its label from the Boston Tea Party (1773) in which American colonists challenging British "taxation without representation" boarded British ships and dumped their cargo of tea into Boston's harbour, an action that helped to inspire the American Revolution.

Tea Party groups arose to challenge "big government"—particularly federal government spending, including the financial stimulus package and bailout of financial institutions introduced to address the financial crisis and recession. The American government's 2010 health care reforms, which require people to purchase health insurance, served as a further irritant among those who considered this to be another threat to individual liberty. Like other social movements, the Tea Party movement mobilized persons with a variety of differing beliefs and perspectives. This includes libertarians who support a pure free-market system and individual freedoms, gun rights advocates, those who advocate abolishing income tax and dismantling social programs, those favouring a returning to the gold standard to prevent the printing of large amounts of paper money, those favouring strict limits on immigration, and states rights advocates, as well as social conservatives who promote traditional Christian moral values. Former Republican vice-presidential candidate Sarah Palin is very popular among Tea Party groups, and supporters of the movement have been active in the Republican party to elect candidates that share their views.

Many of those involved in these movements shared the view that the elites that dominated society and politics needed to be challenged and that major changes in values and institutions were needed to liberate oppressed groups. However, not all social movements are associated with various forms of progressive (leftist) and human rights–oriented politics (see Box 9-3, The Tea Party Movement).

Some of those active in the new social movements had a vision of a "new politics" that differed from conventional politics (Dalton, 2006). In particular, they were critical of the hierarchy and power politics of conventional political organizations and sought to create informal unstructured organizations or networks based on grassroots participation. Likewise, direct action by participants (such as demonstrations, sit-ins, and blockades) is seen as more effective in bringing about substantial change than working through existing political parties and interest groups. By using dramatic actions, activists in the new social movements have been able to gain television coverage for their causes.

The more flexible structures adopted by the new social movements give them real advantages because a broad framework allows a movement to grow and encompass as many people as possible who share its broad objectives. However, this very breadth can harm movements by presenting a confused picture of who they are and what they want.

▶ Some Canadian Aboriginal groups have blockaded railways and highways to draw attention to their grievances.

Changes in Movements

Over time, there is a tendency for organizations based on social movements to become more conventional in nature. The labour and socialist movements that developed in the latter part of the nineteenth century are no longer seen as challenging, unconventional forces in many countries. Likewise, many of the organizations that developed out of the women's and environmental movements have, to a considerable extent, become conventional in their structures and activities. When this happens we speak of the *demobilization, routinization,* or *institutionalization* of a movement (Wilson, 2002). It loses some of its spontaneity and becomes less confrontational in its relations with government. For example, a number of the large environmental organizations in the United States (sometimes referred to as the "Big Ten") became highly institutionalized organizations concerned primarily with fundraising and lobbying government officials. Foundations set up by wealthy business people and, in some cases, individual corporations have provided an important base of financial support, allowing these organizations to hire professional managers to play leading roles in the organizations. For example, over the years the Nature Conservancy has received $10 million from BP (infamous for causing the massive oil spill in the Gulf of Mexico in 2010) while Conservation International received $2 million from BP and in the past included BP's CEO on its board of directors (*The Economist,* 2010, June 5). The leaders of some of the large conservation and environmental organizations have come to prefer working with government and business rather than confrontation. Grassroots activists and local organizations that preferred a tougher stance in defence of the environment tended to be bypassed (Dowie, 1995).

Some view the adoption of conventional interest group strategies as the "selling out" of a movement and its ideals. Others argue that it has increased the possibility of achieving success by influencing the policies of government and business through realistic proposals and by becoming an accepted participant in policy discussions. In some cases, those dissatisfied with the transformation of a movement into more conventional interest groups have established new groups that focus on grassroots mobilization and confrontation. For example, the Sea Shepherd Conservation Society was started by a founder of Greenpeace who favoured more vigorous direct action (such as attacking whaling vessels) and the radical group Earth First! was started by a former Sierra Club employee.

Overall, the continued existence of more "radical" elements within a movement can be useful in preventing the more moderate institutionalized groups from making excessive compromises of the movement's goals and principles. While institutionalized groups may become effective in the policy-making process, it is the more militant thinkers and activists who usually "generate the ideas that ultimately shape political discourse and shift the tides of history" (Bosso, 2005, p. 154). As well, the existence of groups that can mobilize activists in support of a cause can help to provide leverage for the more conventional groups to persuade government to accept their moderate proposals so as to avoid being confronted with more extreme demands and disruptive actions.

Transnational Social Movements

Social movements often migrate across borders and thus can be considered transnational. Older political movements such as the anti-slavery and labour movements were influential in many countries. Some newer social movements such as the women's and environmental movements have global reach, influencing politics in varying ways in many countries in almost all parts of the world as well as seeking to influence various international institutions. For example, organizations associated with the environmental movement such as Greenpeace International, Friends of the Earth International, and the World Wide Fund for Nature have offices and undertake activities in many countries. Although based in the richer countries, they also have a substantial presence in a number of less developed countries. The processes of globalization, particularly advances in communications and transportation, have facilitated the global reach of a number of social movements.

Activities

Those active in social movements often are involved in protest activities because their group has not been successful in achieving its goals through more conventional forms of political activity (see Chapter 10). Nevertheless, those associated with a social movement often establish public interest groups to pursue particular policy objectives related to the vision and perspective of the movement. In addition, some movements have led to the establishment of political parties, including social democratic and labour parties, nationalist parties, and green parties. Other movements, such as the women's movement have exhibited less interest in forming their own political party.[3] Connections of movement activists to different mainstream political parties, beliefs that movement objectives might be better achieved through non-partisan action, a reluctance to expend a movement's energies on electoral politics, and a belief that engagement in party politics will lead to a compromise of the movement's principles often contribute to a reluctance to form a movement-based political party.

THE COMMUNICATIONS MEDIA

The communications media can be considered a major source of political influence. The media not only are important in communicating the concerns and views of various groups and individuals to government, but also have an ability to raise issues, influence both public and politicians, and help shape political debate.

There are differing perspectives about the mass media in contemporary liberal democracies. In the **libertarian perspective**, the media should be free from government control and regulation so that individuals can obtain and assess the information and ideas they want. With different ideas freely competing in a variety of media forums, citizens can use their own judgment as to which ideas are good and which are bad. Further, citizens can use the information provided by the media to hold government accountable for its actions. The **social responsibility perspective** argues that a system of free media does not necessarily result in the public interest being served. In search of profitability, the media may resort to sensationalism rather than live up to their responsibility to be "truthful, accurate, fair, objective and relevant" and to provide a "forum for the exchange of comment and criticism" by the public (McQuail, 1994, p. 124). In this perspective, the media should be a "public trust." This does not necessarily require substantial government regulation or control, but might be achieved through such measures as adopting codes of journalistic ethics, encouraging professionalism among journalists, and establishing press councils to hear citizen complaints about the media (McQuail, 1994). In the **dominant ideology perspective**, "the media serve, and propagandize on behalf of, the powerful societal interests that control and finance them" (Herman &

LIBERTARIAN PERSPECTIVE ON THE MASS MEDIA The idea that if the mass media are free from government control and regulation, individuals will be able to obtain and assess the information and ideas they want.

SOCIAL RESPONSIBILITY PERSPECTIVE ON THE MASS MEDIA The view that the media have a responsibility to the public. Freeing the media from government regulation and control does not necessarily result in the public interest being served.

DOMINANT IDEOLOGY PERSPECTIVE ON THE MASS MEDIA The view that the major media convey the values of the powerful and serve the interests of those who benefit from the status quo.

---

[3] In Iceland, the Women's Alliance elected several female representatives. It later joined with three other leftist parties to form the Social Democratic Alliance, which formed the government in 2009.

Chomsky, 2002, p. 5). Ownership of the mass media by large corporations results in the promotion of capitalist values and the global dominance of capitalist countries rather than facilitating the free exchange of ideas. Reducing or eliminating corporate ownership of the media is needed to serve the common good in this perspective.

Ownership and Regulation

In liberal democracies, newspapers and other print media have usually been privately owned and free of government regulation, except for wartime censorship and the protection of national security. In many countries, there is a mixture of private and public ownership of the broadcast media (radio and television). Fears that privately owned American broadcast networks would move into Canada led to the establishment in 1936 of the Canadian Broadcasting Corporation (CBC), a Crown corporation that is expected to be nonpartisan and independent of government control. Although many European countries began to allow privately owned television stations in the early 1980s, public broadcasting networks are still important. Generally, an independent board appointed by government controls public broadcasting. In several countries, including Germany, Sweden, and the Netherlands, broadcasting is controlled by boards representing different political parties along with business, labour, religious, women's, and other organizations (Norris, 2000). In the United States, government ownership has been avoided; television and radio are almost entirely privately owned and profit-oriented.[4]

CORPORATE OWNERSHIP   In many countries, large corporations now own the majority of mass media outlets. There is a trend toward concentration and cross-media ownership, in which a few large multinational corporations own a variety of different media and related entertainment industries. As a result, the diversity of the mass media has been substantially reduced. Media outlets that are part of large corporate empires may be less likely to report on problems occurring with other branches of the corporation. As well, there may be expectations that the media will promote the interests of their corporate owners (see Box 9-4, Italy: Television and Political Power).

The ownership of much of the mass media by large corporations may result in a bias toward defending and promoting the interests of big business and the values of the capitalist system. Media owners tend to be conservative and oriented to the dominant interests in society. Their choice of executives to run their media outlets will likely reflect, at least to some extent, their ideological orientation. On the other hand, as profit-oriented enterprises, media corporations

---

[4] The non-profit, non-governmental Corporation for Public Broadcasting is responsible for the Public Broadcasting Service (PBS) and National Public Radio (NPR), both of which are small networks that rely primarily on private and corporate donations for their funding.

Italy: Television and Political Power

The Italian government used to have monopoly control of television, with each of the three public networks basically under the control of different political parties. Oversight boards helped to ensure that the public networks were generally impartial.

A 1976 ruling by the country's Constitutional Court changed all that by opening the way for private broadcasters. By the end of the 1980s, billionaire Silvio Berlusconi had gained control of private television, with his holding company Fininvest owning the three major private networks. In 1994, as the leading Italian political parties collapsed due to a major corruption scandal, Berlusconi led his newly formed Forza Italia party to electoral victory. While the public networks were more balanced in their coverage, Berlusconi's television networks devoted much of their campaign coverage to his party's candidates, thus contributing to the victory of Forza Italia and its allies. Subsequently, the management of the public networks was purged and replaced by Berlusconi supporters (Marletti & Roncarolo, 2000). During the 2006 Italian election, Berlusconi's television networks were fined four times by the independent communications authority for being biased in favour of Berlusconi's party. His coalition narrowly lost that election but was returned to power in 2008.

will normally want to attract as large an audience as possible. This may involve avoiding political stances that offend segments of the public and presenting different viewpoints. In addition, journalists and reporters tend to be less conservative than many of the owners and managers of the mass media (Alterman, 2003; Croteau, 1998; Miljan & Cooper, 2003). Nevertheless, the owners and executives still exercise some control over what is reported. Further, some mass media, such as right-wing Fox News (part of Rupert Murdoch's immense global media empire, News Corporation), take a clearly ideological stance. Other media, while trying to give the appearance of objectivity and neutrality, often have more subtle biases. In addition, the dependence of the media on advertising revenues may lead to pressure on the media to avoid or downplay stories that reflect negatively on their major advertisers. Indeed, some interest groups have been able to affect the media by threatening to boycott advertisers if a certain show was broadcast. For example, conservative groups persuaded CBS not to air the docudrama *The Reagans*.

REGULATION   The broadcast media are regulated, to varying extents in different countries, by government or a government-appointed agency to try to ensure that they act in the public interest. In some countries this has involved requirements that a certain amount of time be devoted to news and public affairs programming. Canadian broadcast regulations require that radio and television stations carry a substantial proportion of Canadian content. The broadcast media in many countries are required to be non-partisan and to provide balanced coverage of politics particularly during election campaigns. The Internet has thus far generally avoided regulation (although some non-democratic countries, including China, Iran, and Myanmar, try to block access to many sites and prosecute those who post comments critical of the government).

Objectivity

When an independent commercial press that appealed to the mass public developed in North America in the late nineteenth century, journalists began to view themselves as professionals conveying the objective truth to the public. Editors expected writers to report only the facts without exaggeration, interpretation, or opinion (Hackett & Zhao, 1998). A sharp distinction was made between fact and opinion, with opinions relegated to the editorial page. However, the "facts" do not necessarily speak for themselves. Without background and interpretation, the facts may be largely meaningless for much of the public. Indeed, since the "facts" often come from official sources, the attempt to appear objective has been viewed by some analysts as reflecting a bias in favour of the dominant political forces (Hackett & Zhao, 1998). As well, since reporting inevitably involves selectivity in deciding what to report, objectivity may be impossible to achieve fully.

The ideal of objectivity has not disappeared but, as Robert Hackett and Yuezhi Zhao (1998) point out, it has tended to be treated in the broader sense of allowing background and interpretation, provided that reporters attempt to be impartial, fair, and balanced. However, the interpretation of a news story often involves a subtle form of selectivity known as **framing**: "selecting and highlighting some facets of events or issues, and making connections among them so as to promote a particular interpretation, evaluation, and/or solution" (Entman, 2004, p. 5). For example, during the invasion of Iraq in 2003, the media in the United States framed the story in terms of an effort to liberate Iraqis from an evil dictator who possessed weapons of mass destruction. Alternative interpretations were largely ignored for several years.

FRAMING Selecting and highlighting some facets of events or issues, and making connections among them so as to promote a particular interpretation, evaluation, and/ or solution.

To achieve the appearance of fairness, reporters are expected to seek reaction to a government leader's statement from opposition party spokespersons. When an issue is considered controversial, both sides are often presented. However, this means that complex issues may be simplified into a "pro/con" format, ignoring the reality that there may be more than two sides to an issue. The media may only find it necessary to provide balanced treatment to issues that are matters of dispute among contending political parties. Viewpoints and positions that reflect the leading values of society may go unquestioned. As well, the experts called upon to provide comment and analysis of issues often come from established institutions and organizations, including business-supported think tanks.

The Media as Watchdogs?

The media are often expected not only to provide the political information needed by the public to choose among the contending parties, but also to play a watchdog role. By bringing to public attention abuses of power or the failure of governments to deal with important problems, the media can help to check the power of government and assist citizens in pressuring government to correct problems.

Critics of the mass media argue that the contemporary mass media have often turned from watchdogs into attack dogs by mounting sharp personal attacks on politicians and other prominent persons. Political scientist Larry Sabato (1992) described American journalists as being like sharks engaging in a "feeding frenzy" when they publicize rumours and gossip about politicians and celebrities. For example, the media were obsessed with American President Bill Clinton's relationship with Monica Lewinsky, to the point of obscuring important national and international issues. Likewise, presidential candidate John Edwards was hounded by the media during the 2008 Democratic party primaries about his affair with Rielle Hunter. More generally, the media have a tendency to take an aggressive, confrontational approach to political personalities, perhaps as a reaction to the efforts of governments and political parties to try to manipulate the media (Nadeau & Giasson, 2003).

The prevalence of critical and negative journalism should not be exaggerated. The media can also be seen, to some extent, as lapdogs. There is often a cozy relationship between government and journalists, and much of what constitutes news originates from official sources. In the past, some politicians would hand out cash to journalists in order to encourage them to give favourable treatment to a press release. To this day, some journalists may be influenced by the hope of obtaining employment within government, receiving extra income through speech writing or ghostwriting a book for a politician, or gaining access to gather material for a popular biography of a prominent political figure.

More importantly, journalists who are viewed as sympathetic to the government are more likely to be given the inside story, an exclusive interview with a leading political figure, or a "leak" about an impending government announcement. Even though contemporary journalists generally prefer to avoid too close a relationship with politicians, they rely on politicians and government officials for information to make sense of what is happening within government and to provide anecdotes and gossip for an interesting story. With pressure to report the news as quickly as possible and with media owners trying to produce news at the lowest possible cost, journalists often lack the capability and resources to properly research the news stories they are presenting.

Furthermore, media watchdogs are sometimes asleep or muzzled. For example, the pattern of systematic physical, sexual, and cultural abuse of generations of Aboriginals forced to attend residential schools across Canada did not receive media scrutiny until long after the schools were closed. Likewise, in the case of physical and sexual abuse of boys by the Christian Brothers at the Mount Cashel Orphanage in St. John's, Newfoundland, the leading provincial newspaper apparently suppressed the story under influence from the hierarchy of the Catholic Church and other community leaders (Harris, 1991).

Walking the Dog: News Management

Governments and politicians often try to manage the news so as to avoid gaining negative treatment. **News management**—controlling and shaping the presentation of information—includes such techniques as issuing news releases close to news deadlines so that journalists cannot check the facts or obtain critical comments. Information that reflects negatively on government is often released when a more dramatic news event is occurring, or during the summer and on weekends when many journalists are not working and audiences are small.

Politicians and their media advisers are very concerned with controlling the "spin" put on what they have said—that is, trying to ensure that a favourable interpretation is placed on information. For example, during a leaders' debate, "spin doctors" for each party will try to persuade journalists that their leader has won the debate and explain away any mistakes that their leader has made. The Harper government has been particularly concerned with news management, requiring that every government event, press release, and speech by ministers, Conservative MPs, and senior public servants be scripted to present a consistent, positive image and be approved by the Prime Minister's Office or the Privy Council Office.

To avoid unfavourable framing of their proposals and actions, governments spend large sums of money on advertising to carry their message directly to the public. Although some government advertising is designed to increase awareness of government services and programs, governments have also mounted substantial advertising campaigns to promote their perspective on particular issues, boast about their accomplishments, and present themselves in a positive light.[5]

News management by government is most clearly seen in times of war and, more generally, in much of the coverage of international affairs. The mass media often consider it unpatriotic to question their government's decision to go to war and feel obliged to support their country's troops. Government officials and military leaders usually try to control the media tightly during a foreign conflict and may plant false stories about enemy atrocities.

NEWS MANAGEMENT The controlling and shaping of the presentation of news in order to affect the public's evaluation of news stories.

---

[5] According to Rose and Mellon (2010), Ontario's Government Advertising Act, 2004 is the world's first legislation that regulates government advertising by prohibiting partisan advertising and requiring that all provincial government ads be approved by the independent Office of the Auditor General of Ontario.

▶ In April 2004, investigative reporter Seymour Hersh published articles in *The New Yorker* magazine that included pictures illustrating the abuse and torture of Iraqis in the Abu Ghraib prison. This brought to public attention the evidence of abuse that had been largely ignored by the mainstream media.

The Media and Democracy

Debate exists about whether the mass media provide the political information that is needed for people to participate meaningfully in political life, make intelligent choices among parties and candidates, and hold those in public office accountable for their actions. Citizens require not only a set of facts, but also sufficient background and explanations and diverse opinions about what should be done in order to make sense of political issues.

The growth of the communications media in recent decades has greatly increased the amount of political information that is potentially available to the public. However, criticisms are often raised about the quality of information that the ordinary person obtains from the media. Because the mass media need to attract large audiences to be profitable, they tend to focus on providing entertainment to their audiences. Not only may this mean that news and public affairs programming is given limited resources, it can also result in the merging of information with entertainment. This combination, labelled **infotainment**, is particularly evident in the focus of television newscasts on stories that can be portrayed with dramatic images. As the cynical saying puts it, "If it bleeds, it leads."

For example, Arthur Kent, the Canadian-born journalist who reported on the 1991 Gulf War for American television network NBC, was critical

INFOTAINMENT The merging of information and entertainment in news and public affairs programming of the mass media, particularly television.

◀ Do the media keep us informed about politics?

of NBC and other networks for refusing to run serious stories about foreign affairs. Kent was fired as a result of his outspoken criticisms. However, during his successful lawsuit against NBC, network executives testified that news coverage was affected by a concern to broadcast entertaining stories (Kent, 1996).

Stories that can be portrayed in terms of conflict and controversy receive the most attention. News items have become increasingly short to discourage bored viewers from switching to a different channel. Statements and comments by politicians, experts, or ordinary people are edited to a single, snappy sound bite lasting only a few seconds. It is difficult, if not impossible, to explain an issue meaningfully in the sixty seconds that may be allotted to a television news story. Television news thus tends to be simplistic, and does not generally provide the context or historical background needed to understand the events that it portrays (Postman, 1985). Further, "shock talk" radio programs that feature inflammatory and misleading diatribes that are often racist, homophobic, and misogynist have become popular, particularly in the United States.

Alternative Media

The Internet has provided a vehicle for the expression of diverse political viewpoints and the presentation of information and issues not covered by the conventional media. To some extent, this has democratized the media as ordinary individuals report on events by placing videos on YouTube and disseminating their opinions on blogs and social media. Further, it has become much easier to access a variety of conventional media through their online content. On the other hand, the Internet has also become a vehicle for conspiracy theories, malicious gossip, and the expression of hatred directed at different groups and individuals. Not only is there much misinformation online, but the conventional media have tended to reduce their fact checking as they rush to get stories out quickly to remain relevant.

It is unclear how long the Internet will maintain its libertarian character. Some countries try to filter and censor Internet content. Even in countries where the Internet remains unrestricted, those promoting hatred on the Internet have been prosecuted, security forces have investigated those associated with websites deemed to have some connection to terrorism, and corporations and individuals have begun legal action against those posting material claimed to be libellous or defamatory. As employers screen job applicants by "googling" them, politicians seek to find "dirt" on their opponents, and the websites we visit become tracked and recorded, the public nature of the Internet could have a chilling effect on free expression. In addition, control of the Internet has become concentrated in a small number of huge multinational corporations that may find it in their interest to screen postings.

Summary and Conclusion

The freedom to organize into groups to express one's views and try to affect governing is a crucial element of liberal democracy. Interest groups potentially allow people to try to influence what government does on a day-to-day basis, not just on the infrequent occasions when elections occur. They convey the views, opinions, and problems of various elements of society to government and to other citizens on a regular basis. As well, interest groups often supply government with useful information, research, and advice, and some interest groups are directly involved with government in developing public policies. The development of a large number of public interest groups has challenged the dominance of business influence. Nevertheless, some elements of society are better organized and more influential than others. Large corporations continue to have considerable influence.

Interest groups have sometimes been criticized as threats to the common good and as undemocratic.

Many interest groups seek special privileges for their members or for particular segments of society—privileges that may work against the interests of society as a whole. With a wide variety of groups seeking special privileges, who is concerned about the well-being of the country as a whole? For example, many business groups seek tax breaks or subsidies for their particular sector of the economy. However, if government satisfies these demands, it may mean that the population as a whole will have to pay higher taxes or suffer reduced government services.

Social movements have often developed among segments of society that have been treated unfairly and ignored by government and conventional political institutions, and among those who believe that major changes in society and politics are needed. Even in democratic countries, the conventional channels for achieving desired goals are not always effective, and thus social movements often feel the need to use unconventional means to carry their message to the public and to government.

Finally, the communications media are also very important in the processes of political influence. Not only can they affect the political agenda of government by raising or highlighting issues, but they may affect the general political values and beliefs that are present in a political community. Although the media are often viewed as important in holding the government accountable for its actions, they are also a vehicle for government to try to influence the public. The concentration of media ownership in the hands of large corporations raises concerns about whether this leads to a bias in favour of corporate interests. In addition, the promotion of ideological perspectives favourable to business may affect the thinking of the public and the government and thus be an important, though often subtle, form of general political influence.

Key Terms

Discussion Questions

1. What interest groups are you a member of? Do you think that they reflect your views? Can they be considered democratic in the way they operate?

2. Are interest groups a threat to democracy and the common good?

3. What are the most important factors affecting the success or failure of interest groups and social movements?

4. Do the mass media provide you with a good, unbiased understanding of political issues?

5. Does the Internet provide a means to overcome the problems of the mass media? Should the Internet be regulated by government?

Further Reading

Bennett, W.L., Lawrence, R.G., & Livingston, S. (2007). *When the press fails: Political power and the news media from Iraq to Katrina.* Chicago: University of Chicago Press.

Berry, J.M., & Wilcox, C. (2007). *The interest group society* (4th ed.). New York: Pearson Longman.

Hallin, D.C., & Mancini, P. (2004). *Comparing media systems: Three models of media and politics.* Cambridge, UK: Cambridge University Press.

Herman, E.S., & Chomsky, N. (2002). *Manufacturing consent* (updated ed.). New York: Pantheon Books.

Jordan, G., & Maloney, W.A. (2007). *Democracy and interest groups: Enhancing participation?* Houndmills, UK: Palgrave Macmillan.

Macdonald, D. (2007). *Business and environmental politics in Canada.* Peterborough, ON: Broadview Press.

Moran, M. (2009). *Business, politics and society: An Anglo-American comparison.* Oxford: Oxford University Press.

Nesbitt-Larking, P. (2001). *Politics, society, and the media: Canadian perspectives.* Peterborough, ON: Broadview Press.

Pross, A.P. (1993). *Group politics and public policies* (2nd ed.). Toronto: Oxford University Press.

Rothkopf, D. (2009). *Superclass: The global power elite and the world they are making.* Toronto: Penguin Canada.

Sampert, S., & Trimble, L. (Eds.). (2010). *Mediating Canadian politics.* Toronto: Pearson Education Canada.

Shaiko, R.G. (1999). *Voices and echoes for the environment: Public interest representation in the 1990s and beyond.* New York: Columbia University Press.

Smith, J., & Johnston, H. (Eds.). (2002). *Globalization and resistance: Transnational dimensions of social movements.* Lanham, MD: Rowman & Littlefield.

Smith, M. (2005). *A civil society? Collective actors in Canadian political life.* Peterborough, ON: Broadview Press.

Taras, D. (2001). *Power and betrayal in the Canadian media* (updated ed.). Peterborough, ON: Broadview Press.

Young, L., & Everitt, J. (2004). *Advocacy groups.* Vancouver: UBC Press.

Chapter 10

Unconventional and Highly Conflictive Politics: From Protest to Revolution

PHOTO ABOVE: Thailand's Red Shirts, supporters of former Prime Minister Thaksin Shinawatra who was ousted in a military coup in 2006, occupy downtown Bangkok to demand the resignation of Prime Minister Abhisit Vejjajiva and the holding of an election.

CHAPTER OBJECTIVES

After reading this chapter you should be able to:

1. describe what political protest is and why people use protest as a political tool
2. discuss why not all political protest is democratic
3. understand why protest is an integral part of democratic politics
4. distinguish between insurgency and counter-insurgency
5. describe the characteristics of terrorism
6. discuss whether political violence is ever justifiable

On March 16, 2010, thousands of Thais, all dressed in red T-shirts (thus called the Red Shirts), marched on the home of the country's prime minister, Abhisit Vejjajiva. Once there, several dozen demonstrators were allowed through a police blockade to throw plastic bags full of human blood donated by the protesters against the walls of the residence. The protesters viewed the Abhisit government as illegitimate and were trying to pressure it to resign. Three weeks later, on April 10, Thailand's government moved to expel the protesters, causing twenty-five deaths. The Red Shirts quickly regrouped and occupied an upscale section of Bangkok on April 15. Then, on May 19, after the Red Shirts had maintained their occupation for more than a month, the Thai army moved to disperse the protesters with force. This time, the resulting violence left 83 dead and some 1800 injured ("Thailand: Timeline to conflict," 2010).

This was the latest instalment in a series of protests that began in 2006 after a military coup (the eighteenth in Thailand since 1932) overthrew Prime Minister Thaksin Shinawatra. Since then, Thailand has seen red-clad supporters of Thaksin, backed by the United Front for Democracy Against Dictatorship (UDD) and the Democratic Alliance Against Dictatorship (DAAD), occasionally clash with yellow-shirted demonstrators (called the Yellow Shirts) drawn from the People's Alliance for Democracy (PAD), who oppose Thaksin. In 2008, the Yellow Shirts occupied Bangkok's airports, disrupting hundreds of flights.

Both groups have grievances that have not been met through regular governmental processes. Each has developed a repertoire of protest behaviour built around mass demonstrations and has a clear identity, marked by the colour of the T-shirts its adherents wear. Further, both sides employ powerful symbols to help legitimate their claims: yellow is the colour of royalty in Thailand, while the Red Shirts wanted to spill blood to symbolize the depth of their opposition to the current government ("Thai protesters hurl blood," 2010).

The Red Shirts, Thaksin's backers, are drawn mainly from the ranks of the poor, especially the rural poor, and from the country's less developed north. Thus they have come to represent the political left, those who call for changes to produce greater social and political equality. The Yellow Shirts come from the middle and upper classes and Thailand's better-off south. These people had supported the coup against Thaksin, whose administration was seen as corrupt. The Yellow Shirts are therefore identified with the political right, those who support the status quo and accept as tolerable the inequalities it produces. In Thailand, the coup-prone army has historically backed the political right, as it did again in 2010.

Both sets of protesters in Thailand are practising *contentious politics*. That is, they are making their claims on government or against their opponents through disruptive, direct, and highly conflictive means. Their methods have ranged from peaceful political protest to violent confrontation. This particular protest resulted in violence when the government decided that force was required to end the Red Shirts' occupation of downtown Bangkok and restore political stability to the country. Although we generally think that such highly contentious politics are unusual, especially when they result in violence, in this chapter we discover that they are relatively common and have often been the only way in which democracy could grow.

POLITICAL CONFLICT: PROTEST TO REVOLUTION

To Canadians, political conflict often means Question Period in the House of Commons or a candidates' debate during an election campaign. At its broadest, **political conflict** refers to a state of opposition: someone objects to what someone else is doing or proposes to do. The "someone else" is often the government but can also be groups or individuals who hold positions on public issues different from one's own. Political conflict in Canada frequently takes place within formal governmental institutions, staying within the limits of the law, and is usually peaceful. However, in other settings political conflict can be violent, involving resort to arms. This chapter discusses political conflict that goes on outside formal governmental institutions. That conflict is often disruptive and sometimes violent, but it is a form of political participation. We will examine several types of political conflict: political protest, insurgency and guerrilla war, terrorism, and revolution.

The term *political protest* might conjure up images of helmeted police and rock-throwing demonstrators, but it can also suggest people picketing peacefully in front of city hall or organizing a petition. **Political protest** can be defined as oppositional political action that takes place outside formal channels, generally seeking to have government make significant changes in its policies. Political protest takes many forms (see Figure 10-1). The most moderate of these methods include petitions, legally approved demonstrations, and voluntary boycotts of certain products or firms. Non-violent direct action—for example, civil disobedience, illegal demonstrations, or peaceful occupation of a building or office—is a stronger form of protest. It involves illegal activities but is not violent, as is best exemplified by **civil disobedience**: deliberate lawbreaking that accepts punishment by state authorities as part of the action. This was the strategy chosen by Mahatma Gandhi in India from the 1920s to the 1940s to gain independence from the British Empire, and by Martin Luther King in the United States in the 1950s and 1960s (discussed in Box 10-1, The Civil Rights Movement, on page 245).

Very different is protest that involves violence. Sometimes violence is an unintended consequence of a march or boycott, but it can also be used intentionally as a provocation. In other instances, violence is chosen as the best way to secure a political objective. Assassinations, **guerrilla warfare**, **insurgencies**, **revolutions**, and **terrorism** fall into this category.

Seeking Change

People do not protest, let alone turn to political violence, for no reason. Protest is a means to seek political change. It usually is employed only after conventional approaches, such as lobbying, have failed. In non-democratic systems, though, it may be the only way to get change. This does not mean that everyone involved in a protest or who has joined a protest movement has personally tried other means or would even support trying them. Rather, it points to the most common sequence of events.

POLITICAL CONFLICT A state of opposition, usually involving groups and the state, over something government is doing or proposes to do.

POLITICAL PROTEST Oppositional political action that takes place outside formal channels, generally seeking to have government make significant changes in its policies.

CIVIL DISOBEDIENCE Deliberate lawbreaking that accepts punishment by state authorities as part of the action.

GUERRILLA WARFARE A form of highly political warfare built around lightly armed irregulars who oppose a government and use hit-and-run tactics and political work to take power.

INSURGENCY A rebellion or revolt, especially one employing the tools of guerrilla warfare.

REVOLUTION The use of violence to overthrow a government, especially when the overthrow is followed by rapid, thoroughgoing social, economic, and political restructuring.

TERRORISM The deliberate use of violence designed to induce fear in a population in order to achieve a political objective.

FIGURE 10-1
**THE CONTINUUM OF
PROTEST**

INSTITUTIONAL	MODERATE PROTEST	DIRECT ACTION	VIOLENCE
Voting	Petitions	Unofficial strikes	Unintentional
Lobbying	Legal demonstrations	Illegal demonstrations	Throw rocks,
Interest groups	Boycotts	Peaceful occupations	break windows
		Civil disobedience	Guerrilla warfare
			Assassination
			Terrorism

SOURCE: *Adapted with modifications from Dalton (2006, p. 65).*

ANALYZING CONTENTIOUS POLITICS

To most people, seeking the common good suggests reasoned deliberation and debate, which are hallmarks of democratic politics. However, democracy did not grow just through the use of reason and polite persuasion. Those who hold power, the elite, are rarely keen to see their power diminished. Thus logic has often needed to be supplemented by more **contentious politics**—the usually disruptive, direct, and highly conflictive ways that people advance their claims on elites, authorities, and opponents, ranging from peaceful political protest to wars and other lethal conflicts (Tilly & Tarrow, 2007).

CONTENTIOUS POLITICS
The usually disruptive, direct, and highly conflictive ways that people advance their claims on elites, authorities, and opponents, ranging from peaceful political protest to wars and other lethal conflicts.

Political protest is political action because it aims to affect how public issues are treated. It is oppositional political action because those who protest want government to change its policies. This can mean that a government starts to do something it does not do now, stops doing something it now does, or takes action instead of doing nothing. However, oppositional activity is immensely varied and does not always include protest. We reserve the label *protest* for political actions with the following characteristics:

1. Actions take place outside of formal channels.
2. They are usually carried out by individuals or groups that are not ordinarily important political actors.
3. Protest politics generally aims to have government make significant changes in the policies it pursues.

We will look at each of these three traits separately.

Politics outside Formal Channels

Whether in dictatorships or democracies, politics works in set patterns. There are rules you are expected to follow to get something done. They may not always be formal written rules, but rather norms or unofficial standards. In either case, being politically effective and getting what you want usually requires following those rules and working within channels.

Playing by the rules benefits both governments and the groups and individuals that regularly deal with government. It obviously helps governments because they set the rules. However, keeping within channels also works well for those who deal regularly with government because they master the rules and can use them to their own benefit. But what if going through channels does not produce any results? In that case, there are two options: accept your fate or go outside channels.

When people have an issue that is very important to them, they are not likely to be satisfied with accepting defeat graciously. This is true even when the defeat comes as a result of a democratic process and reflects the will of the majority. Such an outcome is especially likely where the claimants belong to some permanent minority (for example, an ethnic or religious group) that the majority or government has consciously marginalized. Ordinary democracy may not work for those who can never become a majority.

"Unimportant" Actors or Issues

Protest is sometimes called the tool of the marginalized—people without the resources needed to gain political influence. We usually think of political influence as the ability to shape decisions, the ability to control large blocks of votes, or having a lot of money or particularly valuable information. Having these resources makes an individual or group valuable to government, and governments often accommodate those who are valuable to them. Prospects are bleak for those groups or individuals with scarce resources unless they too make themselves important to government.

Beginning in the 1960s, political scientists began to see protest as a political resource (Lipsky, 1968). Protest disrupts government's routines, making the authorities at least see that something is happening. Although government officials often characterize protest as lawlessness, they still know that some part of their community feels strongly enough about an issue to take to the streets. In reality, the marginalized may have little option but to use protest. Largely invisible to those in power before they begin to protest, those on the outside frequently find that the rules of the game do not work for them. However, once a protest movement has caught the authorities' attention, perhaps through a high media profile, it can then mobilize other resources, including the support of some politicians, and further enhance their status.

Marginalization does not refer only to the dispossessed and literally disenfranchised. Issues, too, can be marginalized and only appear on the government's agenda after supporters take extraordinary measures. This explains the apparently contradictory phenomenon of the well-educated, middle-class-or-higher protester (Dalton, 2006) whose activity has been notable from the anti–Vietnam War movement of the 1960s to today's anti-globalization demonstrations. Although these individuals may have other resources that they

MARGINALIZATION Exclusion from the mainstream.

can use to influence government, those resources may not work for a given issue. Thus, protest is another resource that the politically active can add to their arsenals (Opp, 1989). Yet even if protest is often the only tool of the marginalized, sometimes the well placed use it as a tactic to get what they want.

CHALLENGES AND BENEFITS OF ORGANIZING   We should not think, however, that mobilizing people to undertake political protest is the easiest way to enter politics. As discussed in Chapter 9, there is the problem of organizing people to act collectively. It may be rational for a person not to participate in a protest, but rather to wait on the sidelines to see what it accomplishes. These *free riders* share the benefits of other's labour without having to do any work or take any risks.

Beyond the matter of getting people to join, movements engaged in protest activities cannot know how government will respond to their demands. There is no guarantee that time and energy invested in building a movement and organizing protest actions will change the status quo and advance a group's vision of the common good. Nevertheless, over the years, Canadians have seen workers, farmers, women, fishers, Quebec nationalists, Aboriginals, gays and lesbians, and anti-abortion activists use political protest to put themselves and their causes on the public agenda. Many of these groups became regular parts of the political process, and today governments, whether federal or provincial, generally do not question the right of these groups to have a voice in policy-making. Whether events would have turned out this way had the groups not protested is impossible to determine. What we do know is that protest advanced their causes substantially.

Gay and Lesbian Emergence: Out in Canada (CBC Archives)
http://archives.cbc.ca/politics/rights_freedoms/topics/599/

Riseup.net (contemporary progressive movements)
http://lists.riseup.net

Seeking Significant Change

Protesters usually believe that there is something terribly wrong that only government action can correct. Yet they also believe that the ordinary mechanisms of political pressure have failed, leaving protest as their last chance to be heard. This is why protest has been used to gain political rights for the excluded, to try to end wars, and to make absolutely clear the opposition of some part of the citizenry to some government policy. Protest is about changing what government does, and people have taken action to seek political change for a very long time.

PROTEST AND POLITICAL CHANGE

In general, then, people protest because they perceive what Clark, Grayson, and Grayson (1976, p. 3) call "institutional deficiencies"—they think that something is not working right and has to be fixed. Those who decide to protest may risk imprisonment and still not gain their objective. Nevertheless, political protest has secured some dramatic results and contributed greatly to strengthening democracy. In Canada, for example:

- *Women's right to vote.* Until the late 1800s, women everywhere were denied basic political rights. It was only in the twentieth century that political equality between men and women became a generally accepted principle of democratic life. The first step toward equality for women was winning the right to vote. Although we now find it unthinkable that women did not have the same political rights as men, it took Canadian women more than fifty years to gain the right to vote in all provinces. Along the way, the proponents of women's suffrage (women's right to vote) lobbied governments and used various forms of protest, such as staging mock parliamentary debates, to demonstrate that they could argue as persuasively and as rationally as men (Cleverdon, 1974).

- *Making farmers' voices heard.* Farmers in Canada in the late nineteenth and early twentieth centuries felt excluded from power and sought to change the political system to better reflect their needs (Lipset, 1950; Macpherson, 1954; Morton, 1950). Unlike the movement for women's suffrage, farmers' movements decided that they needed to form new political parties. Although farmers were then the largest occupational group in the country, they had little influence. Farmers felt that the parties that existed at the time, the Conservatives and Liberals, ignored their views and listened only to the demands of big business. The parties the farmers' movements founded (United Farmers, Progressives, Co-operative Commonwealth Federation [CCF]) or supported (Social Credit) sought to represent the views of not just farmers, but all ordinary working people against the concentrated power of corporate interests. Although none of these parties ever won power federally, several of them governed provinces. Moreover, a number of them created Crown corporations (government-owned enterprises) that brought electricity and telephone service to many parts of rural Canada. One, the CCF, set up the country's first Medicare system in Saskatchewan.

Votes for women and more political power for farmers were issues that Canada's political establishment of a century past would not put on the public agenda. For these two marginalized groups to have their demands heard, they had to move outside the usual political channels. The mechanisms of ordinary democracy had served them badly, but political protest benefited them and democracy well. Yet we should recall that it took women decades of hard work to win the vote and the CCF's election as Saskatchewan's government in 1944 came 12 years after the party's founding. Protest is not a magic potion that confers immediate success on those who use it.

In fact, there are many cases where protest fails. Canada's peace movement has been active for years but it could not halt the testing of cruise missiles in Alberta in the 1980s and similarly has had little impact on decisions to send troops to Afghanistan. Outside Canada, the record is similar. A study of attempts by poor black citizens of Newark, New Jersey, to use protest to claim their rights and gain power showed how those in power frustrated the protesters at every turn (Parenti, 1970). Similarly, women fighting for the vote in Britain in the early 1900s turned to violence after being consistently rebuffed by government. They smashed the windows of elegant shops along London's Regent Street and, when arrested, they began hunger strikes. The authorities responded with force feeding and, eventually, used the "Cat and Mouse Law": a woman was allowed to starve herself until her health deteriorated. She was then released but would be jailed again on regaining her health. In the end, British women won the vote not due to their protest but rather for their contribution to Britain's efforts in World War I, and even then they did not have the same voting rights as men until 1928 (Castle, 1987).

PROTEST IN DEMOCRACY

Some argue that political protest does not have a place in a democracy. They hold that people have the right to make their feelings known in elections, to work through their elected representatives, and to pressure government. Not everyone gets what they want, but that is not cause to go outside fair, well-known rules and procedures. If you fail to get what you want by working through regular democratic processes, it indicates that you are simply too weak or are pursuing goals that the majority rejects. Rather than protest, you should change your objectives and build a broader base.

The crux of this argument is the belief that democratic politics does not contain any biases. Although this view underlies our most basic beliefs about democracy, it is not entirely accurate. There are certainly many instances in which following established democratic procedures did not help the weak and marginalized. This was the case for African-Americans who turned to protest to challenge the discriminatory system of **segregation** (see Box 10-1, The Civil Rights Movement).

Opportunity Structures

Protest movements have sometimes been able to use more conventional political actions because of the opportunities offered by their political systems. **Political opportunity structures (POS)** refer to the openings that political institutions and processes offer to or withhold from movements (Kitschelt, 1986; Tarrow, 1999). For example, the farmers' movement in Canada was able to build political parties and win power because our electoral system and system of parliamentary government, as well as the fact that farmers formed a majority of voters in several provinces, made this a workable option. More recently, **secessionists** in Quebec have used the same strategy with some success because the supporters of Quebec's independence could unite behind a single separatist party and gain control of the Quebec government.

SEGREGATION The legal separation of blacks and whites, particularly in the southern United States.

POLITICAL OPPORTUNITY STRUCTURES (POS) The openings that political institutions and processes offer to or withhold from movements.

SECESSIONIST A person who favours separation of a territory from an existing state.

BOX 10-1

The Civil Rights Movement

The U.S. civil rights movement is one of the most famous examples of how people without power were failed by the democratic process.

Although Abraham Lincoln declared the abolition of slavery in 1863, for the next century African-Americans suffered systemic discrimination. Conditions were worst in the southern states where segregation, the legal separation of races, was in force. This meant that black children and white children went to different schools, that blacks and whites could not use the same restrooms or drinking fountains, and that blacks even had to give up their seats on buses to whites.

Throughout the first half of the twentieth century, African-Americans worked patiently through their country's courts to have segregation legislation declared unconstitutional. Although they had some significant victories, such as *Brown v. Board of Education,* 1954, which declared segregated education unconstitutional, actually getting states to change their laws proved difficult. Despite a constitutional provision adopted in 1870 establishing that the right to vote cannot be denied on account of race or colour, various means such as literacy tests were used to prevent most African-Americans from voting.

Clearly, the normal channels of influence were of little use in trying to change discriminatory laws and policies. Protest action by the civil rights movement was needed to pressure governments to treat African-Americans fairly. They then would appeal their convictions for violating discriminatory laws to a higher court, arguing that the law they broke

The greatest American proponent of civil disobedience was Dr. Martin Luther King, Jr. (1929–1968), a Baptist minister who lived in the South.

actually violated the constitution and should have no force.

Sit-ins were one of the most effective tactics used by the civil rights movement. Black students would sit in the section of a restaurant or lunch counter that was reserved for whites. They would be refused service and told to leave, but would stay until arrested. Eventually this practice mobilized public opinion in the United States behind the civil rights movement, and legislation outlawing segregation followed.

Had African-Americans tried to keep working within the rules, as they had for many years, segregation might have continued much longer. Politicians were hesitant to change the law, fearing that white voters would not re-elect them. Dramatic action like sit-ins focused the country's attention on the abuses of segregation and hastened that system's demise.

TRANSNATIONAL POLITICAL PROTEST

Social movements and political protest have often migrated across borders. Nineteenth-century examples of transnational movements include the anti-slavery and labour movements. Later, the student movement of the 1960s and the women's rights movement of the 1970s were also international in scope. As well, protestors in one country, such as the Zapatistas in Mexico, have gained support for their cause from sympathizers around the world. Curiously, the anti-globalization movement has been the best recent example of contentious politics on a transnational scale.

Peoples' Global Action
www.nadir.org/nadir/initiativ/agp/en/index.htm

The anti-globalization movement, which often refers to itself as the global social justice movement, has focused on specific elements of globalization, particularly international finance and its effects on the world's economy. This has led the movement to target meetings of the World Trade Organization (WTO) and other forums that promote increased economic integration, such as the G8 and G20 summits of the leaders of the countries with the largest economies, meetings of the International Monetary Fund and World Bank, and the European Union summits, for its protests. Since the movement's first major operation in 1998, in which it brought to the public's view a hitherto secret draft of a proposed Multilateral Agreement on Investment (Clarke & Barlow, 1997), the movement has moved more fully into contentious direct actions. Following the protests in Seattle in 1999, there were many big demonstrations (see Table 10-1), most of them involving clashes with police. One, in Genoa, Italy, saw one demonstrator killed, several hundred injured, and charges of torture levelled against the Italian police. Protests decreased after 2003 but began again in 2007 at a G8 summit in Germany. In March 2009, doubtless prompted by the global economic collapse that began in 2008, there

TABLE 10-1

PARTICIPATION IN ANTI-GLOBALIZATION PROTEST ACTIONS

Note: Estimates of the number of demonstrators varies widely.

PLACE	DATE	ESTIMATED NUMBER OF PARTICIPANTS
Seattle	September 1999	100 000
Washington	April 2000	10 000
Prague, Czech Republic	September 2000	12 000
Quebec City	April 2001	30 000
Genoa, Italy	September 2001	100 000
Barcelona, Spain	March 2002	250 000
Miami	November 2003	10 000
Heilingendam, Germany	June 2007	80 000
London	March 2009	35 000
Pittsburgh	September 2009	5000
Toronto	June 2010	20 000

SOURCE: *Compiled by authors from press estimates, 1999–2010.*

was a significant demonstration at a G20 meeting in London. Protests at the G20 summit in Toronto in June 2010 (which, like other protests, attracted people promoting a variety of causes) were generally peaceful, but included some confrontations between security forces and protestors, damage to businesses and the torching of three police cars, and more than nine hundred arrests. Though not specifically an anti-globalization protest, riots in Iceland in January 2009 brought about the fall of a government that had been fiercely pro-globalization, while Greece was shaken in late 2009 and early 2010 by violent demonstrations protesting austerity measures. The largest global protest demonstrations, however, were held to protest the invasion of Iraq, attracting more than ten million demonstrators worldwide in March 2003, including one million or more in London, Rome, Madrid, and Barcelona.

The anti-globalization movement is particularly adept at making use of modern communications technology. Of special importance is its use of email and the World Wide Web (Earl, 2006). These instruments, themselves part of the phenomenon of globalization, allow the anti-globalization movement to organize effectively without needing complex permanent structures. However, this flexibility also brings costs to the movement. Because there really is no central core institution, any group can adhere to the movement and participate in its demonstrations. As a result, violent anti-capitalist groups who wish to destroy the entire capitalist system mix with far less confrontational groups concerned about social justice on a global scale that focus on what they see as the unfair system of international trade rules. The anti-capitalist and anarchist groups, a small minority within the anti-globalization movement but the part most likely to seek violent confrontations with the authorities, give the entire movement a far more radical appearance than many of its members desire.

◀ In 2003, more than one million people in Madrid marched as part of a global protest against the invasion of Iraq.

POLITICAL VIOLENCE

POLITICAL VIOLENCE The use
of physical force with a political
objective.

Political violence can be defined as the use of physical force with a political objective. Violence can enter politics in several different ways (see Box 10-2, Violence and Politics):

1. *Violence can be a tactic chosen by an organization, be it a protest movement or a guerrilla army, to advance its aims.* Although this is more common in countries that are not democracies and consequently do not allow an open political opposition, even long-established constitutional democracies such as Canada or the United States can harbour groups that feel they must use violence to achieve their goals.

The American Political Science
Association, Task Force on Political
Violence and Terrorism
www.apsanet.org/section_571.cfm

2. *Governments can also use violence against their citizens.* Sometimes this resort to physical coercion is a response to a specific situation. For example, governments may want protests stopped and may even order the police or military to use force against the protesters. While such tactics are common in non-democratic countries, democratic governments sometimes react in the same way. Far less common among democratic governments, though unfortunately not unknown, is using violence systematically as a regular instrument to repress dissent and maintain order. This is called **regime violence**.

REGIME VIOLENCE Political
violence used by a government
against its citizens, generally
as a way to repress dissent and
keep order.

3. *Finally, violence can be an unplanned and undesired side effect of an otherwise peaceful political action, such as a protest march.* Due to some unpredictable event, either the protestors or the police become aggressive and the two sides clash.

Canadians are generally repelled by political violence. A movement that regularly uses violence, as did the Front de libération du Québec (FLQ), a revolutionary separatist group that kidnapped and murdered a Quebec Cabinet minister in 1970 (as discussed later in this chapter), is likely to lose public support. This revulsion also occurs when the police react with excessive force, as happened at the 1997 Asia-Pacific Economic Cooperation (APEC) summit in Vancouver.[1] Canadians, like people in most democratic countries, usually draw the line at premeditated violence.

Although violent, even lethal, political contention has been rare in Canada's past, it is not unknown. The earliest significant cases occurred in what are now Quebec and Ontario during the Rebellions of 1837–1838 (Kilbourne, 1964; Schull, 1971). These democratic revolts challenged elite domination of politics and sought to give more power to the people's representatives in elected assemblies, but were crushed by British troops.

---

[1] RCMP officers and Vancouver riot police used violence against students who were peacefully protesting the presence of the Indonesian dictator Suharto at a meeting of APEC being held at the University of British Columbia in 1997. Although there were suspicions that the prime minister's office had ordered the demonstrators to be forcefully dispersed, a later inquiry found no direct links.

Violence and Politics

British political scientist Bernard Crick argued that politics, which he termed "the political method of rule," is built on negotiation and the reconciliation of differences. As such, it effectively excludes the use of violence as a governing instrument (Crick, 1993).

Nonetheless, we see violence used for political ends every day, both by governments and by groups challenging government's authority. Two questions arise from this: Why do people use violence for political ends? And how can we distinguish political violence from simple criminality?

States may use violence legitimately, either to defend themselves and their citizens or to preserve order. Sometimes, however, dictatorships and other non-democratic governments use violence simply to suppress their opponents and repress dissent. Although democratic governments may do the same, it is far less common than in dictatorships.

In such cases, violence may be the only instrument that citizens can use to protect themselves against the state or to try to change their government's behaviour. Many would consider this a legitimate use of political violence.

Violence becomes explicitly political when it is used to influence, defend, or overthrow government. That seems clear, even if no government would ever say that any use of violence against it was anything but criminal. However, revolutionaries committed to toppling a government often resort to ordinary criminal methods such as robbery or kidnapping to finance their operations or simply to display their strength. In these cases, the line between political and criminal action seems to disappear. A further complication arises when peaceful protest turns violent unexpectedly, or when violent elements, even criminal ones, use ordinary protest as a cover for their illegitimate intentions.

After Confederation came the two Riel rebellions: the Red River Rebellion (1869–1870) and the North-West Rebellion (1885) (Stanley, 1992). Both were led by Louis Riel, a leader of the Metis (Roman Catholics of mixed Aboriginal and European ancestry who lived an essentially Aboriginal lifestyle), in what is now Manitoba. The Metis were concerned that they had not been consulted about the transfer of the Red River colony, now a part of Manitoba, from the Hudson's Bay Company to be administered as a territory by a governor (notorious for his dislike of French-speaking Catholics) appointed by the Government of Canada. They feared that white, Protestant settlers would overwhelm them, take their land, and destroy their way of life.

The Red River Rebellion was successful. The Canadian government agreed to establish a provincial government in Manitoba in 1870, with guarantees for a Roman Catholic school system and the establishment of official status for both French and English languages. However, the North-West Rebellion, centred in what would become Saskatchewan and which tried to get Ottawa to pay attention to the needs all residents of that region (Aboriginal, Metis, and European) failed. Violence ensued and the Metis forces were routed by Canadian troops. Riel was captured, tried for treason, and hanged.

BOX 10-3
Aboriginal Protest in Canada

In recent years, Canada's indigenous people, of whom there are more than one million, have made some important gains in negotiations over land claims and have seen Aboriginal rights enshrined in the constitution. Yet it has been violent confrontations between Aboriginal communities and federal or provincial authorities that most captured public attention. Three of these were especially important:

- *Oka.* In 1990, plans by the town of Oka in Quebec to expand a golf course involved expropriating land that held a local Mohawk cemetery. An armed standoff between Quebec Provincial Police (QPP) and the Mohawk Warriors' Society led to the shooting of a QPP officer. A 78-day standoff with the Canadian army then followed.
- *Ipperwash.* In 1995, Ojibway from the Stony Point First Nation claimed that Ipperwash Provincial Park in Ontario belonged to them. A violent confrontation between the Aboriginals and the Ontario Provincial Police resulted in the death of protester Dudley George. The government of the day refused to order an inquiry into George's death, but after a change of government in 2003, a commission of inquiry was established. The inquiry uncovered evidence of racist and culturally insensitive behaviour by the authorities. Its report in 2007 recommended that the land be turned over to the Ojibway.
- *Burnt Church.* In 1999, a confrontation at Burnt Church, New Brunswick, brought Aboriginal and non-Aboriginal fishermen into conflict. A month before this episode, a Supreme Court decision held that treaties from the 1760s exempted Aboriginals in the Maritimes and eastern Quebec from current fisheries regulations. Non-Aboriginal fishermen objected, fearing that uncontrolled fishing would destroy the resource. The two sides clashed violently at Burnt Church, leading to the destruction of much of the Aboriginals' gear and the burning of three fish-processing plants.

We must remember that both sets of lethal contention in Canada in the 1800s grew from unfulfilled democratic demands. In the Red River Rebellion, the use of force led to talks with the government. In the other three rebellions, it was the failure of regular political processes that resulted in the use of violence.

This pattern of failure to address grievances underlies political scientist Ted Robert Gurr's frustration–aggression hypothesis (Gurr, 1967), which seeks to explain what triggers violent protest. Gurr argued that where levels of frustration are high within a population and have lasted for a long time, these feelings can readily find violent expression. This certainly seems to be what occurred at both Oka and Burnt Church (see Box 10-3, Aboriginal Protest in Canada). However, this theory does not actually explain why people sometimes direct their energies into highly contentious, even violent, politics instead of ordinary political action, such as electoral campaigning, or even ignoring politics altogether.

The Mothers of the Plaza de Mayo

Argentina has had many military dictatorships but none as violent as the regime that ruled the country from 1976 to 1983. Seizing power after an elected government proved unable to contain a wave of violence generated by urban guerrillas, the military waged a "Dirty War" against those it considered subversives and dissidents. Suspects were swept from the streets, taken to interrogation centres, and never heard from again. These were the Disappeared, and there were between ten thousand and thirty thousand of them.

In 1977, the mothers, wives, sisters, etc., of the Disappeared, frustrated by government refusals to release any information regarding the whereabouts of their family members, began to protest. Although the military regime ended in 1983, even now the Mothers of the Disappeared still gather every Thursday in the Plaza de Mayo, a park in downtown Buenos Aires that faces the presidential residence on one side and the Ministry of Defence on another. There they march quietly, partly in memory of their loved ones, partly to press the now democratically elected government to prosecute the architects of the Dirty War and their accomplices.

Their struggle has continued long enough that the Mothers have begun searching for their stolen grandchildren, who were born in captivity and

The Mothers of the Disappeared have held a silent march in the Plaza de Mayo, which faces the presidential palace, every Thursday since 1977 to protest the disappearance of as many as thirty thousand women, men, and children during the military dictatorship that lasted from 1976 to 1983. Some of their family members are still missing.

turned over to the families of military officers. Reynaldo Bignone, the last president under the military regime (1982–1983) was arrested in March 2007 and charged with the theft of the babies of the Disappeared. As Hebe de Bonafini, the president of the Association of the Mothers of the Plaza de Mayo, has said, the struggle will never end.

The frustration–aggression hypothesis also does not address the question of why and when governments regularly use violence against their own citizens, what we have called regime violence. When we think of regime violence we usually think of a police state, one where the security forces—police, military, secret police, intelligence services—have free rein to harass citizens. Their repertoire includes **disappearances**, detaining people without charge, brutality, and torture (see Box 10-4, The Mothers of the Plaza de Mayo). There are too many examples of political systems that have used violence systematically against their own people to list here, but examples include Saddam Hussein's Iraq, the Taliban regime in Afghanistan, the Soviet Union under Stalin, Germany under Hitler, and Argentina during the "Dirty War," 1976–1983.

DISAPPEARANCE The kidnapping by security forces of an individual who is never heard from again.

Project Disappeared
www.desaparecidos.org/arg/eng.html

The former examples were all dictatorships, but sometimes democracies also resort to using regime violence. This most often occurs as a response to political protest. For example, in the 1960s, police forces in American states where the segregation of the races was legal used violence against citizens engaged in peaceful protests demanding that African-Americans receive their full constitutional rights. It can also happen that the authorities turn a blind eye to private citizens who use violence against protesters or other dissidents. Again, the American South offers an example: for many years the Ku Klux Klan terrorized black citizens who sought to exercise their legal rights.

There are several reasons why states might use violence as instrument of government against their own citizens. One is to instill so much fear in the population that it will not dare to act against the government. Another is to maintain in power an individual or group (which can be defined by class, colour, religion, ethnicity, or ideology) that would otherwise be thrown out. In fact, the two often go together.

TYPES OF POLITICAL VIOLENCE

We will analyze three types of political violence. They are either important today or have been prominent during the last century. The first is guerrilla warfare (also called guerrilla insurgency) and its counterpart, counter-insurgency. The second is terrorism and the third is revolution.

Guerrilla Warfare or Guerrilla Insurgency

Like political protest, guerrilla warfare is principally an instrument of the weak. Also called guerrilla insurgency, it is a familiar form of violent political action. This kind of political violence has been practised from time immemorial; we find references to it that date back 3500 years, and it is mentioned in the Bible. Nevertheless, it only received its current name early in the nineteenth century, when it was applied to the Spanish resistance to Napoleon's invasion and occupation (*guerrilla* is Spanish for "little war"). Anthony Joes, an expert on guerrilla warfare, holds that "guerrilla insurgency is quintessentially a *political* phenomenon" (Joes, 2004, 7; emphasis in original), even if those who fight guerrillas often portray them as bandits.

All guerrilla insurgencies share five traits (Beckett, 2001; Joes, 1992, 2004; Laquer, 1977). First, the guerrillas are highly mobile and use hit-and-run tactics rather than set-piece battles. Second, they are fewer in number and less well armed than their adversaries. Third, guerrillas operate in familiar, often difficult terrain, which can be rural or urban (see Box 10-5, Urban Guerrillas), where their enemy loses its edge in technology and numbers. Fourth, the guerrillas know their locale and often have local support, which simplifies the task of gathering intelligence and securing supplies. Finally, guerrilla war is protracted war; if it ends quickly, the guerrillas have probably lost.

Urban Guerrillas

When we think of guerrillas, we imagine men and women in camouflage trekking through a jungle or scrambling over a mountain pass. We do so for two reasons. One is that the successes of rural guerrillas, such as Mao Zedong in China in the 1930s and 1940s and Fidel Castro in Cuba in the 1950s, have shaped our image of insurgent warfare. The other is that most guerrillas have operated mainly in rural areas. Doing so puts distance between them and the government's soldiers that they fight, gives them the advantage of operating in difficult terrain that they know better than their enemy, and puts them in touch with the rural poor, who are often among those guerrillas claim to defend. However, guerrillas can also operate effectively in urban areas.

We have seen this in the Iraq, where most action against the U.S.-led coalition has taken place in the cities. In general, operating in urban areas offers certain advantages to irregulars, another name for guerrillas. They have access to a large base of potential recruits, supplies are easier to gain, urban home turf can be just as difficult for a counter-insurgent to penetrate as any jungle, and the counter-insurgent runs a very high risk of killing civilians, thus raising the insurgents' legitimacy.

Iraq is not the first case of urban guerrilla struggle. In the late 1960s and early 1970s, such groups were very active in Uruguay and Argentina. They were quite violent, robbing banks and kidnapping people for ransom to finance themselves, and provoked military coups in both countries, creating governments that eventually destroyed the guerrillas. The violence in Iraq is even worse. In early 2010, the website Iraq Body Count (www.iraqbody-count.org) estimated that there had been between 95 000 and 104 000 civilian casualties since the U.S.-led invasion in 2003. Many of those deaths—the exact number is unknown but one source estimates 18 500 (Iraq Body Count, 2010)—were caused by suicide bombers.

Although guerrilla warfare has existed for a long time, it became especially well known in the twentieth century (see Table 10-2). Not only did a great number of exceptional guerrilla commanders emerge—for example, Mao Zedong of China, Augusto César Sandino in Nicaragua (discussed in Box 10-6, Guerrilla Violence), Ho Chi Minh in Vietnam, and Fidel Castro in Cuba—but guerrilla insurgency also came to be identified with revolutionary struggle. The question we must ask is why revolutionaries would turn to guerrilla warfare. Although all of the characteristics of guerrilla operations noted above apply in general, there are two additional reasons that apply with special force to revolutionaries.

One of these is that revolutionaries—who could be Marxists, independence fighters, or motivated by religion—generally are persecuted by governments. To survive they must find methods that both let them mount a successful resistance and give them an opportunity to win adherents. Guerrilla operations do both. By emphasizing the use of small units, light arms, and brief engagements, guerrilla tactics allow insurgents to turn their usual liabilities—small size and poor equipment—into advantages. Further, having to operate clandestinely means that the insurgents must mix with the ordinary

TABLE 10-2
SOME GUERRILLA MOVEMENTS OF THE TWENTIETH AND TWENTY-FIRST CENTURIES

WHERE	WHEN	LEADER OR COMBATANTS
China	1920s–1949	Mao Zedong
Nicaragua	1927–1934	Augusto César Sandino
Various	1939–1945	World War II partisans
Algeria	1940s–1958	Independence fighters
Vietnam	1940s–1975	Ho Chi Minh
Malaya	1946–1954	Communists
Mozambique and Angola	1950s–1974	Independence fighters
Cuba	1956–1959	Fidel Castro
Afghanistan	1979–1989	Mujahedeen
Afghanistan	2002–present	Taliban
Iraq	2003–present	Insurgents

people for whom they claim to fight. This allows the revolutionaries to do the slow, painstaking work of convincing people to turn against the government (always a dangerous choice) and back the guerrillas. The guerrillas can fail militarily and still continue to exist if their political work succeeds. If they fail politically, though, military success will not suffice.

Just how do guerrilla revolutionaries do their political work? One objective is to show people that the government cannot protect them, so the guerrillas attack government installations, blow up power lines and bridges, and often kill government officials—police, military, mayors, etc. In general, guerrillas seek to limit the violence used against ordinary citizens, because the insurgents need their aid and it is these people whom the revolutionaries claim to defend. Some groups, however, have chosen to terrorize civilian populations. Among these are the Shining Path (Sendero Luminoso) guerrillas of Peru (Palmer, 1994; Rochlin, 2003) and the Contras or Nicaraguan Resistance, an insurgent group formed and armed by the United States government to attack the revolutionary government of Nicaragua in the 1980s (Grandin, 2006).

COUNTER-INSURGENCY   C.E. Callwell, a nineteenth-century student of guerrilla warfare, said that "when [guerrilla warfare] is directed by a leader with a genius for war, an effective [**counter-insurgency**] campaign becomes well-nigh impossible" (quoted in Joes, 2004, p. 1). Yet guerrillas do not always win. Among the more famous counter-insurgent victories are two by the United States in the Philippines (1899–1902 and 1946–1954), one by the British in Malaya (1948–1960), and one by the democratic Venezuelan government against communist insurgents (1960–1964). On the other hand, even more famous losses were suffered by the United States in Vietnam and by the Soviet Union in Afghanistan. Similarly, after 2003, U.S. forces in Iraq and, perhaps, Canadian troops in Afghanistan found themselves in a quagmire. What does it take to make counter-insurgency work?

COUNTER-INSURGENCY A blend of military and political action taken by a government to defeat an insurgency. The tactics are usually described as a mixture of repression and reform.

Guerrilla Violence

Because they fight foreign occupiers or domestic dictators, we often lionize guerrillas, treating them as ideal democratic heroes. However, they are waging a struggle that has a brutal side and they must sometimes use brutality.

Augusto César Sandino became famous for leading a guerrilla war against the U.S. troops who occupied Nicaragua in the late 1920s. His Ejército Defensor de la Soberania Nacional (Defending Army of National Sovereignty) worked patiently with peasants to win their allegiance but administered rough justice to those who took the government's side. Using machetes, the guerrillas would lop off an offender's head, or slice off his arms, causing him to bleed to death. These methods were used because, as Sandino said, "Liberty is not won with flowers" (Macaulay, 1986, p. 212).

The answer is brief and seemingly simple: repress and reform. Government must control the guerrillas militarily at the same time that it addresses the complaints of those who support the insurgents. Counter-insurgency thus has a political dimension just as insurgency does. This political dimension even slides over into the military side, because government forces have to find a level of violence that is high enough to stop the guerrillas but not so fierce as to alienate the general population.

Despite the centrality of politics in counter-insurgency, governments fighting guerrillas often overlook this element, preferring to rely on their superiority of force (Beckett, 2001; Hoffman, 2004; Joes, 2004). The most recent U.S. Army field manual on counter-insurgency (U.S. Army, 2006) stresses political operations. Yet the United States' experiences in Iraq and Afghanistan suggest how difficult it is for governments and their militaries to adopt a strategy that would maximize their effectiveness against guerrilla insurgents and construct a political system better able to seek the common good.

Terrorism

What particularly sets terrorism apart from other forms of political violence such as war, rebellion, *coup d'état*, and revolution is its conscious targeting of the innocent (see Box 10-7, Terrorism Today). Terrorists use this tactic to sow fear among the population, either simply to demonstrate their power or in the hope that citizens will pressure their governments to meet the terrorists' demands.

Those who defend the use of terror usually assert that when fighting the strong, the weak must use any instrument that advances their cause, including not just violence but the use of violence against any target. This is the logic of total war. It is not surprising, therefore, that terrorists also contend that there are no innocent victims. Everyone who is not on the terrorists' side, fully

BOX 10-7

Terrorism Today

Even before al-Qaeda's terrorist attacks on the United States on September 11, 2001, democracies were acquainted with terrorism. For example:

- North Americans have witnessed terrorist attacks by those who bomb abortion clinics, the bombing of an Air India flight in 1985, the right-wing extremists who blew up the Murrah Building in Oklahoma City in 1995, and Theodore Kaczynski (the "Unabomber"), who sent package bombs to unwitting victims.
- In Ireland and Britain, the Irish Republican Army (IRA) and its various factions used violence in their unsuccessful quest to bring Northern Ireland (Ulster) into the Irish Republic. The same applies to Spain, where the ETA (Euzkadi Ta Askatasuna,

Basque Homeland and Freedom) has waged a decades-long armed struggle to separate the Basque provinces from Spain.

- In the 1970s and 1980s, Germany faced serious episodes of terror by the Baader–Meinhoff Gang (which called itself the Red Army Faction), while Italy suffered terrorist attacks from both the Red Brigades on the extreme left and fascists on the extreme right.
- Continuing into the twenty-first century, Israelis live perpetually with terror, as organizations such as Hamas and Hezbollah have turned to suicide bombers as a regular political tool to press for rights for Palestinians. These tactics provoke strong responses from the Israelis, leaving the Palestinians themselves in a state of terror.

SUICIDE TERRORISM A form of terrorist violence in which the attacker's object is to kill her- or himself as well as the target.

Consortium for Research on Terrorology and Political Violence (CRTPV)
www.publicinterest.ac.uk/working-groups/40-consortium-for-research-on-terrorology-and-political-violence-crtpv

supporting their cause, is an enemy—and in total war, whatever can be done to defeat the enemy must be done.

Of particular concern today is **suicide terrorism**, an attack in which the attacker's object is to kill her- or himself as well as the target. Nearly every day there is news of suicide attacks in Iraq, Afghanistan, and sometimes Sri Lanka that kill dozens. Although these have come to be identified with Muslim extremists, until the wave of suicide bombings began in Iraq in 2003 it was the Tamil Tigers of Sri Lanka, a Marxist organization (active from 1974 to its defeat in 2009) seeking an independent Tamil state in the country's north, that had claimed the greatest number of victims. Further, political scientist Robert Pape (2005) concluded that the best predictor of a country having suicide terrorists was not religion but the presence of an outside force the terrorists could paint as an occupier.

Terrorism is not only a form of violence used by groups fighting against established states.[2] Some states also use terror against their own citizens. Campaigns of ethnic cleansing—systematic attempts to remove all people of a

---

[2] The designation of actions as terrorism is often highly controversial. For example, the Russian government condemns Chechen separatists who have bombed buildings and subway stations and have taken hostages as terrorists. Supporters of the Chechen rebels view the Russian government and military as terrorists for their brutal suppression of the breakaway Chechen Republic.

particular ethnicity from a region, often by killing them (for example, as carried out in Rwanda and Yugoslavia in the 1990s)—qualify as terror.

Police states and totalitarian regimes often resort to indiscriminate arrests, torture, and even murder to intimidate the population they govern. In many Latin American countries, particularly in the 1980s, "death squads" associated with repressive governments terrorized the population. As well, states sometimes sponsor terrorism to achieve international objectives. For example, Libyan intelligence agents were involved in the bombing of Pan-Am Flight 103 over Lockerbie, Scotland, in 1988, killing all on board (Coombes, 2003)—presumably as retaliation for an American attack against Libya's leader.

Terrorism is not unknown in Canada. Between 1963 and 1970, members of the Front de libération du Québec (FLQ) planted bombs, held up banks, and caused at least five deaths by bombs and gunfire. In October 1970, the FLQ kidnapped James Cross, the British trade commissioner in Montreal, and Pierre Laporte, labour minister in the Quebec government. Although Cross was released, Laporte was murdered by the terrorists. However, Canada's worst terrorist attack occurred on June 22, 1985, when bombs were planted by terrorists on board Air India Flight 182 before it left Vancouver. The bombing apparently was in retaliation for the Indian government's attack on the Golden Temple at Amritsar, the most important Sikh shrine. The bombs exploded while the 747 was over the North Atlantic and killed all 329 passengers and crew, the great majority of which were Canadians.

Why is terror used to achieve political objectives? Is it because people see the stakes as being so high that the most extreme measures are justified? Or is it because terror works? Whatever the cause, terrorism is an ever-present concern.

Revolution

Revolution implies radical, far-reaching change. It is a concept that has always fascinated political scientists. We want to know why revolutions happen, why they succeed or fail, and what revolutionaries do once in power. Political science distinguishes between two forms of revolution. The first of these classifies any armed overthrow of a government as a revolution. These are termed *political revolutions* that change rulers but need not affect the basic organization of society. They are the more common form of revolution. The second form involves armed overthrows that bring in fundamental economic, political, and social changes. These are **social revolutions** and are very rare.

We find the best examples of social revolutions among the great revolutions of the modern age, an era that reaches back to the latter part of the eighteenth century. These events reshaped both how people think about the political world and how that world works. They defined new ways to govern, opened new political horizons for large, previously excluded sectors of society,

SOCIAL REVOLUTION A revolution that changes not just who governs but also how a state is organized and how its society and economy are structured.

and recast hierarchies of power and prestige. We usually encounter the following in this pantheon of revolutions:

1. The American, 1776–1783, with its entirely new model of government
2. The French, 1789, which began the end of aristocratic rule in Europe
3. The Haitian, 1791–1804, the first successful slave revolt in the New World
4. The Mexican, 1910–1920, a major social revolution in what we now call the Third World
5. The Russian or Bolshevik, 1917, the first communist revolution
6. The Chinese, 1949, a guerrilla-led communist revolution in the world's most populous country
7. The Cuban, 1959, a guerrilla-led communist revolution in the Americas
8. The Iranian, 1979, a revolution linked to religion
9. The Eastern European, 1989, revolutions against communism

Other revolutions had important consequences for their countries but were of less historic significance. Some were wars of independence, as in Greece (1829), while others emerged from systematic restructurings of state and society that followed military coups, as happened in Chile between 1973 and 1989.[3] Even failed revolutions, like the wave that swept Europe in 1848, can be important because they open the way to later reforms. Finally, there have been revolutions that were nearly non-violent, such as the 1989 Velvet Revolution in Czechoslovakia that brought the downfall of the country's communist regime (Wheaton & Kavan, 1992).

THEORIES OF REVOLUTION   In everyday language, we often separate fact from theory, but in political science we use facts to build theories that we then use to interpret other facts. More formally, a "theory is a systematic explanation for observations that refer to a particular aspect of life" (Babbie, 1995, p. 49). Thus, a theory of revolution takes empirical observations about specific revolutions and derives from them an explanation about revolution in general. It considers why revolutions occur, what influences their evolution, and what results they produce.

The most famous theory of revolution comes from Karl Marx. As discussed in Chapter 4, Marx argued that fundamental changes in the structure of a country's economy, the means of production, lead to class conflict. Concretely, he predicted that capitalism would generate conflict between the capitalists (the bourgeoisie) who owned and directed the economy and the working class (the proletariat) whose labour made the economy function. The outcome he foresaw had the proletariat winning and setting humanity on the road to

---

[3] Although the political, economic, and social changes in Chilean society were brought about by the political right, they can still be classed as revolutionary. There is no reason why revolutions have to bring greater liberty and equality.

communism, a society without systematic conflicts because it would abolish classes.

More recent theorists have taken a more modest tack. Some have described specific revolutions in detail, searching for general patterns (Brinton, 1965). Others have hypothesized that key structural elements—for example, changed patterns of relations among classes, an economic collapse, or a crisis of the state—exist in all successful revolutions and have examined the record of revolutions to test their hypotheses (Skocpol, 1979). All search for a general theory of revolutions that will allow us to predict whether a revolution will happen in a particular setting and how it will develop. Some theorists argue that prediction is impossible. Focusing on the Iranian revolution of 1979, on which she is an expert, Keddie (1995) notes that the structural characteristics visible in Iran before the revolution also existed in other countries where no upheaval occurred. Goldstone (1995), however, believes that careful attention to trends as well as structures allows us to identify situations that will produce revolutions unless significant countermeasures are taken. What we know for certain is that there will be more revolutions, but we are unsure if we can predict where and when.

Summary and Conclusion

Political protest attempts to influence government—it is a form of political participation. It can be the best, or only, political tool available to the excluded. Even in democracies, normal channels can prove ineffective for the weak and marginalized. Yet political protest poses difficult questions for democratic citizens. Most of us usually play by the established rules of politics. We believe that they are basically fair or, if not, that they can be changed by normally available methods. However, we also know that some of our fellow citizens cannot make those rules work for them. We may or may not endorse their aims, but we wonder why our democratic rules make effective political action impossible for some people. We are witnessing a perennial problem of democratic politics.

Very few who live in democratic states accept violence for political ends. At times we may sympathize with guerrilla rebels who wage wars to overthrow brutal dictators and revolutions that promise people a better future. Where reasonable channels of political expression exist, though, it is hard to justify the use of force. It is even harder for citizens of Canada or other well-functioning democracies to countenance the use of terror as a means of protest. While terror unfortunately is used in war (although we should question whether the use of indiscriminate killing of civilians and the use of chemical, biological, and nuclear weapons is ever justified), we are loath to consider it a legitimate instrument of politics. Likewise, we find it troubling that some democratic states have supported and provided assistance to governments, security forces, or rebels who use terrorist tactics.

Key Terms

Discussion Questions

1. Have you ever been involved in a political protest? In what circumstances do you think that you would get involved in protest activity? Would you engage in civil disobedience?

2. Is terrorism ever justified? Are terrorists irrational?

3. What are political opportunity structures and why are they important in understanding political protest?

4. Why do you think political violence has had a relatively limited role in Canadian protest politics?

5. What contemporary cases of political protest can you name? How are they different from older instances? How are they the same?

6. Why do revolutions occur? Why do you think Canada has never had a revolution?

Further Reading

Asprey, R. (1994). *War in the shadows*. New York: W. Morrow.

Bouvard, M. (1994). *Revolutionary motherhood: The Mothers of the Plaza de Mayo*. Wilmington, DE: SR Books.

Davis, M. (2007). *Buda's wago: A brief history of the car bomb*. London, UK: Verso.

Debray, R. (1967). *Revolution in the revolution*. New York: Grove Press.

Galula, D. (1964). *Counterinsurgency warfare: Theory and practice*. New York: Praeger Publishers.

Goldstone, J. (Ed.). (2003). *Revolutions: Theoretical, comparative, and historical studies* (3rd ed.). Belmont, CA: Wadsworth/Thompson Learning.

Guevara, C. (1967). *Guerrilla warfare*. Wilmington, DE: SR Books.

Irvin, C. (1999). *Militant nationalism*. Minneapolis, MN: University of Minnesota Press.

Katz, M. (Ed.). (2001). *Revolution: International dimensions*. Washington, DC: CQ Press.

Mao Zedong. (1961). *On guerrilla warfare*. New York: Praeger.

O'Kane, R.H.T. (2007). *Terrorism*. Harlow, UK: Pearson Longman.

Pape, R. (2005). *Dying to win: The strategic logic of suicide terrorism*. New York: Random House.

Sanderson, S. (2005). *Revolutions: A worldwide introduction to political and social change*. Boulder, CO: Paradigm Publishers.

Smith, J., & Johnston, H. (Eds.). (2002). *Globalization and resistance: Transnational dimensions of social movements*. Lanham, MD: Rowman & Littlefield.

Tilly, C., & Tarrow, S. (2007). *Contentious politics*. Boulder, CO: Paradigm Publishers.

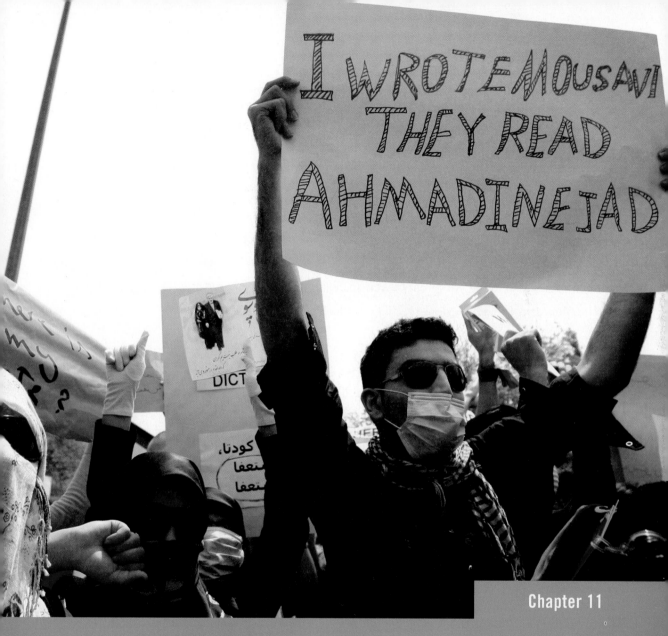

Chapter 11

Democratic and Non-Democratic Government

PHOTO ABOVE: Iranians took to the streets to denounce what was believed to be a fraudulent electoral victory for President Mahmoud Ahmadinejad.

CHAPTER OBJECTIVES

After reading this chapter you should be able to:

1. discuss the arguments for and against democracy
2. understand what attributes a government must have to be deemed democratic
3. distinguish among the various forms of non-democratic or authoritarian governments
4. distinguish between democratic transition and democratic consolidation

The year 2009 was not a good one for democracy. The problems began with presidential elections in Iran. When what was predicted to be a close race between the incumbent, Mahmoud Ahmadinejad, and a reformist candidate, Mir-Hossein Mousavi, turned into a twenty-nine-point landslide for the sitting president, Iranians took to the streets. Through more than a week of protests, Iranians denounced what they saw as electoral fraud. The government responded with force, causing at least thirty-six deaths. In the end, President Ahmadinejad was declared re-elected (BBC, 2010a).

Because Iran puts a great deal of political power in the hands of religious leaders and gives religious law precedence over secular conceptions of human rights, many in Canada are skeptical of that country's democratic credentials. However, Honduras, a country whose political system looks more like ours, produced its own challenge to democracy in June 2009 when soldiers, acting on orders from the nation's Supreme Court, took President Manuel Zelaya from the presidential residence, put him on a plane, and sent him into exile. Although the military immediately handed control of government to Zelaya's constitutionally designated successor, many Hondurans claimed that a *coup d'état* (an illegal overthrow of a government) had taken place. As in Iran, protesters took to the streets and were met with force that produced several deaths. Although Zelaya returned to Honduras in September and was given asylum in the Brazilian embassy, he was never restored to power. At regularly scheduled elections in November 2009, Hondurans chose a new president, Porfirio Lobo of the Nationalist Party. Zelaya went into exile in the Dominican Republic in January 2010 (BBC, 2010b).

Finally, on December 23, 2009, the People's Republic of China (PRC) sentenced long-time democracy advocate Liu Xiaobo to eleven years in prison for "inciting subversion of state power" (CBC News, 2009, December 24). Liu, a former literature professor, "incited subversion" by helping to draft Charter 08, a petition intended to bring his country freedom of speech, free and fair elections, and respect for the rule of law (the principle that not even the state is above the law). Liu received eleven years in jail plus an extra two years' deprivation of political rights—meaning he will be unable to speak about political matters—all because he wanted to move the PRC toward democracy. Although the Chinese government refused to release him, Liu was awarded the 2010 Nobel Peace Prize for his "long and non-violent struggle for fundamental human rights."

Overall, the list of democratic countries has grown over the last three decades. Nevertheless, about two-fifths of the world's population still lives in non-democratic countries. Indeed, some countries that were democratic a few years ago may be moving away from democracy.

We cannot imagine anything similar to the events in Iran, Honduras, and China happening in Canada. However, Canadians face what is called a democratic deficit, or citizens' perception that they have little control over the workings of government. As a result of this perception, voting turnout falls, trust declines in both politicians and politics, and people increasingly believe that the democratic process really has nothing to do with them. While the democratic challenges that Canada faces are less daunting than those in China, Honduras, or Iran, Canadians must acknowledge that challenges do exist and that it is our democratic responsibility as citizens to face up to them.

WHY DEMOCRACY?

Democracy means rule of, by, and for the people. It demands that all adult citizens have an equal and effective voice in the decisions of their political community. It is the only political system that most Canadians can imagine having. Historically, however, democratic government has been the exception and not the rule. Although democracy appeared in Athens some 2500 years ago, it lasted less than three centuries. The world then had to wait more than two thousand years, until the American and French revolutions of the late 1700s, before democracy returned. Then it took another two hundred years, until the early twenty-first century, before even a slim majority of the world's people could be said to live under anything approaching democratic rule.

Why has democracy been so rare in human history? How is it possible to justify restricting the right to govern to a minority? Three arguments have often been used to defend non-democratic government. One focuses on capability and asserts that only a select few are fit to have any say in governing. Note that this does not say that we should look for the best and brightest men and women to lead our governments, something all democrats accept. Rather, it makes the far stronger claim that ordinary people should not take any part in the affairs of state. If the various elites—whether defined by birth, wealth, ethnicity, religion, or some other standard—had not produced so many disasters in the past, this view might merit more serious consideration.

The second case against democracy asserts that if ordinary people govern, they will abuse that power and establish a tyranny of the majority that will persecute the wealthy and other minorities they find offensive and debase cultural and social standards. In other words, democracy produces a levelling effect that destroys the finest achievements of human endeavour. A look at history's despots reveals that no one has a monopoly on vindictiveness and wantonness, just as a review of democratic regimes since the American Revolution shows that democracies have treated minorities more fairly than did authoritarians. Further, democracies were the first to make education universal and have provided environments where the arts have flourished.

The last argument against democracy contends that democracy is impractical. It is all right when times are good, but when tough decisions have to be made rapidly a dictatorship is the answer, a claim that political scientist Karen Remmer (1991) has shown to be ill-founded. Along these lines, the need for democracies to debate issues thoroughly and to negotiate disputed points in order to achieve consensus can be seen as time wasting, as it encourages those involved to hold out until they get what they want. It can also be viewed as a charade, because it disguises the realities of power by letting the weak participate even when the strong will still win.

However, at the heart of the objections to democracy is the fact that it is inconvenient if you are running a government. Under any conditions, governing is hard work and democracy makes the job harder. It demands that citizens be encouraged to participate in politics, even beyond elections, meaning that government has to listen to more people, not just those from whom it wants to hear. Further, democracy insists that government itself be transparent (so the people know what it is doing) and accountable (so the people can judge its performance). Worst of all, democracy allows citizens to vote politicians out of office, taking away politicians' job security (Close, 2004).

As discussed in Chapter 3, those who advocate democracy argue that everyone should have an equal right to a direct say in government. By involving the population as a whole in governing, better policies may result because more views (including the views of those who would otherwise be powerless) are likely to be taken into account. Moreover, democratic procedures such as elections can help to hold politicians accountable to the people and serve the interests of the population as a whole. Citizens can vote corrupt, ineffective, or unresponsive politicians and political parties out of office.

LIBERAL DEMOCRACY A political system based on the ideas that the power and scope of government should be limited, that government should observe the rule of law, and that the rights of the people should be protected.

Liberal democracy, which has been developing in the West for more than two hundred years, combines the ideology of liberalism (discussed in Chapter 4), which advocates a high level of individual freedom, with a democratic system of governing based on the election of representatives. Its great contribution has been to allow countries with large populations, where the highly participatory direct democracy would be impractical, to enjoy the benefits of democratic rule. Liberal democracy is a political system based on the ideas that the power and scope of government should be limited, that government should observe the rule of law, and that the rights of the people should be protected. Because it is based on the rule of law, it is sometimes called constitutional democracy. Further, liberal democracy should be *pluralist*, with many competitors for power, thus implying the existence of a vibrant **civil society**, which presumes that citizens are free to discuss, organize, and act freely.

CIVIL SOCIETY The voluntary groups and organizations that are not controlled by the state.

DEMOCRACY IN THE WORLD TODAY

Freedom House
www.freedomhouse.org

Universal Declaration of Human Rights
www.un.org/en/documents/udhr/

Freedom House, a private American organization dedicated to the promotion of liberal democracy, charts the state of personal freedom around the globe. Its measure of political rights and civil liberties is derived, to some extent, from the Universal Declaration of Human Rights, which was adopted by the United Nations in 1948.[1] Its classification of countries as free, partly free, and not free (see Table 11-1) is based on an assessment of the extent to which the political and civil rights necessary for a country to be considered a liberal democracy are protected in each country. It is safe to assume that free countries (including Barbados, Canada, Chile, France, India, South Africa, South Korea, and the United States) are democratic and that those classified as not free (such as Afghanistan, Belarus, China, Equatorial Guinea, and Libya) are not democratic. However, partly free countries (such as Albania, Fiji, Kuwait, Nicaragua, and Singapore) include those whose classification as democratic or non-democratic is less clear.

---

[1] The principal drafter of the document was John Humphrey, a Canadian international lawyer who taught at McGill University.

YEAR	FREE	PARTLY FREE	NOT FREE
2010	46%	30%	24%
2000	45%	30%	25%
1990	40%	30%	32%
1980	31%	31%	37%
1972*	29%	25%	46%

* First year

SOURCE: *Compiled by the authors from Freedom House (2010).*

TABLE 11-1

FREE, PARTLY FREE, AND NOT FREE COUNTRIES, 1972–2010

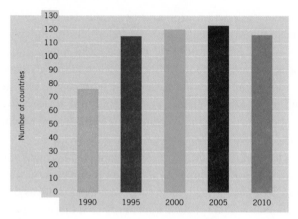

SOURCE: *Compiled by the authors from Freedom House (2010).*

FIGURE 11-1

ELECTORAL DEMOCRACIES IN THE WORLD, BY YEAR

Because some partly free countries possess the basic mechanisms of democracy whereas others do not, it is better to focus on **electoral democracies** (see Figure 11-1). These are countries in which representatives to the national legislature (and, where relevant, the president) are chosen in competitive multiparty and multi-candidate elections, all adult citizens have the right to vote in reasonably free and fair elections, and political parties are able to appeal to voters through the media and election campaigns (Freedom House, 2009). In other words, the opposition has a real chance to replace the government through the election process. There may be other restrictions on personal liberty and there may or may not be programs to secure greater economic and social equality, but citizens can choose those they want to run their government. Figure 11-1 shows that although there were many more electoral democracies in 2010 than twenty years previously, there was a notable decline (5.7 percent) between 2005 and 2010.

ELECTORAL DEMOCRACIES
Countries in which representatives to the national legislature (and, where relevant, the president) are chosen in competitive multiparty and multi-candidate elections, all adult citizens have the right to vote in reasonably free and fair elections, and political parties are able to appeal to voters through the media and election campaigns

LIBERAL DEMOCRATIC GOVERNMENT

Sir Winston Churchill, Great Britain's prime minister during World War II, declared democracy to be the worst form of government imaginable, except for all the others. Churchill harboured no illusions that democracy was perfect or that democratic government would solve all of humanity's ills. Nevertheless, he recognized that democracy brought better government to more people and offered more individuals greater freedom and equality than other systems of rule. What, though, makes a government democratic? Since much of this book analyzes the operation of democratic government in detail, we discuss only some key principles here. Our model is a government based on the liberal democratic principles outlined above, a system such as the one we have in Canada.

Political Pluralism

For a democracy to function properly there must be centres of power that are independent of government. These can be businesses, unions, educational institutions, interest groups, political parties, social movements, the media, and civil society, to name the most obvious. They are able to question what government does and offer alternative policies, which they see as better ways to achieve the common good. Only a handful of these centres of power (namely, political parties) actually aspire to govern, but all compete to exert their influence on government.[2]

POLYARCHY A political system in which there is open competition for power and government actions are freely contested.

The American political scientist Robert Dahl (1971) called a political system in which there is open competition for power and government actions are freely contested a **polyarchy** (literally, "many rule"). Dahl was careful to note that polyarchy is not identical to democracy but rather is a prerequisite for democracy. If all power rests with the state, whoever controls the state—its governor—controls everything. In such conditions, the people cannot rule.

The Rule of Law

Building a government of laws and not of men has long been a central objective of liberal democrats. They seek this sort of system because they believe that a community governed according to laws that are known by all and applied equally to everyone offers the best opportunities to seek the common good. Where power and privilege buy people special treatment from government, the common good is often sacrificed to particular individuals or groups who secure what is best for them, without regard to the community's well-being. Where a government of laws exists, we say that the rule of law prevails and that no one is above the law.

The rule of law places limits on government, as it too is subject to the law. Thus the rule of law is the keystone of a system that protects the people of a community against the arbitrary and abusive use of government power.

---

[2] As discussed in Chapters 1 and 16, there is considerable debate about whether the power of different groups to influence government is actually widely dispersed even in well-established democracies where there is open competition to influence government decisions.

The Rule of Law

John Adams, a leading figure in the American Revolution and the second president of the United States, coined the phrase "a government of law and not of men" to describe his view that government should be based on the rule of law.

The rule of law exists where three conditions are met. First, there is one law and it is known, or at least knowable to all. Second, in principle, the law applies equally to all. Third, even the government that makes the law can be made to obey the law.

Democratic government needs the rule of law for two reasons. One is that, without it, the ideal of equality among citizens on which democracy depends is undermined. That is, without the rule of law, some people will effectively get more rights than others. The other reason is equally basic. If government is above the law, then the rights and liberties that people enjoy in democratic political systems are always liable to be abused and our freedom can always be curtailed.

Although the rule of law is not, by itself, capable of assuring democratic government, as the laws governing society may be undemocratic (see Box 11-1, The Rule of Law), it is difficult to imagine a democratic community functioning well or even existing for long in the absence of the rule of law. Although there is no universal prescription for what is needed to secure the rule of law, having an independent judiciary is essential. This means that the court system is free from political pressure and that judges make their decisions without regard to what the government might want.

Accountability

Perhaps the greatest advantage that democracy bestows on its citizens is the ability to change those responsible for governing. At elections, those chosen by citizens to direct the government have to ask anew for our support. They are accountable to us and need our approval to continue in their jobs. We can allow them to keep governing or we can dismiss them. This is called **vertical accountability**, because government renders an account of its performance to its bosses: the people. Besides elections, citizens use the news media and the citizens' organizations that compose civil society to exercise vertical accountability. This helps to ensure that governments are responsive to the demands of citizens. However, this is only one of two forms of accountability that exist in democracies. The other is horizontal accountability.

Where vertical accountability has citizens restraining government, **horizontal accountability** sees government as restraining itself (Schedler, Diamond, & Plattner, 1999). For example, the courts may be empowered to review the actions of other parts of government to ensure that they conform to the law. Legislatures make executives explain what they are doing, and executives make legislatures do the same. This relationship is especially strong in the United States, with its presidential system of government and its system of

VERTICAL ACCOUNTABILITY
The various ways in which citizens, civil society, and the media seek to ensure that government institutions and public officials work to seek the common good.

HORIZONTAL ACCOUNTABILITY
Sometimes called the requirement of government agencies to report sideways. That is, it refers to how government institutions check the performance of other government institutions to ensure that they work in the public interest.

checks and balances (discussed in Chapter 15). As well, independent auditors responsible to a legislative body ensure that the various departments of government are making efficient use of their funds—funds that come primarily from the people's taxes. In Canada, this is done by the Office of the Auditor General, while in the United States the Government Accountability Office performs the same function. Other independent agencies (such as Canada's Information Commissioner and Parliamentary Budget Officer) are also involved in undertaking horizontal accountability, but unless there is strong vertical accountability from elections, the news media, and civic action, horizontal accountability will be weak.

Transparency

TRANSPARENCY In government, transparency exists to the extent that its operations are visible to the people. People need access to information and to understand how and why governments make decisions to be able to hold governments accountable.

An important corollary of accountability is **transparency**. Obviously, some things that governments do must be kept secret; issues relating to national security are the best example of this. However, citizens of democracies need access to a great deal of information if they are to act responsibly and effectively. Therefore, governments need strategies to get good, useful, and timely information to citizens. This requires governments to admit their mistakes, something they are normally loath to do. But if governments are to be accountable to citizens, they have to be open with them.

Popular Participation

Democratic Audit
www.democraticaudit.com

If someone asked you to choose the most important element of democracy, you would almost certainly select the ability to take part in governing and you would be correct. It is empowering ordinary people to participate effectively in politics that distinguishes all democratic governments from non-democratic ones. As a general rule, liberal democracies place special emphasis on the vote and on free and fair elections. However, as discussed in Chapter 3, different varieties of democracy emphasize different forms of participation. Further, Chapter 6 discusses the fact that some groups of citizens have a higher probability of being active participants in politics, while Chapters 9 and 10 describe modes of political action other than voting.

Participation is obviously a complex question. How much participation must there be for a country to be deemed democratic? Is it enough to let people vote? Must some high proportion of citizens, perhaps 80 percent, vote? Should there be high levels of civic engagement beyond the vote—for example, participation in parties, movements, or other organizations interested in public affairs? What if people's political action breaks the law? Political action was often necessary to secure the extension of the basic rights of citizens to women and to allow Canada's Aboriginal peoples to get more rights that would enable them to determine their own futures as First Nations. Finally, must the political institutions of a country (legislature, executive, parties, elections, courts, etc.)

Participatory Budget-Making in Porto Alegre, Brazil

When Canadians talk about political participation, we generally mean one of two things. In one instance, we are talking about choosing our representatives by taking part in elections as voters or by working in campaigns. In the other instance, we mean working through civil society organizations to persuade government to adapt a policy we support. We almost never think of political participation as directly taking part in formulating policy. This, however, is exactly what Porto Alegre, Brazil (a city of about 1.5 million people), has been doing since 1989, and we can also find examples of this type of political participation in Canada.

In Porto Alegre, the model works like this: The city sets aside between 15 and 25 percent of its budget for municipal projects, with the rest of the money going to pay salaries and other bills. The investment budget, as it is often called, is set after citizens meet to identify needs, discuss options for meeting them, select projects, and set the order in which they will be carried out. The process takes several months and involves large-scale citizen assemblies in each of Porto Alegre's sixteen wards. This system has produced major improvements in the quality of basic services provided to the city's citizens (Gret, 2005).

Because of its success in Brazil, many cities around the world have adopted their own variants of participatory budgeting. In Montreal, for example, local development corporations (Corporations de développement économique communautaire, or CDEC) bring in participants from the community to plan local development projects (Latendresse, 2006).

---

encourage participation, accountability, pluralism, and respect for the rule of law in order for a political system to qualify as fully democratic?

One good example of political institutions that encourage citizens to take an active role in government is found in the process of participatory budget-making in Porto Alegre, Brazil (see Box 11-2). Unfortunately, however, modern democracies do not afford ordinary citizens as extensive a participatory role as direct democracy in ancient Athens did (see Chapter 3). Modern states are much bigger and a much greater proportion of their residents are citizens with the right to participate in politics. Moreover, the range of issues that modern government must consider is so vast that many topics may interest only a small minority of citizens.

The Participatory Budgeting Project
www.participatorybudgeting.org

The Structure of Liberal Democratic Governments

Liberal democratic governments come in many forms but there are three main structural alternatives that dominate: parliamentary systems, presidential systems, and semi-presidential systems. As described in detail in Chapter 14, parliamentary systems, of which Canada is an example, are characterized by a close interrelationship between the political executive (prime minister and Cabinet) and the legislative body (Parliament). The executive is generally composed of members of the elected parliamentary body (in Canada, the House of Commons) and must maintain the support of that body to continue governing. In presidential systems (discussed in detail in Chapter 15), the best known of which is the United States, both the executive (president) and the legislature (Congress) derive their authority from being elected directly by the people and have fixed terms of office. Finally, semi-presidential systems (also discussed in Chapter 15)—adopted by, for example, France and Russia—feature an elected president who shares power with a prime minister and Cabinet. The prime minister and Cabinet usually need to retain the support of the elected legislature to stay in power but the president does not.

Whatever structure of government a democracy takes, however, the state must agree to act democratically—for example, to be bound by the law and to follow the directives its citizens give at elections. The state, which has a monopoly over the legitimate use of force within its territory and which directs the security service and thus controls the instruments of coercion, can only rarely be *forced* to follow democratic procedures. Rather, it must accept the authority of ideas and concepts that make the state accountable to the people. Democracy, then, is a compact between people and their government that is based on trust and shared values.

Finally, although these three basic types of governing structures are normally associated with democratic governments, many non-democratic states use them as well. However, proportionally more non-democratic governments have presidential and semi-presidential systems rather than parliamentary systems.

NON-DEMOCRATIC (AUTHORITARIAN) POLITICAL SYSTEMS

For most of human history, people were not citizens but subjects. They had no voice in government and instead were ruled. Sometimes they were ruled benevolently and wisely, but at other times they were ruled badly. Aristotle listed among the virtuous forms of government ones that sought the common good: monarchy (rule by one person in the interest of the whole) and aristocracy (rule by an elite minority in the interest of all). These were governments *for* the people but neither *of* nor *by* the people. By the end of World War II (1945), however, a new consensus had emerged that viewed non-democratic governments as essentially bad and unable to seek the common good.

Taken as a class, non-democratic (or authoritarian) political systems differ from democratic ones in significant ways. Whereas democratic governments encourage political pluralism, non-democratic systems consciously limit the range of acceptable ideas and actors. Some systems are very restrictive (those called totalitarian) and others are less so, but all try to keep more control over public life than is acceptable in a democracy. Next, whereas democratic systems are expected to respect the rule of law, authoritarian governments have more freedom to ignore the law or to change it to meet their immediate needs. Accountability also suffers under authoritarian governments, which have greater capacity to engineer election results, ignore citizens' complaints, and even persecute those who want accountable government. Finally, authoritarian political systems seek to restrict citizens' participation in politics and to channel such action as does exist into activities the government can regulate. Therefore, non-democratic governments prefer to stage mass pro-government demonstrations, hold elections in which almost all voters appear to support the government, and designate government-controlled organizations (such as labour unions, women's organizations, and environmental groups) as the preferred mechanisms for citizen action. This does not mean that authoritarian states never look after their citizens; many of the wealthier ones do this job reasonably well. However, because non-democratic governments do not give their citizens a political voice, any benefits the people receive come only because the government decides to award those benefits.

TYPES OF NON-DEMOCRATIC POLITICAL SYSTEMS

We often group a variety of non-democratic states under a single label: *authoritarian political systems*. This term was originally employed by Juan Linz (1964) to refer only to those non-democratic governments that, unlike totalitarian states, did not attempt to control all facets of public life in a country. Using it now to describe any political system that is not democratic leaves us unable to distinguish a state that is murderously despotic from one that gains and keeps power through electoral fraud, corruption, and legal manoeuvres designed to hobble the opposition.

Our first step, then, is to unpack the concept of authoritarian political systems in order to view its component parts. Although some of the specific political systems no longer exist, many can still be found today. Far more importantly, the anti-democratic values that underlie these systems have never ceased to exist. Specifically, we examine six types of authoritarian systems to grasp the variety of patterns of anti-democratic government:

- totalitarian systems
- absolute monarchies
- personal dictatorships
- party dictatorships
- military dictatorships
- theocratic dictatorships

Totalitarian Systems

All dictatorships share a common trait: a high level of concentration of political power. Ordinary citizens have no right to select their governors, let alone to participate actively in making the laws that govern them. The distinguishing

Totalitarianism versus Authoritarianism

Jeane Kirkpatrick, an American political scientist who served as her country's ambassador to the United Nations, argued in a famous article that authoritarian and totalitarian dictatorships were intrinsically different (Kirkpatrick, 1979). Authoritarian governments, which she labelled traditional autocracies (one of many synonyms for non-democratic government), were less entrenched, made fewer changes, and could be reformed from within. In contrast, totalitarian regimes (called revolutionary autocracies in Kirkpatrick's parlance) turned their countries upside down but could never be changed from within.

Was Kirkpatrick right? As is so often the case in political science, we must conclude that she was partly right and partly wrong.

The collapse of Eastern European communism a decade after Kirkpatrick's article appeared, followed two years later by the disappearance of the Soviet Union, suggests that totalitarianism was not impervious to internal pressures. In fact, attempts to reform communism by Soviet leader Mikhail Gorbachev are what set the process of change in the Soviet Union in motion.

However, some old-style totalitarian states still exist among the handful of communist systems that remain. Of these, North Korea comes closest to the totalitarian mould, followed by Cuba, while Vietnam and China have moved further away from the old model, especially its economic aspects.

characteristic of a totalitarian dictatorship is that it seeks to control all aspects of life within a country (see Box 11-3, Totalitarianism versus Authoritarianism). Benito Mussolini, the founder of Italian fascism, neatly summed up the nature of totalitarianism with the following slogan: "All within the state, nothing outside the state, nothing against the state!"

Complete domination was probably always a tyrant's dream but before the twentieth century it was impossible. During the last hundred years, however, advances in transportation and communications have made it possible to approximate total control. Carl Friederich and Zbigniew Brzezinski (1956) identified six traits that characterized the totalitarian dictatorships of the first part of the twentieth century. All had

1. an official ideology
2. a single mass party usually led by one man, the dictator, and made up of no more than 10 percent of the population
3. a police state that used terror to control the population
4. a nearly complete monopoly by the party over all means of mass communication
5. a similarly complete monopoly by the party over all means of armed combat
6. an economy planned and controlled by the party

MOST IMPORTANT PRACTITIONERS   The most important practitioners of totalitarian rule were the various fascist and communist movements that reached their highest point between 1920 and 1970. Although they were different in many ways, both communism and fascism sought to unite all people of a country in a common project commanded by an individual leader and a single political party.

Leading the totalitarian states were very powerful, unchecked rulers, dictators such as Benito Mussolini in Italy, Adolf Hitler in Germany, Joseph Stalin in the former Soviet Union, and Mao Zedong in the People's Republic of China. All were able to mobilize their populations and harness them to the needs of the state. As well, they ruled by force and violence. Leading great projects that were supposed to transform society or even remake human nature, totalitarian rulers brooked no interference and wasted no time negotiating with those who opposed them. In this respect, they acted as dictators have always acted. It was their ability to monitor and control the lives of their citizens that made the totalitarians distinctive. Yet all of the totalitarian rulers failed. World War II put an end to Mussolini and Hitler, and while communism in the Soviet Union and China lived on after Stalin and Mao, later rulers generally reduced repression and relaxed to a limited degree their control over their people.

Cuba, which Fidel Castro ruled from 1959 until 2006, when illness caused him to cede power to his brother Raúl, is the totalitarian country Canadians know best, because so many of us vacation there. Although the Castros have looked after Cubans by providing free education and health care and ensuring that no one starves, political opponents are repressed and the Communist Party of Cuba can never be voted from office. In these latter respects, Cuba conforms perfectly to Friederich and Brzezinski's definition.

PATHOLOGICAL TYRANTS   It is not only big, powerful states that have flirted with totalitarianism. Perhaps the most shockingly bloodthirsty totalitarian ruler of our age was Pol Pot, who terrorized Cambodia from 1975 to 1979 (Kiernan, 2002). He and his Khmer Rouge turned the Southeast Asian country into a killing field, murdering 1.5 million of its roughly 8 million inhabitants.

Pathological tyrants are neither new nor especially uncommon. Nineteenth-century Paraguay produced José Gaspar Rodríguez de Francia, who styled himself as *El Supremo* and shut his country off from the rest of the world for almost thirty years (White, 1978). More recently, the tiny African country of Equatorial Guinea had the misfortune to fall under the control of Francisco Macias Nguema, who brutalized and impoverished his nation while persecuting educated individuals (Decalo, 1988).

EMERGENCE FROM A VACUUM   We should note here that totalitarian states, whether ruled by madmen or shrewd dictators, grow out of periods of turmoil and societal chaos. It is as if the vacuum caused by breakdown opens the way to those who would exercise total control over their people. This suggests that societies that are able to function effectively are poor targets for totalitarian rulers.

Absolute Monarchies

Historically, most people have been ruled by monarchs. Some contemporary monarchies (such as the British, Dutch, and Spanish) are constitutional, meaning that the monarch is subject to the law like everyone else and has very limited powers. Constitutional monarchs are the symbolic leaders of their countries and do not have an active role in governing. However, some monarchies, such as Saudi Arabia's, are labelled absolute because the monarch has unlimited power. This was the type of system that the French Revolution toppled in 1789. In fact, much of today's thinking about democratic government was first conceived to serve as an antidote to absolutism.

In absolute monarchies, political activity is constrained. Political parties are often prohibited and there are seldom elections since government positions are filled by royal appointment. If there is a representative assembly, it is more likely to be a council of nobles than an elected body that speaks for the people. There is usually strict censorship and the liberties of those outside the ruling circle are radically circumscribed.

Given those characteristics, it is no surprise to learn that in the twentieth century absolute monarchies were often victims of revolution. This fate befell the Russian empire in 1917, the Ethiopian empire in 1974, and the Iranian empire in 1979. However, in none of these cases was the ensuing regime democratic. Rather, absolutism gave way to other forms of dictatorship. It may be that making political activity illegal forces those who want change into clandestine revolutionary movements. If successful, they may use their tightly disciplined organizations to control the state.

▶ King Abdullah of Saudi Arabia, an absolute monarch, also holds a number of additional positions, including prime minister and commander of the National Guard.

Four Kinds of Dictatorships

There has never been a true democratic dictatorship because all dictatorships vest power permanently in the hands of a ruler who is not accountable to the public. Dictatorships, like totalitarian regimes, often claim to work on behalf of all of their citizens. However, these governments will not put their hold on power to the test of an open and honest election. Dictatorships can be built around one person or around an institution, such as a party, the military, or a religious elite. Thus there are four kinds of dictatorships: personal, party, military, and theocratic.

PERSONAL DICTATORSHIPS   **Personal dictatorships** are harder to find today than they would have been even as recently as 1980. They are distinguished by having a single leader who rules far more according to personal preferences than by following the law. Historically, personal dictators have always been men, but there is no reason why a woman could not fill the role. The great danger in this form of government is that, as in all dictatorships, there are no institutional constraints on the leader, who leaves power only when he dies or is driven out by armed force.

PARTY DICTATORSHIPS   **Party dictatorships** are different in that political life is controlled by a single party rather than by a lone individual. In the most unambiguous cases, only one party has the legal right to exist or, if others do exist, only one party is legally able to exercise power. Communist states have provided the best-known party dictatorships, but they are not the only ones. Besides the obvious instances of Mussolini's Italy and Hitler's Germany, Portugal and Spain also had one-party dictatorships for extended periods in the twentieth century. One-party states were also very common in Africa from independence, usually in the 1960s, to the early 1990s. Rulers of these African states generally justified their turn to one-party rule in terms of unifying the nation. They argued that the best way to build a strong nation out of the many tribes that often coexisted uncomfortably within their countries was to channel all political action through one party. Although this is a logical premise, in practice eliminating other parties led to dictatorship. Throughout history, most dictatorships of this sort have met violent ends, but since the 1970s more of them are negotiating the conditions of their demise with other political forces.

MILITARY DICTATORSHIPS   In **military dictatorships**, the military provides a country's rulers (Fitch, 1998; Janowitz, 1977). These systems are established in the wake of a military seizure of power, usually called a *coup d'état*. Sometimes military dictatorships are run by committees of a country's armed forces, known as military juntas. Most military regimes start with a junta but many are quickly dominated by a single leader. When this happens, the resulting government takes on some of the traits of a personal dictatorship,

PERSONAL DICTATORSHIP An undemocratic government dominated by a single individual. Saddam Hussein's Iraq was a classic example of this kind of system.

PARTY DICTATORSHIP An undemocratic political system that is controlled by one party. The most familiar examples are found in communist political systems.

MILITARY DICTATORSHIP An undemocratic government run by the military.

"The people of this country are going to catch on to this thing called democracy . . . and if they don't we'll make them!"

distinguishing itself mostly by giving the military special benefits. Unlike other dictatorships, however, military governments often leave power of their own volition. It is quite common for the military to oust a civilian government, rule for a few years, and then arrange elections for a new civilian government. Although the military frequently imposes restrictions on who may compete for power, the transition is usually peaceful.

THEOCRATIC DICTATORSHIP
An undemocratic state run by religious elites. The best contemporary example is Iran.

THEOCRATIC DICTATORSHIPS   A **theocratic dictatorship** is run by religious elites (theocracy is government in the name of God or by priests). Iran is the best current example of a theocratic state (see Box 11-4, Theocracy in Iran). Until overthrown in 2001 by U.S.-led forces that included Canada, the Taliban government in Afghanistan was the most extreme theocratic dictatorship of modern times. Basing its governing philosophy on a radical reading of the Quran, the Taliban was infamous for eliminating virtually all rights for women. Both the Iranian and Taliban regimes emerged when a preceding secular authoritarian state was overthrown.

In an authoritarian state, it is common and usually legal for elites to disregard the public's wishes. Such systems often use force with impunity when challenged by their citizens. The fact that in cases like Iran the authorities

BOX 11-4

Theocracy in Iran

Iran's seventy million people have had very little experience with democracy. Only under the Mossadegh government, which ruled for only a few short days in 1953, was there respite from authoritarianism.

Although the 1979 Iranian Revolution promised greater freedom after overthrowing the increasingly repressive and autocratic monarchy headed by the Shah, it soon instituted a theocratic system, an Islamic Republic, headed by the religious leader Ayatollah Ruhollah Khomeini. Best known in the West for its uncompromising application of law based on religious doctrine, Iran's political system has also relied on the country's armed forces, the Revolutionary Guards, to use force to ensure compliance.

By 1997, however, there were signs that Iranians had had enough of strictly enforced religious principles. They elected Muhammad Khatami, a moderate cleric committed to reform, as president of Iran. The reformers were fought at every turn by conservatives who supported a theocratic dictatorship, but the forces of change and moderation made significant gains. The Majlis (legislative) elections of 2000 produced a pro-reform majority and Khatami himself was re-elected in 2001 with a huge majority. A moderation of the radically religious regime seemed in the offing. However, Khatami and his allies in Majlis were not Iran's ultimate authority. That power rested in the hands of a religious leader, Ayatollah Ali Khameni, Iran's "Supreme Leader." The Supreme Leader is chosen by an elected, seventy-member Council of Experts, all of whom currently are clerics. Among his other roles, the Supreme Leader is commander-in-chief of the armed forces and the police, head of the state television and radio company, and the country's top jurist.

In 2003, university students led Iranians to the streets in a call for freedom and democracy. Their demonstrations were broken up not just by the police, but also by vigilantes who used clubs and chains. Then, before legislative elections in 2003, the Guardian Council (a twelve-member chamber, half of whom are appointed by the Supreme Leader and half by the Majlis, with absolute veto powers) struck four thousand reformist candidates from the lists. The remaining reformers boycotted the vote. The conservative candidates, approved by the Guardian Council, won in a landslide. In the 2005 presidential elections, hardliners won again, as Mahmoud Ahmadinejad took power after a convincing win in a runoff election. In his re-election in 2009, President Ahmadinejad, who was best known for trying to make Iran a nuclear state, resorted to fraud to avoid another runoff election (as described at the beginning of this chapter). Protests followed and Ahmadinejad ordered Iran's security forces to repress the demonstrators, causing dozens of deaths.

believe they are acting morally—indeed, in accordance with God's will—may serve only to strengthen their resolve and make movement toward more rights for more people even harder.

Although Islam is the faith underlying today's theocracies, it is important to recall that other religions have been the basis for theocratic rule. North America produced one in the seventeenth-century Massachusetts Bay Colony, which was founded and run by the Puritans, a Protestant sect. As is the case with any religious dictators, the Puritans declared that no one had the right to sin and were zealous in their pursuit of those who violated the colony's rigid moral codes (Parrington, 1987). Immigration and the establishment of

▶ Pakistani children exit their class at a makeshift school on the outskirts of Peshawar, Pakistan. The school was set up privately after militants allegedly blew it up, in an effort to deter girls from attending. The militants consider female education to be un-Islamic, reminiscent of the former Taliban regime in neighbouring Afghanistan, which banned education for girls and forced working women to return to their homes.

Human Rights Watch
www.hrw.org

religious tolerance in neighbouring colonies ended the Puritans' experiment. Thus, dictatorships based on religion can evolve into more democratic political systems.

Final Thoughts on Authoritarian Government

All of the non-democratic governments that we now label authoritarian share two characteristics:

1. All of them give the right to determine what constitutes the common good to a restricted number of people. Thus, in authoritarian systems the common good is less what is good for everyone than what the rulers believe is good. (Skeptics will say that the same thing happens in democracies, because elites set the agenda there as well.)
2. In general, authoritarian governments are more likely to use coercion as a normal governing instrument than are democracies. There are good reasons for this. A government that is unelected and unaccountable does not fear the judgment of its citizens. Therefore, it does not need to convince them that a particular action is good for the country; it is enough to declare it so and punish those who object. In a democracy, persuasion and consultation are government's best and most useful tools. In an authoritarian state, although a government can try to persuade its people, coercion is easier and more effective, at least in the short term.

We can sum up the differences between democratic and authoritarian governments in this way: Democracy aims to be rule by the people. Authoritarianism aims only to rule the people.

FROM NON-DEMOCRATIC TO DEMOCRATIC GOVERNMENT

Any country that is now democratic has an undemocratic past. Even Canada and the United States, which are among the handful of countries never to have known authoritarian rule since they became independent, have all undeniably become far more democratic over the years, for example by eventually extending the right to vote to all citizens (see Box 11-5, Expanding Democracy in Canada).

Democratic Transitions and Democratic Consolidation

A democratic transition occurs when an authoritarian political system is replaced by a democratic one. The American political scientist Samuel Huntington (1991) argued that there had been three waves of democratic transitions since the late 1700s. The latest of these began in Portugal in 1974 and reached a plateau in 2005, when the last of the so-called **Colour Revolutions** took place in Kyrgyzstan. In this third wave, democracies emerged in Southern Europe (Portugal, Greece, and Spain), Latin America (Argentina, Brazil, Chile, and Mexico, among others), Africa (Nigeria and South Africa are the most notable), Central and Eastern Europe (Poland, Hungary, Estonia, and possibly Russia), and Asia (Philippines, South Korea, the Republic of China [Taiwan], and Indonesia).

This third wave was notable because it coincided with the collapse of Soviet communism and saw the fall of authoritarian systems that had lasted for more than forty years in Mexico, Portugal, Spain, and South Africa. There are still some very important countries that are not democracies (the People's Republic of China, Cuba, Vietnam, Kazakhstan, Syria, and Saudi Arabia) and, as discussed below, there are countries that have reverted to less democratic ways. Nevertheless, the world was far more democratic in 2010 than it was forty or fifty years earlier.

Political science devoted a lot of attention to this latest wave of democratic transitions, identifying two very different routes to democracy: democracy negotiated between authoritarian and democratic leaders (known as **pacted democracy**), or democracy achieved by pressure from a popular movement (Bunce, 2003). The governments of democratic countries also played an important role in assisting these transitions through programs to strengthen democracy (Carothers, 1999, 2002, 2007). The United States has been the most active in this regard but Canada has also made significant contributions. In fact, the two countries have worked together with several others to promote democracy in Afghanistan (Canada, 2008).

COLOUR REVOLUTIONS A series of essentially non-violent political movements against authoritarian governments in the Commonwealth of Independent States, whose members are all former Soviet republics, that adopted a colour or flower as their symbols. The Rose Revolution (Georgia, 2003), Orange Revolution (Ukraine, 2004) and the Tulip Revolution (Kyrgyzstan, 2005) all overthrew authoritarian rulers and installed more democratic regimes.

PACTED DEMOCRACY A democratic transition produced by a deal between non-democratic elites from the old regime and democratic reformers.

Expanding Democracy in Canada

It is easy to take Canadian democracy for granted and assume that it has always been a part of this country's political life. Although Canada is one of the few countries in the world never to have suffered under a dictatorship, democracy as it exists today took time to develop. We can see this by looking at restrictions on the franchise, or the right to vote (Elections Canada, 1997).

Until early in the twentieth century, Canada had a property franchise. This meant that those who did not own property worth a certain value or have an income of a specified level were unable to vote. Until the 1940s, some provinces restricted the rights of people of certain non-European ethnic backgrounds, especially Asians, even though those individuals were Canadian citizens. Women were denied the vote federally until 1918, and some Aboriginals were not enfranchised until 1960.

More than voting rights have been extended. Before the 1960s, official bilingualism had a limited reach. It was only in that same decade that laws were adopted promoting and protecting women's rights. Aboriginal rights only arrived on the national agenda in the 1970s, and gay and lesbian rights did not become an important issue until the 1980s and 1990s. Therefore, democracy in Canada is a work in progress and always will be.

Canada is not alone in expanding democratic rights slowly. All of the world's historic democracies have done the same. This should make us question whether we are right to expect newly democratic countries to offer the same rights and freedoms and to have the same institutions as those in Canada, Britain, or the United States.

A successful democratic transition leads to democratic consolidation. A democracy is consolidated when there are no significant forces in a country calling for the restoration of an authoritarian regime. Just when that point comes, however, is hard to determine. To be able to study it effectively and understand its workings correctly, we look for indicators—something that we treat as reflecting or revealing the presence of what we want to study. Perhaps the best indicator of democratic consolidation is persistence, although we then have to decide when a democracy has lasted long enough to be consolidated.

However, a transition can stop short of fully consolidated democracy. Assume that a country holds free and fair elections and all significant political actors accept that elections are the only way to gain power. Once in power, though, a government could pack the courts with its favourites, amend laws to make corruption harder to punish, or change the electoral system to give itself an advantage. It would be an imperfect democracy: not fully authoritarian but far from the democratic ideal.

Democracies established as part of the third wave have often been imperfect. They hold democratic elections but may limit citizen participation to only the electoral sphere or have very weak accountability mechanisms. Their governments can even "undo democracy" (Close & Deonandan, 2004) by consciously weakening democratic structures, which allows them to rule with less accountability and fewer restraints. Although this is undesirable, it is better than the alternative of simply abolishing democracy and establishing a dictatorship. In the past, governments frequently chose that route but today they are more likely just to hobble democracy, because many foreign aid agencies and international organizations will not deal with dictatorships. Whatever the reason, maintaining even a debilitated democracy leaves a foundation on which a future government can build a healthier democracy.

DEMOCRACY'S FUTURE

Is democracy the future political system of every human being? At the height of the third wave many analysts were very optimistic. Francis Fukuyama (1989, 1992), a political scientist who worked for the U.S. Department of State (the American department of foreign affairs), argued that liberal democracy had proven its superiority and would soon be universally accepted. Roughly twenty years later, after the third wave had crested and the democratic tide was going out, Larry Diamond (2008), a political scientist who is recognized as a leading expert on democratic government, was far more cautious. After examining the Freedom House data on electoral democracies that showed democracy being rolled back for the first time in more than three decades (see Figure 11-1), Diamond asked what had happened. His response pointed to a combination of factors that underlie what he called "the democratic recession." Chief among them was the inability of many new democracies "to meet their citizens' expectations for freedom, justice, a better life, and a fairer society" (Diamond, 2008, p. 37). Because of this, voters have turned to strongman rulers who promise dramatic action to address problems instead of the promises that democratic governments made. Diamond suggests that those aiding countries in making democratic transitions gave too much attention to economic growth and establishing a free-market economy and too little attention to government. Although Diamond did not argue that "the most important political distinction among countries concerns not their form of government but their degree of government," as did Samuel Huntington (1968, p. 1), he makes it clear that addressing the weaknesses of democracy anywhere and everywhere must start with government.

Beyond what Diamond noted, there is also the question of the impact that the success of the Chinese development model will have on other countries seeking rapid economic transformation. As discussed in Chapter 17, since the 1980s the People's Republic of China has recorded extremely high levels of economic growth and dramatically modernized its economy by combining capitalist economics with an authoritarian government led by the Communist Party of China. In the past, successful development by authoritarian governments—from South Korea before it democratized in 1989 to the military dictatorship that ruled Chile from 1973 to 1989—has inspired many imitators. In countries that are not democratic, or that have weakly consolidated democracies, the temptation to use undemocratic government to hasten development may again prove irresistible.

DEMOCRATIC DEFICIT In democratic countries, the difference
between citizens' expectations of
how democracy should work and
how it actually works through
existing government institutions,
political organizations such as
parties, and decision-making
processes.

It is not just in new democracies that we find a democratic recession. Even long-consolidated democracies, such as Canada, suffer from a **democratic deficit**. This term is used to describe the disconnect that citizens perceive between how a democratic government ought to function and their actual experience in dealing with their own, supposedly democratic, system. For example, we expect our members of Parliament and provincial legislators to represent the views of their constituents. However, if there is a conflict between what the constituents want and what our representative's party wants, the constituents regularly lose. Governments often operate from the top down, not from the bottom up as democratic principles demand.

The general effect of a democratic deficit is to reduce the legitimacy of democratic government. This is essentially what Diamond saw happening in new democracies, although the problem is not as acute in consolidated democratic states. Nevertheless, a poll conducted in 2006 showed that only 59 percent of Canadians were "very satisfied" or "fairly satisfied" with how our democracy works (Institute of Wellbeing, 2010, p. 6).

Democracy thus remains a work in progress, even in countries that have been considered democratic for a long time. This does not mean that we should abandon universal democracy as a goal. However, it is clear that both citizens and governments have a responsibility to ensure that democratic government remains responsive to its citizens and that citizens participate actively in their own governance.

Summary and Conclusion

It is likely that when most people hear the word *democracy* they think immediately of their right to vote. To be democratic, however, a political system needs more than free elections. First, the rule of law must be observed to ensure that all individuals are equal before the law and that government itself must obey the law. Next, democratic government has to be accountable for its decisions and take responsibility for its actions: it must answer to the people who chose it (vertical accountability) and there must be a system of internal checks that allow one part of government to oversee and control what other parts of government do (horizontal accountability). Finally, for accountability to work, democratic government needs to be transparent, so that citizens can discover what government is doing and have good information on which to base their voting behaviour.

Democracy is a complicated system of government, but it must be if it is to work the way we want it to.

Most Canadians accept that democratic government is superior to any alternative that has ever existed. Nevertheless, even today democratic government is far from universal. Admittedly, there are far more democracies than there were thirty or forty years ago, but there are still many governments that are not convinced of democracy's value. Of more immediate concern to Canadians is the problem of the democratic deficit—democracy not being as accountable, transparent, or responsive to citizens' needs as we would like it to be. Accordingly, citizens must be vigilant and act to guarantee that our governments behave in ways consistent with democratic principles.

Key Terms

Discussion Questions

1. How much importance should we give to the recent decline in the number of electoral democracies? Is it a short-term adjustment or a sign of a longer trend? How could we determine which it is?

2. Why has it taken so long for democracy to extend to the majority of the world's people?

3. Would you argue that any of the four key principles of liberal democracy is more important than the others?

4. Are all other forms of government worse than democracy, as Sir Winston Churchill asserted? Why or why not?

Further Reading

Brooker, P. (2009). *Non-democratic regimes* (2nd ed.). Houndmills, Basingstoke, Hampshire, UK: Palgrave Macmillan.

Diamond, L. (2008). *The spirit of democracy: The struggle to build free societies throughout the world.* New York: Times Books/Henry Holt and Company.

Lipset, S.M., & Larkin, J.M. (2004). *The democratic century.* Norman, OK: University of Oklahoma Press.

Williamson, D.G. (2007). *The age of the dictators.* Harlow, UK: Pearson Longman.

Governing

Chapter 12

The Constitution and the Courts

PHOTO ABOVE: When Kevin Bourassa and Joe Varnell exchanged wedding vows in Toronto's Metropolitan Community Church in 2001, attendees included Ontario's NDP leader and journalists from around the world. Outside, protesters wore devil masks.

CHAPTER OBJECTIVES

After reading this chapter you should be able to:

1. explain the significance of a constitution and constitutional government
2. describe the major characteristics of the Canadian constitution
3. outline the provisions of the Canadian Charter of Rights and Freedoms
4. discuss the political importance of the courts
5. examine the methods used to select judges
6. explain the difference between common law and codified law

When two same-sex couples, Kevin Bourassa and Joe Varnell and Elaine and Anne Vautour, exchanged wedding vows in Toronto's Metropolitan Community Church on January 14, 2001, Ontario's NDP leader attended, along with journalists from around the world. Governor General Adrienne Clarkson sent a congratulatory telegram. Outside, protestors wore devil masks.

The Ontario government refused to register the wedding licences and a legal battle over same-sex marriage ensued. Within a few years, courts in several provinces ruled that the traditional legal definition of marriage—a union of one man and one woman—was discriminatory and violated the equality rights provisions of the Charter of Rights and Freedoms in Canada's constitution. The marriages were officially registered on June 11, 2003, and since then many gay and lesbian couples have been legally married. However, former Alberta Premier Ralph Klein indicated that, if necessary, he would use the "notwithstanding clause," a clause in the Charter that allows the passing of legislation that infringes on certain rights, in order to prevent the legalization of same-sex marriages in Alberta.

In 1999, the Liberals supported a Reform party motion in the House of Commons upholding the traditional definition of marriage. However, following the provincial court decisions, Liberal Prime Minister Jean Chrétien decided to introduce legislation to define marriage as involving two persons. Calgary's Catholic bishop said that Chrétien risked burning in hell, and the Pope reminded Catholic politicians of their obligation to vote according to their faith. Upon becoming prime minister, Paul Martin tried to downplay the issue, hoping that a decision could be delayed until after an election. Toward the end of the 2004 election campaign, however, Martin was facing a possible Liberal defeat and decided to use the issue to attack the Conservatives. The Conservatives, Martin argued, would take away people's rights by using the Charter's "notwithstanding clause." Conservative leader Stephen Harper said that he opposed same-sex marriage and, if his party formed the government, he would hold a free vote (one in which MPs were not expected to vote with their party) in the House of Commons to decide the issue. Although he avoided the question of whether the "notwithstanding clause" should be used to protect a ban on same-sex marriages from court challenges, other Conservatives were more forthright. MP Randy White proclaimed, "To heck with the courts . . . the politicians make the laws" (Hume, 2004).

The Civil Marriage Act, which makes same-sex marriages legal in all parts of Canada, was passed by Parliament in 2005. The Conservative government elected in 2006 reopened the issue through a motion in the House of Commons asking the government to introduce legislation that would restore the traditional definition of marriage. The motion was defeated 175–123. As a result, the question of whether the Conservatives would try to use the "notwithstanding clause" to overrule the interpretation of the Charter by the courts that legalized same-sex marriages was avoided. Prime Minister Harper indicated that he didn't plan to reopen the controversial issue.

The issue of same-sex marriage raises questions about how rights should be protected. Should the courts or legislative bodies have the final say in determining how general constitutional rights such as equality rights should be applied to particular issues?

CONSTITUTIONAL GOVERNMENT

Liberal democracy is based on the perspective that there should be limits on the power and scope of government, that government should abide by the rule of law, and that the rights of the people should be protected from arbitrary actions by government. In other words, liberal democracy is characterized not only by government elected by the people, but also by **constitutional government,** or a government that consistently acts in accordance with established fundamental rules and principles. In a number of countries, governments feel free to ignore or violate the provisions of their constitution. Thus constitutional government requires more than the existence of a constitution; it also means that government acts in accordance with the rule of law such that government is bound by the law, including the fundamental laws and principles that are established in the constitution.

CONSTITUTIONAL GOVERNMENT A government that consistently acts in accordance with established fundamental rules and principles.

WHAT IS A CONSTITUTION?

A **constitution** establishes the fundamental rules and principles by which a state is governed. It determines which institutions have the authority to make laws and governing decisions and the relationships among those institutions. A constitution also lays out the basic relationship between government and the people, including the rights and freedoms of the people (King, 2007).

CONSTITUTION The fundamental rules and principles by which a state is governed.

With the exception of the United Kingdom (see Box 12-1, The British Constitution), New Zealand, and Israel,[1] all countries today have a **codified constitution**—that is, a formal constitutional document or a set of constitutional documents that establishes the major constitutional provisions. Generally, the provisions of a codified constitution are legally superior to laws passed by a country's legislative bodies. Ordinary laws are expected to be consistent with the constitution. However, codified constitutions typically do not provide a complete and detailed description of the governing system. For example, Canada's formal constitution does not mention the position of prime minister even though that person is the central figure in government. In Canada and many other countries, **constitutional conventions**—fundamental principles that are consistently followed even though they are not contained in a legal document and are not generally enforceable in the court—are very important in understanding how the constitution operates. In addition, judicial interpretations of the formal constitution are important in determining the meaning of constitutional provisions. Finally, some important aspects of the governing system (such as the laws concerning elections) are often established in ordinary legislation rather than in the formal constitution.

CODIFIED CONSTITUTION A constitution whose major provisions are set out in a formal constitutional document or a set of constitutional documents.

CONSTITUTIONAL CONVENTIONS Fundamental principles that are consistently followed even though they are not contained in a legal document and are not generally enforceable in the courts.

---

[1] Israel's Basic Laws have been treated as constitutional by the courts, resulting in some laws passed by the Knesset (Parliament) being overturned.

The British Constitution

Although the United Kingdom is generally considered to have one of the oldest constitutional governments, it is often described as having an unwritten constitution. Much of the British constitution consists of constitutional conventions. For example, by convention, the British monarch will always give the assent needed for a bill (proposed legislation) to become an act (also known as a statute) if a majority in Parliament has passed it.

The British constitution is not entirely unwritten, and thus it is more accurately described as an uncodified constitution. A number of important statutes have been passed by the British Parliament concerning various aspects of the system of government. For example, the Bill of Rights (1689) limited the power of the monarch by, for example, requiring that any new taxes be approved by Parliament, guaranteeing free speech in Parliament, and preventing the monarch from interfering with the law. The Act of Settlement 1701 established the independence of the judiciary (and barred Catholics and those who married Catholics

from the throne). More recently, the Scotland Act 1998 established a Parliament for Scotland, the Constitutional Reform Act 2005 provided for the creation (in 2009) of the Supreme Court of the United Kingdom, and the Constitutional Reform and Governance Act 2010 contained various provisions to increase the accountability and transparency of government. Despite the importance of these acts, they can be changed by an ordinary Act of Parliament. The constitution of Britain is thus not legally superior to Parliament.

Some praise the British constitution for its flexibility. Others argue that it would be desirable to establish a codified constitution that would more clearly establish democratic principles and provide stronger guarantees of the rights and freedoms of the people. Despite some important constitutional reforms in recent times that have changed the nature of the British system of government, there has been no serious effort by British governments to codify the constitution (Flinders, 2010).

The United States (1787) and France (1789) pioneered the use of a formal, written, codified constitution. As Heather MacIvor (2006) points out, those who developed the American constitution believed that legitimate authority should be based on the consent of the governed. A written constitution would limit the power of government and allow the courts to ensure that government acted in accordance with the will of the people that was expressed in the constitution. However, the assumption that a written constitution necessarily reflects the will of the people, rather than the views of those who drafted it, can be questioned.

The Canadian Constitution

Like the constitutions of other countries, the Canadian constitution can be considered a combination of a variety of elements:

The **Constitution Act, 1867** (originally known as the British North America Act) is the core, written element of the constitution. This Act of the United Kingdom Parliament established Canada by uniting the colonies of

Constitution Finder
http://confinder.richmond.edu

Canadian Constitutional Documents:
A Legal History
www.solon.org/Constitutions/Canada/English

CONSTITUTION ACT, 1867 An Act of the United Kingdom Parliament that established Canada by uniting the colonies of Canada (Ontario and Quebec), Nova Scotia, and New Brunswick. It also set out many of the features of Canada's system of governing.

FIGURE 12-1

CANADIAN CONSTITUTIONAL TIMELINE

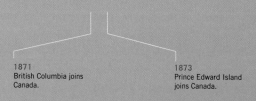

1867
British North America Act (later renamed *Constitution Act*) adopted for union of the province of Canada (Ontario and Quebec) with Nova Scotia and New Brunswick.

1870
Province of Manitoba established.

1905
Provinces of Saskatchewan and Alberta created.

1926
Imperial Conference proclaims Canada and other British dominions as "autonomous."

1871
British Columbia joins Canada.

1873
Prince Edward Island joins Canada.

1927
Attempts begin to find a formula to allow the constitution to be amended in Canada.

Canada (Ontario and Quebec), Nova Scotia, and New Brunswick. It also set out many of the features of Canada's system of governing, including the basic features of Parliament and the federal system. Over the years, there have been a number of amendments and proposed amendments to the Constitution Act (see Figure 12-1). As well, various other historic British statutes and orders-in-council (Cabinet decisions) such as the Terms of Union by which British Columbia (1871), Prince Edward Island (1873), and Newfoundland (1949) joined Canada are part of the formal Canadian constitution.

The **Constitution Act, 1982**, an amendment to the Constitution Act, 1867, made the constitution a fully Canadian document, made it clear that the formal constitution is the supreme law of Canada, and specifically indicated which documents are to be considered part of the codified constitution. As discussed below, it also added the Charter of Rights and Freedoms to the formal constitution and established procedures for amending the constitution.

There are also a variety of ordinary legislative statutes, such as the Supreme Court Act and the Canada Elections Act, which can be considered constitutional because of their fundamental importance.

Constitutional conventions, many of which were inherited from Britain, establish important principles that determine the functioning of the system of governing. For example, the convention that the prime minister and Cabinet can remain in office only if they have the confidence (support) of a majority of the members in the House of Commons is a fundamental principle underlying Canada's system of government. Judicial bodies such as the Supreme Court

CONSTITUTION ACT, 1982
The Act that made the constitution fully Canadian, added the Charter of Rights and Freedoms to the constitution, and established procedures for amending the constitution.

1931
Statute of Westminster confirms that Canada is a sovereign country.

1960-1966
Quebec governments seek constitutional changes.

1976
Parti Québécois elected.

1982
Constitution Act, 1982 adopted making the constitution fully amendable in Canada and adding the Charter of Rights and Freedoms to the *Constitution Act.*

1990
Meech Lake Accord fails to pass in Newfoundland and Manitoba legislatures.

1995
Quebec referendum on sovereignty narrowly defeated.

1940   1950   1960   1970   1980   1990   2000

1949
Most aspects of constitution can be amended in Canada. Supreme Court of Canada replaces the Judicial Committee of the British Privy Council as the highest court of appeal. Newfoundland joins Canada.

1967-1971
Constitutional negotiations end in failure.

1980
Quebec government request for a mandate to negotiate sovereignty-association defeated in a Quebec referendum.

1987
Prime minister and premiers reach agreement on the Meech Lake Accord.

1992
Prime minister, premiers, and Aboriginal leaders reach agreement on Charlottetown Accord. Accord defeated in a national referendum.

2000
Clarity Act setting out conditions for a province to become independent passed by Parliament.

of Canada have made many important decisions that determine how the constitution is interpreted. For example, judicial bodies have had a major role in interpreting the division of law-making powers between the national and provincial legislatures, establishing the rights of Aboriginal peoples, and applying the provisions of the Charter of Rights and Freedoms.

◄ In 1982, Queen Elizabeth II signed the documents that made the constitution entirely Canadian.

CONSTITUTIONAL PROVISIONS

We can analyze constitutions in terms of four basic elements (Newton & Van Deth, 2010):

1. a preamble
2. provisions concerning the institutions of government, including the procedures for passing laws
3. provisions establishing the rights and freedoms of the population
4. procedures for amending (changing) the constitution

Preamble

Many formal constitutions begin with a statement concerning the basic values and goals of the country. For example, the preamble to the American Constitution (1787) proclaims

> *We the People of the United States, in Order to form a more perfect Union, establish Justice, insure domestic Tranquility, provide for the common defence, promote the general Welfare, and secure the Blessings of Liberty to ourselves and our Posterity, do ordain and establish this Constitution for the United States of America.*

The preamble to the Canadian constitution (1867) is more mundane:

> *Whereas the Provinces of Canada, Nova Scotia, and New Brunswick have expressed their Desire to be federally united into One Dominion under the Crown of the United Kingdom of Great Britain and Ireland, with a Constitution similar in Principle to that of the United Kingdom . . . such a Union would conduce to the Welfare of the Provinces and promote the Interests of the British Empire*

The German Basic Law (1949) refers to "the determination to promote world peace as an equal partner in a united Europe," while the French constitution (1958, as amended) affirms the "Rights of Man," the "principles of national sovereignty," and "the rights and duties as defined in the Charter for the Environment." Among the aims of the South African constitution is to "heal the divisions of the past and establish a society based on democratic values, social justice and fundamental human rights."

Governing Institutions

CONSTITUTIONAL MONARCHY A system of governing in which the monarch acts as official head of state but is strictly limited in power by the constitution.

Constitutions establish the basic organization and legal responsibilities of various governing institutions.

In Canada, as in the United Kingdom and other **constitutional monarchies**, executive authority is formally held by the monarch (with her or his powers exercised by the governor general and lieutenant-governors). Government thus acts in the name of the Crown. However, by constitutional convention, the monarch (the official head of state) and her (or his) representatives act only on the advice of the prime minister and Cabinet except in certain exceptional circumstances (see Chapter 14). Thus the monarch's power is strictly limited by the constitution. In Canada, the United States, and other democratic systems, legislative (law-making) authority rests primarily with an elected representative body. However, as discussed in Chapters 14 and 15, parliamentary and presidential systems differ in the constitutional relationship between the executive and legislature. In both parliamentary and presidential systems, the judiciary (court system) is expected to be independent of both the executive and the legislative branches in order to uphold the law in a fair and impartial manner.

Constitutions not only divide governing authority among executive, legislative, and judicial institutions, but also in a number of countries establish the authority and institutions of different levels of government (as discussed in Chapter 13). In countries with federal systems (such as Canada, the United States, and Australia), the constitution divides much of the authority to make laws between the national and provincial or state levels of government.

Rights and Freedoms

Nearly all constitutions contain provisions concerning the rights and freedoms of individuals. In the United States, for example, the Bill of Rights, a set of ten amendments to the constitution, was adopted in 1791. As a result, American governments are prohibited from passing laws that infringe upon such matters as freedom of religion, speech, and association and the right to a fair trial. In addition, constitutions usually establish a variety of political rights, including the right of all citizens to vote and seek public office, and provide protection against discrimination based on a variety of characteristics such as gender, race, and religion. Some modern constitutions also require government to take action to ensure that all persons have various economic, social, and cultural rights so that they can enjoy a basic standard of living and quality of life (see Box 12-2, Economic, Social, and Cultural Rights).

PROTECTING RIGHTS IN CANADA   The original Canadian constitution, the Constitution Act, 1867, did not explicitly protect rights and freedoms, other than the right to use English or French in Parliament, the Quebec legislature, and federal and Quebec courts, as well as the right of denominational schools to receive public funding in some provinces. Instead, following British practice, it was assumed that Parliament and provincial legislatures would not infringe upon traditional liberties and that judicial bodies would, where possible, interpret laws in a manner consistent with those liberties.

The tradition of respecting rights and freedoms was generally followed. However, there were important exceptions, such as the treatment of Aboriginal peoples and the incarceration of Canadian citizens of Japanese descent

International Covenant on Civil and Political Rights
www.hrweb.org/legal/cpr.html

International Covenant on Economic, Social and Cultural Rights
www2.ohchr.org/english/law/cescr.htm

Canadian Civil Liberties Association
www.ccla.org

Economic, Social, and Cultural Rights

Based on the 1948 United Nations Universal Declaration of Human Rights, two international covenants have been adopted by the General Assembly of the United Nations. One, the International Covenant on Civil and Political Rights (1965), has been ratified by sixty-five countries, including Canada and the United States. The other, the International Covenant on Economic, Social, and Cultural Rights (1966), has been ratified by one hundred and sixty countries, including Canada (but not the United States). The economic, social, and cultural rights include the right to adequate food, clothing and shelter, education, physical and mental health, and work. However, given the obstacles to achieving these goals, particularly in developing countries, the Covenant requires government to use the "maximum of its available resources, with a view to achieve progressively the full realization of the rights." Some countries, such as South Africa,

have included these rights in their constitutions. In Canada, however, the set of proposed constitutional amendments known as the Charlottetown Accord (1992), which included some of these rights in a social charter, failed to pass.

International covenants are considered to be legally binding on the countries that ratify them (although some countries have added qualifications or interpretations to their ratification). However, there has been controversy about the desirability of incorporating economic, social, and cultural rights into specific provisions of national constitutions. While some people view binding, constitutional commitments to be desirable so that governments are required to ensure that all persons have access to what is needed for a life of dignity, others argue that governments should be able to determine their own budgetary priorities and the level of services they provide.

CHARTER OF RIGHTS AND FREEDOMS As part of the Constitution Act, 1982, the Charter protects a variety of rights and freedoms. It is superior to ordinary legislation, explicitly allows the courts to invalidate legislation, and applies to the actions of all governments and organizations under the control of government.

Canadian Charter of Rights and Freedoms
http://laws.justice.gc.ca/en/charter

during World War II. Beginning with Saskatchewan in 1947, the Canadian and all provincial governments eventually adopted Bills of Rights, although these did not have the weight of a constitutional provision. In 1982, the **Charter of Rights and Freedoms** was added to Canada's formal, written constitution (see Box 12-3, The Canadian Charter of Rights and Freedoms). The Charter is superior to ordinary legislation, and thus all legislation is expected to be consistent with its provisions. It explicitly allows the courts to invalidate legislation that is inconsistent with the Charter, and it applies to the actions of all governments and organizations under the control of government.[2]

LIMITS TO RIGHTS AND FREEDOMS   Rights and freedoms are not absolute. For example, freedom of expression is an important right, but it does not give a person the right to yell "Fire!" in a crowded theatre when there is no fire. Many countries have laws that prohibit the possession, production, and distribution of pornography, prohibit the expression of hatred directed at various groups, and place limits on advertising directed at children. Although certain limitations to freedoms are necessary to avoid harm, the question of

---

[2] Human rights codes adopted by provincial and national governments provide for a number of human rights, including protection against various forms of discrimination by private employers and other organizations and individuals. These codes are expected to be consistent with the Charter.

BOX 12-3

The Canadian Charter of Rights and Freedoms: Basic Provisions

The basic provisions of the Canadian Charter of Rights and Freedoms include the following:

- *Fundamental freedoms* (Section 2) protect freedom of conscience and religion, and freedom of opinion and expression, including freedom of the media, freedom of peaceful assembly, and freedom of association.
- *Democratic rights* (Sections 3 to 5) include the right of all citizens to vote and hold elected office. The maximum term of Parliament and provincial legislatures is limited to five years.
- *Mobility rights* (Section 6) include the right to move and to pursue a livelihood in any province. However, provinces are allowed to adopt provincial preference policies that improve the conditions of socially or economically disadvantaged individuals if the province has a below-average rate of employment.
- A variety of *legal rights* (Sections 7 to 14), including the right to life, liberty, and security of the person, the right to be secure against unreasonable search or arbitrary detention, the right to a trial within a reasonable period of time, the right to be presumed innocent until proven guilty, and the right not to be subject to any cruel and unusual punishment.
- The *equality rights* clause (Section 15) provides that every person is equal under the law and has the right to the equal protection and equal benefit of the law without discrimination on such grounds as race, origin, colour, religion, sex, age, or mental or physical disability. However, *affirmative action* laws or programs designed to help disadvantaged individuals or groups are permitted.
- *Language rights* (Sections 16 to 23) include the declaration that English and French are the official languages of Canada and New Brunswick and are given equal status in the operations of the Canadian and New Brunswick governments. Canadian citizens whose mother tongue is either English or French have the right to have their children educated in their own language where numbers warrant. In Quebec, this right only applies to parents who received their schooling in Canada.

In general, the Charter includes quite a comprehensive set of individual rights and freedoms. Unlike the American Bill of Rights, equality rights and some provisions relating to group rights and affirmative action are included. Section 25 guarantees that the Charter does not diminish the rights of Aboriginal peoples (including treaty rights and rights established by land claims agreements past, present, and future). Section 27 requires that "the Charter shall be interpreted in a manner consistent with the preservation and enhancement of the multicultural heritage of Canada."

how far governments should go in limiting freedoms to protect people from potential harm is often controversial, as discussed in Chapter 3. Generally, when rights and freedoms are entrenched (included) in the formal constitution, the courts may be called upon to determine whether laws limiting rights and freedoms are justified or excessive (see Box 12-4, The Courts and Freedom of Speech). However, it can be a lengthy process to determine whether a law or government action violates rights and freedoms.

The Courts and Freedom of Speech

In 1919, the U.S. Supreme Court upheld the conviction under the Espionage Act of Charles Schrenck, the secretary of the Socialist Party of America, for distributing flyers urging opposition to the draft in World War I. The Court ruled that there was a "clear and present danger" in times of war that justified restriction of freedom of speech. Then, in 1969, the U.S. Supreme Court struck down the conviction of Ku Klux Klan leader Clarence Brandenburg, who had given a speech calling for revenge against "niggers" and Jews. The Court modified the "clear and present danger" criterion to rule that freedom of speech could not be restricted unless "advocacy is directed to inciting or producing imminent lawless action and is likely to incite or produce such action" (*Brandenburg v. Ohio 395 U.S. 444*).

The U.S. Supreme Court generally has interpreted constitutional protection of free speech in a more libertarian manner than is the case in most other countries. For example, Germany (like many other European countries) has a law prohibiting denial of the Holocaust (or, more generally, genocide). In 2010, British Bishop Richard Williamson was convicted of stating in a Swedish television interview (available in Germany on YouTube) that he didn't believe that millions of Jews had been killed in Nazi death camps. Similarly, the Supreme Court of Canada upheld the conviction of teacher James Keegstra under the provision of the Criminal Code banning "hate speech" for wilful promotion of hatred against Jews. In the view of the majority of Supreme Court judges, there was a "pressing and substantial concern" that justified restricting freedom of speech and that hate speech was "only tenuously connected with the values underlying the guarantee of freedom of speech" (quoted in Russell, Knopff, Bateman, & Hiebert, 2008, p. 282).

In the wake of the terrorist attacks on the United States in 2001, the governments of many democratic countries took strong measures to deal with terrorism. Some of these measures have been criticized for violating the rule of law and individual rights and freedoms. For example, the Parliament of the United Kingdom passed legislation in 2001 that allowed resident foreigners suspected of terrorism to be interned without trial, if they chose not to be deported to their home countries where they could be subject to torture or the death penalty. After this legislation was ruled to be in conflict with the Human Rights Act, the UK Parliament passed the Prevention of Terrorism Act 2005, which allowed judges to authorize house arrest and other control measures for both citizens and foreign nationals suspected of involvement with terrorism. Critics argued that this violated the legal principle of habeas corpus (the right to a court hearing to determine whether a person is detained lawfully), which dates back to the Magna Carta of 1215.

As part of the American "war against terrorism," several hundred foreigners, including juveniles, captured during the conflict in Afghanistan were held for very lengthy periods of time at Guantánamo Bay, a U.S. military base leased from Cuba since 1903 where American law does not apply, without being charged. Prisoners were denied access to their families and to legal counsel

◄ Terrorism and the rule of law: several hundred foreigners were held for very lengthy periods of time at Guantánamo Bay (a U.S. military base on land perpetually leased from Cuba in 1903) without being charged. Allegations of ill treatment and torture of prisoners later surfaced.

and subjected to ill treatment. As well, a number of "enemy combatants" were transported to foreign countries, where allegedly they were tortured.

Canada's anti-terrorism legislation adopted in 2001 allowed individuals suspected of involvement in terrorism to be held for seventy-two hours without a charge being laid, and potentially to be imprisoned for up to twelve months if they did not abide by certain restrictive conditions. Through security certificates endorsed by a federal judge, non-citizens could be held indefinitely without charge based on secret evidence unless they decided to return immediately to their home countries. This provision (which was only used in a few cases) was struck down by the Supreme Court of Canada in 2007. Canadian anti-terrorism legislation also provided that those called before an investigative hearing could be compelled to testify, required lawyers to report in secret to government authorities if they believed that their clients were engaged in suspicious transactions, made it a serious offence to give money or financial or other related services to groups or individuals that the Canadian government declares to be terrorist, and allowed the Canadian Security Establishment to intercept private international communications by Canadians without judicial authorization. Some of these provisions had a "sunset clause," meaning that they expired after six years.[3]

The **reasonable limits clause** of the Canadian Charter of Rights and Freedoms explicitly allows for laws to place reasonable limits on rights and freedoms, provided that the limits can be "demonstrably justified in a free and democratic society" (Section 1). For example, the Supreme Court of Canada has upheld laws prohibiting hate literature and possession of child pornography as reasonable limits on freedom of expression. Canada's reasonable limits clause was the model for a similar clause in South Africa's constitutional Bill of Rights.

REASONABLE LIMITS CLAUSE
A provision in the Charter of Rights and Freedoms that allows for "reasonable limits" to be placed on rights and freedoms, provided that the limits can be "demonstrably justified in a free and democratic society."

---

[3] The opposition parties defeated a renewal of some of these provisions in 2007. Nevertheless, in 2010 the Conservative government proposed a new Combating Terrorism Act that would include provisions similar to those that had expired. At the time this textbook was written, the proposed Act had not been passed.

TABLE 12-1.
THE CHARTER AND THE NOTWITHSTANDING CLAUSE

PROVISIONS THAT CANNOT BE OVERRIDDEN	NOTWITHSTANDING CLAUSE APPLIES TO
Democratic rights	Fundamental freedoms
Mobility rights	Legal rights
Language rights	Equality rights
Male–female equality rights	

NOTWITHSTANDING CLAUSE
A provision in the Charter of Rights and Freedoms that allows a legislative body to explicitly declare that a particular law (related to some parts of the Charter) shall operate *notwithstanding* the provisions of the Charter. Such a declaration is only effective for five years, although it can be re-enacted as often as is desired.

CONSTITUTIONAL AMENDMENT A formal change to the constitution.

Overriding the Charter: The Notwithstanding Clause   The Canadian Charter of Rights and Freedoms was opposed by some premiers who argued that Parliament or provincial legislatures rather than the courts should have the final say in determining the appropriate extent of rights and freedoms.[4] As a compromise, Section 33 of the Charter allows Parliament or a provincial legislature to override some rights by using the **notwithstanding clause** (see Table 12-1). This involves Parliament or a provincial legislature explicitly declaring that a particular law shall operate *notwithstanding* the provisions of the Charter. Such a declaration is only effective for five years, although it can be re-enacted as often as is desired. Box 12-5, The Use of the Notwithstanding Clause, provides an example of how this clause has been used.

Amending the Constitution

Constitutional amendments are needed from time to time because of changing circumstances and the changing values of a country's citizens. Experiences with the constitution may also lead to a desire to improve it. However, to try to ensure that a government does not change the constitution to gain excessive powers or to take away constitutionally protected rights, most countries require a higher level of support to change their formal, written constitution than is needed to pass or change an ordinary law. For example, amendments to the American constitution must be proposed by a two-thirds majority in each of the two Houses of Congress (or by a convention requested by two-thirds of the state legislatures). Three-quarters of the state legislatures (or conventions held in three-quarters of the states) must ratify the proposal.[5] Only twenty-seven amendments to the American constitution have been passed in more than two hundred years. Some countries (such as Sweden, Denmark, and the Netherlands) require that amendments be passed by parliamentary bodies twice—once before and once after an election. Other countries (including

---

[4] As well, the Quebec government opposed a constitutional charter that would apply to the provincial governments.

[5] Proposal by Congress and ratification by state legislatures are almost always used. However, the Twenty-first Amendment overturning the prohibition of alcohol (1933) was ratified by special state conventions rather than by state legislatures.

The Use of the Notwithstanding Clause

The notwithstanding clause in Canada's Charter of Rights and Freedoms has stirred much controversy. Some view it as an unfortunate compromise between the supporters and opponents of the Charter that results in important rights being vulnerable to the whims of the governing party in Parliament or a provincial legislature and to the pressure of public opinion. Others argue that the clause allows flexibility and protects democratic principles by ensuring that responsibility for some political decisions ultimately lies with the elected representatives of the people (Petter, 1990). Although some countries limit rights and freedoms in times of national emergency, Canada is almost unique in having a clause that explicitly allows constitutionally protected rights to be overridden.

The notwithstanding clause has been rarely used by provincial and territorial legislatures and never used by the Canadian Parliament. However, considerable attention was given to its use to protect the French character of Quebec. In 1988, the Supreme Court of Canada struck down the provision in Quebec's Charter of the French Language (Bill 101) that required most public signs in that province to be exclusively in French. The Quebec government then invoked the notwithstanding clause and passed a sign law permitting only French on signs outside stores while allowing French and English on signs inside stores. However, the Quebec government did not renew its use of the notwithstanding clause when the five-year limit ran out. Instead, it passed a new sign law in 1993, consistent with the Supreme Court's ruling, that required French to be given a prominent position on signs in Quebec.

The requirement that legislation must explicitly state that the Charter is being overridden makes it politically risky for a government to use the notwithstanding clause because of the public's strong support for the rights and freedoms included in the Charter.

Australia, Switzerland, and Japan) require approval in a referendum as well as by legislative bodies (Rasch & Congleton, 2006).

AMENDING CANADA'S CONSTITUTION   Some aspects of the Canadian constitution can be changed without any procedural difficulties. The unwritten aspects of the Canadian constitution—conventions and judicial interpretations—evolve over time. Ordinary laws that are of constitutional significance (such as the Canada Elections Act) can be changed by the adoption of a new law by a simple majority in Parliament or a provincial legislature. The procedures adopted in 1982 for amending the Constitution Act are more complex:

- A few provisions of the Constitution Act, such as the offices of the monarch, governor general, and lieutenant-governors, and the composition of the Supreme Court of Canada, are only amendable by the resolution of a majority in Parliament[6] and in all of the provincial legislatures.

---

[6] A majority in each of the chambers of Parliament (that is, the House of Commons and the Senate) is normally needed for any amendments to the constitution. However, if the Senate does not pass the resolution for the amendment, after one hundred and eighty days the House of Commons can repass the resolution, in which case the approval of the Senate is not needed for the amendment.

- Most of the Constitution Act (including the division of law-making authority between Parliament and provincial legislatures) can be changed with the agreement of majorities in the House of Commons and the Senate and majorities in at least two-thirds of the provincial legislatures, provided those legislatures represent provinces containing at least one-half of the population of all the provinces.[7] A province has the right to "opt out" of a constitutional amendment that reduces the powers of its legislature.
- Although a referendum is not required to approve constitutional changes, the use of a referendum in 1992 to seek approval for a major package of changes suggests that there is a political expectation that a referendum be held to approve major changes. British Columbia and Alberta require that a referendum be held before their legislatures approve a constitutional amendment.
- Changes to constitutional provisions that affect only certain provinces (such as the change of the name of the province of Newfoundland to Newfoundland and Labrador in 2001) require the approval of Parliament and only the affected provincial legislatures.

Major amendments to the formal constitution have proven difficult to achieve. The Constitution Act, 1982 was passed over the strenuous objections of the Quebec government and Aboriginal leaders. An attempt to win the support of Quebec for the Constitution Act, 1982 met with failure when the **Meech Lake Accord** failed to win the approval of the Newfoundland and Manitoba legislatures within the required time frame in 1990. Although the Meech Lake Accord initially had the support of the prime minister and all ten premiers, it aroused strong opposition, particularly to the clause recognizing Quebec as a "distinct society," in the rest of Canada. A second attempt, the **Charlottetown Accord** (1992), also gained the support of the prime minister, premiers, territorial leaders, and national Aboriginal leaders for a package of changes that included recognition of the inherent right of Aboriginals to self-government and major changes to the Senate. However, the Charlottetown Accord was defeated in a referendum, with 55 percent of Canadians rejecting it.

Overall, the different views on the nature of Canada held by many English-speaking Canadians, French-speaking Quebecers, and Aboriginals have made major changes to Canada's formal constitution very contentious. With a high level of agreement needed for constitutional changes, it is not surprising that major changes have been difficult to achieve.

MEECH LAKE ACCORD A 1987 package of proposed constitutional changes that was not passed. It contained controversial provisions, including the recognition of Quebec as a "distinct society."

CHARLOTTETOWN ACCORD A 1992 package of proposed constitutional changes, including recognition of the inherent right of Aboriginals to self-government and major changes to the Senate. It was defeated in a referendum.

---

[7] Although this is still the procedure in the Constitution Act, the Canadian Parliament passed legislation in 1996 requiring that proposed constitutional changes introduced into the Canadian Parliament must also have the support of Ontario, Quebec, British Columbia, the Prairies (in effect, Alberta plus either Saskatchewan or Manitoba), and Atlantic Canada (at least two provinces containing at least one-half of the region's population).

JUDICIAL REVIEW

In some countries (including Japan, Australia, Italy, and India), the courts have the authority to strike down legislation or governmental actions that are deemed to be in violation of the constitution. Even though the power of **judicial review** is not explicitly stated in the American constitution, the Supreme Court assumed this power by its ruling in *Marbury v. Madison* (1803) that "Congress can not pass laws that are contrary to the Constitution and it is the role of the federal courts to interpret what the Constitution permits." Likewise in Canada, although the Constitution Act, 1867 did not explicitly include the power of judicial review, judicial bodies early on assumed this role in ruling on disputes concerning the distribution of law-making authority between Parliament and provincial legislatures. The importance of judicial review was enhanced by the Charter of Rights and Freedoms and by Section 52 of the Constitution Act, 1982, which states that the constitution is "the supreme law of Canada" and that "any law that is inconsistent with the Constitution is, to the extent of the inconsistency, of no force or effect."

In many countries (including Germany, Austria, France, and Chile), judicial review is carried out by a special constitutional court rather than by the regular court system. Some countries (including Belgium, the Netherlands, and Switzerland) do not provide for judicial review, or have only a weak version of it (Lane & Ersson, 2000; Newton & Van Deth, 2010). Rather than determining whether legislation is constitutional, the courts in these countries may interpret laws in ways that emphasize individual rights and procedural fairness. In the United Kingdom, the principle of **parliamentary sovereignty** means that Parliament is the supreme law-making body and the courts cannot invalidate an Act of Parliament. However, the courts can declare an Act of Parliament as incompatible with the Human Rights Act (1998). In addition, the United Kingdom is expected to abide by the rules and regulations of the European Union.

Even in countries where judicial review is available, there is considerable variation in the degree to which the courts are active in invalidating legislation and government actions that are inconsistent with the constitution. The United States is often viewed as the best example of **judicial activism**. For example, in the 1930s, the Supreme Court overturned a number of laws that had been passed as part of President Roosevelt's "New Deal" to address the Great Depression. The U.S. Supreme Court also played a major role in ending racial segregation (which it had earlier upheld) by invalidating state laws that prevented black students from attending white schools, overturning laws that made interracial marriages illegal, and ordering that children be bused from one neighbourhood to another to try to achieve racial integration in public schools.

In Canada, the Judicial Committee of the Privy Council (a panel of judges primarily from the British House of Lords) was the highest court of appeal

JUDICIAL REVIEW The authority of the courts to strike down legislation or governmental actions that the courts deem to be in violation of the constitution.

PARLIAMENTARY SOVEREIGNTY A basic principle of the British system of governing, recognizing Parliament as the supreme law-making body such that the courts cannot invalidate an Act of Parliament.

JUDICIAL ACTIVISM The term used when the courts are active in invalidating legislation and government actions that are inconsistent with the constitution.

BOX 12-6

Is Judicial Activism Desirable?

Some commentators have argued that judicial activism has made Canadian courts too powerful. Instead of the elected representatives of the people making decisions about controversial issues, appointed judges who are unaccountable are, in effect, making important decisions concerning issues such as abortion, same-sex marriage, and the legalization of the medical use of marijuana. Because governments have been very reluctant to use the Charter's "notwithstanding clause," there is no check on what some view as the excessive activism of the courts (Morton, 2003). As well, the courts (unlike governments) generally do not have the capability to monitor and assess the consequences of their decisions.

Other commentators argue that by actively using the Charter, the courts have helped to protect the rights of minorities. When it adopted the Charter of Rights and Freedoms, Canada established itself as a true constitutional democracy in which an independent judiciary sets limits to the power of government (Potter, 2003). The courts are more likely to be concerned about the rights of unpopular minorities than elected officials, who may be pressured by majority opinion.

In assessing each argument, it should be noted that the courts have been more active in invalidating legislation at some points in time and more deferential to the wishes of legislative bodies at other points in time, depending on the issues involved and the judges who are hearing the cases. As well, governments and legislative bodies have sometimes preferred to leave some controversial moral issues to the courts to decide.

for many matters until 1949 and had an important effect on the evolution of Canada's federal system, particularly by striking down a number of federal laws that it viewed as infringing upon provincial legislative authority. After the Charter of Rights and Freedoms was adopted in 1982, the Supreme Court of Canada became quite active in invalidating laws and policies that the court viewed as inconsistent with the Charter. For example, in 1988 the Supreme Court struck down a law that (with certain exceptions) made abortion a criminal offence, ruling that the law violated the Charter right to "life, liberty and security of the person." A subsequent attempt to pass a new law specifying the conditions under which abortion would be allowed failed to be approved by Parliament. Similarly, the courts have struck down various laws that discriminate against gays and lesbians by interpreting the equality rights provision in the Charter so as to prohibit discrimination on the basis of sexual orientation even though sexual orientation is not explicitly mentioned in the Charter. As discussed in Box 12-6, Is Judicial Activism Desirable?, there has been considerable controversy about the role of judicial activism in Canada's courts.

Although some European countries allow their constitutional courts to review legislation before it becomes law, Canadian and American courts generally only consider the validity of laws when faced with a particular case. Given the costs of pursuing cases through the court system, many laws and government actions are not reviewed by the courts. The Canadian government can refer a proposed law to the Supreme Court of Canada (and provincial governments to the highest court in their province) for an advisory opinion, as the Canadian government did concerning same-sex marriage. Nevertheless, governments will usually try to ensure that new legislation is "Charter-proof" to avoid the possibility that it will be struck down if a case comes before the courts.

THE INDEPENDENCE OF THE JUDICIARY

To ensure that the rule of law is upheld, the judicial system should be independent of government and other influences. Where a court system is not free from political interference, governments and their agents can intimidate the population, and the principle that all persons should be treated fairly and equally by the law is likely to be undermined.

To protect their independence, judges in Canada and many other constitutional democracies are given a high level of job security, such that they cannot be removed from their position by the government. Federally appointed judges in Canada retain their positions until age seventy-five. Removal can occur only through a resolution passed by a majority in both Houses of Parliament. Further, this action is taken only after the Canadian Judicial Council, which is composed of the provincial chief justices and associate chief justices, conducts an inquiry.

In addition, it is considered improper for politicians or government officials to try to influence a judge (for example, by calling a judge to discuss a case). Judges are expected to refrain from political activity once appointed to the bench.

Selection Process

Although judges are supposed to be completely non-political and non-partisan once appointed, the selection of judges is often in the hands of a political leader who may be tempted to appoint those who have been active in the leader's political party.

The procedure used to appoint Marshall Rothstein to the Supreme Court of Canada in 2006 involved the prime minister and the minister of justice drawing up a confidential list of seven candidates after consultations with leading members of the legal community. An advisory committee then drew up an unranked short list of three names. From this short list, the nominee chosen by the prime minister was questioned by an ad hoc parliamentary committee in a televised hearing (although the committee was told not to ask personal questions or questions about how the prospective judge would rule on particular issues). The decision to recommend the nominee rested with the prime minister; the parliamentary committee did not have the power to confirm or reject the nominee and did not prepare a report or make a recommendation.[8]

---

8 Prime Minister Stephen Harper decided to appoint Thomas Cromwell to the Supreme Court of Canada in 2008 without following this procedure after the opposition parties complained that the inclusion of two Cabinet ministers compromised the independence of the committee.

In choosing other federally appointed judges, the minister of justice makes recommendations to the Cabinet after applicants are assessed by a regional Judicial Advisory Committee. In 2006, a change in the makeup of these committees occurred such that a majority of the members are appointed by the Canadian government and include a representative of the police. This change was criticized by the country's top judges for compromising the independence of the committees (*Globe and Mail Online*, November 10, 2006). A provincial Cabinet minister, the attorney general, makes recommendations to the provincial Cabinet concerning the appointment of judges to the lower provincial courts.

Generally, the appointment of judges, particularly at the Supreme Court level, will tend to reflect the perspective of the prime minister. Some provincial premiers have argued that the appointment of Supreme Court judges on the recommendation of the prime minister jeopardizes the ability of the Supreme Court of Canada to fairly adjudicate disputes between the Canadian government and provincial governments.

In the United States, the president's nominees for the Supreme Court and all other federal judges must face hearings conducted by the Senate Judiciary Committee before the Senate decides whether to confirm the nomination. Some of these hearings have involved extensive investigations into the lives and beliefs of the nominees. Presidents often choose nominees based on their ideological orientations, and the Senate has rejected some nominees whose views differ substantially from that of the Senate majority. For example, President Richard Nixon's nomination of G. Harrold Carswell, who had supported racial segregation and opposed women's rights, was rejected by the Senate by a vote of 45–51. U.S. Supreme Court judges can hold their position for life, as there is no mandatory retirement age.

In more than three-quarters of American states, judges are elected by voters rather than appointed and are subject to re-election at regular intervals. While this provides for some democratic accountability of judges, it also may reduce the willingness of judges to act fairly and impartially when the public is incensed about a particular crime or issue. As well, the reliance of judges on large campaign contributions to get elected or re-elected can raise questions about their impartiality.

In Canada, all federally appointed judges and most provincially appointed judges must have at least ten years of experience as a judge or lawyer. In the United States, there are no formal qualifications for Supreme Court judges (although many have had distinguished legal careers). In a number of Western European countries, judges are selected after completing law school and receive specialized training before beginning their judicial careers. In many countries, a judicial appointments commission (often consisting of judges, lawyers, and parliamentary appointees) is responsible for recommending promotion to higher levels of the court system.

◄ Canadian prime ministers have tried to make the Supreme Court of Canada more representative by appointing women to this important body. Beverley McLachlin is Canada's first female Chief Justice.

In recent times, to varying extents, efforts have been made to appoint judges with more diverse characteristics than in the past. At the time this textbook was written, four of the nine Supreme Court of Canada judges were female, including Chief Justice Beverley McLachlin. Prior to 2009, the nine U.S. Supreme Court judges included one female and one African-American. President Obama's first Supreme Court appointment was a Hispanic woman (Sonia Sotomayor) and his second was a Jewish woman (Elena Kagan). Both appointments were controversial, with most Republican senators voting against confirming these choices.

COURT SYSTEMS

Court systems are generally hierarchical in nature, with appeals from lower courts heard in higher courts. Canada can also be described as having a basically unified court system in that the same court system is used for cases involving most laws under federal or provincial jurisdiction. Federally appointed judges are used in all but the lowest (provincial) courts, while provincial governments are responsible for the organization and administration of all courts except the Supreme Court of Canada. Exceptions to this unified court system are the Federal Court, which adjudicates cases related to certain acts of Parliament (including laws related to copyright and patents and citizenship and immigration), the Tax Court of Canada, and military courts.

The United States has a dual or parallel court system in which the vast majority of cases are tried in state courts. Federal courts deal with federal law, but generally do not hear appeals from state courts unless the death penalty has been imposed. The U.S. Supreme Court hears appeals from the highest level of state courts only if it considers the case to involve substantial constitutional issues, a federal statute, or the actions of a federal official (McKenna, 1990).

LEGAL SYSTEMS

Common law and codified law are the two major legal systems used in most liberal democracies. The common law system originated in the twelfth century as the King's courts in England began to use the "common customs" of the country as the basis for their decisions rather than the traditions of different localities used in the courts presided over by the nobles (Hausegger, Hennigar, & Riddell, 2009, p. 12). The practice developed that judges would use precedents (that is, decisions made in previous similar cases) to guide their decisions. Thus **common law** consists of court judgments that have accumulated over many centuries. However, many areas of common law have been superseded by statutory law (that is, law passed by a legislative body). Nevertheless, common law continues to be an important component of **private law**—that is, law that deals with the relationships among individuals, groups, and businesses that are primarily of private interest rather than of general public interest. **Codified law** involves the adoption of a comprehensive system of principles that judges use to determine the outcome of a particular case. Many systems of codified law have been influenced by the code commissioned by French Emperor Napoleon in 1804 (often referred to as the Napoleonic Code), which was derived from the laws of the Roman Empire as well as sources in French law.

Common law is used in England and most of the former British colonies. Codified law (in various versions) is used in most countries in continental Europe and Latin America. In Canada, nine provinces use common law while Quebec uses the Civil Code of Québec, which was adopted in 1994 and replaced an earlier code established in 1866. Criminal law is the responsibility of the federal government, with most criminal law compiled in an Act of Parliament known as the Criminal Code. American states also use the common law, although Louisiana's Civil Code is based, in part, on the Napoleonic Code. Some jurisdictions (including Scotland and South Africa) use a mixture of common law and codified law.

COMMON LAW A system of law based court judgments that have accumulated over many centuries.

PRIVATE LAW Law that deals with the relationships among individuals, groups, and businesses that are primarily of private interest rather than of general public interest.

CODIFIED LAW A system of law based on the adoption of a comprehensive set of principles that judges use to determine the outcome of a particular case.

Summary and Conclusion

The basic legal framework for governing is provided by the constitution. Ideally, constitutions reflect a fundamental consensus among citizens about the governing of their country. Where the constitution is widely accepted, the power of those in governing positions becomes legitimate authority as long as constitutional rules and procedures are followed. However, because a constitution has a strong effect on the distribution of political power, the constitution and proposals for constitutional change can be very controversial.

The constitutions of most countries potentially limit the power of government by establishing various rights and freedoms for the population. Most countries in modern times have given the courts (whether regular courts or special constitutional courts) the authority to review legislation and government actions to determine whether they are consistent with the constitution. Where the courts are active in exercising that power, this can provide strong protection for rights and freedoms. However, some argue that involving judges in determining the validity of legislation makes the judiciary too powerful and interferes with the principle that the judiciary should be separate from politics. The political significance of the courts makes the process of selecting judges very important.

The protection of rights and freedoms and the promotion of economic, social, and cultural rights may be considered desirable for the promotion of the common good. A free society in which people do not fear arbitrary action by government, have the right to participate in political life, and are able to enjoy a basic standard of living and quality of life will be more likely to foster the good of all than will a society controlled by a dictatorial government concerned with maintaining its control of society. However, terrorist attacks have raised questions in liberal democracies about how to reconcile concerns about security with a commitment to individual rights and freedoms. For some, the threat of terrorism justifies extraordinary measures; others argue that terrorism should be fought without substantial changes to our rights and freedoms.

Some commentators argue that too much emphasis is placed on individual rights without a corresponding concern for the responsibility of individuals to each other and to their community. For example, it can be argued that the right to vote carries with it a responsibility to make an informed judgment about what is good for the community when voting. However if freedoms are only granted to those who act "responsibly," then the freedoms may be so limited as to be meaningless. The point of political freedoms is to allow a diversity of opinions to be expressed so that, through discussion, the best course of action can emerge. Developing a sense of responsibility in all citizens is undoubtedly desirable, but may be best achieved through encouragement and education rather than through legal requirements.

Critics of our "rights culture" also argue that by focusing attention on individual rights, discussion of the common good may be neglected. Going to court to pursue one's rights not only is expensive, and thus more available to the wealthier elements of society, but also detracts from the democratic political activity of trying to convince others that a particular course of action is for the common good. Nevertheless, legal action can be a useful way to ensure that government and public agencies live up to their responsibilities.

The courts are important not only in ensuring that people accused of violating the law receive a fair trial, but also in interpreting and reviewing laws and government actions to ensure that they are compatible with the constitution. To ensure that the judicial system works for the common good and protects the rights of individuals and minorities, it should be independent of government, impartial, and fair. However, the methods used to select judges may raise questions about whether the judicial system is completely independent and impartial.

Key Terms

Discussion Questions

1. Should economic, social, and cultural rights be added to the Canadian Charter of Rights and Freedoms?

2. Should the "notwithstanding clause" be eliminated from the Canadian constitution?

3. Should the rule of law and civil liberties be suspended when a country is faced with terrorist threats?

4. How should judges be chosen?

5. Is judicial activism desirable?

Further Reading

Bogdanor, V. (2009). *The new British constitution*. Oxford: Hart Publishing.

Green, I. (2006). *The courts*. Vancouver: UBC Press.

King, A. (2007). *The British constitution*. Oxford: Oxford University Press.

MacIvor, H. (2005). *Canadian government and politics in the Charter era*. Toronto: Nelson Thomson.

Malleson, K., & Russell, P.H. (Eds.). (2006). *Appointing judges in an age of judicial power: Critical perspectives from around the world*. Toronto: University of Toronto Press.

Russell, P. (2004). *Constitutional odyssey* (3rd ed.). Toronto: University of Toronto Press.

Chapter 13

Multiple Governments

PHOTO ABOVE: On May 16, 2007, Alex Salmond, leader of a party that is committed to holding a referendum on independence for Scotland, became head of the Scottish government.

1. describe and assess unitary, federal, and confederal systems
2. define the meaning of devolution and discuss how it has been applied
3. compare the Canadian federal system to other federal systems
4. outline the basic features of the European Union
5. discuss the significance of local government

On May 16, 2007, Alex Salmond, the leader of the Scottish National Party, which is committed to an independent Scotland within the European Union, was sworn in as First Minister of the Scottish government.

The United Kingdom has often been thought of as a highly centralized country. The principle of parliamentary sovereignty meant that the British prime minister and Cabinet with the support of the majority party in Parliament has had virtually unlimited powers. For example, although there are a large number of local governments, Prime Minister Margaret Thatcher didn't hesitate to eliminate the Greater London Council in 1986 because she viewed it as too left-wing. Nevertheless, the United Kingdom can be considered a multinational country in which England, Scotland, Wales, and Northern Ireland each retain a distinctive identity. Although political authority has been concentrated in London, some laws and policies have reflected the differences among the component units of the country.

As in a number of other countries, there has been a move away from centralized political authority in the United Kingdom in recent times. The rise of nationalism, particularly in Scotland in the 1970s, created pressure for change. The governing Conservative party under Thatcher was perceived as pursuing a centralization of power. This contributed to the Conservative party losing all of its seats in Scotland and Wales. The Labour party, which had considerable support in those areas, adopted the cause of establishing Scottish and Welsh Parliaments. Upon being elected in 1997, the party proceeded to hold a referendum in Scotland and Wales that endorsed the idea of a Parliament for Scotland and an Assembly for Wales. This did not, however, fully satisfy many in Scotland who felt that the powers granted were too limited. Others in the

United Kingdom, however, worried that the creation of Scottish and Welsh governments could eventually lead to the breakup of the United Kingdom.

The Scottish National Party narrowly won the election to the Scottish Parliament in 2007, winning 47 of the 129 seats. Because it formed a minority government with the support of only the two Green party members, its ability to achieve its objectives, including holding a referendum on independence for Scotland, was very limited. To reduce support for independence and prevent the Scottish National Party from winning a majority in the 2011 Scottish election, the British government planned to introduce legislation to increase the powers of the Scottish Parliament.

The devolution of powers to regional parliaments has caused some grumbling in England. Members elected from Scotland, Wales, and Northern Ireland vote on matters in the Parliament of the United Kingdom that affect only England (such as education), but members from England do not have a voice on these matters for other regions. A plan to establish a series of regional assemblies in England was scuttled when voters in northeast England defeated a proposal for a regional assembly in 2004.

Although the United Kingdom, unlike Canada, does not have a federal system, neither is it a purely unitary system. Not only are there three regional governments with the Scottish Parliament seeking greater powers, but the UK is also a member of the European Union (EU). The laws and regulations adopted by the governing bodies of the EU have important effects on the governing of the United Kingdom.

INTRODUCTION

Virtually every country has more than one government. In addition to the central government, often termed the national government, there are usually a variety of local governments. Many countries also have regional (subnational) governments or regional administrative units. This raises several important questions:

- How do governments within a country relate to one another?
- Is the central government the supreme authority, or is authority shared between central and regional governments?
- Do different governments within a country co-operate for the common good of the country, or are the relations between governments characterized by conflict and power struggles?

Furthermore, there are not only various governments within a country, but also a variety of international governmental agreements and organizations (such as the North American Free Trade Agreement) that affect the policies of the member-states. A particularly important development is that most of the independent countries in Europe have agreed to share some of their sovereign powers with the European Union, which to some extent acts as a supranational government (that is, a government above the state).

To understand the relations among governments within a country, a distinction is usually made between unitary systems and federal systems. In a **unitary system**, sovereign authority rests with the central government. In a **federal system**, sovereign authority is divided or shared between the central government and governments representing provinces in Canada and South Africa; states in the United States, India, and Australia; Länder in Germany and Austria; and cantons in Switzerland.

UNITARY SYSTEM A system of governing in which sovereign authority rests with the central government; regional and local governments are subordinate.

FEDERAL SYSTEM A system of governing in which sovereign authority is divided or shared between the central government and regional governments, with each deriving its authority from the constitution.

UNITARY SYSTEMS

Many countries have unitary systems of government (see Table 13-1 for examples). The constitutional relationship among different governments is hierarchical, with regional and local governments subordinate to the central government. Even though the central government typically delegates some responsibilities to other levels of government or to regional and local administrative authorities, the central government is superior to other governments.

Unitary systems generally provide uniformity across the country in terms of common laws and policies. Regional and local authorities may carry out some of the central government's policies and have some ability to adopt regulations and develop programs that do not conflict with those of the central government.

Devolution

The governments of some countries with unitary systems have granted some legislative (law-making) powers as well as administrative responsibilities to

TABLE 13-1
UNITARY AND FEDERAL SYSTEMS

BASICALLY UNITARY	BASICALLY FEDERAL
Bangladesh	Argentina
Bolivia	Australia
Chile	Austria
Czech Republic	Belgium
Denmark	Brazil
Finland	Canada
France	Ethiopia
Greece	Germany
Hungary	India
Ireland	Malaysia
Japan	Mexico
Netherlands	Nigeria
New Zealand	Russia
Poland	South Africa
South Korea	Spain
Sweden	Switzerland
Turkey	United States
United Kingdom	Venezuela

DEVOLUTION A system of governing in which the central government grants some legislative (law-making) powers as well as administrative responsibilities to one or more regional bodies.

one or more regional bodies—a process termed **devolution**. For example, France and Italy have established regional governments with elected assemblies that have significant powers in their region of the country. As discussed in the introductory vignette, the United Kingdom has established regional governments and legislatures for Scotland, Wales, and Northern Ireland, though not for England, which has a large majority of seats in the UK Parliament. These governments are able to legislate on such matters as health, education, law and order, and transportation. However, the powers of these governments concerning taxation are very limited in the case of Scotland and non-existent in the case of Wales and Northern Ireland.

Devolution does not involve sharing sovereignty with regional governments. The Parliament of the United Kingdom could revoke the devolution of powers regardless of the wishes of the regional legislature. Indeed, the Parliament of the United Kingdom suspended the Parliament of Northern Ireland in 1972 (reinstated in 2007) because of the violent conflicts in that territory. Nevertheless, many see Scotland as becoming increasingly self-governing within the United Kingdom. It is very unlikely that the British government would try to take away the powers that have been granted to the Scottish Parliament, particularly because they were supported by a substantial majority of Scottish voters in a referendum.

In some basically unitary countries, certain distinctive regions have extensive autonomy that is constitutionally protected. For example, the former

◀ Bitter opponents Protestant Unionist leader Ian Paisley and Catholic Sinn Fein leader Gerry Adams sit together after agreeing on a historic power-sharing agreement that allowed the reopening of the Northern Ireland Assembly in 2007.

colonies of Hong Kong and Macau are special administrative regions of the People's Republic of China with a high degree of autonomy in accordance with a Basic Law providing for "one country, two systems." Greenland became self-governing in 2009, although Denmark remains responsible for military protection and foreign policy as well as for providing some financial assistance.

Generally, there has been a tendency in recent decades for central governments in unitary systems to devolve powers to regional authorities. In part, devolution has allowed for greater responsiveness to the needs, cultures, and circumstances of different parts of the country and for greater participation of citizens in governing. As well, devolution can be a response to nationalist movements seeking self-government or independence.

FEDERAL SYSTEMS

In a federal system, regional governments—such as provincial governments in Canada and state governments in the United States—are not subordinate to the central (national or federal) government. The federal and provincial governments each derive their authority from the constitution. Provincial governments cannot be abolished by the central government, nor can the federal government be abolished by provincial governments. Constitutional changes, particularly those that affect the powers of the two levels of government, require the agreement of both levels of government. Both the central and the regional governments interact directly with those they govern. That is, citizens directly elect representatives to both their provincial legislatures and the national Parliament, and the laws and policies of national and provincial governments directly affect the people and territory they govern.

Reasons for Adoption

In some cases, federal systems have been established as a way of creating or holding together large countries. Federal systems have also been adopted in some countries to provide regionally based language, ethnic, or cultural groups with a degree of self-government.

The first modern federal system was established in the United States in 1789 when the thirteen states that had fought for their independence from Britain agreed to establish a central government. The founders of the United States believed in the virtues of limited government and wanted the states to continue to be self-governing in many respects (Lyons, Scheb, & Richardson, 1995). As a result, they developed a federal system in which necessary governing powers would be divided between the two levels of government. Subsequently, a variety of other countries (see Table 13-1) have adopted federal systems. At present, about twenty-five countries constituting about 40 percent of the world's population can be considered to have basically federal systems (Watts, 2008).

Canada adopted a federal system because the idea of uniting the British North American colonies that was proposed in the 1860s met with considerable opposition in both Quebec and the Maritimes, where many people feared being dominated by the central government. Maritimers wanted to retain the legislatures they had developed. Quebecers, fearful of the potential consequences of becoming a minority in the new country, wanted to retain control over their own culture.

Division of Powers

Federal systems typically involve a division of powers between national and provincial governments, with the constitution giving some responsibilities to the national government and other responsibilities to provincial governments (see Table 13-2). To varying extents, the constitutions of federal countries also provide for some concurrent policy areas (such as agriculture and immigration in Canada) where both levels of government can pass legislation.

It is virtually impossible to divide legislative authority neatly between the national and provincial governments, and thus there is inevitably some overlap in the responsibilities of each level of government. Through their interpretation of constitutional provisions, the courts or other judicial bodies have often played a significant role in determining the powers of each level of government. For example, Parliament's authority by the Constitution Act, 1867 to legislate for the "peace, order, and good government of Canada" has generally been interpreted quite narrowly rather than giving the Canadian government a general power to act in the interests of the country as a whole.

TABLE 13-2
**THE CONSTITUTIONAL
DIVISION OF POWERS IN
CANADA**

SOME AREAS OF LAW-MAKING THAT ARE THE EXCLUSIVE RESPONSIBILITY OF THE PARLIAMENT OF CANADA	SOME AREAS OF LAW-MAKING THAT ARE THE RESPONSIBILITY OF THE PROVINCIAL LEGISLATURES	AREAS IN WHICH BOTH PARLIAMENT AND PROVINCIAL LEGISLATURES HAVE LAW-MAKING AUTHORITY
Regulation of trade and commerce (interprovincial and international)	Management of public lands	Agriculture
Unemployment insurance	Hospitals	Immigration
Postal service	Municipal institutions	Public pensions
Defence	Education	
Fisheries	Most "local works and undertakings"	
Currency	Laws concerning property rights and the relations among individuals	
Banking	Administration of justice within a province	
Indian affairs	"Generally all Matters of a merely local or private nature in the Province"	
Criminal law	Non-renewable natural resources, forest resources, and electrical energy	
Marriage and divorce		
The "peace, order, and good government of Canada"		
Foreign affairs		

SHARED DECISION MAKING   Some federal systems are characterized primarily by shared decision making. For example, in the German federal system, the national Parliament is responsible for legislation in most fields, although this often involves negotiations between the representatives of the national governing coalition parties and the representatives of the Land (state) governments that sit in the upper chamber of Parliament. The Land governments are responsible for administering most of the legislation passed by the national Parliament, although much of the actual provision is, in turn, carried out by local governments (Courchene, 2007; Swenden, 2006).

Intergovernmental Relations

In what is often termed **classical federalism**, the federal and provincial governments each concern themselves with their own areas of constitutional authority without infringing upon the areas of authority of the other level of government. Thus, classical federalism, which in Canada lasted from the mid 1890s until 1939 (with the exception of the period around World War I), involved a low level of interaction between the two levels of government.

As the activities of governments expanded, particularly with the development of the modern welfare state, the need to coordinate the policies of the

CLASSICAL FEDERALISM A version of federalism in which the federal and provincial governments each concern themselves with their own areas of constitutional authority without infringing upon the areas of authority of the other level of government.

central and provincial governments became more important. Contemporary federal systems typically feature both levels of government involved in many of the same areas of activity, often jointly involved in developing and administering important services. As well, large amounts of financial resources often need to be transferred from the central to the regional governments to carry out their programs. For example, the Canadian government contributes to the financing of many programs that are the constitutional responsibility of provincial governments, including health care, post-secondary education, and social assistance. Generally, Canadian government transfers to provincial governments for these programs (usually on a per capita basis) are unconditional; that is, the money can be spent as the provincial government sees fit. However, in the case of the Canada Health Transfer, provincial and territorial governments are required to follow the principles of public administration, comprehensiveness, universality, portability, and accessibility in providing basic public health care. In addition, the Canadian government provides unconditional **equalization payments** to the governments of the poorer provinces to assist them in providing services to their residents (as discussed in Box 13-1, Equalization Payments).

EQUALIZATION PAYMENTS
Payments made by the federal government to try to ensure that different provincial governments are able to provide an equivalent level of services to their populations without resorting to excessive levels of taxation.

CO-OPERATIVE FEDERALISM
A federal system in which the two levels of government are jointly involved in developing, financing, and administering many government services.

CO-OPERATIVE FEDERALISM   Modern federal systems usually involve a high degree of interaction between the two levels of government, often described as **co-operative federalism**. In Canada, this interaction primarily involves the executives (prime minister and Cabinet and premiers and their Cabinets) as well as senior officials rather than Parliament and provincial legislatures.

Despite the substantial level of co-operation among the two levels of government in developing, financing, and administering many programs, this does not necessarily mean that the relationships between the two levels of government are harmonious. There can be serious power struggles if the central government tries to impose national standards on programs run by provincial or state governments. Each level of government typically wants a larger share of total government revenues so that it can provide popular programs and services or lower taxes. The interests of particular states or provinces may differ from the interests of the country as a whole. The competition between different political parties that may be in control of each level of government can also create tensions in intergovernmental relations.

The Canadian federal system, in particular, often features considerable conflict between national and provincial governments. A number of provincial governments have resented the "interference" of the national government in areas of provincial authority and have wanted increased powers for provincial governments along with a larger share of tax revenues. Many provincial premiers have found that being strong defenders of provincial interests is useful in winning re-election, even if that means challenging a Canadian government of the same political party. Likewise, some Canadian governments have found

Equalization Payments

Most countries, whether unitary or federal, provide some assistance to the poorer regions of their country. In federal systems, particularly those in which provincial governments provide many of the important and costly public services such as health care, education, and social services, the governments of the poorer regions may not be able to afford to provide the same level of services to their citizens without resorting to excessive levels of taxation. Thus a system of equalization is important for the well-being and unity of the country.

The Canadian government, for example, provides equalization payments to the governments of the less prosperous provinces to give them the same financial capability (ability to raise money through taxes) as an "average" province. In the 2010–2011 fiscal year, these payments to six provinces (including Ontario) amounted to about $14.4 billion. Nevertheless, this may have been insufficient to provide equivalent services in provinces where needs are greater or the costs of providing services are higher as a result of a more geographically disperse population or a higher proportion of people needing social services. There have also been controversies concerning the treatment of non-renewable natural resources (particularly oil and gas). Fifty percent of the revenues from non-renewable resources are now included in the equalization formula. Some provinces (notably Newfoundland and Labrador) argue that their revenues from these resources should not be included (as was promised by the Conservative party in the 2006 election) because they are one-time sources of revenue.

In almost all countries, the national government pays for equalization. However, in Germany, the bulk of equalization funding for the poorer Länder comes from the governments of the richer Länder. The United States does not have an equalization system although some federal grants to state governments for particular programs include larger per capita payments to states with low per capita incomes.

it useful to take an adversarial relationship with some provincial governments so as to be seen as a strong defender of the national interest. Co-operative federalism is not really all that co-operative!

Attempts to coordinate the activities of the two levels of government typically involve difficult negotiations between the Canadian and provincial governments. Nevertheless, there has been an increasing level of collaboration among Canadian governments in recent years (Simeon & Cameron, 2002). For example, environmental policy is, to a considerable extent, the product of a consensus among provincial, territorial, and Canadian ministers of the environment and their officials. This was formalized with the adoption of the Canada-wide Accord on Environmental Harmonization in 1998.[1]

---

[1] The Quebec government has not signed the Accord. It has, however, worked out a co-operation agreement with the Canadian government on environmental assessment.

Regional Representation

In most federal countries, the interests of states or their equivalent are represented in the upper chamber (such as the Senate) of the national legislature. In some cases (such as the United States, Brazil, and Australia), each state has the same number of representatives. In other countries (including Canada, Germany, and Switzerland), equal representation does not exist, but less populated units receive more representation than they would if representation was in proportion to population.

In many cases, the members of the upper chamber are elected by voters in each state. Because of the importance of political parties in most countries, this means that representatives of each state will generally tend to vote in accordance with the national perspective of their party rather than the particular interests of their state. In the United States, however, party discipline is weaker, allowing senators more opportunity to represent the interests of their state. In Germany, the head of government and several Cabinet ministers from each Land (state) are members of the Bundesrat (Federal Council, the upper chamber of the national Parliament). This gives Land governments the ability to be involved in national decision making, as about one-half of German legislation requires the approval of the Bundesrat (Oeter, 2006).

The Canadian Senate (the upper house of Parliament) was intended to represent regional interests. However, its members are appointees of present and past prime ministers. Thus, it has not effectively represented provincial interests. To some extent, provincial interests are represented in the Canadian government through the practice of including persons from all, or almost all, provinces in the Canadian Cabinet. However, the ability of Cabinet ministers to represent provincial interests is limited by Cabinet solidarity and Cabinet secrecy (as discussed in Chapter 14).

Centralization and Decentralization

There are considerable differences among federal systems in the extent to which governing is decentralized. In some federal systems (such as that of Australia), the national government can be considered the major government, with considerable control over government finances and with the ability to take a leading role in a wide variety of policy areas. The Canadian federal system, on the other hand, can be viewed as quite decentralized, as it features strong provincial governments whose decisions have a major impact on the lives of their residents. Provincial governments in Canada have control of a larger share of government revenue than in most other federal systems.

The extent to which a federal system is centralized or decentralized is affected not only by the provisions concerning the division of powers in the constitution and how the constitutional division has been interpreted by judicial bodies, but also by various political, social, and economic factors.

Federalism and Multi-Level Governance
www.unc.edu/depts/europe/conferences/mlg/

"We can keep dumping in this river for now . . . it will take years until the federal and provincial governments agree on who should legislate a ban."

Institute of Intergovernmental Relations
www.queensu.ca/iigr/index.html

Individual countries have moved in the direction of centralization or decentralization depending on the circumstances of a particular time. Despite being established as a decentralized federal system, the central government in the United States has come to play a leading role in American politics, although state governments continue to have important constitutional powers. Many Americans look to the central government to solve economic, social, and security problems. The international role of the United States helps to enhance the power of the central government. Despite the rhetoric of national politicians in favour of enhancing the powers of state governments, legislation such as the Homeland Security Act of 2002 and the No Child Left Behind Act has reduced the power of state governments in recent times (Albritton, 2006).

The Canadian federal system, in contrast to the American system, initially concentrated considerable power in the hands of the Canadian government. A number of provincial governments have been assertive in using their powers and have, at times, resisted efforts by the federal government to get involved in matters under provincial jurisdiction. Judicial decisions in the late nineteenth and early twentieth centuries also contributed to decentralization by interpreting the constitution in ways that limited some of the general powers of the Canadian government. In recent decades, the threat of Quebec independence has helped to move the Canadian federal system further toward decentralization. Resource-rich provinces such as Alberta, along with Ontario, have also at times created strong pressures in favour of decentralization.

MODERNIZATION AND GLOBALIZATION   In the past, it was often thought that as countries modernized, they would become more centralized. Regional differences would decline as transportation and communication links tied a country closer together. The increased mobility of people would make ties to a particular place of residence less important. A strong central government would be needed to manage the national economy effectively and to provide a variety of social services to the population. However, the trend in recent decades has often been in the opposite direction. In both unitary and federal systems, there has been a tendency to disperse power from the central government to regional and local governments (Hooghe & Marks, 2001).

Some analysts have suggested that globalization encourages decentralization (Courchene, 1992). In a more globalized economy, the ability of central government to manage the national economy is reduced. Regions and important cities can develop international and global links. For example, the North American Free Trade Agreement has, to some extent, increased economic links between Canadian provinces and neighbouring American states at the expense of economic links across Canada. However, the impact of globalization appears to be mixed: in some cases it has encouraged a trend toward centralization, in others toward decentralization, and in still others has had no apparent effect. One set of studies found that the effects of globalization have not, at least not yet, been powerful enough to change the balance between centralization and decentralization in various federal systems. Changes in the direction of centralization or decentralization appear to be affected more by domestic factors than by external factors such as globalization (Lazar, Telford, & Watts, 2003).

Asymmetrical Federalism

ASYMMETRICAL FEDERALISM
A version of federalism in which some provincial or state governments have a greater degree of self-government than others.

In some federal systems, such as the United States, there is uniformity among state governments in that each has the same legislative powers. In others, such as India, Malaysia, and Belgium, some regional governments have a greater degree of self-government than other regional governments, a system described as **asymmetrical federalism** (Watts, 2008). In some cases, the constitution

Asymmetrical Federalism in Spain and Canada

In the past, Spain was highly centralized. Since it moved from dictatorship to democracy, it has become quite decentralized, although it does not formally call itself a federation. Its constitution adopted in 1978 lists the areas in which its seventeen Autonomous Communities (called *autonomías* in Spanish, equivalent to provinces or states) may elect to exercise their jurisdiction. Each of these Communities proposes an autonomy statute, effectively its constitution, where it lays out the powers it wishes to exercise and which it must negotiate with the national government. Thus, one Autonomous Community, such as the Basque Country, may decide to assume more control over its health care system than does another, such as Castilla y Leon.

In Canada, the question of whether Quebec should be recognized as a distinct society, which could provide a justification for more areas of legislative authority than the other provincial governments have, has been very controversial. For many Canadians outside Quebec, the principle of the equal legal status of the provinces is fundamental. Each provincial government should have the same powers and Quebec should not have any form of different or special status. More powers for the Quebec government, it is argued, would undermine national unity and lead eventually to Quebec independence. Many French-speaking Quebecers, on the other hand, view the Quebec government as representing one of the major founding peoples of Canada and support the desire of the Quebec government to lead the social and economic development of the province.

In the words of former Prime Minister Joe Clark, Canada is a "community of communities." From this perspective, "national" communities such as Quebec and First Nations should have the powers needed to protect and develop their cultures (Gagnon, 2010).

Asymmetrical federalism can make a federal system more flexible by responding to the different political cultures and identities of different areas of the country. However, it tends to reduce the uniformity of programs and policies across the country and to increase the complexity of the federal system.

establishes different powers for different regional governments (as discussed in Box 13-2, Asymmetrical Federalism in Spain and Canada). In other cases, the constitution allows regional governments to opt in or opt out of national programs thus creating asymmetry when some, but not all, regional governments take advantage of that opportunity.[2]

The Canadian federal system has some asymmetrical elements. The Constitution Act, 1867 provided for a different system of private law for Quebec (the Civil Code of Québec). When the Canada Pension Plan was established in 1965, Quebec alone exercised the right of provincial governments to

---

[2] Many unitary systems also feature asymmetry in that certain regional governments have more powers than others. Devolution to some regional governments, as in the United Kingdom, is a form of asymmetry.

control pensions by setting up the Quebec Pension Plan. Through an agreement between the Quebec and Canadian governments, Quebec established a Parental Insurance Plan in 2006 to provide different maternity, paternity, parental, and adoption benefits than are available through the federal Employment Insurance program in the rest of Canada.

Community Self-government

A federal system usually involves a division of authority between the central government and a number of regional governments that represent particular geographical areas. However, a federal system can also involve linguistic, ethnic, or religious communities that have a degree of self-government. For example, the federal system in Belgium involves three communities (corresponding to the Dutch-, French-, and German-speaking groups) that are responsible for linguistic and cultural matters, as well as three regional governments. In Canada, the gradual movement toward Aboriginal self-government may eventually result in a "third order" of government, with substantial authority based on membership in particular Aboriginal communities. Such governments are not necessarily confined to jurisdiction over Aboriginal lands, but could provide education and social services to Aboriginals living in cities. Recent treaty and land claim settlements have provided some Aboriginal nations with quite extensive constitutionally protected governing authority. However, given their small populations and economic weaknesses, it may be difficult for many First Nations to fully exercise their potential powers.

ASSESSING UNITARY AND FEDERAL SYSTEMS

Benefits of the Unitary System

There are several reasons why a unitary system might be the best way to provide for the common good. In a unitary system,

- The governing authorities may be more likely to work for the common good of the whole country, as there are no strong subnational governments promoting the particular interests of their region at the expense of the country as a whole.
- National unity may be promoted because greater attention is likely to be given to national issues and problems. In a federal system, provincial governments may find it politically advantageous to highlight and exaggerate regional grievances so that they can be perceived by voters as defenders of their province.
- The central government can be more easily held accountable by citizens as it cannot easily shift blame for problems to other governments.
- People will be more likely to have the same level of government services available in all regions. Uniform standards for education, health care, and

environmental quality are likely to be adopted. Thus all persons may feel that they are equal citizens of the country.

- Greater efficiencies in governing are possible. With a central government in control, policies can be consistently directed toward certain objectives without different governments pursuing different and possibly inconsistent goals. Costly duplication of services by different governments may be avoided. Total administrative costs will likely be lower if many of the activities of government are centralized.

- People may find it easier to have their professional, technical, and educational qualifications recognized, find employment, and conduct business in different parts of the country.

Benefits of the Federal System

Federal systems also have a variety of positive features:

- Provincial or state governments may be more sensitive to the needs and desires of people in particular areas of the country. The flexibility of a federal system enables provincial governments to adopt policies that reflect the circumstances of their region and the values of the people in that region.

- Less populated and remote areas of the country might be ignored in a unitary system, but can find a voice in their own provincial government.

- Citizens may find it easier to participate in the policy-making process in their own province than in the processes of a distant central government.

- A federal system allows for greater diversity than does a unitary state. Minorities that are concentrated within a particular province can use their provincial government to develop their culture. For example, the French language and culture in Canada has been preserved and developed in part because of the powers of the Quebec government. In this case, a group that is a minority in the country as a whole constitutes a large majority in a particular province, and thus is able to achieve a degree of self-government.

- A federal system helps to limit the concentration of power. Consistent with the ideal of liberal democracy, a federal system places constitutional limits on the powers of each government. Competition between central and provincial governments may serve to check the power of each level of government.

- A federal system can allow for experimentation with different policies and approaches by different governments. For example, the government of Saskatchewan initiated the system of free medical care that was subsequently adopted by other provinces and then turned into a nationwide program funded, in part, by the Canadian government.

CONFEDERAL SYSTEMS

CONFEDERAL SYSTEM A system of governing in which sovereign states have agreed to delegate some of their authority to a joint government with limited authority while retaining their sovereignty.

Independent states generally retain their sovereignty when they interact with each other on the international stage. In some cases, however, sovereign states have agreed to delegate some of their authority to a joint government with limited authority while retaining their sovereignty. In this arrangement, known as a **confederal system**, the institutions of the confederation only have those powers that have been delegated to it by the governments of the sovereign states. Because the member-states retain their sovereignty, they could withdraw from the confederation without necessarily seeking the approval of other member-states. In a pure confederal system, the institutions of the confederation do not interact with citizens directly. Instead, they rely on the member-states to implement the agreements (Swenden, 2006). As well, unlike in federal systems, citizens do not directly elect a confederal government. Instead, it consists of representatives of the governments of the member-states.

Confederal systems are not very common.[3] Switzerland, until 1848, was a confederation of cantons. A loose German confederation of thirty-nine states existed between 1815 and 1866. After the War of Independence, the independent American states established a confederal system in 1781. The Congress of the United States (controlled by representatives of state governments) had very limited powers and there was no head of government or head of state for the country. Congress could declare war and conduct foreign relations, but it did not have the power to levy taxes or prevent states from levying tariffs on goods coming in from other states. Within a few years, agreement was reached to establish a federal system to create "a more perfect union" of the states. In the contemporary world, Benelux (Belgium, Netherlands, and Luxembourg), the Caribbean Community (consisting of fifteen member-states), and the Commonwealth of Independent States (eleven former Republics of the Soviet Union, including Russia) can be considered to be basically confederations (Watts, 2008).

THE EUROPEAN UNION

EUROPEAN UNION (EU) A unique system of governing in which many European countries have pooled some of their sovereignty while retaining their independence.

The **European Union** (EU) is a unique system of governing in which many European countries have pooled some of their sovereignty while retaining their independence. The EU combines features of confederal and federal systems. To some extent, the institutions of the EU are supranational (that is, they provide a level of governing above the state).

The origins of the EU can be traced to the commitment of some European leaders to avoid the repetition of the wars that had devastated the continent. In

---

[3] Although the formation of Canada in 1867 is often described as Confederation, Canada has never had a confederal system. Likewise, Switzerland is officially named the Swiss Confederation, but it has a federal system of governing.

◄ The Louise Weiss Building in Strasbourg, France, is the official location of the European Parliament.

1951, six countries formed the European Coal and Steel Community to manage these materials that are important for warfare. This was followed in 1957 by the establishment of the European Economic Community (later termed European Community), which led to the creation of a common market. It also developed common agricultural and fisheries policies and programs to aid the poorer member-states.

In 1992, the Treaty on European Union (often referred to as the Maastricht Treaty) proclaimed the goal of "creating an ever closer union among the peoples of Europe" based on "respect for human dignity, liberty, democracy, equality, the rule of law, and human rights." Since 1992, the EU has expanded from twelve members to include, as of 2010, twenty-seven European countries.[4] This has made the EU, with a population of about five hundred million and a gross national product of about $19 trillion, the world's largest economy. In 2009, the Treaty of Lisbon brought some important changes intended to strengthen the EU and make it more democratic (see Box 13-3, A Constitution for the European Union?).

Key Features

A key feature of the EU is the free movement of persons, goods, services, and capital throughout the Union. Generally, citizens of the EU have the right to work, set up business, and reside in any country. Through a customs union, duties and other charges and restrictions on goods moving within the EU are prohibited and a common customs tariff is placed on goods originating outside the EU.

The EU has also adopted a common currency, the euro, replacing the use of national currencies. As of January 2011, seventeen countries have adopted

---

[4] There are also three official candidate members (Croatia, Macedonia, and Turkey) and five potential members.

A Constitution for the European Union?

There has often been controversy concerning the future of the EU. Some, such as former German Foreign Minister Joschka Fischer, believe that the EU should work toward becoming a fully federal state. Others, such as former British Prime Minister Margaret Thatcher, fear that moves toward greater European integration will result in the loss of national sovereignty, domination by the leading powers such as Germany, and excessive regulation by Brussels-based EU officials.

In 2004, after lengthy and difficult negotiations, the governments of the member-states unanimously agreed to adopt a formal constitution for the EU. However, it was rejected by voters in referendums in France and the Netherlands (and likely would have been defeated by voters in the UK). Without sufficient popular support to obtain ratification in all member-states, the constitutional proposal was shelved.

In 2007, the leaders of the EU countries reached agreement on the Treaty of Lisbon, which would modify existing treaties but not be a constitution for the EU. Voters in Ireland rejected the Treaty in 2008, despite support for it by the major Irish political parties. However, in a second referendum held sixteen months later, two-thirds of those voting supported the Treaty. A severe recession in Ireland combined with guarantees that the Treaty would not infringe upon Irish sovereignty over taxation, family issues (including abortion), and Ireland's neutrality in international affairs helped to gain support for the Treaty. Because the Treaty of Lisbon is not a constitution, referendums were not held in other countries despite significant public opposition in several countries.

The Treaty of Lisbon came into effect on December 1, 2009, after all twenty-seven member-states ratified it. Nevertheless, the EU still lacks widespread popular support and legitimacy among the citizens of Europe. National identities continue to be much stronger than a European identity. There is considerable reluctance among many about transferring more sovereignty from their own state to the EU and resentment when EU laws challenge national laws.

The EU is often described as having a "democratic deficit" because its institutions and operations seem remote and inaccessible to ordinary citizens. Voter turnout for European Parliament elections in 2009 was the lowest ever, with only 43 percent of eligible voters casting a ballot. Although the Treaty of Lisbon increases the power of the elected European Parliament and increases the transparency of EU governing institutions, voters cannot directly change the government of the EU.

the euro and other member-states are working toward meeting the requirements to adopt it. The UK and Denmark are exempted from the obligation to adopt the euro and Swedish voters rejected its use in a referendum. The adoption of the euro along with the establishment of the European Central Bank to manage monetary policy in the "eurozone" (countries using the euro) involves requirements that member-states implement certain fiscal policies, including a maximum level of government debt and deficit[5] and a relatively low rate of

---

[5] The requirement that a government in the eurozone should not have an annual budgetary deficit exceeding 3 percent of the country's gross domestic product (GDP) and government debt exceeding 60 percent of GDP could not be met in the wake of the recession in 2007 to 2009. Ireland, Greece, and Spain had deficits exceeding 10 percent of GDP in 2009 and other countries exceeded the deficit and debt limits to varying extents.

inflation. Adopting a common currency (and associated conditions) limits the ability of individual countries to manage their own economies. The bailout of the Greek government to avoid it defaulting on its loans in 2010 and the financial problems of several other countries illustrate the serious challenges facing the eurozone.

The powers of the EU as specified in the Treaty of Lisbon are classified in terms of three major areas of competence:

1. Exclusive competence of the EU to legislate on such topics as the customs union, competition policy necessary for the internal market, monetary policy for countries using the euro, and the common trading policy.
2. Shared competence allowing member-states to legislate in some policy areas if the EU does not legislate. These areas include the internal market, various aspects of social policy, agriculture and fisheries, environment, consumer protection, transport, energy, freedom, security and justice, and development and humanitarian aid.
3. Support and coordination in areas where member-states have exclusive competence, including health care, education, industry, culture, and tourism.

Europa: Gateway to the European Union
http://europa.eu/index_en.htm

Despite possessing some important powers, the EU is committed to the basic principle of **subsidiarity**, the idea that decisions and actions should be carried out by the level of governing that is closest to citizens. Thus the EU should act only on matters than cannot be effectively carried out by national, regional, or local governments.

SUBSIDIARITY The idea that decisions and actions should be carried out, if possible, by the level of governing that is closest to citizens.

Institutions and Decision Making

The major institutions of the EU include:

- *The European Parliament.* Voters in the EU countries directly elect the European Parliament. Originally it was only a consultative body, but it now has joint ("co-decision") legislative and budgetary powers with the Council of the EU. It can censure the European Commission and conduct independent inquiries. Members of the European Parliament have organized themselves into seven transnational party groupings reflecting different ideological perspectives.
- *The European Council.*[6] The presidents or prime ministers of the member-states usually meet every six months to set the general direction and priorities of the EU. The European Council also selects the full-time President of the Council of the European Union for a term of two and a half years, which can be renewed once.

---

[6] The European Council should not be confused with the Council of Europe, a larger organization that deals particularly with the protection of human rights.

- *The Council of the European Union* (also known as the Council or the Council of Ministers). The Council, the major decision-making body of the EU, is composed of ministers from each of the member-states. Most of its decisions do not require agreement by all member-states, but rather by a qualified majority (55 percent of Council members representing 65 percent of the member-states[7]). However, some policy areas including taxes, social security, foreign policy, and defence policy require unanimous approval by the members of the Council. Different ministers sit on the Council, depending upon the policy area being considered.
- *The European Commission.* Appointed by the governments of the member-states, the Commission initiates legislative proposals, oversees the implementation of common EU policies (either by the civil service of the EU or by member-states), and acts as guardian of the EU treaties. The president of the European Commission along with one commissioner from each member-state (who are approved as a group by the European Parliament) are appointed for a fixed five-year term.[8] Members of the Commission are expected to act independently of the government of the state that selected them so as to act for the interests of the EU as a whole.
- *The Court of Justice of the European Union.* Composed of one independent judge from each member-state, the Court interprets and applies European Community regulations and directives. It can impose a fine on a country that violates EU law and can invalidate an EU law that violates the EU treaties.
- *The European Central Bank.* The Bank manages the euro and is responsible for the EU's economic and monetary policy.

Confederal or Federal?

Unlike countries with federal systems, the EU has not established a constitution (see Box 13-3, A Constitution for the European Union?). Instead, the EU was established and has been modified by treaties ratified by all of its member-states. Some of the decisions of the EU have to be approved by all member-states. As well, although the EU has established a substantial bureaucracy, the member-states are largely responsible for implementing and administering EU directives and regulations. In addition, the EU (unlike governments in federal systems) does not collect taxes from its citizens. Instead, it relies for its budget (one that is smaller than that of some of its member-states) on a small share of a value-added tax, customs duties, and contributions from its member-states based on a percentage of their gross national product.

---

[7] This new version of a qualified majority will be phased in between 2014 and 2017.

[8] Beginning in 2014, members from a rotation of eighteen countries will serve for a five-year term. Controversy surrounds this provision and therefore it is not clear whether it will be implemented.

The EU also differs from a pure confederal system in several ways. Many of its decisions do not require agreement by all of its members-states and some of its decisions directly affect individual citizens and business enterprises. As well, its Parliament is directly elected by its citizens and its Court of Justice can make decisions based on EU law that take precedence over the laws of member-states.

Challenges

Although the EU is represented in a variety of international organizations, it has been unable to take unified positions and actions on many foreign and military policies. For example, there have been important differences among the member-states of the EU concerning military actions in Iraq and Afghanistan.

The EU also faces considerable challenges as it becomes more culturally diverse, a result of its expansion to include many of the former communist countries of Eastern Europe. Particularly controversial is the potential inclusion of Turkey, a country that is only partly in Europe and, although officially secular, one whose population is primarily Islamic. The inclusion of countries in Eastern Europe creates substantial financial costs in terms of aid to the poorer countries. The right of persons in the poorer countries to move to the richer Western European countries to obtain employment provides economic benefits to the richer countries that face labour shortages as a result of low birth rates, but can cause animosity among those who dislike changes to the ethnic and cultural makeup of their country.

Finally, the economic and financial difficulties faced by Europe in 2010 led some to speculate about the possible abandonment of the euro and the effects of the increasing dissatisfaction in the economically stronger countries about supporting the weaker countries that might potentially lead to the breakup of the EU.

LOCAL GOVERNMENTS

Although attention in political life often focuses on politics and governing at the national and international levels, it is the local communities we live in that are particularly important to our quality of life. The friendliness and safety of our neighbourhoods; the availability of parks, playgrounds, and public places; our ability to commute to work or school within a reasonable period of time; the accessibility of recreational and cultural activities; and the opportunities for involvement in community life are important determinants of our happiness.

United Cities and Local Governments
www.cities-localgovernments.org

Local (municipal) governments are typically responsible for many of the services that affect the quality of life in our communities, such as water, sewage treatment, garbage disposal, roads, public transportation, fire and police protection, land development and zoning, parks, and recreational facilities.

Local governments in some countries have responsibilities for administering welfare and other social services. Local governments are also usually involved in promoting the economic development of their communities.

Local governments often only have whatever authority the central government—or, in the case of federal systems, provincial or state governments—decides to delegate to them. Thus, despite their importance, local governments are generally subordinate to higher levels of government. The actual degree of autonomy of local governments may vary over time depending upon the thinking of the higher levels of government. For example, in Great Britain, which has a long tradition of strong local self-government, both Conservative and Labour governments have moved in recent decades toward greater regulation by the central government. In contrast, France, which has a long tradition of control by the central government, has moved to allow greater autonomy to local and regional communities (Stoker, 2006).

Some countries, including Germany, India, and Switzerland, provide constitutional protection for the powers of local governments. Indeed, Brazil, Venezuela, and South Africa recognize local governments as a distinct "third order of government" alongside the national and state/provincial governments (Watts, 2008, p. 132). In the United States, many state constitutions provide some protection for the powers of municipal governments, with the larger cities often provided with some form of "home rule" that protects their powers and structures from being changed without their consent (Sancton, 2002).

The Canadian Version

In Canada, local governments are the responsibility of provincial governments that have authority over local governments. Indeed, provincial governments can alter the boundaries of municipalities as they see fit. For example, in 1998, the government of Ontario decided to amalgamate the six municipalities of Metropolitan Toronto despite opposition from local political leaders and 73 percent of those who voted in a referendum.

Although local governments make important decisions affecting their communities, they generally have to carry out their activities in accordance with the rules and regulations adopted by their provincial government and have to seek provincial approval for some decisions. Municipal governments often administer some provincial government policies in such areas as the environment, policing, and building standards. However, provincial governments have generally taken over the fields of health, education, and (except in Ontario) social services that used to be primarily the responsibility of local authorities (Young, 2009).

Local governments in Canada (unlike those in the United States) do not have the authority to raise revenues from income or sales taxes. Instead, they depend largely on property taxes and, to a lesser extent, provincial government grants (which are often tied to conditions or purposes set by the provincial

Federation of Canadian Municipalities
www.fcm.ca

government) and various user fees. Although the Canadian government does not have any direct constitutional authority over local governments, it has provided funding from time to time to help pay for special projects such as the development of public mass transit systems. Since 2005, the Canadian government has given local governments a share of gasoline tax revenues for environmentally sustainable municipal infrastructure. Overall, local governments receive only about 8 percent of the taxes raised by governments (Federation of Canadian Municipalities, 2006). This is often inadequate to provide for municipal services and infrastructure.

As cities have grown, they have sought greater political and financial power. Major cities (and their surrounding regions) have become leading forces of national and global economic growth in the knowledge-based economies of the advanced countries. However, they lack sufficient powers and finances to carry out this role effectively (Courchene, 2007). Former Toronto Mayor Mel Lastman suggested that Toronto, which has a greater population than all of the Atlantic provinces plus two of the Prairie provinces combined, should be given provincial government status. Through Ontario's City of Toronto Act, 2006, Canada's largest city has been given broader legislative powers, a greater ability to manage its own financial affairs, and recognition of its right to enter into agreements with the Canadian government.

Complex Governing Authorities

There are often complex sets of governing authorities at the local level. Schools are generally run by elected school boards that may be responsible for all of the schools in a city or in a region of a province. Likewise, there may

◀ The City of Toronto has been seeking greater legislative and financial powers so that it can more effectively carry out its role as a leading force in the national and global economy.

be library boards, police boards, community centre boards, health boards, hospital boards, transit authorities, conservation authorities, parks boards, public utilities commissions, and water and sewage authorities. Such agencies, boards, and commissions are often independent of the municipal government and may service a broader geographical area than a municipal government. This fragmentation of decision-making power at the local level can make it difficult for city politicians and administrators to pursue a coherent set of objectives or respond to the wishes of city residents (Leo & Mulligan, 2006). As well, various local authorities (such as school and hospital boards) have been increasingly subject to control by provincial governments rather than by the local community.

Democracy and Local Government

Are local governments more likely than more distant central or provincial governments to foster the participation of citizens? Given the direct effect of local governments on the people they govern, one might expect citizens to be more likely to participate at the local level. Indeed, some democratic theorists have argued that democracy at the local level is an essential building block of a democratic political system. It may be easier for citizens at the local level (particularly in smaller cities and towns) to develop connections to other citizens, engage in meaningful discussion, learn about the issues that affect them, and actively participate in political life (McAllister, 2004).

Turnout in local elections, however, is almost always lower than in national or provincial elections. Although this generalization is valid for a variety of countries, the lower level of voting in local elections is particularly evident in Canada (see Table 13-3), where the average turnout is about 35 percent (McAllister, 2004).

The low voter turnout is particularly evident in larger cities. For example, turnout in Ontario's local elections averaged 54 percent in places with less

TABLE 13-3
VOTER TURNOUT IN RECENT MUNICIPAL ELECTIONS, SELECTED CANADIAN CITIES

CITY	YEAR OF ELECTION	TURNOUT
Ottawa	2010	44%
Toronto	2010	53%
Montreal	2009	39%
Winnipeg	2010	38%
Halifax	2008	36%
Vancouver	2008	31%
Saskatoon	2009	27%
Edmonton	2010	33%
Victoria	2008	27%

SOURCE: *City election websites.*

than ten thousand people compared to 37 percent in cities with more than one hundred thousand people (Kushner, Siegel, & Stanwick, 1997).

Political parties, which can make voting easier by highlighting issues, presenting different platforms, and mobilizing voters, are not generally involved in local politics in Canada.[9] In some cases, the lack of credible challengers to an incumbent mayor can make a local election uninteresting. Where the Republican and Democratic parties involve themselves in local politics in the United States, voter turnout is higher than in cities that feature non-partisan elections, but still is usually substantially lower than in national and state elections. In Western Europe, higher voter turnout in local elections may reflect the ability of political parties to mobilize voters in local elections on the basis of national political issues and long-standing ideological and social divisions. In these countries there is often not a sharp distinction between national and local politics (Milner, 1997; Morlan, 1984).

The low level of participation in municipal elections in Canada does not necessarily mean that citizens are uninterested in the decisions that affect their local community. Many cities have active community and neighbourhood organizations involved in improving the quality of life in the city. Issue-oriented groups and civic movements have attracted considerable support for efforts such as challenging freeway construction that would go through quiet neighbourhoods, preserving the character of neighbourhoods that are threatened by development projects, protecting green spaces, and promoting the provision of low-cost housing for the poor.

---

[9] Civic parties exist in some cities, including Montreal and Vancouver, and at times the NDP has involved itself in local politics in some cities.

Summary and Conclusion

Almost all countries have multiple governments. The existence of multiple governments adds complexity to political life and makes an understanding of the relationships among governments essential for an understanding of governing processes.

Unitary systems feature a hierarchical relationship among governments, with the central government superior to other governments. Nevertheless, some distinctive parts of the country may be granted a significant level of autonomy and local or regional authorities may have responsibility for delivering many government services. Federal systems feature a substantial level of self-government for provinces or their equivalent and, generally, a shared involvement in a number of policy areas between central and provincial governments. Each citizen is directly affected by both national and provincial governments, and citizens elect both a national and a provincial government.

Confederal systems result when sovereign states join together to establish a central governing agency with limited powers delegated from the member-states. The European Union features a unique combination of confederal and federal features in its evolving system of governing.

Although local governments deliver a variety of important services to their communities, they are often restricted in their capabilities because of controls by "higher" levels of government and limited financial resources. Despite the development of many groups seeking to improve the quality of life in their community, local politics often falls short of the democratic ideal of an active, engaged citizenry.

The existence of multiple governments has important political implications. Coordination and co-operation among different governments within a country are important requirements for effective governing. However, power struggles between national and provincial governments, as well as their different interests and values, can make co-operation difficult to achieve, as is often evident in the Canadian federal system. Ensuring that multiple governments work toward the common good and are responsive and accountable to those they govern presents difficult challenges.

Key Terms

Asymmetrical federalism 320

Classical federalism 315

Confederal system 324

Co-operative federalism 316

Devolution 312

Equalization payments 316

European Union (EU) 324

Federal system 311

Subsidiarity 327

Unitary system 311

Discussion Questions

1. Do the advantages of a federal system outweigh its disadvantages in Canada? Should other countries such as the United Kingdom adopt a federal system?

2. Why has the Canadian federal system tended to become more decentralized?

3. Do you think that the Canadian government should continue to set conditions for provincial health care systems?

4. Should Canada move further in the direction of asymmetrical federalism?

5. Is the European Union an appropriate model for a potential North American Union or for the African Union?

6. Do you think that local governments should have greater authority?

Further Reading

Bakvis, H., Baier, G., & Brown, D. (2009). *Contested federalism: Certainty and ambiguity in the Canadian federation*. Don Mills, ON: Oxford University Press.

Bakvis, H., & Skogstad, G. (Eds.). (2008). *Canadian federalism: Performance, effectiveness, and legitimacy* (2nd ed.). Don Mills, ON: Oxford University Press.

Burgess, M. (2006). *Comparative federalism: Theory and practice*. London: Routledge.

Cini, M., & Borragan, N.P.-S. (Eds.). (2010). *European Union politics* (3rd ed.). Oxford: Oxford University Press.

Gagnon, A.-G. (2010). *The case for multination federalism*. London and New York: Routledge.

Heuglin, T.O., & Fenna, A. (2006). *Comparative federalism: A systematic inquiry*. Peterborough, ON: Broadview Press.

McAllister, M.L. (2004). *Governing ourselves: The politics of local communities*. Vancouver: UBC Press.

McAllister, R. (2010). *European Union: An historical and political survey* (2nd ed.). New York: Routledge.

Sancton, A. & Young, R.A. (Eds.). (2009). *Foundations of governance: Municipal government in Canada's provinces*. Toronto: University of Toronto Press.

Smith, J. (2004). *Federalism*. Vancouver: UBC Press.

Tindal, C.R., & Tindal, S.N. (2008). *Local government in Canada* (7th ed.). Toronto: Nelson Canada.

Watts, R.L. (2008). *Comparing federal systems* (3rd ed.). Montreal: McGill–Queen's University Press.

Parliamentary Systems

PHOTO ABOVE: On April 27, 2010, the Speaker of Canada's House of Commons, Peter Milliken, ruled that Stephen Harper's Conservative government could be considered to be in contempt of Parliament for refusing to let members of Parliament see documents related to the torture of Afghan detainees that had been handed over to Afghanistan's National Directorate of Security by Canadian military police.

CHAPTER OBJECTIVES

After reading this chapter you should be able to:

1. outline the basic characteristics of parliamentary systems
2. define the meaning of majority, minority, and coalition governments
3. describe how the prime minister and Cabinet are chosen in Canada
4. discuss whether there is too great a concentration of power in the Canadian governing system
5. examine the organization and functioning of the Canadian Parliament

On April 27, 2010, the Speaker of Canada's House of Commons, Peter Milliken, ruled that Stephen Harper's Conservative government could be considered to be in contempt of Parliament for refusing to let members of Parliament (MPs) see documents related to the torture of Afghan detainees that had been handed over to Afghanistan's National Directorate of Security by Canadian military police.

Richard Colvin, a senior Canadian diplomat in Afghanistan, repeatedly sent memos warning senior government and military officials that the torture of prisoners was a common practice. However, his warnings were ignored.

In 2007, the Canadian Military Police Complaints Commission started an investigation of the issue. The federal government tried unsuccessfully to prevent the investigation and subsequent hearings and to stop Colvin from testifying. Although military officials denied Colvin's allegations, the Commission had difficulty determining the truth since government censors had redacted (blacked out) most of Colvin's memos and he was forbidden to testify about the redacted material.

In 2009, a special House of Commons committee reported that the government had breached parliamentary privileges by refusing the committee's request for documents. The House of Commons passed a motion ordering the government to release the documents. Although the government tabled thousands of pages of documents, these were heavily redacted and did not comply with the House of Commons order.

In his ruling, Milliken (2010) upheld the centuries-old right of Parliament to hold the government to account:

Before us are issues that question the very foundations upon which our parliamentary system is built. In a system of responsible government, the fundamental right of the House of Commons to hold the Government to account for its actions is an indisputable privilege and, in fact, an obligation. Embedded in our Constitution, parliamentary law and even our Standing Orders, it is the source of our parliamentary system from which other processes and principles necessarily flow. . . . [A]ccepting an unconditional authority of the executive to censor the information provided to Parliament would in fact jeopardize the very separation of powers that is purported to lie at the heart of our parliamentary system and the independence of its constituent parts. Furthermore, it risks diminishing the inherent privileges of the House and its Members, which have been earned and must be safeguarded.

Milliken gave the government two weeks to reach a compromise acceptable to all parties so that the relevant documents would be provided in a way that did not compromise national security. Seven weeks later, an agreement was reached allowing a committee consisting of one MP from each political party to view the documents except for those the government declared to be matters of Cabinet confidence or that contained the legal advice of the Department of Justice. A panel of arbiters would determine which documents could be made public. The NDP, critical of the exemptions, decided to boycott the process.

THE DEVELOPMENT OF THE PARLIAMENTARY SYSTEM

PARLIAMENTARY SYSTEM A system of governing in which there is a close interrelationship between the political executive (prime minister and Cabinet) and Parliament (the legislative or law-making body). The executive is generally composed of members of the House of Commons (the elected parliamentary body) and must maintain the support of the House of Commons.

The development of the **parliamentary system** is associated with the political history of the United Kingdom. In 1215, English nobles upset with the king's tax increases (which were needed to finance a war with France) forced King John I to sign the Magna Carta. Among its provisions was one that established a council of barons separate from the king and his advisers to approve taxes. It also began the establishment of the rule of law, rather than arbitrary rule by the king, by enabling the courts to order (through a writ of habeas corpus) that an imprisoned person be brought before a court for trial and punishment. As need of monarchs for financing continued to increase, knights and local leaders representing the "commons" were invited to what became known as Parliament, which separated into two houses: the House of Lords and the House of Commons. Over time, the convention developed that bills for taxation had to originate in the Commons and that money would only be supplied to the executive after grievances had been dealt with. After Parliament forced Catholic King James II from the throne in the Glorious Revolution, Parliament passed the Bill of Rights (1689), which guaranteed freedom of speech in Parliament, required Parliament's consent for the levying of taxes, and stipulated that the monarch could not make or suspend laws without Parliament's approval. In accepting the Bill of Rights, the new king and queen, William and Mary, swore an oath to govern in accordance with the statutes, laws, and customs of Parliament.

Out of the body of royal officials that advised the king, known as the Privy Council, evolved an inner committee known as the Cabinet. The practice developed that the King's ministers who were responsible for various executive offices would be members of Parliament. The position of prime minister as the chief minister became recognized toward the middle of the eighteenth century. Subsequently, the Cabinet strengthened its position in relation to both the monarch and Parliament by viewing itself as a collective body taking a united stance (Punnett, 1971). After the Reform Act 1832 reduced the ability of the monarch to manipulate elections and a majority of reformers committed to a particular program were elected in 1831, the principle of **responsible government** developed (Birch, 1980). This means that the political executive (the prime minister and Cabinet) is accountable to Parliament for its actions and must retain the support of the elected members of Parliament to remain in office. Parliament thus not only became the supreme law-making body, but also could make or unmake governments. With the development of two disciplined (united) political parties (Conservatives and Liberals, with Labour later replacing the Liberals as a major party), voters could hold the government accountable by supporting or defeating the governing party in an election. As well, the development of cohesive parties made the House of Commons an adversarial body where the governing party defended its actions and Her Majesty's Loyal Opposition held the government accountable.

RESPONSIBLE GOVERNMENT A governing system in which the political executive (the prime minister and Cabinet) is accountable to Parliament for its actions and must retain the support of the elected members of Parliament to remain in office.

◄ The Palace of Westminster, where the Parliament of the United Kingdom meets.

The British parliamentary system, often referred to as the **Westminster system** (because the UK Parliament meets in Westminster Palace), is sometimes characterized as a majoritarian system in which the governing party having a majority of seats in Parliament is able to ensure that its legislative program will be adopted and implemented. However, as discussed in Chapter 8, a governing party's majority in the House of Commons does not usually reflect the votes of the majority of the electorate because of the boost that the single member plurality electoral system usually gives to the leading party. For its supporters, the Westminster system provides efficient and stable government. Due to its simplicity, voters can easily choose to elect or defeat the governing party. Critics point out that the Westminster system heavily concentrates power in the hands of the prime minister and Cabinet, making Parliament as a whole of limited significance in a majority government situation. This can result in the views and interests of various minorities being ignored.

The Westminster system was exported to other parts of the British Empire. The parliamentary systems of many former British colonies, including Canada, Australia, India, and a number of Caribbean countries, are modelled on the Westminster system (although they have various modifications). Many other countries have adopted more consensus-based, power-sharing parliamentary

WESTMINSTER SYSTEM A governing system that developed in Britain, featuring single party majority rule, executive dominance of Parliament, and an adversarial relationship between the governing party and the opposition.

The UK Parliament: About Parliament
www.parliament.uk/works/index.cfm

systems. In part, this is a result of adopting proportional representation electoral systems that typically lead to coalition governments with a greater balance in power between the executive and Parliament. Although people in Canada and the United Kingdom often express a preference for majority government, an analysis by Arend Lijphart (1999) found that consensus-based democracies tend to be superior on a variety of criteria, including the provision of welfare, environmental protection, and the representation of different groups and perspectives.

In this chapter we focus on the Westminster system, particularly as it applies to Canada. Among the modifications of the Westminster system that make the governing of Canada different than that of the United Kingdom are the federal system, the Charter of Rights and Freedoms, and the power of judicial review exercised by the courts. As well, although Canada has retained the single member plurality electoral system, Canada no longer has a two-party system and thus has had frequent periods of rule by minority government. However, with devolution and with the two leading parties gaining less than two-thirds of the vote (and a coalition government formed after the 2010 election), the United Kingdom might no longer be considered a pure Westminster system.

EXECUTIVE–LEGISLATIVE RELATIONS

A basic feature of parliamentary systems is the close interrelationship of Parliament (the legislative body) and the political executive (the prime minister and Cabinet). The members of the political executive are themselves members of Parliament, usually from the House of Commons (see Figure 14-1). The authority of the political executive is based on its ability to maintain the support of the majority of elected members of Parliament. If that support is withdrawn, the executive is generally expected to resign. This will normally result in an election.[1]

Although Parliament has to approve new laws (and changes to existing laws), it is normally the political executive that proposes the laws passed by Parliament. The political executive also presents the government's spending and taxing plans for Parliament's approval. As well, the political executive is responsible for overseeing the implementation and administration of the laws passed by Parliament and for making the day-to-day governing decisions. However, while the political executive is the governing body, it is expected to be responsible (that is, accountable) to Parliament for its actions.

---

[1] In Germany, Spain, and Israel, a motion of non-confidence presented by a member of an opposition party can be passed only if a majority is able to agree on another person to be prime minister. This provision, termed a "constructive vote of confidence," makes it less likely that the government will be forced out of office. In July 2010, the British deputy prime minister proposed that, after a vote of non-confidence, fourteen days be allotted to try to form a new government so as to avoid an election.

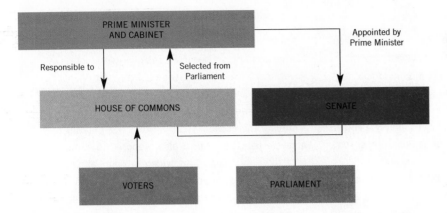

In modern parliamentary systems, political parties play a crucial role in the functioning of the governing system. The ability of the political executive to maintain the support of the elected House of Commons is based on control of its party's members. If a party elects a majority of the members of the House, the prime minister and Cabinet will be the leading members of the governing party and are almost certain to maintain the support of the House and have most of their legislative initiatives passed by the majority in the House. In this **majority government** situation, the prime minister and Cabinet dominate the House of Commons.

If no single party has elected its members to a majority of seats in the House of Commons, one party may, nevertheless, form a **minority government**. As with a majority government, the prime minister chooses the Cabinet from among his or her party's members of Parliament. To pass legislation, gain approval for government's spending and taxing plans, and avoid being defeated on a vote of non-confidence, the prime minister and Cabinet need to gain the support of one or more other parties (unless one or more opposition parties decide to abstain from voting). This support may be on an issue-by-issue basis or be part of a general formal or informal agreement between the governing party and another party. The ability of the political executive to control the House of Commons will be limited, and negotiations with other parties will usually be necessary.

Alternatively, if no one party has a majority of seats, a **coalition government** consisting of two or more political parties may be formed (see Box 14-1, Coalition Governments). In this situation, there will be negotiations among the coalition partners to determine which Cabinet positions each party will receive and the policies the government will pursue. In some cases (as, for example, in contemporary Italy), coalitions among parties will be formed before the election such that the winning coalition will form the government. In other cases, such as Germany, the negotiations among parties seeking to form a coalition government occur after the results of an election are known.

MAJORITY GOVERNMENT
The government formed when the prime minister's party has a majority of the members of the House of Commons; thus, a single party forms the government.

MINORITY GOVERNMENT A single party governs, but that party does not have a majority of members in the House of Commons. Thus, a minority government needs to gain the support of one or more other parties to pass legislation and to stay in office.

COALITION GOVERNMENT A government in which two or more political parties jointly govern, sharing the Cabinet positions.

BOX 14-1

Coalition Governments

Coalition governments are the norm in Western European parliamentary systems, where proportional representation makes majority government very unlikely. However, coalition governments have not been common in many of the Commonwealth countries that have a single member plurality electoral system. The United Kingdom had coalition governments only during the two world wars and during the Great Depression (1931–1939). Although Canada has had thirteen minority governments since 1921, its only coalition government was formed in exceptional circumstances during World War I. Prime ministers have preferred minority government to coalition government in the hope that their party can win a majority in a subsequent election.

When the May 2010 UK election resulted in a "hung Parliament" in which no party held a majority of the 650 seats in the House of Commons, the Liberal Democratic party, which had won 57 seats, negotiated with the Conservative party (306 seats) and the Labour party (258 seats) to form a coalition government. After five days, a deal was struck between the Conservatives and Liberal Democrats. In addition to agreeing on a number of policy positions, the Liberal Democrats were appointed to six Cabinet positions (including the party's leader, Nick Clegg, as deputy prime minister) in Conservative Prime Minister David Cameron's government.

After the 2008 Canadian election, Stephen Harper formed his second Conservative minority government. Shortly afterwards, the government presented a budget update that angered the three opposition parties. Not only did the update fail to stimulate the economy as the world was entering a severe recession, but it also proposed to eliminate the public subsidy provided to political parties. With the government headed for defeat on a motion of non-confidence, the Liberal and New Democratic parties signed an agreement to form a coalition government in which they would share Cabinet positions. The Bloc Québécois promised to support the coalition for eighteen months.

Before the non-confidence motion could be voted on, Harper requested that Governor General Michaëlle Jean prorogue Parliament, thereby ending the session without a vote. Jean agreed to the request and the Conservatives mounted a successful public campaign criticizing the proposed coalition as "undemocratic" and as giving power to "separatists and socialists." Liberal leader Stéphane Dion resigned and Michael Ignatieff was selected as interim Liberal leader. The Liberals subsequently decided not to bring down the government and the Harper government brought in a budget that increased government spending and retained the subsidy for political parties.

Shifts in the parties joining or leaving the coalition may also occur without an election being held, as has often been the case in Israel.

Typically, coalition governments involve parties that are close to each other in ideological terms. In a number of countries, coalition governments are stable such that the coalition remains in office for its full term and is able to govern effectively. This has been the experience of Germany, which has been governed by coalitions since 1949. In some countries, however, coalition governments have been undermined by disputes among the coalition partners. Italy, for example, was characterized by political instability, with sixty-one coalition governments formed after 1945 (although until 1984 all were dominated by the Christian Democratic Party). The establishment of two broad coalitions of parties, one leaning left and the other leaning right, has brought greater stability to Italian politics since 1996.

THE HEAD OF STATE

In addition to the close interrelationship of the political executive and Parliament, parliamentary systems also differ from presidential systems in having different individuals as head of state and head of government. The **head of state** is an important but largely ceremonial position in a parliamentary system. The head of state carries out a variety of official functions but is expected to be "above" politics and thus is not usually involved in making governing decisions. Having a non-partisan head of state can provide a symbol of unity for a country (see Box 14-2, Should Canada Have Its Own Head of State?). The head of state will not be tarnished by government incompetence or scandal because the head of state is not involved in politics and governing. This provides the legitimacy needed for the head of state to act, if necessary, in some unusual circumstances, to ensure that a government is in place or to dismiss a government that is acting unconstitutionally.

In some countries with parliamentary systems, the head of state is a president with a limited term of office. The president may be elected directly by the country's citizens (as, for example, in Austria, Ireland, and Israel) or selected by a vote of members of the national Parliament along with, in some cases, regional representatives (as, for example, in Germany, Greece, and Italy). In a number of countries with parliamentary systems (including the United Kingdom, Sweden, Denmark, Spain, and the Netherlands), a hereditary monarch is the head of state. The powers of the monarch in these democratic countries have been greatly restricted by formal constitutional provisions or "unwritten" constitutional conventions.

The Canadian Governor General

Canadian governments act in the name of the Crown. However, the duties and responsibilities of the monarch have been delegated to the **governor general** at the national level and to lieutenant-governors at the provincial level. The governor general and **lieutenant-governors** are appointed by the monarch on the recommendation of the Canadian prime minister for a five-year term (which is sometimes extended for a year or two).

The governor general has the important responsibility of ensuring that a government (prime minister and Cabinet) is in place at all times. Usually, the choice of prime minister is merely a formality. The governor general is expected to choose the leader of the party that has the support of the House of Commons. In the event of the death, retirement, or resignation of the prime minister, the governing political party will recommend a replacement.

HEAD OF STATE In a parliamentary system, the head of state is an important but largely ceremonial position, but has the responsibility to ensure that a legitimate government is in place.

Commonwealth Parliamentary Association
www.cpahq.org

GOVERNOR GENERAL The person who carries out the duties and responsibilities of the monarch at the national level in Canada.

LIEUTENANT-GOVERNOR The person who carries out the duties and responsibilities of the monarch at the provincial level in Canada.

BOX 14-2

Should Canada Have Its Own Head of State?

In Canada, the British monarch is the official head of state in her role as Queen of Canada. This symbolizes Canada's historic ties to Britain and continuing membership in the Commonwealth, of which the Queen is the ceremonial head. However, because the monarch's responsibilities have been delegated to the governor general at the national level and to lieutenant-governors at the provincial level, the Queen's role is almost entirely symbolic.

For a significant proportion of Canada's population, the use of a foreign monarch as the formal head of state is an outdated relic of the country's colonial past. There was a sizable protest when the Queen visited Quebec in 1964; subsequent royal visits to Quebec have been greeted with indifference.

In 2002, Foreign Affairs Minister John Manley suggested that Canada should have an elected head of state. However, the issue was quickly dropped because it was considered too controversial.

A number of Commonwealth countries including India, Pakistan, and many African countries no longer have the Queen as head of state. Despite opinion polls indicating that a majority of Australians favour ending the monarchy, in a 1999 referendum 55 percent of Australians rejected a constitutional proposal that would replace the Queen with a president chosen by Parliament. While many who rejected the proposal favoured retaining the monarchy, some voted "no" because they did not favour the method proposed for selecting a president.

PREROGATIVE POWERS Powers of the monarch that have not been taken away by Parliament. These are also known as reserve powers.

DISSOLUTION The termination of Parliament followed by the holding of an election for the House of Commons.

PROROGATION The suspension of Parliament and its committees by the governor general at the request of the prime minister. Prorogation (unlike an adjournment) ends a session of Parliament such that the work of committees is ended and bills that have not been passed have to be reintroduced unless Parliament in the next session agrees otherwise.

About Government
www.canada.gc.ca/aboutgov-ausujetgouv/about.html

The governor general must also approve all legislation, a variety of appointments, and various executive decisions, such as the ratification of treaties and a declaration of war. However, in these matters, the governor general always acts on the advice of the prime minister and Cabinet (or, in some cases, the prime minister alone).

The governor general is not entirely powerless. There are some **prerogative powers** (also known as reserve powers)—powers of the monarch that have not been taken away by Parliament—where the governor general in exceptional circumstances can use personal discretion in deciding how to act. These powers include the appointment and dismissal of the prime minister and the **dissolution** of Parliament (termination followed by an election) or **prorogation** of Parliament (ending of a Parliamentary session).[2] For example, if the prime minister and Cabinet are ignoring the constitution or lack the support of the House of Commons, the governor general could be justified in acting independently in dismissing the prime minister.

The use of the prerogative powers can involve the governor general in political controversies. This was the case when Prime Minister Stephen Harper, facing defeat in the House of Commons and replacement with a Liberal–NDP coalition government, requested that the governor general prorogue Parliament. Likewise, there was considerable controversy a year later, when Harper requested prorogation to give the government time to "recalibrate" its policies. The opposition parties argued it was an attempt to muzzle the Commons committee that

---

[2] Lieutenant-governors have essentially the same powers and responsibilities at the provincial level.

was investigating the detainee transfer issue discussed in the opening vignette. As well, the prorogation gave the prime minister time to gain control of the Senate and its committees by filling vacancies that were coming due.

THE PRIME MINISTER AND CABINET

In Canada and many Commonwealth countries, the positions and powers of the prime minister and Cabinet are not specified in the formal constitution, but instead are established by convention. The prime minister, who acts as the **head of government**, is normally the leader of the political party that is able to maintain the confidence of the House of Commons either by itself or with the support of other political parties. The prime minister is almost always a member of the House of Commons representing a particular electoral district, and thus not directly elected by voters in the country as a whole. Usually, but not always, the prime minister's party elected the most representatives to the House of Commons. After an election, a prime minister usually will resign if his or her party did not win the most seats. The governor general would then choose as prime minister the party leader that is most likely to have the support of a majority of members in the House of Commons.[3] However, if a prime minister thinks his or her party can gain sufficient support from other parties, the prime minister and Cabinet can remain in office until defeated in the House of Commons. In some countries such as Germany, the chancellor (prime minister) is elected by the members of the Bundestag (the equivalent of the Canadian House of Commons). In countries where coalition governments are common, the head of state may hold discussions with various party leaders to determine who has sufficient support to head the government. Regardless of the precise procedure used for selecting the head of government in different countries, the prime minister is usually the leader of one of the largest parties.

The prime minister is responsible for recommending the appointment (and dismissal) of the members of the **Cabinet** as well as determining what Cabinet positions they will hold. In Canada, and most other countries, the selection of Cabinet ministers is a prime ministerial responsibility.[4] Together, the prime minister and Cabinet ministers are the political executive with responsibility for governing. Although the prime minister and Cabinet are expected to be responsible and accountable to Parliament for their actions, in reality the prime minister and Cabinet in Canada and other countries that basically follow the Westminster model normally control the dominant party in the House of Commons. Thus, the parliamentary system is often described as a system of

HEAD OF GOVERNMENT The person who heads the executive side of government and is usually responsible for choosing the Cabinet. In Canada, the prime minister is the head of the Canadian government while the heads of provincial governments are known as premiers (in Quebec, *premier ministre*).

CABINET The members of the political executive. The Cabinet in a parliamentary system is led by the prime minister, with many or most Cabinet ministers having the responsibility of heading a government department.

---

3 For example, the Progressive Conservative party won the most seats but less than a majority of seats in the 1985 Ontario election. After the NDP agreed to support a Liberal government (although not establishing a formal coalition), the Liberal leader was appointed premier.

4 In Australia, the Labour MPs elect the Cabinet when their party governs. However, this became a formality when Kevin Rudd became prime minister in 2007.

executive dominance, as it places considerable power in the hands of the prime minister and Cabinet, particularly in a majority government situation.

The Prime Minister and Cabinet in Canada

The prime minister is the leading figure within the Canadian Cabinet. The prime minister determines who will be appointed to the Cabinet and what their responsibilities will be. At any time, the prime minister may change the responsibilities of any Cabinet minister or demand a Cabinet minister's resignation. The prime minister is also responsible for organizing the Cabinet, and thus determines what Cabinet committees there will be and who will sit on those committees. The prime minister chairs Cabinet meetings, sets the agenda for those meetings, and (since votes are not held in the Cabinet) determines the consensus of the Cabinet. In addition to playing a leading role in Cabinet, prime ministers are also party leaders. They take responsibility for their party's election campaigns and play a leading role in defending the government in the House of Commons. The mass media and the public pay far more attention to the prime minister than to any other political figure. Prime ministers make a substantial number of prestigious appointments and thus can reward loyal supporters. Although modern prime ministers do not run a particular department of government, they normally play a leading role in foreign affairs, federal–provincial relations, and constitutional negotiations with provincial governments.

A prime minister cannot govern alone. Nevertheless, prime ministers have tended to become less dependent upon their Cabinets for advice. Instead, they provide central direction or, at least, central coordination to the government. To help achieve this, the size, importance, and activities of the offices that provide advice and assistance directly to the prime minister have increased substantially in recent decades. The **Privy Council Office (PCO)**, an administrative structure that is directly responsible to the prime minister, has a central role in organizing the Cabinet and trying to coordinate and direct the activities of government. It is also very important in providing policy advice to the prime minister. The **Prime Minister's Office (PMO)**, consisting mainly of loyal supporters of the prime minister, not only provides secretarial support such as scheduling appointments and handling correspondence, but also is involved in maintaining the prime minister's power and popularity by providing partisan advice, writing speeches, managing the media, making recommendations concerning patronage appointments, and trying to maintain party unity and loyalty to its leader. Together, the PCO and PMO provide the prime minister with a dedicated source of advice and a capability to direct and coordinate the activities of government. The concentration of power has led some analysts to characterize the governing system in Canada (and various other parliamentary systems such as the United Kingdom and Australia) as **prime ministerial government**, as discussed in Box 14-3, Prime Ministerial Government.

Prime Ministerial Government

Has Canada has developed a prime ministerial government? Have prime ministers become the equivalent of American presidents in the sense that they are the chief executive, rather than the traditional view that they are "first among equals" in the Cabinet?

In his study of governing in Canada, Donald Savoie (1999, pp. 7, 362) concluded that

power has shifted to the prime minister and his senior advisers at both the political and public service levels and away from Cabinet and Cabinet Committees. . . . Cabinet has now joined Parliament as an institution being bypassed. . . . The Canadian prime minister has little in the way of institutional check, at least inside government, to inhibit his ability to have his way.

More recently, Savoie (2008, p. 16) described the governments of both Canada and the United Kingdom as "court governments" in which "effective political power now rests with the prime minister and a small group of carefully selected courtiers."

Others, however, argue that the idea that there has been an almost dictatorial concentration of power in the hands of the prime minister and his senior advisers is a myth. According to Eddie Goldenberg, Prime Minister Jean Chrétien's chief of staff, the prime minister sets the overall tone and priorities of government and makes some critical decisions, but typically leaves the implementation of policy priorities to individual Cabinet ministers and their staff (Goldenberg, 2006). Some prime ministers, however, are more likely to involve themselves as much as possible in all aspects of governing, while others focus on a few key priorities. For example, Prime Minister Stephen Harper has often been described as tightly controlling his Cabinet ministers, even to the extent of approving their speeches.

Having a powerful prime minister is nothing new in Canadian politics. Sir John A. Macdonald and William Lyon Mackenzie King were more than "first among equals" in their Cabinets although they had to work with a few important regional "strongmen." However, particularly with the influence of the media, there has been a "presidentialization" of government with the prime minister (and often spouse and children) becoming highly visible public figures. No longer can a prime minister walk the streets of Ottawa alone at night, as did Mackenzie King, without being recognized and subjected to intense media scrutiny of his or her personal life.

Although some prime ministers (and premiers) have dominated their Cabinets, it should be kept in mind that some Cabinet ministers are also very important in government policy-making because of the departments they control and their popularity within the party or the country. For example, through most of the decade that Jean Chrétien was prime minister, he had to contend with the considerable power wielded by his popular rival, Paul Martin, who held the important position of finance minister. Despite the intense competition for power between Chrétien and Martin, they were usually able to agree on important budget priorities (Goldenberg, 2006). Nevertheless, Martin worked to organize the Liberal party and the caucus to try to replace Chrétien as leader. Faced with a party leadership vote in 2003 that he likely would have lost, Chrétien announced his retirement and Martin easily won a subsequent

▶ Former British Prime Minister Margaret Thatcher's political career was ended by her failure to maintain the support of her party caucus.

leadership contest. Later, the Liberal party changed its rules so that a leader who is prime minister does not need to face a leadership endorsement vote, matching a similar provision in the Conservative party's constitution.

The power of the Canadian prime minister is also limited by the nature of the federal system. Prime ministers often face serious difficulties in their relationships with provincial governments, and may have to compromise to achieve objectives that require the involvement of provincial governments.

The concentration of power in the hands of the prime minister and an inner circle is not unique to Canada. The United Kingdom and other countries that follow the Westminster model have also tended to move from Cabinet government to prime ministerial government (Weller, 1985). Margaret Thatcher, British prime minister from 1979 to 1990, governed with single-minded determination and changed the direction of British politics, overriding opposition within Cabinet and her party's caucus. Eventually, however, she failed to maintain sufficient support of her caucus and resigned when it appeared that she might not win in a leadership contest involving Conservative MPs. Tony Blair, British prime minister from 1997 to 2007, also was a dominant figure within the British government, often ignoring the views of Cabinet and caucus and adopting a presidential style. However, Gordon Brown, Chancellor of the Exchequer (the equivalent of finance minister), had considerable power and independence in determining the economic policies of the government. Brown was able to frustrate Blair's plans to have Britain adopt the euro and was a vocal critic of Blair within the Cabinet (Rhodes, Wanner, & Weller, 2009).

The Cabinet

There are important political considerations that affect the prime minister's choice of Cabinet ministers. Canadian prime ministers devote considerable attention to ensuring that their Cabinets are geographically representative. There is almost always at least one Cabinet minister from each province (except, occasionally, Prince Edward Island and, after the 2008 election, Newfoundland and Labrador), with more Cabinet ministers from the provinces with greater populations. The proportion of French Canadians in the Cabinet has tended to be in proportion to their share of Canada's population. There is also an expectation that French Canadians outside Quebec and English-speaking Quebecers will each have their own representative in the Cabinet.

Before 1957, Cabinets were exclusively composed of men of British, Irish, or French ancestry. In recent times, prime ministers have made an effort to appoint more women and persons of different ethnic and racial backgrounds to the Cabinet. Nevertheless, the Cabinet, like Parliament, is not fully representative of the diversity of Canadian society. For example, the twenty-six Cabinet ministers appointed by Prime Minister Stephen Harper after the election of the Conservative party in 2006 only included six women. In the following years, the Cabinet became larger and included several more women. A problem with selecting a representative Cabinet is that a prime minister is generally limited by the extent to which the party's members of Parliament reflect the diversity of the country. This, in turn, is affected by the party's nomination processes and whether a party makes deliberate efforts to try to ensure that persons with various characteristics are nominated and elected.

DEPARTMENTS   Many of the activities of government are divided among a number of departments (such as justice, health, and national defence), each of which is headed by a Cabinet minister who is expected to take responsibility for the actions of his or her department. Other Cabinet ministers, currently termed **Ministers of State** in Canada, may be given responsibilities for policy areas such as sports, small business and tourism, and seniors, but have no department to oversee.

Because each department is concerned with a particular policy area and the particular set of interests associated with that policy area, there is often some tension among the different departments. For example, the Department of Agriculture has had a more favourable view of the use of certain pesticides than the Department of the Environment. Further, each department will typically seek more money and employees for its programs, while the Department of Finance and the **Treasury Board**, a Cabinet committee responsible for the government's expenditures, will normally try to limit spending.

CABINET ORGANIZATION   The Cabinet has traditionally been viewed as a body that collectively makes governing decisions. Because each member of the Cabinet is expected to maintain **Cabinet solidarity** (that is, fully support

MINISTERS OF STATE
Cabinet ministers who are not responsible for a particular government department.

TREASURY BOARD A permanent Cabinet committee with its own staff and minister that plays a major role in governing in Canada because of its responsibility for the expenditure and management practices of government.

CABINET SOLIDARITY The convention in a parliamentary system that each member of the Cabinet is expected to fully support and defend the decisions and actions that Cabinet takes.

Institute on Governance
www.iog.ca

▶ Prime Minister Stephen Harper chose twenty-six MPs for his first Cabinet, but only six of these were women.

and defend the decisions and actions that Cabinet takes), there is an expectation that the Cabinet as a whole will discuss and deliberate on the key governing decisions. In reality, however, modern Cabinets are too large and Cabinet ministers often have too little time to fully consider all of the decisions that government makes. Thus, discussion of specific Cabinet decisions is typically done in one of the committees of Cabinet. Some prime ministers, including Stephen Harper, have used a select group of Cabinet ministers—the Priorities and Planning Committee that he chairs—to set the strategic direction of the government and make many decisions on behalf of the Cabinet as a whole.

COORDINATION   Although many individual Cabinet ministers are responsible for overseeing a department of government, in recent decades considerable attention has been devoted to trying to coordinate the diverse activities of government. In Canada, this coordination and direction for the government is provided by what are termed **central agencies**. These include the Privy Council Office, the Prime Minister's Office, the Treasury Board, and the Department of Finance (which develops the government's budget and assesses the impact of government activity on the economy).

CENTRAL AGENCIES
Organizations that try to provide direction and coordination to government. In Canada, the key central agencies are the Privy Council Office, the Prime Minister's Office, the Treasury Board, and the Department of Finance.

POWERS   The prime minister and Cabinet are responsible for the executive powers of government. This includes the conduct of relations with provincial and foreign governments, the issuing of a large number of regulations, the making of a substantial number of important appointments, and oversight of the administrative apparatus of government. The prime minister and Cabinet also play a key role in the legislative process. Almost all legislation and proposals for raising and spending money passed by the Canadian Parliament are proposed to Parliament by the Cabinet.

CABINET RESPONSIBILITY   The prime minister and Cabinet are account-able for their actions in governing through their responsibility to the House of Commons. Because the prime minister and Cabinet hold their positions only as long as they have the support of the majority of members of the House of Commons, there is an expectation that the Cabinet as a group will defend, explain, and take responsibility for the actions of the government in Parlia-ment. In a majority government situation, it is highly unlikely that the House of Commons would pass a motion of non-confidence in the government or defeat important legislative and financial proposals presented by the Cabinet. Nevertheless, the rules of the House of Commons provide opportunities for the opposition parties to raise questions about and criticisms of the actions and performance of the government. In particular, Canada's daily Question Period provides for lively, if not always informative, exchanges between the opposition and governing parties.

In addition to the **collective responsibility** of the Cabinet to the House of Commons, there is an expectation that individual Cabinet ministers will take responsibility for the actions of the department they administer. If there are problems within a department, opposition party members typically call for the minister to resign from the Cabinet. However, Cabinet ministers in Canada have not resigned for the errors of officials in the departments they administer. Instead, Cabinet ministers are more likely to promise to look into a problem and try to rectify it. Ministers are more likely to be asked by the prime min-ister to resign for personal failings. For example, Defence Minister Maxime Bernier resigned in 2008 after he mistakenly left secret North Atlantic Treaty Organization (NATO) documents for five weeks at the apartment of his girl-friend, who had connections to biker gangs.

COLLECTIVE RESPONSIBILITY The convention that the Cabinet as a group will defend, explain, and take responsibility for the actions of the government in Parliament.

SECRECY   The accountability of the government is also limited by **Cabinet secrecy**. The Cabinet meets behind closed doors and Cabinet documents nor-mally remain secret for twenty years. Cabinet secrecy helps to maintain Cabi-net solidarity and ensure that the Cabinet is seen as a united team, regardless of the disagreements that undoubtedly exist among individual Cabinet minis-ters. Cabinet discussions can be full and frank because participants know that word of disagreement will not get out to the media or to opposition parties. As well, Cabinet secrecy helps to shield public servants who advise the Cabinet from public criticism (public servants, being politically neutral, do not nor-mally respond to criticisms). However, the principle of Cabinet secrecy can be used to avoid releasing research conducted by the government that would aid in public discussion of an issue and assist the opposition parties and the public in holding the government accountable for its actions.

CABINET SECRECY The convention that the views expressed in Cabinet remain secret to enable full and frank discussion and maintain Cabinet solidarity.

Since 1983, the Access to Information Act has established the right of journalists, interest groups, opposition parties, and the public to obtain gov-ernment information for a small fee. Although government departments are required to respond to requests within thirty days, with an extension only in

Access to Information and Privacy Office
http://justice.gc.ca/atip-aiprp/home-accueil-eng.asp

▶ Prime Minister Stephen Harper's "open government."

limited and specific circumstances, many requests are not responded to until well after the deadline and extensions have often been misused (Office of the Information Commissioner of Canada, 2009). In a number of cases, released information has been heavily redacted (blacked out). As well, the Canadian government has not yet followed the initiatives of the United Kingdom and the United States in making a large amount of information collected by government available electronically to the public at no cost. In overturning the government's attempt to keep some documents secret, Madam Justice Eleanor Dawson ruled that restrictions to access to information should be "limited and specific" so that "citizens can participate meaningfully in the democratic process" and ensure "that politicians and bureaucrats remain accountable to citizens" (quoted in Sallot, 2004).

PARLIAMENT

Parliament is responsible for passing laws and approving the spending and taxing plans of government (see Figure 14-2). In addition, Parliament, particularly the House of Commons, is expected to hold the government accountable

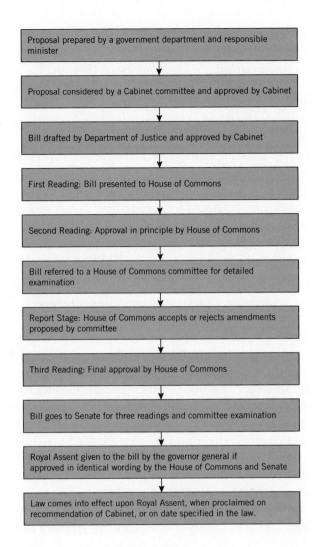

FIGURE 14-2
THE GENERAL PROCEDURE FOR PASSING LEGISLATION IN CANADA

Note: A few bills are presented first to the Senate and then proceed to the House of Commons. Where one chamber proposes amendments to a bill that has been passed by the other chamber, it is returned to the first chamber for further consideration.

for its actions. In this regard, Parliament provides a visible forum in which the opposition can criticize the actions or inactions of government, and the governing party can defend what it is doing. This not only helps to keep the government "on its toes," but also may help voters to make up their minds as to which party to support in the next election. In addition, although the Cabinet oversees the development of most new laws, Parliament can play a useful role by carefully examining proposed legislation and suggesting modifications of some details of proposed legislation to make it more effective. Finally, individual members of Parliament frequently raise issues and concerns of those they represent.

Many countries have two separate chambers ("houses") involved in the legislative process (termed bicameral legislatures). In some cases, this is a carry-over from the non-democratic past, when a body representing privileged interests was seen as necessary to check the power of a body representing the people. For example, the British House of Lords in the past consisted primarily of nobles who inherited their position. Since 1958, the UK prime minister has been able to recommend the appointment of life peers and in 1997 the number of those holding hereditary positions was reduced to 92 (from a total of 733). In the 2010 UK election, the Conservatives advocated a mainly elected chamber while the other two major parties promised a fully elected second chamber. In most federal systems, the second or upper chamber represents the interests of provinces or states.

The Parliament of Canada consists of two chambers: the House of Commons and the Senate. Provincial legislatures have only a single chamber of elected representatives.

The House of Commons

HOUSE OF COMMONS The elected chamber of Parliament, with each member representing a particular electoral district.

The Canadian **House of Commons** is the elected chamber of Parliament, with each member representing a particular electoral district. Representation is by population, with district boundaries drawn so that, in most cases, each member of the House of Commons represents approximately the same number of people. Nevertheless, some rapidly growing districts have much larger than average populations until district boundaries are redrawn after the decennial census. There are some constitutional guarantees to maintain a minimum level of representation from the smaller provinces and the territories. Thus Atlantic Canada, with 7 percent of Canada's population, has 10 percent of the seats in the House of Commons. Ontario and Quebec, with 62 percent of the country's population, hold 59 percent of the seats while the West, with 31 percent of the population, has 30 percent of the seats.

On the surface, the House of Commons controls the executive because the prime minister and Cabinet have to maintain the confidence (support) of the House of Commons. If a majority of members of the House of Commons pass a motion of non-confidence in the government, or if a major proposal made by the Cabinet, such as a budget proposal, is defeated, the prime minister must either request that an election be held or resign. However, in reality it is the prime minister and Cabinet who control the House of Commons, particularly in a majority government situation. **Party discipline** is the basic operating principle of the House of Commons (see Box 14-4, Should Party Discipline Be Relaxed?). That is, members of each party normally vote in accordance with the position that the party has adopted in caucus. The prime minister and Cabinet are usually able to convince their party's members in the House of Commons to support them and their legislative proposals. Therefore, as long as their party elected a majority of members to the House of Commons, the prime minister and Cabinet do not have to worry about losing the confidence of the House of Commons. Nevertheless, the opposition parties can sometimes

PARTY DISCIPLINE The expectation that members of each party will vote in accordance with the position that the party has adopted in caucus.

Should Party Discipline Be Relaxed?

Party discipline has generally been tighter in Canada than in other countries such as the United Kingdom, where strict party discipline is only maintained for votes of non-confidence, votes on the government's budget, and votes on certain issues deemed to be crucial to the government's program.

In the United Kingdom, unlike in Canada, it is not unusual for legislative proposals coming from Cabinet to be defeated in the House of Commons even when the governing party has a majority of seats. Votes in the British House of Commons are designated according to three classifications: one-line whip,* in which MPs, including Cabinet ministers, are free from party discipline; two-line whip, in which party members are encouraged and Cabinet ministers are expected to vote in accordance with their party's position; and three-line whip, in which party discipline is imposed on all members.

In Canada, there have been only a few free votes for which party discipline has been withdrawn—usually on controversial moral issues such as capital punishment and abortion—so that members can follow their consciences.

The tightness of party discipline in Canada has often been criticized. Party discipline reduces the significance of ordinary members of Parliament, who are expected to toe the party line. Members may be expected to vote against the wishes or interests of their constituents. Provincial and regional interests may not be adequately represented in Parliament because parties and their leaders may be concerned about the dominant interests of the country as a whole or those areas viewed as crucial to electoral success.

There are, however, some positive features to party discipline. It helps to ensure that the positions taken by different parties are clear. This makes it easier for voters to choose among competing parties and to hold the governing party accountable for its actions. As well, it means that individual members of Parliament are less subject to pressure from lobbyists and special interests. Further, it means that the government can focus on doing what it considers to be for the common good of the whole country without having to contend with individual members of Parliament seeking special benefits for their constituencies in return for their voting support.

---

* The Whip is the enforcer of party discipline.

persuade the government to change or withdraw a legislative proposal, particularly if the opposition can mobilize public opinion to its side or if the proposal is not a high priority for the government.

PRIVATE MEMBERS   Ordinary members of the House of Commons who are not in the Cabinet (termed **private members**) have generally played a limited role in the development of new legislation. Private members cannot propose laws that involve the imposition of taxes or the spending of money for a new and distinct purpose without the approval of Cabinet. Although private members propose a large number of bills, only a very small number are passed. However, changes to procedures have provided time for a selected number of these bills to be debated and voted upon. For example, in 2010 the House of Commons passed a private members' bill, the Climate Change Accountability

PRIVATE MEMBERS Ordinary members of the House of Commons who are not in the Cabinet.

Act (which would set national greenhouse gas emission targets), that was introduced by NDP MP Bruce Hyer and supported by the three opposition parties. More frequently, ordinary members of Parliament have been successful in making minor modifications to legislation proposed by the Cabinet.

COMMITTEES   **House of Commons committees**, composed of government and opposition party members in proportion to their party's strength in the House of Commons, provide detailed examination of proposed legislation and often suggest modifications to that legislation. As well, they examine the annual estimates of government's proposed spending. At times they investigate or hold public hearings on particular policy issues, thus making a contribution to the development of new policies.

OPPOSITION   The House of Commons is particularly important in providing a public forum for the criticism and defence of the actions of the executive and its legislative proposals. The party with the second-highest number of seats usually is designated as the **official opposition** and leads off the questioning or criticism of government every day that the House is sitting. Other parties with at least twelve seats in the House of Commons have official party status, which, along with other privileges, gives them a budget for hiring research and support staff.

Various opportunities are provided for opposition members to propose **non-confidence motions** in the government. Although non-confidence motions are usually unsuccessful, they provide an opportunity to focus attention on what the opposition parties see as the failings of the governing party.

Although the House of Commons provides a forum for debating proposed legislation, the governing party can put forward a motion of **closure** to limit debate in the House to one day or, more frequently, a time allocation motion to set the amount of time allocated to a bill if an agreement on a timetable for debate cannot be reached with the other parties. Sometimes these limits are used to avoid a **filibuster**, the use of delaying tactics by the opposition.

The Senate

Canada's **Senate** was established, in part, to provide a body of "sober second thought" to check the democratic tendencies of the House of Commons. As well, to allay fears that the House of Commons would be dominated by Ontario and Quebec, or by English Canadians, the Senate provided for equal regional representation.

Although the government does not need to maintain the confidence of the Senate, legislation needs the approval of the Senate as well as the House of Commons. Only in the case of resolutions to approve constitutional changes can the Canadian House of Commons override the opposition of the Senate.

HOUSE OF COMMONS COMMITTEES Committees composed of government and opposition party members in proportion to their party's strength in the House of Commons; they provide detailed examination of proposed legislation and often suggest modifications to that legislation.

OFFICIAL OPPOSITION The party with the second-highest number of seats in the House of Commons; the official opposition leads off the questioning or criticism of government every day that the House is sitting.

NON-CONFIDENCE MOTION A motion put forward by opposition members in a legislature expressing a lack of confidence in the government. If passed, the prime minister is expected to either resign or request that an election be held.

CLOSURE A procedure in a legislative body that cuts off debate if approved by a majority vote.

FILIBUSTER The use of various delaying tactics by those opposed to the passage of a particular piece of legislation.

SENATE (CANADA) The upper chamber of Parliament, appointed on the recommendation of the prime minister. Senators hold their positions until age seventy-five.

As in the House of Commons, senators examine legislative proposals and introduce modifications that are, on occasion, accepted by the government and the House of Commons. Senators usually have been reluctant to block the passage of legislation approved by the House of Commons. However, when Brian Mulroney was prime minister (1984–1993), the Liberal majority in the Senate engaged in confrontation with the Progressive Conservative majority in the House of Commons on such important legislation as the Canada–United States Free Trade Agreement and the imposition of the goods and services tax.

Generally, the Senate does not receive as much media and public attention as the House of Commons. Because of the expertise of many senators, the greater amount of time available for deliberation, and the somewhat less partisan nature of the Senate, this second chamber (particularly through its committees) often makes useful suggestions for improving legislative proposals. Over the years, the Senate has also prepared important reports on such topics as poverty, the mass media, science policy, free trade, terrorism, and aging.

REPRESENTATION   The Senate is designed to provide equal regional representation to offset the representation by population in the House of Commons. There are twenty-four senators from each of Ontario, Quebec, the Maritimes (ten each from Nova Scotia and New Brunswick; four from Prince Edward Island), and the West (six each from Manitoba, Saskatchewan, Alberta, and British Columbia), plus six from Newfoundland and Labrador and one from each of the three territories. However, since senators are not elected by provincial voters nor appointed by their provincial legislature or provincial government, it is questionable whether senators "represent," in a meaningful way, the province for which they are appointed. In most other countries with federal systems, the upper chamber is elected by the people in each province or state. For example, in the United States and Australia, the Senate is elected with each state having the same number of senators. In Germany, however, the Bundesrat (upper house) consists of delegates of the Länder (provincial) governments with each Land having four, five, or six votes depending on the size of its population.

APPOINTMENTS   The prime minister recommends the appointment of senators who have usually been loyal supporters of the prime minister's party. Senators hold their positions until age seventy-five and can only be removed from office for failing to attend two consecutive sessions of Parliament, becoming bankrupt, or being convicted of treason, a felony, or other "infamous crime." Thus when another party forms the government it will typically find that the outgoing party continues to control the Senate. For example, despite losing the 2006 Canadian election, the Liberal party continued to hold a majority in the Senate until 2010.

BOX 14-5
Reforming the Canadian Senate

The Senate has been a perennial topic of Canadian politics, but there are strongly held differences concerning whether there should be minor reforms to improve its operations or major changes to make it more democratic and representative, or whether it should simply be abolished.

In the 1980s, a movement based in Alberta developed to promote the idea of a "Triple-E" Senate (one that is *elected, effective*, and based on an *equal* number of representatives from each province). A Triple-E Senate would give a stronger voice to the smaller provinces. To promote the idea of an elected Senate, the Alberta government has held province-wide elections since 1989 to choose potential senators, although there is no requirement that these "senators-in-waiting" be appointed. Saskatchewan is also planning to hold senatorial elections.

An elected Senate with equal representation from each province would probably quite frequently be controlled by a different party than the House of Commons. Being elected, senators would be less likely to back off from a confrontation with the House of Commons. As a result, negotiation and compromise between the House of Commons and the Senate would be needed to avoid a deadlock in Parliament. In Australia, a deadlock occurred in 1975 between an elected Senate based on equal state representation and the House of Representatives (equivalent to Canada's House of Commons) controlled by different parties, when the Senate refused to approve the appropriations of funds needed to run the government. This resulted in a very controversial decision by the governor general to dismiss the prime minister (who retained the confidence of the House) and appoint the opposition leader as interim prime minister until elections for both houses of Parliament were called.

Changing the number of representatives from each province to create a Triple-E Senate would involve the difficult process of constitutional amendment. It is unlikely that Quebec and Ontario would agree to the reduction in power that would result from the election of an equal number of representatives from each province in an effective Senate. As well, various groups, such as women and Aboriginals, might insist on guaranteed representation in a reconstituted Senate.

One of the promises Conservative leader Stephen Harper made in the 2006 election campaign was that he would only appoint senators who were elected by voters in their province. Despite this promise, he appointed Michael Fortier to the Senate (and to the Cabinet) shortly after becoming prime minister. In 2009, Harper filled twenty-seven vacancies by appointing unelected senators after failing to pass legislation to elect senators for limited terms. In 2010, the Harper government introduced legislation that would limit senators appointed after 2008 to a single non-renewable eight-year term. The government also introduced a bill that would establish a framework for electing potential Senate nominees by any province that wished to do so. The fate of this attempt at Senate reform was not known at the time this textbook was written.

Reform of the Senate has been a staple of Canadian political discussion for many decades, with some such as the New Democratic Party and Ontario Liberal Premier Dalton McGuinty advocating its abolition (see Box 14-5, Reforming the Canadian Senate). The ability of an appointed body to reject legislation passed by an elected, representative body is often viewed as a relic of the non-democratic past.

Summary and Conclusion

Parliamentary systems are often described as having a close interrelationship of legislative and executive powers. Despite the label *parliamentary system*, very considerable power rests with the prime minister and Cabinet, particularly in a majority government situation. The role of the ordinary member of Parliament tends to be limited. Although the prime minister and Cabinet must retain the support of the House of Commons, this is largely a formality in a majority government situation. Nevertheless, they are expected to be responsible to the House of Commons for their actions.

The Westminster version of parliamentary system, in which majority government is the norm, facilitates decisive action by the government. By maintaining tight party discipline, the governing party can act in ways that it believes will be for the good of the country as a whole or, at least, for the re-election of the governing party. It also can facilitate the accountability of the government to the people, as praise or blame for the actions of the government and most of the laws passed by Parliament can be attributed to the governing party.

However, this concentration of power can have negative consequences. A majority government, elected by a minority of voters, may ignore different sections of the population or different viewpoints. Because of strict party discipline, the task of holding the government accountable for its actions rests with the opposition parties in the House of Commons. Although the parliamentary system does provide an opportunity for the opposition parties to question and criticize the prime minister and Cabinet, this does not often lead the government to modify its policies. Further, the secrecy within which government operates and the large number of activities conducted by modern governments can make it difficult for the opposition parties to investigate all actions of government. Effective access to information legislation; independent officers of Parliament able to scrutinize government spending, pursue public complaints, and ensure that those entrusted with power are acting ethically; an independent judiciary; vigilant media; and an attentive public are also important in trying to ensure that government does not abuse its power.

Parliamentary systems feature collective decision making by the prime minister and Cabinet, with Cabinet ministers often chosen to be representative of some of the important segments of society. Ideally, government decisions are based on discussion and deliberation by experienced Cabinet ministers, most of whom have the expertise of their departments of government to provide them with advice. Power has, however, tended to drift from the Cabinet as a whole to the prime minister and a small group of aides, officials, and ministers at the centre. Prime ministerial government may result in a clear direction for a government run by a decisive leader, but it carries the risk of wrong-headed or insensitive decisions made by the head of government without adequate deliberation among those with different ideas and perspectives.

Key Terms

Cabinet 345

Cabinet secrecy 351

Cabinet solidarity 349

Central agencies 350

Closure 356

Coalition government 341

Collective responsibility 351

Dissolution 344

Executive dominance 346

Filibuster 356

Governor general 343

Head of government 345

Discussion Questions

1. Should Canada replace the monarchy with an elected head of state?

2. Does the parliamentary system tend to give too much power to the prime minister?

3. Should party discipline in Parliament be loosened?

4. Is a coalition government preferable to a minority government?

5. Should the Canadian Senate be maintained as is, changed, or abolished?

6. Is the Westminster system of parliamentary government the best way to achieve the common good?

Further Reading

Docherty, D.C. (1997). *Mr. Smith goes to Ottawa: Life in the House of Commons.* Vancouver: UBC Press.

Docherty, D.C. (2005). *Legislatures.* Vancouver: UBC Press.

Franks, C.E.S. (1987). *The Parliament of Canada.* Toronto: University of Toronto Press.

Lijphart, A. (1999). *Patterns of democracy: Government forms and performance in thirty-six countries.* New Haven: Yale University Press.

Lijphart, A. (2008). *Thinking about democracy. Power sharing and majority rule in theory and practice.* New York: Routledge.

Rhodes, R.A.W., Wanna, J., & Weller, P. (2009). *Comparing Westminster.* Oxford: Oxford University Press.

Russell, P.H., & Sossin, L. (Eds.). (2009). *Parliamentary democracy in crisis.* Toronto: University of Toronto Press.

Savoie, D.J. (1999). *Governing from the centre: The concentration of power in Canadian politics.* Toronto: University of Toronto Press.

Seidle, F.L., & Docherty, D.C. (Eds.). (2003). *Reforming parliamentary democracy.* Montreal & Kingston: McGill-Queen's University Press.

Smith, D.E. (2007). *The people's House of Commons: Theories of democracy in contention.* Toronto: University of Toronto Press.

Smith, J. (Ed.). (2009). *The democratic dilemma: Reforming the Canadian Senate.* Montreal: McGill-Queen's University Press.

White, G. (2005). *Cabinets and first ministers.* Vancouver: UBC Press.

Chapter 15

Presidential and Semi-Presidential Systems

PHOTO ABOVE: On March 23, 2010, President Barack Obama signed the controversial Patient Protection and Affordable Care Act to reform the health care system in the United States.

CHAPTER OBJECTIVES

After reading this chapter you should be able to:

1. outline the basic differences between parliamentary and presidential systems of government
2. discuss the relationship between the president and Congress in the United States
3. examine the strengths and weaknesses of presidential systems
4. explain the basic features of semi-presidential systems
5. evaluate semi-presidential systems

On March 23, 2010, President Barack Obama signed the Patient Protection and Affordable Care Act to reform the health care system in the United States over a period of eight years.

In contrast to those who benefit from the universal health care system in Canada and all other wealthy countries, a substantial proportion of the American population is not covered by their country's system of generally private health care insurance. As he campaigned for the presidency, Barack Obama talked often about his mother's battles with insurance companies and her difficulties in paying medical bills as she struggled unsuccessfully with cancer. Health care, he argued, needed to be affordable and available to all. His plan would require employers (except small businesses) to provide health insurance to their employees or at least contribute to the cost, cover all children, and allow people to choose between competing private and public health care plans.

Even though the Democratic party, which favoured health care reform, controlled sixty of the one hundred seats in the Senate and had a large majority in the House of Representatives, achieving major reforms proved difficult. The powerful insurance industry mounted a massive lobbying effort and conservative political figures raised fears that "Obamacare" would lead to "death panels" that would decide whether seniors would live or die. Public health care was labelled "socialized medicine" and a threat to the freedom of Americans.

Democrats in the Senate and the House of Representatives prepared and introduced bills that had different proposals for health care reform. For example, the House bill proposed a public option while the Senate bill did not. A variety of amendments (including provisions to prevent public subsidies for abortions) were adopted to satisfy some and to try to gain the support of a few moderate Republicans.

On November 7, 2009, the House of Representatives passed the Affordable Health Care for Americans Act by a margin of 220–215 (with 39 Democrats opposed and 1 Republican in favour). This was followed on December 24 by the Senate passing its own bill, the Patient Protection and Affordable Care Act with all sixty Democrats voting in favour and thirty-nine Republicans opposed.

Normally, a conference committee of the two Houses works out a compromise bill that both Houses can pass and send to the president for final approval. However, after the death of Democratic Senator Edward Kennedy and the election of a Republican to replace him, the fate of health reform appeared uncertain. In the U.S. Senate, a filibuster can prevent a bill from coming to a vote unless sixty Senators pass a motion of cloture to end debate. To prevent this from happening, the House of Representatives passed the Senate bill and then several days later both Houses passed a second bill incorporating changes to the Senate bill through a special reconciliation procedure that requires only a majority vote in the Senate.

Major changes are difficult to achieve in the American presidential system. The president may try to persuade Congress to act in a certain way, but each of the two Houses of Congress has a major role in the process of developing and passing legislation. In this case change was achieved, but it was much less than the advocates of health reform wanted. As many as thirty million Americans could remain without health insurance, no public option was included, and the health care system will likely remain very costly and complex.

THE PRESIDENTIAL SYSTEM

The **presidential system** of government was developed in the United States. The loose confederation of the thirteen American states created during the War of Independence reflected the general view that a strong central government would threaten individual liberties and the rights of the individual states. However, a group known as the "federalists" argued that the problems faced by the country—including economic weakness, debts from the war, disagreements among the states, and the difficulty in raising an army to put down a rebellion—made it necessary to create an effective central government. In the view of James Madison, a leading federalist, tyranny could be prevented by separating the power of government into different institutions each independent of the others. Based on the assumption that individuals were motivated primarily by self-interest, Madison argued that "ambition must be made to counteract ambition" (*Federalist Papers*, no. 51). In other words, by ensuring that the executive branch (headed by the president), the legislative branch (**Congress**), and the judicial branch were each independent, the ambitions of those in each branch to become more powerful would be checked by those in the other branches who had their own ambition to be powerful. In addition, the power of the American government would be restricted by providing it with a limited range of constitutional powers.

Presidential systems feature a **separation of powers** in which the president and Congress each have separate bases of authority (see Figure 15-1). Unlike a parliamentary system, those holding executive positions cannot be members of the legislative branch. The judicial branch is also considered an independent branch, although its members are recommended for appointment by the president and approved by the Senate. Ideally, the separation of powers creates a system of **checks and balances** that prevents any branch of government or any individual from becoming too powerful.

Unlike in a parliamentary system, the executive (president and the Cabinet) does not need to maintain the support of the legislature to remain in office. Both the president and the members of Congress have fixed terms of office. The president cannot dissolve Congress and order an election in the hope that

PRESIDENTIAL SYSTEM A system of governing in which the president and Congress each separately derive their authority from being elected by the people and have a fixed term of office.

CONGRESS The legislative branch of the American government consisting of the House of Representatives and the Senate.

SEPARATION OF POWERS A basic feature of presidential systems in which the executive, legislative, and judicial branches of government are separate from each other, with each having different personnel and different bases of authority.

CHECKS AND BALANCES A basic principle of the American presidential system in which each of the three branches of government is able to check the actions of the others so that no individual or institution becomes too powerful.

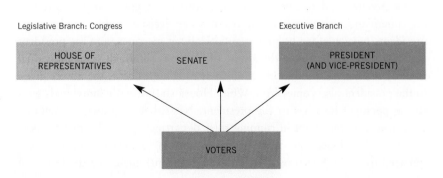

Legislative Branch: Congress

| HOUSE OF REPRESENTATIVES | SENATE |

Executive Branch

| PRESIDENT (AND VICE-PRESIDENT) |

VOTERS

FIGURE 15-1

A SIMPLIFIED DEPICTION OF THE AMERICAN PRESIDENTIAL SYSTEM

this will result in a Congress that is more willing to support the executive. Even though the executive and legislative branches are independent of each other, the passage of legislation involves both branches.

The presidential system has been adopted (with some modifications) by almost all countries in Central and South America as well as by some countries in other parts of the world, including Indonesia, the Philippines, Cyprus, Nigeria, Ghana, and Malawi (Shugart, 2006).

The President

In a presidential system, the president is both head of state and head of government. That is, the president carries out the ceremonial duties associated with the head of state, but also heads the executive branch of government. As chief executive, the president is commander-in-chief of the armed forces, exercises considerable control over foreign policy, helps to shape domestic policy, and exercises some control over the public service. Although the president heads the executive branch of government and thus is responsible for the implementation of laws, the president is also involved in the legislative activity of passing laws. Not only are the president and the executive branch active in proposing legislation to Congress, but the president's ability to veto laws passed by Congress (discussed below) means that Congress has to take into account the president's views in passing legislation.

The president nominates a variety of senior officials and Supreme Court and other federal judges. However, to check the power of the president, many presidential nominations (including Cabinet and senior departmental officials, ambassadors, federal and Supreme Court judges, members of regulatory agencies and advisory boards, and senior military officers) must be approved by the Senate (the upper chamber of Congress). Likewise, although the president has the authority to negotiate treaties, they must be approved by a two-thirds majority in the Senate.

The American President
www.whitehouse.gov

Cabinet and Executive Offices

The Cabinet secretaries who are appointed by the president and confirmed by the Senate head up the various departments of government. However, the American Cabinet as a whole is not a key decision-making body. Some presidents have avoided holding regular Cabinet meetings, and the president does not necessarily follow the advice of Cabinet. Although some individual Cabinet secretaries are important advisers to the president, the advice given to the president also comes from White House staff, usually individuals with strong personal loyalties to the president. Nevertheless, individual Cabinet secretaries are important in running their departments and drafting proposals and regulations. The president also controls various executive offices (referred to as the Executive Office of the President), including the Office of

Management and Budget and the Council of Economic Advisers, which gives the president important sources of advice. Of particular importance is the National Security Council, chaired by the president and including the chair of the Joint Chiefs of (Military) Staff and the Director of National Intelligence, which plays a central role in national security and foreign policy decisions.

Although Congress is responsible for legislation, the president can issue executive orders concerning how laws and policies are to be carried out. Further, by appointing top officials, the president can try to affect how the laws passed by Congress are implemented. For example, President Ronald Reagan tried to eliminate many environmental regulations by appointing like-minded persons to head the Environmental Protection Agency and cutting the funding for the Agency. However, two of his appointees to head the Agency who were critical of environmental policy resigned in disgrace. Subsequently, Congress passed stronger, more enforceable environmental legislation (Kraft, 2011).

Presidential Selection and Term

The president, along with a vice-presidential running mate, is elected by the American people. Although voters in the United States choose among the competing presidential candidates, technically they are voting for members of the Electoral College committed to casting their ballot for a particular presidential candidate. A majority of Electoral College votes is needed to elect a president (see Chapter 8). If no candidate has a majority of Electoral College votes, the president would be elected by the House of Representatives, the lower house of Congress, with each state delegation casting a single vote. Because the United States has a two-party system, this has not occurred since 1824.

Other countries with presidential systems directly elect their president rather than using an electoral college. In many countries (such as Brazil, Chile, and Argentina) a runoff election is held if no candidate has a majority (or, in some countries, a large plurality) of votes. In Mexico and the Philippines, however, the candidate with the most votes on a single ballot wins. For example, in the 2006 Mexican election, the winning candidate (Felipe Calderón) obtained 36.38 percent of the vote compared to 36.34 percent for the second-place candidate.

Because of concerns that excessive power may accumulate in the hands of a long-serving president, presidential systems limit the amount of time that presidents can hold the office. For example, Mexico limits its president to a single six-year term. The president of the United States has a fixed term in office of four years and can be elected to a maximum of two terms. Unlike the prime minister in a parliamentary system, the president holds office regardless of the support of Congress.

IMPEACHMENT   Although presidents have a fixed term of office, Congress does have the ability to remove a president who has engaged in illegal

Presidential Impeachment

Although a number of American presidents have faced impeachment proceedings, no president has ever been removed by this process. Richard Nixon resigned in 1974 before he could be impeached for participating in the cover-up of illegal activities (including breaking into Democratic party offices in Washington's Watergate building). In 1999, Bill Clinton was accused of false testimony and obstructing justice when he stated that he had not had sexual relations with his intern, Monica Lewinsky, in a deposition to a grand jury as part of a sexual harassment civil lawsuit. Although a small majority of the House voted to impeach the president, only one-half of senators voted for conviction, and thus Clinton was able to complete his term. Voting was almost entirely along party lines, indicating the political nature of the impeachment procedure.

The power of impeachment has been successfully used in several other countries to remove a president, particularly for corruption. For example,

President Fernando Collor of Brazil was removed from office in 1992 as a result of allegations by his younger brother that Collor was benefiting from illegal deals engaged in by a friend of the president. The "gifts" from his friend included two ranches, renovations of his apartments in Brazil and Paris, expensive cars for his children, and cash to various family members. Pressure from the public to impeach the president helped to ensure that representatives in Congress voted to impeach despite attempts by the president's friends to bribe representatives (Kara, 2005).

In contrast, President Ernesto Samper of Columbia was able to survive credible allegations that his presidential campaign was funded by the Cali cocaine cartel. Efforts to impeach him were voted down by Columbia's House of Representatives, which also prohibited further investigations. In this case, the popularity of the president discouraged representatives from voting for impeachment (Hinojosa & Pérez-Liñán, 2005).

IMPEACHMENT A process by which a president and other public officials can be removed from office after being accused of criminal behaviour and convicted by a legislative body.

behaviour. The process, known as **impeachment**, is difficult and lengthy. In the United States, the president, other top officials, and judges can be removed from office only if convicted of "treason, bribery or other high crimes and misdemeanours." After an investigation by the Judiciary Committee of the House of Representatives, a majority in the House has to pass articles of impeachment stating the offence(s). Then, after holding a trial, a two-thirds majority in the Senate has to reach a guilty verdict in order to remove the president (see Box 15-1, Presidential Impeachment).

The Vice-President

A candidate for vice-president in the United States is handpicked by a presidential candidate to serve as an election running mate, sometimes providing balance in the sense of appealing to different regions, appealing to persons with a somewhat different ideological perspective, or having different personal characteristics than the president. The vice-president has the constitutional right to preside over the Senate, although does so only occasionally, and can vote only in the case of a tie. Otherwise, the major constitutional role

The Significance of the Vice-President

The office of vice-president has not attracted the most flattering commendations:

- "The most insignificant office that ever the invention of man contrived." (President John Adams)
- "It's not worth a bucket of warm piss; it doesn't amount to a hill of beans." (Vice-President John Nance Garner)
- "About as useful as a cow's fifth teat." (President Lyndon B. Johnson)
- "The only thing the job calls for is waiting: waiting for the president to die or be impeached; waiting for the Senate to wind up in a tie so the vice-president can break it. That's all the vice-presidency is about: waiting. Everything else is make-work." (Lynne Cheney, wife of former Vice-President Richard Cheney, in a 1988 novel)

But is the insignificance of the vice-president exaggerated? In recent decades, vice-presidents have provided advice to the president and been members of the important National Security Council. Although the importance of the vice-president varies from one presidential administration to the next, Vice-President Richard (Dick) Cheney had a major influence on government policies in George W. Bush's administration. Unlike some other vice-presidents in recent decades, however, Cheney, because of his age and health, did not seek to become president at the end of Bush's two terms in office.

Thus, although the significance of the vice-president depends primarily upon the wishes of the president, the vice-presidency has tended to become an important executive institution.

of the vice-president is to be available to take over the presidency in case the president dies or is unable to continue in office (see Box 15-2, The Significance of the Vice-President). Depending on the president, some special tasks may be assigned to the vice-president.

The American Congress

The American Congress is a legislative body composed of two separate bodies:

- The **House of Representatives,** which is elected every two years from districts of approximately equal population size.
- The **Senate,** which is composed of persons elected for six-year terms on a two-per-state basis with one-third of the Senate being elected every two years.

The president does not have the power to dissolve Congress and thus has to live with a Congress that has a different political perspective. Because the president does not need the support of Congress to remain in office, Congress can feel free to reject legislative or budgetary proposals from the president, knowing that it will not lead to a new election. To protect the independence of Congress, the president and the Cabinet secretaries are not allowed to be members of Congress.

HOUSE OF REPRESENTATIVES The lower chamber of the American Congress, elected for a two-year term from districts of approximately equal population size.

SENATE (UNITED STATES) The upper chamber of Congress. Two senators are elected by voters in each state for a six-year term.

Both the Senate and the House of Representatives are active bodies. Because the Senate is smaller, contains elected representatives of states rather than smaller districts, has a longer term of office, and has the authority to approve treaties and reject presidential nominees, the Senate is considered to be the more important of the two chambers. Many members of the House of Representatives are interested in seeking to become senators when the opportunity arises. Nevertheless, both chambers are active in the legislative process. Proposed legislation often contains different provisions when passed by each chamber. A joint conference committee is then established to find a compromise between the two bills. Bills must be passed in identical form in the two chambers before being presented to the president (see Figure 15-2). "Revenue bills" (those involving taxes and, in practice, government spending) must be initiated in the lower chamber, the House of Representatives, although the Senate can propose amendments.

The American president does not attend Congress except to present the annual State of the Union address. Proposals for legislation must be presented by a member of Congress.[1] Although the executive branch prepares many of the legislative proposals that Congress considers, Congress is very active in modifying or rejecting the executive's proposals. Members of the American Congress have sizable staffs that are often involved in drafting and modifying legislative proposals. Congress is therefore active not only in approving legislation, but also in developing it.

PRESIDENTIAL VETO   As a check on the legislative power of Congress, the president has the authority to veto any law passed by Congress. Congress can override the **presidential veto**, but this requires a two-thirds majority in each body of Congress, and thus is quite rare.

The veto power of the president, although important, has limitations. The American president can only veto a bill in its entirety, rather than approving some aspects and rejecting others.[2] Thus, if Congress is passing a bill that the president opposes, members of Congress will often include some provisions that the president wants in order to reduce the likelihood of a veto. Even though the president does not use the veto frequently, the anticipation of a veto will often lead Congress to modify its proposals to try to satisfy the president.

CONGRESS'S OVERSIGHT ROLE   Congress exercises oversight of the activities of the public service because of its powers to investigate government

United States House of Representatives
www.house.gov

United States Senate
www.senate.gov

PRESIDENTIAL VETO The ability to prevent the passage of a bill. The president of the United States has the authority to veto laws passed by Congress, although this veto can be overridden by a two-thirds majority in each body of Congress.

---

[1] In other countries, the president usually has the authority to introduce legislation to Congress and may be able to limit the ability of Congress to amend the proposed legislation.
[2] If the president simply does not sign a bill, it automatically becomes law within ten days. However, if Congress has adjourned within that period, the bill does not become law (termed a "pocket veto"). In some American states, the governor possesses a line-item veto, allowing the governor to reject parts of the proposed legislation. Some countries give their presidents this powerful tool.

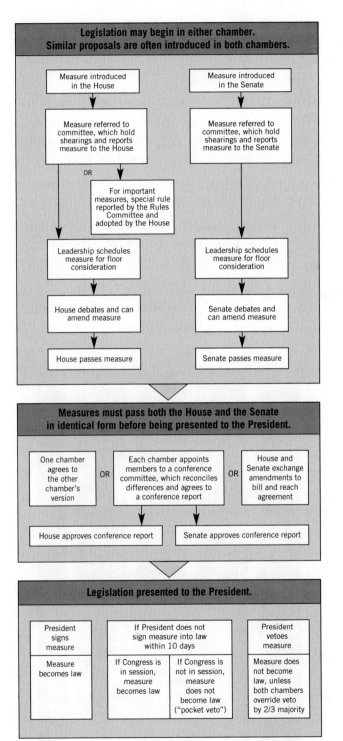

FIGURE 15-2

HOW A BILL BECOMES A LAW IN THE UNITED STATES

activity. Public servants are frequently called to testify before Congressional committees. Both Congress and the president take an active role in determining the government's spending plans (unlike the system in Canada, where parliamentary approval is normally a formality).

PARTY DISCIPLINE   Party discipline in the American Congress has traditionally not been very tight. There has often been quite a broad spectrum of differing perspectives within each of the two parties represented in Congress. Because the president and Cabinet do not need the support of a majority in Congress to stay in power, there is less pressure to maintain party discipline than in a parliamentary system.

Individual members of the U.S. Congress often vote as they see fit, or in the interests of the constituencies they represent, rather than as members of a party team. This means that the president may not be able to get Congress to support his policies even when the president's party controls Congress. For example, when the Republicans controlled Congress from 2002 to 2006, Republican President George W. Bush was unable to get Congress to pass many of his proposals without major modifications, particularly concerning domestic political issues (Brady & Volden, 2006).

► On November 14, 1995, the government of the United States shut down when the president and Congress were unable to agree on the government's budget.

Gridlock

On November 14, 1995, the government of the United States shut down. More than 14.8 million non-essential federal government employees were sent home and many government offices were closed.

The American system of government occasionally suffers from "gridlock," particularly because of tension between the executive and legislative branches. In 1994, the Republican party campaigned on the basis of a "Contract with America"—including tax cuts, a balanced budget requirement, term limits for legislators, and a major reduction in social welfare programs—and won a majority in the House of Representatives and gained control of the Senate. Because of their strongly conservative ideological perspective, the Republican majority rejected the government budget proposed by Democratic President Bill Clinton. While the November shutdown lasted only five days, the continuing inability to reach an agreement between the president and the Republican majority resulted in another shutdown from December 15 to January 6. Eventually, with the majority of the public blaming the Republicans in Congress for the crisis and with Clinton able to convince a substantial proportion of the public that the Republican proposals went too far, a modified version of Clinton's budget was passed. Existing programs were maintained, cuts

to government spending were smaller than the Republicans had demanded, and Clinton vetoed the more radical proposals that the Republican Congress had passed (Brady & Volden, 2006). Clinton was easily re-elected president in 1996; the Republicans continued to have a majority in both Houses of Congress, losing eight seats in the House of Representatives and gaining two in the Senate in the 1996 election. Despite the continuation of "divided government" (a situation where the majority in Congress and the president represent different political parties), agreement on subsequent budgets between the president and Congress were successful in producing a balanced budget and budgetary surpluses (Burden & Kimball, 2004).

The events of 1995–1996 are an extreme example of the gridlock that can make substantial changes difficult to achieve in the American political system. In part, gridlock can be the result of the "divided government" that has frequently occurred in the American presidential system in the past several decades. Even when the president's party has a majority in Congress, gridlock can still occur because individual members of Congress are often more interested in voting in accordance with the wishes and interests of their district or state rather than voting along party lines. Bargaining and compromise are needed to make the system work.

Conversely, a president faced with a Congress that has a majority of opposing party members has some ability to influence individual members of Congress regardless of their party affiliation. For example, in the early 1980s, Republican President Ronald Reagan was able to get much of his program adopted despite the control of Congress by the Democratic party. Reagan persuaded some conservative-minded Democrats of the virtues of his proposals. As well, by making his case directly to the American public, he created a favourable climate of opinion for his proposals, thus putting pressure on members of Congress to pass them. Nevertheless, as discussed in Box 15-3, Gridlock, differences between the president and Congress can potentially lead to "gridlock" (difficulty in getting things done), particularly if Congress is dominated by a political party that has a strongly different perspective than the president.

Although party discipline is not as tight in the United States as it is in most parliamentary systems, it should not be concluded that political parties are irrelevant. Members of a party do tend to vote the same way as the other members of their party. The parties in Congress have become more cohesive in the past few decades as the Democrats have become more consistently liberal or centrist and the Republicans more strongly conservative. For example, an analysis of the voting records of the Senate from 2000 to 2002 found that all but one of the fifty Democratic senators took leftist (liberal) positions on the majority of issues while all but one of the fifty Republican senators took rightist (conservative) positions on the majority of issues. Nevertheless, some moderate Democrats voted with the Republicans when Republicans presented relatively moderate proposals, and some moderate Republicans voted with the Democrats on other issues (Brady & Volden, 2006).

COMMITTEES   A final major feature of the U.S. Congress is the importance of congressional committees. It is in the hundreds of committees and subcommittees of the House and Senate that legislative proposals are most thoroughly debated, modified, or eliminated. In some cases, legislation is drafted by a congressional committee. The chairs of these powerful committees are chosen by the majority party in each House; the chair is often the party member who has served on that committee the longest. The committee chairs are often quite independent-minded and thus do not always feel the need to adhere to their party's positions.

In general, the passing of legislation in the American system is a very difficult process. There are a large number of obstacles to overcome. Presidents have to use all of their persuasive capabilities and negotiating skills in order to have their proposals accepted. As President George H.W. Bush said, perhaps with some exaggeration, it was easier to deal with Iraqi dictator Saddam Hussein than with the U.S. Congress. Within Congress, proposed legislation has to pass a variety of hurdles. For example, a committee chair may refuse to allocate time to discuss a bill. In the Senate, filibusters[3] are quite common, as each senator can speak on a proposal for as long as he or she wants. Senators are quite willing to use this power to express their opposition to a particular piece of legislation. A motion of cloture to limit debate must be passed by a 60 percent majority. Through the use of a filibuster, forty-one of the one hundred senators can prevent legislation from coming to a vote. Thus, in most cases controversial legislation will not likely be voted on in the Senate unless some support can be found in both political parties. To surmount the obstacles, a

---

[3] Filibusters are not allowed for some budgetary and trade bills.

proposed bill, whether initiated in Congress or prepared by the president's staff, will typically be changed considerably as compromises and additions are made to gain the support of various persons and interests.

The Balance between Executive and Legislative Power

Does the presidential system in the United States provide a suitable balance of powers between the executive and legislative branches so that each is able to check the power of the other? At times, the balance has shifted in favour of Congress such that the system might be best described as a congressional system. At other times, the president has been dominant such that some have described the system as having an "imperial presidency," with the president becoming like a powerful monarch. In particular, as the United States became heavily involved militarily in global affairs and as concerns about national security increased, presidents have tended to assume greater powers, as discussed in Box 15-4, War Powers. Nevertheless, Congress is important in determining the country's domestic policies.

Evaluating the Presidential System

Evaluating governing systems is complex. A variety of criteria can be used, and different people are likely to have different views about which criteria are most important. There is considerable variation in how any particular system of governing operates, not only as a result of different specific constitutional provisions, but also as a result of differences in the party system, the electoral system, and political culture as well as the broader circumstances and distribution of power that exists in any particular country. There are not only variations in how a particular system operates in particular countries, but also differences over time within a particular country. Further, in evaluating the presidential system it is important to keep in mind that the United States is the only developed country that maintained a democratic presidential system for a lengthy period of time. Nevertheless, we can discuss some potential strengths and weaknesses in the presidential system by comparing it to the parliamentary system discussed in Chapter 14.

LEADERSHIP AND DECISIVE ACTION   Those who prefer a presidential system often view it as providing strong leadership. The president leads the executive branch of government and is secure in office. Being elected in a national vote, the president can claim to speak for the people of the country as a whole. As head of state, a president can usually count on the respect and support of the people (although recent presidents have often lost the support of the majority of people during their term in office). However, given the independence of Congress, it is difficult for a president to ensure that a coherent set of policies is adopted.

BOX 15-4

War Powers

There is an inherent tension in the American governing system concerning the use of military force. The president is commander-in-chief of the Armed Forces, and there is an expectation that the president will take a leading role in international affairs and matters relating to national security. However, it is the constitutional responsibility of Congress to decide whether to declare war and to provide the funds needed by the military. To circumvent the constitutional requirement concerning a declaration of war by Congress, presidents have, on a number of occasions, ordered military actions without a formal declaration of war.

In 1964, after alleged attacks on U.S. naval vessels by North Vietnam, President Lyndon Johnson convinced almost all members of Congress to pass the Gulf of Tonkin Resolution, which authorized the president to take "all necessary actions to protect our Armed Forces." War was never declared but this Resolution was used to justify sending more than half a million troops to fight in Vietnam and to engage in the secret bombing and invasion of Cambodia. As the lengthy conflict continued and the Senate Foreign Relations Committee found that it had been deceived about some of the attacks on American military vessels, strong opposition to the war effort grew among the public and many members of Congress.

With President Richard Nixon discredited by the "Watergate" scandal and the attempts of his administration to stifle legitimate dissent, Congress decided to restrict the powers of the president by passing the War Powers Act in 1973.

This Act (which was passed by overriding President Nixon's veto) requires that the president notify Congress when troops are to be sent into foreign combat and that troops be brought home within sixty days (or ninety days, if necessary) unless Congress declares war or extends the length of troop involvement. As well, the president is required to answer any questions about the conflict that are raised by Congress and to submit periodic reports.

The War Powers Act, while viewed by the executive as an infringement on its constitutional powers, has not been a serious obstacle to presidents deciding to engage in various foreign conflicts. By raising fears about a threat to national security (real or artificial), presidents have not had difficulty winning support from Congress to take whatever actions the president deems necessary, thus circumventing the power of Congress to declare war (Hess, 2005). For example, in 2002, Congress voted by a large margin to authorize the use of the Armed Forces against Iraq, "to defend the national security of the United States against the continuing threat posed by Iraq." An attempt by the majority in Congress in April 2007 to pass legislation requiring that the president start withdrawing troops from Iraq later that year was vetoed by President Bush. Although Congress could end a conflict by not approving the funds needed for troop engagement, this would be politically risky, as it would be portrayed as not supporting the troops.

In a parliamentary system, the prime minister and Cabinet are capable of decisive action in a majority government situation because of their domination of the legislative branch. However, where no party has a majority, bargaining and negotiating among parties is required to gain majority support for legislative proposals. In some countries, the parliamentary system has been characterized by series of weak and unstable governments because of a highly fragmented party system in which stable coalitions cannot be formed.

◀ American presidents have found ways to avoid the constitutional provision that only Congress has the authority to declare war.

DEMOCRATIC ELECTION   The presidential system is sometimes viewed as more democratic than the parliamentary system, as the president is elected by the people. Instead of voting for a candidate in one's electoral district, which indirectly affects who will be prime minister and which party will govern, Americans have an opportunity to vote for the president as well as for the individuals who will represent their state and district in Congress.

REPRESENTATIVENESS   Members of Congress have greater independence than members of Parliament to represent the population and interests of their district or state, as they are not as tightly bound by party discipline as is the case in most parliamentary systems. In contrast, the party discipline characteristic of parliamentary systems limits the ability of members of the House of Commons to represent their constituents.

RESPONSIVENESS   Individual members of Congress are often very responsive to the voters or important interests in the districts or states they represent. However, the difficulties in passing legislation can make the governing system slow to respond to the wishes of the electorate as a whole. Although the American president may be responsive to the public in order to gain re-election, the term limit means that the president does not have to be responsive to public opinion in the second term. As well, Cabinet secretaries are not elected and may be unresponsive to the public. In parliamentary systems, the prime minister and the governing party have an incentive to be responsive to the voters to secure re-election and, in a majority government situation, have the capability to respond quickly to the views and demands of the citizenry.

ACCOUNTABILITY   The president and Cabinet do not sit in Congress and are not accountable to Congress. Nevertheless, the committees of the U.S. Congress are willing and able to investigate executive actions as part of their "oversight" role to ensure that the executive is acting properly. At times, presidents and other executive officials have claimed "executive privilege" to try to avoid releasing documents and testifying before a congressional committee. The extent of executive privilege has never been clearly established, although the courts have tended to view it as a qualified privilege relevant in certain situations. More generally, the separation of powers allows each branch of government to try to shift blame to the other for any problems, making it difficult for voters to determine who to hold accountable.

A parliamentary system makes government responsible to the House of Commons for its actions. However, in a majority government situation, the governing party doesn't normally need to worry about maintaining the necessary support of the House of Commons. Nevertheless, because the prime minister and Cabinet actively participate in the House of Commons, the public has an opportunity to assess the performance of the government through the ongoing debate between government and the opposition in the House.

OPENNESS   The presidential system tends to be more open than the parliamentary system. Rather than policy choices being made in the secrecy of Cabinet, Congress plays an active and more public role in developing and modifying policy proposals. Policy differences between Congress and the president are often aired publicly. This transparency may facilitate greater public participation in the policy-making process and make the process more inclusive of differing interests and viewpoints. However, the openness of the American political system makes the system more susceptible to influence by groups with specific interests (such as a variety of business interests) that may be able to prevent laws for the common good from being passed.

FLEXIBILITY   Presidential systems tend to be less flexible than parliamentary systems (Linz, 1994). The fixed terms of office in presidential systems can make it difficult to resolve impasses between the executive and legislative branches, as an election cannot be held before the end of the term of each elected politician. In parliamentary systems, a government that is unable to retain the confidence of the majority in the House of Commons can be removed from office. Likewise, prime ministers that lose the support of their party or caucus can be pressured to step down.

EXPERIENCE   The American presidential system often features "outsiders" being elected as president. Former military leaders and popular personalities are sometimes able to appeal to the public at large even if they do not have a strong connection to a particular party. Although this may bring a fresh perspective to national politics, it means that the president may have very limited experience in national politics and international affairs. For example, although Bill Clinton and George W. Bush had political experience as state governors, neither had experience in national politics before becoming president. Barack Obama served less than four years in the U.S. Senate (with part of that time spent campaigning) before being elected president. As well, since a president is unrestricted in the choice of Cabinet secretaries, some of those chosen have had little or no political experience. Prime ministers usually have extensive political experience, although some Canadian prime ministers (for example, Brian Mulroney) have come to office with little or no experience as an elected politician. Unlike parliamentary systems, in which a potential prime minister can gain experience and knowledge by serving as leader of an opposition party, presidential systems offer no formal role for losing presidential candidates.[4]

SEMI-PRESIDENTIAL SYSTEMS

A number of countries have adopted systems of governing involving a mixture of parliamentary and presidential features, which are often referred to as **semi-presidential systems**.[5] France, which adopted this system in 1958, is the best-known example. A number of other European countries, including Russia and several other former communist countries, adopted this system in the 1990s. As well, a number of African countries as well as Peru, Sri Lanka, and Taiwan have also adopted various versions of the semi-presidential system (Shugart, 2006).

SEMI-PRESIDENTIAL SYSTEM
A system of governing in which an elected president shares power with a prime minister and Cabinet, who usually need to retain the support of the elected legislature.

A semi-presidential system generally features an elected president sharing executive power with a prime minister. As in a presidential system, the president has a fixed term in office and can be removed only through an impeachment procedure. Unlike the head of state in a parliamentary system, the president wields substantial powers, including the power to appoint (and, in some countries, dismiss) the prime minister. As well, the president generally has the power (in some cases with limitations) to dissolve the elected legislature and require that an election be held. As in a parliamentary system, the prime minister and Cabinet (the government) are responsible to an elected legislative body and, in most countries, need to maintain the support of that body.

---

[4] An exception is Nicaragua, where the runner-up in the presidential election automatically receives a seat in the National Assembly.

[5] They are also referred to as "mixed," "hybrid," "parliamentary-presidential," or "premier-presidential" systems.

France

In France's previous parliamentary system, governments changed frequently and were often unable to act effectively. In 1958, French army officers unhappy with the government's efforts against the war of liberation in the French colony of Algeria staged a *coup d'état* in Algiers and threatened to overthrow the French government unless Charles de Gaulle (the leader of the Free French in World War II) was made president. The president of France invited de Gaulle to take over as prime minister instead. De Gaulle accepted this invitation on the condition that a new constitution providing for a powerful president was adopted. A referendum approving a semi-presidential system was passed by a large margin in 1958. De Gaulle was then chosen president, a position he held until stepping down in 1969.

Currently, the French president is elected for a fixed five-year term and can serve a maximum of two terms.[6] The president appoints the prime minister, normally from the majority party or a coalition of parties that has the majority in the elected National Assembly. The president, with advice from the prime minister, appoints the members of the Council of Ministers (Cabinet) as well as top public, military, and judicial officials. The president chairs the meetings of the Council of Ministers. As in presidential systems, ministers do not sit in the Assembly. The Assembly, elected for a maximum five-year term, can censure the prime minister and Council of Ministers and force them to resign but cannot censure the president or force a presidential election. However, unlike the American presidential system, the French president can dissolve the Assembly and have a new Assembly election conducted (although another election cannot be held for at least one year). The French president cannot veto laws passed by the Assembly but can refer a proposed law back to the Assembly for reconsideration one time and can also refer the law to the Constitutional Court to determine its validity before signing the legislation.

The French president can call national referendums, determine when the National Assembly meets and what its agenda will be, assume emergency powers, and propose constitutional amendments. As well, the president has a leading role in foreign affairs, is responsible for negotiating and ratifying foreign treaties, and is commander-in-chief of the armed forces (Elgie, 2005).

When the Assembly has a majority of members from the same party as the president (or parties that support the president), the president tends to be the dominant figure in the French government. The prime minister, in this situation, is usually someone who has personal loyalty to the president. Although the president does not have the constitutional authority to dismiss a prime minister, presidents have been able to encourage prime ministers of their own party to resign (in some cases, by requiring them to sign an undated letter of resignation before taking office).

---

[6] Prior to 2007, the president could serve an unlimited number of seven-year terms.

If the majority in the Assembly represents a party that has a different perspective than the president, the president will find it necessary to choose the leader of that party as prime minister, as the government must have the support of the majority in the Assembly. The president can dissolve the Assembly and call an election, but if the election leads to a similar result the president will have to live with a government that has a different political perspective. In this situation, termed **cohabitation**, the president shares power with the prime minister and Cabinet. From 1986 to 1988 and 1993 to 1995, Socialist President François Mitterand shared power with the conservative parties that controlled the Assembly, while from 1997 to 2002, President Jacques Chirac, a conservative, shared power with Socialist Prime Minister Lionel Jospin. In this power-sharing arrangement, the prime minister has a strong ability to determine the domestic policies that will be adopted, regardless of the views of the president (Elgie, 2005). However, beginning in 2007, the election of the Assembly for a five-year term occurs shortly after the election of the president for a similar term. This change reduces the likelihood of cohabitation. For example, the election of President Nicolas Sarkozy in 2007 was followed several weeks later by the election of a majority of his supporters to the Assembly.

COHABITATION The sharing of power between the French president and prime minister that occurs when the Assembly is controlled by a party opposed to the president.

Russia

Following the collapse of the Soviet Union, the Russian Federation (with Boris Yeltsin as president) emerged as an independent state in December 1991. Serious conflicts developed between Yeltsin, who introduced unpopular radical reforms, and the Congress of People's Deputies. After Yeltsin decided to disband the Congress in 1993 and rule by decree, the Congress declared him no longer president. Yeltsin then persuaded Russian military forces to attack and destroy the "White House" where Congress met. Subsequently, Yeltsin oversaw the development of a new constitution (approved in a referendum) that gave the president extensive powers. Nevertheless, the leading parties elected to the new State Duma (the lower house of the Federal Assembly or parliament) were often critical of Yeltsin's policies. However, with support from Russian "oligarchs" (those who had become extremely wealthy as state-owned assets were sold off at bargain prices), Yeltsin managed to get re-elected as president in 1996.

President Vladimir Putin, elected in 2000 with the support of several political parties, became a very powerful and popular president. Indeed, under Putin, Russia reverted to a considerable extent to an authoritarian regime with substantial control of the media and suppression of dissent. Putin has continued to be powerful after his two terms as president as a result of being appointed prime minister by his hand-picked presidential successor, Dmitry Medvedev, and by becoming chair of the dominant political party, United Russia.

▶ Vladimir Putin became a powerful Russian president. When his two terms concluded, he was appointed prime minister by his hand-picked presidential successor and has continued to be the dominant political figure in Russia.

Russia's semi-presidential system gives the president, elected for a fixed six-year term[7] and a maximum of two consecutive terms, considerable power to issue edicts and regulations that have the effect of laws without the approval of the Federal Assembly. The president directs foreign and military policy and negotiates and signs international treaties. The president can also call referendums to gain support for his policies. The president is responsible for appointing the Cabinet, can chair Cabinet meetings, and has an unrestricted power to dismiss the government. The president also has developed a large administrative staff that provides considerable governing capability. The president's nomination of a prime minister (officially labelled the Chair of the Government) has to be approved by the State Duma. However, if the Duma rejects the president's choice three consecutive times, the Duma is dissolved and a new Duma is elected.

Evaluation of Semi-Presidential Systems

Do semi-presidential systems combine the best features of the parliamentary and presidential systems? Or is the dual executive, each with significant

---

[7] A constitutional amendment in 2008 changed the term from four to six years. This will not affect Medvedev's term as president, which ends in 2012. Putin will be able to run for president in 2012, or earlier if Medvedev resigns.

powers, a recipe for instability? An early version of this system, Germany's Weimar Republic (established after World War I), had difficulty dealing with the serious problems the country faced. This contributed to the coming to power of Adolf Hitler and the Nazi party (Linz, 1994). Unlike most contemporary semi-presidential systems, the Weimar constitution gave unlimited power to the president to dissolve Parliament. This allowed the president to ignore the views of Parliament (Morgan-Jones & Schleiter, 2004).

France is typically viewed as a success story, even though its government has functioned in quite different ways depending upon whether the president has the support of the majority in the Assembly. Nevertheless, the French system is sometimes criticized for giving the president excessive power. Russia is a clearer case of a semi-presidential system that can give excessive power to the president. However, in this case, the lack of a strong democratic political culture (resulting from its history of authoritarian and totalitarian government) along with the specific features of the governing system and Putin's popularity have facilitated Putin's exercise of strong powers whether as president or prime minister. On the other hand, in countries such as Poland, Romania, and Taiwan, the powers of the president are quite limited and thus the semi-presidential system leans in a parliamentary direction (Siaroff, 2009).

The governing responsibility of both the elected president and the prime minister and Cabinet that have the support of the Assembly can lead to tension and gridlock. However, there is flexibility in that the president can govern (for example, by appointing a non-partisan Cabinet) when the legislature is fragmented among many parties and thus unable to provide majority support to the government. This has been found to be useful in a number of the newer democracies, particularly those in Eastern Europe, that have adopted this system (Schleiter & Morgan-Jones, 2005).

Summary and Conclusion

The term *presidential system* can be misleading. The president controls the executive branch of government and serves as both head of state and head of government. However, the separation of powers allows each of the three branches of government to check the powers of the other branches. At times, in the United States, the president has tended to be more powerful than Congress. At other times, Congress has asserted its powers and limited the power of the president. Generally, however, although presidents typically dominate in terms of foreign and military policy, power is more diffused in a presidential system than in those parliamentary systems where majority governments are common. The sharing of powers between the president and Congress usually makes bargaining and compromises between the president and Congress necessary in order to make governing decisions. Therefore, some political scientists have suggested that it would be more accurate to describe the American system of government as a presidential–congressional system rather than a presidential system.

To a considerable extent the power of the American president is dependent on the president's ability to persuade the public and individual members of Congress of the merits of a particular policy.

As head of state as well as head of government, a president can successfully claim to speak on behalf of the national interest, as long as the president retains the respect and support of the people. Because individual members of Congress tend to represent state or district interests, it can be difficult for Congress to take coherent action for the common good of the country as a whole.

Semi-presidential systems generally have both a democratically elected president with significant powers and a prime minister and Cabinet that are responsible to an elected legislature. Because the elected legislature can be dissolved before its term is up, there is somewhat greater flexibility than in a pure presidential system, where both the president and the Congress have fixed terms in office.

There is considerable variability in semi-presidential systems in terms of the constitutional provisions of different countries; how these provisions operate in practice; and, within individual countries, whether the president has the support of the majority in Parliament. As with all systems of governing, the actual functioning of semi-parliamentary systems is dependent on such factors as the nature of the political party system, the context within which the governing system was established, and the personalities of the leading political figures (Elgie, 1999).

Key Terms

Checks and balances 363

Cohabitation 379

Congress 363

House of Representatives 367

Impeachment 366

Presidential system 363

Presidential veto 368

Semi-presidential system 377

Senate (United States) 367

Separation of powers 363

Discussion Questions

1. Do you think it would be best for a new democracy to adopt a parliamentary, presidential, or semi-presidential system?
2. What criteria are most important in evaluating different systems of governing?
3. Is Canada's parliamentary system preferable to an American-style presidential system?
4. Is there an appropriate balance between legislative and executive power in the United States?
5. Does the semi-presidential system create a hybrid that contains the best or the worst of the parliamentary and presidential systems?

Further Reading

Aberbach, J.D., & Peterson, M.A. (Eds.). (2005). *The executive branch*. Oxford: Oxford University Press.

Brady, D.W., & Volden, C. (2006). *Revolving gridlock: Politics and policy from Jimmy Carter to George W. Bush* (2nd ed.). Boulder, CO: Westview Press.

Cohen, R.E. (1995). *Washington at work: Back rooms and clean air* (2nd ed.). Needham Heights, MA: Allyn and Bacon.

Elgie, R. (Ed.). (1999). *Semi-presidentialism in Europe*. Oxford: Oxford University Press.

Fiorina, M. (1996). *Divided government* (2nd ed.). Boston: Allyn & Bacon.

Fisher, L. (1998). *The politics of shared power: Congress and the executive* (4th ed.). College Station, TX: Texas A&M University Press.

Kelley, D.R. (Ed.). (2005). *Divided power: The presidency, Congress, and the formation of American foreign policy*. Fayetteville, AK: University of Arkansas Press.

Lijphart, A. (Ed.). (1992). *Parliamentary versus presidential government*. Oxford: Oxford University Press.

Linz, J.J., & Valenzuela, A. (Eds.). (1994). *The failure of presidential democracy*. Baltimore, MD: Johns Hopkins University Press.

Chapter 16

Public Policy and Public Administration

PHOTO ABOVE: On April 20, 2010, BP's oil drilling rig exploded in the Gulf of Mexico. For many months, millions of litres of oil a day gushed from the site, causing an ecological disaster.

CHAPTER OBJECTIVES

After reading this chapter you should be able to:

1. discuss the role of government in the economy
2. examine general perspectives on public policy
3. analyze the policy process
4. describe the characteristics of bureaucracies
5. evaluate public administration reforms

On April 20, 2010, an oil drilling rig working for BP, one of the world's largest petroleum companies, exploded in the Gulf of Mexico, killing eleven workers. A blowout preventer on the 1.5 km deep well failed and for months the leakage of millions of litres of oil a day killed birds, dolphins, and fish and fouled the ecologically sensitive marshes of Louisiana and the coastline of several states.

BP had been granted a "categorical exemption" from the environmental assessment required under the National Environmental Policy Act. BP's application for a drilling permit stated that a spill was "unlikely" and that even if it were to occur it would have "sublethal effects on fish and marine mammals." Less than two weeks before the disaster, BP lobbied the U.S. government to broaden the use of categorical exemptions so as to avoid unnecessary paperwork and time delays (Eilperin, 2010).

The disaster in the Gulf raises issues about government regulation of industry. In recent decades there has been a move to deregulate industry as much as possible. Government regulations are seen by business interests as inefficient and harmful to the competitive free market. In the United States, responsibility for ensuring safety in offshore drilling gradually has been shifting to the oil industry, although various requirements concerning blowout preventers remain. In Canada in 2009, the National Energy Board, which is responsible for regulating the industry, adopted what it termed a "modern, goal-oriented" approach that allows companies to determine what technologies intended to protect the environment are most

appropriate for their particular projects (Mayeda, 2010). Several petroleum companies—including BP, which has three oil drilling licences for the Beaufort Sea—have made requests to the Canadian government to reduce the environmental regulations for Arctic drilling (Suzuki & Moola, 2010). In 2010, Chevron Canada was drilling a 2.6 km deep well (much deeper than BP's well) in the Atlantic Ocean off the shore of Newfoundland.

In the pursuit of profit and multimillion-dollar bonuses for their executives, corporations may take excessive risks and seek to cut costs by pressuring governments to reduce regulation. This is the case not only in the petroleum industry but also in the financial industry, where excessive risk and greed led to the near collapse of the global economy in 2008. Further, because of their financial clout and lobbying efforts, corporations may be able to gain special privileges (such as exemptions from regulations) that may not come to public attention until a disaster occurs.

Rigid and excessive regulations may be harmful to the economy. However, appropriate and carefully administered government regulations are essential to protect the common good.

INTRODUCTION

Many people view government very negatively. Fairly or unfairly, government is often seen as inefficient and ineffective with public servants enjoying secure jobs that do not require hard work and initiative. As American President Ronald Reagan said in his inaugural address in 1981, "Government is not the solution to our problem, government is the problem." Nevertheless, when serious problems arise people generally expect government to "do something" and criticize government if the public interest has not been adequately protected.

In this chapter, we focus on **public policy**, "a course of action or inaction chosen by public authorities to address a given problem or interrelated set of problems" (Pal, 1992, p. 2). In addition to discussing some general policies concerning the regulation and management of the economy and the development of the "welfare state," we examine the processes of policy-making and the different perspectives on the politics of public policy. We also look at the changing nature of public administration that affects the implementation of public policies.

PUBLIC POLICY A course of action or inaction chosen by public authorities to address a given problem or interrelated set of problems.

GOVERNMENT AND THE ECONOMY

In countries such as Canada and the United States, the free-market system[1] is largely responsible for what goods are produced, the prices of goods and services, and the availability and terms of employment. However, public policies have important effects on the functioning of the economic system, how wealth and income are distributed, and the well-being of people in a country. Governments are major economic actors that collect a sizable proportion of a country's income through taxation to fund its operations and services and to transfer to individuals for various purposes. Further, there is state ownership of some businesses. For example, in many Canadian provinces the generation and distribution of electricity is in the hands of a provincial Crown corporation. Likewise, public transit systems and VIA Rail as well as the postal service are publicly owned. In addition, partnerships between government and private businesses or non-profit organizations have become increasingly common.

Public policies in the form of laws, regulations, taxes, and various incentives have important effects on business activities. Governments have often tried to maintain competition in the marketplace. For example, the American and European governments successfully pursued legal action against the anti-competitive practices of Microsoft Corporation that allowed it to dominate the Internet browser and software markets. Likewise, a variety of regulations

---

[1] Free (liberal) market economies are particularly characteristic of countries such as the United States, Canada, and Britain. In addition to the managed economies of many non-Western countries (see Chapter 17), many Western European countries have been described as having "coordinated market economies." For a discussion of the varieties of capitalism see, for example, Hancké (2009).

have been adopted to protect consumers and to try to ensure that they have the information they need to make informed choices in the marketplace. Before such regulations were adopted, few businesses voluntarily provided such information and many products were unsafe.

Environmental policies have also affected business activity. Protection of the natural environment and conservation of natural resources are important for business as well as the public in the long run. However, individual businesses are usually reluctant to take costly measures to limit their negative impact on the environment unless they can be assured that their competitors will be required to take similar actions. Without effective government regulation, businesses can avoid bearing the costs of their pollution.

Labour policies have often helped to reduce bitter conflicts between business and labour. These policies include rules concerning the certification of unions to bargain collectively on behalf of workers and assistance to try to reach agreements without a strike or lockout. As well, to try to prevent workers from being exploited by business, most contemporary governments legislate the minimum wage that workers must receive, set limits on the hours of work, require that vacation time be provided, and establish safety standards for workplaces.

Public policies not only put some limits on what business can do, but also can provide support and assistance to various sectors of the economy. For example, governments often provide subsidies to fledgling industries, to industries that are vital to the country's economy or military capabilities, and to high-technology industries that are considered to be the wave of the future. As well, governments often provide various forms of assistance to sectors of the economy that are experiencing decline, such as textiles, steel, and shipbuilding industries, or that have volatile fortunes, such as agriculture. Governments also often provide loans and subsidies to encourage businesses to locate in the less economically developed areas of a country.

Government involvement in the economy is sometimes described as "interference" with the free market. Excessive regulation can reduce the flexibility of the free-market system. High taxes can reduce the ability of businesses to be competitive in the global marketplace and may result in the emigration of persons with specialized skills. Price controls can lead to shortages and insufficient investment for future demand to be met.

Government involvement in the economy is not necessarily harmful to the free market and the interests of business. Government restrictions on monopolies can help to encourage a competitive market. Government provision or funding of research and development can be of major assistance to business in a technological age. The provision of some public services, such as education, hospitals, and parks, by government removes some activities from the market. However, the general interests of business, as well as the population as a whole, are served by providing a healthy and educated workforce and by ensuring a higher quality of life.

Managing the Economy

Economic activity tends to go through cycles of expansion and contraction. During the Great Depression of the 1930s, when business investment collapsed and unemployment rates skyrocketed, British economist John Maynard Keynes (1883–1946) developed the idea that government could smooth out the ups and downs of the free-market economy. **Keynesian economic policies** involve stimulating the economy (by spending money and/or reducing taxes) when private business investment is low and cooling down the economy (by reducing spending and/or raising taxes) when excessive investment is creating inflation. As well, because the poor tend to spend rather than save their money, government programs that put money into the hands of the poor can help to ensure that there is sufficient demand for the goods and services that business can supply. This in turn can result in full or nearly full employment. In general, Keynesian economic policies reflect the view that government can have a positive role in ensuring the smooth functioning of the free-market capitalist system without directly intervening in business decisions.

Keynesian economic policies were adopted by most of the advanced capitalist countries during and after World War II. They were successful in providing three decades of sustained growth and prosperity. However, Keynesian economic policies fell out of favour among economists and government policy-makers in the mid 1970s when economies suffered from a simultaneous combination of inflation and economic stagnation ("stagflation"). In their place, neo-liberal ideas that viewed the market as efficient and self-regulating became influential. Cutting taxes, reducing regulation, and reducing government spending were seen as the key to economic growth. Particularly influential was the idea of **monetarism** developed by American economist Milton Friedman (1912–2006).

In Friedman's view, Keynesian policies had led governments to increase the supply of money, causing inflation, in order to cover the debts caused by excessive government spending. Friedman argued instead that, each year, governments should have a "balanced budget" (that is, spending should not exceed revenues), even though this means that government will reduce its spending in recessionary times as tax revenues decline. In addition, autonomous institutions such as the Federal Reserve System[2] in the United States and the Bank of Canada should fight inflation by limiting the growth of the money supply and keeping interest rates high when inflationary pressures occur. By keeping government out of direct involvement in managing the economy, the unpopular bitter medicine needed to prevent inflation can be administered.

KEYNESIAN ECONOMIC POLICIES The idea that government can smooth out the ups and downs of the free-market economy by stimulating the economy when private business investment is low and cooling down the economy when excessive investment is creating inflation.

MONETARISM An economic perspective based on the view that government's role in the economy should be largely restricted to controlling the supply of money.

---

[2] The Federal Reserve System consists of a Board of Governors appointed for a fourteen-year term by the president and approved by the Senate and twelve regional independent Federal Reserve Banks. An Open Market Committee that includes the Board of Governors and five of the Reserve Bank presidents is responsible for monetary policy through its regular decisions affecting the cost and availability of money, credit, and basic interest rates.

Friedman also argued that the role of government in the economy should be substantially reduced. With less regulation and lower taxes, there will be greater incentives for investment and production. Economic problems will be resolved by the free market rather than by government. In practice, however, major tax cuts have often not been matched by significant cuts in government spending, even by governments strongly committed to the free market. For example, the substantial tax cuts instituted in the United States after the election of President George W. Bush in 2000 led to large government deficits and mounting government debt as government spending increased.

As noted in Chapter 9, the financial crisis of 2007–2009 was caused to a considerable extent by the lack of adequate regulation of major financial institutions in the United States and Europe. This led to an expensive bailout of banks and other financial institutions and was followed by major government spending programs and exceptionally low interest rates to provide economic stimulus. In 2010, as the government of Greece was about to default on its loans and as several other European countries including Spain, Portugal, Italy, and Ireland[3] faced huge government deficits and debts, the European Union along with the International Monetary Fund and the European Central Bank put together a loan facility of about $1 trillion to assist governments in financial trouble and prevent a collapse of the euro. As German Chancellor Angela Merkl told the German Parliament:

> *The lack of rules and limits can make behavior in financial markets driven purely by the profit motive destructive and lead to an existential threat to financial stability in Europe and even the world . . . The market alone won't correct these mistakes. (quoted in Leonard, 2010)*

The conditions for receiving loans involved the imposition of austerity programs, including major cuts to public programs and to the employment, wages, and pensions of public servants. However, severe austerity programs can lead to unrest (as evidenced by major strikes and demonstrations in Greece in 2010) and carry a risk of leading to a worldwide recession or even a depression. In a globalized economy, the problems of one part of the world can quickly spread to the rest of the world.

The Welfare State

Many modern governments, particularly in the richer, developed countries, have developed a **welfare state** in which "government-protected minimum standards of income, nutrition, health, housing, and education [are] assured to every citizen as a political right, not as a 'charity'" (Wilensky, 1975, p. 1).

WELFARE STATE A term used to describe countries in which government ensures that all people have a minimum standard of living and are provided some protection from hardships resulting from unemployment, sickness, disability, and old age.

---

[3] The problem of large government deficits and debts resulting in part from the financial crisis of 2007–2009 affected not only some of the countries in the "eurozone," but also the United Kingdom and the United States. Iceland was saved from bankruptcy in 2008 by a $4 billion loan from Russia and assistance from Nordic countries.

Criticism of the Welfare State

Critics view the welfare state as substantially increasing the tax burden that people face and contributing to government deficits and debt. Increases in government spending and borrowing crowd out private investment and activity. The welfare state interferes with the "discipline" of the marketplace, particularly by reducing the incentive for people to work if welfare or unemployment benefits are too generous. Instead, the welfare state encourages people to become dependent on government and less likely to take responsibility for their own lives.

Are these criticisms of the welfare state valid? The provision by the Canadian government of basic health care, education, and various social services has contributed to the high quality of life enjoyed by Canadians. Furthermore, the welfare state does not necessarily reduce the competitiveness of an economy. It can allow people to take greater risks, such as finding new jobs, knowing that they have security to fall back on. As well, various social programs help people to adjust as economies change in response to globalization (Atkinson, 2000). In the contemporary knowledge-based economies of the advanced countries, an efficient welfare state combined with major government investments in education, health, and culture can be helpful in developing a highly productive workforce (Castells, 2004).

Welfare state programs contributed to the long period of social peace and economic growth in the decades after World War II by helping to achieve a compromise between the demands of workers and the pursuit of profit by business. Welfare state policies may help to legitimate the free-market capitalist system in the eyes of the public by removing some of the harshness of the economic system.

Overall, a variety of social, health, and educational programs have come to be viewed as rights or entitlements. Once they are established, it can be politically difficult to change these programs to improve their efficiency or effectiveness, particularly if they provide benefits to a substantial proportion of the population. Nevertheless, as many governments at the beginning of the second decade of the twenty-first century faced growing deficits and debts combined with very slow economic growth and aging populations, welfare state programs (along with public sector employment and wages) faced potentially severe cutbacks.

In the past, there was generally an expectation that individuals should be self-reliant. The failure to provide for oneself and one's family was seen as a result of personal irresponsibility rather than a general failure of the economy. This view was challenged by the Great Depression of the 1930s, when millions of people were unable to find work. The Depression also demonstrated the inability of private charities and local governments to deal with the problems faced by the needy. The successful mobilization of society and the economy by governments for World War II increased the capabilities of governments and created more positive attitudes toward an active role for government. There were expectations that governments should take responsibility for the well-being of returning soldiers and the families of those who had sacrificed their lives. As well, the threat of communism and the growing strength of labour and socialist parties created a political climate favourable to the development of the welfare state as a way of protecting the free-market capitalist system from challenges.

The welfare state has been the subject of considerable debate in recent decades, as discussed in Box 16-1, Criticism of the Welfare State. While some programs, such as publicly funded medical care and old age pensions, are popular among the public in many countries, there is less support for social assistance (welfare) and employment insurance. Since the mid 1990s, the Canadian government has substantially reduced the proportion of unemployed persons who are eligible to collect employment insurance, and some provincial governments have reduced social assistance payments and required that the able-bodied work for their social assistance payments. In 1996, the U.S. government adopted a policy limiting welfare to five years in one's lifetime.

Although welfare state programs have helped to improve the lives of the less advantaged members of societies, they have not substantially reduced inequalities in income and wealth. Indeed, there has been a tendency for inequalities to increase in recent decades. In particular, the total income of top corporate executives has risen rapidly while the average wages of workers has tended to be stagnant when inflation is taken into account. Although the norm of two-income rather than one-income families has helped to increase average household incomes, the tens of millions of dollars in annual compensation received by many top executives has become a political issue, particularly where corporate executives have received large bonuses despite making decisions that resulted in huge losses for their businesses and expensive government bailouts.

◀ Inequalities have continued to increase in recent decades, with the incomes of corporate executives rising rapidly while average workers' salaries have remained stagnant. The home of Bill Gates, pictured here, has an assessed value of US$147.5 million.

ANALYZING PUBLIC POLICY

Analyzing the choice of public policies involves looking at the broad set of forces that set the context for public policy and examining the details of the processes that led to the adoption of specific policies. Among the general influences on public policy are the ideas and ideologies that affect how the various individuals and groups that are involved in policy-making decide what problems to address, how those problems are defined, and what general patterns of policies can be found in any political community. Very important as well is the distribution of power and the ways in which different groups attempt to influence public policy. Developing public policy is not only a process through which government officials try to determine which policy is "best" in some technical way, but also a political process that reflects the contending ideas and interests of different groups in society and those in different governing institutions.

General Perspectives

There are a variety of widely differing general perspectives concerning the policy-making process and the outcomes of the policy process in democratic countries. Each of the approaches gives a different answer to why government acts the way it does and who tends to benefit from public policies (Brooks, 1998).

PLURALIST PERSPECTIVE
A perspective that views public policies as the outcome of competition among a wide variety of organized groups that seek to protect and promote the interests of their members with no group having a dominant influence.

The **pluralist perspective** views public policies as the outcome of competition among a wide variety of organized groups that seek to protect and promote the interests of their members. Some groups may be more influential than others on particular issues, but no group has a dominant influence on a wide range of policies. Business interests have many resources that they can use to exert influence, but those who hold the pluralist perspective argue that a variety of other groups and interests have some resources they can use to influence policy if they use those resources skilfully (Graefe, 2007). Further, the pluralist perspective views government as not systematically biased in favour of any particular group or interest. Politicians, it is argued, try to develop policies that satisfy a wide variety of groups.

PUBLIC CHOICE THEORY
A perspective based on the assumption that all political actors are rationally attempting to maximize their own individual interests or preferences. Public policies will generally reflect the choices made by voters.

Public choice theory assumes that all individuals involved in politics (including politicians, government employees, interest group leaders, and voters) are rationally attempting to maximize their own individual interests or preferences. Politicians wanting to maximize their power by winning elections will adopt policy positions preferred by the majority of voters or those voters who are crucial to the outcome of an election. This can lead to excessive government spending as politicians compete with one another by making expensive promises to gain votes. As well, public servants encourage the adoption of policies that expand the activities of government to increase their own status and chances for promotion.

Neo-Marxist theory views politics as reflecting the conflicts that result from the way society is organized to produce goods. Capitalist societies are fundamentally divided along class lines. Based on the unequal power of different classes over how wealth is produced and distributed, people organize themselves to challenge or maintain the capitalist system and the policies that sustain it. Some contemporary neo-Marxists extend this analysis to argue that capitalism also creates relations of inequality among individuals based on gender, race, ethnicity, and sexual orientation (Graefe, 2007).

The state in neo-Marxist theory can be viewed as a space in which the struggle of different social forces occurs, with the policies that are adopted by government reflecting the unequal power relations between the dominant capitalist forces and subordinate groups.[4] Economic globalization further enhances the dominance of capitalist interests and increases the pressure for policies that favour capitalist interests based on the argument that such policies are needed if a country is to be competitive in the global economy (Graefe, 2007).

State-centred theory views public policies as reflecting, to a considerable extent, the preferences and priorities of those in important positions of authority within various state institutions. Disputes over policies often arise out of the struggles and conflicts within and between different state institutions. State officials have considerable autonomy from social forces and an ability to gain support for the policies they prefer. The state-centred perspective tends to view senior public servants as being of particular importance because of their permanence and expertise.

EVALUATION   There is no consensus among political scientists as to which one of the general perspectives (and numerous variants) is most useful for understanding public policy. The pluralist perspective has often been modified by those who argue that business interests have a "privileged position" from which to influence policy because of the importance to government of maintaining the confidence of the business community to create jobs and economic prosperity (Lindblom, 1977).[5] As well, it has been pointed out that the pluralist perspective was developed to provide a description (perhaps idealized) of the American political system and thus may be less applicable in other countries. For example, as noted in Chapter 9, a number of democratic countries (such as Austria, Sweden, and Germany) feature, to varying extents, active collaboration between the state and selected major interests (usually national representatives of business and labour) to set the direction of the political community, particularly in terms of economic and social policies. In such

NEO-MARXIST THEORY A perspective that views politics as reflecting the conflicts that result from the way society is organized to produce goods. Public policies in a capitalist society will reflect the unequal power relations between the dominant capitalist forces and subordinate groups.

STATE-CENTRED THEORY A perspective that views public policies as reflecting, to a considerable extent, the preferences and priorities of those in important positions of authority within various state institutions.

---

4 This differs somewhat from traditional Marxist theory in which the state is often described as an instrument of the ruling class of capitalists to defend their property and interests.

5 This modification is often labelled "neo-pluralism."

neo-corporatist systems, only selected interests have a major influence on key aspects of public policy.

Public choice theory can be criticized for its assumption that citizens determine the policies of government through their voting choices. Political parties often do not adopt clear policy positions during election campaigns. Many voters do not carefully examine the positions of parties in deciding how to vote. As well, governments do not always act in accordance with their election promises and platforms.

Neo-Marxism can be criticized for paying insufficient attention to the effects on public policy of factors other than those that relate to the conflicts generated by the capitalist system. As well, it generally does not pay sufficient attention to the importance of state actors in affecting public policy. State-centred theory has the opposite problem: it tends to downplay the influence of social forces on the policies adopted by government.

Overall, none of the general theoretical approaches, while useful, seems to fully account for the general patterns of public policy. The best explanations of policy may differ from one policy area to another, from one country to another, and from one time to another. For example, foreign and defence policy might be best understood in terms of state-centred theory, while the pluralist, public choice, or neo-Marxist theories may be more useful in understanding economic and social policies. Further, while the general approaches tend to focus on who is powerful in affecting public policy and obtaining the outcomes that are in their interests, the role of ideas, ideologies, and the ways in which policy problems are defined and discussed also require attention.

The International Dimension

Public policy is a product not only of influences and decision-making processes within a country; globalization, international institutions, and international agreements are increasingly important in affecting public policy. For example, the meetings of the heads of government of the countries with the largest economies (the G20) play an important role, particularly in trying to coordinate policies to manage the global economy. Likewise, international financial institutions such as the International Monetary Fund use their financial power and influence to affect the policies of many countries.

International agreements play an increasingly important role in affecting the policies adopted by individual countries. International environmental agreements, for example, require that governments adopt policies to phase out the use of ozone-depleting chemicals and prohibit trade in products made from endangered species. Trade agreements are particularly controversial (see Box 16-2, Turtles and Trade) because they can limit the ability of governments to regulate business and manage economic activity. As well, by protecting the rights of corporations, some trade agreements can make it difficult for governments to use public provision of services as a policy instrument if such

Turtles and Trade

Protesters dressed up as sea turtles were an incongruous sight at the 1999 anti-globalization demonstrations that shut down a meeting of the World Trade Organization (WTO) in Seattle. However, the flamboyant costumes served as a vivid symbol of protesters' concern for an endangered species.

The WTO oversees a set of agreements that create legally binding rules and obligations on most of the countries of the world to achieve the objective of global free trade. The rules prevent countries from discriminating against the goods and services of other member countries. Dispute settlement panels can penalize offending countries for non-compliance with the rules.

In 1997, India, Malaysia, Pakistan, and Thailand took a complaint to the WTO concerning an American law banning the import of shrimp caught by trawlers that did not use devices to prevent harm to sea turtles, an endangered species. A dispute settlement panel of the WTO upheld the complaint, ruling that the American law resulted in a discriminatory trade practice that worked to the advantage of American fishers. The original ruling stated that "like goods" (similar foreign and domestic products) must be treated the same, regardless of whether the good was produced in an environmentally friendly manner. An appeal panel upheld the original ruling on the grounds that the United States had discriminated against Asian countries by providing only Caribbean countries with assistance to deal with the sea turtle problem.

Chapter 11 of the North American Free Trade Agreement (which involves Canada, the United States, and Mexico) goes further than the WTO by allowing businesses to sue the governments of any of the three countries if they adopt trade-restrictive policies that cause them to lose business opportunities or future profitability. For example, Ohio-based S.D. Myers Corporation, a hazardous waste disposal firm, successfully sued the Canadian government to compensate it for a Canadian policy banning the export of PCBs, a potentially toxic chemical. By banning the export of PCBs, the Canadian government reduced the potential profits that S.D. Myers would obtain by processing Canadian PCBs at its American plant.

These cases of sea turtles and toxic chemicals illustrate an important issue: trade agreements can make it more difficult for governments to adopt policies such as strict environmental measures if they are deemed to place undue limitations on trade.

services are already provided by private business. For example, student organizations have expressed concern that international trade agreements might open the door to private profit-oriented universities and reduce the willingness of governments to subsidize public universities.

THE POLICY PROCESS

Moving from broad-scale generalizations about public policy, we can examine the details of the policy process, which is often analyzed in terms of a sequence of steps:

1. agenda setting
2. policy formulation
3. decision making

4. policy legitimation
5. policy implementation
6. policy evaluation

Agenda Setting

In any sizable political community, innumerable problems and concerns could potentially become a subject for public policy. However, only a small number of problems can be dealt with at any time. **Agenda setting** refers to the process by which potential problems come to the attention of and become a priority for policy-makers.

There are a variety of potential influences on agenda setting, including political parties, interest groups, social movements, and the mass media. Crises, particularly crises emphasized by the mass media, can also affect the level of attention given to different problems. For example, the deaths caused by contaminated drinking water in Walkerton, Ontario, in 2000 turned the problem of water safety into a major political issue.

Not all issues on the government's policy agenda originate from the demands of various groups and individuals in society. Various departments and agencies of government may initiate the policy process by raising issues that the public may not necessarily view as serious problems. Individual politi-cians may act as **policy entrepreneurs** by trying to promote a particular issue or cause to advance their political careers. In such cases of "inside initiation," efforts may be made by the department, agency, or individual politician to persuade the public, as well as the government as a whole, that a particular problem should be given priority in the policy process (Hessing, Howlett, & Summerville, 2005).

PUBLIC VERSUS GOVERNMENTAL AGENDA   A distinction is sometimes made between the issues that are considered important by the public (the public agenda) and the issues that are considered important by the government (the governmental agenda). There is usually some relationship between the pub-lic agenda and the governmental agenda, as political leaders want to be seen as dealing with issues that are deemed important by the public. Governments make extensive use of public opinion polling to keep track of public concerns.

However, the relationship between the two agendas is not always a close one. Governments may place a high priority on issues that are of little con-cern to the public at large (such as constitutional issues in Canada) but are of particular importance to the processes of governing. Political leaders may also give high priority to problems that can be easily labelled and have solu-tions that can work to their political advantage. Complex problems with no easy solution may be ignored or downplayed. Likewise, issues that are highly controversial, such as abortion, may be ignored because politicians could risk losing support no matter which position they take.

Furthermore, politicians may give symbolic recognition to a problem or concern of the public without developing a substantial policy. For example, some Canadian political leaders have viewed the provision of subsidized child care as a low-priority issue. Although claiming that they fully support such a policy, many years have been spent in "studying" the issue and providing limited funding.

Policy Formulation

The policy formulation stage of the policy process involves developing and evaluating different courses of action to deal with a problem (Adolini & Blake, 2001). A variety of individuals and groups are typically involved at this point. Public servants in policy-oriented positions often play a leading role in developing possible policy options. Governments also often commission outside experts such as consultants, pollsters, and academics to help in the formulation of policy. Reports of parliamentary committees sometimes provide recommendations that are useful in policy formulation. Interest groups concerned about a particular policy area often provide policy advice to government policy-makers. Think tanks (policy research organizations) also provide analyses of problems and make policy recommendations

Institute for Research on Public Policy
www.irpp.org

Centre for Cyber Citizenship
www.policy.ca

Public Policy Forum
www.ppforum.ca

OPENING THE PROCESS The policy formulation process in advanced democracies has generally moved toward the involvement of a larger number of participants. Rather than a tight and closed relationship between a government department or agency and a small number of leading interest groups, analysts now often characterize the involvement of governmental and non-governmental actors in the development of policies in particular areas as a **policy network**.[6] The membership in the policy network may change from issue to issue, and no one set of actors or interests is in complete control of the policy area (Heclo, 1978). The extent to which governmental actors play a leading or dominant role in policy formulation and the extent to which a variety of different interests have a significant role in policy formulation varies considerably from policy area to policy area and from one country to another (Howlett & Ramesh, 1995). Overall, there has been an increasing interest in having greater public involvement in the policy-making process, particularly by consulting with all "stakeholders" (those affected by a policy decision in the issue area).

POLICY NETWORK The governmental and non-governmental actors that participate in the development of policies in particular areas.

DEFINING THE PROBLEM The problem that needs solving has to be defined before policies are developed, and the way the problem is defined will

---

[6] A distinction is often made between a policy network, consisting of those actors who have a direct interest or involvement in a policy area, and a broader policy community, which also includes all groups and individuals who have a more general interest in a policy area. The assumption is that members of the policy network will tend to be more influential in policy formulation than other members of the policy community (Hessing, Howlett, & Summerville, 2005).

likely affect the type of policy that is developed. Problems are often defined, sometimes in competing ways, at the agenda-setting stage. However, those involved in formulation may modify or transform the way the problem is defined as they develop policy options.

ASSESSING OPTIONS   The formulation of policies often involves the development of different options to deal with the problem being addressed. Those developing policy then have to analyze the pros and cons of the different options. A tool that is often used to assess policy proposals is **cost–benefit analysis,** a technique that assesses whether, and to what extent, the monetary benefits of a policy option exceed the costs. However, assigning a monetary value to all costs and benefits can be difficult or arbitrary. If, for example, the policy option being considered involves allowing forest companies to cut trees in an area of natural beauty, how can a price be put on natural beauty? Is it something more than the number of tourist dollars that might be lost? Likewise, in deciding on a new highway speed-limit policy, what value does one put on the lives that might be saved by a lower speed limit? Is it something more than the expected lifetime earnings of crash victims? Another complication of cost–benefit analysis is that the costs or benefits of a policy often fall unevenly among different groups of people. Consolidating waste disposal in one location may bring cost savings that benefit the political community as a whole—but for the people who live next to the dump, the negative impact may far outweigh the benefits.

POLICY INSTRUMENTS   In formulating a policy, a variety of different policy instruments need to be considered in order to assess which instrument or set of instruments will be most likely to achieve the desired results. For example, in dealing with the problem of industrial pollution, a government may establish regulations that limit the amount of discharge allowed, provide subsidies to help companies pay for pollution control equipment, levy a tax on each unit of harmful emission that is released, or encourage industry to adopt voluntary guidelines on emission reductions. Regulations have been the major approach used by Canadian governments to deal with pollution, although in recent times voluntary guidelines have increasingly been used. Emission taxes (such as a carbon tax to reduce greenhouse gas emissions) have been a more important policy instrument in some European countries than in North America, although British Columbia and Quebec have implemented carbon taxes.

A newer instrument, cap and trade, has been adopted by a number of countries to reduce greenhouse gas emissions. Annual permits to emit a certain quantity of pollutants are issued by government (usually based on current emissions). Industrial facilities that do not use the full amount of their permits can trade or sell their unused allotment. Emissions are reduced by issuing a smaller number of permits to each facility each year. This instrument is viewed as an economically efficient method of dealing with pollution,

COST–BENEFIT ANALYSIS
A technique that assesses whether, and to what extent, the monetary benefits of a policy exceed the costs.

A variety of policy instruments can be used to deal with the problem of industrial pollution.

as each company can calculate whether it is financially better to adopt pollution-reducing measures or to buy permits from other companies. Problems can arise with greenhouse gas trading schemes, however, if companies can obtain credits by investing in emission reduction projects in countries that lack effective monitoring (Schapiro, 2010).

The choice of policy instrument is affected by the nature of the problem that the policy is seeking to address. Some types of policy instruments are more effective in dealing with certain types of problems. As well, the choice of instruments may be affected by the ideological perspective of those in governing positions and in the electorate. Neo-liberals are more likely to favour instruments that provide the least government intervention and distortion of the free market. Social democrats are more likely to favour regulation of business activity. In addition, the choice of instruments may be affected by the ability of different interest groups to influence government. Business interests are more likely to favour voluntary guidelines, while environmental groups are more likely to favour strict government regulations and emission taxes to deal with pollution problems.

Decision Making

The decision-making stage involves choosing among a small number of different options or deciding to postpone the adoption of any policy. Policy decisions are generally made at the executive level, particularly by the prime minister and Cabinet with advice from senior officials. The political effects of different courses of action, such as the effects on the government's popularity, relationships with other governments, and its overall goals, as well as the effects on power relationships within the governing party, are important factors in the minds of government decision-makers and their political advisers. In a minority government situation, the prime minister will have to consider the likelihood of gaining support from one or more other parties. Pressure from interest groups and the opinions of the public also have an influence on decision making.

Policy Legitimation

Laws and authorization for government spending and taxing have to be approved by a legislative body. This approval fulfills important legal requirements and adds legitimacy to the policy. Discussion of a proposed policy in a legislature may help to increase awareness of the policy, and the public may be reassured that there has been an airing of different views before the policy was adopted. As well, the process of legislative approval sometimes results in modifications in the legislation needed to put the policy into effect. This may have the effect of appeasing some groups opposed to the legislation.

Policy Implementation

The formal adoption of a policy is not the end of the process. *Policy implementation* is a very important part of the policy process. The passage of a law to deal with a problem does not necessarily mean that the action is carried out. Typically, programs need to be designed and money, staff, and expertise must be provided. As well, regulations need to be adopted to establish the rules needed to implement and administer the law.

Bureaucratic discretion is often necessary because of the complex, technical nature of policies. Rather than simply applying the words of a law or regulation, public servants often need to apply specialized knowledge to figure out the most appropriate means to achieve the general objective. To help with implementation, government officials may strike compromises and work with the groups affected. For example, regulators often reach agreements with industries being regulated to allow the industry time to adjust its operations to comply with a new regulation.

The implementation of policies does not simply involve senior public servants under the supervision of a Cabinet minister designing a program and providing instructions to public servants to carry it out. To be effective, those responsible for carrying out a policy must be motivated to carry out the policy. Issuing commands and having subordinates carry them out may not work when those providing government services are professionals who believe that they should use their own judgment. For example, a government policy intended to increase the literacy and numeracy of students is likely to succeed only if teachers are committed to the policy.

Enforcement is an important aspect of the implementation of many policies. Although some policies offer encouragement to act in a certain way or provide for voluntary compliance, effective policies often require enforcement of their provisions. For example, it would be naive to expect an industry to voluntarily reduce its emissions of pollutants simply because the government asks it to, if such reductions are costly. However, strict enforcement is sometimes undesirable or unworkable. For example, pollution regulations may result in a major employer closing down because the costs of compliance are too high. Thus, government officials may be willing to give considerable leeway to companies that claim difficulty in meeting emission standards.

Enforcement of a policy may involve difficult and costly monitoring. For example, monitoring fish catches to ensure that quotas are not being exceeded is often difficult and evasion is common. Further, where a law is widely violated (for example, the law prohibiting the possession of cannabis), some police forces may decide that their limited resources are better spent on other offences.

Finally, policy implementation may be difficult if the co-operation and coordination of other levels of government needs to be obtained. For example, the Canadian government has at times faced difficulties in implementing its national health care policy because provincial governments are responsible for the health care system.

Overall, then, policy implementation is not simply a matter of administration—that is, of putting a policy into effect. There can be a considerable difference between the policy as envisioned by decision-makers and the

◀ Marijuana smokers gather in front of the Vancouver Art Gallery to celebrate "420" (April 20), which is dubbed National Pot Smoking Day.

402 Part IV: Governing

policy that is actually put into effect. The implementation stage thus involves a combination of administrative and political decisions.

Policy Evaluation

Policy evaluation involves determining the extent to which a policy is achieving its objectives and how it can be made more effective. Such evaluation can potentially lead to policy change, whether by scrapping an unsuccessful policy or by making modifications to improve a policy's effectiveness.

Policy evaluation is important because few policies are completely successful in solving the problems for which they were designed. However, despite increased attention being given to evaluation, policies do not always receive systematic evaluation by government. Not only is the evaluation of policy often difficult, but governments may be reluctant to fully evaluate policies to which they have become politically committed for fear that the evaluation will reflect badly on them or because they do not want to reopen a controversial issue. Senior public servants may have a tendency to defend the programs that they are responsible for and be reluctant to conduct thorough evaluations that could lead to reductions in the budgets and staff associated with the programs they administer.

WHO EVALUATES? Some evaluation is performed by those involved in carrying out programs, the auditor general, interest groups, and government agencies or other groups through the statistics they gather. Some laws require that government undertake a review within a certain period of time. For example, the Canadian Environmental Assessment Act must be reviewed after five years. Health care agreements between the national and provincial governments in Canada require that each government issue a report on the quality of health care in its jurisdiction according to a standard set of indicators, although there have been problems in achieving this objective.

Various interest groups conduct evaluations of the successes and failures of government policies from their particular point of view. For example, to make their case clearly to the public, some environmental groups issue report cards on government environmental performance. Businesses and business-oriented think tanks often evaluate policies in terms of their effects on business profitability and competitiveness. Some international agencies and non-governmental organizations provide a comparative analysis of the performances of different countries in various policy areas. For example, Human Rights Watch reports on the performance of both non-democratic and democratic countries in terms of human rights abuses.

Human Rights Watch
www.hrw.org

The Policy Cycle

The policy process is often described as a **policy cycle** (see Figure 16-1). This assumes that policies are continually undergoing modification in response to

POLICY CYCLE The analysis of the policy process as a continuous cycle of stages, with policies continually undergoing modification in response to evaluations of the policy.

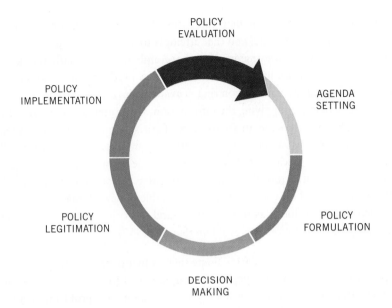

FIGURE 16-1
THE POLICY CYCLE

evaluations of the policies. Evaluations of existing policies may have an agenda-setting effect. Unsuccessful programs will likely lead to demands for change and place a particular problem back on the public and/or governmental agenda. This can potentially make the policy process a continuous, cyclical process.

However, the depiction of the policy process as a smooth, continuous cycle can be misleading. Policy evaluations that would, ideally, lead to policy changes are not always done. Unsuccessful programs have to compete with other policy problems for attention at the agenda-setting stage. If action is taken on a problem, the general public may believe that the problem has been solved, thereby reducing demands for further actions. Nevertheless, the policy process is dynamic and never-ending. New policy actors, new data and arguments, new ways of looking at problems, new expectations, changing circumstances, and new solutions mean that the policy process is a continuous one, with recurring debate over what should be done (Kraft, 2011).

Models of the Policy Process

THE RATIONAL-COMPREHENSIVE MODEL   It is often thought that the ideal policy process (termed the **rational-comprehensive model**) is one in which policy-makers establish clear goals to deal with a problem, examine all alternatives for dealing with the problem in terms of measuring the consequences of each alternative, and choose the best alternative. This alternative is implemented, then monitored and evaluated to assess whether the goals have been achieved, and changed if necessary (Anderson, 1979). Even if this model does not perfectly describe the actual policy-making process, governments have devoted considerable efforts to try to create a more rational policy process.

RATIONAL-COMPREHENSIVE MODEL OF THE POLICY PROCESS A policy-making model that involves establishing clear goals to deal with a problem, examining all possible alternatives, and choosing the best alternative. The policy is then monitored and evaluated to assess whether the goals have been achieved, and changed if necessary.

Critics, however, argue that the rational-comprehensive model of the policy process is unrealistic, and that attempts to apply this model have often been unsuccessful. Governments often have ambiguous or conflicting goals. Policy-makers may not have the information they need for fully rational decision making, and the information that is available is often biased in favour of the interests that are supplying the information. Governing decisions are often made in a hurry, or even in an atmosphere of crisis, because governments tend to react to problems rather than anticipating them (as was the case for the BP oil spill disaster). Because policy-makers lack the resources, time, information, and capabilities to fully examine all possible options and their potential effects, they will likely choose the first acceptable policy alternative presented to them—one that looks as if it will work and meet their goals—rather than the best possible solution to a problem (Simon, 1957).

THE INCREMENTAL MODEL   Some suggest that the policy process usually involves making minor changes to existing practices (termed the **incremental model**). Rather than searching for the best solution to a problem, decision-makers tend to "muddle through" (Lindblom, 1959), trying to cope with problems through a limited response. Policy-makers typically only examine a small number of fairly similar alternatives based on past experience, and do not try to evaluate all possible consequences of each alternative. Rather, by making only minor adjustments to existing policies, policy-makers can rely on past experience to assess the policy options being considered (Doyle & Kellow, 1995).

Because policy-making typically involves reaching compromises among a variety of views and interests, both inside and outside of government, policy-makers tend to avoid the risks involved in taking a new policy direction. Instead, they hope to accommodate different interests by making small adjustments to existing policies.

THE STREAMS AND WINDOWS MODEL   Even if the outcome of the policy process is often only minor, incremental changes to existing policies, there are occasions when major new policies are adopted. The **streams and windows model** depicts the policy process as fluid, rather than a process involving an overall plan or a series of limited steps. Policy, problem, and politics "streams" move independently of each other. The problem stream involves the processes by which "various problems come to capture the attention of people in and around government" (Kingdon, 1995, p. 87). The policy stream refers to the proposals that a variety of individuals and groups interested in a policy area are continually developing. The politics stream includes the campaigns of interest groups and political parties, election outcomes and changes in government, and shifts in the national mood and public opinion. At times the streams meet, resulting in "windows of opportunity" in which policy entrepreneurs—whether interest group leaders, academics, journalists, politicians, or bureaucrats—can successfully push their pet proposals (Kingdon, 1995).

INCREMENTAL MODEL
A policy-making model that suggests that the policy process usually involves making minor changes to existing practices.

STREAMS AND WINDOWS MODEL OF THE POLICY PROCESS A policy-making model that views the policy process as fluid. Changes in the identification of problems, policy proposals, and political circumstances create windows of opportunity in which policy entrepreneurs may successfully push their pet proposals.

The adoption of a national Medicare system in Canada could be analyzed in terms of this model. The Royal Commission on Health Services chaired by Justice Emmett Hall recommended a comprehensive and universal public health care system for Canada in 1964. Unlike the situation in the United States, there was a consensus among those who favoured health care reform that this was the best policy to achieve that objective. The election of a Liberal minority government that leaned in a socially minded direction and was supported by the NDP, which strongly favoured public health care, created a window of opportunity for Canadian government action.[7] Although opposed by private health insurance companies and by many doctors, the public and federal public servants generally saw the existing private insurance system as a problem and supported extending free, public provision of hospital services to physician services. The positive experience of Saskatchewan, which had pioneered public health care and successfully withstood the opposition of doctors (including a doctors' strike in 1962), also helped to facilitate the adoption of a national Medicare policy in 1966.

Policy-making might best be understood in terms of a mixture of the three models. Some policies result from a lengthy and rather comprehensive process of examining and assessing various alternatives. Many government actions involve only minor adjustments to existing policies and programs. Occasionally, however, major shifts in public policy occur. Sometimes these shifts occur with a change of government, particularly when a party with a different ideological perspective comes to power. For example, Mike Harris's Ontario Progressive Conservative government, which replaced an NDP government in 1995, brought in a "Common Sense Revolution" that included major cuts to government programs and tax reductions. At other times, a perceived crisis may lead to major changes in policy direction. For example, the terrorist attacks on the United States in 2001 resulted in many countries quickly adopting national security laws that limited the application of policies protecting civil liberties that these countries had pursued in previous decades.

PUBLIC ADMINISTRATION

How should the many policies, programs, and services of government be carried out? Over the past century, governments have developed large administrative structures staffed primarily by permanent employees (termed public or civil servants) to carry out these activities and to provide advice concerning policies and programs to the political executive.

---

[7] Although the Progressive Conservative party opposed the introduction of Medicare, Justice Hall had been appointed by PC Prime Minister John Diefenbaker, thus making the policy appear less partisan or ideological.

Bureaucratic Organization: A Threat to Democracy?

The organization of the modern public service is often termed a bureaucracy (a term that literally means "rule by offices"). In the view of Max Weber, bureaucratic organizations are a key characteristic of modern societies, reflecting the capitalist system's concern with efficiency and the use of legal–rational forms of rule in modern political systems. Weber characterized a bureaucratic organization as one in which people are hired and promoted based on their qualifications and merit, work is organized in terms of specialized positions (offices), detailed rules and procedures are followed by all members of the organization, and there is a hierarchical chain of command so that those at the top can direct and supervise large numbers of people. These characteristics can make bureaucratic organizations efficient, although their adherence to rules and regulations can also result in these organizations being inflexible and impersonal.

Weber was concerned that powerful bureaucratic organizations controlled by senior officials would dominate the governments of modern societies thereby limiting the democratic ideal of rule by the people (Heywood, 2002). However, while the government bureaucracy has very considerable potential power because of its permanence and expertise, elected political leaders often also draw upon other sources of advice and do not always rely on the bureaucracy to carry out government programs. Those governments that have a firm sense of their goals and priorities may be able to direct the bureaucracy on key issues rather than be directed by the bureaucracy.

Bureaucratic Organization

Given the complex nature of many governing tasks, the public service needs a high level of professional expertise and a specialized form of organization referred to as a **bureaucracy**[8] (as discussed in Box 16-3, Bureaucratic Organization). Instead of government employees being hired largely on the basis of political patronage (that is, based on ties to the governing party), hiring and promotion in modern public services is based primarily on merit (such as qualifications and competitive examinations).[9]

REPRESENTATIVE BUREAUCRACY Staffing the public service strictly based on merit can make the public service unrepresentative of the characteristics of the society as a whole. An emphasis on formal qualifications, such as university degrees and scores on public service examinations, may result in hiring practices that favour people from some parts of society more than others. In Canada, for example, efforts began in the 1960s to increase the relatively small proportion of French-speaking persons in the public service

BUREAUCRACY An organization in which people are hired and promoted based on their qualifications and merit, work is organized in terms of specialized positions, detailed rules and procedures are followed by all members of the organization, and there is a hierarchical chain of command so that those at the top can direct and supervise large numbers of people.

Public Service Commission of Canada
www.psc-cfp.gc.ca

---

[8] Bureaucracy is an attribute of virtually all large organizations, whether governmental, business, or non-profit.

[9] Although the United States has a merit-based public service, a number of top officials are appointed by the president and are usually replaced when a new president takes over.

in order to create a public service that could operate in both official languages and increase French Quebecers' attachment to the Canadian government. Since then, efforts have been made to create a more **representative bureaucracy** by establishing targets for hiring and promoting more women, Aboriginals, visible minorities, and persons with disabilities. Likewise, the United States moved from a non-discrimination policy to affirmative action to create a representative bureaucracy. In 1971, the Civil Service Commission directed federal agencies to ensure full representation of women and racial minorities at all levels. This was confirmed by the Civil Service Reform Act of 1978, which provided that the civil service should reflect the diversity of the country (Watkins-Hayes, 2010).

REPRESENTATIVE BUREAUCRACY A bureaucracy that reflects the characteristics of society, particularly by trying to ensure that all levels of the public service have a proportion of women and various disadvantaged minority groups similar to that of the population as a whole.

Politics and Administration

Public administration is often thought of in terms of the carrying out of the policies adopted by the government. As noted in Chapter 14, each department of government is headed by a Cabinet minister who is expected to oversee and take responsibility for the actions of the department. In Canada, the day-to-day running of a department is in the hands of a **deputy minister**, usually a senior public servant appointed by the prime minister in consultation with the Clerk (head) of the Privy Council Office. The Privy Council Office also plays a major role in coordinating and directing the work of the deputy ministers and senior public servants.

DEPUTY MINISTER The executive head of a department of government appointed by the prime minister in consultation with the Clerk of the Privy Council Office. The deputy minister runs the department with oversight by the Cabinet minister who is the political head of the department.

Because public servants are a key source of information and advice for Cabinet ministers, they often play a major role in the policy-making process. As well, once a law is passed by Parliament and a program needs to be established, it is typically the public servants within a particular department that are involved in recommending how implementation is going to be conducted. Since laws are often fairly general in nature, this leaves considerable room for discretion. Likewise, the regulations needed to determine how the law is to be applied are often drafted by public servants with formal approval by Cabinet. Although the public service is expected to be non-partisan, its advice and actions nevertheless are political in the sense that they have an important effect on how the country is governed.

Criticisms of the Government Bureaucracy

The government bureaucracy has come under considerable criticism in recent decades for several reasons:

- Bureaucratic organization is often viewed as slow moving, rigid, and inflexible rather than efficient.
- The commitment of public servants to the public interest is sometimes questioned.
- Users of government services sometimes receive insufficient attention and respect.

In particular, public choice theory, based on the assumption that individuals always pursue their own self-interest, asserts that public servants seek to expand the programs and expenditures of government so as to enhance their own position, privileges, and power. The effect, compounded by the efforts of government to try to satisfy the demands of a variety of interest groups, is that government has become much larger than necessary. This, it is argued, has stifled the growth of the more dynamic and efficient private sector.

Generally, then, concerns about administrative inefficiencies, the stifling of entrepreneurial initiatives by government "red tape," and excessive rules and regulations have led many governments to undertake major reforms of their administrative structures and practices. These changes are part of a broader tendency to shrink the size of government, privatize state-owned enterprises, contract out the delivery of services to private businesses, reduce regulation of business, and focus on being competitive in the global marketplace.

New Public Management

NEW PUBLIC MANAGEMENT
The adoption of the practices of private business in the administrative activities of government.

The adoption of the practices of private business is a major feature of **new public management,** an idea that has influenced changes to government administration in many countries since the 1980s (see Box 16-4, *Yes Minister*). In particular, this approach emphasizes efficiency by reducing the size of the public service, providing performance incentives to employees, and encouraging competition to provide public services between private and public organizations so that services are provided at the lowest cost. Instead of the hierarchical structure and rules and procedures of the traditional bureaucracy, the emphasis is on decentralized structures in which managers have the autonomy to make managerial decisions and to create a leaner, more flexible operation. Further, like private business, the focus should be on satisfying the customers of public services. Finally, advocates of new public management are often critical of the leading role of the public service in providing policy advice to government.

ALTERNATIVE SERVICE
DELIVERY New methods of delivering government programs, such as the establishment of government service agencies that have considerable autonomy from the normal departmental structures and rules and the establishment of partnerships with business, other levels of government, and voluntary organizations to deliver services.

ALTERNATIVE SERVICE DELIVERY   One aspect of the new public management is the development of new methods of delivering government programs, termed **alternative service delivery.** This may involve establishing government service agencies that have considerable autonomy from the normal departmental structures and rules, for example, Passport Canada, the Canada Revenue Agency, the Canadian Food Inspection Agency, and Parks Canada. Some agencies are expected to be self-financing.

Another form of alternative service delivery involves establishing partnerships with business, other levels of government, and voluntary organizations to deliver services. Alternative service delivery can also involve contracting out government activities to private business or to groups of former public servants. This approach is particularly common in the United States, where private businesses have been contracted not only by a number of cities to manage

BOX 16-4

Yes Minister: Margaret Thatcher and the British Administration

The influential British television series *Yes Minister* featured a negative depiction of the relationship between Cabinet ministers and senior public servants. This coincided with the real-world perspective of Margaret Thatcher, Conservative prime minister from 1979 to 1990. Thatcher viewed the public service as a serious obstacle to implementing her free-market ideological vision.

In *Yes Minister,* a savvy senior public servant manipulated a hapless, inexperienced Cabinet minister. The minister was dependent on the public servant, who really ran the department and ensured that any of the minister's proposals for changes that might be inconsistent with the department's interests were not acted upon (Savoie, 2003).

During the Thatcher years, the government, facing serious economic problems, instituted major changes in the traditional British administration including the establishment of one hundred and thirty-eight independent executive agencies that employ about three-quarters of the public service. These agencies, each headed by a chief executive officer, are provided with performance targets by a Cabinet minister, but are given a considerable level of autonomy to achieve those targets. A Citizen's Charter requires that departments and agencies establish standards for their services and publicly disclose whether these standards are being met. Finally, a system of market testing allows private companies to compete against government agencies and departments for contracts to provide various public services (Borins, 2002).

As for *Yes Minister*, the program ended in the 1980s, a relic of a bygone era in the British civil service. However, Margaret Thatcher made sure the show's writer was awarded with a knighthood!

garbage collection and road maintenance, but also by state and national governments to run prisons and carry out a variety of military functions. For example, in 2006 there were about 100 000 civilians working under contract to the United States government as part of its military and reconstruction efforts in Iraq—not far short of the 140 000 U.S. troops then in that country (*Washington Post*, December 5, 2006, p. D01).

PROBLEMS   A key problem with the efforts to make government more businesslike is that there are inherent differences between government and business. Business is concerned with making a profit; government should be concerned with the common good, even if this means undertaking activities that are costly. The objectives of government are more complex than the simple bottom line of profitability that drives business activity. Indeed, a focus on profitability may conflict with the interests of the public in such goals as environmental protection and social well-being (Paehlke, 2003).

The idea that the leading role of the public service in developing policies should be reduced is also controversial. Based on its experience in administering programs, the public service is able to provide useful advice in developing new policies and modifying existing ones. Further, a knowledgeable,

"Wouldn't it be great if government no longer ran the parks?"

professional public service protected by a high level of job security may be more likely to provide honest, forthright advice than consulting firms and partisan advisers who may tend to tell Cabinet ministers what they want to hear (Savoie, 2003).

The adoption of private-sector methods does not necessarily lead to the most desirable results. Focusing on efficiency and competitiveness may undermine the sense of public service that has been developed among the employees of government in countries such as Canada and the United Kingdom. Privatized services are not always better managed than government-run services. For example, the Ontario government conducted a performance review of a large maximum security prison whose operations had been contracted out to a major American prison management corporation. It found that an equivalent government-run prison had better security and health care and reduced repeat offender rates. Thus, the government decided to take over the running of the prison (CBC News, November 10, 2006). Likewise, an academic study of the privatization of the prison system in Mississippi found that the presumed advantage of greater efficiency was questionable and that privatization can create problems in achieving the public good (Morris, 2007).

Finally, the idea that much of the work of the public service should be done by autonomous agencies, each responsible for a particular program, has been questioned. In looking at Britain and New Zealand, analysts have found that adopting this approach can make it more difficult for governments to deal with complex problems that require coordination among a variety of departments and agencies (Aucoin, 2002). In New Zealand, the pioneer in the adoption of new public management, the establishment of three hundred separate agencies increased administrative costs and made coordination of public services difficult. Since 1996, New Zealand governments have ended pursuing radical market-oriented changes in public administration and instead have been gradually reasserting government control of various public functions (Dunleavy et al., 2006).

Summary and Conclusion

The policies adopted by governments are typically the result of a complex process involving a variety of different political actors. Interest groups, social movements, businesses, political parties, think tanks, and journalists seek to influence the choice of issues that will be the subject of policy-making, as well as trying to affect how policy-makers think about those issues. In addition, policy-making is increasingly affected by forces beyond the state, including international organizations and agreements and the global economy.

Policy-making is not simply a matter of problem solving, or trying to determine the best policy to achieve the common good. Rather, it is a matter of choice in which resources are limited and the goals and objectives of those interested or involved in policy-making differ and cannot easily be weighed against each other. In other words, the policy process is a *political* process in which different goals, interests, and values are involved (Simeon, 1976). The policies that are adopted and implemented do not necessarily reflect the common good, but rather tend to reflect the political interests of the government, the perspectives of those involved in the policy process, and the ability of various groups and individuals to exert influence.

The idea that the government bureaucracy is efficient and dedicated to the public interest has been challenged by those who contend that public servants pursue their own interests by seeking to expand the activities of government. The public service has also been criticized as being too rule-bound, slow to act, and prone to act in established ways. Attempts have been made to adopt a more businesslike approach to administration through the techniques of the new public management. Providing greater autonomy and flexibility for administrative managers may be useful in reducing inefficiency and cutting red tape. However, a strong, professional public service is important in the effort to pursue the common good of a political community. Good public administration involves not only the efficient delivery of services, but also the provision of quality advice to government.

Key Terms

Discussion Questions

1. Can the best public policies be chosen scientifically?

2. Which of the general perspectives do you think is most applicable to understanding public policy?

3. Is greater public participation in the policy process desirable?

4. Is bureaucratic organization undesirable? Is it a threat to democracy?

5. What are the advantages and disadvantages of new public management reforms?

Further Reading

Adolini, J.R., & Blake, C.H. (2010). *Comparing policies: Issues and choices in industrialized societies.* Washington, DC: CQ Press.

Dobuzinskis, L., Howlett, M., & Laycock, D. (Eds.). (2007). *Policy analysis in Canada: The state of the art.* Toronto: University of Toronto Press.

Dunn, C. (Ed.). (2010). *The handbook of Canadian public administration* (2nd ed.). Don Mills, ON: Oxford University Press.

Howlett, M., Ramesh, M., & Perl, A. (2009). *Studying public policy: Policy cycles and policy subsystems* (3rd ed.). New York: Oxford University Press.

Miljan, L. (2008). *Public policy in Canada: An introduction.* Don Mills, ON: Oxford University Press.

Orsini, M., & Smith, M. (Eds.). (2007). *Critical policy studies.* Vancouver: UBC Press.

Osborne, D., & Gaebler, T. (1992). *Reinventing government: How the entrepreneurial spirit is transforming the public sector.* Reading, MA: Addison-Wesley, 1992.

Pal, L.A. (2009). *Beyond policy analysis: Public issue management in turbulent times* (4th ed.). Scarborough, ON: Nelson.

Savoie, D.J. (2003). *Breaking the bargain: Public servants, ministers, and Parliament.* Toronto: University of Toronto Press.

PART V

Global Concerns

Chapter 17

Politics and Development in the World's Poorer Countries

PHOTO ABOVE: The clients of the Grameen Bank in Bangladesh are among the world's poorest people—and the bank's pride and joy. Muhammad Yunus, an economist, believed the country needed a bank that would extend credit to Bangladesh's millions of landless men and women, thereby letting them create their own jobs and look after their families better.

1. identify the terms that are used to depict the poorer countries
2. outline the extent of global inequality
3. discuss the meaning of development and the different development strategies
4. evaluate Canada's foreign aid policies
5. examine the political problems of the Third World

The clients of the Grameen Bank in Bangladesh are among the world's poorest people—and the bank's pride and joy. Ordinary commercial banks would not touch them because they have no collateral to pledge. The difference is that Dr. Muhammad Yunus, the 2006 Nobel Prize winner and creator of the Grameen Bank, believed the country needed a bank that would extend credit to Bangladesh's millions of landless men and women, thereby letting them create their own jobs and look after their families better. The bank, whose name means rural in Bangala, the language of Bangladesh, was founded in 1983 and has now lent to more than three million borrowers.

The Grameen Bank believes that credit for self-employment is a basic human right. It makes small loans limited to about US$400 for business start-ups and US$650 for home building. (Bangladesh has a per capita annual income of US$500, so the sums are not trivial.) To help ensure repayment and the proper use of loans, the bank organizes its customers to use peer pressure. The result has been a default rate of less than 0.5 percent and an on-time repayment record of 98 percent.

Perhaps the most striking thing about the Grameen Bank is its clientele, 94 percent of whom are women. The bank makes women its priority for three reasons. First, they are the society's poorest, thus the least likely to get help from a regular credit institution. Second, when extra cash comes into a home, women are more likely to use the money for the family's good, whereas men tend to spend it on themselves. Finally, it is not uncommon for a man to desert his family, leaving a woman as the sole breadwinner.

The Grameen Bank has become a model for other countries. It does not solve all of the problems of underdevelopment, but is a partial response to one set of the many issues facing poor countries. However, by showing that mixing a lot of local initiative with creative thinking produces better lives for many people, the Grameen Bank has an importance that stretches far beyond Bangladesh.

To many Canadians, "development" means giving a poor country a standard of living that approaches Canada's, complete with personal computers and a car for everyone. In the very poor, extremely under-developed countries of the Third World, that kind of development, which has long been the goal of foreign aid programs, can miss the poorest. Even the most entrepreneurial and energetic of the poor find it almost impossible to get ahead under conventional development projects. That is why the Grameen Bank is so important.[*]

---

[*]For information about the Grameen Bank, see Wood and Sharit (1997), Yunus (1999), and the bank's website at www.grameen-info.org.

THE DEVELOPMENT GAP

Less than one-sixth of the people in the world live in high-income countries like Canada and the United States. The remaining five-sixths have a per capita income less than half that of Canada (see Table 17-1). Canadian governments have trouble funding all of the services that people need, so the situation is obviously worse where the money per person available to fund education, health care, roads, and other important services is far less than that of Canada. We live in a world where the average income of each of the 1.07 billion people living in high-income countries is seventy-five times that of each of the 973 million people living in low-income countries, although the difference falls to twenty-six times greater if we use **purchasing power parity** (PPP) adjusted income figures (World Bank, 2010b, p. 379). Is it meaningful to talk about achieving the common good in the poorest countries? Should Canadians be concerned about the problem of global inequality? How can poor countries develop?

Social scientists have applied a variety of names to the world's poor countries. Among them have been **Third World**, developing, less developed, **underdeveloped,** and the **South** (terms discussed in Box 17-1, Evolution of the Term *Third World*). Political science generally prefers Third World (Green & Luehrmann, 2003; Handelman, 2003) but uses all of the terms noted above. Whatever name is used, it is the mix of the economic and social characteristics of poor states combined with how their political systems function that has drawn the attention of political scientists, policy-makers, and the politically informed public in the wealthy (or developed) countries of what some call the **North.**

WHAT IS DEVELOPMENT?

Terms such as **developing countries,** *less developed countries,* or *underdeveloped countries* are often used to describe Third World countries, but they raise several questions: What exactly does "development" mean? In what ways are poorer countries "less developed" than the richer countries? Are the poorer

PURCHASING POWER PARITY (PPP) A measure of per capita income that shows the purchasing power of an income, instead of its worth at current exchange rates.

THIRD WORLD Less developed countries.

UNDERDEVELOPED COUNTRIES A term often used to describe Third World countries.

SOUTH Less developed, poorer countries.

NORTH The rich, developed countries.

DEVELOPING COUNTRIES Countries that have not reached the same level of development as the richer, advanced countries.

TABLE 17-1
THE WEALTH OF THE WORLD

INCOME GROUP	ANNUAL INCOME RANGE	% WORLD'S INCOME	% WORLD'S POPULATION
High	> US$11 909	72.9%	16.0%
Upper Middle	US$3856–11 909	12.9%	14.1%
Lower Middle	US$976–3855	13.3%	55.3%
Low	< US$975	0.9%	14.5%
Canada	US$41 730 (average annual income)	2.4%	0.49%

SOURCE: *Calculated from World Development Report, by the World Bank (2010b), Washington: The World Bank*

Evolution of the Term *Third World*

Various names have been developed over the years to refer to the world's poorest countries.

The Third World was political scientists' first choice. That name was introduced in the late 1940s, to distinguish what was then a small number of independent countries in Africa, Asia, and Latin America from the blocs linked to the two great powers of the day: the United States and the Soviet Union. The United States and its allies (for example, Canada and Britain) formed the First World and the Soviet Union and its allies (for example, Bulgaria and Mongolia) were termed the Second World. Other countries constituted the "Third World."

Although many of these countries later banded together to form the Non-Aligned Movement, the Third World soon came to symbolize poverty and political instability instead of an independent line in foreign policy.

The South is another label political scientists have used. This emphasizes the fact that most poor countries lie in the tropics, to the south of the rich states of the northern hemisphere. Of course, the name is not literally accurate, because the southern hemisphere includes developed countries such as Australia and New Zealand.

Underdeveloped, developing, and *less developed* are variations on a final theme used to categorize the poor states of the world. The focus here is the low levels of economic well-being that characterize the countries in this group. Nevertheless, there is the implicit assumption that development is possible and that eventually all of the world's countries will do a better job of meeting their citizens' needs.

These countries tend to be new democracies, if they are democratic at all. The nations that broadly fit this description include all of Latin America and the Caribbean; Africa; the Middle East, except Israel; and Asia, except Japan, Singapore, Taiwan (Republic of China), and South Korea. Interestingly, the last three states were considered Third World countries until the 1980s. Now they are labelled *newly industrialized countries* to indicate that they are no longer poor, underdeveloped countries.

countries "developing"? Does that mean that they will become just like the richer "developed" countries?

The less developed countries are often compared to the more developed countries in terms of per capita **gross domestic product (GDP)** (the amount of goods and services produced) and in terms of average incomes (see Table 17-1). Such measures are available for nearly all countries and give us a sense of the economic disparities between rich and poor nations. If countries increase their GDP, we can say that economic growth is occurring. Economic growth, however, does not always result in **development**. For example, economic growth need not lead to a reduction of poverty. Indeed, in some cases, increased poverty has accompanied increased growth (United Nations Development Programme [UNDP], 2003). Because of the great inequalities in wealth and power in many less developed countries, additional wealth often ends up in the pockets of the rich. New oil wells, mines, factories, stores, and dams may result in the dislocation of peasant farmers, urban workers, and indigenous peoples, reducing their ability to eke out a living. The distinction between growth and development is discussed further in Box 17-2, Development versus Growth.

GROSS DOMESTIC PRODUCT (GDP) The market value of goods and services produced in a country, excluding transactions with other countries.

DEVELOPMENT A condition that involves the satisfaction of the basic needs of all of the people as well as the means for them to live fulfilling and productive lives based on the creation of a more diversified, sophisticated, and sustainable economy.

BOX 17-2

Development versus Growth

Imagine living in a country whose economy is based on mining diamonds.

If we mine and sell more diamonds, the economy's GDP will *grow*. But the country has not necessarily developed. Increased diamond mining might simply let the mine owners' buy more imported luxury items or invest their profits abroad. However, processing the diamonds into jewellery or using the profits from diamond mining to develop new industries would lead to a more broadly based economy that would rely less on one commodity. It would also encourage people to develop more skills.

Generally, if more of the profits from increased mining activity remained in the country to buy locally produced goods and services, the economic *development* of the country would rise. Likewise, if government used increased tax revenues to improve roads, schools, and health care, there would be a stronger foundation for future development.

Development may be thought of in terms of three goals:

1. It involves satisfying the basic needs of everyone, such as food, housing, clothing, and clean water, as well as the means to live fulfilling and productive lives, such as education, health care, employment, and security against severe hardships. For example, the United Nations Development Programme has as its objectives the elimination of extreme poverty, often defined as subsisting on less than US$1 per day (UNDP, 2002), and improving the status of women. Improving the status of women, especially ensuring that young women receive an education, tends to result in a healthier population, slower population growth, and a more skilled workforce.

2. It builds a more diversified and sophisticated economy. This requires moving from an economy centred on the production of unprocessed natural resources to one that turns them into finished goods. As well, it develops the scientific, technological, and managerial capabilities needed to compete with the developed countries. Further, it requires moving from being a supplier of low-cost labour to multinational corporations based in the rich countries to developing local entrepreneurial capacity and the banking, legal, and other services needed to support domestic businesses.

3. Development needs to be environmentally sustainable. Economic growth has often come through unrestrained exploitation of natural resources. Indiscriminate logging and fishing may bring short-term economic growth, but they harm long-term development. Indeed, one of the major dilemmas of development is that industrialization and increased wealth often create a heavy burden on the environment. Although the rich countries use a high proportion of the world's resources and produce a substantial share of global pollution, increases in the wealth in heavily

HDI RANK	COUNTRY	GDP PER CAPITA (PPP US$)	% ADULT LITERACY	LIFE EXPECTANCY (YEARS)	GDP RANK MINUS HDI RANK*
4	Canada	35 812	100%	80.6	14
10	Japan	33 632	100%	82.7	16
13	United States	45 592	100%	79.9	−4
51	Cuba	6876	99.8%	78.5	44
53	Mexico	14 104	92.8%	76.0	5
75	Brazil	9567	90.0%	72.2	4
85	Ukraine	6914	99.7%	68.2	9
92	China (PRC)	5383	93.3%	72.9	10
111	Indonesia	3712	92.0%	70.5	10
118	Equatorial Guinea	30 627	87.0%	49.9	−90
123	Egypt	5349	66.4%	69.9	−20
134	India	2753	66.0%	63.4	−6
141	Pakistan	2496	54.2%	66.2	−9
149	Haiti	1155	62.1%	61.0	9
158	Nigeria	1969	72.0%	47.7	−17
171	Ethiopia	779	35.9%	54.7	0
176	Congo (Dem. Rep.)	298	67.2%	47.6	5
181	Afghanistan	1054	28.7%	43.6	−17

TABLE 17-2
HUMAN DEVELOPMENT INDEX, SELECTED COUNTRIES, 2009

Notes: Gross Domestic Product per capita is calculated in terms of purchasing power parity.

* A positive figure indicates that the HDI rank is higher than the GDP per capita rank.

SOURCE: Adapted from United Nations Development Programme, *Human Development Report 2010*, published 2010, Palgrave Macmillan. Reproduced with permission of Palgrave Macmillan.

populated Third World countries have the potential to place great stresses on the world's environment. For example, shifting from bicycles to cars as a major means of transportation is creating serious problems of congestion and air pollution in many Third World cities and also contributes to global climate change. From an environmental perspective, Third World economic growth that brings consumption levels like those of the richer countries would be disastrous. Both richer and poorer countries need to develop in a more sustainable fashion.

Center for Global Development
www.cgdev.org

Measuring Development

Rather than simply measuring a country's wealth, the United Nations Development Programme uses an index based on literacy and education, life expectancy, and per capita GDP to get a broader picture of how well countries are doing in their pursuit of development (see Table 17-2). On this **Human Development Index (HDI)**, rankings do not always correspond exactly to GDP.

Cuba, for instance, ranks forty-four places higher on the HDI than it does on GDP, the largest difference of any country. This indicates that Cuba produces very good human development results for its level of economic activity.

HUMAN DEVELOPMENT INDEX (HDI) An annual index for most countries, calculated by the United Nations Development Programme and based on literacy and education, life expectancy, and per capita GDP.

At the other extreme, Equatorial Guinea, a small African state, has an HDI level ninety places below its income rank. Equatorial Guinea produces and exports oil, so it has a high national income that has not produced benefits for its people (UNDP, 2010).[1]

The good news is that, however it is measured, development has clearly occurred throughout the Third World. Compared to 1960, life expectancy has increased substantially, literacy rates and school enrolment at all levels have jumped, and women in particular have made great gains (UNDP, 1995). The percentage of those living in extreme poverty had fallen from 30 percent in 1990 to 23 percent in 2003 (UNDP, 2003). However, these global figures hide disturbing facts.

First, although a smaller percentage of the world's population qualifies as "extremely poor" (one-quarter of the population of the developing world instead of one-half), more than 1.4 billion people still fall into that category (United Nations, 2009). Further, some parts of the world are doing far worse than others and have even lost ground since 1990. In sub-Saharan Africa, the percentage of the population living in extreme poverty (defined since 2005 as living on US$1.25 or less per day) is greater than 50 percent; in West Asia (which includes war-torn Iraq), the proportion rose from 2 percent in 1990 to 6 percent in 2005 (United Nations, 2009). The rapid growth of the Chinese and Indian economies over the last decade has reduced poverty there. Since these two countries make up three-eighths of the world's population, improvements there cause global poverty figures to drop, even though poverty has worsened throughout Africa. Statistics reveal, but they also conceal.

Clearly, individual countries have made great strides. Forty years ago the countries of Southeast and East Asia were extremely poor, with a short life expectancy and high levels of illiteracy and infant mortality. From China to Thailand, however, conditions are much improved. In fact, aside from North Korea, the region's experience demonstrates that development is not just possible, but can be achieved in a generation.

However, just as there are development success stories, there are also failures. The most dramatic cases of failed development are found in sub-Saharan Africa, followed by the Middle East and parts of Latin America. Recognizing these problems, in 2000, the UN set eight Millennium Development Goals (MDG) to be achieved by 2015: (1) eradicate extreme poverty and hunger; (2) achieve universal primary education; (3) empower women and advance gender equality; (4) reduce child mortality; (5) improve maternal health; (6) combat HIV/AIDS, malaria, and other diseases; (7) ensure environmental stability; (8) develop a global partnership for development (UNMDG, 2005, 2006). However, the 2009 Millennium Development Goals Report notes that

---

[1] The HDI says nothing about a country's political system. Both Cuba and Equatorial Guinea are dictatorships. The difference in their HDI levels shows clearly that not all dictatorships are the same.

◀ Argentina should be rich, but it needs more stable democratic politics, as well as a sound and sustainable economic program, to achieve this.

progress has been very slow and appears to have stalled, due in great part to the economic crisis that began in 2008 (United Nations, 2009).

Despite the disappointing progress toward meeting the MDG, we should not forget that living standards throughout the poor world have improved over the past fifty years. We also need to recall that some countries have reached the ranks of developed nations. However, there are also states that have seen earlier movement toward development reversed and others where development simply has not occurred. Box 17-3, Three Development Scenarios, presents some cases of successful and failed development.

HOW CAN COUNTRIES DEVELOP?

There is no simple solution to the problem of development. Those who study the issue often differ sharply on the causes of underdevelopment and on how best to achieve development. However, there are two principal approaches: market-driven and state-directed.

Market-Driven Approaches

Since at least the 1950s, the dominant model (called a paradigm) of development has emphasized the free market. The advice that the Third World gets from international agencies such as the International Monetary Fund and the World Bank, as well as from many economists, typically is based on the assumption that government involvement in the economy is undesirable. The free-market capitalist economic system, free trade, and unrestricted foreign investment, it is argued, lead to prosperity.

International Monetary Fund
www.imf.org

The World Bank
www.worldbank.org

BOX 17-3

Three Development Scenarios

The Third World presents us with cases of failed development and reversed development as well as successful development:

1. *Failed development.* When the Belgian Congo became independent in 1960, Belgium had not prepared its colony for independence, so there were few well-educated Congolese to exercise power. The new country plunged into civil war, with the Americans backing one faction and the Soviets backing another. The eventual winner of the conflict was Joseph Mobutu, who later changed his name to Mobutu Sese Seko and the country's name to Zaire. From 1965 to 1997, he exercised dictatorial rule, becoming Africa's most corrupt leader. Things did not improve for the Congolese after Laurent Kabila ousted Mobutu and renamed the country the Demo-cratic Republic of the Congo (DR-Congo). It soon was swept up in warfare, and in 2001 Kabila was assassinated. His son then seized power, but in 2006 won the country's first ever multiparty election. Fighting began anew in 2008 as both Tutsi and Hutu militias from Rwanda clashed with the Congolese army. One particularly disturbing aspect of this new conflict is the apparently systematic rape of many thousands of women and girls by both DR-Congo soldiers and the foreign militias (York, 2010). The country's fifty-five million inhabitants have annual per capita incomes of only US$150, but their land is rich in natural resources. The Congolese, however, will not benefit from their gold, silver, and oil until they achieve political stability, which will come only when there is peace in the region.
2. *Reversed development.* Early in the twentieth century, Argentina had a per capita income similar to Canada's. By 2003, it was less than 30 percent of ours. Argentina is a big country, with thirty-eight million well-educated people. It has significant natural resources (agricultural and mineral), a once large but now declining manufacturing base, and modern service industries. However, between 1930 and 1983 the country was almost always ruled by dictatorships, all of which pursued bad policies. Since 1983, the country has been democratic, but this has not solved its problems. In December 2001, Argentina's economy nearly collapsed and sparked a political crisis that saw five presidents governing within two weeks. By 2006 it had recovered much of the lost ground, but the economic crisis that began in fall 2008 has hit Argentina hard. Argentina should be rich, but it needs more stable democratic politics, plus sound and sustainable economic programs, to achieve this.
3. *Successful development.* South Korea (officially, the Republic of Korea) is a developed country today. It is not a large country, but has a population of thirty-eight million. At its founding in 1946, the country's prospects were poor. Formerly a Japanese colony, Korea was divided into a communist north (the Korean Democratic Republic) and a non-communist south. Over the next four decades, while North Korea stagnated, South Korea prospered by using a form of government-managed capitalism (Wade, 1990). It currently has a sophisti-cated economy based principally on manu-facturing. South Korean firms like Samsung and Hyundai are household names in Canada. Until 1988, South Korea was ruled by a series of dictatorships, most of them military. It is now such a sufficiently stable democracy that it weathered a severe economic crisis from 1997 to 1998 without incident.

MODERNIZATION THEORY   There have been two major free-market models. The first, **modernization theory**, was important from about 1950 to 1970. It argued that poor countries had to change their traditional values, institutions, and practices in order to develop. Change could be achieved by copying the ways of developed countries, especially the United States, beginning with their economic policies by bringing in the most modern firms from abroad. That would set in motion a process that would break down old social orders and lead to democratic government, as well as produce more wealth.

Unfortunately, things did not work out that way. Foreign firms did come but they had less impact on local life than expected. As a result, social change was less thoroughgoing than anticipated, meaning that the elites retained power and democracy was stifled. While there was some economic growth, that too was less than promised.

DEPENDENCY THEORY   Indeed, modernization theory was sufficiently disappointing that some theorists proposed a competing theory, called **dependency theory** (Cardoso & Falletto, 1979; Frank, 1979). It saw underdevelopment as a result of unequal power relations between the centre (dominant capitalist countries) and the periphery (poor, dependent countries).[2] Over time, the centre developed at the expense of the periphery, which became underdeveloped (Frank, 1972). Further, dependency theorists asserted that the centre supported non-democratic governments in the periphery because they would maintain the system of dependency. Although much of what dependency theory said was accurate, it offered little in the way of concrete suggestions for improvement, besides turning to socialism. As a result, it had little practical effect.

THE WASHINGTON CONSENSUS   Although modernization theory did not vanquish underdevelopment, the general free-market principles on which it was based retained their strength. Therefore, in the 1980s, when many poor countries found themselves unable to pay even the interest on debts contracted from foreign lenders, another free-market solution was adopted. This new model was called the **Washington Consensus** because it involved the United States Treasury (finance department) and two **international financial institutions (IFI)** headquartered in Washington: the International Monetary Fund and the World Bank. As was true of modernization theory, the Washington Consensus originated in the wealthy countries and prescribed remedies that the governments of wealthy countries thought appropriate.

At the heart of the Washington Consensus were calls for poor countries to generate more revenue for debt repayment by cutting government expenditures—especially on health, education, and other social programs—to balance their budgets, selling off government-owned enterprises (privatization),

MODERNIZATION THEORY
A development model that views the traditional values, practices, and institutions of Third World countries as the basic cause of underdevelopment. To develop, poor countries should change their cultural outlook, social structure, economic organization, and political system based on the model of the advanced Western societies.

DEPENDENCY THEORY
Dependency theory argues that underdevelopment results from unequal power relations between the centre (dominant capitalist countries) and the periphery (poor, dependent countries).

WASHINGTON CONSENSUS
A series of policies put together by the International Monetary Fund and the World Bank that encourage developing countries to generate more revenue for debt repayment by cutting government expenditures to balance their budgets, selling off government-owned enterprises (privatization), and fully opening their countries to foreign goods and investments.

INTERNATIONAL FINANCIAL INSTITUTION (IFI) An organization that has some ability to affect the global economic system; for example, the International Monetary Fund and the World Bank.

---

[2] The centre is also referred to by dependency theorists as *the core* or *metropolitan countries* and the periphery as *satellites*.

STRUCTURAL ADJUSTMENT PROGRAM (SAP) A program administered by international financial institutions, which offers loans at very low interest rates to governments facing problems paying their debt if they adopt the programs endorsed by the Washington Consensus.

and fully opening their countries to foreign goods and investments. These prescriptions form the core of **structural adjustment programs (SAPs)**. SAPs administered by IFIs offer governments loans at very low interest rates ("soft loans") if their countries enacted the programs endorsed by the Washington Consensus. A country that refused to agree to a SAP could easily find itself without access to international credit because private banks will not lend to clients, even sovereign states, that cannot or do not pay their debts. Without such loans, countries might be unable to import such necessary items as light bulbs or spare parts for cars and trucks, since exporters want to be paid in a major international currency, normally U.S. dollars.

The SAPs paid little heed to the social consequences of the economic policies they prescribed. Since 1999, SAPs have been replaced by programs that give more attention to the plight of the poor. One of these, the Enhanced Heavily Indebted Poor Countries Initiative (HIPC), focuses on substantially reducing a poor country's foreign debt. Another new program requires any country seeking assistance from the IFIs to consult with citizens' groups in preparing Poverty Reduction Strategy Papers (PRSP), which map an anti-poverty strategy. Nevertheless, the IFIs and the donor countries that give aid to the Third World are still setting conditions similar to those used under SAPs that the recipients must meet in order to receive funds. This might be acceptable if the programs were sure to produce development, but that has not proven true.

As a result, some conclude that these multilateral initiatives are more about protecting the wealthy countries of the North (for example, by ensuring that countries do not default on their loans and destabilize the global banking system) than developing the South. Although the World Bank and the International Monetary Fund are mandated to assist the poorer countries, control of these organizations rests with the governments of the rich countries, who have a majority of the votes.

SUCCESS?   Overall, free-market approaches have not been spectacularly successful in achieving development. Indeed, no country in the world has ever developed using a *purely* free-market framework. Governments have always taken an active role in shaping the economies of successful developing countries.

State-Directed Approaches

There are two classes of state-directed development approaches: socialist and capitalist. The latter of these has been more successful. In fact, state-directed capitalist approaches have a better record of actually producing development than do market-driven approaches.

SOCIALIST MODELS   Many development models have been labelled "socialist." Some were Marxist and based on the experience of the Soviet Union, while others were either less dogmatically Marxist or built around a democratic socialism. Some were relatively successful but others failed badly, just like the market-driven experiments did. As well, like the free-market experiments, many of these socialist development systems came from outside a country and did not necessarily fit local conditions.

The initial socialist development model originated in the Soviet Union after the Bolshevik Revolution of 1917. It featured collectivized agriculture, a focus on heavy industry, and the use of central planning. This approach turned a semi-industrialized Russia into a highly industrialized Soviet Union, a country that from 1945 to 1991 was, along with the United States, a military super-power. However, the Soviet model had significant limitations that kept living standards fairly low in the Soviet bloc (the Soviet Union and its European satellites: Bulgaria, the former Czechoslovakia, East Germany, Hungary, Poland, and Romania[3]). The Soviet model was also exported to Cuba, Vietnam, Laos, North Korea, and China, though each of these countries made its own modifications. This model did not produce superlative results anywhere, although in most places it did ensure that people had access to education, reasonable health care, and basic housing. The model's greatest failures came in China, Cuba, and North Korea when the governments of those countries tried to make extremely radical and rapid changes.

When we look at models that are social democratic, a name often taken by and applied to democratic socialist parties, the record improves. This is not to say that the economic results are dramatically better, but that social democratic development has produced better levels of human development than is the norm for free market–led development and does not do worse in terms of economic results. There are many examples but we will consider the Indian state of Kerala, at the southwestern tip of the country, which is famous for its high levels of literacy and health care and its promotion of women's rights. The foundation for the state's success began with the election in 1957 of the Communist Party of India (Marxist), or CP(M), a democratic party despite its name. Since then, power has shifted between the CP(M) or a coalition it leads, the Left Democratic Front, and the Indian National Congress Party or the coalition it leads, the United Democratic Front. Nevertheless, Kerala remains a poor place (Biswas, 2010), suggesting that it takes more than a healthy, well-educated workforce to trigger economic development.

STATE-DIRECTED CAPITALIST MODELS   Two development policies, import substitution industrialization (ISI) and the Asian model, were conceived in poor countries. ISI was widely adopted in Latin America and Africa and worked well for several decades. The Asian model is indigenous to East Asia and has registered some spectacular successes since the 1970s.

---

[3] The former Yugoslavia was for a time part of this bloc, as was Albania, but each pursued an independent Marxist path.

**IMPORT SUBSTITUTION
INDUSTRIALIZATION (ISI)**
An economic development
model that involves creating
an industrial sector by placing
tariffs on imported industrial
products.

TARIFF A tax on imports.

Import Substitution Industrialization (ISI)   As its name suggests, **ISI** sought to industrialize countries by setting up businesses to produce manufactured goods that a country already imported. Governments protected these firms with high **tariffs**—taxes on imports—in order to diversify their countries' economies. Work done by the United Nations Economic Commission on Latin America and the Caribbean (ECLAC) suggested that ISI would be a good way to broaden a country's economic base, strengthen its financial system, and improve its prospects for democracy. Although Canada and the United States successfully used tariffs in the nineteenth century, that system was somewhat different from ISI because the North American nations were protecting already established businesses and not attempting to encourage the creation of new ones (Rapley, 2007).

For a while, from the 1940s to about 1970, ISI produced good results in countries such as Mexico, Brazil, and Argentina. However, it eventually failed because of problems inherent in the policy. Many countries applying ISI did build new industries, but these industries never flourished because they kept making expensive goods of poor quality. If governments talked about reducing tariffs to force these firms to become more efficient, their owners warned of foreign takeovers and their workers staged demonstrations to protect their jobs. Governments got the message and backed down.

**EXPORT-LED
INDUSTRIALIZATION (ELI)**
A model of economic
development with a capitalist
system in which government
and the biggest businesses
work very closely to develop
export industries. Government
influences investments, provides
incentives for exports, and can
decide whether firms are allowed
to export products.

Asian Model   Another practical approach to development is **export-led industrialization (ELI)**, the best known form of which is called the Asian model because Asian countries have used it most effectively. It is slightly newer than ISI, but has had a longer run of success, only encountering difficulties after about fifty very good years.

Sometimes called "the governed economy" (Wade, 1990), this model builds export industries. It features a capitalist system in which government and the biggest businesses work closely together. Government influences investments, provides incentives for exports, and even decides whether firms are allowed to export products. Like ISI, parts of the domestic market are typically protected from foreign competition. Conditions are often placed on the involvement of foreign companies, such as requiring them to create partnerships with local companies, transfer technology, and leave some of their profits in the country. As well, by keeping the value of their currency artificially low and by paying very low wages (often by suppressing unions and not enforcing labour laws), the newly industrialized countries can sell goods at very low prices (Martin & Schumann, 1997).

The objective of ELI is to build the strongest economy possible in the shortest time possible. Japan did this twice: in the nineteenth century when it first industrialized, and then when it rebuilt after World War II. South Korea and Taiwan (the Republic of China) followed Japan's lead. The latter two countries created their own variants of the Asian model to develop rapidly and better defend themselves against their communist neighbours (North Korea

◀ Export-led industrialization was particularly successful in Asian countries such as Taiwan.

and the People's Republic of China, respectively) when U.S. economic assistance was reduced in the 1970s. Other countries that have followed this path more or less successfully include Singapore, Malaysia, Thailand, Indonesia, and more recently and spectacularly, the People's Republic of China.

The Asian model has two striking features:

1. *It works with both non-democratic and democratic governments.* South Korea, Taiwan, and Indonesia were all dictatorships when they began their spectacular development, but now have democratic governments. Similarly, although Singapore is formally democratic, it is governed by a party that seldom loses elections, as was Japan until 2009.

2. *It has worked best in Asia.* Some commentators feel that this success reflects cultural factors (called Asian values), including a strong work ethic, family and moral values, thrift, discipline, and an emphasis on social cohesion rather than individualism. Others point to the fact that the Asian countries that grew strong and prosperous using this model were particularly adept at using government to lead the way to development, both by managing their economies and by emphasizing education. Finally, some commentators hold that the Asian model has not spread because the international trade rules now in place discriminate against countries that use government to build their economies. Indeed, ELI was particularly successful in Japan, Taiwan, and South Korea, in part because the United States provided them with billions of dollars in aid and, prior to the 1990s, offered them favourable trading terms as part of a strategy of building a defence against communist countries.

Both Approaches Have Worked   These two homegrown approaches (ISI and ELI) have each worked well for a while, in some countries. This suggests that different development policies may work better in some places and at some times than in others. Intuitively, this makes sense: Canada did not follow the same path to development as the United States or Britain, yet all became developed democracies. Nevertheless, there is still a tendency to search for the magic bullet that will solve every country's economic and even political problems.

TWO "MIRACLE ECONOMIES": INDIA AND THE PEOPLE'S REPUBLIC OF CHINA

Although there is no agreement about exactly how we should define a "miracle economy," the label is applied only to economies that grow very quickly (say, at a rate greater than 5 percent annually) for an extended period (at least five years). The Asian model produced economic miracles in Japan, South Korea, the Republic of China (Taiwan), Singapore, and to some extent Malaysia during the last third of the twentieth century. Now, in the twenty-first century, the miracle economies are the People's Republic of China (PRC) and India. Although both are Asian nations, neither fits the Asian model exactly.

What most interests us about the PRC and India is the difference between their political systems. The PRC is not the first country to combine private enterprise with authoritarian politics, but it is the first communist state to embrace capitalist economics. Like other Communist party states, power in China is concentrated in the central government, which allows Beijing to direct development. India, on the other hand, has been an electoral democracy since becoming independent in 1947. Moreover, it is a federation, so authority is divided between the centre and the states. Therefore, the government based in New Delhi cannot assume a role that parallels Beijing's. Our analysis starts with the PRC.

The People's Republic of China

From the Communist Revolution in 1949 until 1978, the PRC's economic performance was poor. Mao Zedong's revolutionary government began with a drive to build heavy industry, but two highly disruptive political movements launched by Mao himself, the Great Leap Forward (1958–1962) and the Cultural Revolution (1967–1976), set development back substantially, It was only in 1978, two years after Mao died, that Deng Xiaoping (de facto Chinese leader) began to limit the role of communist ideology in economic policy. This led quickly to a return to private agriculture, legalizing private businesses, and allowing foreign firms to invest in the PRC and establish their businesses there. Since 1990 the PRC's economy has grown at more than

9 percent annually, meaning that it has grown to four and a half times its original size in twenty years, and between 1990 and 2009 annual per capita income rose from US$351 to an estimated US$3565 (International Monetary Fund, 2010; Quah, 2008), a tenfold increase.

The PRC has done this by emphasizing export-led growth, the keystone of the Asian model. The PRC has also followed the Asian model by leaving a great deal of power in the hands of an undemocratic state. This path was also followed by South Korea and Taiwan in the first decades of their remarkable economic expansions. Where the PRC departs from the model is in having a communist government; the Communist Party of China is the architect of the PRC's capitalist economic miracle. Beijing's experience has been copied by another Asian communist state, Vietnam. Vietnam's economy is estimated to be sixteen times bigger in 2009 than it was in 1990 and the annual per capita income for Vietnam's eighty-nine million people has risen from US$98 to US$1100 (International Monetary Fund, 2010). Communists appear to make very good capitalists!

China's large, rapidly growing economy has important effects on its foreign policy, particularly as it seeks to secure the natural resources needed for its industrial development (as discussed in Box 17-4, Chinese Foreign Policy).

◀ China seeks African resources to fuel its rapid economic growth.

BOX 17-4

Chinese Foreign Policy

The People's Republic of China (PRC) is not only the world's most populous country with one of the world's fastest growing economies, but also a nuclear power, thus automatically a foreign policy actor of some significance in the world. However, Beijing's military power is not the most striking element of its foreign policy. Rather, it is the role that the PRC is playing in the developing world that really catches the observer's eye. Although the PRC has long played a role in international politics, only since its economic takeoff in the 1990s have its own economic interests become the leading factor in its relations with developing nations.

The PRC has been very active in Africa. It is interested in the continent's raw materials, which the PRC needs to drive its rapidly growing economy. As well, Beijing has begun to offer generous development assistance to African nations. Blessed with ample international reserves (the foreign currency and gold a country holds), the PRC can offer concessional (very low-interest) loans with easy repayment schedules. The PRC is particularly active in financing infrastructure projects, for example, roads, energy development, and ports. Further, unlike the practice of developed democracies, such as Canada, Sweden, or the United States, the PRC does not set political conditions on its development assistance, giving it access to countries like Zimbabwe or Sudan, which Ottawa or Washington would scorn (Brautigam, 2009; Rotberg, 2008).

Similar patterns of trade and aid also characterize the PRC's relations with the nations of both Southeast Asia and Latin America (Roett & Paz, 2008; Sutter, 2008). Once again, Beijing's principal interest is securing access to natural resources and its development assistance focuses on infrastructure, which is necessary to ensure that those resources reach China easily. It is clear that the PRC pumps a great deal of money into the economies of nations that export natural resources. However, this comes at the cost of reconfirming the role of many African, Latin American, and Southeast Asian states as nothing more than suppliers of raw materials to more developed countries.

India

With a population of 1.18 billion, India is only slightly smaller than the PRC. However, its recent history and the nature of its economic miracle are very different. As already noted, India has chosen its leaders, both federal and state, through democratic elections since its independence in 1947. Although Indian politics exhibits high levels of both corruption (Quah, 2008) and political violence between religious groups and castes (Basu & Roy, 2007), it is universally recognized as the world's largest democracy.

India breaks with the Asian model and other state-led development plans because it started its "miraculous" growth when it began to move away from a highly regulated and **protectionist economic policy** in 1991. A series of reforms cut red tape, encouraged foreign investment, and put an end to government monopolies in many areas. The results have been impressive. International Monetary Fund estimates indicate that India's economy is more than four times larger in 2009 than it was in 1990 and that per capita income

PROTECTIONIST ECONOMIC POLICY An economic policy that uses high tariffs to ensure that domestic firms have an edge when competing with foreign companies. Import substitution industrialization is an example.

has risen to US$1033 from US$362 (International Monetary Fund, 2010). Although Indian governments, both federal and state, still play a significant role in the economy, especially in infrastructure development (for example, roads and airports), the country's experience offers another path for countries that are trying to move out of poverty.

Another way in which India diverges from the PRC and the other Asian model countries is that its economic takeoff was powered by services and not manufactured goods. In particular, India has thrived due to its huge pool of well-educated, English-speaking information technology (IT) personnel. Many North American firms have shifted much of their IT work to India to take advantage of the far lower wages available there. However, although services may be the engine driving Indian prosperity, this may not be enough to bring dramatic benefits to the 70 to 75 percent of Indians who live in villages, many still without clean water, electricity, or paved roads. Labour-intensive manufacturing, the option chosen by Asian model countries to build their economies, would seem to offer a better way to lift more people out of poverty and into something more comfortable (Stackhouse, 2000).

Taken together, the Chinese and Indian examples suggest that development can be achieved by both authoritarian and democratic governments, through development policies that give the market either more or less freedom to operate, and by stressing manufacturing or services. For all of their differences, however, both of these successful examples of development work within a capitalist framework that relies heavily on the private sector. Although both countries are growing rapidly, we must not forget that the PRC and India are still poor and have high levels of poverty. Even in the better-off PRC, 51.1 percent of the people live on less than US$2 a day, while in India the figure is 81.7 percent (World Bank, 2010a). There is still a lot do to before the world's two most populous countries can be called "developed."

FOREIGN AID

Less developed countries often need help from richer countries to be able meet the basic needs of their populations. They also need the skills and technology of the richer countries if they are to compete successfully in global markets. Charitable organizations provide humanitarian assistance and supply volunteers to assist with development projects. However, only the governments of the richer countries have the financial resources to provide substantial development assistance to the poorer countries.

Canada's foreign aid to poor countries, formally called **Official Development Assistance (ODA)**, is sometimes purely altruistic, as with disaster relief or humanitarian assistance. Often, however, wealthy countries use ODA to secure multiple objectives. In the case of Canada, it seems that the most important objective is to help Canadian business: more than two-thirds of Canadian aid has been "tied" (World Bank, 2004), meaning that the money

OFFICIAL DEVELOPMENT ASSISTANCE (ODA) Aid to the poorer countries given by the governments of the richer countries.

had to be spent in Canada, on Canadian goods and services,[4] even if these are more expensive or less suited to the needs of the developing countries.

Canada gives less aid than many Canadians think it does. In 1969, former Canadian Prime Minister Lester Pearson proposed that the wealthy countries dedicate 0.7 percent of their GDP to foreign aid. This goal has been accepted by the richer countries and adopted by the United Nations. However, only a few countries (including Sweden, Denmark, and the Netherlands) have met or exceeded this goal. Canadian governments have remained committed to that goal, but in reality, assistance as a proportion of GDP has declined until recently. In 2008, Canada's ODA was about 0.32 percent of GDP, below the average of 0.48 percent for the world's developed countries (OECD, 2010).

Although aid does not seem to be especially generous, since the end of World War II in 1945 more than US$2 trillion has been spent by the developed countries on foreign aid. Supporters of ODA point to increased literacy, longer life expectancies, and greater opportunities throughout the poor world. Further, Jeffery Sachs (2005), an economist and proponent of increased aid, argues that without significant external assistance many countries will be unable to break free from what he calls "the poverty trap" and attain a measure of economic prosperity.

Critics, however, note that 2.5 billion people, some 40 percent of the world's population, subsist on US$2 per day and therefore something is not being done correctly. Robert Calderisi (2006), a Canadian who worked for many years with the World Bank in Africa, argues that aid to individual countries should be cut by half to make recipient governments manage the funds more carefully. William Easterly (2006), another economist, criticizes ODA programs for being paternalistic and unaccountable. He would like to give groups of poor people, not countries, development vouchers that they could use to contract the services of any aid agency or **non-governmental organization (NGO)**.

Paul Collier (2007) takes a different approach. Focusing on the "bottom billion," the poorest of the poor, he argues that neither aid nor trade will be sufficient to bring development to the countries where those billion people live. Collier proposes a series of solutions, one of which is unrestricted access to the markets of rich countries such as Canada for the labour-intensive products exported by the bottom billion.

One point that most agree with is that no country should receive ODA unless its government meets certain standards of **transparency** and **accountability**. Part of ODA's bad reputation comes from the period of the Cold War (1945–1990), when both the West (the United States, Canada, and their allies) and the Communist bloc (the Soviet Union and its allies) gave foreign aid to dictatorships to win their allegiance rather than focusing directly on the poor.

NON-GOVERNMENTAL ORGANIZATION (NGO) A private organization that often delivers public services but is independent of government. NGOs have been very active in international development activities.

TRANSPARENCY The visibility to the public of the governmental decision-making processes.

ACCOUNTABILITY Having to be responsible for one's actions and having to accept the consequences of failure to perform as expected.

---

[4] In 2008, the Canadian government announced a plan to untie aid by 2012–2013.

Nevertheless, large amounts of aid are still given to some countries that do not meet standards of transparency and accountability.

Economic Discrimination

Seen from the perspective of the South, the reluctance of the North to send more aid is only part of the problem. Equally serious is the reluctance of the rich countries to open their markets fully to the Third World and to accept fair global trading rules.

Canada and the rest of the world's wealthy countries talk about free trade and levelling the international economic playing field. But when it comes to trading with poor countries, the richer countries find ways to discriminate against the products that poor countries produce more cheaply, primarily foodstuffs and textiles, in order to protect their own producers. As well, the richer countries heavily subsidize many exports, which then have a major competitive advantage over Third World products. However, we insist that Third World countries must not protect their producers from our products. We can do this because we are stronger and the poorer countries need to trade with us so desperately that they often accept an unfair deal.

Trade Pacts

There are numerous trade agreements involving both rich and poor countries. One hundred and fifty-three countries (as of 2010) are members of the World Trade Organization (WTO), an international organization dealing with the rules of trade between countries and the only international organization concerned with economics that does not assign member countries votes based on the size of their economies (see Chapter 18). There are also many regional free-trade agreements such as the North American Free Trade Agreement (involving Canada, the United States, and Mexico) and bilateral agreements such as the Canada–Chile Free Trade Agreement.

Free-trade agreements establish binding trade rules and sometimes set up impartial panels to settle trade disputes. In theory, this helps weaker countries, as the arbitrary power of stronger countries can be constrained by the rules. The products of the poor countries can potentially gain access to the large, rich markets of the world's developed countries without facing discriminatory tariffs and quotas. However, many poor countries argue that trade agreements are biased toward the richer countries and do not lead to fair trade relations. For example, agriculture is the major economic activity in many less developed countries, with a large proportion of the population often engaged in farming. However, agriculture in the less developed countries faces severe challenges that the WTO, whose task is to facilitate international trade, has had trouble addressing.

The rich countries provide about US$1 billion a day in subsidies to their own farmers. Agricultural products are then exported at very low prices, making it difficult for farmers in poorer countries to sell their products. Indeed, it has been estimated that the rich, developed countries spend six times more on subsidizing their agricultural production than they spend in development assistance (Oxfam, 2003). Because poor countries are dependent on access to the markets of rich countries, they are vulnerable to pressure to accept rules that may be more beneficial to the rich.

POLITICS IN THE THIRD WORLD

Few Third World countries have been able to develop effective democratic systems. Politics in most of these states has been characterized by instability, military rule, violence, and corruption. These traits have contributed to the problems of development.

As discussed in Chapter 11, many less developed countries in the last quarter of the twentieth century embraced democratic government. Yet only a minority of countries that made **democratic transitions** has succeeded in forming strong, stable democracies (termed **consolidated democracies**). How can we explain this?

DEMOCRATIC TRANSITION
A process of change involving abandoning authoritarian government for democratic rule.

CONSOLIDATED DEMOCRACIES
Countries with democratic governments that are stable, well accepted by both ordinary citizens and political elites, and unlikely to be overthrown.

In one sense, politics in the Third World is no different from politics anywhere. People want to control the state, to make rules that they think are good, and to enforce those rules as they think best. However, Third World politics diverges from politics in consolidated democracies, such as Canada, in three important ways:

1. Liberal democracies have been rare in the Third World.
2. Third World countries have weak governmental institutions.
3. Violence plays a much bigger part in Third World politics than in developed, consolidated democracies.

Few Liberal Democracies

Had we looked at the governments of the Third World in 1980, we would have found only a handful of liberal democracies where the rule of law is respected, rights and freedoms are protected, and citizens have a voice in governing. These would have included India in Asia, Botswana in Africa, Costa Rica in Latin America, and Barbados in the Caribbean. There were also countries that were semi-democracies or marginal cases, such as Singapore and Sri Lanka, but most Third World countries would not have been considered democratic in 1980. Now, 66 of the 119 countries that Freedom House (2010) identifies as electoral democracies (countries that choose their leaders through free elections) are developing nations. Since the overall sample of countries examined by Freedom House includes 132 states that can be considered developing nations, one half of them can be considered democratic, although many of these countries do not fully match the definition of liberal democracy.

Authoritarian governments (another name for a non-democratic system of government, as discussed in Chapter 11) failed and were replaced in many countries by democratically elected governments. Some of the failures resulted from the authoritarian government's mismanagement, while others resulted from the breakdown of communism, which left some Third World dictatorships without patrons. A few transitions resulted from external pressure by the United States and the international financial institutions. Most of the transitions were completed by the early 1990s.

However, it takes more than dismantling an authoritarian state and holding elections to build a strong, stable democracy. The transition to democracy has been difficult for many countries. A number of countries have the form but not the substance of democracy. In particular, there are often very few institutional limits on the executive's power. Once elected, a president or prime minister often has the power to govern without restraint until the next election.

Weak Institutions

Strong, **personalistic leaders** have historically dominated politics in poor countries. Almost always men, they are called *caudillos* in Latin America, *big men* in Africa, and *bosses* just about everywhere. Giving one leader too much power can be a problem anywhere, even in the United States (Schlesinger, 1973), Britain (Weir & Beetham, 1999), and Canada (Simpson, 2001). Consolidated democracies, however, generally have counterweights to executive power that seldom exist in new democracies.

These counterweights include **political institutions** inside and outside of government, such as legislatures, courts, the public service, the media, organized interests, political parties, and groups independent of government. Democracies need to have both sets of institutions working well. Having strong political institutions lessens the risk that one person, group, or organization will become too powerful in two different ways. A multiplicity of robust institutions disperses power among many centres, each having some ability to counter the actions of the others. Further, having several powerful institutions in a political system gives citizens more chances to present their views to government.

Almost all countries have at least one strong governmental institution: the executive. In Canada, the executive refers to the prime minister or premier, the Cabinet, and the public service. In much of the Third World, however, the president or prime minister monopolizes executive power. As a result, there is little accountability and corruption is often a serious problem. Political corruption exists in all countries. However, poor countries appear especially vulnerable to this problem. Why?

PERSONALISTIC LEADER
A political leader whose claim to rule is based on some presumed inherent personal qualities. It also implies a government in which all important decisions are made by the leader and according to the leader's wishes.

POLITICAL INSTITUTIONS
Behavioural patterns or established organizations associated with politics and governing.

In part, poor countries are vulnerable to corruption due to weak political institutions that cannot protect the public. Corruption is also a sign that politics is a winner-take-all game, with no place left for opponents. Making matters worse is a failure of legitimacy. Citizens do not trust government because government excludes many interests and concentrates control in the hands of those who are already powerful. Governments then use force to repress their opponents, and those opponents use force to try to change the government. Although this oversimplifies the situation, it does give us a sense of the dynamics that produce political violence in the Third World.

The Role of Force and Violence

Violence has always characterized politics in the developing world (as it once did in developed countries). Even nations with long histories of democratic rule, such as Costa Rica, experienced coups, revolutions, and insurgencies in the past. Other democracies, such as Jamaica and India, still have a lot of political violence, especially during election campaigns. And the non-democratic countries face even graver challenges, as violence is often a standard instrument of rule.

The clearest contemporary instances of political violence and its devastating effects on a country are found in a number of sub-Saharan African states. In the continent's east, Rwanda and Burundi have been racked by ethnic warfare that spilled over their borders and affected neighbouring states. One of those neighbours, the Democratic Republic of Congo, has itself been the scene of violent conflict almost continuously since 1997. Governments in the West African states of Sierra Leone and Liberia have collapsed at times, leaving their citizens to be plundered and murdered by marauding armed bands. Development is obviously impossible in these settings. Why, though, has violence been so common throughout the Third World?

CHANGING TIMES   The main agent of political violence in the Third World has been a politically active military. Recently, however, those militaries have taken a less prominent role, thus there are fewer **coups d'état** (forcible seizures of power by the armed forces or occasionally the police). Militaries in poor countries have long been politicized; that is, they have regularly taken clear political stances and often seized government to run it themselves. They have done this because they have the guns, but also because they are commonly the best organized institution in a country, with the highest concentration of technically skilled, well-trained personnel. Accordingly, when civilian politicians have been corrupt or incompetent, or have gone against the military's wishes, the soldiers would step in and take over (see Box 17-5, Military Coups).

Through the 1980s, it seemed that there was no general solution to the problem of politically active militaries. However, the wave of democratic transitions that began then has coincided with a sharp fall in the frequency

COUP D'ÉTAT A forcible seizure of power by the armed forces or occasionally the police.

BOX 17-5

Military Coups

Military takeovers of government do not just happen. Studies of coups and how they work help us understand this phenomenon (Farcau, 1994; Fitch, 1977; Luttwak, 1969).

- First, the army will almost certainly be involved because, of all the armed services, it has the resources that are best suited to toppling a government: armed troops, tanks, and other armour. The air force can strafe buildings and opposing troops, while the navy can shell shorelines and block harbours, but the army secures the area.
- Second, although some coups have been led by sergeants and generals, many coups are led by majors and colonels because they are in direct command of large numbers of soldiers.
- Third, coups succeed or fail based on whether key figures oppose or support them. For example, an attempted coup failed in Spain in 1981 because the king opposed it publicly, causing military commanders to fall in line behind him.
- Fourth, successful coups capture not only government leaders, but also the communications media. When a coup succeeds, it often forms a governing committee or junta (a Spanish word meaning "board" or "committee"). The junta contains all of the key players in coups.
- Finally, some coups are bloodless, because they are essentially unopposed, but others spur civil wars or lead to cruel dictatorships.

of coups. This may reflect a heightened democratic consciousness among soldiers, but there are several other explanations to consider.

One explanation is that citizens in many countries have become dissatisfied with military governments. This is especially true of four South American countries (Argentina, Brazil, Chile, and Uruguay) that saw particularly brutal and long-lasting military regimes in the late twentieth century. Another is that militaries around the world have recognized their nearly uniform failure as governors. Militaries can impose order and throw out inept rulers, but with only a handful of exceptions they have not presided over extended periods of development. Finally, the international community no longer tolerates military governments. International financial institutions now are very reluctant to make loans to military regimes and often demand that civilian governments cut military budgets to qualify for loans.

The military will always be a political actor and there will likely always be some military regimes. However, current trends suggest that there will be many fewer governments run by generals than in the past.

PUTTING PROBLEMS INTO PERSPECTIVE Why do the political conditions just described affect the Third World? The fact that today's wealthy democracies have pasts as unsavoury and unpromising as what we find in today's developing world tells us that improvement is possible. We often forget that democratization—in its social and economic manifestations of less rigid class barriers and a more equal distribution of wealth as well as in its political form—has been under way for more than two hundred years in the historic democracies of northwestern Europe and North America. To expect Africa, Asia, and Latin America to cover the same distance in a decade or even a generation is unrealistic. Nevertheless, ever more countries are offering their citizens increasingly accountable, honest, and efficient governments. This signifies progress toward building states that can pursue the common good.

We must recognize, however, that poverty makes good government difficult. In poor countries, controlling the state may offer the surest road to wealth. Where that is the case, keeping the power to govern may seem too important to risk by holding elections, allowing a free press, and encouraging citizens to participate actively in politics. Such conditions also work against building strong state institutions other than the presidency and the security forces because strong organizations can become independent and work toward the common good instead of the ruler's interests. In addition, poor countries often have difficulty in establishing an honest, efficient, and knowledgeable staff for government and its agencies. Because government may not be able to pay adequate salaries, public servants may look to other sources of income, such as soliciting bribes or holding multiple jobs, to make a decent living.

Foreign Intervention

The political problems that many Third World countries face are not all of their own making. To a considerable extent, they are a product of a history of domination and exploitation.[5]

The control and colonization of most of the world by the European powers often left Third World countries ill-prepared for governing after becoming independent. In a number of cases, the boundaries of the new countries made little sense, as they combined groups of people of different ancestries, cultures, languages, and religions. To make matters worse, the imperial powers frequently stimulated ethnic divisions within their colonies as part of a divide-and-rule strategy. In other cases, the descendants of the European colonists tried to maintain their economic and political power after independence against the challenges of indigenous peoples.

POST-INDEPENDENCE   Further, although most of the Third World was able to achieve independence in the decades following World War II, this did not end foreign intervention in their affairs. During the Cold War, the Western and Soviet blocs struggled to gain the support of Third World governments. This involved not only giving their supporters economic and military aid, but

---

[5] Domination and exploitation have been associated not only with Western powers. Imperialism, colonization, slavery, forced religious conversion, and the massacre of conquered peoples have been carried out at various times by the powerful, whether Western or non-Western.

also overthrowing unfriendly governments; supporting repressive regimes, revolutionary movements, and terrorist groups; and even encouraging wars among Third World countries.

The end of the Cold War reduced these negative forms of foreign intervention that disrupted the political development of Third World countries. However, concerns about international terrorism, the rise of militant **Islamism**, the security of oil supplies, and the international trade in illegal drugs keep powerful countries intervening in the politics of the Third World.

Recently, another apparently more benign form of political intervention has emerged: humanitarian intervention in failed states. *Failed states* are those that no longer have the capacity to maintain order. This is not a new phenomenon, but we have only recently given it a name. Examples of failed states in recent years include Sierra Leone, Liberia, Somalia, and Haiti. In all of these cases, troops from several countries were dispatched under United Nations authority to restore order. One hundred years ago, either the disorder in a country whose government had ceased functioning would have been ignored or, more likely, a powerful state such as Britain, France, or the United States would have taken over.[6]

ISLAMISM The perspective often associated with those seeking to purge "degenerate" foreign elements from Muslim society and base government on Islamic principles.

The North–South Institute
www.nsi-ins.ca

---

[6] As discussed in Chapter 2, foreign military invention has also been used occasionally to protect part of a population that is severely threatened by its own government or security forces. This "responsibility to protect" has been controversial, particularly when such intervention has not been authorized by the United Nations Security Council.

Summary and Conclusion

Although there have been improvements in living standards throughout much of the Third World, particularly in the newly industrialized countries of East Asia, differences between the richest and the poorest countries continue to increase. About 1.4 billion people in the developing world, about one-quarter of the total population in the developing world, live in extreme poverty, with incomes of less than US$1.25 a day. This is down from 1.9 billion, one-half of the total population in the developing world, in 1981 (World Bank, 2008). Feeding growing populations, creating employment, and providing housing and other services to those who have flocked to the slums of congested cities pose difficult challenges for many countries.

The problems of the world's poorest states are everyone's problems. A world of great wealth for

some and grinding poverty for others is, potentially, a very unstable place. Political violence in Third World countries is not just local, but can affect people in all countries. Poverty, unemployment, or violence in underdeveloped countries leads to migration, legal or illegal, to the richer countries. Environmental problems, such as the destruction of rainforests to achieve rapid economic growth, affect the ecosystems of the world as a whole.

We do not fully understand how countries develop successfully. There does not seem to be a single, universally applicable route to solving the economic, social, and political problems of underdevelopment. We know that some policies have worked for a while but that none has fully delivered on its promises. Adopting the free-market policies of the United States and other rich Western countries has not generally been very successful. In the past, the adoption of the state socialist approach of the Soviet Union failed. Although several Asian countries have achieved high rates of economic growth through export-led industrialization, it is unclear whether this approach can be replicated successfully elsewhere or, indeed, if the successes of some Asian countries can be maintained. Despite improvements in the living standards of the Third World, only the city-state of Singapore has fully entered the ranks of the richest developed countries, while South Korea and Taiwan can also be considered economically developed countries.

Development is a political and social issue as well as an economic one, thus abstract economic theories need to be qualified by an understanding of the political, social, and cultural realities of particular underdeveloped countries. Political problems such as corruption, wars, instability, ineffective government administration, and poorly regulated economic activity create serious obstacles to development. Political institutions, both governmental and non-governmental, need to be strengthened and reformed to involve the people in the process of development, to hold government accountable for its actions, and to ensure that sound policies are designed and implemented. The development of Third World countries can also be promoted by pressuring various international institutions to provide fairer opportunities for countries that are weak and poor. Social and cultural changes such as improving the status of women and encouraging the involvement of local communities in the development process can be very helpful.

Overall, the poorer countries face difficult problems in seeking the common good of their citizens. With limited wealth, it is difficult to meet even the most basic needs of the population. Governments often lack the resources needed for effective governing. The great inequalities found in many poor countries let the wealthy wield enormous political power, which hinders needed reforms. Further, underdeveloped countries face not only internal problems, but also problems resulting from global inequities in power. The poorer countries have faced domination and exploitation by the powerful wealthy countries, whether through imperialism or the global economic system. Various forms of assistance to the poorer countries are often insufficient to overcome the challenges they face.

In sum, if we want to achieve the common good of humanity, addressing global imbalances in economic and political power as well as providing meaningful assistance to developing countries is necessary. A key problem is that governments and citizens typically are concerned primarily with the good of their own countries.

Key Terms

Accountability 432

Consolidated democracies 434

Coup d'état 436

Democratic transition 434

Dependency theory 423

Developing countries 416

Development 417

Export-led industrialization (ELI) 426

Gross domestic product (GDP) 417

Human Development Index (HDI) 419

Import substitution industrialization (ISI) 426

International financial institution (IFI) 423

Islamism 439

Modernization theory 423

Non-governmental organization (NGO) 432

North 416

Official Development Assistance (ODA) 431

Personalistic leader 435

Discussion Questions

1. Why is global inequality so severe?
2. What should a poor country do to develop?
3. Why have some countries in the Third World prospered while others remain poor?
4. Should wealthy countries provide greater assistance to poor countries?
5. Should developed countries help less developed countries to become consolidated democracies?
6. Should poor countries have to meet certain standards of transparency and accountability before they can receive official development assistance?

Further Reading

Anderson, R., Seibert, R., & Wagner, J. (2008). *Politics and change in the Middle East* (9th ed.). Upper Saddle River, NJ: Prentice-Hall.

Charlton, E. (2009). *Comparing Asian politics: India, China, and Japan* (3rd ed.). Boulder, CO: Westview Press.

Chazan, N., Lewis, P., Mortimer, R., Rothchild, D., & Stedman, S.J. (Eds.). (1999). *Politics and society in contemporary Africa.* Boulder, CO: Lynne Rienner Publishers.

Close, D. (2010). *Latin American politics: An introduction.* Toronto: University of Toronto Press.

Collier, P. (2009). *Wars, guns and votes: Democracy in dangerous places.* New York: HarperCollins.

De Rivero, O. (2001). *The myth of development: The non-viable economies of the 21st century.* London, UK: Zed Books.

Handelman, H. (2010). *The challenge of third world development* (5th ed.). Upper Saddle River, NJ: Pearson/ Prentice-Hall.

Huntington, S. (1968). *Political order in changing societies.* Boston: MIT Press.

Menon, N., & Nigam, A. (2007). *Power and contestation: India since 1989.* Halifax: Fernwood Publishing.

North–South Institute. *Canadian development report.* Ottawa: North-South Institute [annual].

Seligson, M., & Passe-Smith, J. (Eds.). (2008). *Development and underdevelopment: The political economy of global inequality* (4th ed.). Boulder, CO: Lynne Rienner Publishers.

Sen, A. (1999). *Development as freedom.* New York: Knopf.

Thompson, A. (2004). *An introduction to African politics.* London, UK: Routledge.

Tsai, K. (2007). *Capitalism without democracy: The private sector in contemporary China.* Ithaca, NY: Cornell University Press.

United Nations Development Programme. *Human development report.* New York: Oxford University Press [annual].

World Bank. *World development report.* Washington: The World Bank [annual].

Chapter 18

Politics and Governance at the Global Level

PHOTO ABOVE: The international conflict known as the turbot war broke out in March 1995. The Canadian Coast Guard seized the Spanish trawler *Estai* on the Grand Banks off Newfoundland, accusing it of contravening measures to conserve fish stocks.

CHAPTER OBJECTIVES

After reading this chapter, you should be able to:

1. discuss the differences between national politics and international politics
2. explain the differences between various theoretical approaches to the study of international politics
3. analyze contemporary international political issues and policy-making recommendations using various theoretical approaches
4. assess the chances of international peace and the possibilities of order and governance at the global level

The international conflict known as the turbot war broke out on March 9, 1995, when the Canadian Coast Guard seized a Spanish trawler, the *Estai*, on the Grand Banks off Newfoundland, accusing it of contravening measures to conserve fish stocks.

The Grand Banks used to be one of the richest and most popular fishing grounds in the world. By the 1970s, it became clear that unless rigorous fisheries conservation measures were adopted, its fish stocks would collapse. On January 1, 1977, Canada declared a 320 kilometre exclusive economic zone and imposed strict controls on fishing inside the zone. However, about 10 percent of the Grand Banks are beyond Canada's limit. In 1979, the conservation of the fish stocks outside the 320 kilometre limit became the responsibility of an international organization, the Northwest Atlantic Fisheries Organization (NAFO). In February 1995, NAFO announced its allocation decision for the total allowable catch for turbot for 1995, with a breakdown for Canada, the European Union (EU), and other countries that left the EU dissatisfied. Since NAFO procedures so allow, the EU unilaterally set itself a higher quota.

In part because of NAFO's inability to enforce its own quotas and conservation measures, Canada decided to act in defence of its interests. In May 1994, following the collapse of the cod stocks and the consequent adoption of a moratorium, the Canadian government decided to search, and if necessary seize, any foreign vessels suspected of fishing in violation of conservation measures. The Canadian government announced a turbot fishing moratorium of sixty days and, at the same time, added Spain and Portugal to the list of states whose ships could be searched and seized.

The EU refused to impose the moratorium. On March 9, 1995, the Canadian government seized the *Estai* in international waters and accused it of fishing with nets smaller than those permitted under conservation measures and of purposely misreporting its fish landings. The Spanish government brought a case against Canada before the International Court of Justice (ICJ) in The Hague, accusing it of piracy. Eventually, Canada dropped its charges and the ICJ decided not to act on Spain's request.

A similar incident occurred in May 2004 when the Canadian Coast Guard boarded two Portuguese vessels and gathered evidence of their illegal fishing. According to Article 18 of the NAFO Convention, however, prosecution of vessels suspected of illegal fishing is the responsibility of the flag state acting on the basis of evidence gathered by inspectors upon boarding. In this case, the Portuguese authorities considered the evidence gathered by Canada to be insufficient and did not take legal action against the two vessels.

These two episodes exemplify the predicament in which states find themselves in international politics, namely whether to entrust the defence of their interests to a weak international regime with limited enforcement abilities or to rely on themselves, which might at times require the use of force. This chapter examines politics at the global level, first pointing out the major differences between national and international politics and then illustrating the differences between various approaches to the study of international politics.

INTERNATIONAL POLITICS AND GOVERNANCE

There is a major difference between national politics (politics within one state) and international politics (politics at the global level). States are entities composed of a population, a government, and a territory. They are sovereign, meaning that their governments have the final authority to make and enforce rules on the population living within their territorial boundaries. The world as a whole does not have such a central authority. There is, in other words, no world government; states live in an **anarchic** world.

This means that the organization of authority within the world is horizontal rather than vertical (that is, hierarchical), as within a state. The world has as many authorities as there are sovereign states—almost two hundred of them. The fact that the world is anarchic does not mean, however, that there are no rules in relations among states. Rules do exist. They are based on customary practices that have often been codified into law. They are also the result of agreements negotiated and signed by states directly (international treaties) or negotiated and agreed upon within the framework of international governmental organizations, which are associations of sovereign states created to facilitate co-operation among them in specific issue areas. International rules also derive from interpretations of existing international law provided by the courts.

Because the world is anarchic, though, there is no certain mechanism to enforce international rules. An individual who breaks the law within a state will, more often than not, be apprehended by police, tried in a court of law, and punished. A state that chooses to ignore international rules either because it interprets them in a different way than other states, or simply because it is in its interest to do so will, more often than not, escape punishment. Individuals cannot claim that certain rules do not apply to them or refuse to appear in court if summoned. A state can refuse to be bound by some rules by choosing not to be part of the treaty establishing them. A state may also refuse to submit to a court when accused of violating international law. The International Court of Justice (ICJ), which has the task of settling disputes among states (either in accordance with international law or, if so requested by the parties, *ex aequo et bono*—that is, simply on the basis of justice and equity), has no compulsory jurisdiction. This means that the ICJ cannot summon a state to appear before its fifteen judges who sit in The Hague in the Netherlands unless that state has voluntarily agreed to recognize the jurisdiction of the court and submit itself to its judgment.

Although the world as a whole does not have a government, it can be said to have **global governance**, which can be defined as the process whereby a number of different actors compete and co-operate to provide a certain degree of order and predictability to relations among states.

All scholars of international politics agree in defining the world as anarchic (that is, lacking a central authority). They also agree in recognizing that,

---

ANARCHY A situation in which there is no central authority.

International Court of Justice
www.icj-cij.org

GLOBAL GOVERNANCE The process whereby a number of different actors (mainly states and international governmental and non-governmental organizations) compete and co-operate to provide a certain degree of order and predictability to relations among states.

anarchy notwithstanding, a certain degree of governance exists. When it comes to assessing the significance of anarchy, identifying its consequences, and making policy suggestions, however, scholars divide themselves into a number of different schools. Each one starts from different assumptions, adopts a different theoretical approach, and ends up making different policy recommendations. This chapter focuses primarily on the two major approaches: realism and liberal–internationalism.[1]

REALISM

The realist school assumes that since the world is anarchic, states find themselves in the same predicament as that of individuals in the state of nature before the establishment of government imagined by English philosopher Thomas Hobbes (1588–1679). According to Hobbes, life in the state of nature is "solitary, poor, nasty, brutish, and short" (1651/1968, p. 186). Individuals have to fend for themselves in this competitive and dangerous environment.

Realism also assumes that the main objective of states is their own security, understood primarily as the defence of their territorial borders and form of government and the protection of their population from external threats. This objective is the core of what is usually called the **national interest**, which realists view as the most important common good that governments pursue when conducting foreign policy—that is, when acting in relation to other states or actors outside their national territories.

For realists, the pursuit of the national interest is a central and constant feature of the foreign policy of any state, regardless of changes of governments or political leaders. So, at least in regard to the quest for national security, realists regard each state as a unitary actor that makes decisions as if it were a single person, even if decisions are made by different individuals and institutions acting on behalf of the state.

If states have to rely only on themselves for their security, it follows that they must seek to preserve and accumulate their power. Power—that is, the ability of a state to get its way in the international arena when its interests or preferences clash with those of other states—derives from a variety of resources or capabilities. These may be tangible and measurable, such as economic and military resources, or intangible and unquantifiable, such as ideological and cultural resources. The European Union, for instance, believes that its security and that of its member-states depends primarily on its ability to attract other states to copy its own political, economic, and social model. Thus, its security strategy calls for "spreading good governance, supporting social and

REALISM An approach to the study of international politics that assumes that because the international system is anarchic, security is the major preoccupation of states. Peace rests primarily on deterrence, and the possibility of international governance is limited because states are reluctant to put constraints on their sovereignty.

NATIONAL INTEREST The goals a state pursues in the conduct of its foreign policy. The term is multi-faceted and, besides the quest for power and security, includes goals ranging from the pursuit of economic growth and wealth to the preservation and expansion of national culture.

---

[1] The most prominent representatives of the realist school are Carr (1939/2001), Morgenthau (1948), Waltz (1979), and Gilpin (1981). The work of Keohane and Nye (1977) and Keohane (1984) have shaped the liberal–internationalist school. For an overview of all theoretical approaches, see Sterling-Folker (2006).

political reform, dealing with corruption and abuse of power, establishing the rule of law and protecting human rights" (European Council, 2003). Tangible resources or capabilities are usually defined as constituting hard power, whereas intangible resources are usually referred to as soft power. Both are important.

Since all states are sovereign, they are equal from a legal point of view. Equal in law, however, does not mean equal in fact. Some states have more power than others. This means, as first pointed out by the Greek historian Thucydides some 2400 years ago, that "the strong do what they have the power to do and the weak accept what they have to accept" (Thucydides, 1972, p. 4). According to the realist school,[2] a world divided into sovereign states constitutes an **international system**. How power is distributed among states affects the way the system works, that is, how states tend to relate to one another in it (see Box 18-1, Power Distribution in the Classroom and at the Pub).

The modern international system dates from the treaties of Münster and Osnabrück signed in 1648. They are collectively known as the Peace of Westphalia and hence the system is sometimes referred to as the Westphalian system. The treaties put an end to the so-called wars of religion that had devastated Europe since the Protestant Reformation of 1517. Even more importantly, it recognized and incorporated the concept of state sovereignty, which had been developed by the French jurist Jean Bodin (1503–1596). Since then, sovereign states have been the major units of the international system. The distribution of power among the states in the system has undergone changes, however.

We distinguish among different types of international systems based on how power is distributed among states. Because each concentration of power is called a **pole**, we talk about multipolar, bipolar, and unipolar international systems (see Figure 18-1).

Multipolarity

From the Peace of Westphalia until the beginning of the twentieth century, the international system was **multipolar**, meaning that it contained at least four, and sometimes more than four, major poles.[3]

INTERNATIONAL SYSTEM
A concept referring to both the most important international actors (states and international governmental organizations) and the pattern of interactions among them. The latter depends primarily on how power is distributed among actors.

POLE A concentration of power in the international system. It could be a state or an alliance.

MULTIPOLAR SYSTEM
A type of international system containing four or more major powers.

---

[2] To be more precise, one should make a distinction between two trends within the realist school. Traditional realism looked at the behaviour of states in the international system the way Hobbes speculated about the behaviour of individuals in a state of nature. The most representative work of this phase is Morgenthau (1948). Later, a group of scholars, called neo-realists, concentrated on examining the dynamics of different types of international systems and their impact on the behaviour of states. Their most representative work is Waltz (1979).

[3] Note that scholars do not regard a tripolar system, of which there is no historical example, as a type of multipolar system. The reason is that the policy of balancing, which is the central characteristic of a multipolar system, would be difficult to pursue since two states could ally and prevail on the third. A tripolar system is therefore considered a distinct type and inherently unstable.

Power Distribution in the Classroom and at the Pub

A university class—a group of students and their lecturer—can be regarded as a type of system. Its components or units in this case are not states but individuals. When these individuals move out of their normal environment, say to a local pub to celebrate the end of the academic year, the distribution of power among them will change.

When the class meets in a classroom, power is concentrated in one individual, the lecturer, while the students are in a subordinate position. When they meet at the pub at the end of the academic year, their behaviour will change. Most likely it will be much less formal and predictable than in the classroom.

In a classroom, the lecturer will speak most of the time and occasionally call upon students who signal their desire to speak. While some students will be listening attentively, others will be letting their minds wander or even fall asleep. In the pub, the lecturer will no longer shape the interaction between himself or herself and the students and among the students themselves. Some students might continue debating the topic that occupied them in class, but they will be more willing to express their views and will not ask formal permission from the lecturer to intervene in the conversation. Others will strike up side conversations, maybe on a different topic.

Because the distribution of power among them has changed, the behaviour of the components of the system changes. Outside the classroom, power is no longer concentrated in one individual, the lecturer, but is equally distributed among all components of the system—students and lecturer. In the pub, the lecturer no longer has any official authority over students and consequently their behaviour is no longer constrained in the same way as in the classroom. The same thing happens in the international system. The range and type of foreign policy actions that states can prudently pursue in an international system in which power is more or less equally distributed will be much larger, and less predictable, than those they can pursue in a system in which power is concentrated in one state, for instance.

States in a multipolar system tend to maintain what is called a **balance of power**—that is, they tend to behave in such a way as to prevent the emergence of a dominant power. On the one hand, a state must try to preserve or even increase its power in order to guarantee its security. On the other hand, it must be careful not to be perceived by other states as representing a threat to them because in such a case it would eventually face a confrontation with them. States thus face what is called a **security dilemma**: they need power to feel secure, but the accumulation of power might undermine rather than increase their security if it leads other states to feel in danger and form an alliance to meet the perceived threat.

Power, in fact, can be augmented not only through an increase in capabilities, but also through the formation of alliances. Indeed, in a multipolar system, the formation of alliances plays a key role in the maintenance of a balance of power (see Box 18-2, Anatomy of Alliances).

BALANCE OF POWER
A situation in which no state is dominant in the global system.

SECURITY DILEMMA The dilemma that arises when states need power to feel secure, but their accumulation of power might undermine rather than increase their security if it leads other states to feel that they are in danger and form an alliance to meet the perceived threat.

FIGURE 18-1

TYPES OF INTERNATIONAL SYSTEMS

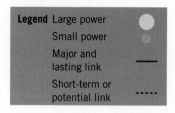

Legend Large power

Small power

Major and lasting link

Short-term or potential link

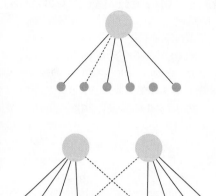

Unipolarity

One state (usually referred to as superpower or hyperpower) has a dominant or hegemonic position in the system.

Bipolarity

Two superpowers have a number of lesser powers as allies or satellites. This was the type of international system during the Cold War.

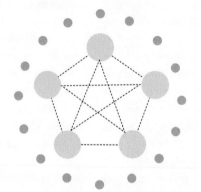

Multipolarity

Four or more great powers compete and co-operate with one another to make sure that none of them emerges as a superpower. Smaller powers do not play a significant role.

SOURCE: *Adapted from Rourke, J.T. (2003).* International Politics on the World Stage, *9th edition. Boston: McGraw Hill, page 65. Reproduced with the permission of The McGraw-Hill Companies.*

Bipolarity

The distribution of power in the international system may change. This can occur when some states are unable to continue producing the power resources and capabilities needed to sustain their position in the system, or when changes in technology such as the development of the nuclear bomb lead to the rise of new powers. At the end of World War II, the international system that had been multipolar since its inception became **bipolar**. The United States and the Soviet Union emerged as rival superpowers, so called because of their formidable nuclear arsenals, which no other country could match.

Their rivalry might have been compounded by the differences in their economic and political regimes—the United States was a liberal democracy with a free-market economy whereas the Soviet Union had a communist dictatorship with a command economy (an economy under the total control of the state). Realists, however, argue that in a bipolar system, the two superpowers are

BIPOLARITY A type of international system in which two superpowers compete with one another. The other states in the system fall within the sphere of influence of one or the other of the two superpowers.

BOX 18-2

Anatomy of Alliances

Alliances in the realist perspective are not based on friendship or a commonality of ideology or views but on interest. In other words, alliances are formed whenever they are needed to meet a common threat. There are two main characteristics of alliances:

1. To be effective as a mechanism to balance power, they must not be permanent but be able to shift according to needs.
2. If war becomes necessary to prevent one state from becoming dominant, the defeated state

is not eliminated from the map, but simply cut down to size and reinstated in the system so that it can participate in the formation of any new alliance that may become necessary to maintain a balance of power in the system. For instance, this is how European powers dealt with France after they had defeated Napoleon at the beginning of the nineteenth century.

bound to compete with one another. The other states in the system will fall within the sphere of influence of one or the other of the two superpowers, and thus two opposing blocs will be formed. Some states might be able to remain non-aligned, but competition between the two superpowers and their respective blocs will be the major issue in a bipolar system and overshadow all others. Each superpower will try to keep the other in check, and at the same time try to increase its own power. They will also try to recruit new members to their respective bloc, while trying to prevent others from joining the rival one.

In the past, the rivalries between Sparta and Athens in the ancient Greek city state system and between Rome and Carthage ended in a direct military confrontation and the defeat (and, in the case of Carthage, destruction) of one of the two rivals. This was not the case with the confrontation between the United States and the Soviet Union, which is why the period between 1946 and 1989 is known as the Cold War. Realists argue that two superpowers did not clash militarily because of the presence of nuclear weapons. As Robert Oppenheimer, one of the scientists who worked on the development of the atomic bomb in the United States, put it, the two superpowers were like two scorpions in a bottle—if one attacked the other, it must do so at the price of its own destruction (Oppenheimer, 1953, p. 529). While avoiding direct military confrontation, however, the two superpowers did fight each other by proxy. Military confrontation took place between some of their client states and even within one state that they were both trying to bring to their respective bloc, in the form of a civil war.

Unipolarity

The economic collapse of the Soviet Union and its subsequent political disintegration at the beginning of the 1990s left the United States as sole superpower

▶ At the end of World War II, the international system became bipolar. The United States and the Soviet Union emerged as rival superpowers: no other country could match their formidable nuclear arsenals. With the economic collapse of the Soviet Union, the United States became the sole superpower and the system transformed from bipolar to unipolar.

UNIPOLARITY An international system with a single superpower.

and transformed the system from bipolar to **unipolar.** Given its overwhelming military superiority and economic size, no other state is capable of matching the United States in terms of power.

On the one hand, a sole superpower has the ability to act unilaterally (that is, without the formal approval of international organizations and even in defiance of international law) to suppress any perceived threat to its status. On the other hand, it has an incentive to build as vast a consensus as possible around its choices. Thus, the sole superpower has an incentive to exercise power through authority (that is, through multilateral procedures that are perceived as legitimate by other states in the system) and persuasion rather than solely through coercion. In other words, the sole superpower must act as much as possible as a hegemon. The repeated use of coercion might solve problems in the short run, but in the longer run it will invite the formation of a countervailing bloc, and thus erode its position in the system as well as its security. It seems highly unlikely that France, Germany, Russia, and China, for instance, would be able to form a lasting coalition capable of rivalling the United States, at least in the short term. Yet their collective attempt to hold the United States back from intervening in Iraq in the winter of 2002–2003 provides an example of how a countervailing bloc might originate.

The Limits of International Co-operation

Realists recognize that during the twentieth century, **international governmental organizations (IGOs)** have come to play an increasingly more visible and important role in the international system. They also recognize that IGOs can, and often do, constrain the action of states.

Iraq, for instance, did not get away with its invasion and forced annexation of Kuwait in August 1990. Acting through its Security Council, the **United Nations (UN)** (see Box 18-3, The United Nations), the most visible and ambitious among IGOs, immediately called for Iraq's withdrawal (Security Council Resolution 660 of August 2, 1990). Since Iraq ignored this and subsequent resolutions, the Security Council, through Resolution 678 of November 29, 1990, called for Iraq's ousting by inviting member-states "to use all necessary means" (a euphemism for military force). Based on this resolution, a number of countries led by the United States assembled a military coalition, defeated Iraq in the 1991 Gulf War, and forced it to withdraw from Kuwait. What happened to Iraq, however, could not happen to any of the five permanent members of the Security Council, without whose vote no resolution could be approved. It would also be unlikely to happen to any state that is a close ally of any of the permanent five.

Realists also underline the fact that the UN is not a supranational body. Its members are sovereign states and the respect of state sovereignty is one of the core principles on which the UN is based. The UN, in the realist view, is simply a multilateral political arena that states have set up and in which they pursue their national interests, as they do in bilateral relations. Inevitably, therefore, the big powers enjoy as privileged a position within the UN as they do outside it.

IGOS AS TOOLS AND ARENAS   Realists point out that IGOs usually have been set up through the initiative of big powers. Their institutional structure and the way they work reflect the distribution of power in the international system, or at least the distribution that existed when they were founded. This means that the big powers occupy a key position and play a key role in the functioning of the organization. Thus, for example, the so-called Big Five, victors in World War II (the United States, the Soviet Union, Great Britain, China, and France), gave themselves a permanent seat on the UN Security Council as well as the ability to block any of its resolutions through a veto. In the International Monetary Fund, each country has a number of votes proportional to the reserve funds it has contributed, which means that the United States has 371 743 votes, corresponding to 16.74 percent of the total number of votes, while the microstate of Palau has 281 votes, corresponding to 0.01 percent.

According to the realists, IGOs are best regarded as tools that big powers create in order to help them fulfill their responsibilities for the maintenance of

INTERNATIONAL GOVERNMENTAL ORGANIZATION (IGO) An organization created by states to facilitate co-operation among them.

UNITED NATIONS (UN) An international governmental organization representing almost all of the world's states.

United Nations
www.un.org

International Monetary Fund
www.imf.org

BOX 18-3

The United Nations

The name United Nations was first used during World War II in the so-called Declaration by United Nations of January 1, 1942, when representatives of twenty-six countries pledged their willingness to continue fighting together against the Axis powers (Germany, Japan, Italy, and their allies).

In 1945, representatives of fifty countries met in San Francisco at the United Nations Conference on International Organization to draw up the United Nations Charter. The Charter, which is the international treaty that established the UN, was signed on June 26, 1945, and its ratification completed by October 24, 1945. The forerunner and model on which the United Nations was based was the League of Nations, an organization conceived in similar circumstances during World War I, and established in 1919 to promote international co-operation and to achieve peace and security.

The principal organs of the UN are:

- *The General Assembly*, which seats the permanent diplomatic representatives of all UN member countries (192 as of July 2010). The General Assembly can debate any topic that falls within the provisions of the Charter. Each member has one vote. Its decisions, called General Assembly Resolutions, have no legally binding force for member-states. They simply carry the weight of that body's opinion on major international issues and, since the General Assembly is the nearest thing the world has to a global Parliament, perhaps can also be said to carry the moral authority of the world community. The "perhaps" seems necessary since, according to Freedom House, only 88 UN member-states

(corresponding to 45.84 percent of the total) are full-fledged democracies; therefore, the views of a majority of UN member-states cannot necessarily be considered to represent the views of a majority of the world's people.

- *The Security Council*, which is the body responsible for peace and security issues. It is supposed to identify aggressors and situations that represent a threat to peace and decide on enforcement measures. It has fifteen members, five of which are permanent (the United States, Russia, China, Britain, and France). The other ten rotating members are selected for a two-year period. A Security Council resolution needs nine votes, including those of the five permanent members or their abstention, to be approved. This means that any of the permanent five can block a resolution, and with it the activity of the Security Council. Security Council resolutions are binding on all UN members, but this does not mean that they can always be enforced. In case of non-compliance on the part of the state to which the resolution is addressed, in fact, enforcement depends on the willingness of other UN members to heed the provisions of the resolution, which might also mean readiness to put some of their military forces at the UN's disposal.

- *The Secretariat*, which is the administrative organ of the organization. It has some eight thousand international civil servants headed by the secretary-general, who is elected for a five-year renewable term by the General Assembly and the Security Council.

international order. The role of IGOs is primarily to help foster international consensus, and thus provide legitimacy for an order that inevitably reflects more closely the interests and preferences of the big powers than those of other states in the system.

IGOs, once formed, might impose some constraints on the big powers, but such constraints are largely self-imposed. Even in the current unipolar system, the United States prefers to act either with the approval of the UN or at least with the political support of a coalition of allies. Realists, however, focus on the fact that when states perceive that a certain action is necessary for their own security, they will act—if they have the power to do so—even without UN approval, as the United States did in the spring of 2003 with regards to Iraq.

These cases might be infrequent but, according to realists, they prove that, in the final analysis, states are the main players in the system, not least because they have a monopoly on the use of force. The UN might authorize the use of coercion (whether in the form of economic sanctions or military intervention) against one of its members, but the UN has no ability to enforce its own resolutions and depends on the willingness of other member-states to do so. According to realists, therefore, states work with IGOs when it is in their interest to do so, but do not delegate responsibility for their own security to the UN or any other IGOs.

War and Peace in the International System

Realists view competition and rivalry, and hence conflict, as the normal mode of interaction among states. The fact that the international system is anarchic, moreover, means that there is no authority capable of taming conflict and that, consequently, the latter can easily lead to war. To maintain peace, one cannot, and need not in any case, replace competition and rivalry with co-operation and friendship or eliminate anarchy through the creation of a central authority in the system. For realists, the problem is how to make sure that competition and rivalry stop short of war. Their solution is to make war too costly an option for a would-be aggressor to choose. It follows that peace can be attained only through strength. Wolves cannot be turned into lambs, but they can be deterred from attacking if it is made clear to them that they cannot possibly prevail.

MAINTAINING PEACE IN MULTIPOLAR AND BIPOLAR SYSTEMS

What keeps peace in a multipolar system is the relatively equal distribution of power among its "great powers" (the term *great power* is usually used instead of *big power* when talking about multipolar systems), which deters any of them from taking aggressive action. If one great power increases its power capabilities and begins to be perceived as a threat by the other great powers, an alliance will be formed between two or more of the latter to counter the would-be aggressor. In other words, formation of flexible alliances keeps a balance of power among the great powers and hence maintains peace in the system.

The balance of terror, also known as the doctrine of mutual assured destruction (MAD), kept peace during the Cold War, or to be more precise, prevented a direct military confrontation between the United States and the Soviet Union. The two contenders had accumulated such vast arsenals of nuclear weapons that neither had an incentive to launch an attack since the initiator could not hope to survive a retaliatory strike from the adversary. War would mean mutual assured destruction, no matter who initiated it.

Global Security Institute
www.gsinstitute.org

Bulletin of the Atomic Scientists
www.thebulletin.org

The knowledge that peace rested only on the balance of terror or mutual assured destruction led the two states to sign the 1972 Anti-Ballistic Missile (ABM) Treaty, which purposely limited to two (later reduced to one) the number of strategic defence systems each country could deploy. Since ABM systems were supposed to neutralize incoming missiles while still in the air, it was thought that their deployment would destabilize the balance of terror and hence increase the probabilities of a nuclear exchange. The superpower that would succeed first in protecting all of its territory with such systems might in fact be tempted to launch an initial strike in the hope of being able to withstand the retaliatory one and escape from the exchange relatively unscathed.[4] The signing of the treaty was an implicit acknowledgment that maintaining peace did not depend on the simple desire for it—because in this case the two superpowers could have agreed to disarm completely. Peace rested instead on tying one's hands or, to put it differently, resisting any temptation one might have to resort to war by eliminating all advantages one might derive from an attack.

MAINTAINING PEACE IN A UNIPOLAR SYSTEM   It is more difficult to analyze how peace can be maintained in a unipolar system since such a system has been around only for about two decades, and hence there are few data on which to base any conclusion. It would appear, however, that in a unipolar system the sole superpower confronts a rather difficult task. On the one hand, it has primary responsibility for maintaining stability and order in the international system. On the other hand, any initiative the superpower takes for this purpose risks being perceived by other actors as nothing but the blatant pursuit of its national interests and hence an aggressive action.

The UN, for instance, could hardly undertake any military operation with respect to breaches of the peace, threats to the peace, or acts of aggression (the

---

[4] The United States has continued to work on the technology needed for ABM systems and intends to deploy a type of ABM system designed to protect its territory and that of its allies from the threat represented by the missiles of the so-called "rogue" states, mainly North Korea and Iran.

so-called Chapter 7 operations) if it could not rely on the willingness of the United States to provide its military forces for such operations. This means, however, that the United States has to be involved in all activities executing mandates under Chapter 7 of the UN Charter. As the United States also desires to retain command and control of its own troops in such operations, the impression is inevitably given that these interventions are not the duly authorized execution of a UN mandate but American wars.

The 1950–53 Korean War and the 1991 Gulf War are often thought of as American wars and not as UN-mandated interventions. When the UN mandate is acknowledged, the suggestion is often made that the United States coerced and cajoled the members of the UN Security Council to obtain its authorization in order to legitimize an intervention it was ready to undertake unilaterally. Things are even worse, of course, when the sole superpower takes initiatives without an explicit UN authorization, as was the case in 2003, when the United States and some of its allies invaded Iraq.

The provisional conclusion seems to be that in a unipolar system peace depends not only on the willingness of the superpower to intervene to maintain stability and order, but also on its ability to forge consensus around such order and the actions it undertakes to maintain it. In other words, a superpower in a unipolar system must act as a hegemon. Without willing partners and eager followers, **hegemony** deteriorates into domination and a dominant

HEGEMONY OR HEGEMONIC SYSTEM A type of unipolar system in which the superpower exercises power primarily through leadership and persuasion and thus creates a large consensus around its actions.

◀ The United States tries to persuade the UN Security Council to participate in the latest war.

power invites the formation of countervailing alliances, which leads to turbulence and war.

The Realist School and the Limits of Governance

Realists are skeptical about the possibility of global governance. They regard it at best as limited and based on the ability and willingness of big powers to take the lead in shaping and providing it. There are two reasons for such skepticism:

1. Realists focus primarily on the issue of security, which they assume to be the central concern of sovereign states and therefore unlikely to be completely delegated to any IGO, the UN included.
2. States are generally unwilling to put constraints on their sovereignty. Hence, the international system might change in terms of its distribution of power among states, but it is unlikely to change in terms of its organization of authority. In other words, the system is likely to remain anarchic.

For realists, therefore, the possibility of global governance depends on the ability of bigger powers (whether many, two, or one) to develop rules and institutions, which, while conferring privileges on them, also enjoy a minimum of legitimacy among lesser powers in the international system. For realists, in other words, global governance means at best the benign rule of hegemons.

LIBERAL–INTERNATIONALISM

LIBERAL–INTERNATIONALISM
An approach to the study of international politics that assumes that increased cultural and social connections as well as economic interdependence are leading to the emergence of a global civil society in which co-operation, the rule of law, and peace are valued and global governance is spreading both functionally and geographically.

INTERNATIONAL NON-GOVERNMENTAL ORGANIZATION (INGO) An international organization whose members are not states but rather representatives of civil society.

The liberal–internationalist school has a less sombre view of the consequences of international anarchy and is more optimistic about the possibilities of global governance. **Liberal–internationalism** differs from realism in a number of ways (see also Table 18-1):

- Liberal–internationalists believe that while states might still be the most important actors in the international arena, they are not the only ones. Other actors, such as IGOs, **international non-governmental organizations** (INGOs)—examples include Greenpeace and Amnesty International[5]—specific state institutions such as parliaments and bureaucracies, societal groups, multinational corporations (MNCs), and even individuals, play an important role.
- For liberal–internationalists, states and societies interact in many different issue areas—political, economic, social, and cultural. Each of these issue areas affects the others and none is dominant all of the time.

---

[5] INGOs are distinguished from IGOs because they are established and controlled by individuals and/or groups in civil society rather than by national governments.

TABLE 18-1
**MAJOR DIFFERENCES
BETWEEN REALISM
AND LIBERAL–
INTERNATIONALISM**

	REALISM	LIBERAL–INTERNATIONALISM
Key actors	States	States, IGOs, INGOs, groups, individuals
View of the state	Unitary actor, power seeking, moved by national interest	Network of different actors, competing national interests
View of the international system	Anarchic	Interdependence of actors, international society
Views on peace	Attainable through strength, deterrence, balance of power	Attainable through law
Views on possibility of international governance	Weak; provided by hegemonic powers	Strong; governance is spreading fast

For this reason, liberal–internationalists tend to speak of international relations (conceived of as a vast array of interactions between states and societies) as opposed to simply international politics (which suggests primarily power relations). Hence, national security, although important, cannot be examined in isolation.

- Liberal–internationalists do not regard states as unitary actors but as a network of different actors—individuals, socio-economic groups, and governmental institutions and departments—each with different interests, priorities, and preferences. These actors interact with similar actors across national borders on many different issue areas, each of which is of primary importance to some actors and of lesser importance to others. Unlike realists, liberal–internationalists do not believe that there is a constant national interest. Instead, there are many different, shifting, and competing national interests. Thus, even if everyone might agree on the primacy of national security (that is, the need to defend one's state from external threats), disagreements will inevitably occur concerning the means that should be used to defend oneself from such threats. Therefore, how a state behaves on the international scene is always the result of a bargaining process among competing domestic groups and institutions.
- Liberal–internationalists believe that individuals, groups, and institutions learn from their experiences and mistakes, and hence are capable of modifying their behaviour accordingly.

An International Society in the Making

Liberal–internationalists agree with realists that the world is made up of sovereign states and that there is no authority above them. They disagree, however, on the question of how significant anarchy is for the functioning of the international system and the behaviour of its members. According to them, the principle of sovereignty, which has traditionally regulated interstate relations, is constantly evolving.

The idea has recently gained ground, for instance, that sovereign states have a responsibility to protect their own citizens from avoidable catastrophes as well as to guarantee their enjoyment of human rights. As discussed in Chapter 2, when states are unwilling or unable to do so, that responsibility must be borne by the international community as a whole. Thus, under certain circumstances it is appropriate for a state, a coalition of states, or an IGO to take action—including military action—against another state in order to protect the latter's population or part of it. This is, of course, an important limitation on state sovereignty.

INTERDEPENDENCE   Liberal–internationalists also point out that the range of international interactions is so vast and its reach so deep that all actors in the international system are interdependent—that is, each is affected by the actions of others. The interdependence of actors, the fact that all of them face an increasing number of common challenges, such as environmental degradation, increasing global population, climate change, and the shrinking of the time–space dimensions due to technological advances in communication and travel, have slowly led, according to liberal–internationalists, to the development of a common identity, a sense of "we-ness" on planet Earth.

For all of these reasons, liberal–internationalists think that the international system is not an almost immutable structure constraining the behaviour of its units, but an evolving one. The international system does constrain the behaviour of its units, but the latter—states, groups, and individuals—are constantly modifying the system itself through their own ideas and actions. The increasing number and relevance of INGOs, moreover, is evidence of the rapid emergence of a vibrant global civil society, which will eventually give birth to a global and democratic political society. Thus, for liberal–internationalists the world is more than a system of independent sovereign states. It is also an **international or global society** in the making.

INTERNATIONAL OR GLOBAL SOCIETY The idea that the increasing number and importance of international interactions and the rising degree of interdependence is creating a global common identity and leading to the development of a global society.

Why States Co-operate

Liberal–internationalists point out that, although there are occasional exceptions, states usually comply with international law even in the absence of a central authority capable of enforcing it. They do so for two reasons:

1. States wish to do what is considered right and moral, and do not wish to lose prestige in the eyes of international public opinion.
2. Even more importantly, states have learned over time that it is in their interest to abide by international law because it is preferable to live in an ordered and predictable world rather than in a lawless, uncertain, and dangerous one.

Order and predictability allow states not to have to worry too much about the behaviour of other states, since it can be assumed that their behaviour will fall within the parameters allowed by the law.

JOINING IGOS   The desire to reduce uncertainty in interstate relations has pushed states to establish and join an increasing number of IGOs. Although IGOs can rarely enforce rules on states unwilling to abide by them, they are useful because they provide a context in which it is easier for states to co-operate with one another. That is, they can help to find a mutually satisfying adjustment in situations of conflicting interests or preferences.

Membership in IGOs does not weaken state sovereignty; it simply provides a different context in which to exercise it. More precisely, the context provided by IGOs reduces the costs of negotiating agreements by providing clear rules, better information, and opportunities for compromises and side payments through issue linkages. When different issues are on the table, in other words, states are more willing to make concessions on some if at the same time they get what they want on others. Membership in IGOs also improves the chances of voluntary compliance since the costs of defection (or non-compliance), in terms of reputation and credibility, are higher than they would be in a bilateral relationship. This explains why smaller powers like Canada seem to value membership in IGOs more than big powers do. Their sovereignty is enhanced because they gain more voice and hence influence, especially when acting in concert, than they would have in bilateral relationships with bigger powers.

The analysis of liberal–internationalists is undoubtedly very convincing when applied to the technical and even economic issue areas of international relations (Keohane, 1984). For example, an effective **international regime**—defined as a set of principles, norms, and procedures that regulates (usually, but not necessarily, through IGOs) international activity in a specific issue area—exists in the area of telecommunications. International trade also has an increasingly effective regime centred on the World Trade Organization (see Box 18-4, The World Trade Organization). Indeed, as interdependence has increased, so have the need for IGOs and international regimes and the eagerness of states to form them. The proliferation of IGOs and international regimes reinforces the habit of co-operation, and this, according to liberal–internationalists, bodes well for an increasingly peaceful future (Brown, 1995).

The Problem of Security and the Search for Peace

Unlike realists, who think that states can rely only on self-help for their security, liberal–internationalists believe that states can, and should, rely on IGOs and law. For them, state security is better achieved through a collective approach. The principle of **collective security** posits that states pledge to intervene on behalf of a member whose security is threatened by the aggressive actions of another state.

INTERNATIONAL REGIME
A set of principles, norms, treaties, and IGOs that regulates international activity in a specific issue area.

World Trade Organization
www.wto.org

COLLECTIVE SECURITY The principle that all members of the collectivity of states (or simply a number of them) are jointly responsible for the security of each of them and therefore pledge to intervene on behalf of a member whose security is threatened by the aggressive actions of another state.

The World Trade Organization

Based in Geneva, Switzerland, the World Trade Organization (WTO) is the international organization charged with managing trade relations among its one hundred and fifty-three members. At the same time, the WTO is an organization aimed at promoting free trade through the progressive dismantling of tariff and non-tariff barriers, a forum for governments to negotiate trade agreements, and a place and mechanism for them to settle trade disputes.

The WTO was established in 1995 but its origins date back to 1947, when twenty-three states negotiated a General Agreement on Tariffs and Trade (GATT) aimed at overcoming economic nationalism, which was perceived as one of the factors responsible for the outbreak of World War II, and promoting freer international trade. To this end, GATT sponsored a series of trade negotiations called "rounds" that reduced tariffs and non-tariff barriers and increased the total value of world exports from $53 billion in 1948 to $11 069 billion in 2004. At the end of the last successful round—the Uruguay round—the WTO was formed.

The current round of trade negotiations—the Doha round, launched in November 2001—has tackled trade in services and agricultural products, particularly the issue of subsidies that hurt the less developed countries. It is on this issue, however, that talks stalled in 2006. Trade liberalization is supposed to take place according to the principle of the "most favoured nation," which means that concessions granted to one WTO member must be extended to all other members. Exceptions exist, however, in the case of regional free-trade areas and in favour of less developed countries. Trade liberalization, moreover, can also be suspended when domestic industries face severe injury.

The WTO's top-level decision-making body is the Ministerial Conference, which is formed by member-states' ministers of international trade and meets at least once every two years. Day-to-day operations are conducted by the heads of national delegations, which meet as the General Council. Each member-state has the right to have one representative on the Council, whose work is supported by a Secretariat who is headed by a Director General and has about six hundred staff members.

An important innovation of the WTO as compared with GATT is its dispute-resolution mechanism. It provides fixed timetables for the various steps in the procedure, which means that any dispute is solved in a maximum of fifteen months. Disputes are submitted to the General Council, which then selects a panel to hear the dispute and submits a report for adoption. The procedure is repeated if there is an appeal of the first report. What is new with respect to the old GATT procedure is that disputes cannot be prolonged indefinitely and no party to a dispute can block or veto the adoption of a report. Now, a report can be blocked only if every member agrees to do so. The procedure has changed, in other words, from negative to positive consensus and, as a result, the international trade regime has been strengthened.

Among other things, the UN is a system of collective security, as was its predecessor, the League of Nations. The principle of collective security is also consistent with the realist reliance on deterrence to discourage aggression and maintain peace. If states can be certain that aggression will be punished by collective action, they will refrain from engaging in aggressive behaviour.

For a system of collective security to work, however, one must assume that participating members can always agree on establishing who the aggressor is when two states come to blows. Unfortunately, this is not always easy since states, much like individuals, are more likely to listen sympathetically to the arguments of friends than to those of foes. For collective security to work, one must also assume that participating members are always ready and willing to act against the aggressor. The historical record on this point is not too comforting. When Japan invaded Manchuria and Italy conquered Ethiopia in the 1930s, members of the League of Nations did not make good on their promise to intervene. Thus, the system of collective security effectively collapsed, leading to further aggression by Germany against Czechoslovakia and Poland and in the end to World War II.

Things did not fare any better with the UN Security Council during the Cold War, since the ideological and political rivalry between the United States and the Soviet Union effectively paralyzed the Council until the end of the Cold War. Only two acts of international aggression met with a collective response by the UN between 1945 and 1991:

- *The intervention against North Korea for its invasion of South Korea in 1950.* The UN was able to intervene only because, at the time, the Soviet Union was boycotting the meetings of the Security Council to protest the fact that Taiwan (the Republic of China) and not the People's Republic of China had a seat at the UN. Had the Soviet Union been present, it would almost surely have vetoed an intervention against its North Korean ally.
- *The 1991 intervention against Iraq following its invasion of Kuwait.* The end of the Cold War rekindled liberal–internationalist hopes that the UN could finally fulfill its collective security responsibility, but these hopes did not last very long.

As the debate over what to do with Iraq's protracted defiance of the disarmament terms imposed by UN Security Council Resolution 687 at the end of the 1991 Gulf War showed, disagreements among Security Council members resurfaced almost immediately and manifested themselves dramatically during the period immediately preceding the 2003 intervention against Saddam Hussein's regime. Such disagreements were due partly to the ambiguity of the evidence available to decide whether Iraq represented an immediate threat to regional and world peace, and partly to the desire of some permanent members of the Security Council—France and Russia, in particular—to try to constrain the range of action of the lone superpower.

Reducing the Likelihood of War:
The Role of Economic Interdependence

Some liberal–internationalists believe that, as a method of solving interstate conflicts, war is losing legitimacy, just as the duel has lost legitimacy as a way of solving interpersonal disputes (Mueller, 1989). Indeed, states formally renounced recourse to war for the solution of international controversies and as an instrument of national policy in 1928 when they signed the General Treaty for the Renunciation of War (better known as the Briand-Kellogg Pact, from the names of the French and American foreign ministers instrumental in negotiating it). The treaty had little practical effect but was significant at the level of ideas since it indicated a rapidly changing attitude toward state-sanctioned violence. Liberal–internationalists, moreover, argue that interests, rather than just sensibilities, are changing. The high degree of economic inter-dependence that characterizes liberal democratic states has made war a very costly mechanism to solve disputes because it entails economic disruptions, both commercial and financial, and hence economic costs for most warring states.

For example, France and Germany went to war three times in less than a century, but war between the two countries—or any two European countries, for that matter—would be unthinkable today given their high degree of eco-nomic interdependence. Indeed, economic interdependence has also led to the building of a network of common political institutions (the countries belong-ing to the European Union being those who have gone the farthest in this direction), which has made war an even more remote possibility.

Some liberals argue that the European Union (see Chapter 13) represents an example of a **postmodern state**—that is, a state in which the meaning and practice of sovereignty has been redefined since tools of governance are shared, foreign and domestic policies have become inextricably intertwined, and security is no longer based on control of borders and deterrence (Cooper, 2000). The idea is that the example of the European Union could be replicated in other parts of the world, until the entire world would become a postmodern state.

Given also the traditional liberal idea—whose origins go back to the German philosopher Immanuel Kant (1724–1804)—that states with liberal democratic governments are less likely than states with other types of gov-ernment to wage war, especially toward one another, liberal–internationalists believe that international peace can be promoted by fostering the development of free-market economies and democratic institutions around the world. Such a policy, however, if not pursued subtly and carefully, might lead, at least in some parts of the world, to resentment and resistance, and thus end up trigger-ing, rather than preventing, disorders and even military hostilities.

The Liberal–Internationalist Promise of Governance

Liberal–internationalists are more optimistic than realists about the possibil-ity of global governance. The world, they argue, does not resemble Hobbes's mythical state of nature. It also appears to be increasingly acquiring the fea-tures of a global civil society, as evidenced by a growing network of connec-tions across national boundaries (Lipschutz, 2000).

European Union
http://europa.eu

POSTMODERN STATE A state in which the meaning and practice of sovereignty have been redefined since tools of governance are shared, foreign and domestic policies have become inextricably intertwined, and security is no longer based on control of borders and deterrence.

These connections, which have traditionally linked organized groups, now involve single individuals thanks to the World Wide Web. One can see the slow but nevertheless sure emergence of a global consciousness that is increasingly bringing challenges to, and slowly eroding, the traditional primacy of the sovereign states. To be sure, the world does not yet have a central authority—and it might never have one. Yet it exhibits an increasing number of functional areas (for example, telecommunications or international trade) and geographic areas (for example, the European Union) in which the rule of law prevails. Such a trend, moreover, is self-reinforcing, and hence unlikely to be reversed.

OTHER THEORETICAL APPROACHES

Besides realism and liberal–internationalism, other approaches to the study of international politics include the radical and the constructivist approaches.[6] Largely drawing inspiration from the writings of Karl Marx, the radical approach (or approaches, since there are more than one) shares some characteristics with realism but also differs from it in significant ways. Radicals regard social classes and particularly transnational economic elites as the key actors in international politics. For radicals, in fact, states are simply agents acting in the interests of these elites. Likewise, the most significant feature of the international system is not that it is anarchic but its capitalist structure. For radicals, the international system is organized hierarchically between a developed, exploiting core and an economically exploited and dependent periphery. If for realists the existing international order reflects more closely the interests and preferences of the big power, for radicals it serves the interests of transnational economic elites. The difference between the two approaches is that, whereas realists limit themselves to describing the existing order and regard it as an inescapable feature of how international politics works, radicals also denounce it as inequitable and oppressive and argue that it should be changed. Unlike liberal–internationalists who regard liberal democracy as a carrier of peace, radicals argue the opposite. They believe that the free-market capitalist economy that typically characterizes liberal democracies is exactly what causes conflict and war, both nationally and internationally. For radicals, therefore, the possibility of global governance and the promotion of the common good rest upon overcoming the current liberal–capitalist system.

If radicals consider international politics as driven primarily by economic interests, constructivists regard it as being the result of ideas and norms, especially those of the social and political elites. The national interest

---

[6] On radicalism, see Cox (1987) and Wallerstein (1974–1980); on constructivism, see Wendt (1999) and Zehfuss (2002). There is also a feminist approach to the study of international relations; see, for instance, Enloe (1989) and Sylvester (1994).

is not determined by the fact that the international system is anarchic (realism) or results from the competing interests of domestic groups (liberal–internationalism), nor is it merely economic (radicalism). National interests are instead "constructed" by social and political elites and are based on their "identities"—that is, their beliefs about what is worth pursuing (values) and how it should be pursued (norms). Indeed, constructivists argue that power in international politics is based primarily on, and derives from, ideas and not material structures; as Wendt (1992) put it, "Anarchy is what states make of it." Consequently, constructivists argue that the behaviour of actors in the international system changes, sometimes even very quickly, as a result of interactions and socialization. It also follows that, given the increasing degree of international interactions brought about by economic globalization and the strength and attraction of liberal democratic ideas, the international system is constantly evolving. Most constructivists hold robust expectations about the eventual emergence of a reliable system of global governance for at least three reasons. First, since World War II, European states have rejected power politics and instead developed a system of widely shared norms. Second, these states have been relatively successful in projecting this new system in their immediate neighbourhood (Central and Eastern Europe). Third, these developments are expected to be replicated in other parts of the world. Overall, the major contribution of the constructivist approach—so far, at least—seems to be reminding students of international politics that ideas, norms, and culture are not simply dependent variables, as assumed by radicals in particular, but can play a significant and independent role.

FOREIGN POLICY ANALYSIS

All of these theoretical approaches capture some aspects of international relations. The liberal–internationalist analysis is certainly very effective in explaining the evolution of the international system in the twentieth century and is particularly convincing when applied to state relations in economic issue areas. The realist analysis is instead more effective in explaining security relations.

It should be remembered, however, that all of these theoretical approaches offer an explanation of how the international system as a whole works and of how states tend to behave in it over time. The approaches, however, do not claim to explain how states make specific foreign policy decisions. In order to do that, one needs to open the so-called "black box," that is, the complex processes by which decisions are made within states. In other words, one needs to move beyond the assumptions that the state is rational and unitary (realism) or rational and made up of different actors (liberal–internationalism) and examine in more detail how actors—individuals, groups, and institutions—work to arrive at specific decisions (see, for instance, Box 18-5, The U.S. Decision

BOX 18-5

The U.S. Decision to Intervene in Iraq

Iraq's protracted failure to comply with the disarmament terms imposed by UN Security Council Resolution 687 at the end of the 1991 Gulf War was met throughout the 1990s by a policy of containment centred on the imposition of economic sanctions. The terrorist attack of September 11, 2001, although not immediately related to Iraq, changed policy thinking, at least in the United States. The Bush administration came to the conclusion that Iraq's defiance needed a more resolute response, a military one if necessary (Pollack, 2002).

The official rationale provided by the U.S. administration for its new course of action was that Iraq, rather than disarming, might be enhancing its chemical and biological capabilities and even developing nuclear weapons. Given Saddam Hussein's past willingness to use chemical weapons against his enemies both at home and abroad, Iraq was perceived as representing a threat to regional and international security. To those critics (among whom were realist scholars) who argued that the Iraq threat did not appear imminent enough to justify pre-emptive military action, the Bush administration answered that the concept of "imminent threat" needed to be adapted "to the capabilities and objectives of today's adversaries." Prudence, in other words, called for action before terrorists or rogue states obtained weapons of mass destruction (WMD).

The rationale for action, however, was not entirely based on (realist) security considerations. It also rested on a good dose of (liberal–internationalist) interventionism. The Bush administration, in fact, also argued that the replacement of Saddam Hussein's dictatorship with a liberal democratic regime would bring similar changes in other countries in the region and thus promote peace regionally and internationally. The administration also justified the intervention in "humanitarian" terms. However, this argument was used sparingly since the Iraqi regime had committed its worst atrocities against Kurds and Shia Muslim groups between 1987 and 1991.

The option of moving from a policy of containment to one of regime change in Iraq had already been seriously considered by the Clinton administration at the end of the 1990s. Before September 11, 2001, however, it would have been difficult to convince the American public that a military intervention in Iraq was required for national security. After September 11, all that was needed was to emphasize the possibility that Saddam's WMD might be passed on to, or simply fall into the hand of, Islamic terrorists. Before the policy change could be implemented, the Bush administration had to overcome the skepticism of the State Department and some members of the uniformed military who thought that a military intervention in Iraq required a bigger allocation of military resources than senior people in the administration thought necessary (Wallack, 2006). Finally, before the new policy was implemented, the United States tried to obtain an explicit UN approval. When this failed, it moved to the second-best option, that is, building a large political alliance—the so-called "coalition of the willing"—and arguing, not unconvincingly, that its intervention was in line with existing UN Security Council resolutions.

to Intervene in Iraq). This is the task of a branch of the study of international relations called foreign policy analysis.

The study of foreign policy decisions involves examining variables at different levels of analysis. At the individual level, it examines the preferences of key decision-makers—for example, presidents or prime ministers and foreign ministers—as expressed, for instance, in parties' electoral platforms or speeches. These preferences, whether initiatives or responses to other states' actions, must pass various tests and go through a number of stages before they can become foreign policy decisions or choices.

At the systemic level, the foreign policy choices must be consistent with the structure of the international system—that is, they must be within the range of actions the state can comfortably take given the constraints represented by the distribution of power in the system. Thus, during the Cold War, a satellite of the Soviet Union or of the United States could not reasonably and safely pursue a foreign policy objective that was perceived as damaging to the interests of the superpower in whose sphere it orbited.

At the national level, implementation of foreign policy choices cannot require more power capabilities than the country has at its disposal. There is little practical use in giving oneself the objective, as Canada did when Lloyd Axworthy held the position of minister of foreign affairs, of promoting "human security," understood as the general improvement of the quality-of-life conditions experienced by individuals worldwide (Axworthy, 2003). Canada does not have the capabilities to improve "human security" worldwide; it could at best only bring attention to such an issue.

Preferences must also enjoy domestic consensus and hence be perceived as consistent with national identity and effective in promoting the country's national interest, however the latter might be defined. Before they become foreign policy decisions, they must also go through a complex policy process whose institutional characteristics depend on the type of political system of the country in question. In general, it can be said that the more liberal democratic, and hence open, the political system is, the more likely it is that the original preferences are adjusted and modified during the policy-making process. For all of these reasons, a democratic country's foreign policy has a built-in bias in favour of continuity. A new foreign policy is likely to emerge only in the wake of a major change in the structure of the international system and/or in the country's capabilities, two events that happen rarely.

Once decisions are made and implemented, they will have an impact on the external environment and on other states that are likely to react and hence begin the whole process anew.

Summary and Conclusion

This chapter has examined the difference between national politics and international politics: the fact that the respect of rules at the international level depends more on voluntary compliance on the part of states than on enforcement. It has also examined the differences between various theoretical approaches to the study of international politics, focusing in particular on realism and liberal–internationalism.

Realists argue that the fact that states are sovereign makes the international system anarchic and hence very similar to Hobbes's state of nature. In such a world, security, which is the major preoccupation of states, depends on self-help and hence on power. Peace depends on deterrence, namely making it clear to potential aggressors that the costs of aggression outweigh the potential benefits. Because states are jealous of their sovereignty, the possibilities of international governance are limited.

Liberal–internationalists argue that although the world is still politically organized in states, each of whose governments claims to be the ultimate authority over its territory and population, increased cultural and social connections and economic interdependence are leading to the emergence of a global civil society—one that values co-operation, the rule of law, and peace. A world political federation might never emerge, but international governance is spreading both functionally and geographically.

Overall, international politics raises difficult issues for the pursuit of the common good. Given the problems that the world faces (such as war, global climate change, global inequality, international terrorism, and the protection of basic human rights), it would be desirable for the common good to be considered, at least in part, in terms of the common good of humanity or of the entire planet.

However, the realist perspective alerts us to the continuing importance of national interests. The common good of humanity can, at best, be achieved only to a limited degree in an anarchic world. In contrast, liberal–internationalists have a more optimistic outlook on achieving the common good. In their view, the development of international organizations and agreements, along with increased interaction among the peoples of the world in areas such as trade and communications and the spread of democracy, make progress toward a more peaceful and prosperous world possible. But international organizations and trade agreements do not necessarily lead to the global common good, as they may reflect the interests of the powerful. As well, international governmental organizations are often not particularly democratic. Achieving the global common good, therefore, presents us with difficult challenges.

Key Terms

Anarchy 444

Balance of power 447

Bipolarity 448

Collective security 459

Global governance 444

Hegemony or hegemonic system 455

International governmental
   organization (IGO) 451

International non-governmental
   organization (INGO) 456

International or global society 458

International regime 459

Discussion Questions

1. What are the major differences between the realist and liberal–international approaches to the study of world politics? What are the implications for policy suggestions?

2. What are the policy options and the dilemmas a state confronts in trying to guarantee its own security?

3. Can the United Nations be considered a world government? How significant is the lack of a central authority in world politics?

4. Is a peaceful world a realistic objective? How might a more peaceful world be achieved?

Further Reading

Baylis, J., Smith, S., & Owens, P. (Eds.). (2007). *The globalization of world politics: An introduction to international relations* (4th ed.). Oxford: Oxford University Press.

Baylis, J., Wirts, J., & Gray, C.S. (Eds.). (2009). *Strategy in the contemporary world: An introduction to strategic studies*. Oxford: Oxford University Press.

Jackson, R., & Sørensen, G. (2006). *Introduction to international relations: Theories and approaches* (3rd ed.). Oxford: Oxford University Press.

Kennedy, P. (1987). *The rise and fall of the great powers: Economic change and military conflict from 1500 to 2000*. New York: Vintage Books.

Ravenhill, J. (Ed.). (2007). *Global political economy* (2nd ed.). Oxford: Oxford University Press.

GLOSSARY

Accountability Having to be responsible for one's actions and having to accept the consequences of failure to perform as expected.

Affirmative action/employment equity Policies designed to increase the proportion of persons from disadvantaged or under-represented groups in various positions.

Agenda setting The process by which potential problems come to the attention of and become a priority for policy-makers.

Alternative service delivery New methods of delivering government programs, such as the establishment of government service agencies that have considerable autonomy from the normal departmental structures and rules and the establishment of partnerships with business, other levels of government, and voluntary organizations to deliver services.

Anarchism An ideology that views the state as the key source of oppression and seeks to replace the state with a system based on voluntary co-operation.

Anarchy A situation in which there is no central authority.

Anthropocentrism The focus on human well-being that is at the centre of most political thought.

Asymmetrical federalism A version of federalism in which some provincial or state governments have a greater degree of self-government than others.

Authority The right to exercise power that is accepted by those being governed as legitimate.

Balance of power A situation in which no state is dominant in the global system.

Binational and multinational states States whose populations are composed of two or more nations.

Bipolarity A type of international system in which two superpowers compete with one another. The other states in the system fall within the sphere of influence of one or the other of the two superpowers.

Brokerage party A party that attempts to find compromises to accommodate a variety of interests (particularly regional and ethnic/cultural divisions) so as to try to build broad support across the country in a non-ideological manner.

Bureaucracy An organization in which people are hired and promoted based on their qualifications and merit, work is organized in terms of specialized positions, detailed rules and procedures are followed by all members of the organization, and there is a hierarchical chain of command so that those at the top can direct and supervise large numbers of people.

Cabinet The members of the political executive. The Cabinet in a parliamentary system is led by the prime minister, with many or most Cabinet ministers having the responsibility of heading a government department.

Cabinet secrecy The convention that the views expressed in Cabinet remain secret to enable full and frank discussion and maintain Cabinet solidarity.

Cabinet solidarity The convention in a parliamentary system that each member of the Cabinet is expected to fully support and defend the decisions and actions that Cabinet takes.

Cadre party A loosely organized party usually established by members of a legislative body with the support of local notables. Cadre parties are concerned primarily with electing members of the party to legislative bodies, rather than with building a strong, centralized, membership-based organization outside of the legislature.

Central agencies Organizations that try to provide direction and coordination to government. In Canada, the key central agencies are the Privy Council Office, the Prime Minister's Office, the Treasury Board, and the Department of Finance.

Charismatic authority Authority based on the perception that a leader has extraordinary or supernatural qualities.

Charlottetown Accord A 1992 package of proposed constitutional changes, including recognition of the inherent right of Aboriginals to self-government and major changes to the Senate. It was defeated in a referendum.

Charter of Rights and Freedoms As part of the Constitution Act, 1982, the Charter protects a variety of rights and freedoms. It is superior to ordinary legislation, explicitly allows the courts to invalidate legislation, and applies to the actions of all governments and organizations under the control of government.

Checks and balances A basic principle of the American presidential system in which each of the three branches of government is able to check the actions of the others so that no individual or institution becomes too powerful.

Citizenship The idea that a country's permanent residents are full members of the political community with certain duties and rights.

Civic nationalism Nationalism based on the shared political values and political history of those who are citizens of a country.

Civil disobedience Deliberate lawbreaking that accepts punishment by state authorities as part of the action.

Civil society The voluntary groups and organizations that are not controlled by the state.

Classical federalism A version of federalism in which the federal and provincial governments each concern themselves with their own areas of constitutional authority without infringing upon the areas of authority of the other level of government.

Classical liberalism A form of liberalism that emphasizes the desirability of limited government and the free marketplace.

Cleavage A social division that involves those associated with each grouping having a distinct collective identity and distinct interests that can lead to the development of organizations such as political parties that reflect the different sides of the social division.

Closure A procedure in a legislative body that cuts off debate if approved by a majority vote.

Coalition government A form of government in which two or more parties jointly govern, sharing the Cabinet positions.

Codified constitution A constitution whose major provisions are set out in a formal constitutional document or a set of constitutional documents.

Codified law A system of law based on the adoption of a comprehensive set of principles that judges use to determine the outcome of a particular case.

Cohabitation The sharing of power between the French president and prime minister that occurs when the Assembly is controlled by a party opposed to the president.

Collective responsibility The convention that the Cabinet as a group will defend, explain, and take responsibility for the actions of the government in Parliament.

Collective security The principle that all members of the collectivity of states (or simply a number of them) are jointly responsible for the security of each of them and therefore pledge to intervene on behalf of a member whose security is threatened by the aggressive actions of another state.

Colour Revolutions A series of essentially non-violent political movements against authoritarian governments in the Commonwealth of Independent States, whose members are all former Soviet republics, that adopted a colour or flower as their symbols. The Rose Revolution (Georgia, 2003), Orange Revolution (Ukraine, 2004) and Tulip Revolution (Kyrgyzstan, 2005) all overthrew authoritarian rulers and installed more democratic regimes.

Common good What is good for the entire political community.

Common law A system of law-based court judgments that have accumulated over many centuries.

Communism A system in which private property has been replaced by collective or communal ownership and everyone is free to take from society what they need.

Confederal system A system of governing in which sovereign states have agreed to delegate some of their authority to a joint government with limited authority while retaining their sovereignty.

Congress The legislative branch of the American government consisting of the House of Representatives and the Senate.

Conservatism A perspective or ideology that emphasizes the values of order, stability, respect for authority, and tradition, based on a view that humans are inherently imperfect, with a limited capacity to reason.

Consolidated democracies Countries with democratic governments that are stable, well accepted by both ordinary citizens and political elites, and unlikely to be overthrown.

Constitution The fundamental rules and principles by which a state is governed.

Constitution Act, 1867 An Act of the United Kingdom Parliament that established Canada by uniting the colonies of Canada (Ontario and Quebec), Nova Scotia, and New Brunswick. It also set out many of the features of Canada's system of governing.

Constitution Act, 1982 The Act that made the constitution fully Canadian, added the Charter of Rights and Freedoms to the constitution, and established procedures for amending the constitution.

Constitutional amendment A formal change to the constitution.

Constitutional conventions Fundamental principles that are consistently followed even though they are not contained in a legal document and are not generally enforceable in the courts.

Constitutional government A government that consistently acts in accordance with established fundamental rules and principles.

Constitutional monarchy A system of governing in which the monarch acts as official head of state but is strictly limited in power by the constitution.

Contentious politics The usually disruptive, direct, and highly conflictive ways that people advance their claims on elites, authorities, and opponents, ranging from peaceful political protest to wars and other lethal conflicts.

Co-operative federalism A federal system in which the two levels of government are jointly involved in developing, financing, and administering many government services.

Corporate state A system associated with fascist Italy in which business and labour work harmoniously to achieve goals established by the state to advance the good of the nation.

Cost–benefit analysis A technique that assesses whether, and to what extent, the monetary benefits of a policy exceed the costs.

Counter-insurgency A blend of military and political action taken by a government to defeat an insurgency. The tactics are usually described as a mixture of repression and reform.

Coup d'état A forcible seizure of power by the armed forces or occasionally the police.

Deep ecology An environmentalist perspective that views anthropocentrism as the fundamental cause of environmental degradation and advocates the cultivation of an environmental consciousness and a sense of oneness with the world that recognizes the unity of humans, plants, animals, and the Earth.

Deliberative democracy A political system in which decisions are made based on discussion by free and equal citizens rather than by elected representatives alone.

Democracy Rule by the people.

Democratic deficit In democratic countries, the difference between citizens' expectations of how democracy should work and how it actually works through existing government institutions, political organizations such as parties, and decision-making processes.

Democratic socialism The perspective that socialism should be achieved by democratic rather than revolutionary means, and that a socialist society should be democratic in nature with political rights and freedoms respected.

Democratic transition A process of change involving abandoning authoritarian government for democratic rule.

Dependency theory Dependency theory argues that underdevelopment results from unequal power relations between the centre (dominant capitalist countries) and the periphery (poor, dependent countries).

Deputy minister The executive head of a department of government appointed by the prime minister in consultation with the Clerk of the Privy Council Office. The deputy minister runs the department with oversight by the Cabinet minister who is the political head of the department.

Developing countries Countries that have not reached the same level of development as the richer, advanced countries.

Development A condition that involves the satisfaction of the basic needs of all of the people as well as the means for them to live fulfilling and productive lives based on the creation of a more diversified, sophisticated, and sustainable economy.

Devolution A system of governing in which the central government grants some legislative (law-making) powers as well as administrative responsibilities to one or more regional bodies.

Direct democracy A system in which citizens themselves make the governing decisions.

Disappearance The kidnapping by security forces of an individual who is never heard from again.

Dissolution The termination of Parliament followed by the holding of an election for the House of Commons.

Dominant ideology perspective on the mass media The view that the major media convey the values of the powerful and serve the interests of those who benefit from the status quo.

Ecocentrism The view that nature has intrinsic value and should not be valued only in terms of its use for human beings.

Ecofeminism A combination of environmentalism and feminism that views male dominance as the basic cause of the degradation of the Earth.

Electoral College A body that elects the president of the United States. Members of the Electoral College from each state are expected to vote for the presidential candidate who has won the most votes in their state.

Electoral democracies Countries in which representatives to the national legislature (and, where relevant, the president) are chosen in competitive multiparty and multi-candidate elections, all adult citizens have the right to vote in reasonably free and fair elections, and political parties are able to appeal to voters through the media and election campaigns

Electoral system The system used to translate the votes that people cast into the composition of the legislature and the selection of the government.

Electoral–professional party A political party whose dominant concern is winning elections and that relies on professional experts to market the party to voters.

Empirical analysis Analysis that involves explaining various aspects of politics, particularly by using careful observation and comparison to develop generalizations and testable theories.

Enlightenment An intellectual movement that developed in the mid eighteenth century, emphasizing the power of human reason to understand and improve the world.

Environmentalism A perspective based on the idea that humanity needs to change its relationship to nature so as to protect the natural environment and ensure that it can sustain all forms of life.

Equal rights The same legal and political rights for all persons.

Equality of opportunity The equal chance for all persons to get ahead in life, regardless of their backgrounds or characteristics.

Equality of outcome An equal distribution of wealth, income, power, and other goods.

Equalization payments Payments made by the federal government to try to ensure that different provincial governments are able to provide an equivalent level of services to their populations without resorting to excessive levels of taxation.

Ethnic nationalism Nationalism based on common ancestry along with the cultural traditions and language associated with a particular ethnic group.

European Union (EU) A unique system of governing in which many European countries have pooled some of their sovereignty while retaining their independence.

Executive dominance A parliamentary system that places considerable power in the hands of the prime minister and Cabinet through their ability to control the House of Commons, particularly in a majority government situation.

Export-led industrialization (ELI) A model of economic development with a capitalist system in which government and the biggest businesses work very closely to develop export industries. Government influences investments, provides incentives for exports, and can decide whether firms are allowed to export products.

Failed state A state that is unable to enforce laws, maintain order, protect the lives of citizens, or provide basic services.

Fascism An ideology that combines an aggressive form of nationalism with a strong belief in the naturalness of inequality and opposition to both liberal democracy and communism.

Federal system A system of governing in which sovereign authority is divided or shared between the central government and regional governments, with each deriving its authority from the constitution.

Feminism A perspective that views society as patriarchal and seeks to achieve full independence and equality for women.

Filibuster The use of various delaying tactics by those opposed to the passage of a particular piece of legislation.

Framing Selecting and highlighting some facets of events or issues, and making connections among them so as to promote a particular interpretation, evaluation, and/or solution.

Free rider problem A problem with voluntary collective action that results because an individual can enjoy the benefits of group action without contributing.

Free-market environmentalism The perspective that holds that guarantees of the rights of private property and a free-market economy are crucial to environmental protection.

Generational effect The effect on attitudes and behaviour of the views of different generations that persist throughout the life cycle.

Gerrymander The manipulation of the division of the country into electoral districts so as to benefit a particular party.

Global governance The process whereby a number of different actors (mainly states and international governmental and nongovernmental organizations) compete and co-operate to provide a certain degree of order and predictability to relations among states.

Globalization The processes that are increasing the interconnectedness of the world.

Government The set of institutions that makes decisions and oversees their implementation on behalf of the state for a particular period of time.

Governor general The person who carries out the duties and responsibilities of the monarch at the national level in Canada.

Gross domestic product (GDP) The market value of goods and services produced in a country, excluding transactions with other countries.

Guerrilla warfare A form of highly political warfare built around lightly armed irregulars who oppose a government and use hit-and-run tactics and political work to take power.

Head of government The person who heads the executive side of government and is usually responsible for choosing the Cabinet. In Canada, the prime minister is the head of the Canadian government while the heads of provincial governments are known as premiers (in Quebec, *premier ministre*).

Head of state In a parliamentary system, the head of state is an important but largely ceremonial position, but has the responsibility to ensure that a legitimate government is in place.

Hegemony or hegemonic system A type of unipolar system in which the superpower exercises power primarily through leadership and persuasion and thus creates a large consensus around its actions.

Historical materialism The view that historical development and the dynamics of society and politics can be understood in terms of the way society is organized to produce material goods.

Holocaust The systematic extermination of six million European Jews by the Nazis during World War II.

Horizontal accountability Sometimes called the requirement of government agencies to report sideways. That is, it refers to how government institutions check the performance of other government institutions to ensure that they work in the public interest.

House of Commons The elected chamber of Parliament, with each member representing a particular electoral district.

House of Commons committees Committees composed of government and opposition party members in proportion to their party's strength in the House of Commons; they provide detailed examination of proposed legislation and often suggest modifications to that legislation.

House of Representatives The lower chamber of the American Congress, elected for a two-year term from districts of approximately equal population size.

Human Development Index (HDI) An annual index for most countries, calculated by the United Nations Development Programme and based on literacy and education, life expectancy, and per capita GDP.

Impeachment A process by which a president and other public officials can be removed from office after being accused of criminal behaviour and convicted by a legislative body.

Import substitution industrialization (ISI) An economic development model that involves creating an industrial sector by placing tariffs on imported industrial products.

Incremental model A policy-making model that suggests that the policy process usually involves making minor changes to existing practices.

Individualist perspective A perspective that views human beings as acting primarily in accordance with their own interests.

Infotainment The merging of information and entertainment in news and public affairs programming of the mass media, particularly television.

Initiative A procedure that gives citizens the right, by obtaining a sizable number of signatures on a petition, to have a proposition that they have drafted put to a vote by the electorate for approval.

Inside strategies Strategies in which interest group leaders develop close contacts with key decision-makers in government and the public service in order to influence public policies.

Institutionalized interest group A group that has developed a formal organization, including such features as a well-established membership base, paid professional staff, permanent offices, and the capability to keep its members and the public aware of its views and activities.

Insurgency A rebellion or revolt, especially one employing the tools of guerrilla warfare.

Interest group An organization that pursues the common interests of groups of people, particularly by trying to influence the development, adoption, and implementation of public policies.

International financial institution (IFI) An organization that has some ability to affect the global economic system; for example, the International Monetary Fund and the World Bank.

International governmental organization (IGO) An organization created by states to facilitate co-operation among them.

International non-governmental organization (INGO) An international organization whose members are not states but rather representatives of civil society.

International or global society The idea that the increasing number and importance of international interactions and the rising degree of interdependence is creating a global common identity and leading to the development of a global society.

International regime A set of principles, norms, treaties, and IGOs that regulates international activity in a specific issue area.

International system A concept referring to both the most important international actors (states and international governmental organizations) and the pattern of interactions among them. The latter depends primarily on how power is distributed among actors.

Iron law of oligarchy A generalization that claims that all organizations, even those that appear democratic, inevitably become dominated by a small group of leaders.

Islamism The perspective often associated with those seeking to purge "degenerate" foreign elements from Muslim society and base government on Islamic principles.

Issue-oriented interest group An interest group that spontaneously develops to express the views of people on a particular issue, concern, or grievance.

Judicial activism The term used when the courts are active in invalidating legislation and government actions that are inconsistent with the constitution.

Judicial review The authority of the courts to strike down legislation or governmental actions that the courts deem to be in violation of the constitution.

Keynesian economic policies The idea that government can smooth out the ups and downs of the free-market economy by stimulating the economy when private business investment is low and cooling down the economy when excessive investment is creating inflation.

Laissez-faire economic system A system in which privately owned businesses, workers, and consumers freely interact in the marketplace without government interference.

Left The general ideological position associated with advocacy of greater social and economic equality, laws based on universal human rights rather than traditional morality, and opposition to state support for religious institutions.

Legal–rational authority The right to rule based on legal rules and procedures rather than on the personal qualities or characteristics of the rulers.

Legitimacy Acceptance by the members of a political community that those in positions of authority have the right to govern.

Leninism The version of Marxism that includes the belief that the capitalist system can be overthrown only by force, by means of a tightly disciplined party controlled by a revolutionary vanguard.

Liberal democracy A political system based on the ideas that the power and scope of government should be limited, that government should observe the rule of law, and that the rights of the people should be protected.

Liberal feminism A version of feminism that advocates equal opportunities for women in such areas as education and employment as well as equal legal and political rights.

Liberal, representative democracy A political system that combines a high level of individual freedom and the election of representatives to a legislative body.

Liberal–internationalism An approach to the study of international politics that assumes that increased cultural and social connections as well as economic interdependence are leading to the emergence of a global civil society in which co-operation, the rule of law, and peace are valued and global governance is spreading both functionally and geographically.

Liberation Freeing the human potential that has been stifled by the organization and values of society.

Libertarian perspective on the mass media The idea that if the mass media are free from government control and regulation, individuals will be able to obtain and assess the information and ideas they want.

Lieutenant-governor The person who carries out the duties and responsibilities of the monarch at the provincial level in Canada.

Life cycle effect The effect of one's age on one's attitudes and behaviour. As people grow older, their attitudes and behaviours may change due to changing circumstances (such as education, marriage, employment, and retirement) related to age.

Lobbying An effort to persuade legislators, executives, or public officials, particularly through direct personal contact, to adopt and implement policies or decisions favoured by an individual, business, or group.

Majority government The government formed when the prime minister's party has a majority of the members of the House of Commons; thus, a single party forms the government.

Marginalization Exclusion from the mainstream.

Mass party A party that draws its support from a regular dues-paying membership and features a strong party organization outside of the legislature.

Meech Lake Accord A 1987 package of proposed constitutional changes that was not passed. It contained controversial provisions, including the recognition of Quebec as a "distinct society."

Military dictatorship An undemocratic government run by the military.

Ministers of state Cabinet ministers who are not responsible for a particular government department.

Minority government A single party governs, but that party does not have a majority of members in the House of Commons. Thus, a minority government needs to gain the support of one or more other parties to pass legislation and to stay in office.

Mixed member proportional (MMP) system An electoral system in which voters cast one vote for the party they prefer and one vote for the candidate they prefer. Some legislators are elected to represent particular electoral districts based on gaining the most votes in that district, while others are elected based on the popular vote received by their parties.

Modernization theory A development model that views the traditional values, practices, and institutions of Third World countries as the basic cause of underdevelopment. To develop, poor countries should change their cultural outlook, social structure, economic organization, and political system based on the model of the advanced Western societies.

Monetarism An economic perspective based on the view that government's role in the economy should be largely restricted to controlling the supply of money.

Multiculturalism The idea that different cultures within a country should be recognized and respected and provided with encouragement and support to help them retain their cultures and traditions.

Multiparty system A political party system featuring several parties that are significant actors in the competition for political power.

Multipolar system A type of international system containing four or more major powers.

Nation A group of people who have a sense of common identity and who typically believe they should be self-governing within their homeland.

National interest The goals a state pursues in the conduct of its foreign policy. The term is multi-faceted and, besides the quest for power and security, includes goals ranging from the pursuit of economic growth and wealth to the preservation and expansion of national culture.

National self-determination The idea that nations should have the right to determine their political status, including choosing to have their own sovereign state.

Nationalism The idea that the nation-state is the best form of political community and that a nation should have its own self-governing state.

Nation-state A sovereign state based on people living in a country who share a sense of being a member of a particular nation.

Nazism A version of fascism associated with Adolf Hitler, the Nazi leader of Germany, emphasizing racial conflict and the superiority of the "Aryan race."

Negative freedom The absence of physical and legal restraints on the actions of individuals.

Neo-corporatism A political system in which the state actively collaborates with selected major interests (particularly the national organizations of business and labour) to seek a consensus concerning the country's major economic and social policies.

Neo-fascism A revival of fascism in contemporary times.

Neo-liberalism A perspective based on a strong belief in the free marketplace and opposition to government intervention in the economy.

Neo-Marxist theory A perspective that views politics as reflecting the conflicts that result from the way society is organized to produce goods. Public policies in a capitalist society will reflect the unequal power relations between the dominant capitalist forces and subordinate groups.

New public management The adoption of the practices of private business in the administrative activities of government.

New Right A perspective that combines, in various ways, the promotion of free-market capitalism and limited government and traditional cultural and moral values.

New style of citizen politics A set of changes including greater citizen activism, the questioning of authority, the development of new political parties and new social movements, the raising of new types of issues, and the development of more liberal social values.

News management The controlling and shaping of the presentation of news in order to affect the public's evaluation of news stories.

Non-confidence motion A motion put forward by opposition members in a legislature expressing a lack of confidence in the government. If passed, the prime minister is expected to either resign or request that an election be held.

Non-governmental organization (NGO) A private organization that often delivers public services but is independent of government. NGOs have been very active in international development activities.

Normative analysis Analysis that includes examining ideas about how the community should be governed and what values should be pursued through politics.

North The rich, developed countries.

Notwithstanding clause A provision in the Charter of Rights and Freedoms that allows a legislative body to explicitly declare that a particular law (related to some parts of the Charter) shall operate *notwithstanding* the provisions of the Charter. Such a declaration is only effective for five years, although it can be re-enacted as often as is desired.

Official Development Assistance (ODA) Aid to the poorer countries given by the governments of the richer countries.

Official opposition The party with the second-highest number of seats in the House of Commons; the official opposition leads off the questioning or criticism of government every day that the House is sitting.

One-party dominant system A party system in which a single party rules for long periods of time and the opposition parties are not likely to gain the support needed to successfully challenge the dominant party for control of the government.

Outside strategies Strategies in which interest group leaders appeal to the public for support and mobilize members in order to put pressure on decision-makers concerning public policies.

Pacted democracy A democratic transition produced by a deal between non-democratic elites from the old regime and democratic reformers.

Parliamentary sovereignty A basic principle of the British system of governing, recognizing Parliament as the supreme law-making body such that the courts cannot invalidate an Act of Parliament.

Parliamentary system A system of governing in which there is a close interrelationship between the political executive (prime minister and Cabinet) and Parliament (the legislative or law-making body). The executive is generally composed of members of the House of Commons (the elected parliamentary body) and must maintain the support of the House of Commons.

Participatory democracy A democratic system in which all citizens are able to participate directly in the decisions that affect their lives.

Party caucus A closed-door meeting of the party's parliamentary members.

Party convention A meeting of delegates from party constituency associations as well as the party's legislators and party officials.

Party dictatorship An undemocratic political system that is controlled by one party. The most familiar examples are found in communist political systems.

Party discipline The expectation that members of each party will vote in accordance with the position that the party has adopted in caucus.

Party identification A long-term psychological attachment to a particular political party.

Patriarchy A system in which power is in the hands of men and many aspects of women's lives are controlled by men.

Personal dictatorship An undemocratic government dominated by a single individual. Saddam Hussein's Iraq was a classic example of this kind of system.

Personalistic leader A political leader whose claim to rule is based on some presumed inherent personal qualities. It also implies a government in which all important decisions are made by the leader and according to the leader's wishes.

Personalistic party A party established to promote the election of a particular individual as prime minister or president.

Plebiscitary democracy A form of democracy in which citizens have greater control through the use of such devices as referendums, initiatives, and recall elections.

Pluralist perspective A perspective that views public policies as the outcome of competition among a wide variety of organized groups that seek to protect and promote the interests of their members with no group having a dominant influence.

Pluralist system A political system in which a large number of groups representing a wide variety of interests are able to influence the decisions of government. Government tries to satisfy as many groups as possible and no group has a dominant influence on government.

Pole A concentration of power in the international system. It could be a state or an alliance.

Policy analysis Analysis that involves evaluating existing policies and assessing possible alternatives to deal with particular problems.

Policy cycle The analysis of the policy process as a continuous cycle of stages, with policies continually undergoing modification in response to evaluations of the policy.

Policy entrepreneur Someone who is ready to push a pet policy proposal whenever an opportunity arises.

Policy network The governmental and non-governmental actors that participate in the development of policies in particular areas.

Political agenda The issues that are considered important and given priority in political deliberations.

Political conflict A state of opposition, usually involving groups and the state, over something government is doing or proposes to do.

Political culture The fundamental political values, beliefs, and orientations that are widely held within a political community.

Political efficacy The attitude that individuals can have an impact on political decisions and that government is responsive to what people want.

Political ideology A package of interrelated ideas and beliefs about government, society, the economy, and human nature that inspire and affect political action. Each ideology provides a different perspective that is used to understand and evaluate how the world actually works. Most ideologies also provide a vision of what the world should be like and propose a means of political action to achieve their objectives.

Political institutions Behavioural patterns or established organizations associated with politics and governing.

Political opportunity structures (POS) The openings that political institutions and processes offer to or withhold from movements.

Political party An organization that has a central role in the competition for political power in legislative bodies, and in governing.

Political protest Oppositional political action that takes place outside formal channels, generally seeking to have government make significant changes in its policies.

Political science The systematic study of politics.

Political socialization The processes by which the values, attitudes, and beliefs of the political culture are transmitted to members of the political community.

Political violence The use of physical force with a political objective.

Politics Activity related to influencing, making, or implementing collective decisions for a political community.

Polyarchy A political system in which there is open competition for power and government actions are freely contested.

Positive freedom The capacity to do something worth doing or enjoying.

Postmaterialist theory A theory that modern societies are undergoing a fundamental change in value priorities because generations that grew up in the relative security and affluence of the Western world since World War II are more likely to give priority to postmaterialist values than to materialist values.

Postmaterialist values Non-materialist values such as freedom of expression, participation, concern about the quality of life, and appreciation of a more beautiful environment.

Postmodern state A state in which the meaning and practice of sovereignty have been redefined since tools of governance are shared, foreign and domestic policies have become inextricably intertwined, and security is no longer based on control of borders and deterrence.

Power The ability to achieve an objective by influencing the behaviour of others, particularly to get them to do what they would not have otherwise done.

Preferential voting An electoral system in which voters rank candidates in order of preference. If no candidate has a majority of first preferences, the candidate with the least votes is dropped and the second preferences of those who voted for that candidate are added to the votes of other candidates. This process continues until one candidate has a majority.

Prerogative powers Powers of the monarch that have not been taken away by Parliament. These are also known as reserve powers.

Presidential system A system of governing in which the president and Congress each separately derive their authority from being elected by the people and have a fixed term of office.

Presidential veto The ability to prevent the passage of a bill. The president of the United States has the authority to veto laws passed by Congress, although this veto can be overridden by a two-thirds majority in each body of Congress.

Primary election A state-run election in which citizens select the candidates for the party they support prior to the general election.

Prime Minister's Office (PMO) The office that provides support and political advice to the prime minister.

Prime ministerial government The view that the prime minister has become the dominant member of the political executive, rather than "first among equals" in the Cabinet.

Private law Law that deals with the relationships among individuals, groups, and businesses that are primarily of private interest rather than of general public interest.

Private members Ordinary members of the House of Commons who are not in the Cabinet.

Privy Council Office (PCO) An administrative structure that is directly responsible to the Canadian prime minister, has a central role in organizing the Cabinet and trying to coordinate and direct the activities of government, and provides policy advice to the prime minister.

Programmatic party A party that has a distinct ideological perspective or a coherent set of policy goals that are consistently followed over time.

Proportional representation (PR) system An electoral system in which the proportion of seats a party receives in the legislature reflects the proportion of votes it has obtained.

Prorogation The suspension of Parliament and its committees by the governor general at the request of the prime minister. Prorogation (unlike an adjournment) ends a session of Parliament such that the work of committees is ended and bills that have not been passed have to be reintroduced unless Parliament in the next session agrees otherwise.

Protectionist economic policy An economic policy that uses high tariffs to ensure that domestic firms have an edge when competing with foreign companies. Import substitution industrialization is an example.

Public choice theory A perspective based on the assumption that all political actors are rationally attempting to maximize their own individual interests or preferences. Public policies will generally reflect the choices made by voters.

Public interest group A group that seeks to achieve goals that the group views as being for the good of the community as a whole rather than specific benefits for their members.

Public policy A course of action or inaction chosen by public authorities to address a given problem or interrelated set of problems.

Purchasing Power Parity (PPP) A measure of per capita income that shows the purchasing power of an income, instead of its worth at current exchange rates.

Radical feminism A version of feminism that views society as based fundamentally on the oppression of women and seeks to liberate women through the fundamental transformation of social institutions, values, and personal relationships.

Rational–comprehensive model of the policy process A policy-making model that involves establishing clear goals to deal with a problem, examining all possible alternatives, and choosing the best alternative. The policy is then monitored and evaluated to assess whether the goals have been achieved, and changed if necessary.

Reactionary A conservative who favours a return to the values and institutions of the past.

Realism An approach to the study of international politics that assumes that because the international system is anarchic, security is the major preoccupation of states. Peace rests primarily on deterrence, and the possibility of international governance is limited because states are reluctant to put constraints on their sovereignty.

Reasonable limits clause A provision in the Charter of Rights and Freedoms that allows for "reasonable limits" to be placed on rights and freedoms, provided that the limits can be "demonstrably justified in a free and democratic society."

Recall A procedure that allows citizens to remove representatives from office. By gaining a sufficient number of signatures on a petition, citizens can require that their representative seek re-election before the term of office is over.

Referendum A vote by citizens on a particular issue or a proposed law.

Reform environmentalism A perspective that views the solution to environmental problems primarily in terms of better science, technology, and environmental management.

Reform liberalism A version of liberalism that combines support for individual freedom with a belief that government action may be needed to help remove obstacles to individual development.

Regime violence Political violence used by a government against its citizens, generally as a way to repress dissent and keep order.

Representative bureaucracy A bureaucracy that reflects the characteristics of society, particularly by trying to ensure that all levels of the public service have a proportion of women and various disadvantaged minority groups similar to that of the population as a whole.

Responsible government A governing system in which the political executive (the prime minister and Cabinet) is accountable to Parliament for its actions and must retain the support of the elected members of Parliament to remain in office.

Revolution The use of violence to overthrow a government, especially when the overthrow is followed by rapid, thoroughgoing social, economic, and political restructuring.

Right The general ideological position associated with opposition to imposing greater social and economic equality and with maintaining traditional (usually religious-based) moral values and institutions.

Rule of law The idea that people should be subject to known, predictable, and impartial rules of conduct, rather than to the arbitrary orders of particular individuals. Both the rulers and the ruled should be equally subject to the law.

Runoff election An election held if no candidate receives a majority of votes; generally, only the top two candidates appear on the ballot to ensure that the winning candidate has a majority of the votes cast.

Secessionist A person who favours separation of a territory from an existing state.

Security dilemma The dilemma that arises when states need power to feel secure, but their accumulation of power might undermine rather than increase their security if it leads other states to feel that they are in danger and form an alliance to meet the perceived threat.

Segregation The legal separation of blacks and whites, particularly in the southern United States.

Selective incentive A particular benefit that is made available to members of an interest group but is not available to the public as a whole.

Self-interest group An interest group whose primary objective is to promote the interests of the group and its members and to seek benefits that are primarily or exclusively for their members.

Semi-presidential system A system of governing in which an elected president shares power with a prime minister and Cabinet, who usually need to retain the support of the elected legislature.

Senate (Canada) The upper chamber of Parliament, appointed on the recommendation of the prime minister. Senators hold their positions until age seventy-five.

Senate (United States) The upper chamber of Congress. Two senators are elected by voters in each state for a six-year term.

Separation of powers A basic feature of presidential systems in which the executive, legislative, and judicial branches of government are separate from each other, with each having different personnel and different bases of authority.

Single member plurality (SMP) system An electoral system in which voters in each electoral district elect a single representative to the legislature. The candidate with the most votes is elected, even if that candidate did not receive the majority of votes.

Single transferable vote (STV) system An electoral system in which voters mark their preferences for candidates in a multimember electoral district. Candidates who receive a certain proportion of the vote are declared elected. The second preferences of voters that are surplus to what the winning candidates need are then transferred to candidates who have not reached the quota. The process is continued until all seats in the district are filled.

Social Darwinism The use of Darwin's theory of evolution to argue that competition and conflict allow humanity to evolve through the "survival of the fittest."

Social ecology A perspective that views social, economic, and political relationships of hierarchy and domination as the cause of both human and environmental problems.

Social movement A network of groups and individuals that seeks major social and political changes, particularly by acting outside of established political institutions.

Social responsibility perspective on the mass media The view that the media have a responsibility to the public. Freeing the media from government regulation and control does not necessarily result in the public interest being served.

Social revolution A revolution that changes not just who governs but also how a state is organized and how its society and economy are structured.

Socialism An ideological perspective based on the view that human beings are basically social in nature and that the capitalist system undermines the co-operative and community-oriented nature of humanity. Socialism advocates the establishment of an egalitarian society.

Socialist feminism A version of feminism that views women as oppressed by both the male-dominated character of society and the capitalist system. The liberation of women is connected to the transformation of capitalism into a more co-operative and egalitarian socialist system.

South Less developed, poorer countries.

Sovereignty The principle that states are the highest authority for their population and territory and are not subject to any external authority.

State An independent, self-governing political community whose governing institutions have the capability to make rules that are binding on the population residing within a particular territory.

State-centred theory A perspective that views public policies as reflecting, to a considerable extent, the preferences and priorities of those in important positions of authority within various state institutions.

Streams and windows model of the policy process A policy-making model that views the policy process as fluid. Changes in the identification of problems, policy proposals, and political circumstances create windows of opportunity in which policy entrepreneurs may successfully push their pet proposals.

Structural adjustment program (SAP) A program administered by international financial institutions, which offers loans at very low interest rates to governments facing problems paying their debt if they adopt the programs endorsed by the Washington Consensus.

Subsidiarity The idea that decisions and actions should be carried out, if possible, by the level of governing that is closest to citizens.

Suicide terrorism A form of terrorist violence in which the attacker's object is to kill her- or himself as well as the target.

Sustainability Maintaining the integrity of ecosystems by ensuring that renewable resources are not being used at a rate that exceeds the ability of ecosystems to regenerate them, developing renewable substitutes to replace the consumption of non-renewable resources, and ensuring that the emission of pollutants does not exceed the ability of the ecosystem to handle them without damage.

Sustainable development Meeting the needs of the present without compromising the ability of future generations to meet their own needs; it involves development to ensure that the needs of the poor are fulfilled and protecting the environment for the well-being of future generations.

Tariff A tax on imports.

Terrorism The deliberate use of violence designed to induce fear in a population in order to achieve a political objective.

Theocratic dictatorship An undemocratic state run by religious elites. The best contemporary example is Iran.

Third World Less developed countries.

Traditional authority Authority based on customs that establish the right of certain persons to rule.

Transparency In government, transparency exists to the extent that its operations are visible to the people. People need access to information and to understand how and why governments make decisions to be able to hold governments accountable.

Treasury Board A permanent Cabinet committee with its own staff and minister that plays a major role in governing in Canada because of its responsibility for the expenditure and management practices of government.

Two-party system A party system in which two major parties contend to control the government. Two-party systems are competitive in the sense that a single party does not govern for a lengthy period of time.

Underdeveloped countries A term often used to describe Third World countries.

Unipolarity An international system with a single superpower.

Unitary system A system of governing in which sovereign authority rests with the central government; regional and local governments are subordinate.

United Nations (UN) An international governmental organization representing almost all of the world's states.

Universal suffrage The right of all adult citizens to vote regardless of such characteristics as gender, ethnicity, wealth, or education.

Utilitarianism The view that humans seek to maximize pleasure and minimize pain and that government should act to achieve the greatest happiness for the greatest number.

Valence issues Issues on which there is a general consensus.

Vertical accountability The various ways in which citizens, civil society, and the media seek to ensure that government institutions and public officials work to seek the common good.

Washington Consensus A series of policies put together by the International Monetary Fund and the World Bank that encourage developing countries to generate more revenue for debt repayment by cutting government expenditures to balance their budgets, selling off government-owned enterprises (privatization), and fully opening their countries to foreign goods and investments.

Welfare state A term used to describe countries in which government ensures that all people have a minimum standard of living and are provided some protection from hardships resulting from unemployment, sickness, disability, and old age.

Westminster system A governing system that developed in Britain, featuring single party majority rule, executive dominance of Parliament, and an adversarial relationship between the governing party and the opposition.

REFERENCES

Adams, I. (2001). *Political ideology today* (2nd ed.). Manchester, UK: Manchester University Press.

Adams, J., & Merrill, S. (2005). Candidate policy platforms and electoral outcomes: The three faces of policy representation. *European Journal of Political Research, 44*, 881–896.

Adolini, J.R., & Blake, C.H. (2001). *Comparing policies: Issues and choices in six industrialized countries.* Washington, DC: CQ Press.

Albritton, R.B. (2006). American federalism and intergovernmental relations. In G. Peele, C.J. Bailey, B. Cain, & B.G. Peters (Eds.), *Developments in American politics 5.* Houndmills, Basingstoke, Hampshire, UK: Palgrave Macmillan.

Alcoba, N. (2009, October 19). Prostitutes argue for safer work conditions. *National Post.*

Almond, G., & Verba, S. (1963). *The civic culture: Political attitudes and democracy in five nations.* Princeton, NJ: Princeton University Press.

Alterman, E. (2003). *What liberal media? The truth about bias and the news.* New York: Basic Books.

Anderson, J.E. (1979). *Public policy-making* (2nd ed.). New York: Holt, Rinehart & Winston.

Anderson, T.L., & Leal, D.R. (2001). *Free market environmentalism* (revised ed.). Houndmills, Basingstoke, Hampshire, UK: Palgrave Macmillan.

Ansolabehere, S., Iyengar, S., Simon, A., & Valentino, N. (1997). Does attack advertising demobilize the electorate? In S. Iyengar & R. Reeves (Eds.), *Do the media govern? Politicians, voters, and reporters in America* (pp. 195–207). Thousand Oaks, CA: Sage Publications.

Appleby, T. (2010, January 16). Toronto police: A force of difference. *Globe and Mail.*

Arrow, K., et al. (1995). Economic growth, carrying capacity and the environment. *Science, 268*(5210), 520–521.

Atkinson, A.B. (2000). Can welfare states compete in a global economy? In R.V. Ericson & N. Stehr (Eds.), *Governing modern societies* (pp. 259–275). Toronto: University of Toronto Press.

Aucoin, P. (2002). Beyond the "new" public management reform in Canada: Catching the next wave? In C. Dunn (Ed.), *The handbook of Canadian public administration* (pp. 37–52). Don Mills, ON: Oxford University Press.

Axworthy, L. (2003). *Navigating a new world: Canada's global future.* Toronto: Alfred A. Knopf.

Babbie, E. (1995). *The practice of social research* (7th ed.). Belmont, CA: Wadsworth Publishing Company.

Bachrach, P., & Baratz, M. (1962). The two faces of power. *American Political Science Review, 56*, 947–952.

Baer, D., Curtis, J., & Grabb, E. (2001). Has voluntary association activity declined? Cross-national analysis for fifteen countries. *Canadian Review of Sociology and Anthropology, 38*, 249–272.

Baldini, G., & Papalardo, A. (2009). *Elections, electoral systems and volatile voters.* New York: Palgrave Macmillan.

Ball, T., & Dagger, R. (2004). *Political ideologies and the democratic ideal* (5th ed.). New York: Pearson Longman.

Barnard, F.M. (2001). *Democratic legitimacy: Plural values and political power.* Montreal: McGill–Queen's University Press.

Barry, B. (1996). Political theory, old and new. In R.E. Goodin & H.-D. Klingemann (Eds.), *A new handbook of political science.* Oxford: Oxford University Press.

Basu, A., & Roy, S. (Eds.). (2007). *Violence and democracy in India.* Calcutta, India: Seagull Books.

BBC. (2010a). Iran crisis. Retrieved February 10, 2010, from http://news.bbc.co.uk/2/hi/in_depth/middle_east/2009/iran/default.stm

BBC. (2010b). Retrieved February 10, 2010, from www.bbc.co.uk/search/honduras

Beckerman, W. (1992). Economic growth and the environment: Whose growth? Whose environment? *World Development, 20*, 481–496.

Beckett, I. (2001). *Modern insurgencies and counter-insurgencies: Guerrillas and their opponents since 1750.* London, UK: Routledge.

Bell, D. (1998). The end of ideology revisited. *Government and Opposition, 23*, 131–150; 321–328.

Bell, D.V.J. (2004). Political culture in Canada. In M. Whittington & G. Williams (Eds.), *Canadian politics in the 21st century* (6th ed.). Toronto: Nelson.

Bellini, E. (2004). The robustness of authoritarianism in the Middle East: Exceptionalism in comparative perspective. *Comparative Politics, 36*(2), 139–157.

Benedicto, J. (2004). Cultural structures and political life: The cultural matrix of democracy in Spain. *European Journal of Political Research, 43*(3), 287–307.

Birch, A.H. (1980). *The British system of government* (4th ed.). London, UK: George Allen & Unwin.

Biswas, S. (2010, March 17). Conundrum of Kerala's struggling economy. *BBC News*. Retrieved March 25, 2010, from http://news.bbc.co.uk/2/hi/south_asia/8546952.stm

Black, R. (2006). Carbon emissions show sharp rise. BBC News website, November 27, 2006. Retrieved November 27, 2006, from www.bbc.co.uk.

Blais, A., Gidengil, E., Dobryznska, A., Nevitte, N., & Nadeau, R. (2003). Does the local candidate matter? Candidate effects in the Canadian election of 2000. *Canadian Journal of Political Science, 36*, 657–664.

Blais, A., Gidengil, E., Nadeau, R, & Nevitte, N. (2002). *Anatomy of a Liberal victory: Making sense of the vote in the 2000 Canadian election.* Peterborough, ON: Broadview.

Blais, A, Gidengil, E., Nevitte, N., & Nadeau, R. (2004). Where does turnout decline come from? *European Journal of Political Research, 43*, 221–236.

Blais, A., & Loewen, P. (2009). Youth electoral engagement in Canada. Retrieved from www.elections.ca/loi/youeng/youth_e/electoral_engagement_e.pdf

Blais, A., & Massicotte, L. (2002). Electoral systems. In L. LeDuc, R.G. Niemi, & P. Norris (Eds.), *Comparing democracies 2: New challenges in the study of elections and voting* (pp. 40–69). London: Sage.

Blais, A., Massicotte, L., & Dobrzynska, A. (2003). *Why is election turnout higher in some countries than others?* Retrieved May 26, 2004, from www.elections.ca.

Blais, A., Turgeon, M., Gidengil, E., Nevitte, N., & Nadeau, R. (2004). What matters most? Comparing the impact of issues and the economy in American, British and Canadian elections. *British Journal of Political Science, 34*(3), 555–563.

Blasing, T.J. (2009). Recent greenhouse gas concentrations. Carbon Dioxide Information Analysis Center. Retrieved September 1, 2009 from http://cdiac.ornl.gov/pns/current_ghg.html

Boatright, R.G. (2009). Campaign finance in the 2008 election. In J.M. Box-Steffensmeier & S.E. Schier (Eds.), *The American elections of 2008*. Lanham, MD: Rowman & Littlefield.

Borins, S. (2002). Transformation of the public sector: Canada in comparative perspective. In C. Dunn (Ed.), *The handbook of Canadian public administration* (pp. 3–17). Don Mills, ON: Oxford University Press.

Bosso, C.J. (2005). *Environment, Inc.: From grassroots to beltway.* Lawrence, KS: University Press of Kansas.

Boyd, D.R. (2003). *Unnatural law: Rethinking Canadian environmental law and policy.* Vancouver: UBC Press.

Bozeman, B. (2007). *Public values and public interest: Counterbalancing economic individualism.* Washington, DC: Georgetown University Press.

Bradshaw, L. (1991). Political rule, prudence and the "woman question" in Aristotle. *Canadian Journal of Political Science,24*(3), 557–573.

Brady, D.W., & Volden, C. (2006). *Revolving gridlock: Politics and policy from Jimmy Carter to George W. Bush* (2nd ed.). Boulder, CO: Westview Press.

Brautigam, D. (2009). *The dragon's gift: The real story of China in Africa.* New York: Oxford University Press.

Brinton, C. (1965). *The anatomy of a revolution.* New York: Vintage.

Broadbent, E. (2001). Social democracy—The way ahead. Conference on the future of social democracy in Canada. Retrieved August 26, 2006, from www.misc-iecm.mcgill.ca/socdem/ebeng.htm.

Brodie, J., & Jenson, J. (1988). *Crisis, challenge and change: Party and class in Canada revisited.* Ottawa: Carleton University Press.

Brooks, S. (1998). *Public policy in Canada* (3rd. ed.). Toronto: Oxford University Press.

Brown, S. (1995). *New forces, old forces and the future of world politics.* New York: HarperCollins.

Brownmiller, S. (1975). *Against our will: Men, women and rape.* New York: Simon & Schuster.

Bryson, V. (2003). *Feminist political theory: An introduction* (2nd ed.). Houndmills, Basingstoke, Hampshire, UK: Palgrave Macmillan.

Bunce, V. (2003). Rethinking recent democratization: Lessons from the postcommunist experience. *World Politics, 55*(1), 167–192.

Burden, B.C., & Kimball, D.C. (2004). *Why Americans split their tickets: Campaigns, competition, and divided government.* Ann Arbor, MI: University of Michigan Press.

Burke, E. (1955). *Reflections on the revolution in France.* (T.H.D. Mahoney, Ed.). Indianapolis, IN: The Liberal Arts Press. (Original work published in 1790.)

Cairns, A.C. (1968). The electoral system and the party system in Canada, 1921–1965. *Canadian Journal of Political Science, 1*(1), 55–80.

Cairns, A.C. (2000). *Citizens plus: Aboriginal peoples and the Canadian state.* Vancouver: UBC Press.

Calderisi, R. (2006). *The trouble with Africa.* New York: Palgrave Macmillan.

Canada. (2008). *Independent panel on Canada's future role in Afghanistan.* Retrieved February 10, 2010, from http://dsp-psd.pwgsc.gc.ca/collection_2008/dfait-maeci/FR5-20-1-2008E.pdf

Canadian Broadcasting Corporation. (2004). *CBC/Radio Canada pre-election poll.* Retrieved May 26, 2004, from www.cbc.ca/canadavotes/thepolls/democracypoll.htm.

Cardoso, F.H., & Falletto, E. (1979). *Dependency and development in Latin America.* Berkeley: University of California Press.

Carens, J.H. (2000). *Culture, citizenship, and community: A contextual exploration of justice as evenhandedness.* Oxford, UK: Oxford University Press.

Carothers, T. (1999). *Aiding democracy abroad.* Washington, DC: Carnegie Endowment for International Peace.

Carothers, T. (2002). The end of the transition paradigm. *Journal of Democracy, 13*(1), 5–22.

Carothers, T. (2007). *Confronting the weakest link: Aiding political parties in new democracies.* Washington, DC: Carnegie Endowment for International Peace.

Carr, E.H. (1939/2001).*The twenty years' crisis: 1919–39: An introduction to international relations.* New York: Harper and Row.

Carter, N. (2007). *The politics of the environment: Ideas, activism, policy* (2nd ed.). Cambridge: Cambridge University Press.

Castells, M. (2004). *The information age: Economy, society and culture. Volume II: The power of identity* (2nd ed.). Malden, MA: Blackwell.

Castle, B. (1987). *Sylvia and Cristabel Pankhurst.* New York: Penguin Books.

Caul, M.L., & Gray, M.M. (2000). From platform declarations to policy outcomes: Changing party profiles and partisan influence over policy. In R.J. Dalton & M.P. Wattenberg (Eds.), *Parties without partisans: Political change in advanced industrial democracies* (pp. 208–237). Oxford: Oxford University Press.

CBC News. (2009, September 29). Polygamy charges in Bountiful, B.C., thrown out. Retrieved from www.cbc.ca/canada/british-columbia/story/2009/09/23/bc-polygamy-charges-blackmore-oler-bountiful.html

CBC News. (2009, December 24). Chinese dissident jailed. Retrieved February 10, 2010, from www.cbc.ca/world/story/2009/12/24/chinese-dissident-jailed.htm

Charter of the Global Greens. (2001). Global Greens. Retrieved from www.global.greens.org/au/Charter2001.pdf

Clark, S.D., Grayson, J.P., & Grayson, L. (1976). General introduction: The nature of social movements. In S.D. Clark, J.P. Grayson, & L.M. Grayson (Eds.), *Prophecy and protest: Social movements in twentieth-century Canada* (pp. 1–38). Toronto: Gage.

Clarke, H.D., Jenson, J., LeDuc, L., & Pammett, J.H. (1996). *Absent mandate: Canadian electoral politics in an era of restructuring* (3rd ed.). Toronto: Gage Educational Publishing.

Clarke, H.D., Kornberg, A., & Scotto, T.S. (2009a). *Making political choices: Canada and the United States.* Toronto: University of Toronto Press.

Clarke, H.D., Kornberg, A., & Scotto, T.S. (2009b). None of the above: Voters in the 2008 federal election. In J.H. Pammett & C. Dornan (Eds), *The Canadian federal election of 2008.* Toronto: Dundurn Press.

Clarke, T., & Barlow, M. (1997). *MAI: The multilateral agreement on investment and the threat to Canadian sovereignty.* Toronto: Stoddart.

Cleverdon, C.L. (1974). *The woman suffrage movement in Canada* (2nd ed.). Toronto: University of Toronto Press.

Close, D. (2004). Undoing democracy in Nicaragua. In D. Close & K. Deonandan (Eds.), *Undoing democracy: The politics of electoral caudillismo* (pp. 1–15). Lanham, MD: Lexington Books.

Close, D., & Deonandan, K. (Eds.). (2004). *Undoing democracy: The politics of electoral caudillismo.* Lanham, MD: Lexington Books.

Close, D., & Mintz, E. (2005). State sponsorship and community environmental groups: The Atlantic coastal action program in Newfoundland. *American Review of Canadian Studies, 35*(4), 621–639.

Code, L. (1988). Feminist theory. In S. Burt, L. Code, & L. Dorney (Eds.), *Changing patterns: Women in Canada.* Toronto: McClelland & Stewart.

Collier, P. (2007). *The bottom billion: Why the poorest countries are failing and what can be done about it.* New York: Oxford University Press.

Consumer Education Foundation. (2009). Sold out: How Wall Street and Washington betrayed Americans. Retrieved from www.wallstreetwatch.org/reports/sold_out.pdf

Coombes, C. (2003). *Terrorism in the twenty-first century* (3rd ed.). Upper Saddle River, NJ: Prentice-Hall.

Cooper, R. (2000). *The post-modern state and world order.* London: Foreign Policy Centre.

Coupland, R. (1964). *The British anti-slavery movement.* London: Frank Cass

Courchene, T.J. (1992). *Rearrangements: The Courchene papers.* Oakville, ON: Mosaic Press.

Courchene, T.J. (2007). Global futures for Canada's global cities. *Policy Matters, 8*(2).

Cox, R.W. (1987). *Production, power, and world order: Social forces in the making of history.* New York: Columbia University Press.

Crick, B. (1993). *In defence of politics* (4th American ed.). Chicago: University of Chicago Press.

Cross, W. (2004). *Political parties.* Vancouver: UBC Press.

Cross, W., & Young, L. (2002). Policy attitudes of party members in Canada: Evidence of ideological politics. *Canadian Journal of Political Science, 35*(4), 859–880.

Croteau, D. (1998). *Examining the "liberal media" claim: Journalists' views on politics, economic policy, and media coverage.* Retrieved November 15, 2003, from www.fair.org/reports/journalist-survey.html.

Crozier, M., Huntington, S.P., & Watanuki, J. (1975). *The crisis of democracy.* New York: New York University Press.

Dahl, R.A. (1961). *Who governs? Democracy and power in an American city.* New Haven: Yale University Press.

Dahl, R.A. (1984). *Modern political analysis* (4th ed.). Englewood Cliffs, NJ: Prentice-Hall.

Dalton, R.J. (2000). The decline of party identifications. In R.J. Dalton & M.P. Wattenberg (Eds.), *Parties without partisans: Political change in advanced industrial democracies* (pp. 19–36). Oxford: Oxford University Press.

Dalton, R.J. (2006). *Citizen politics: Public opinion and political parties in advanced industrial democracies* (4th ed.). Washington, DC: CQ Press.

Dalton, R.J., & Wattenburg, M.P. (2000). Partisan change and the democratic process. In R.J. Dalton & M.P. Wattenberg (Eds.), *Parties with partisans: Political change in advanced industrial democracies* (pp. 261–285). Oxford: Oxford University Press.

Daly, H.E., & Cobb, J.B. (1994). *For the common good: Redirecting the economy toward community, the environment, and a sustainable future* (2nd ed.). Boston: Beacon Press.

Decalo, S. (1988). *Psychoses of power: African personal dictatorships*. Boulder, CO: Westview Press.

Devall, B., & Sessions, G. (1998). Deep ecology. In D. VanDeVeer & C. Pierce (Eds.), *The environmental ethics and policy book: Philosophy, ecology, economics* (2nd ed.) (pp. 221–226). Belmont, CA: Wadsworth.

DeWeil, B. (2000). *Democracy: A history of ideas.* Vancouver: UBC Press.

Diamond, L. (2008, March–April). The Democratic rollback. *Foreign Affairs, 87*(2), 36–48.

Dicker, R.C., & Piepmeier, A. (2003). Introduction. In R.C. Dicker & A. Piepmeier (Eds.), *Catching a wave: Reclaiming feminism for the 21st century.* Boston: Northeastern University Press.

Dietz, T., Ostrom, E., & Stern, P.C. (2003). The struggle to govern the commons. *Science, 302*(5652), 1907–1912.

Dobson, A. (2000). *Green political thought* (3rd ed.). New York: Routledge.

Dobson, A. (2007). *Green political thought* (4th ed.). New York: Routledge.

Domhoff, G.W. (2009). *Who rules America? Challenges to corporate and class dominance.* New York: McGraw-Hill.

Dowie, M. (1995). *Losing ground: American environmentalism at the close of the twentieth century.* Cambridge, MA: MIT Press.

Downs, A. (1957). *An economic theory of democracy.* New York: Harper.

Dowty, A. (2005). *Israel/Paelstine.* Cambridge, UK: Polity.

Doyle, T., & Kellow, A. (1995). *Environmental politics and policy making in Australia.* Melbourne: Macmillan.

Dryzek, J. (1997). *The politics of the earth: Environmental discourses.* Oxford: Oxford University Press.

Dunleavy, P., *et al.* (2006). New public management is dead—long live digital-era governance. *Journal of Public Administration Research and Theory, 16*(3), 467–494.

Duverger, M. (1964). *Political parties: Their organization and activity in the modern state* (3rd ed.). London: Methuen.

Dyer, G. (2008). *Climate wars.* Toronto: Random House.

Earl, J. (2006). Pursuing social change online: The use of four protest tactics on the Internet. *Social Science Computer Review, 24*, 362–377.

Easterly, W. (2006). *The white man's burden.* New York: The Penguin Press.

Easton, D. (1953). *The political system: An enquiry into the state of political science.* New York: Knopf.

Eatwell, R. (1995). *Fascism: A history.* New York: Penguin Books.

Eckersley, R. (1992). *Environmentalism and political theory: Towards an ecocentric approach.* Albany, NY: State University of New York Press.

The Economist. (2010, February 13). Old dogs and new tricks. pp. 63–64.

The Economist. (2010, May 8–14). Many wives' tales. p. 55.

The Economist. (2010, June 5). Reaching for a longer spoon. pp. 69–70.

Ehrenreich, B., & English, D. (1979). *For her own good: 150 years of the experts' advice to women.* New York: Anchor Press.

Eilperin, J. (2010, May 5). U.S. exempted BP's Gulf of Mexico drilling from environmental impact study. *Washington Post.* Retrieved from www.washingtonpost.com/wp-dyn/content/article/2010/05/04/AR2010050404118.html

Elections Canada. (1997). *A history of the vote in Canada.* Ottawa: Minister of Public Works and Government Services.

Elections Canada. (n.d.). Estimates of voter turnout by age group at the 2008 federal general election. Retrieved from www.elections.ca/loi/res/estim/estimation40_e.pdf

Elgie, R. (1999). Semi-presidentialism and comparative institutional engineering. In R. Elgie (Ed.), *Semi-presidentialism in Europe.* Oxford: Oxford University Press.

Elgie, R. (2005). The political executive. In A. Cole, P. Le Galès, & J. Levy (Eds.), *Developments in French politics 3.* Houndmills, Basingstoke, Hampshire, UK: Palgrave Macmillan.

Elkins, D.J. (1993). *Manipulation and consent: How voters and leaders manage complexity.* Vancouver: UBC Press.

Elster, J. (1998). *Deliberative democracy.* Cambridge: Cambridge University Press.

Engelhart, K. (2010, April 26). The return of Hitler. *Maclean's,* 30–34.

Enloe, C. (1989). *Bananas, beaches and bases: Making feminist sense of international relations.* London: Pandora.

Entman, R.M. (2004). *Projections of power: Framing news, public opinion, and U.S. foreign policy.* Chicago: University of Chicago Press.

Ersson, S., & Lane, J.-E. (2008). Political culture. In D. Aramani (Ed.), *Comparative politics.* Oxford: Oxford University Press.

European Council. (2003). *A secure Europe in a better world: European security strategy.* Retrieved August 15, 2007, from www.consilium.europa.eu/uedocs/cmsUpload/ 78367. pdf.

Faludi, S. (1991). *Backlash: The undeclared war against American women.* New York: Crown.

Farcau, B.W. (1994). *The coup: Tactics in the seizure of power.* Westport, CT: Praeger.

Federation of Canadian Municipalities. (2006). *Building prosperity from the ground up: Restoring municipal fiscal balance.* Retrieved June 22, 2007, from www.fcm.ca.

Fischer, D.H. (2004). *Liberty and freedom.* Oxford: Oxford University Press.

Fitch, J.S. (1977). *The military coup d'etat as a political process.* Baltimore, MD: Johns Hopkins University Press.

Fitch, S. (1998). *The armed forces and democracy in Latin America.* Baltimore, MD: Johns Hopkins University Press.

Flinders, M. (2010). Bagehot smiling: Gordon Brown's "new constitution" and the revolution that did not happen. *Political Quarterly,81*(1), 57–73.

Fournier, P. (2002). The uninformed Canadian voter. In J. Everitt & B. O'Neill (Eds.), *Citizen politics: Research and theory in Canadian political behaviour* (pp. 92–109). Don Mills, ON: Oxford University Press.

Frank, A.G. (1972). The development of underdevelopment. In D. Cockcroft, A.G. Frank, & D. Johnson (Eds.), *Dependence and underdevelopment.* New York: Anchor Books.

Frank, A.G. (1979). *Dependent accumulation and under-development.* New York: Monthly Review Press.

Freedman, J. (2001). *Feminism.* Buckingham, UK: Open University Press.

Freedom House. (2009). *Freedom in the world.* Retrieved from www.freedomhouse.org

Freedom House. (2010). *Freedom in the world, 2010: The erosion of freedom.* Retrieved from www.freedomhouse.org/uploads/fiw10/FIW_2010_Tables_and_Graphs.pdf

Friedan, B. (1963). *The feminine mystique.* New York: Dell.

Friedan, B. (1998). *It changed my life: Writings on the women's movement.* Cambridge, MA: Harvard University Press.

Friederich, C., & Brzezinski, Z. (1956). *Totalitarian dictatorship and democracy.* Cambridge, MA: Harvard University Press.

Friedman, M., & Friedman, A. (2001). *Free to choose: A personal statement.* Boston: Houghton Mifflin Harcourt.

Friedman, T. (2000). *The Lexus and the olive tree.* New York: Anchor Books.

Frum, D. (1996). *What's right: The new conservatism and what it means for Canada.* Toronto: Random House.

Fukuyama, F. (1989). The end of history? *The National Interest, 16,* 3–18.

Fukuyama, F. (1992). *The end of history and the last man.* New York: Free Press.

Gagnon, A.-G. (2010). *The case for multinational federalism: Beyond the all-encompassing nation.* New York: Routledge.

Gamble, A. (1994). *The free economy and the strong state: The politics of Thatcherism* (2nd ed.). Houndsmills, Basingstoke, Hampshire, UK: Macmillan.

Gardner, J.A. (2009). *What are campaigns for? The role of persuasion in electoral law and politics.* New York: Oxford University Press.

Garrett, G. (1998). *Partisan politics in the global economy.* Cambridge: Cambridge University Press.

Gidengil, E., Blais, A., Everitt, J., Fournier, P., & Nevitte, N. (2006a). Back to the future? Making sense of the 2004 Canadian election outside Quebec. *Canadian Journal of Political Science, 39*(1), 1–25.

Gidengil, E., Blais, A., Everitt, J., Fournier, P., & Nevitte, N. (2006c). Is the concept of party identification applicable in Canada? A panel-based analysis. Presented at the ECPR 34th joint session workshop, Nicosia. Retrieved August 11, 2007, from www.ces-eec.umontreal.ca/ECPRGidengiletal.pdf

Gidengil, E., Blais, A., Nadeau, R., & Nevitte, N. (2003). Women to the left? Gender differences in political beliefs and policy preferences. In M.Tremblay & L.Trimble (Eds.), *Women and electoral politics in Canada* (pp. 140–159). Don Mills, ON: Oxford University Press.

Gidengil, E., Everitt, J., Blais, A., Fournier, P., & Nevitte, N. (2006b). Gender and vote choice in the 2006 Canadian election. Paper prepared for the annual meeting of the American Political Science Association. Retrieved August 10, 2007, from www.ces-eec.umontreal.ca/Gidengiletal/APSA2006.pdf.

Gidengil, E., Fournier, P., Everitt, J., Nevitte, N., & Blais, A. (2009). The anatomy of a Liberal defeat. Paper prepared for the annual meeting of the Canadian Political Science Association, May 2009. Retrieved from http://ces-eec.mcgill.ca/publications.html

Gilley, B. (2006). The meaning and measure of state legitimacy: Results for 72 countries. *European Journal of Political Research, 45,* 499–525.

Gilligan, C. (1982). *In a different voice.* Cambridge, MA: Harvard University Press.

Gilpin, R. (1981). *War and change in world politics.* Cambridge, UK: Cambridge University Press.

Global Footprint Network. (n.d.). Retrieved from www.footprintnetwork.org/en/index.php/GFN/page/world_footprint/

Goerres, A. (2007). Why are older people more likely to vote? The impact of ageing on electoral turnout across Europe. *British Journal of Politics and International Relations, 9,* 90–121.

Goldenberg, E. (2006). *The way it works.* Toronto: McClelland & Stewart.

Goldstone, J. (1995). Predicting revolution: Why we could and (and should) have foreseen the revolutions of 1989–1991 in the U.S.S.R. and Eastern Europe. In N. Keddie (Ed.), *Debating revolution* (pp. 39–64). New York: New York University Press.

Grabb, E.C., & Curtis, J. (2005). *Regions apart: The four societies of Canada and the United States.* Toronto: Oxford University Press.

Graefe, P. (2007). Political economy and Canadian public policy. In M. Orsini & M. Smith (Eds.), *Critical policy studies.* Vancouver: UBC Press.

Grandin, G. (2006). *Empire's workshop: Latin America, the United States, and the rise of the new imperialism.* New York: Metropolitian Books.

Green, D., & Luehrmann, L. (2003). *Comparative politics of the Third World*. Boulder, CO: Lynne Rienner.

Gret, M. (2005). *The Porto Alegre experiment: Learning lessons for better democracy*. London, UK: Zed Books.

Grofman, B. (1996). Political economy: Downsian perspectives. In R.E. Goodin & H.-D. Klingemann (Eds.), *A new handbook of political science* (pp. 691–701). Oxford: Oxford University Press.

Gunther, R., & Diamond, L. (2001). Types and functions of parties. In L. Diamond & R. Gunther (Eds.), *Political parties and democracy*. Baltimore, MD: Johns Hopkins University Press.

Habermas, J. (1975). *Legitimation crisis* (T. McCarthy, Trans.). Boston: Beacon Press. (Original work published 1973.)

Hackett, R.A., & Zhao, Y. (1998). *Sustaining democracy? Journalism and the politics of objectivity*. Toronto: Garamond Press.

Hagopian, M.N. (1985). *Ideals and ideologies of modern politics*. New York: Longman.

Hallowell, J.H., & Porter, J.M. (1997). *Political philosophy: The search for humanity and order*. Scarborough, ON: Prentice Hall Canada.

Hancké, B. (Ed.). (2009). *Debating varieties of capitalism: A reader*. Oxford: Oxford University Press.

Handelman, H. (2003). *The challenge of Third World development*. Upper Saddle River, NJ: Prentice-Hall.

Hardin, G. (1968, December 13). The tragedy of the commons. *Science, 162*, 1243–1248.

Hardin, G. (1974). Lifeboat ethics: The case against helping the poor. *Psychology Today*, September.

Harmes, A. (2004). *The return of the state: Protestors, power-brokers and the new global compromise*. Vancouver: Douglas & McIntyre.

Harris, M. (1991). *Unholy orders: Tragedy at Mount Cashel*. Toronto: Penguin.

Harty, S., & Murphy, M. (2005). *In defence of multinational citizenship*. Vancouver: UBC Press.

Hartz, L. (1964). *The founding of new societies*. Toronto: Longmans.

Hausegger, L., Hennigar, M., & Riddell, T. (2008). *Canadian courts: Law, politics, and process*. Toronto: Oxford University Press.

Hay, C. (2002). *Political analysis: A critical introduction*. New York: Palgrave.

Heberle, R. (1951). *Social movements*. New York: Appleton, Century, Crofts.

Heilbroner, R. (1974). *An inquiry into the human prospect*. New York: W.W. Norton.

Herman, E.S., & Chomsky, N. (2002). *Manufacturing consent* (updated ed.). New York: Pantheon Books.

Hess, G.R. (2005). Authorizing war: Congressional resolutions and presidential leadership, 1955–2002. In D.R. Kelley (Ed.), *Divided power: The presidency, Congress, and the formation of American foreign policy*. Fayetteville, AR: The University of Arkansas Press.

Hessing, M., Howlett M., & Summerville, T. (2005). *Canadian natural resource and environmental policy* (2nd. ed.). Vancouver: UBC Press.

Heywood, A. (2002). *Politics* (2nd ed.). Houndmills, Basingstoke, Hampshire, UK: Palgrave.

Heywood, A. (2003). *Political ideologies: An introduction* (3rd ed.). Houndmills, Basingstoke, Hampshire, UK: Palgrave.

Hinojosa, V.J., & Pérez-Liñán, A. (2005). Presidential impeachment and the politics of survival: The case of Columbia. In J.C. Baumgarner & N. Kada (Eds.), *Checking executive power: Presidential impeachment in comparative perspective*. Westport, CT: Praeger.

Hobbes, T. (1968/1651). *Leviathan*. C.B. Macpherson (Ed.). Harmondsworth, UK: Penguin.

Hoffman, B. (2004). *Insurgency and counterinsurgency in Iraq*. RAND Corporation Occasional Paper OP-127. Santa Monica, CA: Rand Corporation; www.rand.org/pubs/occasional_papers/2005/RAND_OP127.pdf.

Hooghe, L., & Marks, G. (2001). *Multi-level governance and European integration*. Boulder, CO: Rowman and Littlefield.

Horowitz, G. (1966). Conservatism, liberalism and socialism in Canada: An interpretation. *Canadian Journal of Economics and Political Science, 32*(2), 143–171.

House of Commons Library. (2005). 2005 general election. Research Paper 15/33. Retrieved from www.parliament.uk/commons/lib/research/rp2005/RP05-033.pdf

Hume, M. (2004, July 12). For whistle blower, it got personal. *Globe and Mail*, A4.

Huntington, S. (1968). *Political order in changing societies*. New Haven, CT: Yale University Press.

Huntington, S.P. (1991). *The third wave*. Norman, OK: University of Oklahoma Press.

Huntington, S.P. (1993). The clash of civilizations? *Foreign Affairs, 72*(3), 22–49.

Huntington, S.P. (1996). *The clash of civilizations and the remaking of world order*. New York: Simon & Schuster.

Inglehart, R.I. (1977). *The silent revolution: Changing values and political styles among Western publics*. Princeton, NJ: Princeton University Press.

Inglehart, R.I. (1990). *Culture shift in advanced industrial society*. Princeton, NJ: Princeton University Press.

Inglehart, R.I., & Norris, P. (2003). *The true clash of civilizations*. Retrieved on August 10, 2004, from www.globalpolicy. org/globaliz/cultural/2003/0304clash.htm.

Inglehart, R.I., & Welzel, C. (2005). *Modernization, cultural change and democracy: The human development sequence*. New York: Cambridge University Press.

Institute of Wellbeing. (2010). *Democratic engagement: Report highlights*. Retrieved February 7, 2010, from www.ciw.ca/en/TheCanadianIndexOfWellbeing/DomainsOfWellbeing/DemocraticEngagement.aspx

International Commission on Intervention and State Sovereignty. (2001). *The responsibility to protect: Report of the International Commission on Intervention and State Sovereignty*. Retrieved August 20, 2004, from www.dfait-maeci.gc.ca/iciss-ciise/pdf/Commission-Report.pdf.

International Institute for Democracy and Electoral Assistance. (2007a). *Global database of quotas for women*. Retrieved July 10, 2007, from www.quotaproject.org/system.cfm

International Institute for Democracy and Electoral Assistance. (2007b). *Voter turnout: Main findings*. Retrieved July 12, 2007, from www.idea.net/vt

International Institute for Democracy and Electoral Assistance. (n.d.). Voter turnout: A global survey. Retrieved from www.idea.int/vt

International Monetary Fund. *World economic database*. Retrieved March 25, 2010, from www.imf.org/external/pubs/ft/weo/2009/02/weodata/weorept.aspx?pr.x=72&pr.y=13&sy=1990&ey=2009&scsm=1&ssd=1&sort=country&ds=.&br=1&c=924&s=NGDPDPC&grp=0&a=

IPSOS Reid/Dominion Institute. (2007). *National citizenship exam: 10 year benchmark study*. Retrieved July 12, 2007, from www.dominion.ca/Dominion_Institute_Press_Release_Mock_Exam.pdf

Iraq Body Count. (2010). Retrieved March 20, 2010, from www.iraqbodycount.org

Jamieson, K.H. (1992). *Dirty politics: Deception, distraction, democracy*. New York: Oxford University Press.

Janowitz, M. (1977). *Military institutions and coercion in the developing nations*. Chicago: University of Chicago Press.

Jennings, M.K. (1984). The intergenerational transfer of political ideologies in eight Western nations. *European Journal of Political Research 12*, 261–276.

Jennings, M.K., & Niemi, R.G. (1968). The transmission of political values from parent to child. *American Political Science Review, 62*, 169–184.

Jennings, M.K., & Niemi, R.G. (1981). *Generations and politics: A panel study of young adults and their parents*. Princeton, NJ: Princeton University Press.

Joes, A. (1992). *Modern guerrilla insurgency*. Westport, CT: Praeger Publishers.

Joes, A. (2004). *Resisting rebellion: The history and politics of counterinsurgency*. Lexington, KY: University of Kentucky Press.

Johnson, S. (2009, May). The quiet coup. *The Atlantic*. Retrieved from www.theatlantic.com/magazine/archive/2009/05/thequiet-coup/7364/2/?

Kara, N. (2005). Impeachment as punishment for corruption? The cases of Brazil and Venezuela. In J.C. Baumgarner & N. Kada (Eds.), *Checking executive power: Presidential impeachment in comparative perspective*. Westport, CT: Praeger.

Katz, R.S. (2008). Political parties. In D. Caramani (Ed.), *Comparative politics*. Oxford: Oxford University Press.

Katz, R.S., & Mair, P. (1995). Changing models of party organization and party democracy: The emergence of the cartel party. *Party Politics, 1*, 5–28.

Keating, M. (1996). *Nations against the state: The new politics of nationalism in Quebec, Catalonia and Scotland*. Houndmills, Basingstoke, Hampshire, UK: Macmillan.

Keddie, N. (1995). Can revolutions be predicted; Can their causes be understood? In N. Keddie (Ed.), *Debating revolution* (pp. 1–26). New York: New York University Press.

Kenig, O. (2009). Democratization of party leadership selection: Do wider electorates produce more competitive contests? *Electoral Studies, 28*(2), 240–247.

Kent, A. (1996). *Risk and redemption: Surviving the network news wars*. Toronto: Penguin Books Canada.

Keohane, R.O. (1984). *After hegemony: Cooperation and discord in the world political economy*. Princeton, NJ: Princeton University Press.

Keohane, R.O., & Nye, J.S. (1977). *Power and interdependence: World politics in transition*. Boston: Little, Brown.

Kiernan, B. (2002). *The Pol Pot regime: Race, power, and genocide under the Khmer Rouge*. New Haven, CT: Yale University Press.

Kilbourne, W. (1964). *Firebrand: William Lyon Mackenzie and the rebellion in Upper Canada*. Toronto: Clarke, Irwin.

Kinder, D.R., & Kiewiet, D.R. (1981). Sociotropic voting: The American case. *British Journal of Political Science, 11*(2), 129–161.

King, A. (2007). *The British constitution*. Oxford: Oxford University Press.

Kingdon, J.W. (1995). *Agendas, alternatives and public policies* (2nd ed.). New York: Longman.

Kirchheimer, O. (1966). The transformation of West European party systems. In J. LaPalombara & M. Weiner (Eds.), *Political parties and political development* (pp. 177–200). Princeton, NJ: Princeton University Press.

Kirkpatrick, J. (1979). Dictatorships and double standards. *Commentary, 68*(5), 34–45.

Kitschelt, H. (1986). Political opportunity structures and political protest: Anti-nuclear movements in four democracies. *British Journal of Political Science, 16*(1) 57–79.

Korten, D.C. (1996). *When corporations rule the world*. West Hartford, CT: Kumarian Press.

Kraft, M.E. (2011). *Environmental policy and politics* (5th ed.). Toronto: Longman.

Kushner, J., Siegel, D., & Stanwick, H. (1997). Ontario municipal elections: Voting trends and determinants of electoral success in a Canadian province. *Canadian Journal of Political Science, 30*, 539–559.

Kymlicka, W. (1991). *Liberalism, community and culture*. Oxford: Clarendon Press.

Ladd, E.C. (1999). *The Ladd report*. New York: Free Press.

Lane, J.-E., & Ersson, S. (2000). *The new institutional politics: Performance and outcomes*. London, UK: Routledge.

Laquer, W. (1977). *Guerrilla: A historical and critical study*. London, UK: Weidenfeld and Nicolson.

Latendresse, A. (2006). Les expériences de CDEC montréalaises et du budget participative de Porto Alegre à la lumière de leur contribution au renouvellement de la démocratie urbaine. *Nouvelles pratiques sociales, 18*(2), 55–72.

Lau, R., Sigelman, L., Heldman, C., & Babbitt, P. (1999). The effects of negative political advertisements: A meta-analytic assessment. *American Political Science Review, 93*, 851–875.

Lazar, H., Telford, H., & Watts, R. (2003). Divergent trajectories: The impact of global and regional integration on federal systems. In H. lazar, H. Telford, & R. Watts (Eds.), *The impact of global and regional integration on federal systems.* Montreal & Kingston: McGill-Queen's University Press.

Leftwich, A. (1983). *Redefining politics: People, resources and power.* London: Methuen.

Leggett, W. (2007). British social democracy beyond new Labour: Entrenching a progressive consensus. *British Journal of Politics and International Relations, 9*, 346–364.

Leo, C., & Mulligan, S. (2006). City politics: Globalization and community democracy. In J. Grace & B. Sheldreck (Eds.), *Canadian politics: Democracy and dissent.* Toronto: Pearson Education.

Leonard, A. (2010, May 19). Germany's blitzkrieg against short-sellers. *Salon.* Retrieved from www.salon.com/technology/how_the_world_works/2010/05/19/the_german_blitzkrieg_against_short_sellers.

Lewin, L. (1991). *Self-interest and public interest in Western politics* (D. Lavery, Trans.). Oxford: Oxford University Press.

Lijphart, A. (1999). *Patterns of democracy: Government forms and performance in thirty-six countries.* New Haven, CT: Yale University Press.

Lindblom, C.E. (1959). The science of muddling through. *Public Administration Review, 19*(2), 79–88.

Lindblom, C.E. (1977). *Politics and markets: The world's political-economic systems.* New York: Basic Books.

Linz, J. (1964). An authoritarian regime: Spain. In E. Allardt & Y. Littunen (Eds.), *Cleavages, ideologies, and party systems: Contributions to comparative political sociology. Transactions of the Westermarck Society, 10*, 291–342.

Linz, J. (1994). Presidential or parliamentary democracy: Does it make a difference? In J.J. Linz & A. Valenzuela (Eds.), *The failure of presidential democracy: Vol. 1. Comparative perspectives* (pp. 3–87). Baltimore, MD: John Hopkins University Press.

Lipschutz, R.D. (2000). *After authority: War, peace and global politics in the 21st century.* Albany, NY: State University of New York Press.

Lipschutz, R.D. (2004). *Global environmental politics: Power, perspectives, and practice.* Washington, DC: CQ Press

Lipset, S.M. (1950). *Agrarian socialism.* Berkeley, CA: University of California Press.

Lipset, S.M. (1990). *Continental divide: The values and institutions of the United States and Canada.* New York: Routledge.

Lipset, S.M., & Rokkan, S. (1967). Cleavage structures, party systems and voter alignments: An introduction. In S.M. Lipset & S. Rokkan (Eds.), *Party systems and voter alignments: Cross-national perspectives.* New York: Free Press.

Lipsky, R. (1968). Protest as a political resource. *American Political Science Review, 62*(4), 1144–1158.

Liptak, A. (2010, January 21). Justices, 5–4, reject corporate spending limit. Retrieved from www.nytimes.com/2010/01/22/us/politics/22scotus.html

Lobe, J. (2002. September 27). The arrogance of power. *Foreign Policy in Focus.*

Lukes, S. (1974). *Power: A radical view.* London: Macmillan.

Luttwak, E. (1969). *Coup d'etat.* New York: Alfred A. Knopf.

Lutz, M.A. (1999). *Economics for the common good: Two centuries of social economic thought in the humanist tradition.* New York: Routledge.

Lyons, W., Scheb, J.M., & Richardson, L.E. (1995). *American government: Politics and political culture.* St. Paul, MN: West Publishing.

Macauley, N. (1986). *The Sandino affair.* Durham, NC: Duke University Press.

Macdonald, N. (2010, July 26). How to really fuel discontent. *Maclean's.*

MacIvor, H. (2006). *Canadian politics and government in the Charter era.* Toronto: Thomson Nelson.

Mackenzie, H. (2010). *A soft landing: Recession and Canada's 100 highest paid CEOs.* Ottawa: Canadian Centre for Policy Alternatives.

Macpherson, C.B. (1954). *Democracy in Alberta.* Toronto: University of Toronto Press.

Macpherson, C.B. (1965). *The real world of democracy.* Toronto: CBC Publications.

Macpherson, C.B. (1980). *Burke.* Toronto: Oxford University Press.

Mahoney, C. (2008). *Brussels versus the Beltway: Advocacy in the United States and the European Union.* Washington, DC: Georgetown University Press.

Mahoney, C., & Baumgartner, F. (2008). Converging perspectives on interest group research in Europe and America. *West European Politics,31*(6), 1253–1273.

Mann, M. (2004). *Fascists.* New York: Cambridge University Press.

Market and Opinion Research International. (2005). How Britain voted in 2005. Retrieved from www.ipsos-mori.com/researchpublications/researcharchive/poll.aspx?oItemID=2252&view=wide

Marletti, C., & Roncarolo, F. (2000). Media influence in the Italian transition from a consensual to a majoritarian democracy. In R. Gunther & A. Mughan (Eds.), *Democracy and the media: A comparative perspective* (pp. 195–240). Cambridge, UK: Cambridge University Press.

Marshall, T.H. (1950). *Citizenship and social class.* Cambridge: Cambridge University Press.

Martell, L. (1994). *Ecology and society: An introduction.* Amherst, MA: University of Massachusetts Press.

Martin, H.-P., & Schumann, H. (1997). *The global trap: Globalization and the assault on democracy and prosperity.* Montreal: Black Rose Books.

Mayeda, A. (2010, May 12). Canadian offshore drilling regulations relaxed last year. *The Western Star.*

McAllister, M.L. (2004). *Governing ourselves: The politics of local communities.* Vancouver, BC: UBC Press.

McGovern, J. (2007). The emergence of the modern state. In E. Cudworth, T. Hall, & J. McGovern (Eds.), *The modern state: Theories and ideologies* (pp. 20-36). Edinburgh: Edinburgh University Press.

McKenna, G. (1990). *The drama of democracy: American government and politics.* Guilford, CT: Dushkin Publishing.

McQuail, D. (1994). *Mass communication theory: An introduction* (3rd ed.). London, UK: Sage.

Meadows, D., Randers, J., & Meadows, D. (2004). *Limits to growth: The 30-year update.* White River Jct, VT: Chelsea Green Publishing.

Meadows, D.H., Meadows, D.L., Randers, J., & Behrens, W.H. (1972). *The limits to growth.* New York: Universe Books.

Medcalf, L.J., & Dolbeare, K.M. (1985). *Neopolitics: American political ideas in the 1980s.* Philadelphia, PA: Temple University Press.

Meisel, J. (1979). The decline of party in Canada. In H.G. Thorburn (Ed.), *Party politics in Canada* (4th ed.). Scarborough, ON: Prentice Hall Canada.

Meisel, J., & Mendelsohn, M. (2001). Meteor? Phoenix? Chameleon? The decline and transformation of party in Canada. In H.G. Thorburn & A. Whitehorn (Eds.), *Party politics in Canada* (8th ed.). Toronto: Prentice Hall.

Michels, R. (1962). *Political parties: a sociological study of the oligarchic tendencies of modern democracy* (E. Paul & C. Paul, Trans.). New York: Collier. (Original work published in 1911.)

Miljan, L.A., & Cooper, B. (2003). *Hidden agendas: How journalists influence the news.* Vancouver: UBC Press.

Mill, J.S. (1912). *On liberty. Representative government. The subjection of women. Three essays.* London, UK: Oxford University Press. (*On Liberty* originally published in 1859.)

Miller, W.L., & Niemi, R.G. (2002). Voting: Choice, conditioning, and constraint. In L. LeDuc, R.G. Niemi, & P. Norris (Eds.), *Comparing democracies 2: New challenges in the study of elections and voting* (pp. 169–188). London: Sage.

Millett, K. (1985). *Sexual politics.* London: Virago.

Milliken, P. (2010, April 27). Ruling on the question of privilege. *House of Commons Debates (Hansard).*

Mills, C.W. (1956). *The power elite.* New York: Oxford University Press.

Milner, H. (1997). Electoral systems, integrated institutions and turnout in local and national elections: Canada in comparative perspective. *Canadian Journal of Political Science, 30*(1, March), 89–106.

Milner, H. (2002). *Civic literacy: How informed citizens make democracy work.* Hanover, NH: University Press of New England.

Mintz, E. (1993). Two generations: The political attitudes of high school students and their parents. *International Journal of Canadian Studies,* (special issue), 59–71.

Mishler, W., & Clarke, H.D. (1995). Political participation in Canada. In M.S. Whittington & G. Williams (Eds.), *Canadian politics in the 1990s* (4th ed.) (pp. 129–151). Toronto: Nelson Canada.

Mitchell, K. (2003). Educating the national citizen in neoliberal times: From the multicultural self to the strategic cosmopolitan. *Transactions of the Institute of British Geographers, 28*(4), 387–403.

Mittelstaedt, M. (2010, May 17). Canada's long-time adversaries poised to announce peace pact, switch to partnership model. *Globe and Mail.* Retrieved from www.theglobeandmail.com/report-on-business/loggers-environmentalists-reach-truce/article1571684/

Moberg, D. (2008, November 10). Obama and the union vote. *In These Times.* Retrieved from www.inthesetimes.com/article/4035/obama_and_the_union_vote

Montpetit, É. (2004). Governance and interest group activities. In J. Bickerton and A-G. Gagnon (Eds.), *Canadian politics* (4th ed.). Peterborough, ON: Broadview Press.

More, T. (2004). *Utopia.* In T. Ball & R. Dagger (Eds.), *Ideals and ideologies: A reader* (5th ed.). New York: Pearson Longman. (Original work published in 1516.)

Morgan, R. (1977). *Going too far: The personal chronicle of a feminist.* New York: Random House.

Morgan-Jones, E., & Schleiter, P. (2004). Governmental change in a president-parliamentary regime: The case of Russia 1994–2003. *Post-Soviet Affairs, 20*(2), 132–163.

Morgenthau, H.J. (1948). *Politics among nations: The struggle for power and peace.* New York: Knopf.

Morlan, R.L. (1984). Municipal vs. national election voter turnout: Europe and the United States. *Political Science Quarterly, 99*, 457–70.

Morris, J.C. (2007). Government and market pathologies of privatization: The case of prison privatization. *Politics & Policy, 35*(2), 318–341.

Morton, F.L. (2003). Can judicial supremacy be stopped? *Policy Options, 24*(9), 25–99.

Morton, W.L. (1950). *The Progressive Party in Canada.* Toronto: University of Toronto Press

Mueller, J. (1989). *Retreat from doomsday: The obsolescence of major war.* New York: Basic Books.

Myers, R.A., & Worm, B. (2003). Rapid worldwide depletion of predatory fish communities. *Nature, 423*(6937), 280–283.

Nadeau, R. (2002). Satisfaction with democracy: The Canadian paradox. In N. Nevitte (Ed.), *Value change and governance in Canada* (pp. 37–70). Toronto: University of Toronto Press.

Nadeau, R., & Giasson, T. (2003). Canada's democratic malaise: Are the media to blame? *Choices, 9*(1, February), 3–32.

Naess, A., & Sessions, G. (1993). The deep ecology platform. In B. Devall (Ed.), *Clearcut: The tragedy of industrial forestry.* San Francisco: Sierra Book Club & Earth Island Press.

Needler, M.C. (1996). *Identity, interest, and ideology: An introduction to politics.* Westport, CT: Praeger.

Nelson, B.R. (2006). *The making of the modern state: A theoretical evolution.* New York: Palgrave Macmillan.

Neocleous, M. (1997). *Fascism.* Minneapolis, MN: University of Minnesota Press.

Nevitte, N. (1996). *The decline of deference: Canadian value change in cross-national perspective.* Peterborough, ON: Broadview Press.

New York Times. (2008, November 5). Election results 2008. Retrieved from http://elections.nytimes.com/2008/results/president/national-exit-polls.htm

Newton, K., & Van Deth, J.W. (2010). *Foundations of comparative politics: Democracies of the modern world* (2nd ed.). Cambridge: Cambridge University Press.

Norris, P. (2000). *A virtuous circle: Political communications in postindustrial societies.* Cambridge, UK: Cambridge University Press, 2000.

Norris, P. (2002). Campaign communications. In L. LeDuc, R.G. Niemi, & P. Norris (Eds.), *Comparing democracies 2: New challenges in the study of elections and voting* (pp. 127–147). London, UK: Sage.

Nye, J.S., Jr. (2004). *Soft power: The means to success in world politics.* New York: Public Affairs.

O'Neill, B. (2002). Sugar and spice? Political culture and the political behaviour of Canadian women. In J. Everitt & B. O'Neill (Eds.), *Citizen politics: Research and theory in Canadian political behaviour* (pp. 40–55). Don Mills, ON: Oxford University Press.

Obama, B. (2006). *The audacity of hope: Thoughts on reclaiming the American dream.* New York: Vintage Books.

OECD. (2010). Statistical annex of the 2010 Development Co-operation Report. Retrieved March 25, 2010, from www.oecd.org/document/9/0,3343,en_2649_34447_1893129_1_1_1_1,00.html

Oeter, S. (2006). Federal republic of Germany. In K. Le Roy & C. Saunders (Eds.), *Legislative, executive, and judicial governance in federal countries.* Montreal & Kingston: McGill-Queen's University Press.

Office of the Information Commissioner of Canada. (2009). Report card 2008–2009: Out of time. Retrieved from www.infocom.gc.ca/eng/rp-pr_spe-rep_rap-spe_rep-car_fic-ren_2008-2009_2.aspx

Ohmae, K. (1995). *The end of the nation state: The rise of regional economies.* London, UK: HarperCollins.

Olson, M. (1965). *The logic of collective action: Public goods and the theory of groups.* Cambridge, MA: Harvard University Press.

Opp, K.-D. (1989). *The rationality of political protest.* Boulder, CO: Westview Press.

Oppenheimer, J.R. (1953). Atomic weapons and American policy. *Foreign Affairs, 31*(4), 525–535.

Ostrom, E. (2000). *Governing the commons: The evolution of institutions for collective action.* New York: Cambridge University Press.

Owen, D. (2009). The campaign and the media. In J.M. Box-Steffensmeier & S.E. Schier (Eds.), *The American elections of 2008.* Lanham, MD: Rowman & Littlefield.

Oxfam. (2003). *Running into the sand: Why failure at the Cancun trade talks threatens the world's poorest people.* Retrieved May 9, 2004, from www.oxfam.org.uk/what_we_do/issue/trade/bp53_cancun.pdf

Paehlke, R. (2003). *Democracy's dilemma: Environment, social equity and the global community.* Cambridge, MA: MIT Press.

Pal, L.A. (1992). *Public policy analysis: An introduction* (2nd ed.). Scarborough, ON: Nelson Canada.

Pal, L.A. (1993). *Interests of state: The politics of language, multiculturalism and feminism in Canada.* Montreal: McGill-Queen's University Press.

Palmer, D. (1994). *Shining Path of Peru.* New York: St. Martin's Press.

Pammett, J.H., & LeDuc, L. (2003). *Explaining the turnout decline in Canadian federal elections: A new survey of non-voters.* Retrieved May 26, 2004, from www.elections.ca.

Panebianco, A. (1988). *Political parties: Organization and power.* Cambridge, UK: Cambridge University Press.

Panitch, L.V. (1995). Elites, classes, and power in Canada. In M.S. Whittington & G. Williams (Eds.), *Canadian politics in the 1990s* (4th ed.) (pp. 152–175). Toronto: Nelson Canada.

Parrington, V. (1987). *Main currents in American thought* (Vols. 1–2). Norman, OK: University of Oklahoma Press.

Pape, R.A. (2005). *Dying to win: The strategic logic of suicide terrorism.* New York: Random House.

Parenti, M. (1970). Power and pluralism: A view from the bottom. *Journal of Politics, 32*(3), 501–530.

Petter, A. (1990). When rights go wrong. *Policy Options, 11*(3), 33–34.

Pew Research Centre. (2009). Independents take centre stage in the Obama era: Trends in political values and core attitudes: 1987–2009. Retrieved from http://people-press.org/report/517/

Pharr, S., Putnam, R.D., & Dalton, R.J. (2000). A quarter century of declining confidence. *Journal of Democracy, 11*(2), 5–25.

Pierson, C. (1996). *The modern state.* London, UK: Routledge.

Plasser, F., with Plasser, G. (2002). *Global political campaigning: A worldwide analysis of campaign professionals and their practices.* Westport, CT: Praeger.

Pollack, K.M. (2002). *The threatening storm: The case for invading Iraq.* New York: Random House.

Postman, N. (1985). *Amusing ourselves to death: Public discourse in an age of show business.* New York: Penguin.

Potter, S.V. (2003). Judging the judiciary: The rule of law in the age of the Charter. *Policy Options, 24*(9), 34–38.

Pross, A.P. (1993). *Group politics and public policies* (2nd ed.). Toronto: Oxford University Press.

Punnett, R.M. (1971). *British politics and government* (2nd ed.). London, UK: Heinemann Educational Books.

Putnam, R. (2000). *Bowling alone: The collapse and revival of American community*. New York: Simon & Schuster.

Putnam, R.D. (1993). *Making democracy work: Civic traditions in modern Italy*. Princeton, NJ: Princeton University Press.

Quah, J.S.T. (2008). Curbing corruption in India: An impossible dream? *Asian Journal of Political Science, 16*(3), 240–259.

Qualter, T.J. (1986). *Conflicting political ideas in liberal democracies*. Toronto: Methuen.

Rapley, J. (2007). *Understanding development: Theory and practice in the Third World* (3rd ed.). Boulder, CO: Lynne Reinner Publishers.

Rasch. B.E., & Congleton, R.D. (2006). Amendment procedures and constitutional stability. In R.D. Congleton & B. Swedenborg (Eds.), *Democratic constitutional design and public policy: Analysis and evidence*. Cambridge, MA: MIT Press.

Rees, W., & Wackernagel, M. (1996). *Our ecological footprint: Reducing human impact on earth*. Gabriola Island, BC: New Society Publishers.

Remmer, K. (1991). The political impact of economic crisis in Latin America in the 1980s. *American Political Science Review, 85*(3), 777–800.

Resnick, P. (1997). *Twenty-first century democracy*. Montreal: McGill-Queen's University Press.

Rhodes, R.A.W., Wanner, J., & Weller, P. (2009). *Comparing Westminster*. Oxford: Oxford University Press.

Rihoux, B., & Frankland, E.G. (2008). Conclusion: The metamorphosis of amateur-activist newborns into professional-activist centaurs. In E.G. Frankland, P. Lucardie, & B. Rihoux (Eds.), *Green parties in transition: The end of grass-roots democracy?* (pp. 250–287). Farnham, UK: Ashgate Publishing.

Rochlin, J. (2003). *Vanguard revolutionaries in Latin America: Peru, Colombia, Mexico*. Boulder, CO: Lynne Reinner Publishers.

Roett, R., & Paz, G. (Eds.). (2008). *China's expansion into the western hemisphere*. Washington, DC: Brookings Institution Press.

Rose, J., & Mellon, H. (2010). When the message is the meaning: Government advertising and the branding of states. In S. Sampert & L. Trimble (Eds.), *Mediating Canadian politics*. Toronto: Pearson Canada.

Rotberg, R. (Ed.). (2008). *China into Africa: Trade, aid, and influence*. Washington, DC: Brookings Institution Press.

Rothkopf, D. (2009). *Superclass: The global power elite and the world they are making*. Toronto: Penguin Canada.

Rousseau, J.-J. (1968). *The social contract* (M. Cranston, Trans.). Harmondsworth, UK: Penguin. (Original work published in 1762.)

Russell, P.H., Knopff, R., Bateman, T.M.J., & Hiebert, J. (2008). *The court and the constitution: Leading cases*. Toronto: Emond Montgomery.

Sabato, L. (1992). *Feeding frenzy: How attack journalism has transformed American politics*. New York: Free Press.

Sachs, J. (2005). *An end to poverty*. New York: Penguin.

Sallot, J. (2004, March 27). Information commissioner wins access to documents. *Globe and Mail*, A11.

Sancton, A. (2002). Municipalities, cities, and globalization: Implications for Canadian federalism. In H. Bakvis & G. Skogstad (Eds.), *Canadian federalism: Performance, effectiveness, and legitimacy* (pp. 261–277). Don Mills, ON: Oxford University Press.

Sandbrook, R. (2003). Introduction: Envisioning a civilized globalization. In R. Sandbrook (Ed.), *Civilizing globalization: A survival guide*. Albany, NY: State University of New York Press.

Sartori, G. (1976). *Parties and party systems*. New York: Cambridge University Press.

Savoie, D. (2008). *Court government and the collapse of accountability in Canada and the United Kingdom*. Toronto: University of Toronto Press.

Savoie, D.J. (1999). *Governing from the centre: The concentration of power in Canadian politics*. Toronto: University of Toronto Press.

Savoie, D.J. (2003). *Breaking the bargain: Public servants, ministers and Parliament*. Toronto: University of Toronto Press.

Scarrow, S.E. (2000). Parties without members? Party organization in a changing electoral environment. In R.J. Dalton & M.P. Wattenberg (Eds.), *Parties without partisans: Political change in advanced industrial democracies* (pp. 79–101). Oxford, UK: Oxford University Press.

Scarrow, S.E., Webb, P., & Farrell, D.M. (2000). From social integration to electoral contestation: The changing distribution of power within political parties. In R.J. Dalton & M.P. Wattenberg (Eds.), *Parties without partisans: Political change in advanced industrial democracies* (pp. 129–153). Oxford, UK: Oxford University Press.

Schapiro, M. (2010, February). Conning the climate: Inside the carbon-trading shell game. *Harper's*, 31–39.

Schedler, A., Diamond, L., & Plattner, M.F. (Eds.). (1999). *The self-restraining state*. Boulder, CO: Lynne Rienner.

Schleiter, P., & Morgan-Jones, E. (2005). *Semi-presidential regimes: Providing flexibility or generating representation and governance problems?* Centre for the Study of Democratic Government, *Working Paper Series Paper No. 01*.

Schlesinger, A.E. (1973). *The imperial presidency*. Boston: Houghton Mifflin.

Schull, J. (1971). *Rebellion: The rising in French Canada, 1837*. Toronto: Macmillan of Canada.

Schumacher, E.F. (1973). *Small is beautiful: A study of economics as if people mattered*. London, UK: Sphere Books.

Shaiko, R.G. (1999). *Voices and echoes for the environment: Public interest representation in the 1990s and beyond.* New York: Columbia University Press.

Shub, D. (1966). *Lenin: A biography.* Baltimore, MD: Penguin Books.

Shugart, M.S. (2006). Comparative executive-legislative relations. In R.A.W. Rhodes, S.A. Binder, & B.A. Rockman (Eds.), *The Oxford handbook of political institutions.* Oxford, UK: Oxford University Press.

Siaroff, A. (2009). *Comparing political regimes: A thematic introduction to comparative politics* (2nd ed.). Toronto: University of Toronto Press.

Siaroff, A. (2009). The decline of political participation: An empirical overview of voter turnout and party membership. In J. DeBardeleben & J.H. Pammeett (Eds.), *Activating the citizen: Dilemmas of participation in Europe and Canada.* New York: Palgrave Macmillan.

Simeon, R. (1976). Studying public policy. *Canadian Journal of Political Science, 9*(3), 548–580.

Simeon, R., & Cameron, D. (2002). Intergovernmental relations and democracy: An oxymoron if there ever was one? In H. Bakvis & G. Skogstad (Eds.), *Canadian federalism: Performance, effectiveness, and legitimacy* (pp. 278–295). Don Mills, ON: Oxford University Press.

Simon, H.A. (1957). *Administrative behavior: A study of decision-making processes in administrative organization.* New York: Macmillan.

Simon, J.L., & Kahn, H. (1984). *The resourceful earth.* New York: Basil Blackwell.

Simpson, J. (2001). *The friendly dictatorship.* Toronto: McClelland & Stewart.

Skocpol, T. (1979). *States and social revolutions: A comparative analysis of France, Russia, and China.* New York: Cambridge University Press.

Small, T.A. (2008, November). The Facebook effect? On-line campaigning in the 2008 Canadian and United States elections. *Policy Options, 29*(10), 85–87.

Smith, A. (2004). An inquiry into the nature and causes of the wealth of nations [excerpt]. In T. Ball & R. Dagger (Eds.), *Ideals and ideologies: A reader* (5th ed.) (pp. 104–106). New York: Pearson Education. (Original work published in 1776.)

Sniderman, P.M., Fletcher, J.F., Russell, P.H., & Tetlock, P. (1996). *The clash of rights: Liberty, equality, and legitimacy in pluralist democracy.* New Haven: Yale University Press.

Spector, N. (2009, August 27). More harmonizing than harmonized. *The Globe and Mail.*

Stackhouse, J. (2000). *Out of poverty and into something more comfortable.* Toronto: Vintage Canada.

Stanley, G.F.G. (1992). *The birth of Western Canada: A history of the Riel rebellions.* Toronto: University of Toronto Press.

Stephan, A., & Robertson, G.B. (2003). An "Arab" more than a "Muslim" electoral gap. *Journal of Democracy, 14*(3), 30–44.

Stern, D.I. (2004). The rise and fall of the environmental Kutznets curve. *World Development, 32*(8), 1419–1439.

Sterling-Folker, J. (Ed.). (2006). *Making sense of international relations theory.* Boulder, CO: Lynne Rienner.

Stoker, G. (2006). Comparative local governance. In R.A.W. Rhodes, S.A. Binder, & B.A. Rockman (Eds.), *The Oxford handbook of political Institutions.* Oxford, UK: Oxford University Press.

Strategic Counsel. (2008). A report to *The Globe and Mail* and CTV: 2008 federal election pre-election national poll. Retrieved from www.thestreategiccounsel.com/our_news/polls/2008-10-12%20National%20Poll%20(reporting%20Oct10-11)f.pdf

Sunderlin, W.D. (2003). *Ideology, social theory, and the environment.* Lanham, MD: Rowman & Littlefield.

Suny, R.G. (2006). Nationalism, nation making and the postcolonial states of Asia, Africa, and Eurasia. In L. Barrington (Ed.), *Making and protecting the nation in postcolonial and postcommunist states.* Ann Arbor, MI: University of Michigan Press.

Sutter, R.G. (2008). *Chinese foreign relations: Power and policy since the Cold War.* Lanham, MD: Rowman & Littlefield.

Suzuki, D., & Moola, F. (2010, May 15). What the Gulf oil disaster tells us. *The Western Star.*

Swenden, W. (2006). *Federalism and regionalism in Western Europe: A comparative and thematic analysis.* Houndmills, Basingstoke, Hampshire, UK: Palgrave Macmillan.

Sylvester, C. (1994). *Feminist theory and international relations in a postmodern era.* New York: Cambridge University Press.

Tarrow, S. (1999). *Power in movement: Social movements and contentious politics.* Cambridge, UK: Cambridge University Press.

Taylor, D.M. (1992). Disagreeing on the basics: Environmental debates reflect competing world views. *Alternatives, 14*(3), 26–33.

Tessler, M. (2002). Do Islamic orientations influence attitudes towards democracy in the Arab world? Evidence from Egypt, Jordan, Morocco, and Algeria. Retrieved August 21, 2003, from www.worldvaluessurvey.org/Upload/5_TessIslamDem_2.pdf.

"Thai protesters hurl blood at Thai PM Abhisit's home." (2010, March 17). Retrieved from http://news.bbc.co.uk/2/hi/asia-pacific/8571592.stm

"Thailand: Timeline to conflict." (2010, May 19). *ReutersAlertNet.* Retrieved from www.alertnet.org/thenews/newsdesk/IRIN/61c10a18c8dec960b7c511c3cb6f1e80.htm

Thiele, L.P. (1997). *Thinking politics: Perspectives in ancient, modern, and postmodern theory.* Chatham, NJ: Chatham House.

Thompson, D. (1984). *The Chartists.* New York: Pantheon.

Thucydides (1972). *History of the Peleponnesian war.* London: Penguin.

Tilly, C., & Tarrow, S. (2007). *Contentious politics.* Boulder, CO: Paradigm Publishers.

Tocqueville, A. (2000). *Democracy in America* (H.C. Mansfield & D. Winthrop, Trans. & Ed.). Chicago: University of Chicago Press. (Original work published in 1835.)

Tremblay, R.C., et al. (2004). *Mapping the political landscape: An introduction to political science.* Toronto: Thomson Nelson.

Trudeau, P.-E. (1993). *Memoirs.* Toronto: McClelland & Stewart.

UNDP [United Nations Development Programme]. (1995, 2002, 2003, 2010). *Human development report, 1995, 2002, 2003, 2010.* New York: Oxford University Press.

United Nations. (2009). *Millennium development goals report: 2009.* New York: United Nations.

UNMDG [United Nations Millennium Development Goals]. (2005). *MDG Info 2005.* www.devinfo.org/facts.htm?IDX=13

UNMDG. (2006). *Millennium Development Goals Report 2006.* http://mdgs.un.org/unsd/mdg/Resources/Static/Products/Progress2006/MDGReport2006.pdf

US Army. (2006). *Counterinsurgency.* Field Manual 3-24. Washington: Department of the Army. Available at http://usacac.army.mil/cac/repository/materials/coin- fm3-24.pdf.

Valaskakis, K. (2001, April 19). It's about world governance. *Globe and Mail*, A15.

Verba, S., Nie, N., & Kim, J.O. (1978). *Participation and political equality.* New York: Cambridge University Press.

Wade, R. (1990). *Governing the market.* Princeton, NJ: Princeton University Press.

Walker, J.L. (1991). *Mobilizing interest groups in America: Patrons, professions, and social movements.* Ann Arbor, MI: The University of Michigan Press.

Wallack, M. (2006). From compellence to pre-emption: Kosovo and Iraq as U.S. responses to contested hegemony. In O. Croci & A. Verdun (Eds.), *The transatlantic divide: Foreign and security policies in the Atlantic Alliance from Kosovo to Iraq* (pp. 109–125). Manchester, UK: Manchester University Press.

Wallerstein, I. (1974–1980). *The modern world system* (Vol. 1–2). New York: Academic Press.

Waltz, K.N. (1979). *Theory of international politics.* Reading, MA: Addison-Wesley.

Ware, A. (1987). *Political parties: Electoral change and structural response.* Oxford: Basil Blackwell.

Warren, M. (2002). Deliberative democracy. In A. Carter & G. Stokes (Eds.), *Democratic theory today: Challenges for the 21st century* (pp. 173–202). Cambridge, UK: Polity Press.

Watkins-Hayes, C. (2010). Human services as "race work"? Historical lessons and contemporary challenges of black providers. In Y. Hasenfeld (Ed.),*Human services as complex organizations* (2nd ed.). Thousand Oaks, CA: Sage Publications.

Watts, R.L. (2008). *Comparing federal systems* (3rd ed.). Montreal & Kingston: McGill-Queen's University Press.

Weale, A. (1992). *The new politics of pollution.* Manchester, UK: Manchester University Press.

Weber, E. (1976). *Peasants into Frenchmen: The modernization of rural France, 1870–1914.* Stanford, CA: Stanford University.

Weber, M. (1958). In H.H. Gerth & C.W. Mills (Eds. & Trans.), *Max Weber: Essays in sociology.* New York: Oxford University Press.

Weber, M. (1970). In H.H. Gerth & C.W. Mills (Eds. & Trans.), *From Max Weber: Essays in sociology.* London: Routledge and Kegan Paul.

Weir, S., & Beetham, D. (1999). *Political power and democratic control in Britain.* London, UK: Routledge.

Weller, P. (1985). *First among equals: Prime ministers in Westminster systems.* Sydney: George Allen & Unwin.

Wendt, A. (1992). Anarchy is what states make of it: The social construction of power politics. *International Organization,46*, 391–425.

Wendt, A. (1999). *Social theory of international politics.* Cambridge, UK: Cambridge University Press, 1999.

West, D.M. (2010). *Air wars: Television advertising in election campaigns, 1952–2008* (5th ed.). Washington, DC: CQ Press.

West, H.R. (2006). *The Blackwell guide to Mill's* Utilitarianism. Malden, MA: Blackwell Publishing.

Wheaton, B., & Z. Kavan (1992). *The Velvet Revolution: Czechoslovakia, 1988–1991.* Boulder, CO: Westview Press.

Whitaker, R. (1997). Canadian politics at the end of the millennium: Old dreams, new nightmares. In D. Taras & B. Rasporich (Eds.), *A passion for identity: An introduction to Canadian studies* (3rd ed.) (pp. 119–137). Toronto: ITP Nelson.

White, R. (1978). *Paraguay's autonomous revolution: 1810–1840.* Albuquerque, NM: University of New Mexico Press.

Wilensky, H. (1975*). The welfare state and equality: Structural and ideological roots of public expenditure.* Berkeley, CA: University of California Press.

Wilkinson, R., & Pickett, K. (2009). *The spirit level: Why equal societies almost always do better.* London: Penguin.

Wilson, J. (2002). Continuity and change in the Canadian environmental movement: Assessing the effects of institutionalization. In D.L. VanNijnatten & R. Boardman (Eds.), *Canadian environmental policy: Context and cases.* Don Mills, ON: Oxford University Press.

Wolf, M. (2001). Will the nation-state survive globalization? *Foreign Affairs,80*(1), 178–190.

Wolin, S.S. (1960). *Politics and vision: Continuity and innovation in Western political thought.* Boston: Little, Brown.

Wood, G., & Sharit, I. (1997). *Who needs credit? Poverty and finance in Bangladesh.* London, UK: Zed Press.

World Bank. (2004). *World development report, 2004.* Washington, DC: The World Bank.

World Bank. (2008). *World development report, 2008.* Washington, DC: World Bank Publications.

World Bank. (2010a). *World Bank updates poverty estimates for the developing world.* Retrieved March 25, 2010, from http://econ.worldbank.org/WBSITE/EXTERNAL/EXTDEC/EXTRESEARCH/0,,contentMDK:21882162~pagePK:64165401~piPK:64165026~theSitePK:469382,00.html

World Bank. (2010b). *World development report, 2010.* Washington, DC: The World Bank.

World Commission on Environment and Development. (1987). *Our common future.* Oxford: Oxford University Press.

York, G. (2010, March 27). The war that won't end. *Globe and Mail,* F1, F6–F7.

Young, L., & Everitt, J. (2004). *Advocacy groups.* Vancouver: UBC Press.

Young, R. (2009). Conclusion. In A. Sancton & R. Young (Eds.), *Foundations of governance: Municipal government in Canada's provinces.* Toronto: University of Toronto Press.

Yunus, M. (1999). *Banker to the poor: Micro-lending and the battle against world poverty.* New York: Public Affairs Press.

Zehfuss, M. (2002). *Constructivism in international relations: The politics of reality.* Cambridge, UK: Cambridge University Press.

PHOTO CREDITS

INDEX